Adventures in Financial Data Science

The Empirical Properties of Financial and Economic Data

Second Edition

World Scientific Series in Finance
(ISSN: 2010-1082)

Published:*

Vol. 19 *Adventures in Financial Data Science: The Empirical Properties of Financial and Economic Data*
Second Edition
by Graham L. Giller (Giller Investments, USA)

Vol. 18 *Sports Analytics*
by Leonard C. Maclean (Dalhousie University, Canada) &
William T. Ziemba (University of British Columbia, Canada)

Vol. 17 *Investment in Startups and Small Business Financing*
edited by Farhad Taghizadeh-Hesary (Tokai University, Japan),
Naoyuki Yoshino (Keio University, Japan),
Chul Ju Kim (Asian Development Bank Institute, Japan),
Peter J. Morgan (Asian Development Bank Institute, Japan) &
Daehee Yoon (Korea Credit Guarantee Fund, South Korea)

Vol. 16 *Cultural Finance: A World Map of Risk, Time and Money*
by Thorsten Hens (University of Zurich, Switzerland),
Marc Oliver Rieger (University of Trier, Germany) &
Mei Wang (WHU – Otto Beisheim School of Management, Germany)

Vol. 15 *Exotic Betting at the Racetrack*
by William T. Ziemba (University of British Columbia, Canada)

Vol. 14 *Dr Z's NFL Guidebook*
by William T. Ziemba (University of British Columbia, Canada) &
Leonard C. MacLean (Dalhousie University, Canada)

*To view the complete list of the published volumes in the series, please visit:
www.worldscientific.com/series/wssf

World Scientific Series in FINANCE vol. 19

Adventures in Financial Data Science

The Empirical Properties of Financial and Economic Data

Second Edition

Graham L. Giller
Giller Investments, USA

World Scientific

NEW JERSEY • LONDON • SINGAPORE • BEIJING • SHANGHAI • HONG KONG • TAIPEI • CHENNAI • TOKYO

Published by

World Scientific Publishing Co. Pte. Ltd.
5 Toh Tuck Link, Singapore 596224
USA office: 27 Warren Street, Suite 401-402, Hackensack, NJ 07601
UK office: 57 Shelton Street, Covent Garden, London WC2H 9HE

Library of Congress Cataloging-in-Publication Data
Names: Giller, Graham L., author.
Title: Adventures in financial data science : the empirical properties of financial and economic data / Graham L Giller, Giller Investments, New Jersey.
Description: Second Edition. | Hackensack, NJ : World Scientific, 2022. | Series: World scientific series in finance, 2010-1082 ; Vol. 19 | Revised edition. | Includes bibliographical references and index.
Identifiers: LCCN 2021058959 | ISBN 9789811250644 (hardcover) | ISBN 9789811251818 (ebook) | ISBN 9789811251825 (ebook other)
Subjects: LCSH: Financial services industry--Data processing. | Investments--Data processing.
Classification: LCC HG4515.5 .G55 2022 | DDC 332.640285--dc23/eng/20220131
LC record available at https://lccn.loc.gov/2021058959

British Library Cataloguing-in-Publication Data
A catalogue record for this book is available from the British Library.

For any available supplementary material, please visit
https://www.worldscientific.com/worldscibooks/10.1142/12678#t=suppl

Desk Editors: Soundararajan Raghuraman/Pui Yee Lum

Typeset by Stallion Press
Email: enquiries@stallionpress.com

For my wife, for her support,
our children, who put up with my "idiosyncracies,"
and for my parents, who inspired me to share.

In loving memory of
Jack and Lorna Baugh & Gordon and Alice Giller.

I am grateful to the many friends I have found over my years working in the financial services industry, including those who agreed to take a look at drafts of this work and provide feedback. In particular: Winston Featherly-Bean, Pete Kyle, Claus Murmann, Yuri Malitsky, Alex Ribeiro-Castro, Sutesh Sharma, Adrian Schofield and Jaipal Tuttle.

Preface

This revised second edition of *Adventures in Financial Data Science* is being written as over half of America has been vaccinated against the Coronavirus, and life may be returning to normal in parts of the United States, although the δ-variant is also continuing its deadly spread, particularly in The South. As a long read with a potentially narrow audience, the book has surprised me with its success and led to me finding new friends throughout the world. As a personal experience, it has been immensely enriching to write it.

I decided to take the opportunity to refresh some of the charts, particularly those relevant to financial and economic data, from the viewpoint now possible *after* the onset of the Coronavirus recession. For the chapter on the Coronavirus itself, I have chosen to analyze the accuracy of the extrapolations made from the data, freezing the model in the Autumn of 2020 but grading it's performance one year later.

This book features mostly my empirical work, although I did include some theory at the end. It will now be followed by a second, smaller, volume *Essays on Trading Strategy*, that outlines my view of the analytic framework that a trader ought to use to make decisions under uncertainty. That book will be entirely devoted trading strategy theory and will have only slight overlap with this one.

Many parts of this work can be viewed as a plea against the use of the Normal distribution in places where it has no business being used. Finance is one of them.

Graham L. Giller
Holmdel, NJ, 2021

About the Author

Graham Giller is one of Wall Street's original data scientists. Starting his career at Morgan Stanley in the UK, he was an early member of Peter Muller's famous PDT group and went on to run his own investment firm. He was Bloomberg LP's original data science hire and set up the data science team in the Global Data division there. He then moved to J.P. Morgan to take the role of Chief Data Scientist, New Product Development, and was subsequently Head of Data Science Research at J.P. Morgan and Head of Primary Research at Deutsche Bank. He is currently CEO of Giller Investments (New Jersey), LLC, a private research firm.

Contents

List of Figures

List of Tables

Chapter 1

Biography and Beginnings

1.1. About this Book

1.1.1. *What this Book is?*

This book is not a biography, as I am not a famous person, and it is not a textbook either. It is a narrative of analytic work that I have done, structured around both my professional career and some of the things that just interested me. I am hoping to share with you what Richard Feynman described as "The Pleasure of Finding Things Out" [40]. For roughly half of my career I've run my own businesses, strongly focused on analytical work, and when I needed a metric to judge myself I fell back on a simple question: *Did I learn something today?* That is my personal goal, to learn things about the Universe, and what I hope to do here is share some of the things I've learned in my pursuit of practical data science. Nevertheless, I will start by giving you some insights into my background, so you can better understand who I am and how I think about things.

1.1.2. *What this Book is Not?*

There are many books on data science that are essentially compendiums of code snippets that exhibit various elementary analyzes. This book does not follow that format. There is value to pedagogic work, but I believe strongly that understanding comes from figuring out the quirks of each individual data set you work with, and no reader will gain that by merely copying my work. I will show you some results

I have found and discuss what I think they mean, and whether science tells us they are believable. I will provide some links to the public data sets I have accessed, some of which require small fees to access. Financial data has never been free because people use it to make a lot of money, and the data generators are well aware of that.

1.2. Family

1.2.1. *About Me*

I am English and grew up in the West Midlands. First in Coventry, and later in a small village called Church Lawford. I now live in New Jersey on my in-law's family farm, just outside New York City on the Jersey Shore. For the majority of my career I've been professionally involved in what is now called "data science," but for me that started much, much, earlier. I have a doctorate in Experimental Particle Physics, from Oxford University, where I also did my undergraduate work. My work featured very large scale (for the time) computer based data analytics in the field of Cosmic Ray Astronomy. For some reason both time-series analysis and statistics "clicked" for me, and I've spent a lot of my professional career organically applying those tools to data from more "social" sciences. I've worked in proprietary trading at Morgan Stanley in London, as a "quant," and in New York, as a strategy developer and portfolio manager in the now famous and very successful *Process Driven Trading* unit. I ran my own investment fund for about a decade, a small effort for "friends and family," not some giant world shaping enterprise, and subsequently spent time as a consultant data scientist before joining Bloomberg LP's Global Data unit as their first data science hire. I set up the data science group there before joining J.P. Morgan as Chief Data Scientist in a unit called New Product Development (N.P.D.). From there I moved to take the role as Head of Primary Research at Deutsche Bank before that firm decided it no longer wanted to be in the equity business. At the time of writing, I am sitting at home, as the COVID-19 outbreak appears to be entering a third wave.

1.2.2. *Grandad and the Oil Tanker*

One of the questions I'm often asked is "why did you decide to enter finance?" I usually respond with the story about Grandad and the

Figure 1.1: The author at The Blue Coat School, Coventry, 1987. *Photo Credit Phillip Shipley.*

oil tanker. My grandfather was Jack Baugh and he had a great effect on me. I figured out that he didn't always see eye-to-eye with my Father, which I guess is not unusual, but generally we all got on and spent many Christmases and Summers together. When I was a child I knew that it was expected that one aspire to some kind of career, and my choices followed the typical paths of children. The first thing I announced I wanted to be was a professional cricketer. I am not very good at sport, as everybody who knows me well can testify to, but my Grandad was very keen on cricket, having played for his work's team, and that rubbed off on me. When I found out that only native born Yorkshiremen were permitted to play for Geoff Boycott's team my aspirations crashed to the ground, and I was puzzled as to why a professional sports team would have such a rule.

My second announced choice was "Chartered Accountant." This, again, was influenced by my Grandad. His official title was "Chief Cashier of the South Yorkshire Passenger Transport Executive," but what he was was a management accountant and what he did was, with his buddy, run the state owned bus company that provided public transport to the city of Sheffield. In modern times his title would have been Chief Financial Officer. I guess he could see that his grandson was good at maths, so he would try to interest me in his work. Once he took me with him to the Midland Bank in Sheffield, on some personal business, and I was pleasantly surprised to see the manager of that institution come out from the backs of the banking hall to personally greet him. For that was where the bus company also did its banking business. That was when I realized that he was, relatively, important.

When your grandfather wants to entertain you he puts you on his knee and tells you stories, and most of Jack's framing experiences were those from his service in the Royal Air Force during the Second World War. His role was to help airbases install and use a groundbreaking technology called *RADAR*, which I found fascinating, especially as what he was describing was nothing like what I had seen in films. He described two cathode ray tubes showing a straight line with a "blip" on it. The first represented vertical distance and the second horizontal distance and the blip was the reflected signal from an enemy plane. I was expecting the sweeping lines with lingering dots that we are used to from images of air traffic control and ship radar, but this was before that time.

Once he told me about the bus company having "too much money to keep in the bank over the weekend," and so they needed to figure out what to do with it. I guess they had good insights as to what was happening to oil prices, which would arise from running a bus company and, presumably, being in receipt of regular phone calls from commodities brokers, but I was startled when his response to my question "so what are you going to do?" was "we're going to buy an oil tanker off the coast of South Africa and sell it back on Monday morning." I think this is what you tell your grandchild when you want them to be interested in "high finance" when they grow up.

I don't know when this transaction took place, but it was probably in the late 1970s or early 1980s. Periods in which inflation was running hot in the United Kingdom and a time when the prices of physical commodities appreciated in real terms. I now know that that's a fairly unusual circumstance, when spot prices for crude oil are expected to appreciate due to the contango of the forward curve, and that "normal backwardation" would make this a money losing trade. On the other hand, in the 1970s, there was probably a lot more value to being on the receiving end of brokers' phone calls than now, so likely the information they were receiving was more useful in a less efficient market. Of course, I didn't know at the time that

I would become directly involved in plays on the structure of forward curves, many years later.

1.2.3. *Grandma, Bletchley Park, and Partial Differential Equations*

Jack was married to Lorna, and their hallway telephone table always carried a black and white photo of them from their wedding day, with him in his R.A.F. uniform. Unlike Grandad, Grandma didn't talk much about the war. She had strong political opinions and I occassionally witnessed them arguing over policy issues of the day. She was good at crosswords, and made cakes and pies, and the sort of comfort food we all look to their grandparents for and remember fondly after they are gone. When I stayed with them for a week or so over the long summer holidays, she made the picnics that we took to watch cricket.

Crosswords, played a much more significant role in her life than that of many people. While Jack was serving overseas in the R.A.F., Lorna was doing something altogether different at home. She told me that one day, when she was in a Mathematics class at university, a "man from the ministry" (as the English used to say) came into the lecture theatre and asked if anybody in the room was good at crosswords. She raised her hand and a few days later was no longer a student but a codebreaker at Bletchley Park. There is a scene in the movie *The Imitation Game* that refers directly to this recruitment strategy [133]. The movie, very early on, also includes a scene where people were sliding sheets of celluloid over each other looking for a coinciding light patch. This is exactly what she told me she did. To me, at the time, this sounded nothing like what "codebreaking" ought to be, but I was impressed nonetheless.

My mother tells me that earlier on she was less forthcoming about her work. In fact, everybody at Bletchley Park had been sworn to secrecy and "signed the *Official Secrets Act*." And, like many of her peers, she kept those secrets. Later, when people finally started talking about what is probably Great Britain's biggest contribution to winning that war, and it was covered in the press and on television, she apparently turned to her family after a feature on the evening news and said "well now you all know what I did in the war."

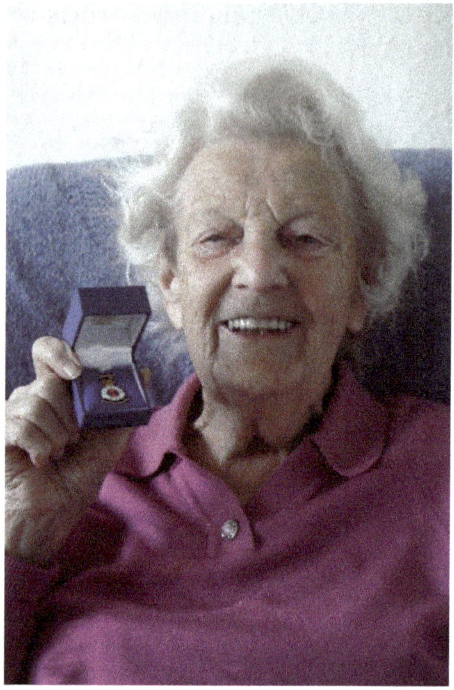

Figure 1.2: Lorna Baugh with her Bletchley Park Service Medal.
Photo Credit Carole Baugh.

I have another memory about Grandma Baugh and maths, one that I'll never forget. In my first year at Oxford, I struggled to keep up with the work not having had the grounding in more advanced mathematics in secondary school that many of my peers had had, and that the Oxford Physics programme assumed. In Hilary Term, I think, we were studying partial differential equations, the key tool of classical physics. I just didn't get it. I understood the general principal of separation of variables as a method of solution, that seemed clear, but the wave equation was bothering me. The wave equation is

$$\frac{\partial^2 f}{\partial t^2} = c^2 \frac{\partial^2 f}{\partial x^2} \tag{1.1}$$

and the solutions are $f(x + ct)$ and $f(x - ct)$. To me that didn't seem to actually "solve" anything! When solving *ordinary* differential equations one finds actual solutions, not generic expressions.

The solutions to the Harmonic Oscillator equation, for example,

$$\frac{d^2f}{dt^2} = -\omega^2 f \tag{1.2}$$

are $\sin \omega t$ and $\cos \omega t$. Those are actually solutions, they tell you what the form of the unknown function, f, actually is. At the time, I was struggling to process what to *do* with such much more general solution, and then in walks Grandma with my parents, come to take me to tea on a Saturday afternoon in Oxford.

"What are you doing?" ask Grandma, so I showed her my work. "Oh, P.D.E.'s. I love them. I used to make them up and do them for fun." This succeeded in making me feel even more out of place. My mother, who was a school teacher and history enthusiast and no form of scientist whatsoever, always told me her mother was "not the best teacher," due to her tendency to declare "Oh that's easy, I don't understand why you don't understand this!"

1.2.4. *Grandpa, Dad, and Caring about People*

My father's family were somewhat different. My father was first a minister and later a school teacher, starting with Religious Education and moving on to "high school" mathematics. His father was also a minister, but that was not his first career, which was Organ Building. That is the construction of musical instruments for churches, and he was a talented pianist and lover of music. This was a "reserved profession," meaning exempt from the draft, so he wasn't called up into military service. However Grandpa, and we always called him "Grandpa" to distinguish him from "Grandad," did not sit aside. He lived and worked in the East End of London (my father was born within the sound of Bow Bells making him an genuine Cockney), so he volunteered to join the London Fire Service and fought fires during the nights in the London Docklands. An area that I would later return to, in my financial career.

Growing up with a parent who is a practicing minister is an experience. One trait that the entire family seems to share is liking the sound of their own voices, and I have always enjoyed public speaking. This seems to be something that started early as, one Sunday, my mother was surprised to find me standing in the pulpit of the

Figure 1.3: Gordon Pryce Giller (center), and his family, taken in London. It was only after seeing this photo that I realized the origin of my somewhat unruly hair. *Photo via Susan Giller.*

church, just reading the numbers of the hymns into the microphone and being broadcast on the P.A. system.

We all have complicated relationships with our parents and I feel that I get on much better with my father now, when I am 52 and he is almost 81, than I did when I was a child. However, my most important memory of him is only tangentially about me, and it dates from when I was at home from college as a student. I woke, late at night, to hear my father saying into the telephone "... and why do you want to talk to Graham Giller?" It turned out that a schoolfriend's father had found a note, with my name and home phone number, in his wife's purse and was calling to challenge a suspected boyfriend. That note must have been there for several years, for it dated from when our schoolteachers were on strike and we had to leave school at lunchtimes because the custodial staff were on strike. This was a common occurrence in the 1980s. Every day, on the way from school to the bus stop where I began my hour-long journey home, I walked under a railway bridge on which somebody had spray-painted "I am the 1 in 10," a reference to the 10% unemployment in the West Midlands during the early years of the Thatcher governments and the UB40 song with that title [134]. During the strike, at lunchtime, we would walk to my friend's mother's employer's office, and eat in their cafeteria.

This all happened several years after I had left school for college, putting my schoolfriends behind me and moving on to a different phase of my life. I hadn't spoken to the friend for over 2 years, and would not again for decades. I knew my reaction would have been to slam the phone down and go back to bed, but my father took at least 30 minutes to listen to this stranger's problems, calm him down, provide an alternate narrative, and generally care about somebody he'd never met and likely never would. I knew that this was something I could not and would not do, and it impresses me to this day.

1.2.5. *My Family*

I always felt that my own children would likely not experience the severe economic dislocation that I grew up with, in the 1970s and 1980s, but, due to the Coronavirus outbreak in 2020, that has not been the case. I am very comfortable with the decision to abandon "mainstream" finance for about a decade, which permitted me to be at home almost every day of my young children's lives. If I had not done that I doubtless would be considerably wealthier than I am now, but it was the right decision.

I am married to Elizabeth and currently we both live and work from home on her family's small nursery farm in New Jersey. At 30 acres, it is not the sort of operation most people think of you when you say "farm," but it is sufficiently large to require machinery to operate and is a tranquil space in busy times. We met on a blind date, which was my first but not hers. In the era before online hookups, this was a traditional introduction. I had recently told my boss, Peter Muller, that after 2 years in New York, a city I really didn't like in comparison to London, I wanted to go home. He decided that what I really needed was a girlfriend, and so set us up with the help of one of his friends. We met at the Metropolitan Museum, and I was astonished to find somebody who was impressive, good looking, and seemed similarly aligned to my thoughts and opinions. Peter had asked me "What kind of girls do you like?" and my reply had been "Somebody I can have a conversation with." I think he had been more expecting something along the lines of "blond with a big chest." I never did go home, and we have spent over 20 years together at this point. We have three children together.

1.3. Oxford, Physics and Bond Trading

1.3.1. *Physics*

After school, I was fortunate to be admitted to read Physics at Lincoln College, Oxford. I stayed there for almost 7 years, three doing my bachelors degree in Physics and three and a half more doing a doctorate in experimental Elementary Particle Physics. I wasn't the best in my class when I arrived, but I got better every year, and gained an Exhibition (a kind of junior scholarship), which entitled me to wear a longer gown to dinner, and First Class Degree. I was then painfully shy, which is something I've struggled with my whole life, and probably did not have as much fun as I could have. I'm sure I came across as a little weird, but I definitely did have a lot of fun there. It was a marvelous experience both in terms of intellectual and social life, and I made lifelong friends.

I loved physics as a subject, and learned it to a depth that was satisfying. For my research, I wasn't drawn to the easy win of the era, which was accelerator physics at the Large Electron Positron collider (LEP) at CERN. It just wasn't appealing to me to measure the ninth decimal place in some parameter of electroweak theory and find that it was entirely consistent with observations. I wanted to do something more "weird," and so chose to join the Soudan II Proton Decay Experiment, which was also conducting research into neutrino physics and cosmic rays.

It was this that got me truly into statistical data analysis, and exploratory data analysis, and created the skills I've used every day for the last 20 years. I ran data analysis jobs that took all night to execute and a simulation of the statistical analysis I used that required a month of CPU time. I found that the Fisherian view of statistics meshed extremely well with what was required of me as an observational scientist and became the person that other grad. students in the department looked to understand statistical issues with their work. As an undergraduate, Dirac had become my scientific "hero" and this was augmented by Fisher.[a] I found it incredible that he had done so much, very much as you become in awe of Feynman as a physicist when you truly understand how much of the subject he influenced.

I had to learn to manage the relationship with my doctoral supervisor and had some truly great intellectual experiences, such as spending time in the lounge at the Nuclear Physics Laboratory with some of the truly best physicists in the world trying to solve real world problems without known solutions. Unfortunately, the contingent of my experimental collaboration team from Argonne National Laboratory let me down by blocking the authorship of a paper based on my D.Phil. research, which was very frustrating personally and one of the reasons I decided to leave academia once my doctoral program was completed. Since my intention had always been to be a professional academic physicist, that was quite a change in career aspiration. It is satisfying to me now, even if slightly small-minded, to see some of the work I have authored while a professional data scientist rank higher in Google Scholar than some of the blander grad-student papers they did permit to emerge [56].

1.3.2. *Bond Trading*

The process of becoming academically attracted to the finance industry started with reading books and magazine articles. As now, I've always been very "hands on" about working with data, so I decided to take a look at some. Every Saturday, I would purchase a copy of the *Financial Times* from the branch of W.H. Smith on Oxford's Cornmarket and take it up to the N.P.L. to enter the data from the bond pricing pages into a database I'd created on our VAX minicomputers. I started looking at the term structure of the UK Government bond markets ("Gilts" as they are known), which was unusual in that it possessed an "infinity-point," since the UK had issued irredeemable bonds. The attraction to past times was interesting, and they included the "War Loan" from the First World War and the "Consols," or Consolidated Annuities, that represented the

[a]In saying this, I am aware of the nastier aspects of his personality, and temper my admiration by them.

Figure 1.4: On a punt in Oxford with my good friend Eu Jin (and others not in the shot).
Photo Credit Chua Eu Jin.

transition of government funding from selling annuities to individuals to an institutional bond market.

I built a yield curve model, using the analytical tools available for doing High Energy Physics, and noticed anomalies in pricing existed. At the time it was probably pretty unusual to be using data tools tuned for samples in the sizes of millions of particle physics events to process this kind of data. I would purchase bonds with yields that were too high and sell them back when they returned to normal pricing. This was the exact opposite of high-frequency trading, as it required going to the Oxford Post Office on Monday and filling out paperwork to purchase a bond over the counter. Around a week later I would get a certificate in the mail and check what had happened to the prices. The reversion time seemed to be around a month, and then you went back to the Post Office and filled out another form to sell the bond, making a profit. During this time, the UK was forced out of the European Exchange Rate Mechanism, or E.R.M., and I was fortunate to be doing this work in a time of volatility in the markets. It made me sufficient money that I ended my studies with a surplus in my bank account, rather than being in debt, and was a lot of fun. A lot more fun that fighting with the bureaucrats from Argonne National Laboratory.

1.3.3. *Electronics*

During my time at Oxford I also wrote a textbook on electronics [46], which was published in 1991 while I was a graduate student. I had introduced to the subject by my Physics teacher, Mr. Singh, who suggested I sit for the "A" level even though the school could not allocate teaching time for me so I had to work on it in my spare time. I did so, and got an A grade on the exam, which probably helped with my entrance to Lincoln. I am profoundly grateful to Mr. Singh (alas, I do not know his first name) for the great support he showed to me and the help he gave me.

At Oxford, I did Electronics as a final year undergraduate option (in addition to Electricity and Magnetism, Nuclear and Particle Physics, and Theoretical Physics) and was surprised to find it was not much more challenging than the "A" level. I also felt that many of the books didn't treat the subject to my standard, so I decided to write my own. I did so over the summer between my second and final years as an undergraduate, and worked on the manuscript as a graduate student, seeing it published part way through my tenure there.

As an undergraduate, I had developed a method of working that involved the synthesis of many authors views of a subject to shape my understanding of a matter, and I had no hesitation to criticize one book's approach in one area and another's elsewhere. I would then write myself a briefing on the subject which I would basically memorize, along with working through problem sets, before tackling my exams. I liked to operate with as full an understanding as I could muster, often from first principles, and so writing a book on a subject didn't seem that challenging to me. As a child, one of my proposed career's had also been "author," although I could not seem to write fiction, so it didn't seem odd to me that a 19 year-old would write a book on a technical subject.

1.4. Morgan Stanley and P.D.T.

1.4.1. *The Japanese Warrants Desk*

In my final year as a graduate student I interviewed at Morgan Stanley, at Canary Wharf in the London Docklands that my Grandpa had known. During the interview Derek Bandeen, who went on to be Global Head of Equities for Citibank, asked me why I was interested in finance. I told him about my experiences with Gilts, and I'm pretty sure that's why I got the job. The other interviewer was Sutesh Sharma, for whom I would be indirectly working, and his most important question was different. Having learned that we both hailed from the same town of Coventry, and that my father was working as a maths teacher, he was very concerned that he wasn't interviewing *his* maths teacher's son.

I joined in 1994, just after submitting my doctoral thesis, and I landed at Canary Wharf as the guy able to do the math and also the coding to support the Japanese Warrants and Convertible Bonds desk, which operated an offshore market for derivatives on Japanese companies. The desk was losing money, and Sutesh's job included trying to figure out why, although he was also trying to set up a proprietary trading business based on deconstructing Convertibles into their component risks. I started out with I.T., on a higher floor of the Morgan Stanley building at 25 Cabot Square, but soon Sutesh called me and told me "I don't know why you're up there, you have a desk downstairs" on the trading floor. This was an interesting time, as we witnessed the death of a business filled with traditional "barrow boy" traders. I was partnered at Morgan Stanley with Jaipal Tuttle, who became a good friend and eventually the best man at my wedding. Jaipal and I were trying to usher in a new era of fully automatic trading and Jaipal claims that, at a party in the Docklands with the desk traders, I apparently claimed that they were all going to be replaced by computers resulting in me being punched in the face by a trader. I have absolutely no memory of this.

I built several things for Sutesh, including a Convertible bond pricing model that fused a binomial tree for stock prices with a trinomial tree for interest rates and was able to value the embedded interest rate optionality within the bonds he was seeking to trade. The idea was to create trades that stripped the bonds into their component risks, remove the undesired ones, and leave behind a pristine, but incorrectly priced, call option on a Japanese company. The only problem with this was that it involved Morgan Stanley buying and holding the credit risk of the issuers of these bonds, and the Equity Division was not permitted to do such a thing. Once day, Sutesh came in and announced that he had found "a guy who wants to buy all our credit risk" who "wants to do a weird kind of swap." We weren't sure why, and I remember discussing whether he was trying to assemble a diversified portfolio of idiosyncratic credit risks on the assumption that they were undervalued. I think what we were really experiencing was the inception of the Credit Default Swaps market.

I worked long days, 7 a.m. to 7 p.m., and was very impressed by the people I found around me. Coming out of the Oxford Physics program with a D.Phil., I hadn't really known what to expect and Sutesh, Derek and Vikram Pandit were clearly very smart. I also flew to New York several times on Concorde for meetings, which was quite an experience as it used afterburners and got you there in around 3 hours total. I liked Morgan Stanley, and learned a lot.

1.4.2. *Creating a Global Instant Messaging Infrastructure by Accident*

My original role at Morgan Stanley was to be the quant who could code. In the era before Python, this meant a lot of hacking in Unix shell scripts and Perl scripts. At Oxford I had worked primarily on a Digital VAX minicomputer, which was in an air conditioned computer room with reel-to-reel tape machines and VT100 data entry terminals, just like you saw in movies. At the end of my time I had progressed to an *Alpha* workstation, but it was still old fashioned "big iron" in its approach.

At Morgan Stanley we used Sun's *Sparc 10* and *Sparc 20* workstations and, on the trading desks, had two or three 27″ cathode ray tube monitors that pumped out a lot of heat. Sutesh would get a lot of calls, and was often away from his desk, so I had to take messages for him. I would write on *PostIt Notes* and stick them on his screen, but the heat would dry out the adhesives and they always fell off.

As I was pretty good at hacking scripts, one day in 1994 or 1995, I decided to write a simple program, called `memo`, which would open up a window on somebody else's computer displaying a message. The intention was to create an *electronic PostIt Note*. One would type

```
memo sutesh Call John at Barclays
```

and a brightly colored window would pop up on his screen. It would stay there until one of three buttons was pressed: `Ok`, `Yes`, `No`. The first cleared the window and the second relayed the reply message to the sender.

This required two technologies that had been implemented by Morgan Stanley IT. First, the *Xwindows* protocol had been set up not to require permissions to open windows on another computer's screen — this was always the default, so that itself may not have been a conscious choice. I was familiar with it because I was used to remotely accessing computers as part of the global Particle Physics infrastructure. The second, which was a very smart decision, was to alias everybody's computer to their account names. Thus, my computer could be reached by the name "`ggill`," Derek's was "`dband`," etc. Older hands had simpler names — Sutesh's was just "`sutesh`" and Vikram Pandit was, I believe, simply "`vik`." We were all very familiar with these account names because we used them to send emails many times a day. Finally, because the system ran on your computer, not on the recipients, it didn't require any software to be installed by the recipient before they could *receive* messages or reply to them. Thus the barriers to use were very small.

So, very simply, you could send a message around the world from any computer. The windows that showed up were displayed in a randomly chosen color that was fairly saturated and they sat on your screen until you clicked a button. Graphically, they were not subtle, which made them get your attention in an era when continuously checking your *Facebook* or *Twitter* feed wasn't yet a habit. I added a "group" functionality, where messages could be broadcast to whole teams, and soon after that Sutesh asked me if this was something they could deploy to the whole desk. I passed the script to an intern from the IT department and returned to being a user not a developer.

Later on, while in New York, Peter Muller and I made a trip down to the Equity trading floor to interview a trader who was being considered to manage a momentum based futures trading system that we had "adopted" after Morgan Stanley management fell out with it's creator.[b] I was startled to see my "memos" on almost every one of hundreds and hundreds of computer screens across the entire, football field sized, trading floor. I told Peter this was probably the most value accretive thing I'd delivered for the firm, which he wasn't particularly happy about because he wasn't very keen on us having careers that were integrated into Morgan Stanley's normal operations. I realize

[b]I was actually fairly familiar with the system as I had been asked to audit it and concluded that deal between the creator of the system and the firm was pretty asymmetric in nature.

now that this was a global "instant messaging" system and that it was adopted "virally" throughout the firm, although we were many years from that term being used to in the context of computer networks. I'm kind of proud of it, although I never received any official credit or acknowledgement for creating it.

1.4.3. *Statistical Arbitrage*

After working on Convertible Bond Arbitrage for Sutesh, Jaipal and I started building a statistical arbitrage business, with Michael Feldshuh who had joined Morgan Stanley from the massively successful hedge fund D.E. Shaw. This company was founded by David Shaw who had previously worked at Morgan Stanley in the A.P.T., or Advanced Pair Trading, group. Michael referred to Shaw as "the Death Star." Stat.Arb., as it is known, is a business that chooses large portfolios by ranking the stocks based on "alpha" and essentially making a very large number of low signal-to-noise ratio bets on companies. In many cases, mean-variance optimization is done to pick the portfolio with the highest *ex ante* Sharpe Ratio, and several notable groups including that run by Peter Muller in New York, as well as D.E. Shaw itself, and Princeton–Newport Partners, run by Ed Thorp, were making a lot of money in this business.

The Sharpe Ratio is a measure of the risk-adjusted returns of a portfolio, and numerically it is the expected return (minus a risk-free-rate) divided by the expected standard deviation of returns. Operationally it is very similar to the Z-scores and t-statistics that I was familiar with from statistical estimation in experimental physics. Stat.Arb., done as well as the best, held out the promise of essentially riskless returns. A perpetual motion machine for money.

Peter Muller had apparently persuaded Vikram Pandit, who was head of the Global Equity Derivatives unit and would go on to be C.E.O. of Citigroup, to shut down all the disparate systematic trading units throughout the firm and concentrate their resources in New York. In addition, as the Warrants desk was being shut down, Jaipal and I needed a place to work. Derek came to me and said I would need to move to New York for "probably a few months." I was very keen to do this, and looking forward to a flush ex-pat lifestyle in corporate apartments and other amenities. Peter wanted his existing team to interview us, and so we were shipped off to New York by plane.

We drove to the airport with Vikram, where he explained that Peter didn't share any of his secrets with Morgan Stanley's management and they wanted to know what was going on. Our job would be to find out that, and they would check in with us from time to time. When Peter interviewed me, I remember him saying that "he saw a reason to hire me, but not Jaipal, so why should he take both of us?" He probably asked Jaipal the same question about me, he had a tendency to do things like that. My mother remarked that I was "probably going to meet a blond American and she'd never see me again." The former part of that turned out to be true.

1.4.4. *Process Driven Trading*

When I joined P.D.T. in 1996, the rift between Vikram and Peter had apparently been healed over in the six or seven odd months it took to get an immigration visa. I was an "L1-B," which is an intracompany transferee. I did not get the ex-pat lifestyle I was looking for, because somebody decided to hire me as a "local" exactly as if I had been recruited from Brooklyn and not from three thousand miles away. Essentially I was just scooped up and dropped into a foreign country with zero support and I wasn't particularly happy. Finding socializing quite difficult, I wasn't the kind of person who would just go out into bars and meet people on a Saturday night. Instead, I would have a drink at home.

P.D.T. at the time was just starting to become quite successful, and comprised Peter himself, Kim Elsesser, who had joined with Peter to set up the group, Mike Reed who ran "Japan" and execution operations, Jason Todd and Frank Buquicchio who created the technology. Few people knew how to pronounce Frank's last name, and we frequently had to explain it to visitors. Steve Geyer was my office mate and the sys.admin., Amy Wong was building a "Fundamental" system and Davilyn Tabb was executing futures trades to hedge the Stat.Arb. book that was created by the algorithms developed by Shakhil Ahmed and Ken Nickerson. Nickerson, who had been at Princeton with Peter, was the lead developer of the systems that made money, which were called "Midas" and "O.T.C." Midas traded the NYSE, and the other system the NASDAQ, or "over the counter" stocks as they were still known at that time. There was also a crew of consultants from various academic fields, including computer science, finance, and operations research, all building systems and all of us operating in isolation, with Peter sitting in the middle controlling the information flow.

After working for Sutesh, who was open, intellectually curious and cultured, Peter was quite a contrast. To me he seemed petty, imperious, and jealous. Every week was dominated by a "strategy review" meeting in which he would tear down our work. He really did have a very good intellectual grasp of the business, having run the research team at Barra prior to being hired into Morgan Stanley by Derek, but did not spend much time teaching us what to do — or at least not me. I would say that Peter's success is entirely down to his intelligence but, at least based on my experiences, he was a horrible manager and I wanted to leave pretty much as soon as I got there.

When P.D.T. was really humming it was an amazing machine but, since I was made responsible for trading systems based on futures and non-equity options, I was mostly a bystander to that experience. The Stat.Arb. systems would make between 1 and 3 million dollars a day, every day from 1996 to 2000 when I left, with only a handful of down days per year. It was like nothing I had ever seen before. My systems were exposed to much more systematic risk and the profit and loss (P/L) curves consequently way more volatile. I learned a lot and met some good people, such as Mike, Jason and Jaipal who are still good friends, but personally I wanted to leave and, after my L1-B and then L1-A visas had expired and Morgan Stanley was working on getting me a green card, I told Peter that. What happened next, I've already explained.

The Quant who didn't hit Enter: When I joined P.D.T., Mike Reed was one of the people I got on best with. His first words to me were "Aren't you glad you're now in America?" but, in general, we shared the same outlook around life and our jobs, and we both wished Peter was a better person. Unlike Shakhil, who liked to have the last word in every conversation and would do things like lecture me on the defects of the British state educational system — the system under which I got to Oxford, and through which I became his peer — we got on well and shared plenty of time together.

One day, very early into my tenure, Mike asked if I could cover for him running "Japan" as he had to wait at his apartment for something. This system ran during the evenings, due to the time-zone mismatch. Under the rules of the time, program trades, which meant large lists of trades sent to an exchange and *not just* computer generated trades, could be entered automatically into the systems of the Tokyo Stock Exchange but required a "manual approval" step to be executed. Mike explained that all I had to do was sit at his workstation and, when it asked "Do you want to trade?" in a terminal window respond by "hitting Y." I agreed.

I normally wrapped up at around 5:30 to 6 p.m., and by the time the system was ready to trade at 7:30 p.m., everybody had gone. Sure enough, the scrolling text stopped, the question was asked, and I pushed the "Y" button on the Sun Sparc 20 workstation he was using. Nothing happened! I tried a few more times. The screen displayed

```
Do you want to trade? YYY_
```

Now this was a stat.arb. system that was long around ¥10 Billion of stock and short around ¥10 billion of stock. The gross risk was about $250 million and I wasn't about to go fooling around with that. I called Mike on his cell phone and he told me "don't worry, I'm almost there." In 5 minutes he arrived, looked at the screen, and hit `ENTER`. The system proceeded to send its orders, now around half an hour late, to the exchange.

This story ended up in Scott Patterson's book *The Quants* [112], without attribution to the involved parties. It's fun to wonder about the nerds that made such a foolish mistake, but I always take it as a lesson to use precise language. If Mike had said "enter Y" rather than "hit Y," the keystrokes I would have entered would have been `Y-ENTER` not just `Y` alone, and everything would have worked first time!

Return on Equity: One of the things senior management asked us to do in 1999 was compute the return on equity of our businesses. As futures trading is very capital efficient, if you are successful you should have a high R.O.E. Mine turned out to be around 85%. This told Morgan's managers how much money they got for their invested capital, but you could turn the numbers upside down and work out how much capital you needed to generate a given income. In 1998, I had been paid $500,000 and $350,000 in 1999, as we had a loss associated with the market volatility connected to the failure of the Long-Term Capital Management hedge fund. I was living pretty nicely on that income and it turned out I did have sufficient capital to make a go of things myself. With the support of Elizabeth, rather than leaving for another firm I decided to set up my own shop.

Decoding Jim Simons: In the late 1990s, Jim Simons' hedge fund *Renaissance Technologies* was very well known in the "hyper-quant" investment world I occupied but not elsewhere. I had been introduced to Jim via one of Elizabeth's friends, and sat next to his wife Marilyn at a birthday dinner. She encouraged me to seek him out and talk about my Grandmother's experiences at Bletchley Park. Jim had worked as a codebreaker for the N.S.A., and was interested.

Toward the end of my time at P.D.T., I was invited to *Rentech*'s building in Long Island to give a seminar to his team of quants and interview with his staff. I wasn't interested in a job, I was more looking for seed capital for the fund I intended to launch, but I jumped at the opportunity.

I gave a talk on simulating execution microstructure in futures markets, and using this work to understand how "slippage," which is the difference between the price at which you decided to trade and the price you executed at, was a function of volatility. After the talk I spent some time with Jim in his office, and then he offered to give me a ride back to Manhattan in his Lincoln Town Car.

In his office was a green blackboard on which somebody had drawn the diagram shown in Figure 1.5. For years afterwards, as Jim's success became more public, I would wonder what secrets were embedded in that simple diagram! I initially suspected that it was the

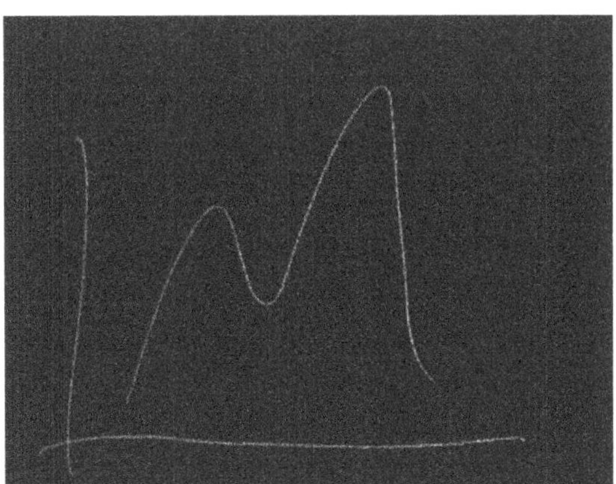

Figure 1.5: Sketch from Jim Simons' office, circa 1999, reproduced from memory.

distribution of *prices* of a security, which would represent the *wrong* way to analyze the markets from the perspective of P.D.T. and those trained by Peter Muller. We always worked with returns or, in the case of my work, rate changes.

Later on, when I spent some time working on statistical Natural Language Processing (N.L.P.) as it is known, I learned that *Hidden Markov Models* were used by codebreakers to model language as a sequence of words. This is a system in which an observed process is controlled by a hidden or "state space" model, which randomly switches its character from time-to-time, and which Jaipal and I had often talked about it being a better description of financial markets than the simple linear models we used at P.D.T. over time, I became convinced that this sketch was of the unconditional distribution observed from such a system, which Jim had likely been explaining to another office visitor. This seems to be confirmed upon reading Greg Zuckerman's book about Renaissance, *The Man who Solved the Market* [142].

The other thing I remember from my *one-on-one* time with Jim was what he said when we were driving in his car. He asked me what I was working on "at the moment" and I observed that my system sometimes worked and sometimes didn't and I was trying to figure out whether I could predict which state it was in and adjust my risk exposure accordingly. His reply was

> *Sometimes it's just random.* — Jim Simons, 1999 [124]

At the time I thought that this could be parsed to mean that performance is not smooth and that I should not worry about such "meta-analysis." This is very true, and advice worth remembering by any trader. On any given day, the most likely driver of your P/L is not you but random chance. It could have been a calculated remark to throw me off the right track (although I don't personally believe this), as Peter Muller might have done. Finally, it can also be viewed as the parsing of my experience in terms of a Hidden Markov Model, which does randomly change its state. Perhaps it's a little overwrought to dwell on such fragments, but there is a lesson here. Sometimes you don't have the skills to analyze the data you encounter — but it's always worth investing in them so that the next time you do.

1.5. Self Employed

I left Morgan Stanley in 2000, the day after my bonus for 1999 cleared (January 2nd) as a newly married man itching to set up a hedge fund, and immediately did so, registering myself as a Commodity Trading Advisor (C.T.A.), and getting an office in the Garment district of New York. I built systems to trade financial futures, using Lehman Brothers as my broker and experienced the automation of the futures market first hand. When I started orders were placed person to person by telephone, and I read them out from a print-out generated by the computer. That then became sending orders by fax and then by email and finally direct market access, computer to computer. I traded from my office, from home, from the lobby of the Four Seasons hotel in Chicago, and from various apartments in New York City. I was long Eurodollar Futures on 9/11 and flat during the blackout of the East Coast a year later. In my first year I cleared a few $100,000, in the second year 1 million, but in the third I made 5 million dollars which changed everything. However, the market anomaly I had found stopped working and, after moving from strategy to strategy, by the time the 2008 financial crisis came along I had a family of three children and was taking too much risk for everybody to be happy. I decided to stop trading my own capital.

1.6. Professional Data Science

1.6.1. *Consulting*

Winding up my own businesses in 2009, I needed something to do. Around this time the press had started talking about "data science," as companies like Google, Facebook, and Amazon were showing large profits from data driven businesses. Netflix had created a stir with *The Netflix Prize*, a million dollar competition awarded to the team that could improve their algorithms.

I spent a few years still working as a "quant," building alphas (meaning predictive models for prices) as a consultant and working with partners in a couple of startup hedge fund ventures. But by 2011, I had become disenchanted with finance and I decided to rebrand myself as a "data scientist" — after all, predictive analytics based on data generated by humans and recorded by machines was something I'd been doing for my entire professional career. I had been a data scientist before the term was coined.

I worked as a consultant to an internet marketing business based in Long Island. This was incredibly useful to me. I massively widened my skill sets, adopted new technologies such as the programming languages R and Python, and entered new fields such as demographics and quantitative geography. It was an essential learning experience, but the commute was unbelievable, even when done just 1 day a week, and I was not getting paid enough to cover decent health insurance. When Bloomberg LP called me up to ask whether I would be interested in leading their data science efforts I lept at the opportunity.

1.6.2. *Bloomberg*

Bloomberg was great. The people really seemed to like me and I had some great opportunities. Around once a month, it seemed, I was giving a presentation to a senior board member such as Peter Grauer, Tom Secunda or Mike Bloomberg himself. Mike was a very impressive person, with strong opinions, and at one time we spent around 20 minutes in a meeting arguing about correlation and causality. Eventually he said "we have to move on," but then pointed directly at me and stated "I want you to follow up with me on this later." This resulted in me giving Mike Bloomberg what was essentially a tutorial on time-series analysis, and he was very interested and asked very relevant questions. Once he got the hang of what I was explaining (Granger Causality), he was really on the ball. I was very impressed.

I always tell everyone that all of the cliches you read about Bloomberg are true. It is a firm with no private offices, and with the elevators disabled strategically to make you walk up and down staircases and interact with people. There are fish tanks filled with colorful tropical fish on every floor, and free food all over the place. This includes plenty of soda, despite Mike's known disenthusiasm for large cups of it. When I was talking to him, explaining the technicalities of information and forecasting skill, he turned to the side and yelled "Melissa, do you have any crackers?" His assistant showed up, and dumped a handful of the small packages of saltine crackers you get with chicken soup in a New York diner onto the table. There were about five of us there, including my boss's boss, and he scattered the packages around the table as if we were going to chow down on

Mike's crackers. About 5 minutes later, he called out again "Melissa, do you have any jams or jellies?" Melissa returned, with a handful of the packages of grape jelly that you get with your toast at breakfast in a New York diner. As I continued to explain causality theory, he buttered his saltine crackers with grape jelly and they splintered into pieces.

1.6.3. *Artificial Intelligence*

I am writing this in an era where extravagant claims have been made about "artificial intelligence" (A.I.) and many firms insist they are deploying A.I. in their day-to-day operations. I know from personal experience that his is absolutely not true and that most the claims that they are doing any kind of advanced analytics is simply marketing spin. Due to the changes to the industry following the 2008 financial crisis, the firms that are prospering are ones that have the largest balance sheets and they succeed not by deploying that capital "intelligently" but by merely having the capital to deploy. Firms that, in the 1990s, were full of intelligent people doing advanced analytics have replaced their staff with program management bureaucrats and entry level employees whose idea of research work is cutting and pasting other peoples' code together. I have encountered more fools and charlatans at advanced levels in companies over the past few years than at any point in the last 20.

To me intelligence means creativity, the ability to invent solutions by abstraction, and to create new things. The domain of outcomes in problems tackled by machine learning algorithms is restricted to simple and well explored spaces. Even the current "gold standard" for machine intelligence, the *AlphaGo* system developed by Google is solving a problem with a binary outcome — either one or other of the players will win. The fact that the number of paths to those outcomes is very large doesn't replace the fact that the space of outcomes is tiny. Compare that to the physical world we live in, where the space of outcomes of the interactions of human beings and physical systems is likely immeasurably large. Machine learning algorithms cannot extrapolate, they can only interpolate, or do brute force enumeration of combinatorial problems that real people tire from. To extrapolate you need to build a model of the universe, which is exactly what human intelligence does. Humans build models, current machines do not. They optimize models that are given to them exogenously. They optimize them very well, and very quickly, but they do not invent them.

In his book, *Deep Thinking*, Garry Kasparov wrote about the realization that Chess was winnable not by artificially intelligent machines but computers that were dumb but much faster than human beings and so could construct better searches of the space of future moves rather than having to invent new strategies [79]. In fact the operation of winning a chess game requires no intelligence whatsoever, just brute force computational scale. Similarly, we seem to be learning that the operation of driving a car also does not require intelligence. Can we get a computer to drive a car? Yes. Can we get a computer to invent a new form of transport? I think we are a very long way from that.

In addition, I think the concept of "Strong A.I." — that when sufficiently large numbers of artificial neural elements are connected together then general intelligence will spontaneously emerge from the machine — is staggeringly naive and full of hubris. We don't yet truly understand human intelligence, or dog intelligence, or even goldfish intelligence. Why would we think that superintelligence is just around the corner?

1.6.4. *Data Science is Actually Science*

There has been a radical transformation to data processing technologies over the past 20 years. My iPhone has more memory (512 GB) than any computer I ever used academically. The first computer I used extensively was a VIC-20, with just five kilobytes of RAM. The internet has radically changed access to code and information, and more and more businesses are learning about the values of data driven reasoning.

However, we have begin to have a tendency to think of research work as a process in which people compile lists of technologies without understanding them. To use technologies because they are there not because they are the right tool to solve the job, to think that coding is basically about downloading packages from the internet, and to generally dismiss a scientific approach to analysis.

We invented science not because we could, but because we needed to. Because things like confounding variables and causality are real issues that need to be dealt with. Neither of those issues have been eliminated with faster computers. As Ronald Fisher wrote "designing an experiment is like gambling with the devil" [10]. Both "A.I." and machine learning are predictive algorithms where the prediction is a deterministic function of the current inputs and a training set. That is no different to the problems of statistical inference dating from a century ago. Now we use nonlinear non-parametric methods, and often they do better than traditional ones, but the general framework of inference, causality and the design of experiments still applies.

On that basis, the way you see me work[c] in this empirical discipline will follow a script that will become familiar:

(i) First, we will talk about the data, and when it is directly visible, *look at the data.* Data science begins and ends with data, and you must be familiar with it.

(ii) Second, we will construct a predictive model to test. This may be based on a theory, or an observation, but it will be a formula that expresses a description of how the data generating process we are studying operates — and it will include a random stimulus, or "innovation" in the language of time series analysis, that is drawn from a specified probability distribution.

(iii) This allows us to establish all three of:

  (a) in the Fisherian manner, a well defined, but hopefully reasonable, "Null hypothesis" [42];
  (b) a method for estimating any free parameters (if required); and,
  (c) a method for testing whether the data supports the Null hypothesis.

(iv) The Null hypothesis will be tested by computing a test statistic, say $\hat{X}$, and computing the probability of measuring a larger value of the test statistic by chance if the Null hypothesis is true. This value, $\Pr(X > \hat{X})$, is the so-called p value, which is the probability of making the Type I Error of rejecting the Null

[c]You will also notice a preference for using Greek letters for variables. That is the legacy of an Oxford education. In addition I use the standard notations $\hat{x}$ to mean "the estimated value of x" and $\bar{x}$ to mean "the average of observed values of x."

hypothesis when it is true. This is also called the "false positive rate." The value of $\hat{X}$ alone is worthless without this value.

(v) If relevant, the distributional assumptions underlying the computation of the p value will be validated.

(vi) If possible, and because many time-series in finance do seem to have properties that are confounded by time itself, we will also examine how the estimates vary through time. If they are consistent with each other, we will accept that they are "constant," but not if otherwise.

This latter step, (vi), is a mistake that is very easy to make and one we all make all the time (I did yesterday). It seems that financial and economic time series are almost *designed* to lead the analyst down this path. If, for example, $a_t = a_{t-1} + \varepsilon_t$ and $b_t = b_{t-1} + \eta_t$, where a_t and b_t are two observed time-series and ε_t and η_t are both *independent sequences of random numbers*, then we will find we can perform a linear regression of a_t onto b_t with apparently significant results much of the time. The result is true of the past data, but it has no predictive value. This is something I demonstrated personally to Michael Bloomberg, it demonstrates not that statistics doesn't work but that time series analysis is difficult.

This methodology, the Scientific Method, is well established and well researched. It represents a valid and useful tool for investigators. Online, there is much "Sturm und Drang" around statistical hypothesis testing and "p hacking." This is because many results have been published when one of the following is true:

(i) the distributional assumptions are absolutely not valid;

(ii) much undocumented research has been carried out before finding a result "worthy of reporting" is found (this is p-hacking); or,

(iii) the *critical values*, α_{crit}, against which p is judged are frankly just too small. A critical value of 0.05 means that a Type I Error will occur in one of every twenty reported results — no physical scientist would change their standard model of the universe under such marginal evidence, and that also assumes the result has not been hacked.

Just because bad science has been executed in the past, and will be in the future, does not mean that science is not relevant to the examination of empirical data and the associated data generating processes. Science is used because it works. An employee of mine at J.P. Morgan once stated, in response to me doubting the veracity of his model:

> *In machine learning these methods aren't relevant.* — [106]

I believe strongly that this is a self-serving falsehood, designed to promote careers over truths. Ultimately, I believe in science, even in business.

1.6.5. *Statistics and the Multiverse*

Proponents of harsh Bayesian Statistics may object to how I describe data. They insist on a probability being only a metric of belief and not a measure of frequency of random events — essentially denying the existence of randomness. They say that the events that unfold are all certain, it's just that we don't know what they will be, and the laws of probability allow us to judge the likely outcomes. That the concept of confidence intervals representing the proportion of experiments in which a true value of a parameter is found to be within the stated range *when the experiment is repeated multiple times in an ensemble of parallel universes* is a fantasy.

As a student of Quantum Mechanics, the concept of fundamental randomness is not alien. It is a tool that apparently predicts the outcomes of experiments extremely accurately and repeatably. Physical scientists also know that experiments *are* independently repeatable, both sequentially and in parallel, in the one Universe we experience and that the calculus of confidence intervals works very well in describing their results. When I was an undergraduate the LEP Experiment at CERN was able to strongly make statements about the number of neutrino families by measuring the "cross-section," which is a kind of normalized reaction rate, for reactions that produced the Z_0 particle [101]. These measurements are decorated with error bars computed as confidence intervals from statistical theory and the curve passes through them exactly as we would expected it to. In the world of physics the mapping between probabilities and observed rates of events in experiments is very sound. Just like Quantum Mechanics, we might find the underlying message of the theory too *emotionally* difficult but it is also very hard to deny its utility.

Even without having to enter the esoteric world of elementary particles, though, it is easy to discover venues in which statistics and probability work together as expected in repeatable trials. In horse racing is it easy to find repeatable experiments that demonstrate that betting odds, which are probabilistic degrees of *belief*, accurately map into the *rates* at which horses are observed to win races. This is a subject that has been *extensively* studied, for example in the work of Bill Ziemba [68] with Hausch and others.

1.6.6. *We Learn as We Work*

My toolkit of of methods is much larger than it was when I emerged from Oxford in 1994. I learned to use the tools I needed to tackle problems that arose while working on data. Because I am not writing a text book, I am not going to present a comprehensive inventory of analytical methods for data science. I am going to mention the methods I needed to learn to tackle the data and analyzes I describe. It is my hope that readers will notice these developments and pursue some of them outside of my analytical narrative, in more instructional works. I will note the books that I have used, or papers I have read, but the bibliography will not be as large as that found in a traditional academic paper, where the purpose is to demonstrate that the authors are well read. I hope you will look at some of these references because they are interesting to read.

Chapter 2

Financial Data

2.1. Modeling Asset Prices as Stochastic Processes

2.1.1. *Geometric Brownian Motion*

This chapter is mostly about my investigations into the properties of financial and economic time-series. A common theme that runs through this work is that the assumptions behind continuous time finance, which are that asset prices follow Normal diffusion processes, are not supported by the data. The canonical process for stock prices is

$$\frac{dS}{S} = \mu\, dt + \sigma\, dX, \tag{2.1}$$

where dX is a Wiener Process. This is a fundamental mathematical object that can be thought of as the limit of a random variable $\delta X \sim N(0, \delta t)$ as $\delta t \to 0$. Since modern mathematics doesn't deal with infinitesimals, it is actually defined in terms of Ito Calculus which talks only about the value of the integral of the process over a finite interval, and requires that *this* be lognormally distributed. The notation $N(\mu, \sigma^2)$ indicates a Normal distribution with a mean of μ and a variance of σ^2. This probability density has the form

$$N(\mu, \sigma^2)\colon f(x|\mu, \sigma) = \frac{e^{-\frac{(x-\mu)^2}{2\sigma^2}}}{\sqrt{2\pi}\sigma}. \tag{2.2}$$

Such a process generates a lognormal distribution[a] for stock prices and is usually termed a "geometric Brownian motion." It represents stock prices as unpredictable random walks about a long-term growth and interval returns as normally distributed in a manner where the mean and variance both scale linearly with the temporal extent of the interval. It assumes that the interval is infinitely divisible and that the process is never constant in expectation.

This type of model is actually is a very good model for genuine Brownian motion, which models the motions of macroscopic objects like pollen grains under the impact of the atoms or molecules of a liquid or gas, and was one of Einstein's discoveries published in his "Miraculous Year" of 1905 [28]. Pollen grains range in size from around $1\,\mu$m to 0.1 mm, but most are typically about $20\,\mu$m (20×10^{-6}m). Water molecules, on the other hand, are around 100 pm (10^{-10} m) in size. If a water molecule were to randomly walk in steps roughly equal to its own size, it would take around 200,000 steps for it to travel the diameter of a pollen grain. So the motions of the water molecule, when measured on the scale established by the pollen grain, are reasonably well modeled by such a *stochastic process.*

On the other hand, this is not such good model for stocks. Its principal attraction seems to be that it gives rise to easy mathematics, not empirical accuracy. The distribution of their daily returns is distinctly non-Normal, and they become less so as the time-scale is reduced from daily to intraday and then tick-by-tick. The reason why we use the Normal distribution to model the infinitesimal returns is because the Central Limit Theorem makes it pointless to do anything else. If δX is drawn from *any* distribution for which the mean and variance exist, then their sum will become progressively closer the Normal as more and more of them are added together, and the limiting process we are considering involves a sum of an infinite number of infinitesimally small random variables — the exact situation that

[a]The reason why it is a *log* Normal distribution and not a regular Normal distribution is because it is written in terms of $dS/S = d(\ln S)$. This produces an non-negative variable that exhibits exponential growth and for which the standard deviation of interval price changes scales with the magnitude of the price at the beginning of the interval. The associated returns, dS/S, are Normally distributed.

the CLT models. That is, whatever the distribution of the underlying infinitesimal impulses that a finite change in prices is built out of, the macroscopic sum (product) of them must follow the Normal (or lognormal) distribution. This model was proposed by Bachelier [3] in 1900, and brought to prominence in the work of Robert C. Merton [98] leading to the development of the Black–Scholes option pricing model [8].

2.1.2. *Randomness in Finance*

Many critics of this work focus their ire on the idea that price changes, or returns, are modeled as "random" events. They argue that this is non-sensical, that stock prices change for real reasons, from the pressure of supply and demand during the trading day, and not because somebody is playing dice with the stock market.

I don't have a problem with that idea, which I feel stems from in incorrect association of "random" with "meaningless." To me "random" means "unpredictable from currently available information" and that is something that, with my training in Quantum Mechanics which models the universe as driven by the fundamentally random behaviours of elementary particles, doesn't seem a problem at all. In almost all of the work I describe here, I will propose models for data generating processes that contain some mixture of deterministic, conditionally random, and entirely random elements.

A concrete way to describe this is in terms of the hierarchies of information sets. Suppose $\mathcal{I}_s$ is the set that contains absolutely everything that is known about the universe at time s, and I seek to predict some measure of the universe at a later time t (i.e. $s < t$). My predictive function is $\alpha(\mathcal{I}_s)$ and what I seek to predict is $m(\mathcal{I}_t)$. If the prediction is useful then it should be coincide with the expected value of the stochastic quantity $m(\mathcal{I}_t)$. Therefore, $\alpha(\mathcal{I}_s) = E[m(\mathcal{I}_t)|\mathcal{I}_s]$, which is sometimes written $E_s[m(\mathcal{I}_t)]$. We will restrict ourselves to such "useful" functions.

Clearly the future information set is not smaller than the past one as no information can be destroyed, which we write as $\mathcal{I}_s \subseteq \mathcal{I}_t$. Also the incremental information, $\Delta\mathcal{I}_t = \mathcal{I}_t \setminus \mathcal{I}_s$, is not deterministic. This must be so, because any deterministic part of $\Delta\mathcal{I}_t$ would be knowable at time s and so would already be part of $\mathcal{I}_s$ by definition.

By iteration, any deterministic information must therefore have existed at the beginning of time,[b] and so be equal to $\mathcal{I}_0$.

2.1.3. *The Golden Rule of Prediction*

The required Normality of the world of continuous time finance, though, just doesn't seem to have much support in actual data and the fact that a global market can be internally self-consistent pricing off such a model doesn't, in fact, mean that it is right. Only examining the data can tell us that, and it does not appear to be doing so! I will mostly not be assuming that the random elements of data generating processes are Normally distributed and will only do so when there is no other choice.

However, certain very useful techniques are only viable with what are called "stable" probability distributions, meaning those for which the convolution with themselves generates the same distribution, i.e.

$$\int f(s)f(t-s)\,ds \propto f(t) \quad \text{or} \quad f * f = f, \tag{2.3}$$

for some probability density function f. The Normal distribution is the only distribution with a finite variance that has this property, which is why the distributions under the Central Limit Theorem converge to the Normal.

You might argue that I am trying to have it both ways here, but I assert that I am not. Since my job is to build predictive models for yet to be observed data, I am actually free to do *absolutely anything I want* with causally valid data to create my prediction. But I am absolutely not allowed to take any liberties with evaluating predictions made with actual future data. This I call *The Golden Rule of Prediction.*

2.1.4. *Linear Additive Noise*

Since $\Delta\mathcal{I}_t$ as defined in Section 2.1.2 is stochastic, it must follow that $m(\mathcal{I}_t)$ contain some stochastic element. One construction that

[b]One could be cheeky here, and call $\mathcal{I}_0$ God (iff $\mathcal{I}_0 \neq \emptyset$).

satisfies all of our conditions is the Linear Additive Noise model[c]

$$m(\mathcal{I}_t) = \alpha(\mathcal{I}_s) + \varepsilon_t, \tag{2.4}$$

where ε_t is random with mean zero and independent of $\mathcal{I}_s$. In the universe we've described, there is only one way to evaluate the accuracy of the predictive function, $\alpha(\mathcal{I}_t)$, and that is through the methods and disciplines of mathematical statistics, as first stated by Fisher. Many of these were explicitly designed for an expression like Equation (2.4). None of the above cares whether you are using linear regression, machine learning, "A.I.," or just plain guessing, to discover α — you get to chose that however you want, but we follow the rules when it comes to measuring your forecasting skill and evaluating the significance of your predictions.

To return to the issue of the behaviour of stock prices and option pricing theory, I'm saying that traders can feel free to use the Merton–Black–Scholes framework to value options if they like, but even if they are successful in that practice we have to look at the actual evidence the universe provides to use to evaluate whether the *hypothesis* that financial prices follow a geometric Brownian motion is accurate. The latter does not follow from the former.

2.2. Abnormality of Financial Distributions

In the prior section, I have asserted many times that the data does not support the idea that stock market returns are Normally distributed. Let's begin our work by looking at the data.

2.2.1. *Calendars and Returns*

In the following we're going to look at daily returns, meaning:

$$r_t = \frac{S_t}{S_{t-1}} - 1, \tag{2.5}$$

often expressed in percent.

[c]The Multiplicative Noise Model $m(\mathcal{I}_t) = \alpha(\mathcal{I}_s)\varepsilon_t$ also works, where ε_t is positive with mean 1.

The t in S_t, is a sequential label indicating the trading day number, and this calculation skips over holidays, weekends, and other exchange closings. After taking account of US holidays, there are approximately 252 business days in a US year and approximately 40 working weeks. Note that a calendar year contains either 52 or 53 weeks and either 365 or 366 days. The latter is due to leap years, and is familiar to everybody, but the former is because years don't necessarily start on the first day of a week, and so years can have fractional "stub" weeks at the beginning and the end. When dealing with financial data over long horizons it's important to be precise about such "day counting" issues, or you will readily make data processing errors.

When data is "daily," yet may refer to something that changes intraday, it is normal practice to assume that we are referring to the value at the end of the day — which in finance will be some kind of "official closing value." US stock markets have historically closed at 4 p.m. New York time, and this is the value referred to. Trading which occurs after the close will be booked to the following business day. There may also be an official "open" of the market, but that has become less important as trading has moved from open outcry auctions to electronic venues. Daily index data is typically computed from these official closes, and it is important to know if these represent actual transaction prices or some kind of average. When modeling daily data, one must be aware that you cannot trade on the closing price and tomorrow's opening price might be substantially different. Many quants don't seem to realize that you can trade just before the close without making too large of an error, thus a system that works on daily data isn't necessarily required to execute its trade the next day. The idea that you must trade with the same code you developed a system with is, I think, a false one. Why wait a day to trade a system on tomorrow's close when you could trade at 3:55 p.m. effortlessly?

Fiscal periods are often expressed with a label such as "2020 $Q1$," meaning the first quarter of fiscal year 2020. It is important when dealing with accounting data[d] to know that this means the fiscal year *ending* in 2020. Retailing companies often have their fiscal years

[d]Also referred to as "fundamental" data or "reference" data.

ending in January, so for such a company this period would represent data from 2019. This may be confusing and it is important to get it right! It is very important to know that not all companies end their fiscal years on the same date.

2.2.2. *Martingales and Markov Processes*

In time-series analysis, the study of Markov Processes is a huge field. A Markov Process has the property that the state of a system in period t is determined solely by the state of that system at time $t-1$ (and a stochastic element). Anything that can be written:

$$a_t = f(a_{t-1}) + \varepsilon_t, \tag{2.6}$$

where the various $\{\varepsilon_t\}$ are independent of each other, is a Markov Process. Thus, Equation (2.1) is a Markov Process.

A "Martingale" is a stochastic process where the expected future value at any given time is equal to the value at that time. A Markov Process may be a Martingale.

$$E_s[a_t] = a_s \quad \forall\, t > s. \tag{2.7}$$

Many models for financial time series assume that they satisfy this property. This does not require that $a_t = a_s$, merely that the conditional expectation of a_t evaluated at time s is equal to a_s. This is, in fact, an excellent model for stock prices. Any predictive model of the stock market should always be compared to this baseline model. It will be hard to beat.

Referring back to the Linear Additive Noise model of Equation (2.4), we see that this is a Martingale when $\alpha(\mathcal{I}_t) = m(\mathcal{I}_t)$. The Wiener Process on its own, dX, is a Markov Process and a Martingale and the Geometric Brownian Motion Process is a Markov Process and is a Martingale when the drift, μ, is zero.

2.2.3. *Daily Returns of the S&P 500 Index*

The S&P 500 Index is the gold standard against which the performance of fund managers in the United States are measured. It is "value weighted," meaning that the index is a scaled sum of the capitalization of companies and not an average share price. In the finance community, this value weighting is generally regarded as the best way to make an index but, in fact, it has several flaws:

(i) it overemphasizes the returns of the biggest stocks;
(ii) it does not represent the "average" return of the market in the sense that the average is the value to be expected when a member of the index is picked at random; and,
(iii) it does not represent the so-called "Market Portfolio" of the *Capital Asset Pricing Model*, which it is often taken to do so.

Nevertheless, it is widely followed and useful and, because stocks returns turn out to be extremely correlated cross-sectionally (meaning between themselves over the same time-frame), its errors in turn are tolerable.

Daily data is available for free from a wide variety of sources. The official index has been published since March 4, 1957. A smaller index dates back to the 1920s and S&P Indices have reconstructed an index that is equivalent to the 500 share index to those dates, but the index itself was not circulated before the 1950s. The ticker symbols *SPX*, *^SPX*, or *$SPX* are often used.

Figure 2.1 shows the daily closing values of the S&P 500 Index since its inception. You can see that it shows strong growth that, were

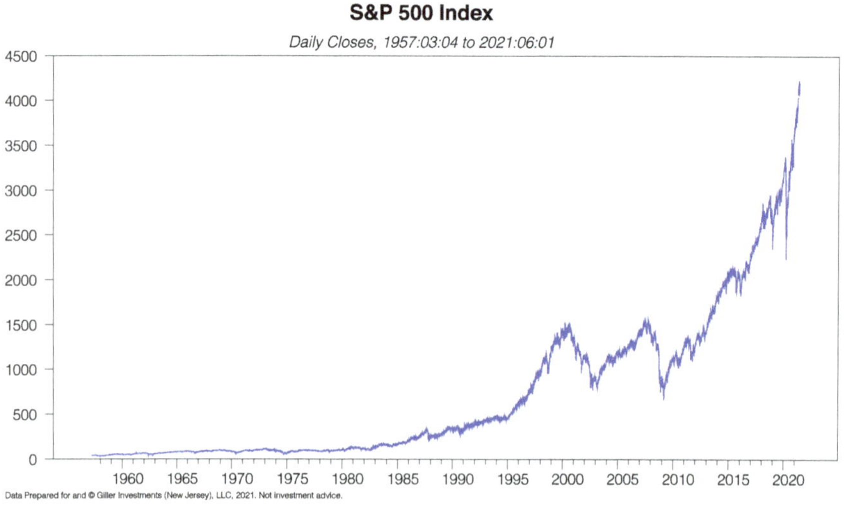

Figure 2.1: Daily closing values of the S&P 500 Index since inception.

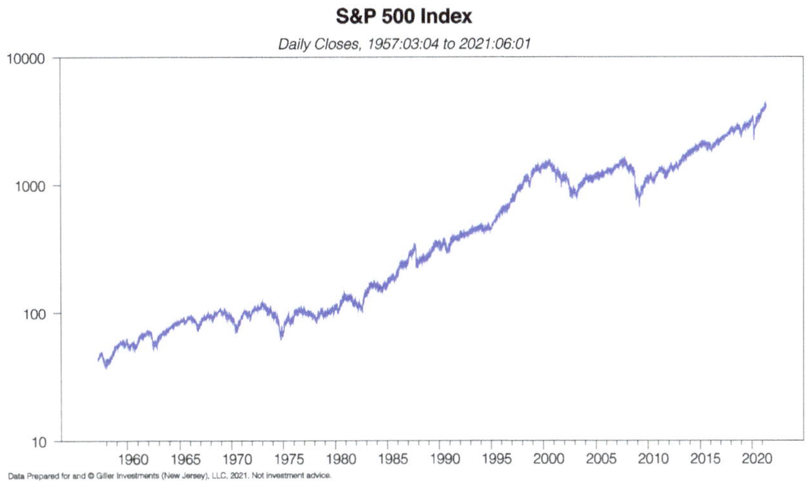

Figure 2.2: Daily closing values of the S&P 500 Index since inception with a logarithmic vertical axis.

it not for the volatility, roughly matches an exponential. This can be more clearly seen by plotting it on a logarithmic scale, which shown in Figure 2.2. That transformation delivers an approximately constant gradient over some 60 years, confirming that models featuring exponential growth are reasonable.

Figure 2.3 shows a histogram of those daily returns together with the best fitting Normal distribution curve. It is clear that the fit is incredibly bad and we cannot accept the hypothesis that the data is Normally distributed. It is my usual practice not to make such statements without referring to properly defined statistical tests, but the results here are self-evident. Ernest Rutherford, the Nobel Prize winning discoverer of the atomic nucleus, apparently said "If you need to use statistics to analyze your experiment then you should have done a better experiment" [4].

When discussing a frequency distribution such as the one observed for stock index returns, the phrase "fat tails" is often used. The statistician's description is "leptokurtosis." This data exhibits more weight in the tails than warranted (the regions in excess of 3 standard deviations from the mean), but it also exhibits a sharper peak and thinner sides. For this data, there are 16,115 observations at the time of writing. The mean is close to zero, but positive at 0.034% or 3.4 "basis points," and the standard deviation is about 1.0% per day.

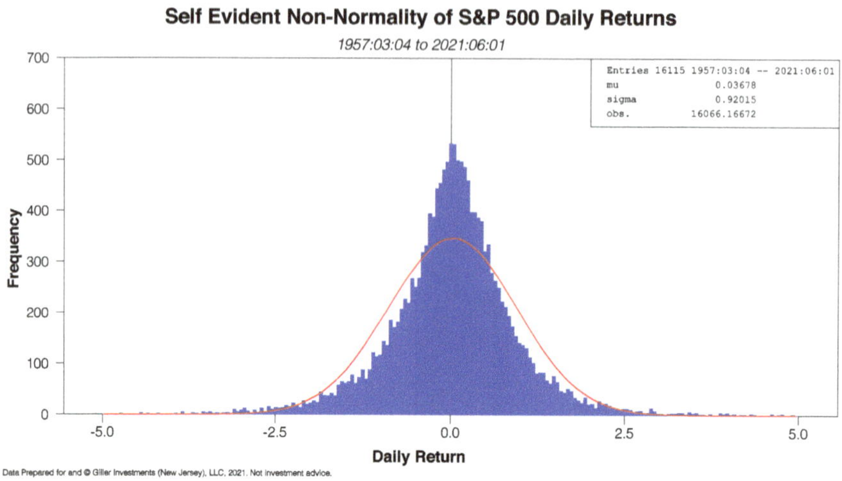

Figure 2.3: Histogram of the daily returns of the S&P 500 Index since inception. The blue bars represent the observed frequencies and the red curve is the best fitting Normal distribution, the famous "bell shaped" curve.

The skewness is -0.6 and the excess kurtosis is 21.3. Using the t-test to evaluate whether this data is consistent with having a mean of zero we find a t statistic of 4.2 which has a significance (p-value) of 0.000025. It is safe to conclude that, on any given day, the stock market is more likely to have gone up than down.[e] The departure from the Normal distribution may be assessed with the Jarque–Bera test [130], which has a statistic of 305,137 and a p value approaching zero, i.e. the data is not Normally distributed.

If not Normal, then what? For most of the history of the subject of *Quantitative Finance*, academics and practitioners would respond to these facts with an answer that can be characterized as "yes, we know, but it's not *that* bad, and what else can we do?" I feel the answer to that question is *be a better empirical scientist.* This is, in fact, a terrible fit to the data and, since the earliest work on Statistics, we have had access to a large menu of univariate distributions we could try instead of the Normal — and some do radically better jobs.

[e]Compounding this 3.4 b.p. daily return over the 252 days the market is open for an average year, the total return is 8.9% annually. This is why authors suggest investing in [118].

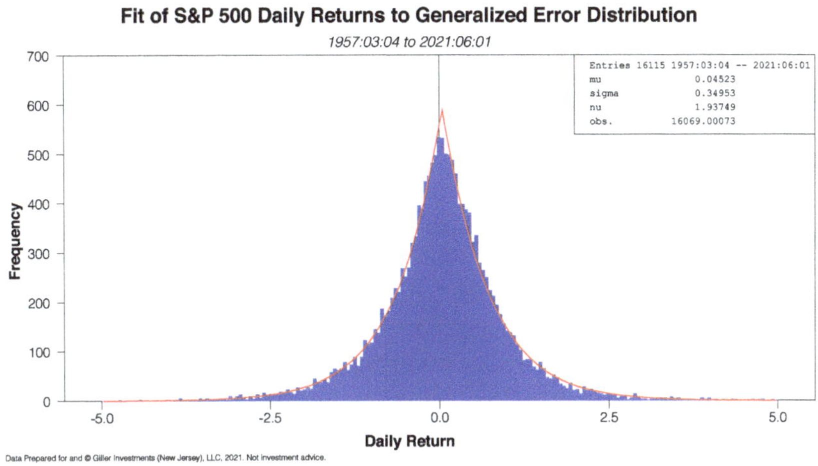

Figure 2.4: Histogram of the daily returns of the S&P 500 Index since inception. The blue bars represent the observed frequencies and the red curve is the best fitting GED curve. The parameter ν is 2κ, which is an alternate parameterization of the distribution used by the software I have.

The one I particularly like is the *Generalized Error Distribution* (GED) [49]. Figure 2.4 shows the same histogram with this curve fitted. It is plain to see that the fit is better. Much, much, better — I feel that Rutherford would approve. The probability density function, $f(x)$, for it is given by

$$\text{GED}(\mu, \sigma, \kappa) \; : \; f(x|\mu, \sigma, \kappa) = \frac{e^{-\frac{1}{2}\left|\frac{x-\mu}{\sigma}\right|^{\frac{1}{\kappa}}}}{2^{\kappa+1}\sigma\Gamma(\kappa+1)}. \tag{2.8}$$

The value of this functional form is that it smoothly deforms from the Normal itself (the case $\kappa = 1/2$) through a range of shapes including those that are leptokurtotic ($\kappa > 1/2$) and those that are the opposite, or platykurtotic ($\kappa < 1/2$). It can even take on the shape of a Uniform distribution.

2.2.4. *Temporal Invariance*

A valid criticism of the work presented in Section 2.2.3 is that I am lumping together 60 years of data. Perhaps it is unreasonable to expect the growth rate, μ, and volatility, σ, of the stock market index to have stayed the same over such a long period? After all, the 1970s and the 2020s bear little resemblance sociopolitically, as I can personally testify to. Perhaps the data is locally Normal, but not with globally constant parameters?

If that were so, one thing we know is that it is not the mean of the distribution that is creating the kurtosis we observe in the data in Figure 2.3. If $\mu \to \mu_t$, with μ_t following *some kind* of stochastic process the effect would be to blur out the distribution creating *platykurtosis*, or "thin tails." The mechanism must be one in which $\sigma \to \sigma_t$ to create the kind of distributional shape we observe.

With such a large data sample, this is pretty easy to examine. Of course, there is a test for comparing the sample variances of two groups of data and it is called the *F-test*, where the "*F*" stands for Fisher. If R_1 is a set of n_1 observations of returns that are Normally distributed with a sample variance s_1^2, and R_2 a second group, then the statistic

$$F = \frac{s_1^2}{s_2^2} \tag{2.9}$$

follows the F distribution with $(n_1 - 1, n_2 - 1)$ degrees of freedom. This test *assumes* the actual data is Normally distributed, so it is not necessarily the best test solely for constancy of variance (known as "homoskedasticity" in statistics), but we are attempting to address the hypothesis presented above.

Figure 2.5 shows the result of performing such an F-test on every pair of sequential years from 1957 to 2021. One can see that in 25 of the 64 years presented the test is a failure with a critical value of 0.05, rejecting the null hypothesis that the variances in the 2 years are equal and Normally distributed with 95% confidence. Either the data are not normal, or they are not homoskedastic, or both!

It would be nice to combine the successive F statistics for each year pair into a composite statistic that addresses the 25 failures in 64 tests, but we can't do that. The Binomial probability of getting 25 *or more* failures when the null hypothesis is true at critical value 0.05 is readily computable to be around 10^{-16}, but the tests are not independent. Consider $F_t = s_t^2/s_{t-1}^2$. Clearly F_t and F_{t-1} are negatively correlated because they both contain s_{t-1}^2 but in the former it is the denominator of the fraction and in the latter the numerator. A tactic to avoid that might be to skip every year, but now we are exposing ourselves (even more) to the charge that our arbitrary

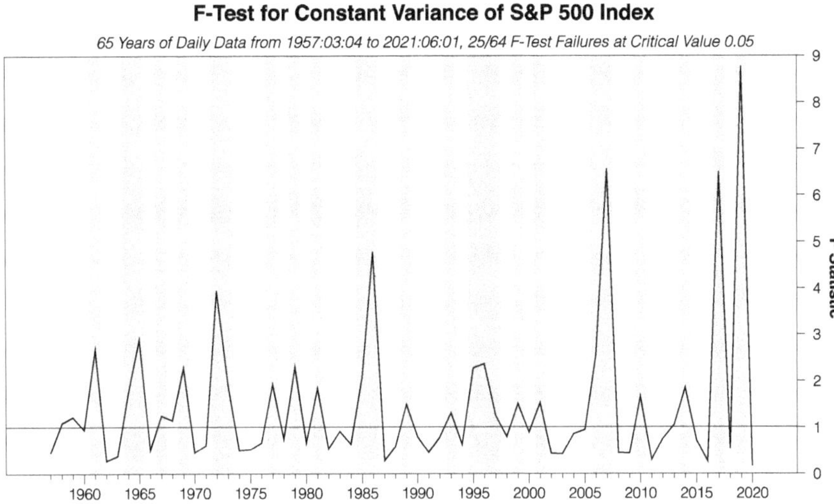

Figure 2.5: Results of a set of successive F-Tests for Normal Distributions of S&P 500 returns with Constant Variance for 1957 to 2021 inclusive. Shading indicates years which failed the test with a critical value of 0.05.

divisions of the data into different temporal regions *by year* does not match the real variance regimes the data contains.

So how can we, as Fisher said, beat the devil that is conspiring to ruin our analysis? We have to turn to a different methodology.

2.2.5. *Heteroskedasticity*

Figure 2.6 shows a time series of the daily returns of the S&P 500 Index, represented as a series of spikes. This suggests that there are episodes of higher and lower variance and that they are also quiescent periods. There appear to be some very sharp spikes, the most prominent being the Wall Street crash of 1987, and episodes of enhanced volatility appear to follow a spike and then ebb away. This suggested to Robert Engle [30] that we should consider a latent, or hidden, variance time-series that wasn't directly observable and in which today's variance was directly proportional to the prior day's variance — that it was autoregressive.

Figure 2.7 shows a scatter plot of tomorrow's daily return squared versus today's daily return squared for every pair of days in this S&P 500 daily dataset. I've plotted it with logarithmic axes to expose

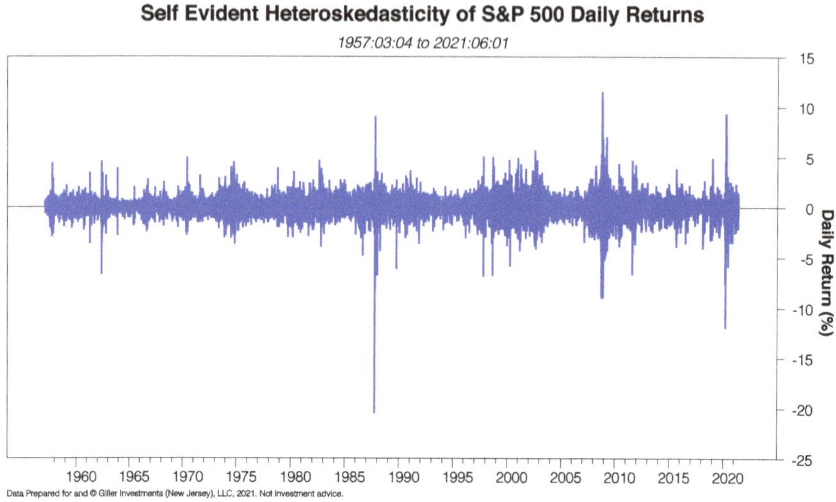

Figure 2.6: Time series of daily returns of the S&P 500 Index since inception in 1967 to date. This data appears to show episodes of higher and lower variance.

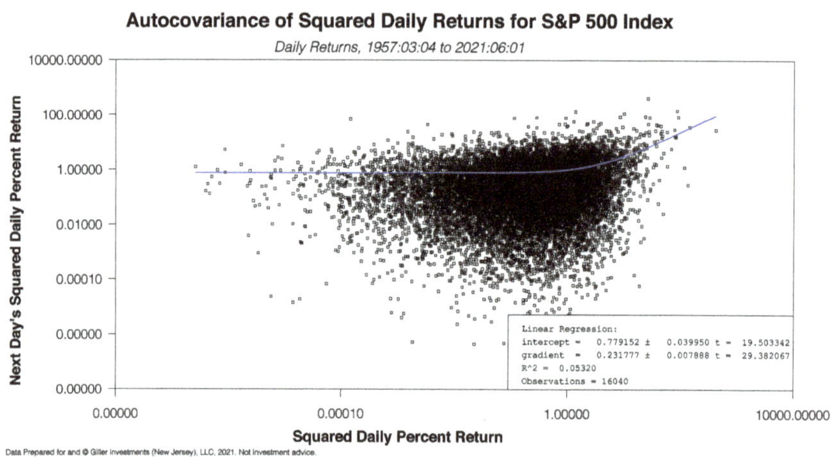

Figure 2.7: Scatter plot of squared daily return of the S&P 500 Index (in percent) versus that quantity for the prior day, with a fitted linear regression line. The axes are logarithmic.

the "data blob" in the middle of the diagram, but that distorts the linear regression line to look like a curve. There are a lot of dots there, are subtle features are hard to see, but there doesn't seem to be any direct evidence for regions of the plot that are dramatically different in their nature. This does support Engle's hypothesis of a linear autoregressive relationship. The relationship tested is

$$r_t^2 = \alpha + \beta r_{t-1}^2 + \varepsilon_t, \tag{2.10}$$

and we find $\alpha = 0.78 \pm 0.05$, $\beta = 0.232 \pm 0.008$, which are a t-statistics of 20 and 29 respectively, and the overall regression F statistic is 863.3 for 1 and 15,365 degrees of freedom.[f] Both statistics have vanishingly small p values — this is a very significant regression!

Let's now return to Fisher's devil, who in Section 2.2.4 is saying that we cannot accept our rejection of the Normal distribution in the F test for heteroskedasticity because we've actually been testing the compound hypothesis of both Normality and homoskedasticity, and we don't know which part of the compound we ought to reject.

With Engle's result, assuming the Normal distribution hypothesis is valid, we would have found way out if α had been zero, or close to it, for that would have meant that r_t^2/r_{t-1}^2 times a suitable constant would have had an $F_{1,1}$ distribution under the assumption of Normal distributions. But the large and significant value of α rules this out, we still need an additional method.

2.2.6. *GARCH*

Having been forced to eliminate a simple scaling model for squared returns we have to go even further with our modeling to try to accommodate the Normal distribution. Engle's model was enhanced by Tim Bollerslev into the *Generalized Autoregressive Conditional Heteroskedasticity* model, known more simply as *GARCH* [9]. This posits a state-space model with an unobserved autoregressive variance process.

$$r_t = \mu + \varepsilon_t \sigma_t, \tag{2.11}$$

$$\sigma_t^2 = C + A r_{t-1}^2 + B \sigma_{t-1}^2, \tag{2.12}$$

$$\varepsilon_t \sim \text{Normal}(0,1), \text{ independently } \forall\, t. \tag{2.13}$$

---

[f] I use $a \pm b$ to represent an estimate with a central value of a and a 68% confidence region of width $2b$ about the center.

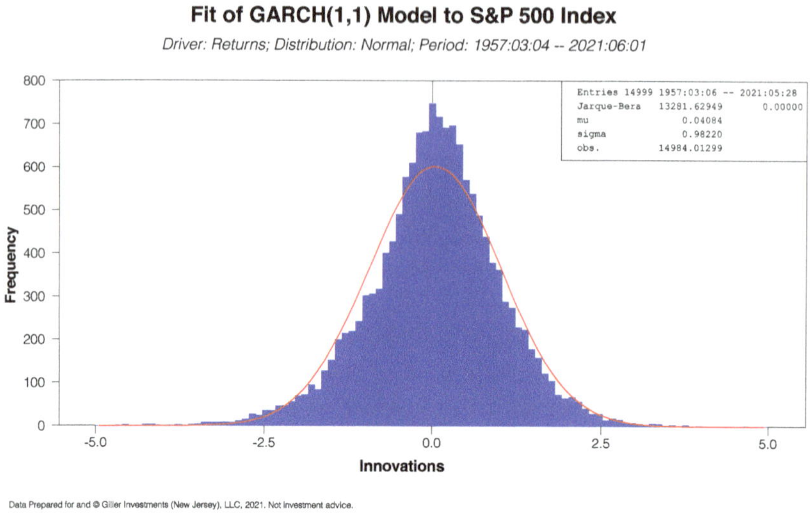

Figure 2.8: Distributions of innovations for a $GARCH(1,1)$ model for the daily returns of the S&P 500 for 1957 to 2020 inclusive. A Normal distribution for the innovations is used in the modeling.

This is clearly much more complex and it requires specialized software to fit it to the data. Nevertheless, bending over backwards to accommodate Fisher's devil, we can estimate this model from the data. The output of the analysis includes the time series σ_t, from which we can extract the *innovations* $\varepsilon_t = (r_t - \mu)/\sigma_t$, which Equation (2.12) tells us should be Normally distributed with a mean of 0 and a variance of 1. The $GARCH$ model contains four free parameters and is fitted using Fisher's method of maximum likelihood. The mean daily return is now 5.5 $\pm$ 0.6 b.p. which is over 70% larger than the prior estimate and the variation is not explained by sampling error. Why is this so? If you look back at Figure 2.6, we can see that several periods with above average volatility exists. The *ordinary linear regression* method minimizes the sum of the squares of the errors and so pays more attention to these volatile periods than the intermixed quiescent ones. The $GARCH$ model does not do this, as maximum likelihood attempts to deliver the parameters most likely to generate the data not strictly the smallest errors. Since a regression that overweights those periods also delivers a lower mean return, it must be the case that *the returns during the volatile periods are lower*. This is actually a very interesting result.

Visually the fit is better, but it's still bad. Maybe the improvement is good enough? We can also fit a $GARCH(1,1)$ model with innovations drawn from the Generalized Error Distribution. Since that provided a radically better description of the data in Figure 2.4, and the parameterization allows us to include the case of the Normal distribution naturally, it is an obvious choice. Again, the fit is definitely much better. It is even accommodating the "blunter peak" observed in the histogram but not the fitted curve in Figure 2.4. But the test would be to examine the shape coefficient, which is κ in Equation (2.8). My software outputs the value 0.73 ± 0.01 which is absolutely inconsistent with the value of 0.5 required to deliver a Normal distribution. Having gone through this procedure to find an excuse to include the Normal distribution, we still cannot do so!

The A and B coefficients are estimated to be 0.092 ± 0.006 and 0.902 ± 0.006, respectively. These are also nowhere near the values required for constant variance, or homoskedasticity. Without a doubt we can reject that model too.

2.2.7. *Stock Market Returns are Not Normally Distributed*

In Section 2.2, we have gone through increasingly complex analysis to defend the key assumption of continuous time finance, which is that interval returns of stock markets are Normally distributed. Based on the evidence presented here, I hope you will agree with me that this hypothesis is incredibly weakly supported.

Under the standard hypothesis testing regime of mathematical statistics we can only reject the null hypothesis if we have an alternate hypothesis to replace it. Very unlikely things are allowed to happen, but only if we can find an explanation under which they are not so very unlikely, but to be expected, should we reject the null hypothesis. It seems very clear to me, based on the evidence presented here, that the hypothesis that daily returns follow a GED is very well supported in contrast to the Normal distribution. Therefore, I chose to unambiguously reject the Normal distribution as a working hypothesis for these returns. Whether the GED is the best alternate choice is not certain, as there are other alternatives to try, but it seems pretty good.

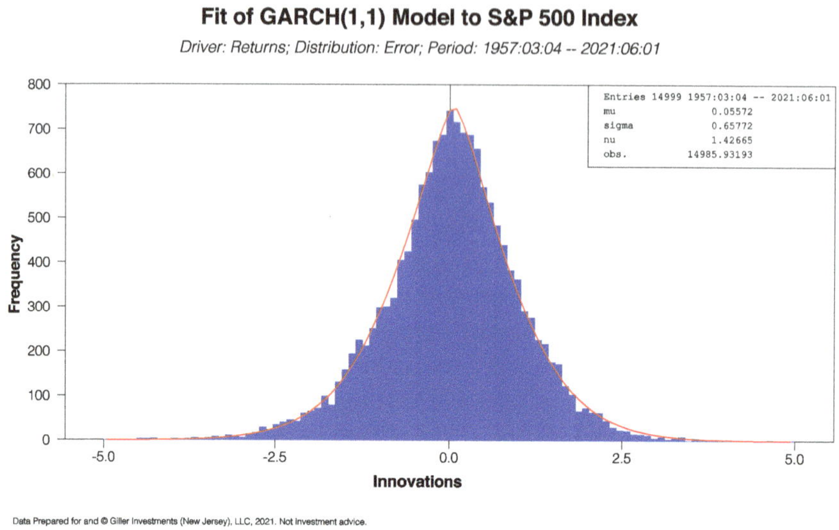

Figure 2.9: Distributions of innovations for a $GARCH(1,1)$ model for the daily returns of the S&P 500 for 1957 to 2021 inclusive. A Generalized Error Distribution for the innovations is used in the modeling.

It's important to understand that all of this effort to pin down the appropriate data generating process is not just an exercise in academic purity. When a time series has regimes of different volatility, or is drawn from a non-Normal distribution, and is processed in a manner that is blind to those facts, then the analysis is listening much more strongly to the more volatile periods and less to the quiescent periods. When building predictive models, we seek to build a model which is right most of the time and not one that is tuned to regimes that occur infrequently and are unpredictable.

2.3. The US Stock Market Through Time

Now that we have access to what appears to be a reasonable description of the gross structure of the data representing the S&P 500, the $GARCH(1,1)$ of Section 2.2.3 with innovations that are fundamentally leptokurtotic and well modeled by a GED, we have a decent analytic microscope to start examining more of the longer-term properties of this data.

2.3.1. *Drift and Momentum*

The first thing that's interesting is to take a look at the average daily return by year. To do this I have extended the S&P 500 Index data using the values back-calculated by S&P Indices from 1928 to the actual start of the index and performed the $GARCH(1,1)$ regressions independently, year-by-year. I augmented the model to include a possible autoregressive term, as follows:

$$\begin{aligned} r_t &= \mu_{y_t} + \varphi r_{t-1} + \varepsilon_t \sigma_t, \\ \sigma_t^2 &= C + A r_{t-1}^2 + B \sigma_{t-1}^2, \\ \varepsilon_t &\sim \text{GED}(0, 1, \kappa), \text{ independently } \forall\, t. \end{aligned} \tag{2.14}$$

Figure 2.10 represents a powerful affirmation that, most of the time, the stock market goes up. To the eye, there doesn't seem to be much relationship between these growth rates and the NBER's[g] (retroactively assigned) labels that the US economy was in recession, although we now have the tools to tackle that analysis quantitatively

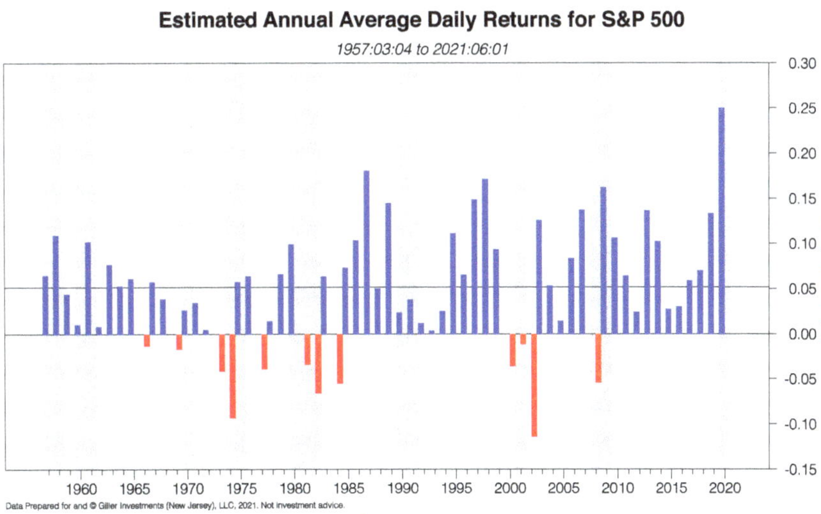

Figure 2.10: Time series of the estimated average daily return of the S&P 500 Index by year from independent $GARCH(1,1)$ regressions with innovations from the Generalized Error Distribution. Shading indicates NBER recessions.

[g]The National Bureau of Economic Research.

(in Section 2.3.3). The official tool to investigate whether those different values for μ are driven by *sampling error* or genuine variation explained by the "year" label is Fisher's Analysis of Variance, or *ANOVA*. Unfortunately, though, this method does assume the data is Normally distributed, and so is problematic to apply to real stock market data such as this.

In an equation such as Equation (2.14), a term like φr_{t-1} represents the part of an expected return that is dependent on prior information and not on original information. This is a literal expression for the prediction function of Equation (2.4), as modified to take account of heteroskedasticity. This is what we call "an alpha" in quantitative finance.

$$m(\mathcal{I}_t) = r_t, \tag{2.15}$$

$$\alpha(\mathcal{I}_{t-1}) = \varphi r_{t-1}, \tag{2.16}$$

$$\mathcal{I}_0 = (\mu, A, B, C, \kappa). \tag{2.17}$$

When $\varphi > 0$ we refer to this as "momentum," meaning that returns tend to be followed by returns of the same sign, and when negative "mean reversion," meaning that returns tend to be followed by returns of an opposite sign.

There is a substantial body of literature suggesting momentum exists in the stock-market [15], and also a substantial body of literature asserting that it shouldn't be there [89]. The basic idea behind the *Efficient Markets Hypothesis* is that there is a paradox between accurate predictive information being readily available and simultaneously exploitable by any investor. Of course, there is also a substantial body of literature suggesting that human beings don't necessarily make rational decisions based on readily available information [78].

Figure 2.11 shows a time series of this estimated autocorrelation factor. Apart from a period in the late 1960s/early 1970s the coefficient has wriggled around between the 95% confidence region defined by Fisher's estimate [41] of the sampling error of a correlation coefficient with a sample size of 252. The period in which strong positive correlation persisted is that of the bull market in the growth stocks know as the *Nifty-Fifty* [39]. The other notable feature is the sharp negative coefficient found (at the time of writing) half-way through 2020. This is associated with the market volatility around the COVID-19 pandemic.

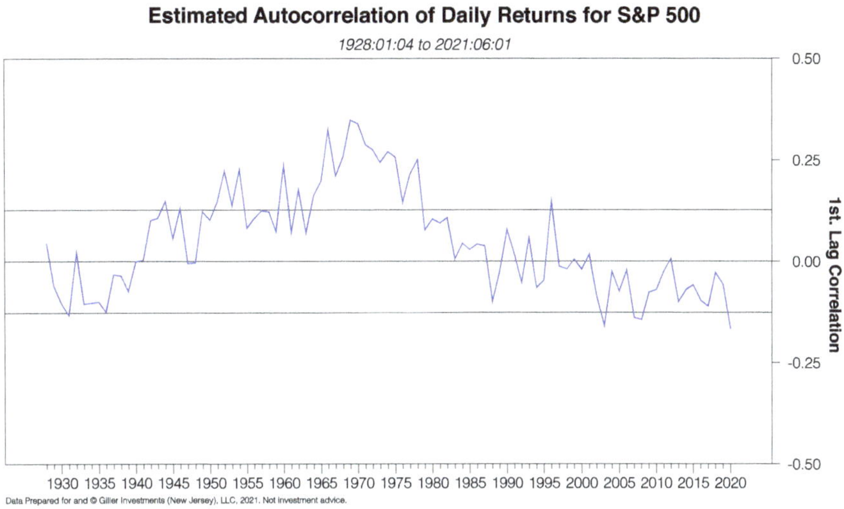

Figure 2.11: Time series of the estimated first lag autocorrelation coefficient of the daily returns of the S&P 500 Index by year from independent $GARCH(1,1)$ regressions with innovations from the GED. The horizontal lines indicate the 95% confidence region around 0.

The momentum chart shows the perils of working with financial data. Any analyst fitting a model to the entire period is going to measure a coefficient that is positive. The average value of the individual by year estimates is 0.047 and a whole sample regression must give back a value consistent with this number. For reference, Carhart's paper on Momentum was published in 1995 and the estimated coefficient turned negative shortly afterwards, and has stayed negative since then.

2.3.2. *Kurtosis*

Finally, let's take a look at the stability of the kurtosis as expressed through the estimated distributional parameter κ. Figure 2.12 shows the time series by year of the independent estimates of this parameter. Although the estimates do move around, they're almost never in the region of the 0.5 required to model the Normal distribution and it seems that a value of around 0.75 would not be too wrong a lot of the time.

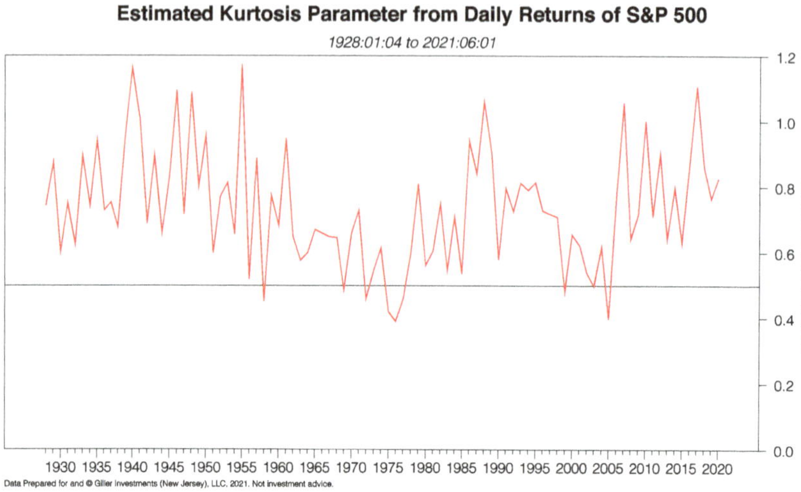

Figure 2.12: Time series of the estimated kurtosis parameter, κ, from daily returns of the S&P 500 Index by year from independent $GARCH(1,1)$ regressions with innovations from the GED. The horizontal line indicates the value equivalent to a Normal distribution.

2.3.3. *Recessions*

In Section 2.3.1, we raised the idea that NBER classified recessions might explain the variation in the growth parameter μ. Since the NBER indicator is either 0 or 1, this is a natural candidate for Fisher's ANOVA analysis, but that assumes the data are Normally distributed — and we've discussed at great length that that assumption is not supported by the data. So, we cannot do ANOVA on the returns themselves, but we can use the method in a *meta-analysis* of the series of fitted parameters.

The sampling errors in maximum likelihood estimates have been shown to be asymptotically Normally distributed with a mean of $\mathbf{0}$ and covariance matrix given by the inverse of the Fisher Information Matrix divided by the square root of the sample size [108]. This is the matrix of the expected value of the second derivatives of the log-likelihood with respect to the parameters. Since our sample is 93 years long, it should qualify as a "large sample," certainly by the perspectives of early 20th. Century statistics, but let's test that assumption. There's a very precise, distribution and bin free test, the *Kolmogorov–Smirnov Test* [97], named after the mathematician who established a rigorous foundation for probability theory. It uses empirical distribution functions, defined to be the proportion of a sample that is less than its argument, which is

$$\mathrm{EDF}(x) = \frac{1}{N}\sum_{i=1}^{N} I[x_i \le x], \tag{2.18}$$

for a data sample $\{x_i\}_{i=1}^N$. $I[x]$ is an *indicator* function that takes the value 1 if its argument is true and 0 otherwise. Kolmogorov provided theorems that showed that $E(x)$ converges to the actual cumulative distribution function (CDF), given by

$$\mathrm{CDF}(x) = \int_{-\infty}^{x} f(y)\,dy \tag{2.19}$$

for probability density function $f(x)$. The test examines the extremum of the absolute difference $D(x) = |\mathrm{EDF}(x) - \mathrm{CDF}(x)|$, and Kolmogorov calculated the sampling distribution of the test statistic, D_{max}.

Figure 2.13 shows both the empirical and cumulative distribution functions, which appear consistent within sampling error. Testing

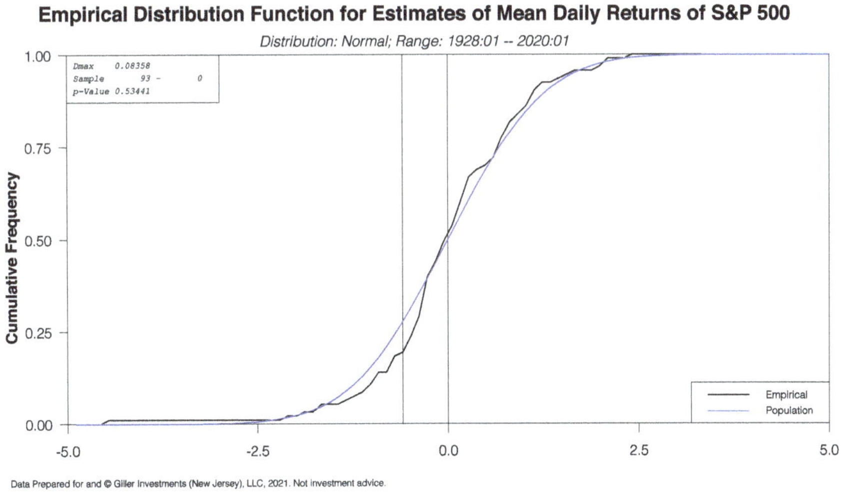

Figure 2.13: The empirical distribution function for standardized estimates of the average daily return of the S&P 500 Index by year, and the cumulative distribution function of the Normal distribution to which it should converge. The vertical line indicates the location of the test statistic, d_{max}.

Table 2.1: Single factor ANOVA table for estimated daily returns of the S&P 500 Index by year.

Groups	Count	Sum	Mean	Variance
Summary statistics				
Growth	64	3.699	0.05780	0.00440
Recession	29	0.887	0.03060	0.01227

Source of variation	*SS*	*df*	*MS*	*F*	*p* value
Analysis of variance					
Between groups	0.01477	1	0.01477	2.1211	0.1487
Within groups	0.63367	91	0.00696		
Total	0.64843	92			

Note: The two groups are based on whether the NBER indicated any month in a given year was in recession or not.

Table 2.2: Single factor ANOVA table for estimated autocorrelation of daily returns of the S&P 500 Index by year.

Groups	Count	Sum	Mean	Variance
Summary statistics				
Growth	64	2.833	0.04426	0.01557
Recession	29	1.554	0.05360	0.02505

Source of variation	*SS*	*df*	*MS*	*F*	*p* value
Analysis of variance					
Between Groups	0.0017	1	0.001739	0.09407	0.7598
Within Groups	1.6823	91	0.018486		
Total	1.6840	92			

Note: The two groups are based on whether the NBER indicated any month in a given year was in recession or not.

against the Normal distribution, $D_{\max} = 0.083$ for a sample of 93 independent measurements. The p value is 0.53, indicating a 50:50 chance of getting a larger value under the null hypothesis that the distribution is Normal. Thus, we cannot reject that hypothesis with any credible level of confidence — these estimates are Normally distributed. Table 2.1 shows the single factor ANOVA table worked out for the data shown in Figure 2.10. The average growth is found to be

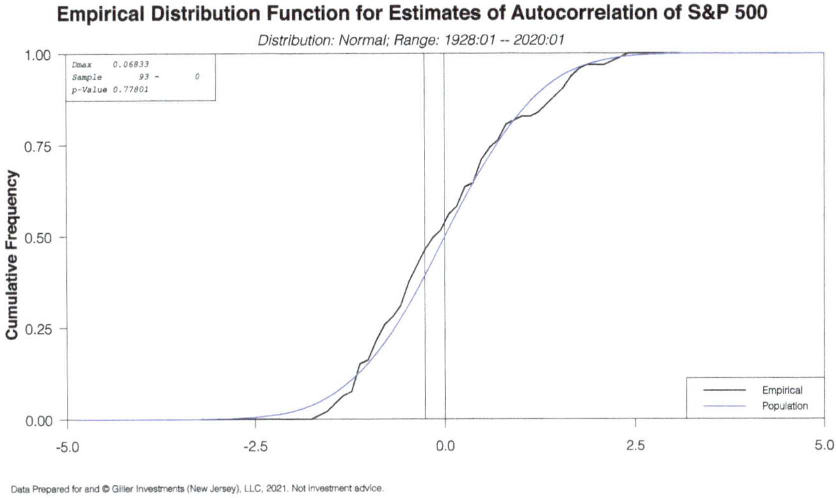

Figure 2.14: The empirical distribution function for standardized estimates of the correlation of daily returns of the S&P 500 Index by year, and the cumulative distribution function of the Normal distribution to which it should converge. The vertical line indicates the location of the test statistic, $d_{\max}$.

lower for the recession years but that factor, "in recession," doesn't significantly explain the variance between the groups.

Let's repeat this analysis for the autocorrelation coefficient. Firstly, we can validate whether the estimated regression coefficients appear to have a Normal distribution about their sample mean by again applying the Kolmogorov–Smirnov Test. This time $D_{\max}$ is 0.068 with a p value of 0.7781, so again we do not reject the null hypothesis of Normally distributed estimates.

2.3.4. *The Basic Properties of Index Returns*

I will return to index returns in Sections 2.6 and 2.8 but, before taking a detour into the analysis of interest rates, let's summarize what appear to be the basic properties of stock market returns — at least, as observed through the lens of a major market index, the S&P 500 Index.

(i) Daily returns are not Normally distributed!
(ii) Daily returns seem to be well described by a Generalized Error Distribution, with a kurtosis parameter κ somewhere between 0.75 and 1.00.

(iii) The average daily return is positive most of the time and doesn't seem to be related to the state of the macroeconomy, as measured by the NBER's *ex post* recessions indicator. Put simply, you should expect the stock market to go up!
(iv) Long term regressions find positive autocorrelation ("momentum") over the long term but this is not stable and the data seems to suggest that it is a phenomenon from the *past*.
(v) The volatility of daily returns exhibits strong momentum and seems to be very well described by a $GARCH(1,1)$ model with fundamentally leptokurtotic innovations.

2.4. Interest Rates

The rate of interest that the US government pays on its debts is the lodestone for all financial prices. They are widely regarded as "risk free," although technically that distinction is restricted to very short term instruments and is talking about default risk not price risk. The idea is that, since government debt is denominated in a fiat instrument, the US Dollar, and the Treasury can theoretically instruct the Bureau of Engraving and Printing to print as many as they want, there can never be a default on an instrument's nominal value. This risk-free nature is, of course, not true for several reasons:

(i) They might *arbitrarily* decide to default.
(ii) The true long-term value of the debt is measured in *real terms*, i.e. after inflation, not *nominal terms* without inflation.
(iii) In practice, most people are not interested in overnight instruments. The price paid for short term debt, such as three month treasury bills, can fluctuate.

"Bonds are about math," so said Michael Lewis in *Liar's Poker* [86]. The math contains a lot of arbitrary and confusing details, a slew of differing conventions, and textbook formulæ that omit real world details. I will not delve into all of this here — I will assume my readers are familiar with the concept of an interest rate, and explain only what details I need to. The classic reference for the mathematics is Fabozzi's book [36].

2.4.1. *The Long-Term Properties of Three Month Treasury Bill Rates*

2.4.1.1. *The Time Series of Rates*

Treasury bills are short term debt instruments issued by the United States government that do not pay installment interest (coupons). Consequently, they are traded on a "discounted" basis. You buy them for less than their face value and the resulting appreciation delivers the rate of return to you. Different maturities are issued, usually three months (technically 91 days), six months and one year. These are calendar days, not trading days — in the bond market you get paid interest over the weekends and holidays. The rates are annualized through conventions in which interest accrues without compounding, but is compounded when reinvested, so that the rates on different maturities may be compared. These rates form a "yield curve," which is a graph of the snapshot of interest rate versus maturity on any given day.

Figure 2.15 shows the time series of US Treasury Bill discount rates for three month (91 day) bills. This is daily data and shows the average rate demanded by investors in these instruments on that day. The data look nothing like the stock market data, exhibiting no general growth. Prior to the 1980s rates were generally increasing, and after that time they were generally decreasing. For a remarkable period of about 10 years following the Global Financial Crisis of 2008 rates were effectively zero, and they have been brought back to zero in the COVID-19 era. Throughout this entire history, which starts in 1954, the average rate is 4.3% with a standard error of 3.1%. There is slight positive skewness (0.9) and excess kurtosis (1.1).

2.4.1.2. *The Distribution of Changes in Interest Rates*

There are many stochastic process models for interest rates, and there is a good summary on the Wikipedia page [17]. Every single one of them incorporates a Wiener process, introducing a stochastic element in continuous time with a Normal distribution, although many of them model the log of the interest rates to restrict the process to positive values (and lognormal distributions), which should be ruled out as we now know interest rates can be zero or negative. Their

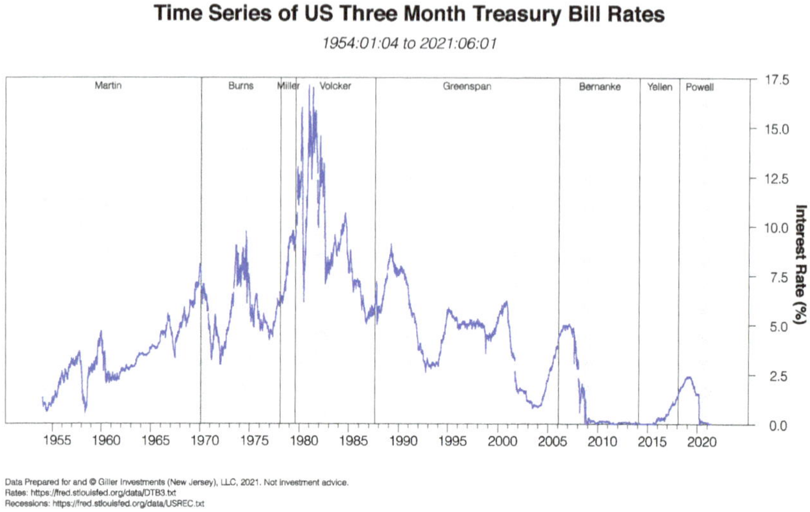

Figure 2.15: Time series of 3-month (91 day) US Treasury Bill discount rates. This series is one of the fundamental benchmarks for the global economy. NBER recessions are indicated by shading and the tenure of various Chairmen of the Board of Governors of the Federal Reserve are indicated.

profusion is likely indicative of the lack of utility over a long time scale.

None of them would produce a distribution of the daily change in interest rates that looks anything like the actual distribution we find, which is shown in Figure 2.16. The observed data has an excess kurtosis of 34 — it is massively fat tailed and utterly unlike a Normal distribution, but it does appear to be well described by the *Generalized Error Distribution*. This data is much more fat tailed than even stock market returns.

Following Engle's advice [32], and our prior experience with stock market models, we should definitely investigate a $GARCH(1,1)$ as the possible origin of the observed leptokurtosis in the changes in rates $\delta r_t = r_t - r_{t-1}$. It is the go-to model for financial time-series volatility. However, the data doesn't seem to be exhibiting any kind of unrestricted growth or decay, as we would find in a pure Brownian Motion, so some kind of mean-reversion term, such as that suggested by the Vasicek Model [137] is required.

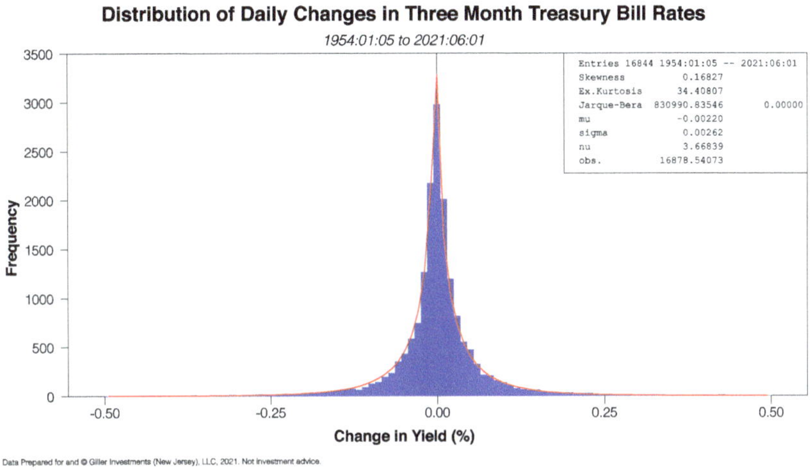

Figure 2.16: Distribution of daily changes in the discount rate of 3-month (91 day) US Treasury Bills. The blue bars show the frequency counts and the red curve is the best fitting *Generalized Error Distribution*.

A candidate structure is shown in Equations (2.20), (2.21), and (2.22).

$$\delta r_t = \mu + \theta r_{t-1} + \varphi\,\delta r_{t-1} + \sigma_t\varepsilon_t, \tag{2.20}$$

$$\sigma_t^2 = C + A\,\delta r_{t-1}^2 + B\sigma_{t-1}^2, \tag{2.21}$$

$$\varepsilon_t \sim \mathrm{GED}(0, 1, \kappa), \tag{2.22}$$

where $\mathcal{I}_0 = \{\mu, \theta, \varphi, A, B, C, \kappa\}$ are free parameters to be determined.

When you estimate this model from the data the analysis converges but the residuals, as seen in Figure 2.17, look very peculiar. They should look like some less leptokurtotic version of the input data, but there is a massive spike exactly at 0 and a deficit around it. What does this mean? It means that the data is much more likely to contain $\delta r_t = 0$ than it should if the probability distribution was correct! This data comes from the Federal Reserve Bank of New York and, for either reasons of quantization (it is only reported to two decimal places, i.e. to the basis point) or a lack of willingness to report small changes or something else, it definitely isn't the infinitely divisible real number the model is expecting.

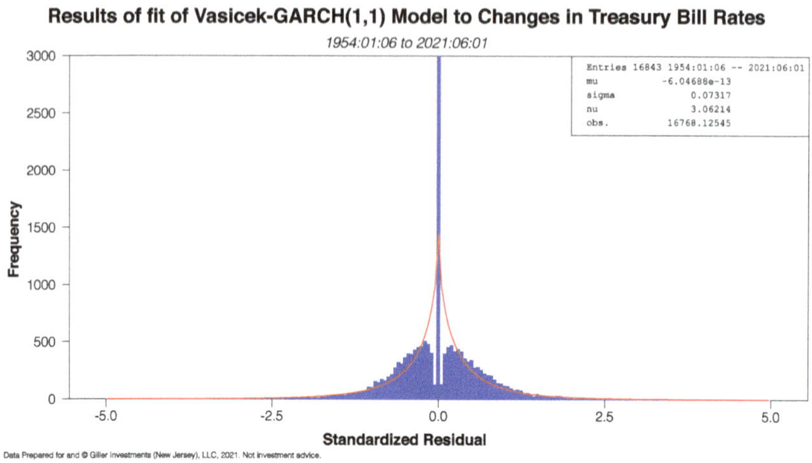

Figure 2.17: Distribution of standardized residuals from fitting the daily changes in the discount rate of 3-month (91 day) US Treasury Bills to a Vasicek-$GARCH(1,1)$ model. The blue bars show the frequency counts and the red curve is the best fitting *Generalized Error Distribution.*

So, what can be done about that? We can either change the time scale, since variance likely increases with $\sqrt{H}$ for data horizon H, making the changes bigger, or we can assume there is some kind of composite process that avoids $\delta r_t \approx$ "small." The former strategy is a conscious attempt to hide the problem whereas the latter ignores it. It's probably best to try both.

2.4.1.3. *A Daily Vasicek-GARCH*(1, 1) *Model with Quiet Days Censored*

By *censoring* the days where $\delta r_t = 0$ we are assuming that the problem is in the reporting of the data and not in its actual dynamical process. Structurally, we leave everything the same and omit any days on which the reported interest rate didn't change *as if they never even happened* so the process definition Equations (2.20, (2.21), and (2.22) become

$$\delta r_t = \mu + \theta r_s + \varphi\,\delta r_s + \sigma_t \varepsilon_t, \tag{2.23}$$

$$\sigma_t^2 = C + A\,\delta r_s^2 + B\sigma_s^2, \tag{2.24}$$

$$\varepsilon_t \sim \mathrm{GED}(0, 1, \kappa), \tag{2.25}$$

$$s = \underset{u<t,|r_u|>0}{\arg\max}\, u. \tag{2.26}$$

As seen in Figure 2.18, the distributions are a lot closer but still very wrong. We have not succeeded in "healing" the data, and still see a deficit of small changes. The distribution is not narrowly missing density exactly at 0, but is bimodal, with slightly higher rates of negative moves than positive moves.

Interestingly, the kurtosis parameter, κ, has been estimated to be 0.71, which is remarkably similar to the values we were seeing for the stock market in Figure 2.12. The Vasicek parameter, θ, is estimated to be negative, as it should be for mean reversion, but is very close to zero and not significant. Interestingly we find a large momentum parameter, $\hat{\varphi} = 0.11 \pm 0.01$, which is highly significant and does qualify as an "alpha" for interest rates. The imputed volatility time series is shown in Figure 2.19.

Figure 2.20 shows the value of the momentum term, $\varphi\,\delta r_t$ in Equation (2.23), estimated independently year-by-year. This is a very interesting plot. It shows a progressive decline in the momentum

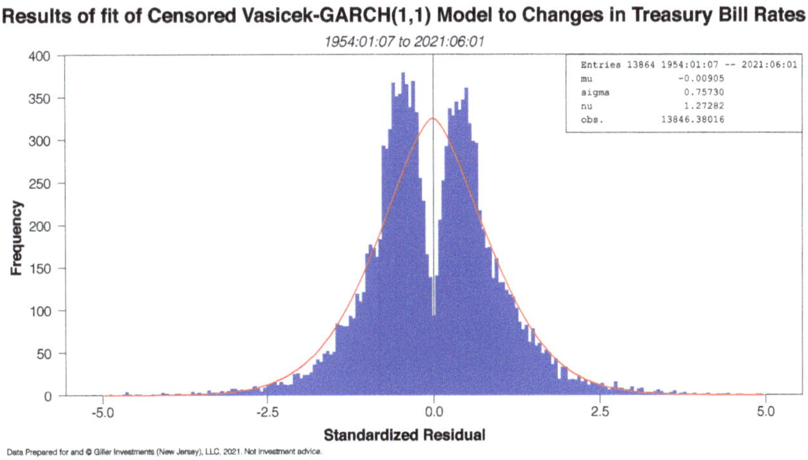

Figure 2.18: Distribution of standardized residuals from fitting the daily changes in the discount rate of 3-month (91 day) US Treasury Bills to a censored Vasicek-$GARCH(1,1)$ model. The blue bars show the frequency counts and the red curve is the best fitting *Generalized Error Distribution.*

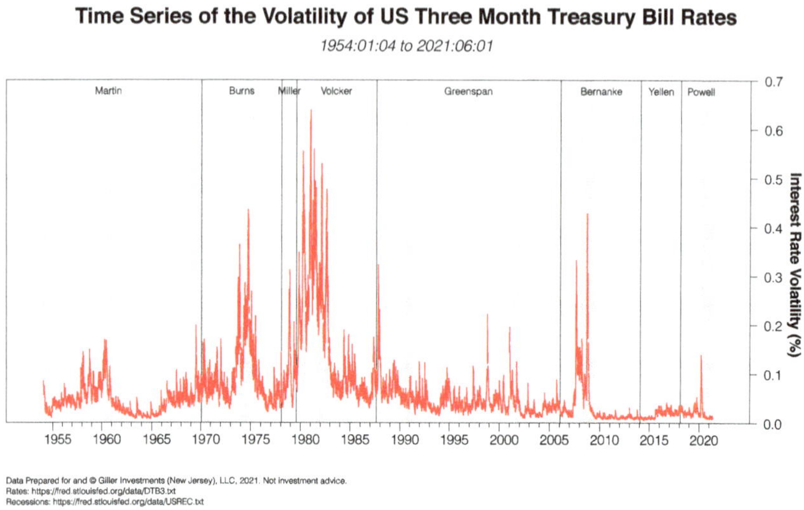

Figure 2.19: Imputed daily interest rate volatility for daily changes in the discount rate of 3-month (91 day) US Treasury Bills estimated from data in which no-change days have been removed.

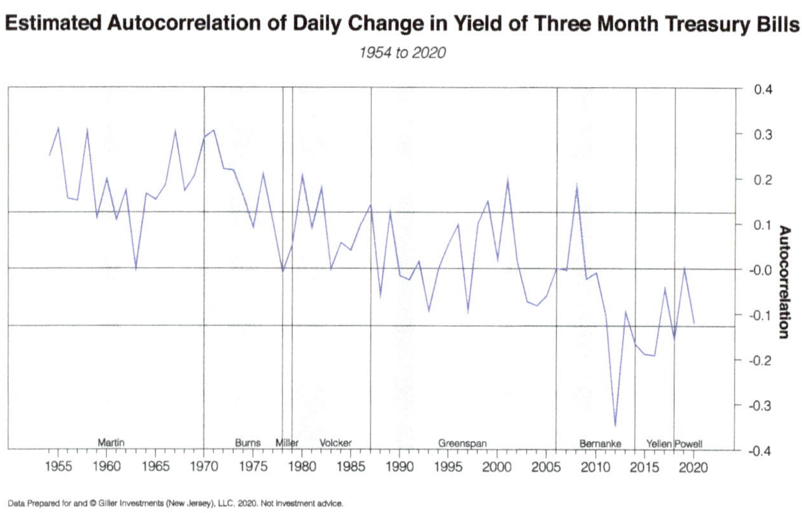

Figure 2.20: Estimated first lag autocorrelation of the daily changes in the discount rate of 3-month (91 day) US Treasury Bills from data in which no-change days have been removed, by year. Vertical lines indicate the dates on which the Federal Reserve Chairman changed and shading indicates NBER recessions. Horizontal lines indicate 95% confidence region about the null hypothesis of zero autocorrelation.

of these rates, from strong values of order 25% through the 1950s to the 1980s, to essentially zero values from the 1980s onward, which a short period of highly reversive markets toward the end of the Bernanke period. In fact through most of the Volker–Greenspan–Bernanke period it would be fair to conclude there was no momentum in these markets. As the coefficient has been positive more often than negative, a whole sample regression would give a positive result, as found above.

2.4.1.4. *Testing for Independence in the Direction of Changes of Interest Rates*

To further understand this distribution, let's take a step away from continuous variables. Let $s_t = \operatorname{sgn}\delta r_t$, the direction of each day's change, so the actual return be modeled as the product of a random direction and a random scale[h] i.e. $\delta r_t = \gamma_t s_t$, for some currently unspecified, but strictly positive, γ_t, which is independent of s_t.

Under these conditions, how might s_t behave? One possibility is that the sequence $s_t, s_{t+1} \dots$ be represented by a system called a Markov Chain, which are discussed in many books on probability and random processes such as the one by Grimmet and Stirzaker [128]. This is a well known probabilistic system in which the transition from state i to state j occurs randomly with probabilities given by the matrix P_{ji}.

There are three states for the three possible values of s_t, representing that the direction of the change in interest rates is one of up, unchanged, or down, respectively. This may be written out with a set of state vectors

$$\mathcal{S} = \{\boldsymbol{S}_1, \boldsymbol{S}_2, \boldsymbol{S}_3\} = \left\{ \begin{pmatrix} 1 \\ 0 \\ 0 \end{pmatrix}, \begin{pmatrix} 0 \\ 1 \\ 0 \end{pmatrix}, \begin{pmatrix} 0 \\ 0 \\ 1 \end{pmatrix} \right\}. \tag{2.27}$$

Associated with each s_t is a vector $\boldsymbol{s}_t$. If s_t is observed, then $\boldsymbol{s}_t$ must take only one of the permitted values $\boldsymbol{S}_i$. If s_t has not been observed, then its elements are the probabilities that the system will be observed to be in the state in which that element is 1. Finally,

[h] "Random" meaning unpredictable from prior public information, as always.

the future probabilities are only dependent on the current state, and not on prior states nor any exogenous stimuli. From this assumption, known as the *Markov Property*, it follows that

$$\Pr(\boldsymbol{s}_{t+f}|\boldsymbol{s}_t) = P^f \boldsymbol{s}_t. \tag{2.28}$$

Such a system allows us to model the temporal evolution of s_t as possessing either momentum, in which states are "sticky" and an up day tends to be followed more by another up day, reversion, in which states are more likely to be different than equal and so an up day is likely to be followed by a down day, etc., and independent, in which the states do not depend on their prior history. An interesting question is then: are the states independent?, i.e. Is the direction of the change of interest rates from day-to-day predictable from prior information or not?

Fortunately, there is a test to address exactly that question. The procedure is called the Whittle Test [6] which involves performing a χ^2 Test on the observed frequencies of state transitions. The null hypothesis of this test is independence, which is equivalent to the *Efficient Markets Hypothesis*. This means that[i] $E[\boldsymbol{s}_t|\boldsymbol{s}_s] = E[\boldsymbol{s}_t]$. Note that this doesn't require them to have the same observed frequencies, just that those frequencies not be dependent on the prior state that is occupied.

Again there is a lot of daily data, so we are able to perform this test year-by-year from 1954 to date. The computed p values are shown in Figure 2.21. At the 95% confidence level, the test fails 22 times in 67 years of data. As the p value of a test is the probability of getting a test statistic at equal to or larger than that observed, which is a cumulative probability, the observed p values from a set of independent tests, such as these, should be uniformly distributed between zero and one. That means there should be 3 such false positives expected, but clearly we see a lot more than that. Since there are many years in which we reject the hypothesis of independence, it will clearly be rejected for the entire dataset as a whole. Nevertheless, we can drill into the time-series and see that independence was,

[i]In this expression, the left-hand side of the equality is the conditional expectation and the right hand side the unconditional expectation vector. If the states are independent, these are equal.

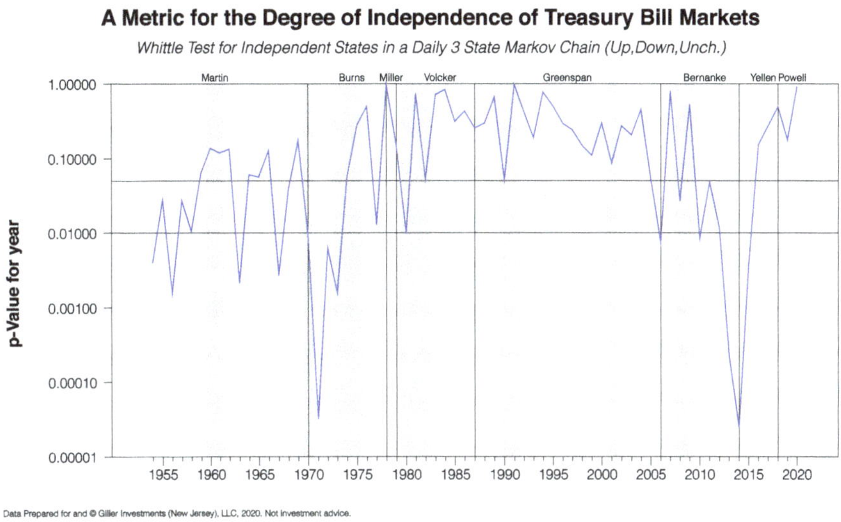

Figure 2.21: Time series of p values from performing Whittle's Test for state dependence on the direction of daily changes in the discount rate of 3-month US Treasury Bills. NBER recessions are indicated by shading and the tenure of various Chairmen of the Board of Governors of the Federal Reserve are indicated. Horizontal lines indicate the critical values of $\alpha = 0.05$ and $\alpha = 0.01$.

in fact, a pretty good description of most of the Volcker–Greenspan–Bernanke period, but not at the start, when, inflation was a concern, nor at the end, when the global financial crisis occurred.

Observing these results, it seems more likely to me that the "stickiness" of interest rates, leading to the observed excess of "no change" datapoints in the data set exhibited in Section 2.4.1.2, is not due to a rounding error but more due to policy responses. The "policy" interest rate of the United States is the rate on Federal Funds, which are monies deposited by banks for regulatory purposes with the Federal Reserve. Federal Funds, Treasury Bill and Treasury Bond rates may be market rates but the Federal Reserve targets the funds rate so that the monthly average is equal to the announced policy rate.[j]

[j]Operationally, The New York Fed. is able to use its balance sheet to execute trades that move the targeted rate to the desired value.

2.4.1.5. *A Compound Model for Interest Rate Changes*

How might these two *stylistically* different models of rate changes be resolved? Figure 2.22 shows the distributions of the magnitude of the innovations imputed from the model of Equation (2.24). These two histograms are remarkably similar, but not statistically indistinct. A Gamma distribution is fitted to both data sets independently, and the parameters of the Gamma distribution[k] are estimated to be $\hat{\mu} = 0.48 \pm 0.01$ and $\hat{\sigma} = 1.60 \pm 0.02$ for the positives and $\hat{\mu} = 0.43 \pm 0.01$ and $\hat{\sigma} = 1.72 \pm 0.03$ for the negatives, respectively. These parameters are not consistent within standard errors, but they are fairly close. The biggest difference is in the counts, as there are more negatives than positives. It's clear that these distributional choices are *not right* but we are learning more about the underlying data generating process.

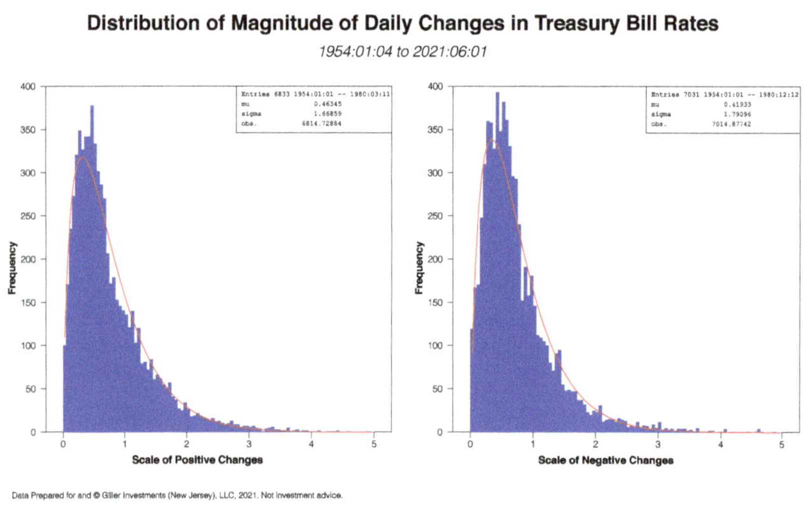

Figure 2.22: Distributions of scale of the innovations imputed when estimating the model of Equation (2.24) from the daily changes in the discount yield of US 3-month Treasury Bills. The left panel shows the distribution for positive change days and the right panel that for negative change days. In both cases the blue bars are a histogram and the red line is the best fitting Gamma distribution.

---

[k]In a parameterization in which the mean of the Gamma distribution is $\mu\sigma$ and the variance is $\mu\sigma^2$.

A model that is wrong, will always try to accommodate the data you fit it to, so a critical eye must be taken to the extracted distributions of residuals to guide us toward the correct distributional choice for our model. From the various models that generated Figures 2.17, 2.18 and 2.22, it seems that daily changes in interest rates have the following properties:

(i) There are a lot of no-change days.
(ii) A $GARCH(1,1)$ is working reasonably well (it succeeds in standardizing the rate changes).
(iii) The distributions of $|\delta r_t|/\hat{\sigma}_t$ are quite similar irrespective of the sign of δr_t.
(iv) The description of a continuous random variable with a mean that is non-zero doesn't seem to explain the data, as the non-zero mean of the data seems to arise from different quantities of similarly distributed data that differ only in the sign.

Putting this all together, a composite model for both the daily change in interest rates and its variance may look something like this

$$\delta r_t = s_t \gamma_t, \tag{2.29}$$

$$\boldsymbol{s}_t \sim \text{Discrete}(\mathcal{S}, P\boldsymbol{s}_{t-1}), \tag{2.30}$$

$$\sigma_t^2 = C + A\,\delta r_{t-1}^2 + B\sigma_{t-1}^2, \tag{2.31}$$

$$\gamma_t \sim \begin{cases} \text{Gamma}(\kappa^2, \sigma_t/\kappa) & \text{if } s_t \neq 0 \\ \text{undefined} & \text{otherwise,} \end{cases} \tag{2.32}$$

with $\mathcal{I}_0 = \{A, B, C, P, \kappa\}$ parameters to be determined.[1] Equation (2.32) defines a system in which the mean of γ_t is $\kappa\sigma_t$ and the variance is σ_t^2. The skewness of γ_t is $2/\kappa$ and the excess kurtosis is $6/\kappa^2$, thus κ plays the role of a kurtosis parameter for the composite distribution of rate changes.

[1]Using the notation Discrete$(\mathcal{S}, \boldsymbol{p})$ to mean a discrete distribution with support over the set $\mathcal{S}$ and state probabilities $\boldsymbol{p}$.

2.4.1.6. *Estimation of the Markov Chain for Rate Change Direction*

As s_t and γ_t are independent by construction the two elements of the model may be estimated separately. The log-likelihood for the Markov Chain system is

$$\mathcal{L}_{\text{MC}}(P) = \sum_t \ln \boldsymbol{s}_t^T P \boldsymbol{s}_{t-1} \tag{2.33}$$

and is straightforward to estimate. The Markov transition matrix $P_{ij} = \text{Prob}(i|j)$ is known as a "row stochastic" matrix, in which the row-sums are all unity, and so the 3×3 matrix in fact only contains six free parameters

$$P = \begin{pmatrix} 1 - P_{12} - P_{13} & P_{12} & P_{13} \\ P_{21} & 1 - P_{21} - P_{23} & P_{23} \\ P_{31} & P_{32} & 1 - P_{31} - P_{32} \end{pmatrix}. \tag{2.34}$$

The matrix is estimated to be

$$\hat{P} = \begin{pmatrix} 0.259 & 0.361 & 0.380 \\ 0.150 & 0.705 & 0.145 \\ 0.391 & 0.343 & 0.266 \end{pmatrix}. \tag{2.35}$$

with the full regression results in Table 2.3. The matrix is not consistent with independence between the successive states, which should be no surprise given the results of Section 2.4.1.4. It shows an interesting symmetry between the positive ($\boldsymbol{S}_1$) and negative ($\boldsymbol{S}_3$) states, and a different form for the no-change ($\boldsymbol{S}_2$) state. No-change is quite persistent, with a 70% chance of remaining in that state and a 15% chance of leaving the state for either of the others. For both the positive and negative change states, rates are more likely to enter that state from another state than they are to remain in the state, i.e. there is momentum in the no-change state and reversion in the change states.

2.4.1.7. *Estimation of the Scale Distribution for Rate Changes*

Estimation of the parameters of the scale distribution is also fairly straightforward. It is necessary to calculate the imputed variance

Table 2.3: Maximum likelihood regression results for the Markov Chain model for the direction of the daily change in the discount rate of 3-month US Treasury Bills.

Regression results

Variable	Estimate	Std. error	t statistic	p-value
P_{12}	0.361	0.007	4.0	6×10^{-5}
P_{13}	0.380	0.005	9.2	0
P_{21}	0.150	0.005	−38.3	0
P_{23}	0.145	0.005	−40.4	0
P_{31}	0.391	0.005	11.1	0
P_{32}	0.343	0.007	1.4	0.16

Overall significance

Statistic	Value	Deg. free	p-value
MLR	2586	6	0

Note: State 1 is "up," state 2 is "unchanged," and state 3 is "down." t Statistics and the MLR are evaluated relative to the null hypothesis of $P_{ij} = \frac{1}{3}$.

series σ_t^2 on the fly, but that is possible as it is a *deterministic* function of prior data (specifically δr_{t-1} and σ_{t-1}^2) providing that the series is initialized with a suitable value. It is common to use the unconditional variance. For estimation, the log-likelihood of the scale distribution system is

$$\gamma_t = |\delta r_t|, \tag{2.36}$$

$$\sigma_t = \sqrt{C + A\delta r_{t-1}^2 + B\sigma_{t-1}^2}, \tag{2.37}$$

$$\mathcal{L}_{\text{SD}}(A, B, C, \kappa) = \sum_t \ln \left\{ \frac{\gamma_t^{\kappa^2-1} e^{\gamma_t \kappa/\sigma_t}}{\Gamma(\kappa^2) \left(\frac{\sigma_t}{\kappa}\right)^{\kappa^2-1}} \right\}. \tag{2.38}$$

This regression converges and is somewhat successful on the basis that we model the scale distribution with a Gamma distribution and we find that the data crudely matches that distribution, which was not the experience previously. However, it is far from "correct." The parameter estimates for the scale distribution are in Table 2.4. Of these four parameters, we may test for the hypothesis that A and B

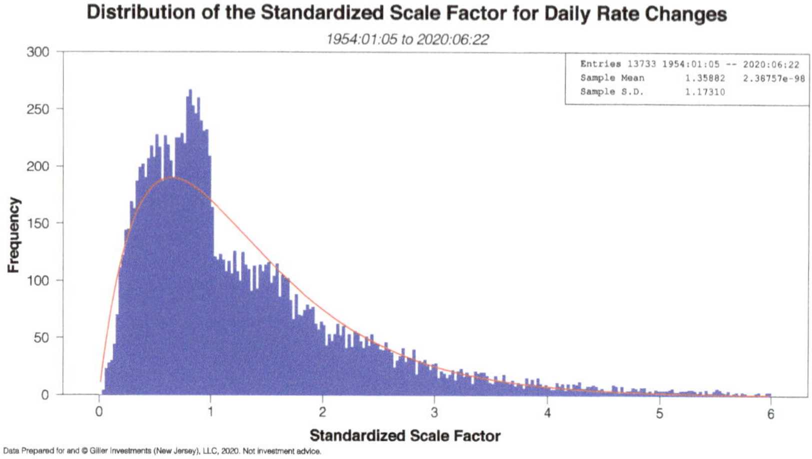

Figure 2.23: Distribution of standardized daily rate change scales for the model specified in Section 2.4.1.5. The blue bars represents the counts of data and the red line is the best fitting Gamma distribution. The data is the daily change in 3-month (91 day) US Treasury Bill discount rates.

Table 2.4: Maximum likelihood regression results for the scale of daily changes 3-month US Treasury Bill Rates with a $GARCH(1,1)$ structure and a Gamma distribution for the innovations.

Variable	Estimate	Std. error
Regression results		
A	0.207	0.004
B	0.747	0.005
C	0.000062	0.000001
κ	1.149	0.005

should be 0 using the Maximum likelihood ratio test, which convincingly rejects that hypothesis with a vanishing p value, but those results cannot be regarded as definitive due to the lack of distributional fit. The unconditional standard deviation of the daily changes is given by $\sqrt{C/(1-A-B)} \approx 0.035\%$ which, based on personal experience trading interest rate derivatives, seems like a very plausible value.

2.4.2. *The Basic Properties of Interest Rates*

As observed through the lens of US Treasury Bill rates, the following properties of interest rates seem to be true.

(i) The distribution of Daily changes in rates does not in any way resemble either the Normal or Lognormal distributions!
(ii) Daily changes in rates are extremely leptokurtotic, so both big changes and quiescent periods are quite likely to occur.
(iii) When the $\delta r_t = 0$ days are censored, daily changes in rates are somewhat similar to a Generalized Error Distribution but with a deficit of small changes.
(iv) Historically, there has been significant momentum in interest rate markets, which exhibits itself both through the autocorrelation of the daily changes and the lack of independence of the signs of those changes on prior values, but this seems to be a phenomenon from the past.
(v) The daily changes in rates appear to be well described by a composite process that is the product of a change direction, that follows a Markov Chain, and a scale that is described by a Gamma distribution with the variance modulated by a $GARCH(1,1)$ model.

2.5. LIBOR and Eurodollar Futures

2.5.1. *LIBOR*

LIBOR, or the *London Interbank Offered Rate*, was for most of my career the world's most important commercial interest rate. It was determined by members of the *British Banker's Association* with good credit participating in a daily survey of the rates they would expect to borrow from each other in US Dollars external to the regulated US markets. It didn't represent actual transaction rates, or even, average transaction rates, but hypothesized transaction rates. Over time it became the global reference for commercial lending transactions, with many US mortgages and other derivative securities contracts being defined in reference to it. Thus large sums of money would flow in and out of bank balance sheets based on these daily indicative quotes, and it became the subject of substantial manipulation that ended up in criminal cases and is well documented in David Enrich's excellent book *The Spider Network* [33].

2.5.1.1. *My impressions of LIBOR from the 1990s*

My interactions with LIBOR began when Peter Muller asked me to build a model for Eurodollar Futures, after joining PDT at Morgan Stanley in 1996. Although the Eurodollar Futures markets are derivative of LIBOR, I remember in my development of systems to trade them, that I concluded that the LIBOR quotes were not a useful guide to the performance of the futures over the short term. For the purposes of trading on the prices of Eurodollar Futures, it was more productive to infer the spot interest rate from the forward curve found in the futures market, which represented actual transaction prices with substantial liquidity behind them, rather than from such banker's quotes that were "indicative" only. In particular, I felt that the LIBOR quotes were too "sticky" — meaning that they didn't appear to change as much as they should if they were a naturally evolving, essentially stochastic, process.

Early on I had a conversation that lead me to conclude that "indicative" quotes held little value. I was looking at the US Treasury Yield Curve on a Reuters screen and noticed that one of the quoted maturities appeared way out of line with the rest of the curve (the quoted interest rate was off by a factor of 10, a simple keystroke error most likely). I went so far as to call Reuters' customer service and complain about it, thinking maybe their system had some kind of bug, and was told that those were the quotes from the brokers and that was that. So I replied "ok, well which broker is giving you that price because I want to deal with them?" Reuters then insisted that they could not possibly identify the broker responsible for the bad data and it was left to stand, even though it clearly was wrong.

2.5.1.2. *LIBOR as a Time Series Compared to Treasury Rates*

LIBOR represents a commercial interest rate and is referenced to Three Month Treasury Bill rates via the *TED spread*, which represents the additional interest commercial banks have to pay to borrow money relative to the US Treasury due to their credit being less good. It was made famous in the opening scenes of Michael Lewis's *Liar's*

Poker [86]. From the viewpoint of stochastic processes, LIBOR rates should be more random than treasury bill rates at the same maturity, i.e.

$$L_t = r_t + \Delta_t, \tag{2.39}$$

$$\Rightarrow \mathrm{Var}[\delta L_t] = \mathrm{Var}[\delta r_t] + \mathrm{Var}[\delta \Delta_t] + 2\ \mathrm{Cov}[\delta r_t, \delta \Delta_t], \tag{2.40}$$

where L_t is LIBOR, r_t are the Treasury Bill rates as before, and Δ_t is the TED Spread. Assuming that bank credit quality doesn't improve when treasury bill rates go up, i.e. that $\mathrm{Cov}[\delta r_t, \delta \Delta_t] > 0$, then it should be generally true that LIBOR is more random than Treasury Bill rates.

$$\mathrm{Var}[\delta L_t] > \mathrm{Var}[\delta r_t]. \tag{2.41}$$

This does not appear to be the case. The unconditional variances of daily changes in 3-month LIBOR and Treasury Bill rates are $18\%^2$ and $26\%^2$, respectively, for daily data from 1986 to date. However, we have learned from the results presented in Section 2.4 that it is a mistake to treat interest rate time-series as if there are merely a continuous random variable. It is also interesting to determine whether the states of the rate change directions are independent.

2.5.1.3. *Whittle Test for Independence of the Sequences of Direction of Daily Change of LIBOR Rates*

It is straightforward to apply the Whittle Test analysis presented in Section 2.4.1.4 to the LIBOR data, and present the results side by side. This data is exhibited in Figure 2.24, with shading to indicate years when the Whittle Test for independence fails with 99% confidence. For Treasury Bill rates the data is mostly from the Volcker–Greenspan–Bernanke period of essentially free interest rate markets, but the LIBOR data fails the test for independence in the majority of periods. There are a total of 19 failures in 35 years of data, or 54%, with a critical value of 0.01. Less than one is expected (0.4). Since these are independent tests, we can compute the binomial probability of getting this number of failures when the expected rate is equal to the critical value, and it is vanishingly small. It is safe to conclude that the LIBOR state sequences are not independent.

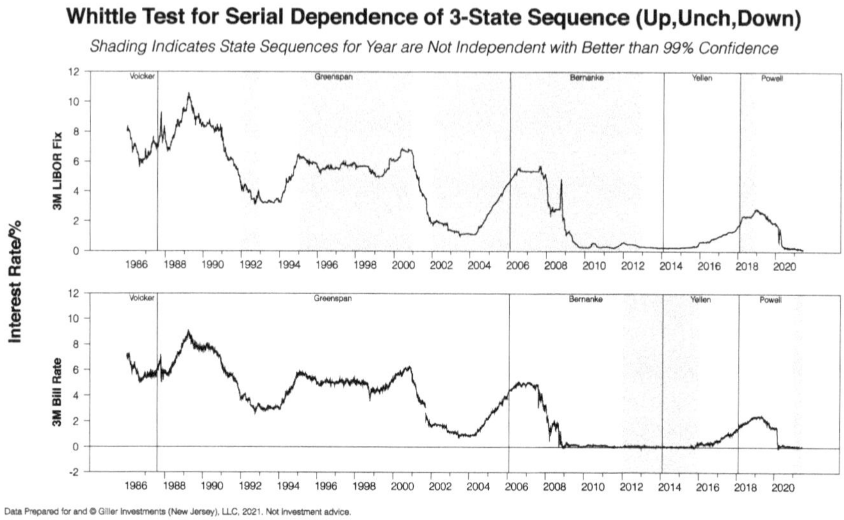

Figure 2.24: Time series of both 3 month LIBOR rates and 3-month (91 day) US Treasury Bill discount rates for the period over which data coincides. The vertical lines indicate the change of tenure of the various Chairmen of the Federal Reserve and the shading indicates years in which the state-sequence of change directions failed the Whittle Test with a critical value of $\alpha = 0.99$.

Even more than that, though, the visual appearance of the curves is radically different. The "hairiness" of the curve exhibits the day-to-day volatility of the rates and, after the mid-90s, this has all but vanished. Even though the LIBOR data is generally following the shape of the Treasury Bill Rates over the long term, on a day-to-day basis they are not comparable.

2.5.1.4. *Estimated Markov Chain Transition Matrix for Direction of Daily Change of LIBOR Rates*

Similarly, the analysis of Section 2.4.1.6 can be repeated for the LIBOR rates. The estimated Markov Chain transition matrix is

$$\hat{P} = \begin{pmatrix} 0.523 & 0.192 & 0.285 \\ 0.174 & 0.627 & 0.199 \\ 0.261 & 0.188 & 0.551 \end{pmatrix}, \tag{2.42}$$

Table 2.5: Maximum likelihood regression results for the Markov Chain model for the direction of the daily change in the 3-month LIBOR rates.

Regression results

Variable	Estimate	Std. error	t statistic
P_{12}	0.192	0.007	−21.2
P_{13}	0.285	0.009	−5.7
P_{23}	0.199	0.008	−17.7
P_{21}	0.174	0.007	−22.0
P_{31}	0.261	0.008	−9.1
P_{32}	0.188	0.007	−22.0

Overall significance

Statistic	Value	Deg. free
M.L.R.	2164	6

Note: State 1 is "up," state 2 is "unchanged," and state 3 is "down." t Statistics and the MLR are evaluated relative to the null hypothesis of $P_{ij} = \frac{1}{3}$. All p values are vanishingly small.

with the full regression results in Table 2.5. The matrix is not consistent with independence between the successive states, which should be no surprise given the results of Section 2.5.1.3, but is also different in form from that of Equation (2.35). This matrix exhibits strong momentum for all three states, unlike the reversion seen in the no-change states previously.

2.5.2. *Biased Expectations in Eurodollar Futures*

A futures contract is a security that gives the owner the right to receive an asset, which was historically a quantity of a commodity, at a future date at the price paid on the purchase date. For example one might pay 300 ¢/bushel to buy a Corn Futures contract for December delivery. That means that, in December, you will be able to collect an order of 5,000 bushels of corn from one of the Chicago Board of Trade's warehouses and will have to pay $15,000 for it. However, all you have to do now is put up the "initial margin," which is a good faith deposit to ensure you are able to cover potential losses between now and December. Margins vary, but are around \$1,000 per contract, giving access to 15:1 leverage for speculators.[m] There are many subtleties to trading physical commodities, but this does not concern us there.

2.5.2.1. *Futures Pricing Relationships*

Eurodollar Futures are futures contract's that historically have been settled to $100 - L_T$, where L_T is the 3-month LIBOR rate on the delivery date, T, in percent. A futures contract is typically purchased several months, or in the case of Eurodollar Futures up to 10 years, before the delivery date, and settled on the last trading day before delivery to a reference price called the settlement price.

When the commodity underlying the futures contract exists, the price is simply determined by *arbitrage pricing*. The price of the future must equal the price of purchasing the commodity (with borrowed money), storing it until the delivery date, and then delivering it. This kind of pricing is relevant for physical commodities that exist, e.g. corn after the harvest, and for equity index futures and other futures which have a liquid market for the "spot" commodity,[n] such as metals. Let's say corn is available to buy now for C_t ¢/bushel and the futures price is $\mathcal{F}_{t,T}$ for delivery at time $T > t$. If I can borrow money at the annualized rate[o] r_t for the period of $T - t$ years, then the pricing relationship

$$\mathcal{F}_{t,T} = \{1 + r_t(T - t)\}\, C_t, \tag{2.43}$$

means that I break even on the trade — that the futures contract is fairly priced relative to the spot commodity. In general the "carrying costs," r_t, include additional positive factors, such as warehouse fees for storing the commodity, and negative terms that reflect the loss of "convenience yield" from holding the future and not the spot commodity. Thus the futures *basis*, $\mathcal{F}_{t,T} - C_t$, might be either positive or negative.

[m] You get the price swings associated with a \$15,000 asset for just \$1,000.

[n] In futures markets, the market for the underlying asset is known as the "spot market" and its price the "spot price."

[o] Assuming interest accrues linearly per calendar day.

When the commodity does not exist, such as an agricultural commodity *before* the harvest or financial futures such as Eurodollar Futures prior to delivery, the best we can say is that the prices would be "fair" if they matched the expected future price of the underlying, corrected for carrying costs and perhaps a risk premium. In the case of Eurodollar Futures, that is

$$\mathcal{F}_{t,T} = 100 - F_{t,T} = E_t[100 - L_T] \Rightarrow F_{t,T} = E_t[L_T], \tag{2.44}$$

where we have written the future's price in terms of the implied forward interest rate, $F_{t,T}$. This is known as the *Expectations hypothesis*.

Subtracting the current LIBOR rate from Equation (2.44) leads to pricing relationship that matches the linear additive noise framework of Equation (2.4)

$$L_T - L_t = F_{t,T} - L_t + \varepsilon_{t,T}, \tag{2.45}$$

$$\text{with } m(\mathcal{I}_T) = L_T - L_t, \tag{2.46}$$

$$\text{and } \alpha(\mathcal{I}_t) = F_{t,T} - L_t, \tag{2.47}$$

so the critical test is clearly: *is the mean of* $\varepsilon_{t,T}$ *zero?* Although that would seem to be relatively straightforward to evaluate, the problem is that the noise term, $\varepsilon_{t,T}$ is a function of both the reference date, t, and the maturity date, T.

Eurodollar Futures trade for settlement every month, but the overwhelming majority of the open interest[p] is concentrated on the four quarterly deliveries toward the middle of the last month of each calendar quarter. This means there have been 153 settlements since trading started in February, 1982, which gives 153 values of T for a test, but there have been over 9,600 trading days so which ones should be used for t? Clearly using $t = T - 1$ will give a mean error close to zero, as futures are not generally dramatically wrong the day before delivery, and $t = T - 2$ a similar value with, perhaps, a variance larger by a factor of 2. However, it's clearly reasonable to expect that adjacent days have very similar errors, i.e. $\text{Cor}(\varepsilon_{t,T}, \varepsilon_{t+1,T}) \approx 1$, and so any analysis that uses *all* of the available trading days is likely to need substantial correction for this correlation of errors.

[p]The net number of contracts outstanding.

2.5.2.2. *A Simple Test for Biased Expectations for Near Quarterly Eurodollar Futures*

In this section, I'll restrict analysis to the closest quarterly future to delivery. The settlement price determined by the value of LIBOR from "a special survey executed two London business days before the third Wednesday of the month." In practice, that is around the 15th of the month. For ease of calculation,[q] we can test for the accuracy of Equation (2.45) with T chosen to be those delivery dates and t taken to be the day on which the contract that settles on that date became the "near contract." Almost always, that is 90 calendar days prior, so $t = T - 90$.

If we consider Equation (2.45) to be a linear regression equation for the relationship between the change in LIBOR and the change in the implied rate from the nearest Eurodollar Future then it is making a very precise statement about form of the relationship:

(i) the intercept is zero; and
(ii) the slope is one.

That is

$$\begin{aligned} L_T - L_t &= \alpha + \beta(F_{t,T} - L_t) + \varepsilon_{t,T}, \\ &\text{where } \alpha = 0, \\ &\text{and } \quad \beta = 1. \end{aligned} \tag{2.48}$$

Both conditions must be true for the Expectations hypothesis to hold. Data is readily (and cheaply[r]) available and so the test is easy to perform.

Figure 2.25 shows a scatter plot of the change in LIBOR over this set of 90 day intervals for the contracts from the June, 1982, delivery to the June, 2020, delivery. Clearly there is a strong, positive, correlation between these variables, and the Expectations hypothesis seems well supported. Performing an F test against the null hypothesis as stated, the F-statistic is $F(2, 135) = 4.63$ with a p value of 0.011, and so we cannot reject this hypothesis with 99% confidence. However,

[q]Which is seldom the correct decision!
[r]This has not always been the case.

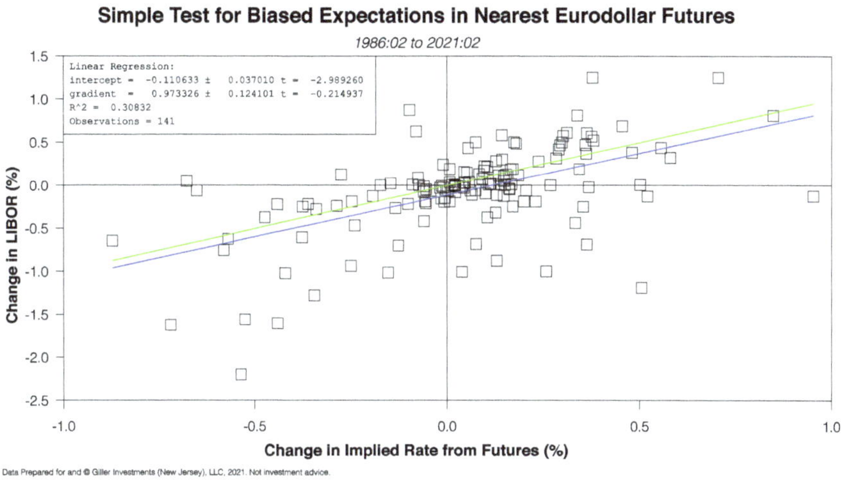

Figure 2.25: Cross-sectional regression between the 3-month (90 day) change in LIBOR and the expected change based on the Eurodollar Futures price 90 days prior. Regression statistics are quoted relative to the Null hypothesis that the Expectations hypothesis for Futures is true.

the intercept is individually significantly different from zero at the 99% level. As this is over ten times the historic minimum price increment of the contract, this is an inefficiency that cannot be brushed under the carpet of transaction costs. It might pay to examine other contract periods.

2.5.2.3. *Tests for Biased Expectations for Other Quarterly Eurodollar Futures*

The analysis of Section 2.5.2.2 can clearly be extended to other intervals, $T - t$, than the original 90 days. The longest history exists for strips of futures up to eight deliveries deep, which corresponds to 720 days forward. Regression results are illustrated in Figure 2.26 and the individual regressions are exhibited in Figure 2.27.

Several things are apparent from this analysis:

(i) There is a decreasing trend for $\hat{\alpha}$ and only the estimate for $T = 90$ is marginally consistent with 0. For all of the other horizons, the Null hypothesis is rejected.

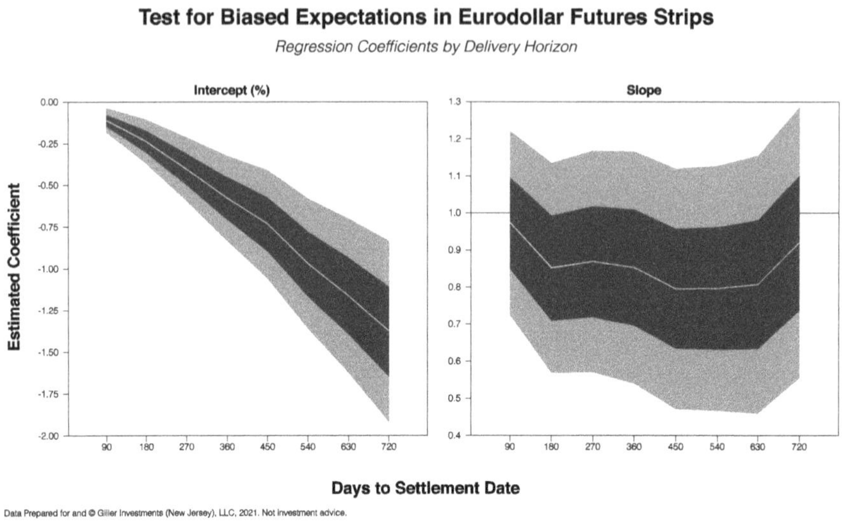

Figure 2.26: Plots of estimated coefficients for the regression model of Equation (2.48) with the final dates, T, taken to the be settlement dates of the Eurodollar Futures. Data is from 1986 to date. Shading indicates 68% and 95% confidence regions.

(ii) The slope coefficient, $\hat{\beta}$, is consistently in the region of ≈ 0.85, independent of the maturity and this term alone is not inconsistent with the Null hypothesis value for each of the estimates. Thus the failure of the Null hypothesis must be attributed to $\hat{\alpha}$ alone.

(iii) The trend in $\hat{\alpha}(T-t)$ is in fact linear in $T-t$, which is presumably how the variance of $L_T - L_t$ scales and so suggestive of this intercept representing a *market price of risk* under the Mean–Variance Efficiency concepts of Harry Markowitz's *Modern Portfolio Theory* [95].

2.5.2.4. *A Model for the Daily Change in Eurodollar Futures Prices*

It would appear that Equation (2.48) should be written in terms of some effective rate, $F'_{t,T} = F_{t,T} - \lambda(T-t)$, which is the implied forward interest rate corrected downwards for a risk premium which depends on the time to delivery and progressively vanishes as the time-to-delivery approaches. In other words, the implied forward

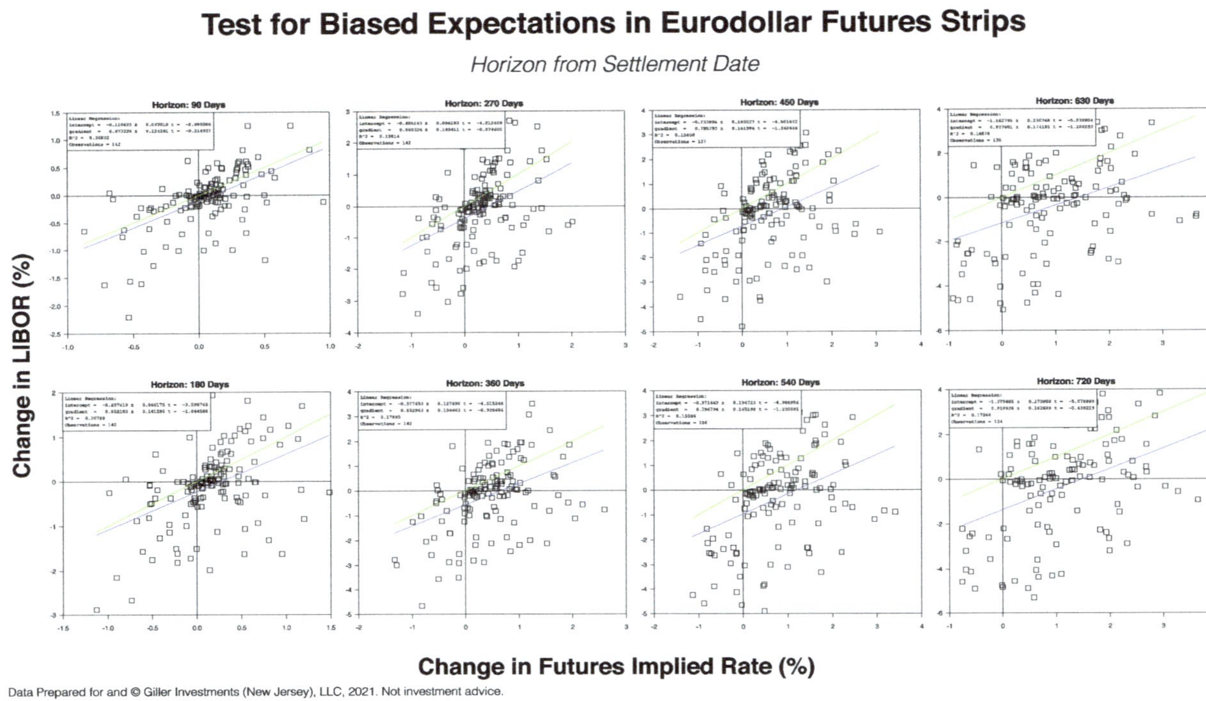

Figure 2.27: Scatter plots and regression lines for the model of Equation (2.48) with the final dates, T, taken to be the settlement dates of the Eurodollar Futures. Data is from 1986 to date. The blue lines are the best fitting linear regression line for each plot and the green lines is the relationship expected under the Expectations hypothesis.

rates are higher than they would be were it not for this maturity dependent term and, due to the way the futures are priced, the futures prices are *lower* than they would be. An investor willing to accept this risk would, therefore expect to be compensated for it if they were to hold longer horizon futures to delivery.

Thus one might propose a model such as

$$\delta\mathcal{F}_{t+1,T} = \mu_T + \varepsilon_{t,T}\sigma_{t,T}, \tag{2.49}$$

$$\sigma_{t,T}^2 = C_T + A_T\,\delta\mathcal{F}_{t,T}^2 + B_T\sigma_{t,T}^2, \tag{2.50}$$

$$\varepsilon_{t,T} \sim \mathrm{GED}(0, 1, \kappa_T), \tag{2.51}$$

$$\mathcal{I}_0 = \{\mu_T, A_T, B_T, C_T, \kappa_T\}_{T=1982Q1}^{2020Q2}, \tag{2.52}$$

to describe the short term changes in Eurodollar Futures prices contract by contract. In these equations, the settlement date, T, is essentially just a label for each of the individual contract apart from its appearance in the risk premium term. One way to examine the validity of this model is to fit it contract-by-contract and compare the coefficients. If the hypothesized parameters $\{\mu_T, A_T, B_T, C_T, \kappa_T\}$ are very similar, this would give us confidence that the system is a reasonable representation of the data.

2.5.2.5. *Estimation of the Eurodollar Futures Variance Model Contract by Contract*

We begin by iteratively fitting the model, contract by contract. The contract specific intercept, μ_T, will just represent the average change in price of each contract over the analysis period. Since this is a maximum likelihood fit to a nested model with no degeneracies the maximum likelihood ratio test may be used to assess the significance of permitting the A_T, B_T, and κ_T values to depart from the Null hypothesis of 0, 0, and $\frac{1}{2}$ respectively.

Figure 2.28 shows the test statistic, χ_1^2, for each contract, by delivery period, from March, 1986, to date, September, 2020, when the model of Equations (2.49)–(2.51) is estimated by maximum likelihood. The test is for the estimated value $\hat{\kappa}_T$ versus the Null hypothesis of Normally distributed innovations ($\kappa_T = \frac{1}{2}$). For all but a few

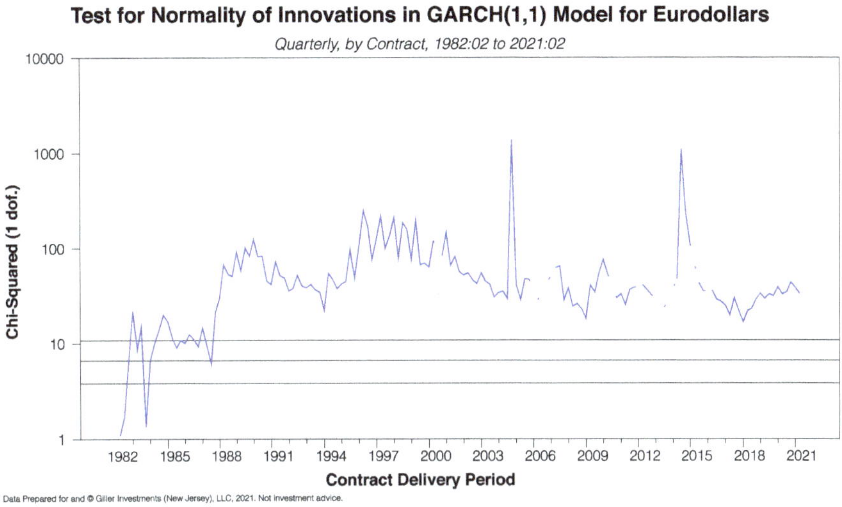

Figure 2.28: The test statistic, χ_1^2, for testing the hypothesis that daily price changes for Eurodollar Futures are Normally distributed. A $GARCH(1,1)$ model is estimated by maximum likelihood and used to test for $\hat{\kappa} = \frac{1}{2}$. The horizontal lines represent the critical values of the statistic for $\alpha_{\text{CRIT}} = 0.05,\ 0.01,\ 0.001$.

of the earliest deliveries, the test clearly rejects the Null with a confidence of over 99.9%. Figure 2.29 shows the estimated parameter, $\hat{\kappa}_T$, for all of the contracts, indexed by settlement date T, for which the regression procedure was able to converge.

It's is pretty clear, and should at this point be no surprise to the reader, that the data clearly and almost uniformly rejects the hypothesis that a Normal distribution should be use to describe the changes in the prices of financial data. The estimated parameter does seem to wander around prior to 2000 but, apart from a spike around 2014, it seems to be reasonable to assert that the parameter should be somewhere in the region of $\frac{3}{4}$ whatever the delivery period of the future considered, with a few exceptions. It is interesting to note that the Federal Reserve exited its *Zero Interest Rate Policy* regime shortly after the observed anomaly [38]. The estimates are clearly serially correlated, judged by the smoothness of their evolution as a time-series, but that is not unsurprising given the method of analysis.

Figures 2.30 and 2.31 show a similar analysis for the $GARCH(1,1)$ parameters $\hat{A}_T$ and $\hat{B}_T$. It is even more clear that homoskedasticity is

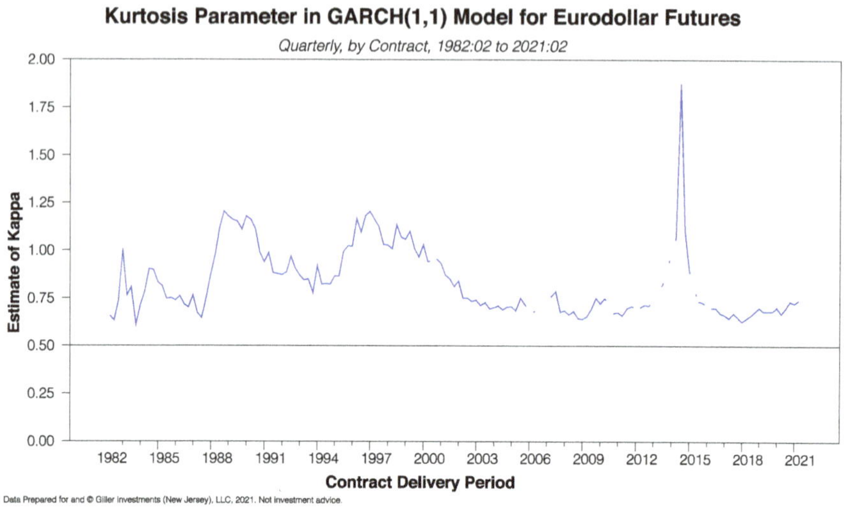

Figure 2.29: The estimated value of the kurtosis parameter, κ, when a $GARCH(1,1)$ model for the daily price change of Eurodollar Futures is estimated contract by contract.

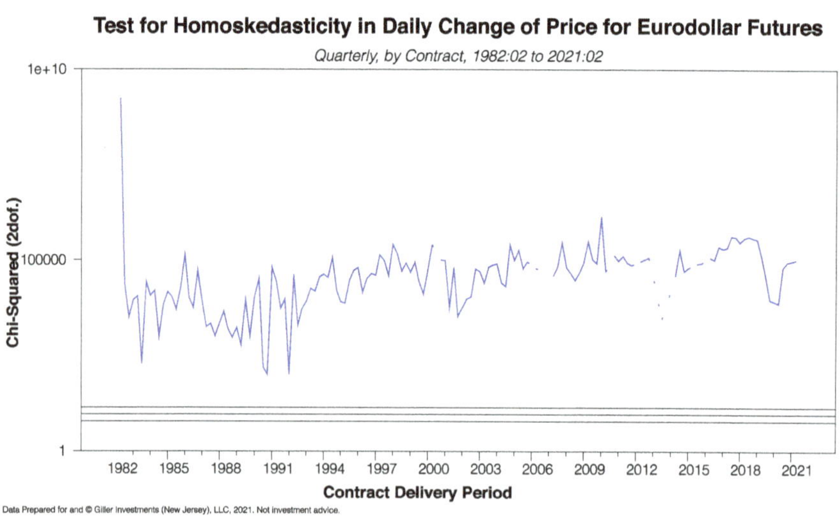

Figure 2.30: The test statistic, χ_2^2, for testing the hypothesis that daily price changes for Eurodollar Futures are homoskedastic A $GARCH(1,1)$ model is estimated by maximum likelihood and used to test for $A_T = 0$ and $B_T = 0$. The horizontal lines represent the critical values of the statistic for $\alpha_{\text{CRIT}} = 0.05, 0.01, 0.001$.

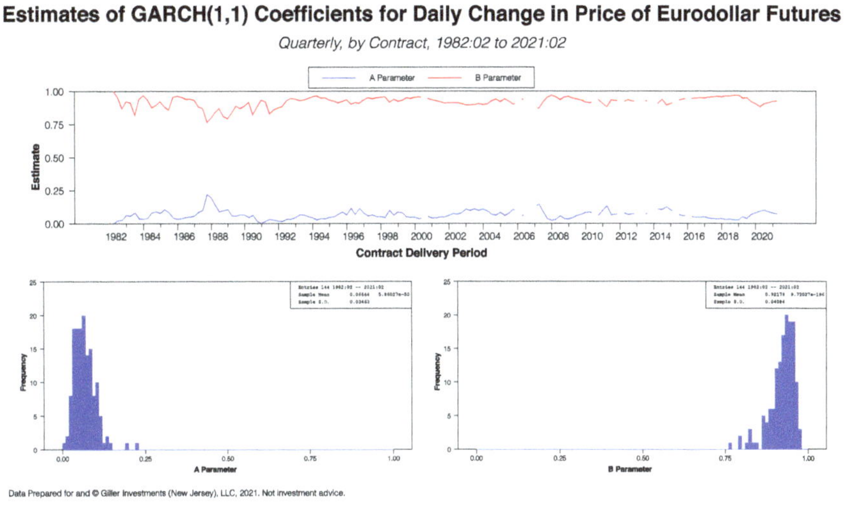

Figure 2.31: The estimated values of the $GARCH(1,1)$ parameters, $\hat{A}_T$ and $\hat{B}_T$ when a model for Eurodollar Futures is estimated contract by contract.

emphatically ruled out for all settlement dates on which the contract by contract analysis converged. The estimated values are clustered around $\hat{A}_T \approx 0.066$ and $\hat{B}_T \approx 0.92$, with a small number of outliers.

My conclusions from these results are that:

(i) Daily price changes for Eurodollar Futures are absolutely not Normally distributed.

(ii) Daily price changes for Eurodollar Futures are absolutely not homoskedastic and are well modeled by a $GARCH(1,1)$ model with innovations drawn from the Generalized Error Distribution and which are leptokurtotic, with a shape intermediate between the Normal distribution and the Laplace Distribution.

(iii) Distributional shape may have varied through time, as indexed by the contract settlement date, but the heteroskedasticity parameters are remarkably uniform through time.

It appears very reasonable to replace the individual parameters, A_T, B_T, with universal constants, and perhaps κ_T as well. Decreasing the degrees of freedom in a fit will also increase ability of a system to converge, so we are likely not to have the problems with the model as exhibited in the data presented.

2.5.2.6. *Test of a Model for Eurodollar Futures Price Changes Including a Risk Premium and Momentum*

Incorporating the results of Section 2.5.2.5, we modify the process proposed to describe the daily changes in price for Eurodollar Futures as follows:

$$M = \left\lceil \frac{T-t}{W} \right\rceil, \tag{2.53}$$

$$\delta\mathcal{F}_{t+1,T} = \mu_M + \varphi\,\delta\mathcal{F}_{t,T} + \varepsilon_{t,T}\sigma_{t,T}, \tag{2.54}$$

for the price process and

$$\sigma^2_{t,T} = C + A\,\delta\mathcal{F}^2_{t,T} + B\sigma^2_{t,T}, \tag{2.55}$$

$$\varepsilon_{t,T} \sim \mathrm{GED}(0,1,\kappa), \tag{2.56}$$

for the variance. This is then a forecasting system in the manner of Equation (2.4) where

$$m(\mathcal{I}_{t+1}) = \delta\mathcal{F}_{t+1,T}, \tag{2.57}$$

$$\alpha(\mathcal{I}_t) = \mu_M + \varphi\,\delta\mathcal{F}_{t,T}, \tag{2.58}$$

$$\text{and } \mathcal{I}_0 = \{\mu_M\}_{M=1}^{24} \cup \{A,B,C,\kappa\}. \tag{2.59}$$

To capture the risk premium effects observed in Figure 2.26, the parameters μ_T have been replaced by a piecewise constant function that buckets the days to settlement, $T-t$, into groups that are W days wide. I use $W = 90$ days as this (almost) evenly divides the forward intervals into calendar quarters. This really should be a function, $\mu(T-t)$, but there is insufficient data to estimate this accurately without some form of smoothing. The alpha is built out of μ_M and $\varphi\,\delta\mathcal{F}_{t,T}$ for momentum, although μ_M is an “alpha” in the manner described by Pete Kyle:

> *All alphas are betas onto risk factors not yet named.* — Pete Kyle, 1998 [84]

The estimates, $\hat{\mu}_M$, are independent and represent the mean daily change for the maturity bucket averaged over the history of all contracts that traded at that maturity and weighted appropriately by the volatility experienced. The Null hypothesis is that these estimates should have a mean of zero and be Normally distributed about that mean.[s] The estimates have a mean of 0.005516 price points per day and sample of values have a Jarque-Bera test statistic of 2.12 with a p value of 0.346, which gives us no reason to reject the hypothesis of Normality. On that basis, we can apply the t test for a Zero Mean to these estimates. The standard error of the mean is 0.00147 and the t statistic is 3.92, which has a p value of 0.0007 versus the Null hypothesis, i.e. We can fairly confidently reject the hypothesis of a zero mean.

If this data represents a risk premium for holding futures versus the spot interest rate instrument there should be no "term structure" within the estimates, meaning that $\hat{\mu}_M$ should not *systematically* depend upon M. The data are illustrated in Figure 2.32, and there doesn't appear to be any clean systematic dependence visible. Although the data does fit a slowly decaying exponential structure, it's hard to conclude that there is any clearly apparent trend here.

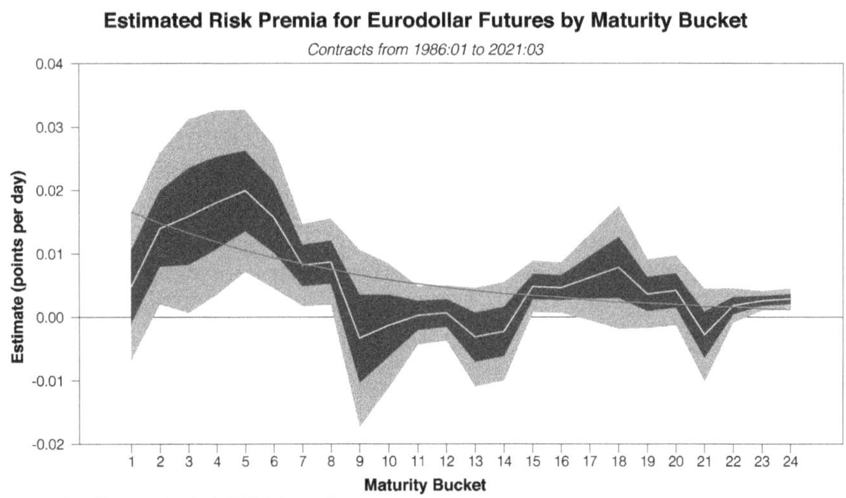

Figure 2.32: Estimated average daily change in the price of Eurodollar Futures for consecutive 90-day wide maturity buckets. The values are estimated using the leptokurtotic $GARCH(1,1)$ model of Equation (2.54). The shaded regions are the 68% and 95% confidence regions about the central estimate, which is the light blue line. The fitted trend is the purple line.

[s]This is based on the asymptotic Normality of maximum likelihood estimators.

Finally, let's look at the momentum term, the term in φ. This is estimated to be $\hat{\varphi} = 0.0619 \pm 0.0069$, which has a t statistic of over 8.9. This is substantial evidence that there is momentum in this data in addition to the non-zero expected return, implying that a profitable trading strategy could be built for Eurodollar Futures — which is, indeed, how I occupied around a decade of my professional career.

2.6. Asymmetric Response

In the previous parts of this chapter I've introduced the $GARCH(1,1)$ model of Engle and Bollerslev [31,9] and shown that it gives an empirically useful description of the observed heteroskedasticity of the returns of stock indices and of changes in US government and commercial interest rates. In this section, we will examine the nature of this heteroskedasticity in more detail.

2.6.1. *Motivation*

If you walked onto a trading floor in the 1990s, you would see many televisions tuned to the channel *CNBC*. For me, and others, it became a habit to listen to this droning accompaniment to the price action occurring in markets as if it was something of value. Particularly when Maria Bartiromo, the so called "money honey," [140] was on the floor of the New York Stock Exchange, which used to be a venue for actual trading before it was replaced with a data center in Mahwah, NJ.

Friends have observed that one of my defects in commercial life is my desire for precision in the use of language, and for years I railed against the market commentators who would talk about "volatility" only when markets went down. I had seen the $GARCH(1,1)$ model with leptokurtotic innovations provide much needed clarity into the description of financial data generating processes, and knew that the embedded relationship was agnostic with respect to direction. Why didn't anyone talk about "volatility" when markets rose? After all the basic relationship has a simple structure

$$\Delta\sigma_t^2 \propto r_{t-1}^2, \tag{2.60}$$

where price changes (or returns) would induce future increases in variance irrespective of direction. Yet any regular observer of stock markets soon comes to the conclusion that this is not so. Volatility does appear to mainly increase following market falls and markets don't appear to ever crash upwards, as Equation (2.60) would suggest should happen.

Figure 2.33 shows the level of the S&P 500 Index[t] around three significant market disruptions: the 1929 and 1987 stock market crashes and the COVID-19 Crisis. These are all events of significant market volatility but the onset of the volatility is abrupt: the stock market doesn't get volatile and go up, it goes down and gets volatile.

2.6.2. *The Functional Form of* $\Delta\sigma_t^2(r_{t-1})$

The asymmetric response suggested by these observations suggests that $\Delta\sigma_t^2(-x) > \Delta\sigma_t^2(+x)$ for positive x, but how should that be introduced into the Bollerslev model of Equation (2.12)? It seems clear that $\Delta\sigma_t^2(x)$ should be a *continuous* function of x, but need it be smooth? Glosten *et al.* [59] suggested a piecewise quadratic form, now known as the *GJR* model.

$$r_t = \mu + \sigma_t \varepsilon_t, \tag{2.61}$$

$$\sigma_t^2 = C + Ar_{t-1}^2 + B\sigma_{t-1}^2 + Dr_{t-1}^2\, I[r_{t-1} < 0] \tag{2.62}$$

($I[x]$ is an indicator function that is 1 when its argument is true and 0 otherwise).

This is the "classic" form of the $GARCH(1,1)$ model we have been using, modified by adding an additional term that is only present when returns are negative and only serves to increase the impact of the return without changing the structural form of the relationship, i.e.

$$\frac{\partial\sigma_t^2}{\partial r_{t-1}^2} = \begin{cases} A & r_{t-1} \geq 0 \\ A + D & r_{t-1} < 0. \end{cases} \tag{2.63}$$

[t]Reconstructed for the 1920s.

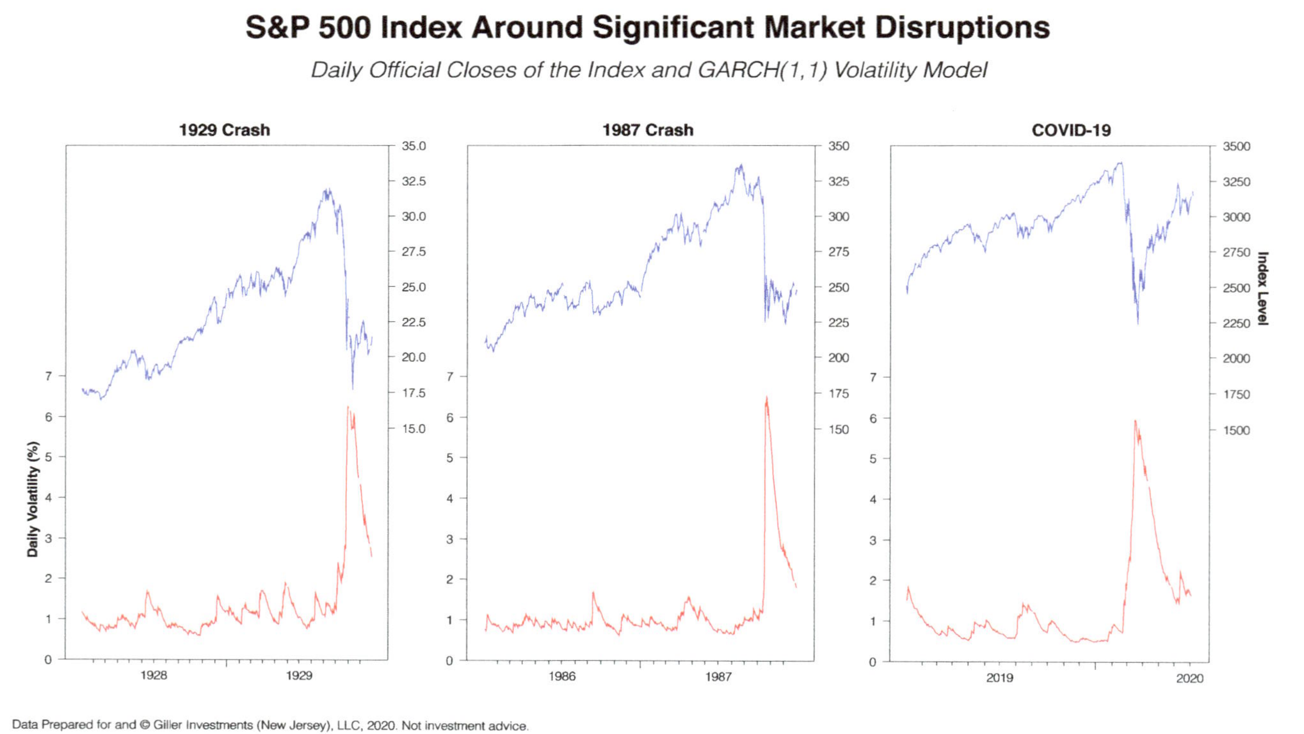

Figure 2.33: The level of the S&P 500 Index around three major market disruptions and the associated daily volatility of returns obtained by fitting a $GARCH(1,1)$ model with innovations drawn from the Generalized Error Distribution.

This form has the value of not only being simple but also being structured so that the maximum likelihood ratio test may be executed to test the hypothesis $D = 0$.

2.6.3. *Asymmetric Response in Index Returns*

2.6.3.1. *Fitting the GJR Model to the Entire History of the S&P 500 Index*

Let's start with the simplest possible thing to do, which is to fit a *GJR-GARCH*(1, 1) model to the entire history of the daily returns of the S&P 500 Index, from 1928 to date — which is 92 years of data. Such a large data sample should eliminate the possibility of the effect being marginal as the sampling errors on the parameters should be quite small. Of course, I will use the Generalized Error Distribution for the process as using the Normal distribution would be unlikely to model the data well.

The fit is straightforward in most time-series analysis software, and the results are presented in Table 2.6. Of course the model clearly rejects Normal homoskedasticity in favor of a GED driven *GARCH*(1, 1) structure. Every single p value in the fit is vanishingly small. The asymmetry, or downside response, term, D is very well

Table 2.6: Maximum likelihood regression results the fit of a *GJR-GARCH*(1, 1) model to the daily returns of the S&P 500 Index from 1928 to date.

Regression results

Variable	Estimate	Std. error	t statistic
μ	0.0483	0.00442	10.9
C	0.00945	0.000993	9.5
A	0.0369	0.00384	9.6
B	0.910	0.00454	200.5
D	0.0909	0.00649	14.0
κ	0.769	0.00915	29.4*

Note: The Generalized Error Distribution is used for the innovations.
*t Statistic computed relative to the Null hypothesis of $\kappa = \frac{1}{2}$.

supported with $\hat{D} = 0.0909 \pm 0.0065$ and t statistic of 14. The data most definitely wants the D term to be added to the model.

These results are very convincing, but what is quite surprising is how strong the downside response term is, at just under three times the size of the "regular" symmetric response term $\hat{A} = 0.0369 \pm 0.0038$. Clearly asymmetry is not a small correction to the classic model of Bollerslev — it is the dominant phenomenon and the commentators on *CNBC* seem to be onto something!

2.6.3.2. *Piecewise Quadratic GARCH*

Although Equation (2.62) is structured to permit the hypothesis $D > 0$ to be easily tested, it has the defect that it is *collinear* in A and D for the negative returns. Colinearity in regression is never a good thing as the two estimators can substitute for each other leading to large negative correlation in their estimates. Although the estimate of the sum $\hat{A} + \hat{D}$ is likely correct, the individual values may be misestimated.[u] This situation is mitigated by the fact that it only applies to around *half* of the data, but it still means that this is not the best way to know what the values of A and D actually are.

Having accepted the empirical fact that the index returns have an asymmetric response to returns, we can restructure Equation (2.62) to remove the collinearity effect as follows:

$$r_t = \mu + \sigma_t \varepsilon_t, \tag{2.64}$$

$$\sigma_t^2 = C + B\sigma_{t-1}^2 + Dr_{t-1}^2 \, I[r_{t-1} < 0] + Er_{t-1}^2 \, I[r_{t-1} > 0], \tag{2.65}$$

$$\varepsilon_t \sim \mathrm{GED}(0, 1, \kappa). \tag{2.66}$$

In Equation (2.65), which I call *Piecewise Quadratic GARCH* or *PQGARCH*, the symmetric response term, A, is deleted from the model and replaced with a downside response only term, D as before,

[u]The sampling error in $\hat{A}$ or $\hat{D}$ depends on the inverse of the covariance matrix of the estimators. The matrix will be singular if the estimators are linearly dependent, and that is exactly the situation that arises with collinearity. If the matrix is singular their sampling errors have infinite variance and so cannot be determined precisely.

and a new upside response only term,[v] E. This model is not collinear as the responses are

$$\frac{\partial \sigma_t^2}{\partial r_{t-1}^2} = \begin{cases} E & r_{t-1} > 0 \\ 0 & r_{t-1} = 0 \\ D & r_{t-1} < 0, \end{cases} \tag{2.67}$$

and under the regular Bollerslev structure we have the null hypothesis $D = E$.

The first thing we should do with such a model is see if it is a reasonable representation of the data. Since I did this analysis toward the start of the 2010s, let's fit the model to the prior decade — 2000 to 2009. That's over 2500 data points with both volatile and quiescent regimes, including a period of substantial market decline (the 2008 financial crisis). It should be a good test of the model.

When I first saw the results exhibited in Table 2.7, I was astonished. The downside response (the D coefficient) dominates the upside response in magnitude (the E coefficient) and the upside response coefficient is actually negative! Not only does the data say that volatility increases when the market drops, it adds to that that volatility actually *decreases* when the market rises. The data rejects the hypothesis that $D = E$ with very high confidence.

2.6.3.3. *Visualization of the Form of* $\Delta\sigma_t^2(r_{t-1})$

Moving away from tables, let's plot the form of these functions. But before doing that, a little work is necessary. The unconditional variance of a $GARCH(1,1)$ system[w] is $\sigma^2 = C/(1 - A - B)$. Assuming $\sigma_{t-1}^2 \approx \sigma^2$, gives

$$\Delta\sigma_t^2(r_{t-1}) \approx A\left(r_{t-1}^2 - \frac{C}{1 - A - B}\right). \tag{2.68}$$

---

[v]Note that here E is not the expectation operator $E[\cdot]$, in this context it is a parameter of the model (a number).

[w]If $\sigma^2 = E[\sigma_t^2]$, with $E[x]$ the meaning the unconditional expectation of x, then Equation (2.12) leads to $\sigma^2 = C + A\sigma^2 + B\sigma^2$ as $E[r_t^2] = \sigma^2$ by definition. The result follows from this expression.

Table 2.7: Maximum likelihood regression results the fit of a *PQ-GARCH*(1, 1) model to the daily returns of the S&P 500 Index from 1928 to date.

Regression results

Variable	Estimate	Std. error	t statistic
μ	0.0138	0.00177	0.8*
C	0.00827	0.00202	4.1*
B	0.950	0.00968	98.1
D	0.116	0.0158	7.3
E	−0.0265	0.00756	−3.5
κ	0.621	0.0256	4.7†

Significance tests

Test	Statistic	Value	p-value
Normal distribution	χ_1^2	22.5	0.000002
Homoskedasticity	χ_3^2	180,560	Negligible
Symmetry	χ_1^2	76.7	Negligible

Note: The Generalized Error Distribution is used for the innovations.
*$\hat{\mu}$ measured in Percentage, $\hat{C}$ in Percentage^2.
†t Statistic computed relative to the null hypothesis of $\kappa = \frac{1}{2}$.

The corresponding expression for a $PQGARCH(1,1)$ system is

$$\Delta\sigma_t^2(r_{t-1}) \approx (DI[r_{t-1} < 0] + EI[r_{t-1} > 0])r_{t-1}^2 - \frac{a(D,E)C}{1 - a(D,E) - B}, \tag{2.69}$$

where E is the constant from Equation (2.65) and $a(D,E)$ is the average of D and E weighted by the proportion of time the market is moving up or down.

Figure 2.34 shows what Equations (2.68) and (2.69) actually look like with data estimated from the first decade of this century. Although the downside responses are roughly similar for losses smaller than 5% in magnitude, the upside is quite different.

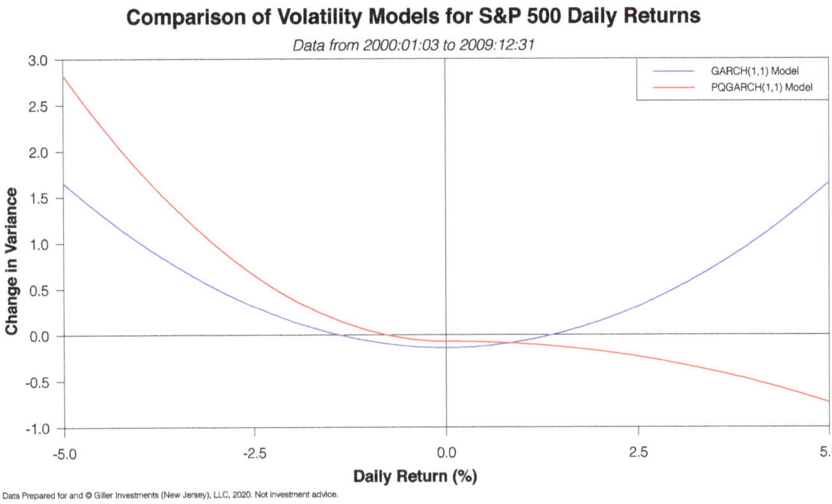

Figure 2.34: The implied variance response functions for $GARCH(1,1)$ and $PQGARCH(1,1)$ models estimated from the daily returns of the S&P 500 Index using data from 2000 to 2009.

2.6.3.4. *Asymmetric Response in Index Returns through Time*

The results of Section 2.6.3.2 were startling to me, but they are for a profoundly unusual decade. The financial crisis of 2008 seems a long time ago now, but it was a severe disruption of the markets. It's necessary, as we did for stock market momentum and interest rates, to study how stable these results are through time. Fortunately, the 93.5 years of S&P 500 history we have provides an excellent laboratory for such an analysis and we have already formed the hypothesis to test: Does $D_y = E_y$ over the long term?

Sweeping through the data, year by year, and accepting values only when the software indicates the model has converged gives a total of 78 fully independent pairs of estimates[x] $\{(\hat{D}_y, \hat{E}_y)\}_{y=1928}^{2021}$, which are shown in Figure 2.35. The mean value of $\hat{D}_y$ is 0.207 and the mean value of $\hat{E}_y$ is -0.018. Their standard errors are 0.175 and 0.086, respectively.

[x]Convergence can be obtained for the missing years by making the data windows overlap, but then the estimates are not independent!

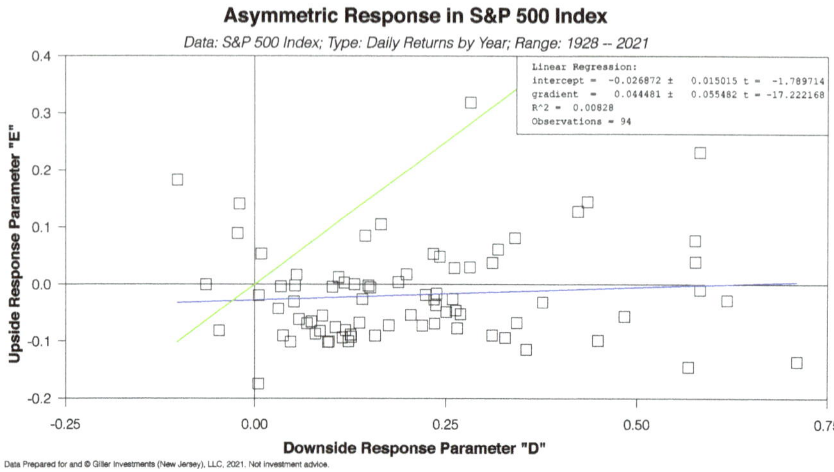

Figure 2.35: Scatter plot of the estimated upside and downside response variables $\hat{D}_y$ and $\hat{E}_y$ for daily return of the S&P 500 Index for the years 1928 to 2021. The blue line is the best fitting regression line and the green line shows the expected relationship if $D = E$.

It is tempting to test the hypothesis $D = E$ directly from the linear regression exhibited but, because both of these variables are estimates, we violate the assumption that the independent variable (D) is known without error. This is the so-called "errors in variables" problem or "regression dilution" and is discussed in texts such as Greene's [63]. Furthermore, such an analysis would assume that the value of E_y in some way "responds" to the input D_y, which doesn't seem like a reasonable model of the data.

A better test is the Kolmogorov–Smirnov test for two samples, which is similar to that previously applied in Section 2.3.3 but in this case compares two empirical distribution functions and asks whether they are consistent with each other. This can be readily computed and the two empirical distribution functions are shown in Figure 2.36. It is unambiguous from this that the hypothesis $D = E$ is rejected with a high level of confidence.[y]

The final datum we can extract from this analysis is to ask whether the observed sets of values, $\{\hat{E}_y\}_{y=1928}^{2021}$, are in fact statistically distinct from zero. Applying the t test for a zero mean

[y]The Kolmogorov–Smirnov test statistic $D_{\max} = 0.671$ with a vanishing p value.

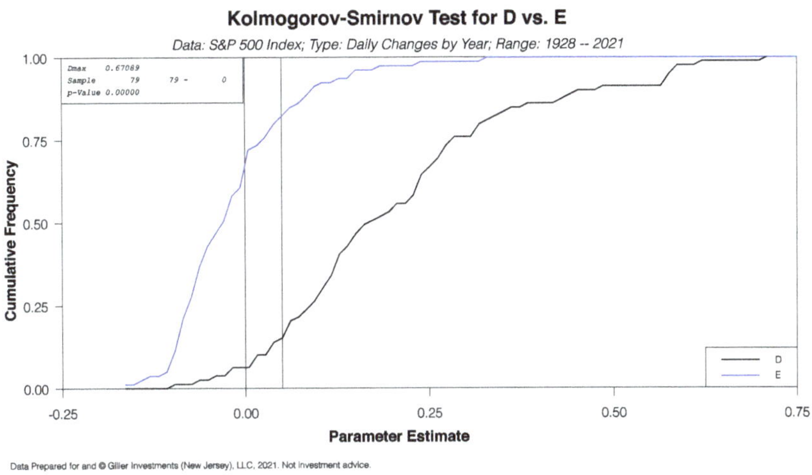

Figure 2.36: Empirical distribution functions for the estimates $\hat{D}_y$ and $\hat{E}_y$ from a fit of the $PQGARCH(1,1)$ model to the daily returns of the S&P 500 Index year by year. The Kolmogorov–Smirnov test rejects the hypothesis $D = E$ with high confidence.

gives a test statistic of −1.8, which is not significant. It seems that the response function could be completely asymmetric, possessing a downside response only. In which case it is not only qualitatively useful to talk about "volatility" only on down days, it is also quantitatively correct!

2.6.4. *Asymmetric Response in Rates*

Having found that the volatility process for stock indices is asymmetric, it is interesting to see if this phenomenon also exists in other assets. The obvious candidates are Treasury Bill rates, as we've built up a substantial experience working with them in Section 2.4, and exchange rates. The toolkit to do the analysis exists, and the only thing that needs to change is to switch from returns to daily changes of the interest rate.

2.6.4.1. *Treasury Bill Rates*

From this analysis we have $\hat{D} = 0.242 \pm 0.184$ and $\hat{E} = 0.326 \pm 0.129$, where the quoted data are the sample mean plus-or-minus the

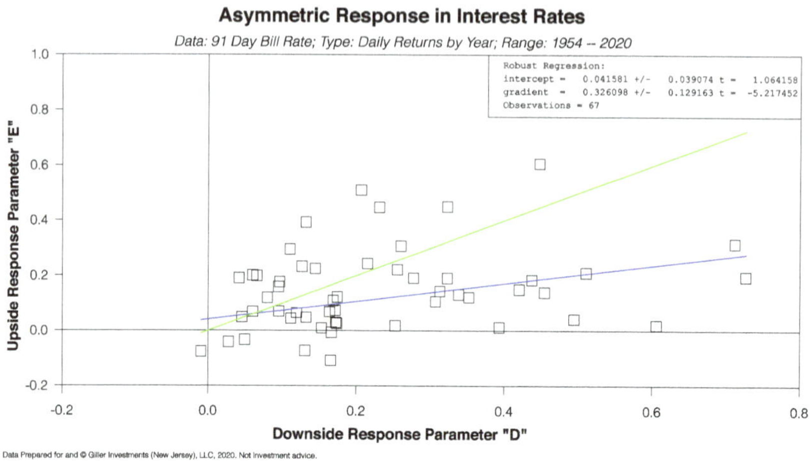

Figure 2.37: Scatter plot of the estimated upside and downside response variables $\hat{D}_y$ and $\hat{E}_y$ for daily changes in 3-month (91) US Treasury Bill rates for the years 1954 to 2020. The blue line is the best fitting regression line and the green line shows the expected relationship if $D = E$. t statistics are relative to the Null hypothesis of $D = E$.

standard error. The scatter of Figure 2.37 shows a distribution that exhibits some correlation but could also (by eye) be consistent with the $D = E$ line. Applying the two sample Kolmogorov–Smirnov test as before, we find that the weight of evidence is insufficient to reject the hypothesis $D = E$ as the observed p value of 0.08 is definitely too large. Thus, on this aspect of their behaviour, interest rates do seem to be different to stock indices.

2.6.4.2. *Exchange Rates: British Pounds*

Applying the same analysis to exchange rates is, again, a matter of "turning the handle." Daily data for the dollar-pound exchange rate, which is quoted in "dollars per pound," is available from many online sources for periods starting in 1971. I used returns not changes for the metric of interest, but everything else about the analysis is the same as that for interest rates.

Here we find that the means of the estimated coefficients are $\hat{D} = 0.129 \pm 0.177$ and $\hat{E} = 0.075 \pm 0.204$ respectively. Figure 2.39 reveals a scatter of $\hat{E}_y$ versus $\hat{D}_y$ that is quite unlike those seen in

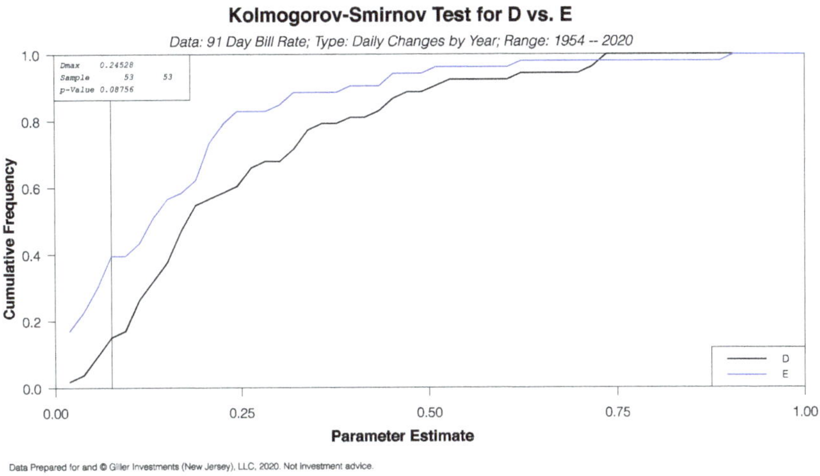

Figure 2.38: Empirical distribution functions for the estimates $\hat{D}_y$ and $\hat{E}_y$ from a fit of the $PQGARCH(1,1)$ model to the daily changes in 3-month (91 day) US Treasury Bill Rates year by year. The Kolmogorov–Smirnov test does not reject the hypothesis $D = E$.

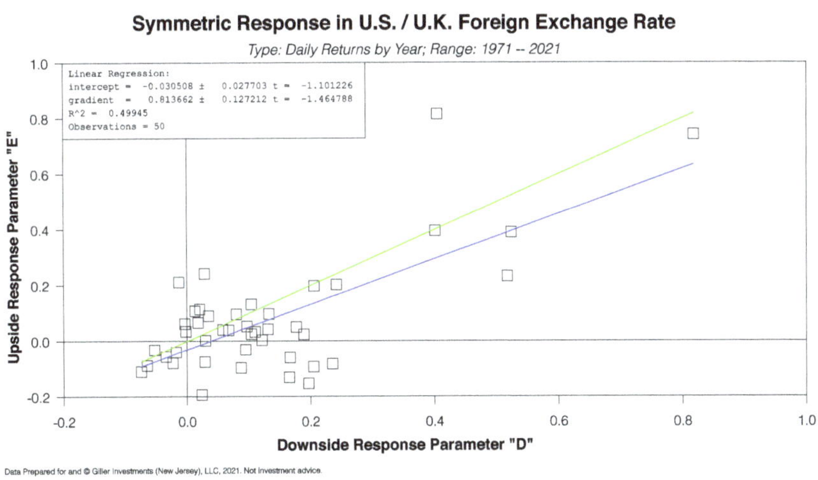

Figure 2.39: Scatter plot of the estimated upside and downside response variables $\hat{D}_y$ and $\hat{E}_y$ for daily returns of the US dollar–British pound exchange rate for the years 1971 to 2021. The blue line is the best fitting regression line and the green line that expected under the hypothesis $D = E$.

Figures 2.35 and 2.37, respectively. This plot does seem to provide much more convincing evidence that $D = E$ in this exchange rate.

To investigate that proposition with a sharper pencil, we can go back to the sequence of maximum likelihood regressions done to estimate the coefficients of the $PQGARCH(1,1)$ model and ask whether the data supports the linear constraint $D - E = 0$ in the estimated parameters.[z] We use the Wald Test [138], which computes a χ_1^2 statistic for each year, and we can compute the p value $\Pr(\chi_1^2 \geq X_y^2)$ for the sequence of observed values $\{X_y^2\}$.

As we have the powerful tool of the distribution free Kolmogorov–Smirnov Test available to us, we can use it to examine whether the distribution of observations is appropriate. As to what distribution these values should be compared to, that is straight forward. A p value, by definition, is a *right*-cumulative probability distribution function and it is well established that cumulative distribution functions, as a statistic, are uniformly distributed [22] on the interval $(0, 1)$. Thus we can test for that exact proposition, which is illustrated in Figure 2.40. It is clear from this that the values are consistent with

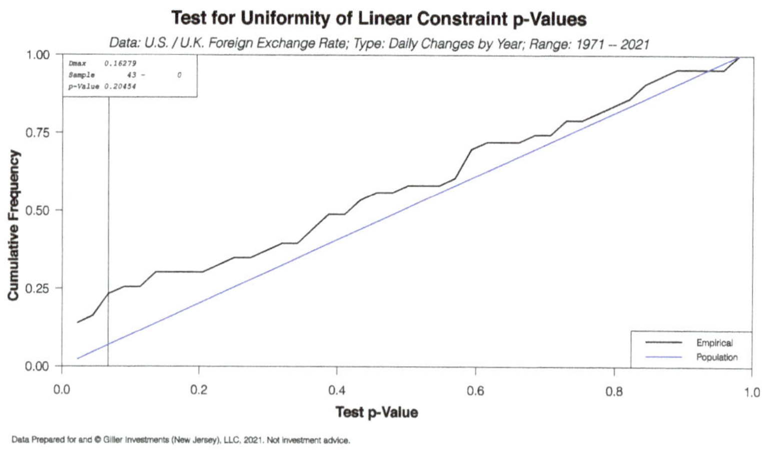

Figure 2.40: Empirical Distribution Function for the p value of a test of $D = E$ for the US dollar–British pound exchange rate, and the expected PDF from a Uniform Distribution. The Kolmogorov–Smirnov test is used to estimate the agreement of these two curves.

[z]That is, $D = E$

being distributed uniformly as expected. The weight of evidence is clearly in favor of $D = E$ for the Dollar–Pound exchange rate.

2.6.5. *Asymmetric Response in Individual Stock Returns*

From the prior sections it seems clear that the asymmetric response of volatility to returns is most strongly an aspect of stock markets. As we have found the phenomenon in stock market *indices*, let's take a look at the constituent companies themselves. To do that we'll take the current members of the S&P 500 that have at least three years of trading history and fit our now familiar $PQGARCH(1,1)$ model with innovations drawn from the Generalized Error Distribution.

To be specific, the model is as follows:

$$r_{it} = \mu_i + \beta_i R_t + \varphi_i r_{it-1} + \varepsilon_{it}\sigma_{it}, \tag{2.70}$$

$$\sigma_{it}^2 = C_i + B_i\sigma_{it-1}^2 + (D_i I[r_{it} < 0] + E_i I[r_{it} > 0])\, r_{it-1}^2, \tag{2.71}$$

$$\varepsilon_{it} \sim \mathrm{GED}(0, 1, \kappa_i). \tag{2.72}$$

This is the model of Section 2.6.3.2 adapted to have company specific parameters and with the added market return term $\beta_i R_t$ which expresses the (readily observable) general covariance of all stocks with a common "market" factor. For the market return we will use the returns of the S&P 500 Index itself as a proxy. The method is to fit the model via maximum likelihood to the available history of all companies currently in the index that have at least three years daily price history available. As this analysis is not about finding an alpha or demonstrating a market factor exists, which is the normal analytic followed on such baskets of stocks, I will not be performing any kind of Panel Regression analysis or Fama–MacBeth regression [37].

2.6.5.1. *A Note on Survivorship Bias*

The analysis in this section is going to use the set of companies that the S&P 500 Index is currently computed from. When we do analysis on the historic performance of a universe of stocks, we need to be careful how that universe is selected. The problems arise when the *ex ante* returns of a universe of securities that has an *ex post* selection criterion are analyzed. The reason being that these companies, by definition, did not fail during the analyzed period. Furthermore, an index such as this one which is selected from the companies with the largest market capitalization (their value) is a list of companies that prospered. Therefore we should expect their average return to be higher than the average return of a similar universe selected at the start of the analysis period. This is commonly called *survivorship bias*.

In this section, however, we are looking at properties of variance. Members of the index are not selected on the basis of the vagaries of a time-series model of their volatility. Although Fisher's devil might assert this study is just about the current index members, and generalization to all stocks should be done with caution, the fact remains that as a forward looking statement about this set of stocks it is useful.

2.6.5.2. *Abnormality of Individual Stock Returns*

In all 387 of 505 Index members were selected for which there was at least 3 years of daily price history and the maximum likelihood regression to fit the model converged. Figure 2.41 shows the distribution of estimated kurtosis parameters, $\{\hat{\kappa}_i\}$, for these companies and, as before, the Null hypothesis of Normally distributed returns would require $\hat{\kappa}_i = \frac{1}{2}$. In fact, this set of estimators has a mean of 0.930 and a standard error of 0.118. The t Test for Mean $\frac{1}{2}$ has a statistic of 72. This data is in no way consistent with the hypothesis of Normally distributed innovations, which should be no surprise to the reader at this point. The typical stock has a higher kurtosis than the index itself, which is not unsurprising as the index is merely a weighted sum of the individual stock returns and so, provided that the mean and variance exist, is subject to the Central Limit Theorem. This means that the index should be "closer to Normal" than its members, which is indeed the case.

2.6.5.3. *Heteroskedasticity in Individual Stock Returns*

Having unambiguously, but unsurprisingly, rejected the Normal distribution, let's look at whether this data supports homoskedasticity.

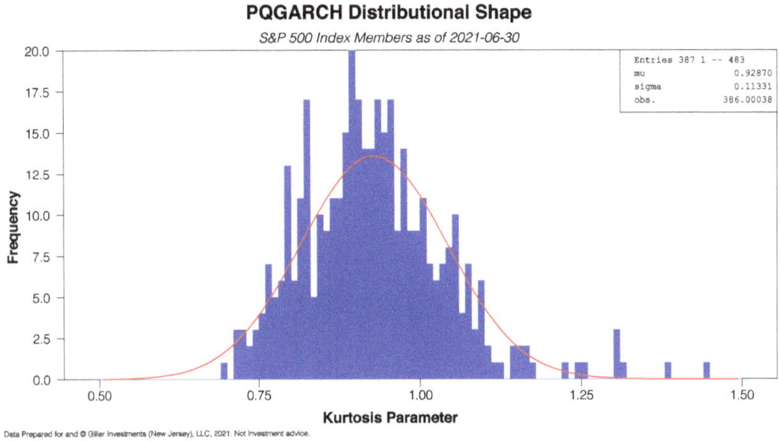

Figure 2.41: Distribution of the stock specific kurtosis parameter, $\hat{\kappa}_i$, for fitting a $PQGARCH(1,1)$ model to the daily returns of S&P 500 Index member stocks. For a Normal distribution this value should be $\frac{1}{2}$, so this hypothesis is emphatically ruled out by the data.

The distributions of the estimates of the variance model parameters, $\hat{B}_i$, $\hat{D}_i$, and $\hat{E}_i$, are exhibited in Figure 2.42. Again we have convincing results. All of these parameters should have zero values for homoskedastic data, and all of them convincingly do not. The actual data for the t test for zero mean is shown in Table 2.8.

Although we see some dispersion in these estimates, they are, in the main, clustered around their means. The key features seem to be that the downside response parameters are larger than the upside response parameters but, in contrast to the results of Section 2.6.3.2, very few of the $\{\hat{E}_i\}$ are negative.

2.6.5.4. *Asymmetric Response in Individual Stock Volatility*

To test for asymmetry, we again evaluate whether the data supports the linear constraint $D - E = 0$ for each regression using the Wald Test to assess significance stock by stock, and using the Kolmogorov–Smirnov Test, as before, to compare the calculated values to the Uniform distribution. From the data already exhibited for $\{\hat{D}_i\}$ and $\{\hat{E}_i\}$, it should come as no surprise that the data unambiguously rejects $D = E$ through this test.[aa]

[aa]The Kolmogorov–Smirnov test statistic $D_{\max} = 0.705$ with a vanishing p value.

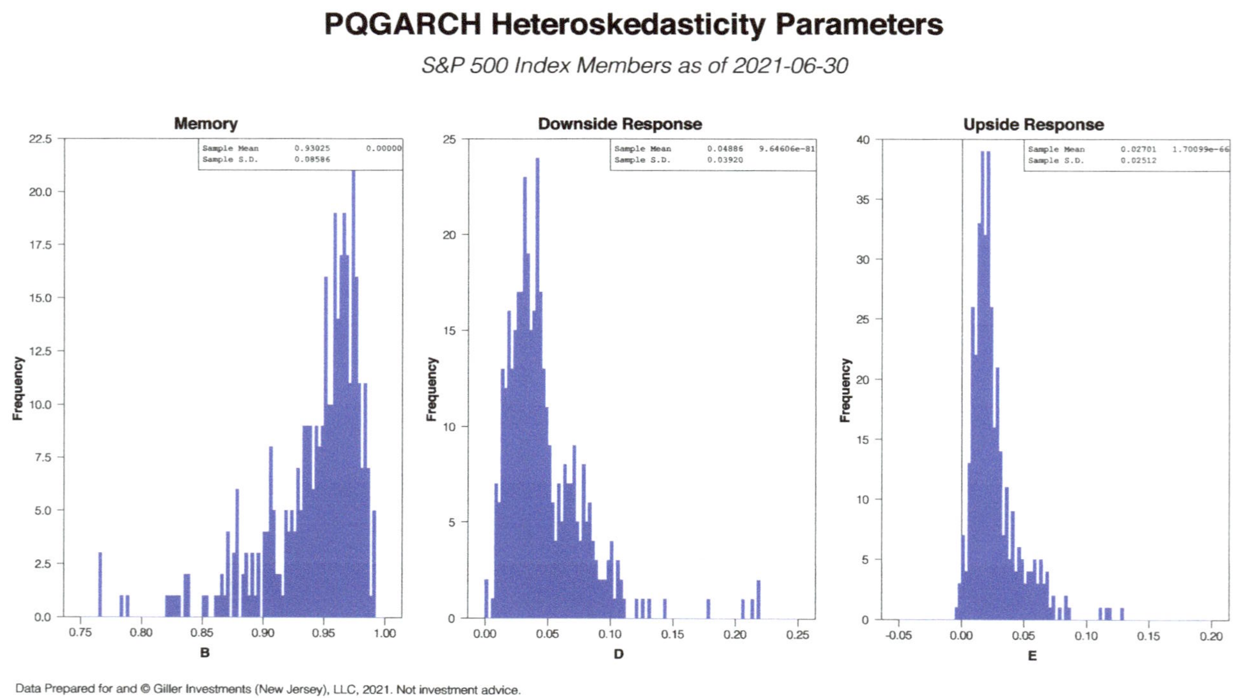

Figure 2.42: Distribution of the stock specific heteroskedasticity parameters $\hat{B}_i$, $\hat{D}_i$, and $\hat{E}_i$, for fitting a $PQGARCH(1,1)$ model to the daily returns of S&P 500 Index member stocks. For homoskedasticity, all parameters should be zero. For symmetric response $D = E$. Neither of these hypothesis are supported by the data.

Table 2.8: Table of values for the t Test for Zero Mean applied to the heteroskedasticity parameters obtained when fitting a $PQGARCH(1,1)$ model to current members of the S&P 500 Index that have at least 3 years of data history.

t **test for zero mean**			
Parameter	Mean	Std. error	t statistic
B	0.930247	0.085860	213
D	0.048864	0.039196	25
E	0.027009	0.025120	21

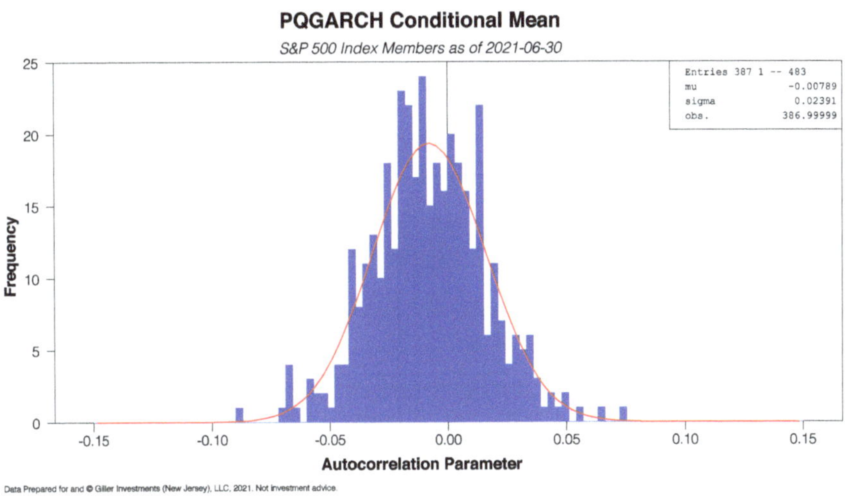

Figure 2.43: Distribution of the stock specific autocorrelation parameter, $\hat{\varphi}_i$, for fitting a $PQGARCH(1,1)$ model to the daily returns of S&P 500 Index member stocks where the conditional mean includes this term and a market return. For efficient markets this parameter should be zero.

2.6.5.5. *Autocorrelation in Individual Stock Returns*

Figure 2.43 shows the distribution of the estimated autocorrelation parameters, $\{\hat{\varphi}_i\}$. The Efficient Markets Hypothesis would require that these values be zero within sampling variation. We see a Normally distributed set of estimates with a mean slightly below zero at -0.008. This mean is significantly distinct from zero with a t statistic of -6.5. Thus, at the individual stock level we see the presence of a small mean-reversion phenomenon once the effect of the market has been removed.

2.6.5.6. *The Market Factor in Individual Stock Returns*

Figure 2.44 shows the distribution of the stock specific market covariance parameters, $\{\hat{\beta}_i\}$. This data has a mean of 0.910 and a standard error of 0.264, indicating that all of these stocks have returns that are positively correlated with the index. The estimators are, clearly, Normally distributed. In addition we see that this "factor" explains as much as 20% of the variance in daily returns of a typical stock, and in some cases as much as 50%.

Although I appear to have introduced this term *ex nihilo*, it is well justified in both theoretical and empirical finance [94]. In time series analysis a "factor" is sequence of random numbers that the time series of interest is dependent on contemporaneously. Factors are not "alphas" because they are not known *ex ante* and so cannot be used in a forecasting function.

2.6.5.7. *The Basic Properties of Individual Equity Returns*

Gathering the results of this section together, we see that the basic properties of stock returns are:

(i) They are not Normally distributed, being well described by a Generalized Error Distribution with a kurtosis parameter, κ, of around 0.9. This makes them *individually* more leptokurtotic than the S&P Index itself, but that is not surprising as such an average will be more "Normal" than its members due to the Central Limit Theorem.
(ii) They are not homoskedastic, and the response of variance to returns is asymmetric with a larger downside response than upside response. This is different to the index, which has a *negative* upside response.
(iii) Individual equity returns are positively correlated with the index and, consequently, positively correlated with each other.
(iv) There seems to be a small, but statistically significant, mean reversion effect where the *residual return*, meaning that part left after accounting for covariance with the market, is negatively

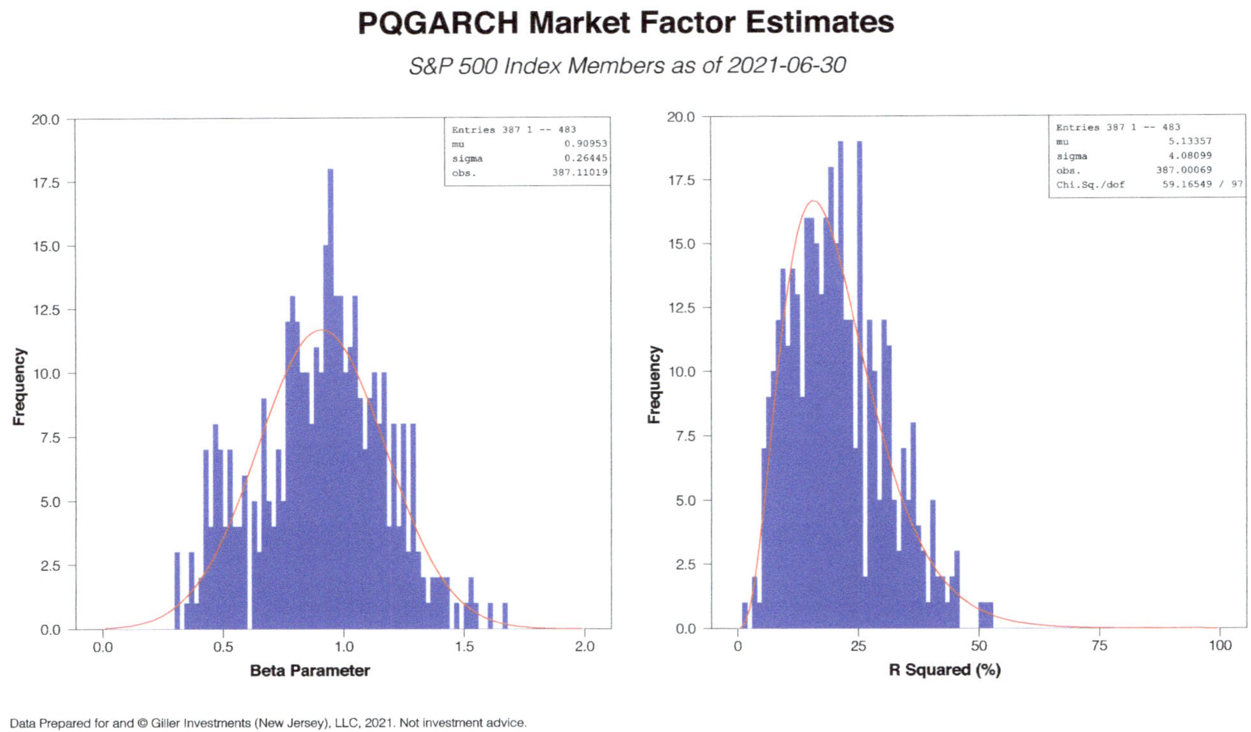

Figure 2.44: Distribution of the stock specific market covariance parameter, $\hat{\beta}_i$, for fitting a $PQGARCH(1,1)$ model to the daily returns of S&P 500 Index and distribution of the variance explained (R^2) by that model. The red curves are the best fitting Normal and Gamma distributions, respectively.

correlated with the prior day's individual stock return. This is inconsistent with the Efficient Markets Hypothesis.

2.6.6. *An Agent Based Model for Asymmetric Response*

These results present us with a conundrum. Variances combine according to the formula $\mathrm{Var}[x+y] = \mathrm{Var}[x] + \mathrm{Var}[y] + 2\,\mathrm{Cov}[x,y]$ and the only way to add two random variables and have the variance of the sum be less than the sum of the variances is for the correlation of the variables to be negative. Yet the results of Section 2.6.5.6 imply that the correlations of stocks are positive in general, which aligns with our experience as well.

Even though we find that stock returns do exhibit an asymmetric response to returns, the asymmetry is exhibited through the upside response having a smaller *positive* value than the downside response. This is quite distinct to the observation for the index that the upside response coefficient is *negative* as shown in Section 2.6.3.2. Since the return of the index is no more than a weighted average of the returns of its constituents, how can the sign of the E coefficient change through this averaging? I will attempt to reconcile these observations by diving deeper into how variance itself is created and, following Pete Kyle [83] construct a model of *skedastophillic noise traders.*[bb]

In the following I will introduce some changes in notation, which I hope are not too indigestible, to prevent confusion between the *PQGARCH* parameter E, which is a scalar representing the response of variance to positive returns, and the expectations operators $E[x]$, meaning the unconditional expectation of x, and $E[x|y]$, meaning the expected value of x given y. Similar to that introduced by Dirac [21], and in common use in Physics, I will use $\langle x \rangle$ to mean the expected value of x and $\langle x|y \rangle$ to mean the expected value of x given y. I may also write this as $\langle x \rangle_y$ for compactness. I will also use h_{it} to refer to the variance process σ^2_{it}, as is done by many authors including Bollerslev [9].

[bb]By this I mean traders that actively seek out volatile stocks to trade without possessing accurate private information on the value of future returns.

2.6.6.1. *Stock Returns with Volatility Generated by Noise Traders, Stock Specific News and the Market*

In this model, I assume that noise traders cause individual stocks' returns to be volatile and that the presence of noise traders increases the variance of daily returns in a manner proportional to the number of noise traders who are trading that stock on a given day. For simplicity, assume that the returns and conditional variance process for an individual stock may be written

$$r_{it} = \beta_i R_t + \varepsilon_{it} h_{it}^{1/2}, \tag{2.73}$$

$$\text{and} \quad h_{it} = v_i \nu_{it} + \eta_{it} + \beta_i^2 H_t. \tag{2.74}$$

Here, ε_{it} is the innovation and h_{it} is the conditional variance of the individual stock, v_i is the stock specific variance per noise trader, ν_{it} is the number of noise traders involved in the stock, η_{it} represents news related idiosyncratic variance, and R_t the returns and H_t the conditional variance process for a single common factor. This simple model does not contain any alphas or rewards for taking idiosyncratic risk, assuming all returns arise from the exposure to market risk that the stock delivers through the $\beta_i R_t$ term.

The returns process of Equation (2.73) is simpler than those discussed previously. By definition $\langle \varepsilon_{it} \rangle_{t-1} = 0$, but there is no such constraint on $\langle R_t \rangle_{t-1}$. However, I assume that $\langle R_t \rangle^2 \ll \langle H_t \rangle$ — meaning that investing in a single stock is a low *Sharpe Ratio* activity.

2.6.6.2. *An Autoregressive Model for the Number of Noise Traders*

In addition to the impact of traders on individual stock volatility, we assume that the behaviour of traders is such that they can be ascribed the following properties: trader's like to trade stocks that

(i) respond strongly to the presence of traders;
(ii) have experienced a positive return; and,
(iii) they have previously traded.

These three properties will be familiar to anybody who has spent any time in financial chat rooms! These properties are created mathematically by writing the process for the stock specific number of noise traders as

$$\nu_{it} = \upsilon_i + \chi\nu_{it-1} + \psi J_{it-1} r_{it-1}^2. \tag{2.75}$$

In Equation (2.75), υ_i, χ and ψ are non-negative constants by definition and J_{it-1} is the indicator function $I[r_{it-1} > 0]$. As the stochastic stimulus $J_{it-1}r_{it-1}^2$ is also non-negative, ν_{it} is guaranteed to be positive. We treat ν_{it} as an *unobservable virtual process*, so the fact that it is a real number and not an integer is not problematic.[cc] Thus we permit the traders to change their focus to the stocks that experience positive returns and also allow the total number of traders to change in response to these shocks. In the model, the traders are "momentum traders" even though there is no *actual* momentum in the returns, which is why they are described as "noise traders."

Taking unconditional expectations, and assuming that $\langle r_i \rangle \simeq 0$, we then find

$$\langle \nu_i \rangle = \frac{\upsilon_i + \psi \langle J_i \rangle \langle h_i \rangle}{1 - \chi}. \tag{2.76}$$

In the above we have used the definition of J_{it-1} to write $\langle J_i r_i^2 \rangle = \langle J_i \rangle \langle r_i^2 \rangle$. Equation (2.76) then confirms that our model captures the tendency of traders to distribute themselves in equilibrium amongst tradable stocks in a manner that favors those that respond to their presence and that are volatile. Note that in order that we satisfy the constraint that $\langle \nu_i \rangle \geq 0$ we require that $\chi \in (0, 1)$.

2.6.6.3. *A Model for Downside Response in Variance*

Consider a corporation who's enterprise value is dependent of the net present value of the effect on the company of a stochastic sequence of news shocks. Since the company itself has control over the release of much of the news that might adversely effect its value, and as the net present value of a slowly disseminated set of negative shocks is less than the net present value of those same shocks immediately disseminated, it is rational for an officer of a corporation who seeks to maximize the return to shareholders to attempt to withhold the

[cc] In the real-world there would be an observable number of noise traders, n_{it}, related to this process by a link function such as $n_{it} = \lfloor \nu_{it} \rfloor$.

release of some part of bad news until a later date. Thus, we expect a downside shock to shareholder value to be followed by a similar shock in the future and so expect the conditional variance of a stock to increase in response to a downside move in the stock price. If this phenomenon is the origin of the downside response of variance observed in Section 2.6.5.4, then Equation (2.74) may be augmented with

$$\eta_{it} = \kappa_i + \phi K_{it-1} r_{it-1}^2 + \lambda \eta_{it-1}. \tag{2.77}$$

As before, in Equation (2.77), κ_i, ϕ and λ are non-negative constants by definition and K_{it-1} is the indicator function $I[r_{it-1} < 0]$. Taking unconditional expectations, we have

$$\langle \eta_i \rangle = \frac{\kappa_i + \phi \langle K_i \rangle \langle h_i \rangle}{1 - \lambda}. \tag{2.78}$$

2.6.6.4. *The Aggregate Individual Stock Variance Process*

The aggregate individual stock variance process is then given by

$$h_{it} = v_i^2 + \chi v_i \nu_{it-1} + \lambda \eta_{it-1} + \phi K_{it-1} r_{it-1}^2 + v_i \psi J_{it-1} r_{it-1}^2 + \beta_i^2 H_t. \tag{2.79}$$

At this point we have made no statements about the form of the factor variance process H_t. However, based on our experience of market data so far in this work, it's likely that if follows some form of autoregressive heteroskedasticity. Without making any strong specifications of this model, we note that this form requires that

$$H_t = \delta H_t + B H_{t-1} \quad \text{where } B \in [0, 1) \tag{2.80}$$

and empirical experience indicates that B is likely to be in the region 0.85–0.95. If we require that $\chi \approx \lambda \approx B$, this allows us to write

$$h_{it} \approx v_i^2 + B h_{it-1} + \phi K_{it-1} r_{it-1}^2 + v_i \psi J_{it-1} r_{it-1}^2 + \beta_i^2 \, \delta H_t. \tag{2.81}$$

We see that this model is a $PQGARCH(1,1)$ model for individual stock returns augmented with a response to *changes* in the factor variance. In terms of our prior notation, we have $C_i = v_i^2$, $D = \phi$, and $E_i = v_i \psi$.

2.6.6.5. *Index Variance Reduction due to the Response of Noise Traders to Positive Return Shocks*

I will now demonstrate how a variance reduction can occur within this structure due solely to the rearrangement of the distribution of traders in response to a positive return shock. Consider an index formed by taking a weighted combination of N_S tradable stocks. For weights $\{w_i\}$ this index has variance

$$\mathcal{H}_t = \sum_{i=1}^{N_S} w_i^2 \left(v_i \nu_{it-1} + \eta_{it} \right) + H_t \sum_{i,j=1}^{N_S} w_i w_j \beta_i \beta_j, \tag{2.82}$$

$$= \sum_{i=1}^{N_S} w_i^2 v_i \nu_{it-1} + \mathcal{H}'_t. \tag{2.83}$$

In the above expression, I have isolated the variance due to the noise traders from the other sources of variance, which are encapsulated in $\mathcal{H}'_t$. From this it follows that

$$\delta\mathcal{H}_{t+1} = \sum_{i=1}^{N_S} w_i^2 v_i (\nu_{it} - \nu_{it-1}) + \delta\mathcal{H}'_{t+1} \tag{2.84}$$

by differencing the equation.

Consider a positive perturbation, $\delta\nu > 0$, in which the number of traders active in some stock $j \in [1, N_S]$ is increased and that number is drawn equally from all of the other stocks, i.e.

$$\nu_{it} = \nu_{it-1} - \delta\nu \left(\delta_{ij} - \frac{1}{N_S} \right). \tag{2.85}$$

Here δ_{ij} is the Kronecker Delta.[dd] Such a change would occur when a stock has a particularly strong upward move that is noticed by the crowd of noise traders. Substituting Equation (2.85) into Equation (2.84) and summing over all stocks gives

$$\delta\mathcal{H}_{t+1} = \delta\mathcal{H}'_{t+1} - \frac{\delta\nu}{N_S} \sum_{i \neq j} w_i^2 v_i. \tag{2.86}$$

This demonstrates that an internal rearrangement of noise traders to follow a positive price shock on a single stock does, in fact, lead to a

[dd] $\delta_{ij} = 1 \; \forall \; i = j$, 0 otherwise.

decrease in the future index variance. If many companies shares prices experience these types of shock, then the net effect will be aggregated. I call this *adiabatic cooling* by analogy to the thermodynamic process from physics.

2.6.7. *Concluding Remarks*

I feel in many ways the results of this section are similar to those presented earlier regarding the use of the Normal distribution. The data clearly and strongly supports the concept of an asymmetric response of the volatility process to the stimulus of underlying returns for equity indices and for individual equities themselves. The mathematical tools to analyze data under such a model empirically are not particularly complex to use. Doing analysis that appears to reject this simple property of market data seems, to me, quite hard to justify. It is factually incorrect and cannot be defended on the basis that the alternative is too hard. In addition, the model I developed in Section 2.6.6 shows that the empirically observed behaviour can be explained in terms of the behaviour of noise traders who follow momentum and bring volatility with them.

2.7. Equity Index Options

People like me, physicists, mathematicians and engineers, were first recruited *en masse* into finance to help trading teams work with options. Options are securities that give the purchaser the right, but not the obligation, to purchase, or sell, a security at an agreed price at a future date. They are, in a way, like futures with the ability to not go through with the transaction if it is nominally unprofitable. To get this privilege, of course, one pays a fee or *premium*, so it is still possible to loose 100% of your investment. Many books describe options in great detail, and the canonical one has become Hull's [73]. To proceed I'll need to use some option specific terminology:

- A call option gives you the right to buy a security at a future time at a future price.
- A put option gives you the right to sell it.
- The agreed upon price is the *strike price* of the option.
- The amount of money you pay for the option is called the *premium*.

- Options that are "in-the-money" are those for which you will be profitable if you exercise your rights and buy or sell the security.
- Options that are "out-of-the-money" are those for which you would be unprofitable if you exercise. "near-the-money" means out-of-the-money options that are very close to being in-the-money.

Another critical term is "implied volatility," which we will discuss later.

Options, it turns out, have a dual personality. Professionals are taught to think of them as plays on volatility, whereas many retail investors know them to provide high leverage at low cost. There are very few instruments that permit the purchaser to balance potential losses of 100% with potential gains of 600%–700% and, if you don't stake your entire balance on a single trade, that can be an appealing return profile.

The work presented here around the performance of option strategies will not involve option theory, so there will be no profit and loss curves based on "delta hedging" nor knowledge of option pricing methodologies. The first part will treat options as simple, contingent securities, and the latter will focus on the *empirical* properties of the *VIX Index* and how that time-series itself behaves and interacts with others.

2.7.1. *The Returns of Basic Option Strategies*

2.7.1.1. *Definition of Strategies*

In this section we're going to take a look at the returns available to traders who buy-and-hold index options. I'm going to consider three basic strategies on S&P Index Options:

(i) Buy near-the-money call options at the start of each month for settlement at the end of the month.
(ii) Buy near-the-money put options in the same manner.
(iii) Buy strangles, which is both the put and the call option above, and so is a play on volatility not direction.

The performance of these strategies will be compared to just buying the index itself.

For each option strategy the profit is either the difference between the spot price of the underlying security on the settlement date and the strike price, or zero, whichever is larger minus the premium paid upfront for the option. Thus,

$$\text{profit} = \begin{cases} \max(S_T - X, 0) - C(t, X, T) & \text{for calls} \\ \max(X - S_T, 0) - P(t, X, T) & \text{for puts.} \end{cases} \tag{2.87}$$

The profit or loss for a strangle is the sum of those two terms.[ee] Here $C(t, X, T)$ is the price, at time t, of a call option for settlement at time T with strike price X and $P(t, X, T)$ is the same thing for put options. The famous Black–Scholes formula [8] tells you what these prices should be if you also input the current risk-free interest rate, r_t, and the volatility of the underlying security, σ_t, that is *expected* for the period $[t, T]$. However, here I am just considering the market-prices of these options.

2.7.1.2. *Distributions of Basic Option Strategy Monthly Returns*

Computing the profitability of the various strategies defined is then straightforward. If X_t is the strike price of the out-of-the-money call option closest to the money on a given date, the net profit of a sequence of investments made once a month is then

$$\sum_T \left[\max\{S_T - X_{T-30}, 0\} - C(T - 30, X_{T-30}, T)\right], \tag{2.88}$$

with a similar expression for the puts and strangles strategies. In the above it is assumed that purchases are made thirty days prior to settlement each month and the sum is over the monthly settlement dates. In reality we use the first and last Cboe[ff] trading dates in each month and, to compare this fairly to the index, the buy-and-hold strategy will be computed for the same investment periods. We assume zero transaction costs, which is currently a reasonable assumption for retail traders.

[ee] With different strike prices for the two options. When the strike prices coincide the position is called a "straddle" instead.

[ff] The Chicago Board Options Exchange, (CBOE) recently renamed itself to just the "Cboe."

To compute the *return* of such an option buying strategy one needs to specify how much capital is to be invested. If you invest 100% of your capital in a strategy you will almost certainly loose money, because future returns are uncertain. Thus the size of the trade needs to be adjusted to accommodate a tolerable risk profile. I often work with the "7% solution," to size positions so that the expected annual drawdown is no more than 7% of initial capital. There is no magic here — it is a number that can produce actual drawdowns of up to 21% of capital, due to the leptokurtotic nature of real market returns — but that is a level I can live with. Options, actually, provide a more precise tool. One can guarantee that 7% as a long option position cannot deliver a loss of more than the premium invested. For monthly trading, the position sizes would be adjusted to deliver no more than an *annual* loss by compounding. For the purposes of this analysis, however, I will scale the strategies so that the variances are all equal.

Figure 2.45 shows the distributions of monthly returns for the four strategies discussed over the period for which PM Settled options on the S&P Index are available at the Cboe. The best performing strategy is actually the simple buy-and-hold one, with a Sharpe Ratio of 0.84, the second best is the call buying strategy, and both buying puts and buying strangles do not make money. What is very clear is how the option strategies have transformed the shape of the returns distributions, sharply limiting the downside to a loss of around 2.5% in single month, whereas the buy-and-hold investor has suffered a 15% down month and several in the region −10% to −5%. The mean monthly returns are 0.990% and 0.789% for the profitable strategies.

As to whether these means are meaningfully distinct, that is hard to judge directly from this data. The t test for zero mean likely cannot be used on the distribution of returns for the call buying strategy as the data is so massively skewed. However, one thing that is vividly true from these histograms is that the most likely outcome for a trader following a simple option strategy is to lose money. Figure 2.46 shows these returns accumulated over the investment period.

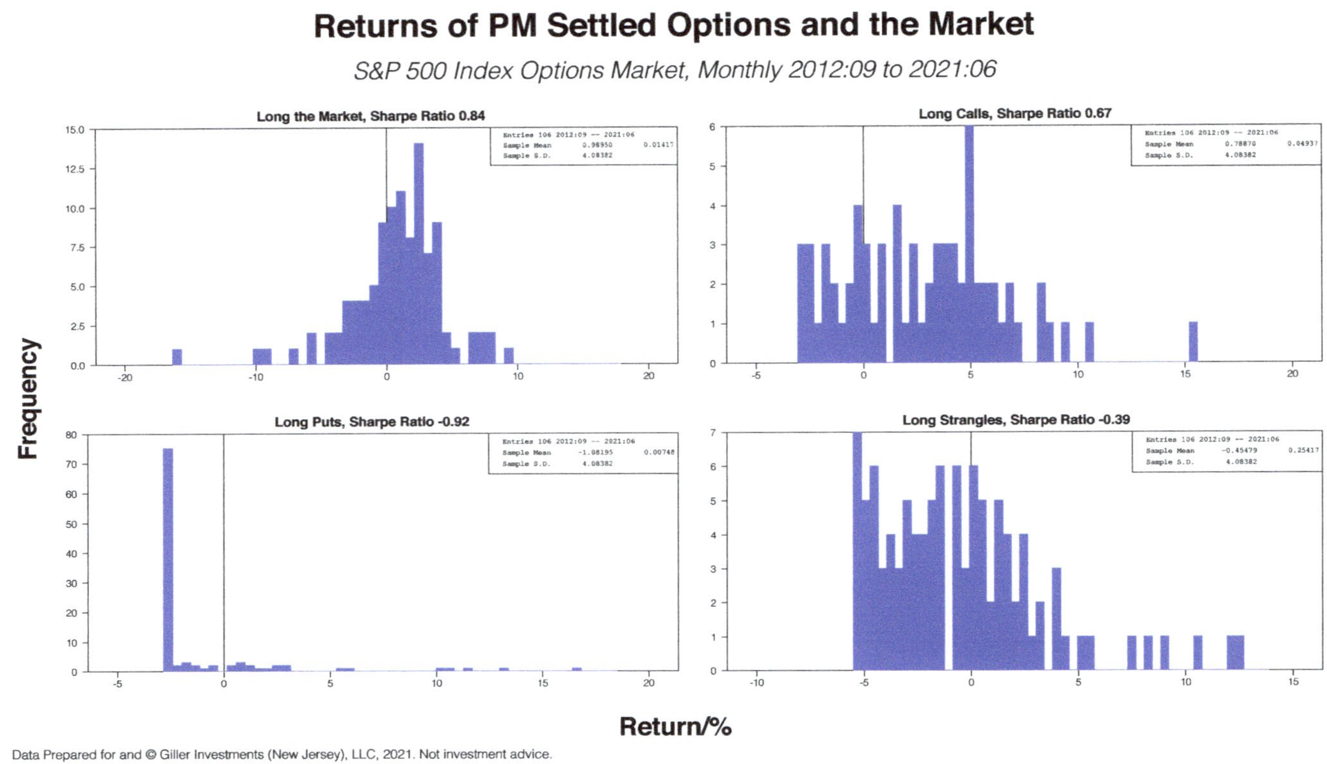

Figure 2.45: Distributions of monthly returns for equal variance investment in three basic option strategies on the S&P 500 Index and buy-and-hold investing in the index itself.

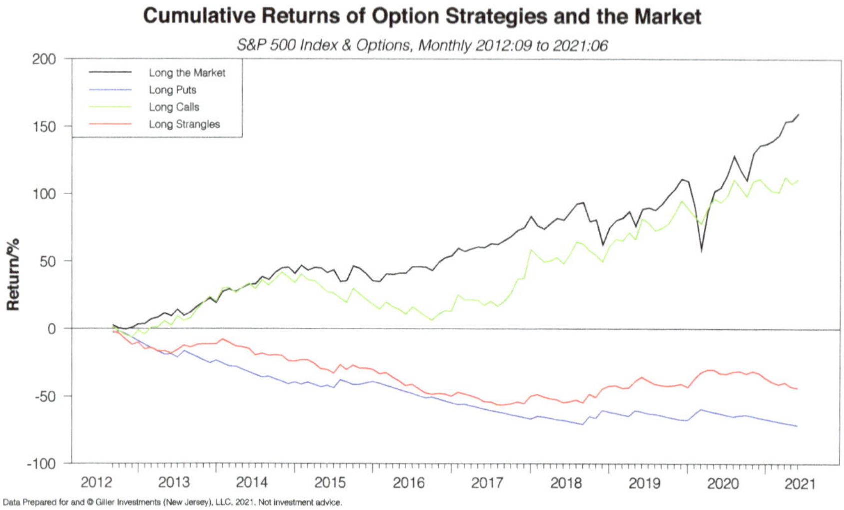

Figure 2.46: Time series of total returns for equal variance investment in three basic option strategies on the S&P 500 Index and buy-and-hold investing in the index itself.

2.7.1.3. *Bootstrapping the Excess Return of a Call Buying Strategy*

If the t Test cannot be used to determine whether the performance difference we observe in Section 2.7.1.2, how can we evaluate whether the performance difference observed in Figure 2.45 is significant? This is a relevant question as it addresses which of the two strategies an investor should adopt.

One method I really like, and which is the real product of the era of computational data analysis, is Bradley Efron's "Bootstrap" [27]. This creates the sampling distribution of a statistic by simulation via random resampling (with replacement) of the actual data. For large data sets this can be done in a number of ways that is so vast that it is, in practice, unlimited and the result is a simulated distribution function for the statistic from which we can answer questions such as: what's the probability that the average monthly return of the call strategy is larger than that of the buy-and-hold strategy? Because the number of bootstrap simulations can be made very large without any risk of violating the assumption that the measured statistics from

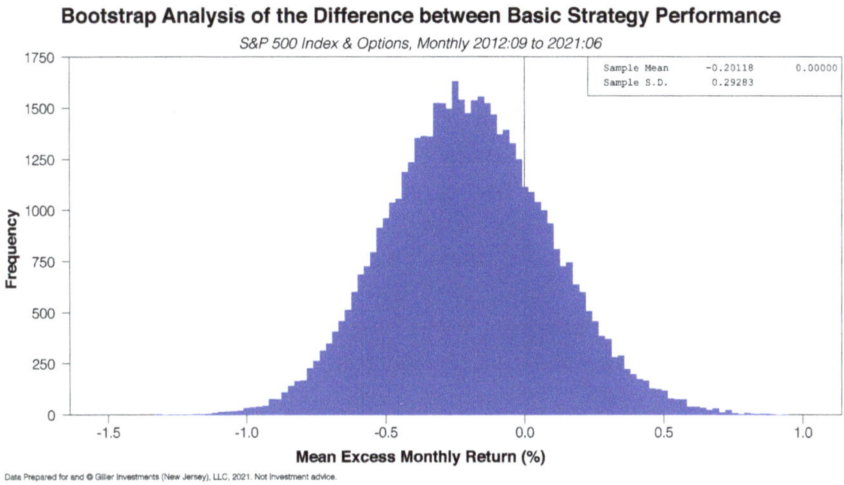

Figure 2.47: Distribution of the test statistic, the mean difference in monthly returns between a call buying strategy and a buy-and-hold strategy for the S&P 500 Index, from 50,000 bootstrap simulations.

the simulations are independent of each other, the sampling error in these computations is negligible.

As the difference in the mean monthly return is mathematically identical to the mean of the differences in monthly returns, that is the statistic I decided to bootstrap. Doing this 50,000 times produces the well behaved distribution exhibited in Figure 2.47, from which we can compute the probability that the average monthly return of the call buying strategy exceeds that of the buy and hold strategy is 0.242. As this is not significant, there is no message from the data as to what the "best" strategy of the two actually is and so the decision must be left to personal choice. Which is to say how much the differences in the skewness and kurtosis of the distributions, or their extreme values, are important to the investor.

2.7.2. *The Price at which the Entire Option Market Breaks Even*

In Section 2.7.1.1, I mentioned the Black–Scholes formula for pricing options. This formula is the product of a number of empirically false assumptions about the behaviour of financial data,[gg] yet it manages to provide a "reasonable ball-park" for pricing options. This arises because the Black–Scholes formula is describing the profit that arises from a hedged strategy and that structure, in a way like the renormalization operation in Quantum Field Theory, means that it doesn't suffer from these defects to first order. We should not conclude, however, from its relative success that this means that its assumptions are empirically sound — to answer that question we must look to actual data.

Black–Scholes, or one of a zoo of similar formulæ, is a function of the parameters of the option contract considered (strike price, settlement date, method of exercise, type of contingent claim) and of the particulars of the market environment it is traded in. Principally those are the interest rate at the time and the volatility expected for the price of the underlying security between the purchase and the settlement date. To price an option one must input this volatility. Alternatively. one may take the prices as given and estimate the volatility necessary to arrive at that price. This is what's known as the "implied volatility."

The normal thing done when looking at the set of all options on a security is to use this ensemble of data to estimate the so-called volatility surface, which is the implied volatility as a function of depth-into-the-money and time-to-maturity: $\sigma(S_t - X, T - t)$. In this section we will attempt something different.

2.7.2.1. *The Market Clearing Price for an Option Market*

For every tradable option on a security there is a current price and an open interest, which is the number of contracts that have been traded and not offset. As before, let $C(t, X, T)$ represent the price of call options at time t, with strike price X and settlement date T, and $P(t, X, T)$ the price of put options on the same underlying. If the open interest in those options are $D(t, X, T)$ and $Q(t, X, T)$ respectively, then the current state of the market represents a bet by the crowd of traders on the future value price of the underlying security on the settlement date. For whatever that price, S_T, actually

[gg] Continuous time, Normal distributions, continuous trading, frictionless trading, constant volatility....

is, some of those traders will make money and some will lose money. Overall the net cashflow of the market, with respect to these options, on the settlement date will be

$$\mathcal{M}(S_T,t,T) = \sum_X \left[Q(t,X,T)\left\{\max(X - S_T, 0) - P(t,X,T)\right\}\right] + \sum_X \left[D(t,X,T)\left\{\max(S_T - X, 0) - C(t,X,T)\right\}\right]. \tag{2.89}$$

Every trader who owns calls has bet that $S_T > X$ on the settlement date, and every trader who owns puts has bet that $S_T < X$. Traders who are short have made the opposite wagers. We can ask, on any give day, what the price, $\mathcal{S}(t,T)$, that minimizes the net cashflow of the whole market on the settlement day is. This is the price that balances, or clears, the market, and is defined by

$$\mathcal{S}(t,T) = \arg\min_S |\mathcal{M}(S,t,T)|. \tag{2.90}$$

This price, $\mathcal{S}(t,T)$, is a forward price for the settlement date, T, implied by the current valuations of all of the trades done by market participants. If the option market, as a whole, is fair then we would expect

$$E_t[S_T] = \mathcal{S}(t,T). \tag{2.91}$$

2.7.2.2. *The Average Discount between Option Market Forward Prices and Spot Prices*

In Section 2.5.2.3, we showed that for *LIBOR* Futures markets the Expectations hypothesis does not hold. Equation (2.91) is a statement of an Expectations hypothesis for Equity Index Options. It is interesting to see not only what the relationship is between $\mathcal{S}(t,T)$ and S_T but also how it is related to S_t, the spot price on the same day.

One figure of merit relevant to that is the discount

$$\mathcal{D}(t,T) = \frac{S_t - \mathcal{S}(t,T)}{S_t}. \tag{2.92}$$

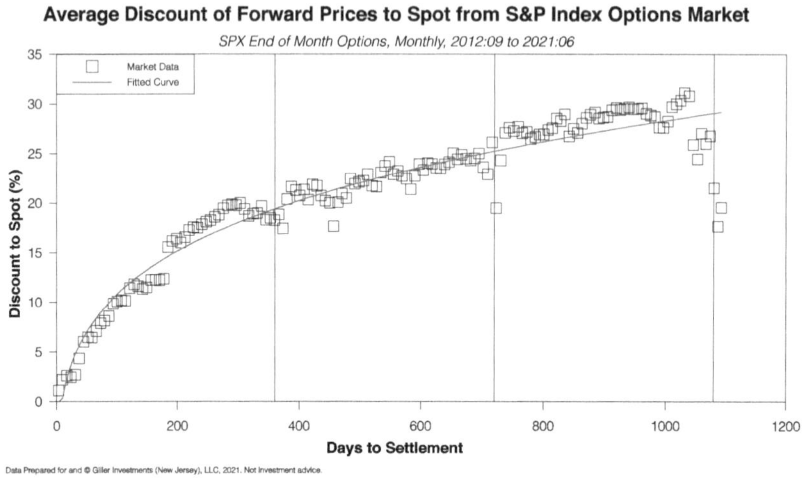

Figure 2.48: Average value of the discount of the forward price of the S&P 500 Index, $\mathcal{S}(t,T)$, implied by the option market to the spot price, S_t, as a function of the forward interval, $T-t$.

This is relatively straightforward to compute, if a little time consuming. Figure 2.48 shows the structural relationship that is observed when this discount is plotted against the number of days to settlement, $T-t$. It appears to be reasonably well modeled by

$$\bar{\mathcal{D}}(t,T) = a + b(T-t)^c. \tag{2.93}$$

The most striking feature of this plot is that the average discount is substantial for long option maturities, reaching as much as $\approx$30% for three year forward options. The plot shows residuals that also appear to be strongly correlated with their neighbors, so this plot is not the right venue from which to estimate the actual functional form of Equation (2.93). What is clear, though, is that the average relationship between the forward price of the S&P 500 Index, as implied by the entire options market over time, and the actual value is a substantial discount. We know that what actually happened to the index over the period covered by this plot is that it rose strongly[hh] and so it is very clear that the Expectations hypothesis for Equity Index Options does not hold for this data.

[hh]In fact more than doubling from 1,405 at the start of September, 2019, to 4,297.50 at the time of writing (June 30, 2020), see Figure 2.1.

2.7.2.3. *Properties of the Risk Premium Rate of Option Market Forward Prices*

The existence of a systematic discount to the forward price that is not predictive means that it must represent a risk-premium accrued by the holders on long-dated options, very much as we identified for holders of Eurodollar Futures in Section 2.5.2. On any given day, t, the average risk premium rate can be computed as

$$b_t = \frac{1}{N_O} \sum_T \frac{\mathcal{D}(t,T)}{\sqrt{T-t}} \tag{2.94}$$

for N_O options with settlement date T. Here I have *asserted* that the parameters a and c from Equation (2.93) take the values 0 and 1/2, respectively. These values are close to, but not exactly equal to, the parameters observed from Figure 2.48. This time-series is plotted in Figure 2.49.

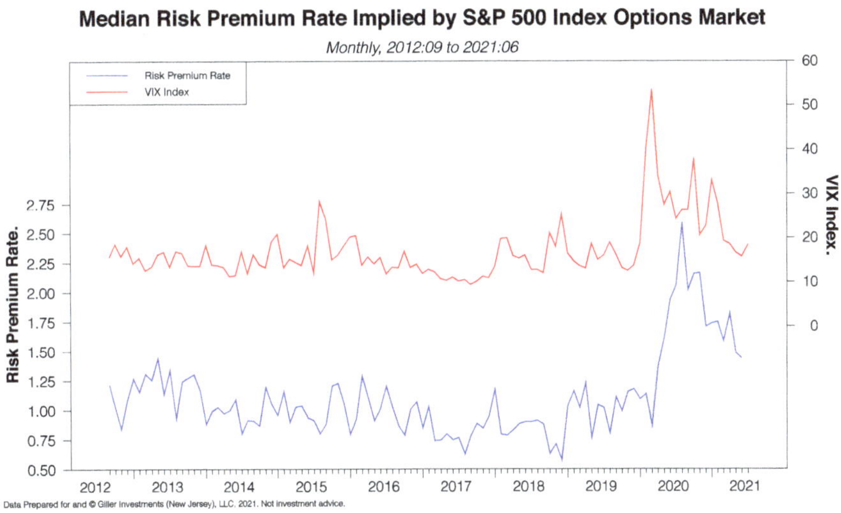

Figure 2.49: Median value of the rate at which the S&P 500 Index Options discount the forward price, $\mathcal{S}(t,T)$, relative to the spot rate, S_t, from September, 2012, to date. The *VIX* Index is display for reference and shading indicates the recession associated with COVID-19.

2.8. The VIX Index

The *VIX Index* is likely familiar to people with more than a casual engagement with finance. At any given time, it is an index, meaning a weighted average, of the *implied volatility* of S&P 500 Index options for delivery over the next 30 days. Implied volatility is the volatility one needs to input into the Black–Scholes equation to arrive at a theoretical valuation consistent with market observed prices. Thus it is a statement that the current price of the option embeds a prediction of the future volatility of the index. Originally calculated by numerical solution of the equations, a slow and cumbersome process, it was later realized that it could be more straightforwardly calculated as the weighted average of the prices of out-of-the-money options, due the work of Emmanuel Derman and others [20].

2.8.1. *The Relationship between Implied Volatility and Empirical Volatility*

The *VIX* is explicitly computed to be an implied forward volatility for the S&P 500 Index over the next thirty days. In this chapter, I have fairly exhaustively dived into developing empirically accurate forecasts for the volatility of the index for the next day alone. As a time series, the *GARCH* models we've used represent a volatility with *mean reverting* properties.

2.8.1.1. *Mean Reverting Nature of GARCH Models*

This is easiest to demonstrate for the classic $GARCH(1,1)$ model, and is treated by many authors. Kuhe provides a clear example [82]. By writing the equations in terms of the residual $r_t^2 - \sigma^2$, where as before $\sigma^2 = E[\sigma_t^2] = C/(1 - A - B)$, we have

$$E_t[r_{t+k}^2 - \sigma^2] = (A + B)^k (r_t^2 - \sigma^2), \tag{2.95}$$

$$\Rightarrow E_t[\sigma_{t+k}^2] = \sigma^2 + (A + B)^k (r_t^2 - \sigma^2). \tag{2.96}$$

Thus, the expected value of the variance at lead k is equal to the unconditional mean plus an exponentially decaying[ii] disturbance due

[ii] Since $A + B < 1$.

to the shock $r_t^2 - \sigma^2$ and, what ever that shock is, the future path is toward the mean.

2.8.1.2. *Computing the Average Forward Variance over 30 Days*

The mean value of this series over the next N days is

$$\bar{\sigma}_t^2 = \frac{1}{N}\sum_{k=1}^{N} E_t[\sigma_{t+k}^2] = \sigma^2 + \frac{A+B}{N}\frac{1-(A+B)^N}{1-A-B}(r_t^2 - \sigma^2), \quad (2.97)$$

where the latter step is obtained by summing the geometric series in $(A+B)^k$. Although this expression is a mouthful, it can be compactly expressed as

$$\bar{\sigma}_t^2 = \sigma^2 + \xi(A+B)(r_t^2 - \sigma^2), \quad (2.98)$$

where ξ is a positive number less than or equal to unity.[jj] From this a very important relation between the next day's expected variance and the forward average is found:

$$\bar{\sigma}_t^2 = (1-\xi)\sigma^2 + \xi\sigma_{t+1}^2. \quad (2.99)$$

2.8.1.3. *Comparison of the VIX with an Empirically Valid Volatility Model*

Equation (2.99) is telling us what to expect should we compare the *VIX* to the $PQGARCH(1,1)$ models developed in this chapter, which have been demonstrated to be excellent descriptions of the distributions of index returns over very long time periods. For a one month forward average it should be true that $\bar{\sigma}_t^2$ is linear in σ_{t+1}^2.

Figure 2.50 shows the two time series side-by-side. The predicted daily volatility from the empirical model should be annualized by multiplying by $\sqrt{252}$, for the average of 252 trading days in a year, but I have allowed the data to chose this parameter to be 283 days. It is very clear from this plot that both series are quite similar, that on the most extreme moves the $PQGARCH(1,1)$ model spikes higher than the *VIX* but, most of the time is systematically smaller. To a

[jj]That being the limiting case for $N = 1$.

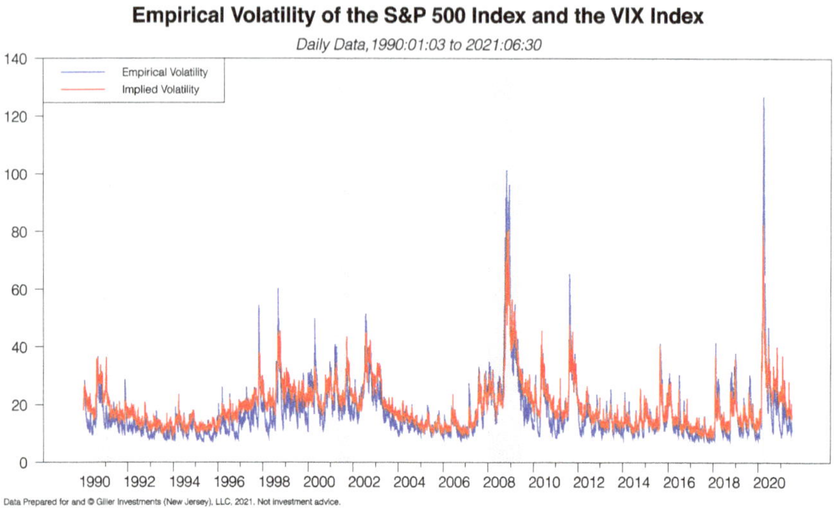

Figure 2.50: Time series of the *VIX* Index and the daily volatility computed by fitting a $PQGARCH(1,1)$ model to the daily returns of the S&P 500 Index. Volatility is annualized for both series. Shading indicates NBER recessions.

trader, this means the options market is systematically rich relative to empirically accurate volatility and that it should be profitable *most of the time* to sell options and eliminate the acquired market risk by dynamically hedging in the manner described by Black and Scholes in their derivation of their equation [8]. However, this strategy will not be profitable around severe market dislocations.

2.8.1.4. *Test of the Variance Linearity Hypothesis for the VIX*

The *VIX* is clearly *very* close to the scaled empirical variance model, but not exactly equal. If it is not systematically different in some way, as distinct from stochastically different due to unknown but unbiased disturbances, then there should be no "polynomial" terms in the expansion

$$v_t^2 = \alpha + \beta_2\sigma_{t+1}^2 + \beta_4\sigma_{t+1}^4 + \beta_6\sigma_{t+1}^6 + \cdots, \tag{2.100}$$

where v_t^2 is the *square* of the *VIX*. The absence of these terms would indicate that the *VIX* and the $PQGARCH(1,1)$ model are completely consistent and there is no more information about the future path of index volatility embedded in one or the other of them.

This hypothesis may be tested by linear regression followed by the Wald Test for the Null hypothesis $\{\beta_2 = 0, \beta_3 = 0, \dots\}$. For this case, I chose to use a robust regression procedure[kk] as the data clearly contains very extreme outliers. As we clearly cannot test all terms for even powers of σ_{t+1} greater than two, we will add terms until the next term added is not statistically significant and then test the model composed up to that point. As none of the higher order terms would cause the Wald Test to reject the Null hypothesis, by construction, this procedure is equivalent to the unlimited version. This procedure is independent of our introduction of the scaling factor described above, as the coefficients in the linear part of the expansion are free to vary and correct any errors associated with that step.

The regression results are shown in both Table 2.9 and Figure 2.51. There is a clear rejection of the linearity hypothesis for the relationship between the squared *VIX* and the $PQGARCH(1,1)$ model. This implies an inconsistency between the *VIX* and the

Table 2.9: Robust linear regression results for fit of the square of the *VIX* to the lead 1 variance predictor from a $PQGARCH(1,1)$ model for the daily returns of the S&P 500 Index for 1990 to date.

Regression results

Variable	Estimate	Std. error	t statistic
α	80.6	3.5	23.1
β_2	0.945	0.009	105.4
β_4	-0.877×10^{-4}	0.023×10^{-4}	−37.8
β_6	0.341×10^{-8}	0.014×10^{-8}	25.2

Wald test for zero coefficients (β_4 and β_6)

Statistic	Value	Deg. free	p-value
F	1517	(2,7645)	Negligible

[kk]Least absolute deviations.

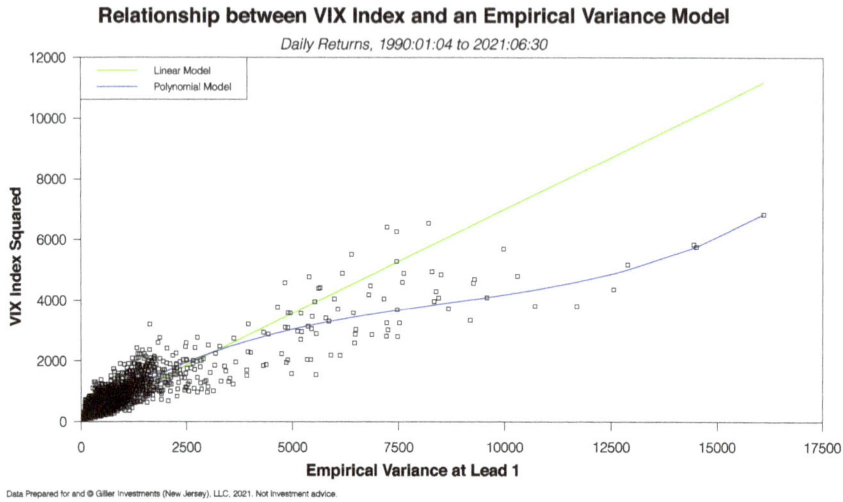

Figure 2.51: Data used to examine the variance linearity of the *VIX* relative to the lead 1 variance forecast obtained by fitting a $PQGARCH(1,1)$ model to the daily returns of the S&P 500 Index. The green line is the best fitting linear relationship and the blue line the best fitting polynomial relationship.

empirically valid volatility model which should be exploitable by traders, depending on the transaction costs.

2.8.2. *The Relationship between Market Returns and Implied Volatility*

At this point we've created a fairly sophisticated understanding of the relationship between the *VIX* and empirical volatility models, but there is a missing piece: the relationship between the change in the *VIX* and market returns *on the same day*. This is not addressed by any of the work above, as all of the empirical models examined are forecasting models — they tell you about how today's returns affect *tomorrow's variance*.

2.8.2.1. *Simple Cross-Sectional Regression between Returns of the VIX and the Market*

Based on the classic, and our preferred augmented, *GARCH* models, we expect there to be a relationship between today's index returns and tomorrow's value of the *VIX*. However, there should be no contemporaneous linkage and that is exactly what is seen. The relationship is not only massively significant but also, apparently, nonlinear. Of course, this data is exhibited for *closing* prices and markets trade *intraday*, so it is very unlikely both that the day's return of the market is established at the very last moment of the trading day or that the option prices that determine the *VIX* move only at the end of the day. Market watching makes it pretty clear that these things accumulate progressively during the day.

Estimated regression coefficients, and their significance, are shown in Table 2.10. As in the previous section, due to the presence of very large outliers, I have used a robust regression procedure rather than *ordinary least squares*.

It is worth noting that the particular procedure used, Least Absolute Deviations, is the correct procedure under maximum likelihood regression when the distribution of the residuals is drawn from the Laplace Distribution.[11] The Laplace Distribution is a special case of our (by now) usual friend the Generalized Error Distribution, with a kurtosis parameter of $\kappa = 1$. Similarly, ordinary least squares is the correct procedure under maximum likelihood regression when

Table 2.10: Robust linear regression results for fit of the daily change in the *VIX* onto the daily return of the S&P 500 Index for 1990 to date.

Robust regression results

Variable	Estimate	Std. error	t statistic	p-value
α	−0.0304	0.0118	−2.6	0.010
β_1	−0.9616	0.0117	−82.2	Negligible
β_2	0.0329	0.0024	13.8	Negligible
β_3	−0.0050	0.0003	−15.5	Negligible

Wald test for zero coefficients (β_2 and β_3)

Statistic	Value	Deg. free	p-value
F	216.2	(2,7601)	Negligible

[11]This is straightforward to demonstrate.

the distribution of residuals is drawn from the Normal distribution ($\kappa = 1/2$). As we have frequently estimated $\hat{\kappa} \approx 0.75$ for financial data, this represents somewhat of a "halfway house" between these extremes. Thus the results of these regressions likely penalize outliers a little harshly.

2.8.2.2. *A Word of Caution on Polynomial Models*

The sort of nonlinear relationship between two time series as exhibited by Figure 2.52 is something that has caused many traders to lose money. The problem is that we need to aggregate a lot of data to capture the larger outliers and that means using long time series. The reader will have noticed by now that I am trying to describe the properties of financial data that are not *locally* valid but are valid over the entire history of the data, that are *generally* valid. In the figure, the overwhelming majority of the data is in the core, where a linear response function is a reasonable representation of the reality of that data. It is on the edges of the data where we see the curvature, and that is the region where not only are the coefficients less

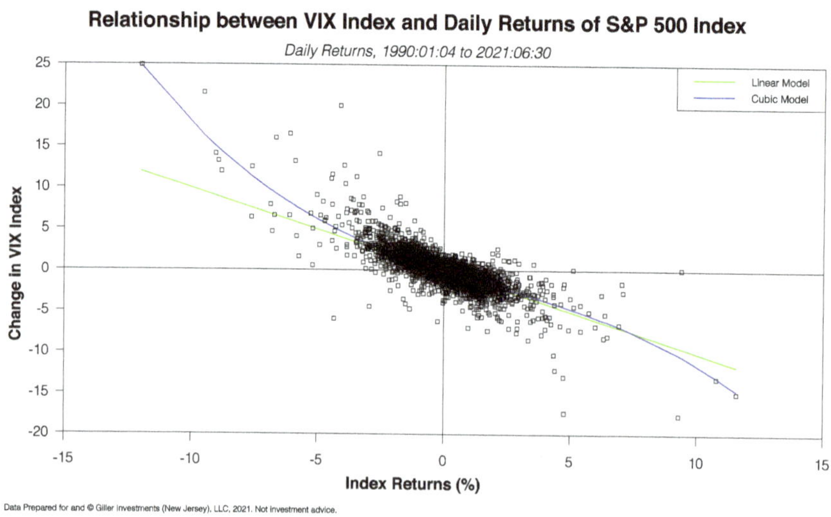

Figure 2.52: Data used to examine the covariance linearity of the *VIX* relative to the daily returns of the S&P 500 Index. The green line is the best fitting linear relationship and the blue line the best fitting polynomial relationship.

well estimated but the consequences of getting them wrong are more significant.

Suppose our information set metric, $m(\mathcal{I}_t)$, is predicted from a polynomial function of an observable and that polynomial is estimated with error. The alpha function is something like

$$E_t[m(\mathcal{I}_{t+1})] = \alpha(\mathcal{I}_t) = \hat{\theta}_0 + \hat{\theta}_1 x_t + \hat{\theta}_2 x_t^2. \tag{2.101}$$

For this simple polynomial, the sensitivity of the forecast to errors in the parameters depends on the order of the term. The propagation of errors gives

$$\mathrm{Var}[\alpha(\mathcal{I}_t)] \simeq \sum_i \left(\frac{dm}{d\theta_i}\right)^2 \mathrm{Var}[\theta_i], \tag{2.102}$$

$$= \sum_i x_t^{2i}\,\mathrm{Var}[\theta_i]. \tag{2.103}$$

In this we assume the errors in the estimators are uncorrelated and that the signal is known precisely at time t. Thus an estimation error on a linear term has much less impact than an estimation error of the same size on a higher order polynomial term. If those higher order terms require a fine balance to get the *historical* curvature right it becomes quite easy to make the wrong decision. The model risk associated with an incorrect, but simpler, linear model is not as high.

2.9. Microwave Latency Arbitrage

I will end this section on financial data by taking a quick look at some of the work I did almost a decade ago on arbitrage possibilities available over microwave links between Chicago and New York. Unlike everything else in this chapter (and most of the work in following chapters), I no longer have access to this data and can only show you what the results *used* to look like. Nevertheless, the analysis is appealing because it is so *physical* in nature.

The subject addressed is whether one can profit from observing trades in the S&P Index Futures[mm] that trade at the Chicago

[mm]Technically *e-mini* futures that trade on the CME's electronic platform *GLOBEX*.

Mercantile Exchange (with the ticker *ES*) and using them as information for the future moves of the *SPY* Exchange Traded Fund that tracks the S&P Index and trades on the *NASDAQ*. In our modern times the CME is a datacenter in Aurora, IL, and the *NASDAQ* is a datacenter in Carteret, NJ, which is a twenty minute drive up the Garden State Parkway from my home.

Both exchanges permit traders to rent "colocated" computer equipment space and attach the necessary antennas and links to permit high-resolution recording of trade data. This data is the full order book, which is a stream of *FIX* messages relating to orders that are placed, modified, withdrawn or filled on the various exchanges. This data occupies an *Alice Through the Lookinglass* world not at all like the sedate feed one sees stream across the business news channels. Every day many millions of order messages are transported to and from the exchange's matching engines — the computers that fulfill the role of executing trades — and brokers and traders colocated computers. This is where the modern world of trading occurs.

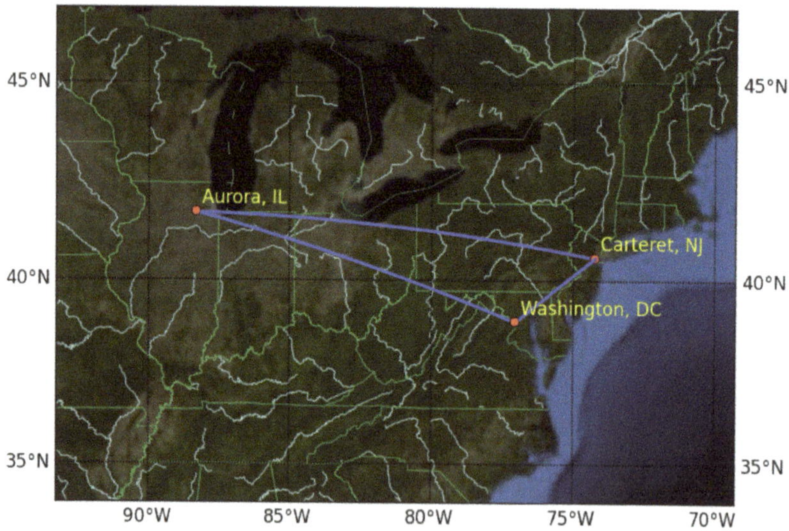

Figure 2.53: Topographic map illustrating the location of Aurora, IL, and Carteret, NJ. The blue lines indicate the *Great Circle Paths* between the locations, which is the shortest possible distance taken over the curved surface of the Earth. This is the path that microwave signals transmitted between installed relay towers could travel along.

Nobody trades "on the floor" any more and if you want to understand what price your order will get filled at, and why, you need this data.

2.9.1. *The Signal*

The idea I was asked to investigate was whether advanced knowledge of the state of the market in S&P Index Futures could be used to profitably trade the *SPY* ETF. My contact had a colocated computer in Aurora from which he was collecting the full *trades and quotes* datafeed with microsecond timestamping for the *ES* futures that are cash settled to the level of the index. He also had a computer in Carteret, doing the same thing for the *SPY*. At this resolution, in busy market periods, multiple trades or order revisions could be observed within a single microsecond but we could not accurately timestamp them because it was beyond the precision of the data feed. Instead we would label them by their microsecond and a sequence number. Both computers were connected to clocks that were synchronized via *GPS* receivers to a resolution of one hundred nanoseconds, which is a tenth of a microsecond and so we believed that the timestamps were reliable enough to compare the two data feeds.

2.9.1.1. *Basic Metrology*

Data would take 3.94 milliseconds to travel from the CME to the *NASDAQ* via the microwave link, which is determined by the speed of light, a fundamental constant. Slower market participants, relying on fibre optic cables, would get the same information in 8.75 ms. Market moving economic news from Washington, DC, would take around 1 ms to travel to the *NASDAQ* and 4 ms to reach Chicago. Thus, the idea was that price changes in the futures caused by supply and demand effects — the ebb and flow of customer orders — could be anticipated from the fast data feed before the majority of *SPY* traders were able to react to them. However, market moving news would hit the *NASDAQ* first and so we would avoid that. The extra four milliseconds is an ocean of time in which to make a trade decision and place an order, should the trader be in possession of (relatively) private information.

2.9.1.2. *Price Changing Ticks*

Both exchanges operate *Limit Order Markets*, which means instructions such as "I will buy five contracts at no higher than 3,125" are transmitted to the exchange computers and rest there until somebody else sends "I will sell three contracts at no lower than 3,125" or similar. At that point the matching orders are removed and a trade ticket issued: the first trader bought three contracts from the second. As thousands of market participants enter orders all the matching ones are removed and we end up with a gap between the best bid (highest unmatched buy order) and the best ask (lowest unmatched sell order). This is called the bid-ask spread and is disseminated to market participants. Associated is the mid-price which is the average of these two prices.

Knowing the bid-ask spread, if a third party wants to trade they can chose whether to take the offered prices or rest orders at (currently) non-competitive prices. If the decision is made to "cross the spread" then a trade will be issued and the market may adjust to reflect the new information or it may absorb that trade without changing the midprice. A "price changing tick" is a trade that resulted in the midprice of the market moving, indicating that all of the orders resting at the best bid (or ask) were matched to the order that came in and the best bid (or ask) moved one price increment lower (or higher, respectively).

2.9.1.3. *Response of SPY to Price Changing Ticks in ES Futures*

With the data sets described, there were approximately twenty thousand price changing ticks on *ES* futures in the one day sample of data I was asked to look at. For every one I computed the response of the midprice of *SPY* from before the trigger to after and averaged those traces in a manner conditioned on the direction of the price move. I also computed the average unconditioned on direction, so I would be able to control for the average price move on this specific day around these events.

To be concrete, I defined a set of times $\{t_i\}$ at which price changing ticks occurred at the CME. This is done by simply looking at the trade reporting feed for trades that occur at a different price to the prior trade. I then compute the volume weighted average price, or *VWAP*, that would be paid to sell a given number of shares in the ETF at the current bid on the *NASDAQ* by "hitting bids." I also compute the same *VWAP* for "lifting asks," or buying at the current ask. The effective midprice is the average of those prices. It is done this way to model realistic execution — merely taking the National Best Bid and Ask, or *NBBA*, exposes the trader to underpricing the effective bid and ask prices due to the presence of small orders at tighter spreads than the actual tradable volume.

This procedure gives a time series $M(t - t_i)$ which shows the motion of the midprice around the time of the price changing tick. We then compute averages of $M(t - t_i) - M(t_i)$ and $\{M(t - t_i) - M(t_i)\} \times \operatorname{sgn} \Delta P_{t_i}$, which is the price move at the *NASDAQ* adjusted by the direction of the trade that occurred at the CME. Figure 2.54 shows the form of these functions.

There are clear differences between these two time series, and the signal is so strong we do not need to do a statistical test to distinguish between them. Rutherford would approve. There is a lot going on in these plots, so let's go through the features in detail.

(1) The unconditional data shows an upwards price trend through the sample period. The day analyzed, 02/16/2020, was in fact an up day for the index and so we would expect to see such a result. On average the market went up so the trend around a randomly chosen time should be an up trend.

(2) I have marked a vertical region to identify ± 5 ms around the event times, $\{t_i\}$. The signed average appears to start moving upwards before this time. It is not unreasonable to suggest that some of these ticks were driven by traders trading at the CME in response to price moves at the *NASDAQ*, leading to a two way trip for price impact triggers and a market in New Jersey that was already in motion when the signal from Chicago arrived.

(3) The midprice move appears to top out at +\$0.005. This is an important number. The SEC's Regulation NMS, that creates the National Market System, requires that posted limit orders on exchanges be separated by a *minimum price increment* of \$0.01. Thus the bid-ask spread in a very liquid market, such as that for *SPY*, is usually as small as possible. The midprice is halfway between the bid and the ask, which is \$0.005 away from either.

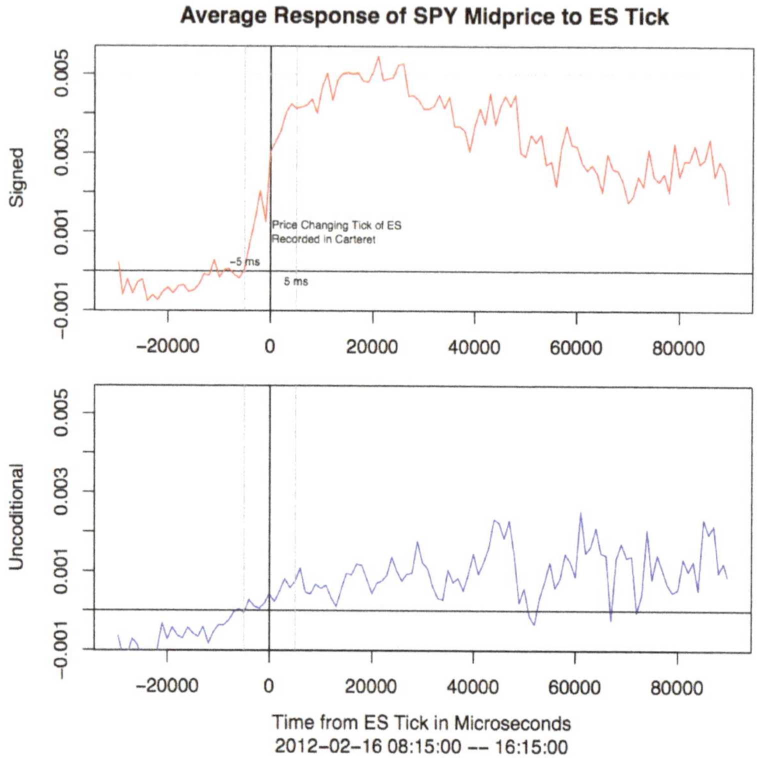

Figure 2.54: Conditioned and unconditioned average price moves at the *NASDAQ* around the times of price changing ticks on *ES* futures at the CME. This data recorded at very high resolution for a single day in 2012.

(4) Overall, there is a signal which reaches a peak of \$0.005 around 25 ms after the trigger. This is real, but insufficient to make money.

2.9.1.4. *The Effect of Book Imbalance*

When analyzing the order books on exchanges we find a wealth of information in addition to just prices. One statistic of interest is the balance of the order book, whether the same quantities of securities are offered to buy and to sell. Sometimes called "book pressure," that has been used successfully to predict short term moves in markets as it is literally telling you about the balance between supply and demand. It therefore makes sense to also condition our analysis on

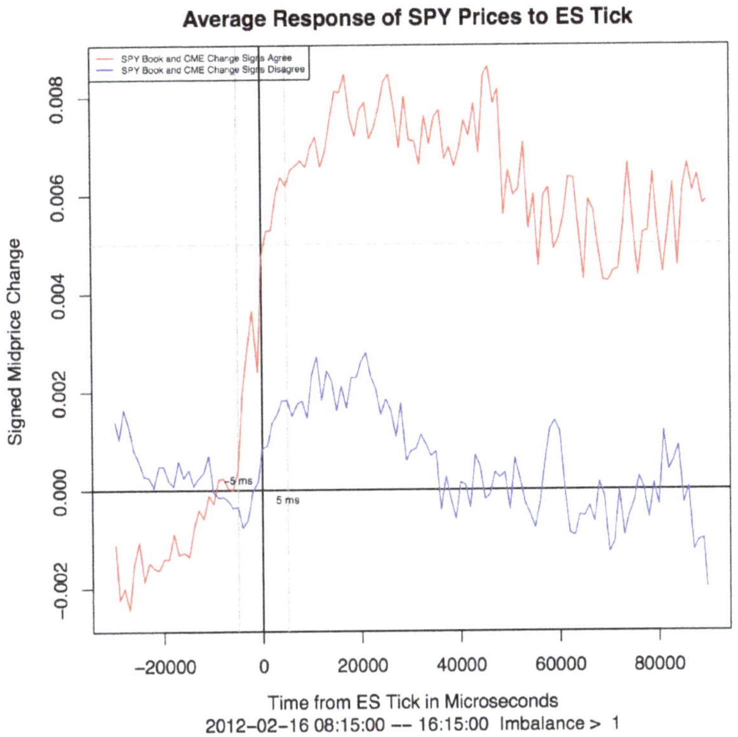

Figure 2.55: Conditioned and unconditioned average price moves at the *NASDAQ* around the times of price changing ticks on *ES* futures at the CME when the order book imbalance is accounted for. This data recorded at very high resolution for a single day in 2012.

whether the observed price changing tick from the CME is aligned with the state of the market.

Figure 2.55 exhibits the results of this analysis. We clearly see that the signal is enhanced even more, while the control series appears even more random. This data is from conditioning on market conditions that would make it easy to move up (or down) and then looking for a signal that is in that direction. Now the move after the trigger is approaching 80% of the spread.

2.9.1.5. *Microstructure is the Key*

I found this analysis very satisfying. It was the closest thing I had done in finance to the sort of work I was doing as a Particle Physicist many years before. There was a physically real reason for the signal to exist and it did not need fancy statistical analysis to tease it out. This work convinced me of the importance of modeling trade execution processes accurately, just as the earlier work in this chapter convinced me of the importance of abandoning the false assumptions of the Normal distribution and homoskedasticity.

At PDT, in the mid. 1990s, Mike Reed and others were routinely using such *Trades and Quotes*, or *TAQ*, data in their model development. We would receive hundreds of CD-ROMs from the *NYSE* and the *NASDAQ* containing such data, before distribution was switched to physical hard-drives due to capacity limitations. I regarded this as an essential step and, later in my career, was astonished to find trading groups at other institutions apparently blissfully unaware of the fact that they had no real idea of the state of the market. Following the golden rule, you can do whatever you want to create an alpha, but if you want to model execution you *must* use a realistic microstructure simulation to work out the market impact, or slippage, of your trades. I knew that was what PDT did, but the lesson was not brought home to me until I did this work.

2.10. What I've Learned about Financial Data

This chapter is the largest in this book and represents work drawn from things I was doing at various points during my career. As I sought to build predictive models in finance I came back, again and again, to the same two basic points: financial data is not Normally distributed; and, financial data is not homoskedastic. At first, earlier on, I did what everybody else did. I acknowledged this facts, hoped that the methods I was using were "probably ok" despite the failure of the assumptions they were based upon, and pressed on regardless.

It was only through time, as my skills built up, that I began to recognize that not only that there were regularities associated with the "abnormality" of this data but that there were also available methods and solutions to deal with these problems. We don't have to stick with ordinary least squares because we don't have an alternative, we do have an alternative. We don't have to stick to homoskedasticity because we don't have an alternative, we do have an alternative.

The rest of this book is about other things I've worked on, and the chapters will be smaller because, for most of my career, I've worked in finance. But I've always sought to build skills by tackling "out-of-domain" problems. In fact, I don't think I've yet failed to find an application in finance for skills developed to tackle problems in other fields.

Chapter 3

Economic Data and Other Time-Series Analysis

The way I approach the analysis of time-series is to try to model as much of the data as possible. To build a "universal" model. As a physicist by training, I'm interested in enduring truths. I don't require that all properties of data are eternally constant, but I do want to know what the "stylized facts" are, as they say in finance.

In this chapter, we have to do something different. Throughout my career, many people who built models they believed in but that subsequently lost money, turn to the crutch of "the market changed." Those with a little more sophistication describe it as "non-stationary." Following Occam's Razor, I adopt the more likely explanation — we assumed some property of the data to be true when it wasn't.

The *Coronavirus* pandemic of 2020 has thrown a wrench in to the wheels of the subject of econometrics. What has happened to some of the variables people work with is so severe that it cannot be accommodated by methods based on the Normal distribution, or even the relatively tame leptokurtosis models we've seen so far in this book. In the analysis of NFP that follows here, I will show what happened to a pretty good model due to COVID-19, and how I've tried to adapt to that.

As the theme in this chapter is non-financial data, I will also be including some other analysis from my career that I have found interesting.

3.1. Non-Farm Payrolls

In the United States and the United Kingdom, from the time of my childhood up until the Reagan-Thatcher era, the biggest driver of economic performance was inflation. The monetary experiments then implemented by people like Paul Volcker are credited with slaying inflation [60]. Since then, until the current COVID-19 pandemic, focus has switched to *Non-Farm Payrolls* (NFP) as the driving factor in moving markets.

The seasonally adjusted change in NFP, has become the talisman for the state of the US economy and is watched by many market participants. To truly understand the impact of unexpected news on markets, one needs to watch interest rate sensitive instruments, such as Three Month Treasury Bills or Eurodollar Futures, during the period from just before 8:30 AM (Eastern time) on the first Friday of every month. This is the time when the NFP data for the prior calendar month is released. The data is derived from a survey run by the Bureau of Labor Statistics of employers and is a count of "payroll" employees, meaning those working regularly and issued with paychecks not paid cash over the counter. The "non-farm" part is because this survey avoids farm laborers as, in the United States, data for farms is collected by the United States Department of Agriculture (the USDA) and not the BLS, which is a bureau of the Department of Commerce. However, this also neatly avoids a source of very seasonal employment — farming.

3.1.1. *Time-Series Prediction of Non-Farm Payrolls before COVID-19*

Figure 3.1 shows the result of fitting the "usual suspects" model to the month-on-month relative change, which we can informally call the "return," in the seasonally adjusted NFP series from 1939 to 2015. That is a model that:

(i) assumes a simple heteroskedasticity structure;
(ii) assumes fundamentally leptokurtotic innovations (drawn from the Generalized Error Distribution, GED);
(iii) permits an asymmetric response; and
(iv) assumes a constant month-on-month average growth rate.

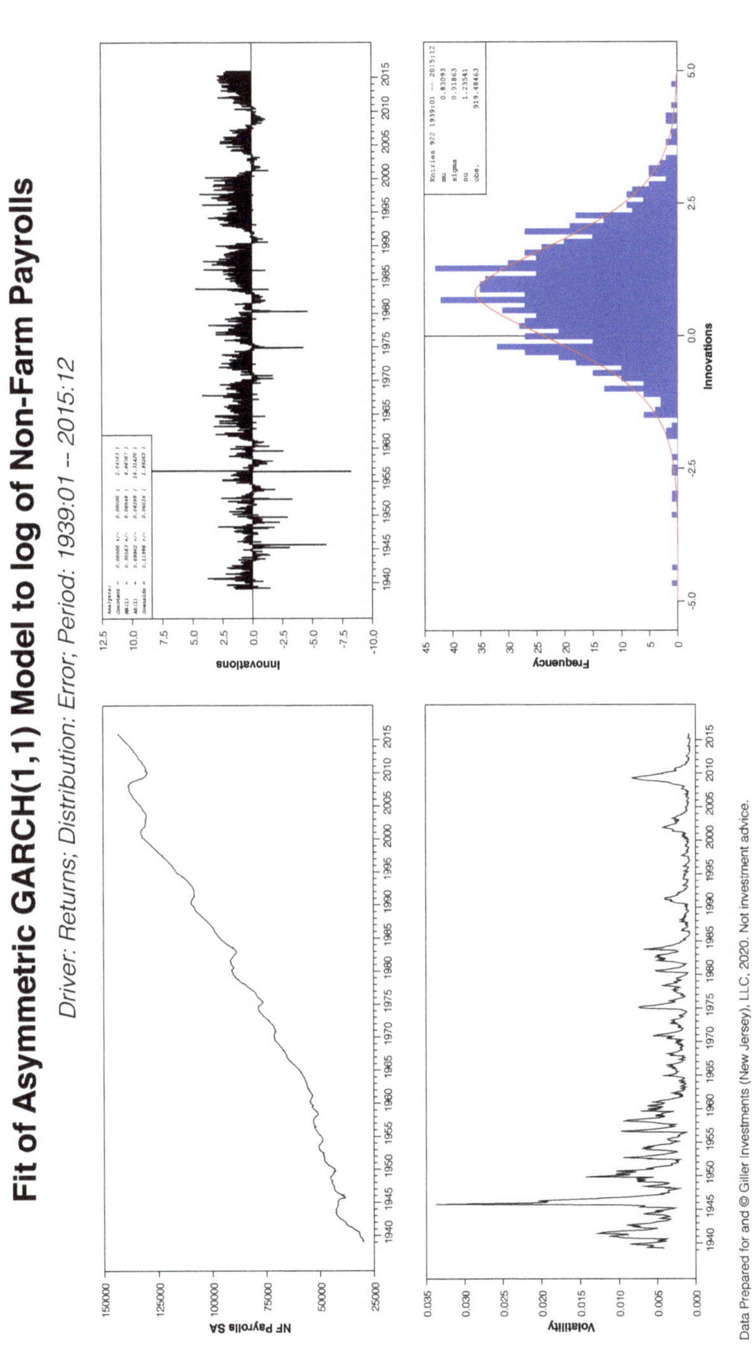

Figure 3.1: Results of fitting a $GJRGARCH(1,1)$ model to the monthly 'return' of US NFP. Data is from 1986 to 2015. The assumed distribution is the Generalized Error Distribution.

This last assumption, item (iv), is perhaps the weakest, but it is a baseline. In the graphic the four panels represent the time-series of the payrolls number itself and of the imputed volatility; the time-series of the innovations; and, a histogram of the standardized innovations.

Just "eyeballing" this data this seems like a pretty reasonable model. Volatility in unemployment is associated with several easy to identify features including:

(i) The end of the Second World War.
(ii) The boom-bust economies of the 1950s and 1960s.
(iii) An extended and notably more quiescent period following the end of the Volcker era and the tenure of Alan Greenspan at the Fed.
(iv) The Great Recession associated with the Global Financial Crisis of 2008.
(v) In addition there is a curious vertical line in the 1956 in the plot of innovations. In fact this is a back-to-back pair of data points due to a strike that caused significant drop in payrolls followed by a reversal the next month. This is a classic example of mean-reversion (negative serial correlation) which we will need to address.

3.1.2. *Details of the GJR-GARCH Model*

Table 3.1 shows the estimated coefficient for the model

$$R_t = \frac{P_t - P_{t-1}}{P_{t-1}} = \mu + \sigma_t \varepsilon_t \tag{3.1}$$

$$\sigma_t^2 = C + (A + D\, I[R_{t-1} < 0])\, R_t^2 + B\sigma_{t-1}^2 \tag{3.2}$$

$$\varepsilon_t \sim \text{GED}(0, 1, \kappa), \tag{3.3}$$

where P_t is the series of seasonally adjusted NFP and all the other terms have their usual roles.

The data emphatically rejects the Normal distribution and homoskedasticity, but the endorsement of asymmetric response is more tepid, only marginally rejecting the Null hypothesis of Symmetry ($D = 0$) with just better than 95% confidence. I, personally,

Table 3.1: Maximum likelihood regression results the fit of a GJR-$GARCH(1,1)$ model to the monthly "returns" of NFPs (seasonally adjusted) from 1940 to 2015.

Regression results for GED

Variable	Estimate	Std. error	t statistic
μ	0.1643	0.00646	35.4*
C	0.0011	0.000513	2.1*
A	0.3061	0.062469	4.9
B	0.6985	0.041117	17.0
D	0.1211	0.058801	2.1
κ	0.7104	0.03523	6.0†

Significance tests

Test	Statistic	Value	p-value
Normal distribution	χ_1^2	223.4	Negligible
Homoskedasticity	χ_3^2	2,210.9	Negligible
Symmetry	χ_1^2	4.2	0.03938147

Notes: The Generalized Error Distribution is used for the innovations.
*$\hat{\mu}$ measured in %, $\hat{C}$ in $\%^2$.
†t Statistic computed relative to the Null hypothesis of $\kappa = \frac{1}{2}$.

would not regard this as sufficiently strong evidence were it not for all the results seen in Chapter 2.

3.1.3. *Student's t Distribution*

Another distribution that possesses the fat tails we seek when describing real-world financial and economic data is Student's t distribution. This has the form

$$\text{Student}(\mu, \sigma, \nu)\colon f(x|\mu, \sigma, \nu) = \frac{\Gamma\left(\frac{\nu+1}{2}\right)}{\sqrt{2\pi}\sigma\Gamma\left(\frac{\nu}{2}\right)\left\{1 + \frac{(x-\mu)^2}{\nu\sigma^2}\right\}^{\frac{\nu+1}{2}}}. \tag{3.4}$$

Although most people will have encountered this distribution in its original context, that of estimating the deviation of a sample mean from zero when the variance of the data must be estimated from the data itself and for which the degrees of freedom, $\nu = n - 1$, is an integer, in fact it is a useful, leptokurtotic, probability distribution. It does have one noxious property that makes it awkward to use in finance: the moments, or expected values of x^k, do not exist when $k \geq \nu$.

This is a problem because if a moment does not exist, measuring a statistic associated with the moment doesn't help you know it. For example, if $\nu \leq 2$ the distribution doesn't have a variance and, even though a finite sample of data will always have a finite sample variance, the sample variance is not a predictor of the dispersion of the distribution. In a financial context, if the returns of an asset and are distributed according to Student's t with $\nu \leq 2$ then risk management is not possible. If neither $E[x]$ nor $E[x^2]$ exist the distribution will not satisfy the Central Limit Theorem and if $E[x]$ does not exist it will not satisfy the Law of Large Numbers (LLNs). Both of these theorems make our lives as data analysts considerably simpler, I often characterize the LLN with the simple statement "averaging works."

Like the GED, Student's t distribution also possesses a Normal limit. Unfortunately, though, that limit occurs when $\nu \to \infty$ and so we cannot use the fitted model to test for Normality. There isn't a statistical test we can construct to detect whether $\hat{\nu} = \infty \pm \delta_\alpha$, where δ_α defines a confidence region with probability content α. Technically, this expression isn't even a legitimate mathematical sentence!

3.1.4. *A GJR-GARCH Model with Student's t Distribution*

Table 3.2 shows the estimated coefficient for the model

$$R_t = \mu + \sigma_t \varepsilon_t \tag{3.5}$$

$$\sigma_t^2 = C + (A + D\,I[R_{t-1} < 0])\,R_t^2 + B\sigma_{t-1}^2 \tag{3.6}$$

$$\varepsilon_t \sim \text{Student}(0, 1, \nu), \tag{3.7}$$

Table 3.2: Maximum likelihood regression results the fit of a *PQ-GARCH*(1, 1) model to the monthly "returns" of NFPs (seasonally adjusted) from 1940 to 2015.

Regression results for Student's *t*

Variable	Estimate	Std. error	t statistic
μ	0.1676	0.00620	27.0*
C	0.0015	0.000592	2.6*
A	0.3840	0.075618	5.1
B	0.6138	0.047556	12.9
D	0.1227	0.075966	2.3
ν	6.9875	1.2512	n/a

Significance tests

Test	Statistic	Value	p-value
Homoskedasticity	χ_3^2	1,238.6	Negligible
Symmetry	χ_1^2	5.2	0.02

Note: Student's t distribution is used for the innovations.
*$\hat{\mu}$ measured in %, $\hat{C}$ in %^{2}.

which is exactly the same as the previous one, but with Student's t substituted for GED in the process for the innovations.

From this table we see that the estimates of the parameters of the *GJR-GARCH*(1, 1) model are essentially the same, and that the results of the significance test are also similar. Clearly this is also a "reasonable" representation of the actual data. The estimated kurtosis parameter, $\hat{\nu}$ favors a value low enough for means and variances to exist, and to be measurable as well, but it is not large enough to generally confuse this distribution with the Normal.

3.1.5. *Bootstrapping the Change in Akaike Information Criterion*

Through statistical diligence we have introduced some confusion into our modeling. Having shown that two candidate distributions both give reasonable descriptions of the data, which should be used? I do not write "which is right," because I don't think that's a meaningful statement. Both are reasonable representations of reality, but I'm a skeptic whether a statement that either is *actually true* is useful. Nevertheless, we need to make a decision based upon evidence as to which we will proceed with.

Since both estimates were made via the method of Maximum Likelihood, it is tempting to look at the Maximum Likelihood Ratio (MLR) for a test. Unfortunately, that fails as we cannot construct a proper *nested model* with the two distributions. A mixture model can be built but, if it chooses one distribution over the other, the associated kurtosis parameter cannot be estimated and so the conditions for Wilk's Theorem, which states that twice the change in the log-likelihood has a χ^2 distribution with degrees of freedom equal to the number of additional model parameters [139] when a model is augmented, do not apply. The change in log likelihood is computable, but the number of additional parameters is zero.

We need a statistic that is sensitive to goodness of fit and meaningful in the way it discriminates between the two cases. The Akaike Information Criterion [12] is such a statistic, and its large sample approximation is very similar in application to the MLR test. It is based on the information loss that occurs when the wrong probability distribution is used to model a data set, and so is rigorously based in Information Theory.

The change in A.I.C.(c)[a] is found to be −54.9 for the Student t version of the model versus the GED version, indicating a preference for that model. But we don't know how significant that change is. If we knew the true distribution of the data that could be computed but we don't. Bootstrapping can be used to investigate that providing it is done in such a manner that the serial correlation of the data is not disrupted. The usual technique for this is to sample overlapping blocks of data, which is known as the "block bootstrap." We see from Figure 3.2 that we are quite unlikely to draw a dataset for which the difference in AIC(c) between the Student's t and GED models would

[a]Meaning the corrected statistic which takes account of sample size more accurately. Akaike's original work was a large sample result.

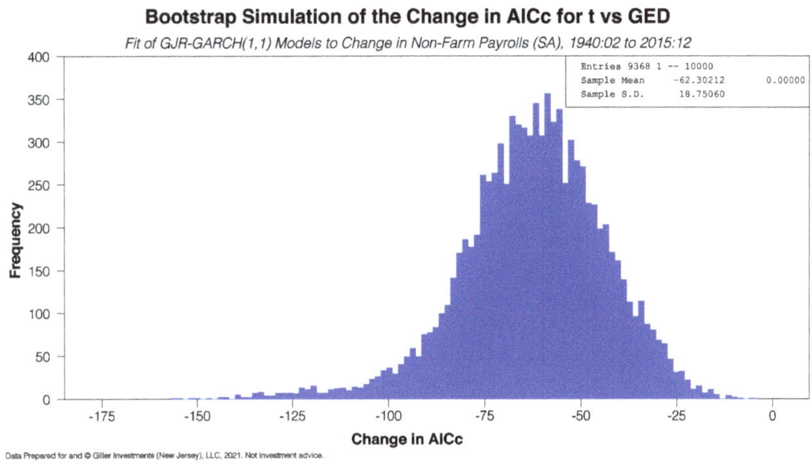

Figure 3.2: Block bootstrap distribution of the change in A.I.C.(c) for fitting a $GJR\text{-}GARCH(1,1)$ model to monthly "returns" of NFP (seasonally adjusted). The mean of an indefinitely large bootstrap sample must coincide the statistic computed from the original data sets, however the dispersion is indicative of how significant that value is.

lead not to chose the former option, so I will proceed with that choice in the rest of this section.

3.1.6. *Predictive Model Selection Using the AIC*

It's reasonable to ask why I decided to bootstrap the change in AIC rather than just the likelihood ratio? Since the change in AIC is the (negative of the) statistic that would be used in the MLR Test penalized for the additional degrees of freedom of a more complex model, the result is actually identical given that the total degrees of freedom is the same for both the GED and Student's t based systems. In this section, the AIC will be used to determine the order of autoregression used in a model for the relative change in NFP.

The procedure is straightforward. One fits a model with zero lagged variables, then $1, 2, 3, \ldots$, etc., and computes the change in AIC for each model. The model with the minimum AIC is selected. For Box–Jenkins style *ARIMA* models we could just as well use the MLR test, as these form appropriately "nested" models, but the AIC does not have that requirement. To fully understand it, I recommend

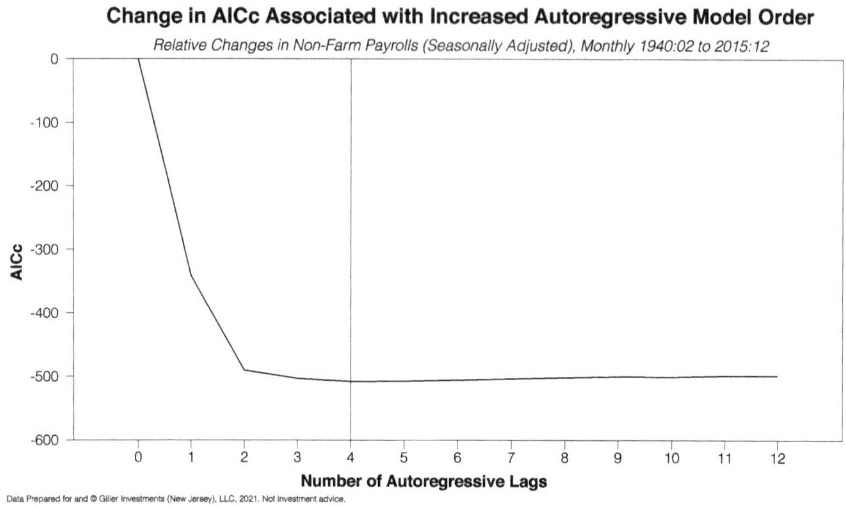

Figure 3.3: Scan of the change in AIC(c) for fitting an $AR(n)$-GJR-$GARCH(1,1)$ model to monthly relative changes of NFP (seasonally adjusted). The scan is for 0 to 12 lags, and the favored model order is $AR(4)$. Student's t distribution is used for the innovations.

reading Burnham and Anderson's excellent book *Model Selection and Multi-Model Inference* [12].

The final regression results are shown in Table 3.3. Key features are that the rate of change in payrolls has considerable momentum; asymmetric autoregressive heteroskedasticity is strong; and, fundamental leptokurtosis is present. The fitted model is

$$R_t = \mu + \sum_{l=1}^{4} \varphi_l R_{t-l} + \varepsilon_t \sigma_t. \tag{3.8}$$

3.1.7. *Out-of-Sample Performance of the Model*

With considerable effort put into model optimization, one thing we can be sure of is that it is likely overfit to some extent, and explaining variance that it has no business doing. We could bootstrap this entire procedure, which would estimate the confidence in the results, but a better approach may be to test it on data it's never seen — that's one

Table 3.3: Maximum likelihood regression results the fit of an $AR(4)$-GJR-$GARCH(1,1)$ model to the monthly relative changes of NFPs (seasonally adjusted) from 1940 to 2015.

Regression results for optimized model

Variable	Estimate	Std. error
μ	0.0222	0.00604*
φ_1	0.3310	0.03411
φ_2	0.3059	0.03133
φ_3	0.1029	0.02962
φ_4	0.0830	0.02918
C	0.0011	0.00057*
A	0.1002	0.07270
B	0.7798	0.07128
D	0.3001	0.09611
ν	4.0207	0.47436

Note: Student's t distribution is used for the innovations. The ϕ_l coefficients are the autoregressive lags.
$^*\hat{\mu}$ measured in %, $\hat{C}$ in $\%^2$.

reason why I withheld the data from 2016 onwards from the model.[b] Predicting from an autoregressive model such as Equation (3.8) one time-step forward is very easy.[c] All known quantities are input and all stochastic quantities replaced with their (conditional) expectations. Since $E_t[\varepsilon_{t+1}] = 0$ by construction, we just get

$$E_t[R_{t+1}] = \mu + \sum_{l=1}^{4} \varphi_l R_{t-l+1} \tag{3.9}$$

$$E_t[\sigma_{t+1}^2] = C + (A + D\, I[R_t < 0])R_t^2 + B\sigma_t^2. \tag{3.10}$$

[b]The other reason is that I originally did this work in September 2015, and the data ended then. I subsequently ran the model out of sample until the current period.

[c]Predicting more than one step ahead is also easy as the Law of Iterated Expectations, $E_t[E_{t+1}] = E_t$, can be used to related expected future predictions to values computable deterministically at the current time.

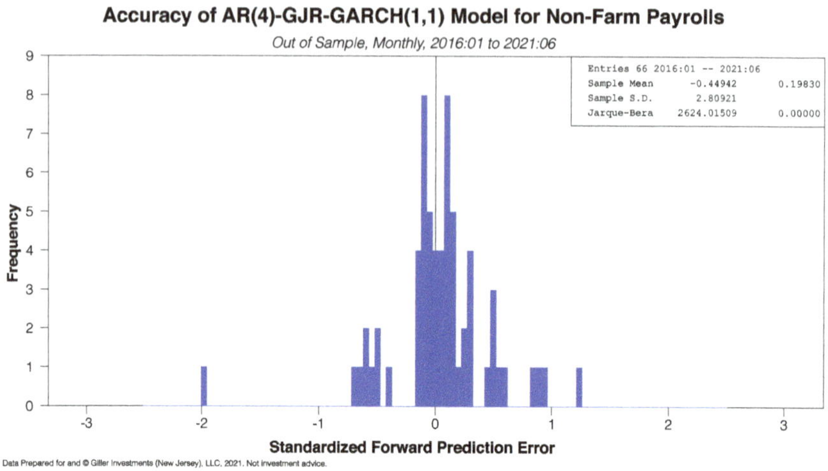

Figure 3.4: Out of sample standardized forward prediction errors for an $AR(4)$-GJR-$GARCH(1,1)$ model for the monthly relative changes in NFP.

If the process evolves as expected, then we can evaluate a standardized score variable

$$Z_{t+1|t} = \frac{R_{t+1} - E_t[R_{t+1}]}{\sqrt{E_t[\sigma_{t+1}^2]}}. \tag{3.11}$$

For this quantity, it should be true that $E[Z_t] = 0$ and $\mathrm{Var}[Z_t] = 1$.

A histogram of the standardized forward prediction error is exhibited for the period 01/2016 to 06/2021 in Figure 3.4. Although we can say that the data is not Normally distributed with high confidence, based on the Jarque–Bera test, it is still plausible to assume that this error is not significantly different from zero. The model seems to work.

3.1.8. *Time-Series Prediction of Non-Farm Payrolls During the Coronavirus Outbreak*

There is, of course, a reason why the analysis of the prior section has ended in February 2020, and did not run all the way to date. That reason is the COVID-19 outbreak and what happened to an apparently excellent, traditional, model is a salutary lesson to all of us in the prediction business.

Equation (3.9) is a linear additive noise model, in the manner of Equation (2.4), and so the linear regression[d] below follows:

$$m(\mathcal{I}_{t+1}) = R_{t+1} \tag{3.12}$$

$$\alpha(\mathcal{I}_t) = \mu + \sum_{l=1}^{4} \varphi_l R_{t-l} \tag{3.13}$$

$$\Rightarrow m(\mathcal{I}_{t+1}) \sim a + b\alpha(\mathcal{I}_t) \tag{3.14}$$

$$\text{where } E[(\hat{a}, \hat{b})] = (0, 1). \tag{3.15}$$

This is a testable hypothesis, of course. The data is shown in Figure 3.5, and it is clear that the model has failed spectacularly. April, 2020's drop in NFPs by approximately 14%, as the US economy shut down, was clearly unprecedented. How are we to react to this data? I think the first thing to say is that is is not true that

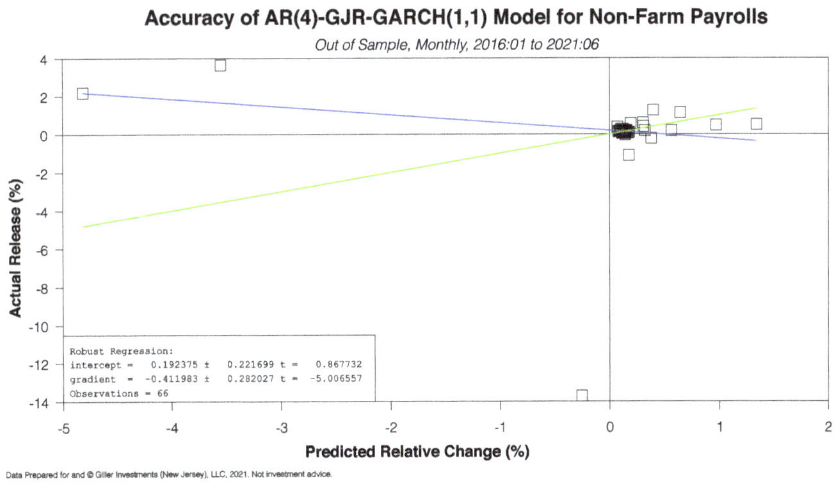

Figure 3.5: Out of sample regression of forward predictions for an $AR(4)$-GJR-$GARCH(1,1)$ model onto the monthly relative changes in NFP. The blue line is the best fitting linear regression line and the green line is the expected relationship under Equation (3.14). t statistics are evaluated relative to that hypothesis.

[d]Here, we use $y \sim \alpha + \beta x$ to represent a linear regression relationship.

the Universe is now different. The world before 2020 contained the capacity for such shocks and, perhaps if our data went back to the 1917 pandemic we would have seen a similar event? We don't know and, although it's certainly a worthy task, I don't have the resources to *reconstruct* NFP for the period 1900–1938. This is one of the problems of working with time series of historical data — the only way to manufacture more data is to wait.

> "The model is good, but the world changed." — disappointed quants.

My model, as constructed, was built to capture both extreme outliers and dynamically changing variance. Let's take a deeper dive into how it actually performed. Table 3.4 shows the actual predictions and reported data, together with the Z scores and p values computed from the fitted $AR(4)$-GJR-$GARCH(1,1)$ model (the p values are *bidirectional*). Also tabulated is the number of events of similar size, or larger, expected in the series of approximately 1,000 data points.

What we see for March and April 2020, are extreme outliers that are very unlikely to have occurred on any given month. Yet, in a series as long as this, they are actually not that unlikely. The March result is expected 0.10 times, which shouldn't really raise eyebrows when observed — after all 9:1 shots do win horse races. The April number is expected just 0.07 times, which is rare but we would not reject a model with 95% confidence on the basis of observing such an event. Perhaps the model is not as bad as it seems? For the mathematics of probability and statistics to actually work, unlikely events must be observed from time-to-time in the real world and predictions will be wrong *almost certainly.*

> "How often have I said to you that when you have eliminated the impossible, whatever remains, however improbable, must be the truth?" — Sherlock Holmes [23].

3.1.9. *A Distribution with Even Fatter Tails*

Lurking within Equation (3.4) is a monster that is often encountered in the context of *pathological* distributions. That is the Cauchy

Table 3.4: Predictions and reported data for the monthly relative changes of NFPs (seasonally adjusted) for 2019–2020. Z Score is computed from the fitted $AR(4)$-GJR-$GARCH(1,1)$ model and p values are bidirectional under the assumption of innovations drawn from Student's t distribution.

Seasonally Adjusted Relative Change in NFP for 2019–2020

Period	Predicted (%)	Reported (%)	Pred. std. dev. (%)	Z score	p-value	Expected
1/2019	0.11	0.16	0.09	0.48	0.66	649.55
2/2019	0.14	−0.03	0.09	−2.00	0.12	115.14
3/2019	0.08	0.11	0.14	0.22	0.84	827.12
4/2019	0.08	0.15	0.13	0.53	0.63	619.79
5/2019	0.11	0.04	0.12	−0.61	0.58	569.66
6/2019	0.09	0.12	0.12	0.23	0.83	824.54
7/2019	0.10	0.13	0.11	0.27	0.80	789.77
8/2019	0.12	0.13	0.10	0.12	0.91	899.30
9/2019	0.12	0.15	0.10	0.27	0.80	789.15
10/2019	0.13	0.13	0.09	−0.04	0.97	957.09
11/2019	0.13	0.15	0.09	0.24	0.82	815.06
12/2019	0.14	0.11	0.08	−0.38	0.72	713.39
1/2020	0.13	0.21	0.08	0.92	0.41	404.51
2/2020	0.15	0.19	0.08	0.47	0.66	654.72
3/2020	0.17	−1.10	0.08	−15.44	0.00	0.10
4/2020	−0.25	−13.71	0.81	−16.59	0.00	0.07
5/2020	−4.82	2.18	8.54	0.82	0.46	454.17
6/2020	−3.55	3.64	7.86	0.91	0.41	407.61
7/2020	0.39	1.25	7.31	0.12	0.91	902.77
8/2020	0.64	1.13	6.46	0.08	0.94	932.96
9/2020	1.34	0.51	5.70	−0.15	0.89	882.54
10/2020	0.97	0.48	5.06	−0.10	0.93	918.44
11/2020	0.56	0.19	4.48	−0.08	0.94	928.55
12/2020	0.38	−0.21	3.97	−0.15	0.89	879.88
1/2021	0.10	0.16	3.52	0.02	0.99	976.47
2/2021	0.07	0.38	3.11	0.10	0.93	917.10
3/2021	0.19	0.55	2.75	0.13	0.90	893.58
4/2021	0.32	0.19	2.43	−0.05	0.96	950.07
5/2021	0.30	0.40	2.15	0.05	0.97	955.39
6/2021	0.30	0.59	1.90	0.15	0.89	878.55

Note: Expected counts are based on the observed sample size (from 1/1939 to 6/2021).

distribution which is obtained by putting the kurtosis parameter, ν, to unity. This has an apparent simplicity in the density

$$\text{Cauchy: } f(x) = \frac{1}{\pi(1+x^2)}, \tag{3.16}$$

yet for this distribution the tails are so fat that even the mean doesn't exist and so the LLN fails. Could this beast be responsible for our misbehaving payrolls data?

Fortunately, this can be ruled out. As Student's t distribution may be smoothly transformed into the Cauchy distribution by taking $\nu \to 1$, we can ask whether the observed datum, $\hat{\nu}$, for the fitted model is consistent with that value. Taking the values from Table 3.3, Wald's Test may again be used to evaluate this proposition. We find a test statistic of 40.5, which should be distributed as χ^2 with one degree of freedom and has negligible probability. This idea is comprehensively rejected, which is somewhat of a relief for the tractability of our work.

3.2. Initial Claims

One of the features of US economic data is that there are many agencies collecting statistics that should be nominally constructable from each other but which are processed separately without any overarching effort to guarantee consistency. NFPs is published by the Bureau of Labor Statistics monthly, but Initial Claims (for Unemployment Insurance) is published weekly by the Employment and Training Administration. These are separate agencies within the Department of Labor. Payrolls is determined from a survey of employers whereas Initial Claims comes from data reported by state Departments of Labor through their processing of actual claims for Unemployment Insurance made by unemployed people.

Since changes in NFPs represents changes in the count of the employed and changes in claims for unemployment insurance represent changes in the count of the unemployed there should be (and is) a strong negative correlation between these statistics. The relationship is not exact for reasons that are both fundamental, as some people leave unemployment for reasons not causing them to claim benefits, and operational, as the unemployed may wait to claim or be ineligible for various reasons.

3.2.1. *Predicting Initial Claims from Google Search Trends*

In the prior section we have seen the effect of the COVID-19 outbreak on NFP. My interest in Initial Claims was actually stimulated by extreme movement in the Payrolls number during this time. I was seeking an alternate measure of unemployment from alternative data — meaning data generated by, or observable directly from, the actions of people in the economy, potentially in real-time and not from official government sources, with its associated release latencies and seasonal adjustment effects. The US economy was losing jobs rapidly during the weeks of March and April, 2020, and waiting for the payrolls number to be released a whole week after the end of the month meant that it was not a reliable indicator of where the economy was moving *right now.* Initial Claims is released at higher frequency, but it still has latencies coming out on the Thursday of the week after the week it refers to. I wanted something I could observe in *real time.*

3.2.2. *Google Trends*

Google Trends is a product that Google makes available for public interest use, and commercially as part of its advertiser tools. It tracks the relative frequency of keyword searches entered into their search engine system. Figure 3.6 illustrates the user interface. The effect of the COVID-19 unemployment recession is clearly visible.[e]

This data may be downloaded manually and has two features that, for somebody in my business, are annoying:

(i) the data is always scaled between 0 and 100 and
(ii) requesting a longer history results in data with a lower temporal resolution being returned.

To make the data useful for my purposes of high-resolution prediction of Initial Claims I had to overcome these two problems.

[e]Although not so strongly when I first started using this data, in the first weeks of March 2020.

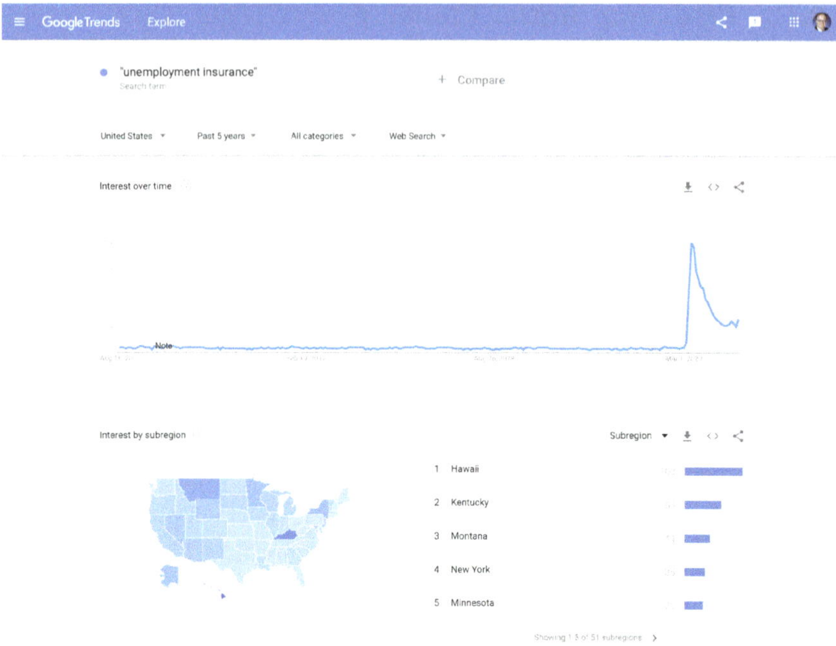

Figure 3.6: Screenshot of the *Google Trends* user interface taken in August 2020. The screen shows a search for the keyword "unemployment insurance" within the United States over the prior 5 years.

The solution I adopted was to programmatically access the data[f]; to request the largest window I could that would return daily data; and, to request overlapping periods always ending in the current date. This would allow me to renormalize a historic activity peak (of 100) when a subsequent higher activity level caused that prior peak to be reported at a lower relative strength (e.g. 85) relative to the new peak (which was 100).

Another item that would have to be tackled was that official economic statistics are usually seasonally adjusted but I would not be able to apply the canonical seasonal adjustment procedure, the *X13-ARIMA* procedure developed by the BLS [100], to the Google data. This was firstly because the Google series would not be long

[f]Via the widely available `pytrends` package for the *Python* programming language.

enough for any kind of seasonal modeling to be reliable, but mostly because the adjusted data released by the government agencies uses an adjustment that is computed using the data about to be released — so there is no way at all to know that adjustment before the release date. Instead, I would have to predict the adjustments from their own history and use that series as a predictor of the target seasonally adjusted Initial Claims series.

3.2.3. *Details of the Covariance between Google Trends and Initial Claims*

My first step in the analysis of a time-series that will be used as a predictor of public numbers is usually to plot the data side by side, and perform a linear regression. I often iterate between regular and logarithmic axes — this is based on my early training as a physicist, where I learned to analyze the basic form of a relationship based on which axis transformations deliver a linear plot. The time-series are shown in Figure 3.7.

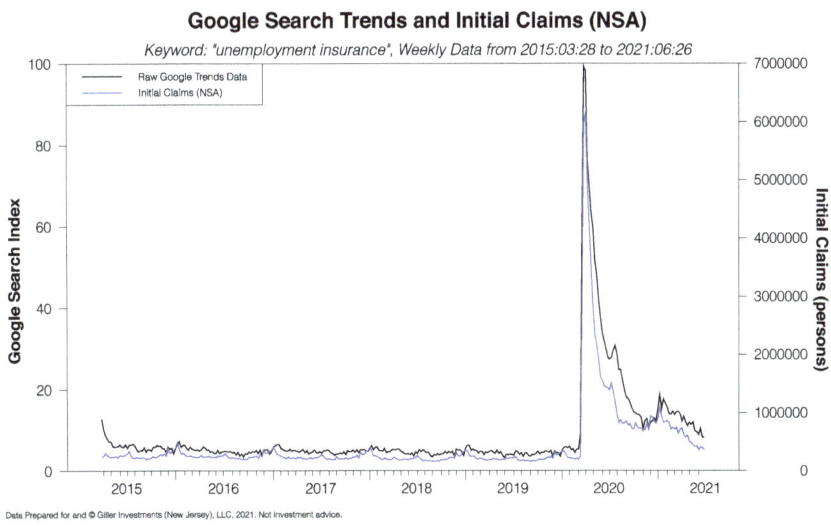

Figure 3.7: Time-series of Google Trends activity index for the keyword "unemployment insurance" and Initial Claims (not seasonally adjusted). The Google data is normalized as described in the text and the Initial Claims are measured in persons.

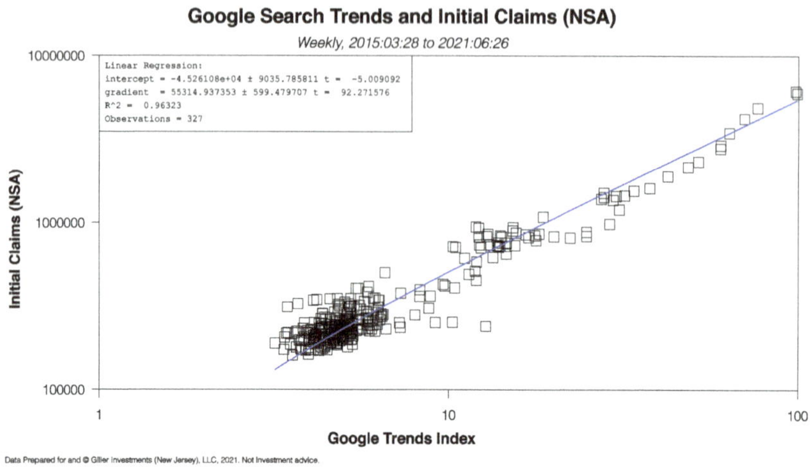

Figure 3.8: Linear regression of Initial Claims (not seasonally adjusted) onto Google Trends activity index for the keyword "unemployment insurance." The Google data is normalized as described in the text and the Initial Claims are measured in persons. Axes are logarithmic.

The dynamic ranges of both time series are so dramatic that it's hard to tell whether there is genuine covariance. Both series have a long period of low values and a short period of high values, apparently exhibiting two distinct regimes, and that would induce a positive correlation across the whole data set even if the correlation *within* the regimes were, in fact, negative.[g] Figure 3.8 shows the scatter plot of Initial Claims (NSA) versus the Google Trends activity index and associated linear regression. Although the fit is very good, the data clearly shows two separate regions.

3.2.4. *Time Varying Coefficients Models*

There are two methods I've found useful when data clearly exhibits different regimes. The first is the *Hidden Markov Model* that proposes a data generating process that randomly switches between different regimes but has constant parameters *within the regimes.* The second, which we will use here, is the *Time Varying Coefficients*,

[g]This phenomenon is often exhibited in *panel* data and is easy to demonstrate via elementary analysis.

which models the parameters as randomly evolving synchronously with the data. Both of these are forms of what are called *State Space Models*.

TVC models are very easy to obtain from traditional Linear Additive Noise models. One merely replaces the constants with time series themselves. However, so that the system is solvable, we need to constrain the evolution of the parameters through time in some way. A remarkably successful methodology is to model the parameters as generated by a random walk, which permits the system to be solved with the *Kalman Filter* [25]. This, necessarily, requires us to abandon the assumption of non-Normal distributions — which may cause my readers to be concerned, given the well justified assault on both the assumptions of Brownian Motion and the use of the Normal distribution I presented in Chapter 2. Nevertheless, I have no other model to offer as there are a very restricted set of distributions for which a Kalman Filter may be used.[h] As always, I assert the Golden Rule — I can use whatever method I want to build forecasts, but I must evaluate their performance according to the rules of the scientific method.

For the linear regression

$$y_t = \alpha + \beta x_t + \varepsilon_t \tag{3.17}$$

$$\varepsilon_t \sim N(0, \sigma^2), \tag{3.18}$$

with static parameters $\{\alpha, \beta, \sigma\}$, we substitute the system

$$y_t = \alpha_t + \beta_t x_t + \varepsilon_t,\ \varepsilon_t \sim N(0, \sigma_t^2), \tag{3.19}$$

with dynamic parameters

$$\alpha_t = \alpha_{t-1} + \eta_t,\ \eta_t \sim N(0, H_t^2) \tag{3.20}$$

$$\beta_t = \beta_{t-1} + \chi_t,\ \chi_t \sim N(0, X_t^2). \tag{3.21}$$

This system models variance created by both measurement noise and the stochastic evolution of the parameters, and permits those noise processes to change through time. However, for the system to

[h]In addition to the Normal distribution, the Cauchy distribution may also be used.

be solvable via linear algebra, the Normal distribution is required. This is because the Normal is a "stable distribution," meaning that[i] $N(m_1, s_1^2)+N(m_2, s_2^2) = N(m_1+m_2, s_1^2+s_2^2)$. Neither the Generalized Error Distribution nor Student's t distribution are stable.

3.2.5. *Fitting a Simple Linear Model and a TVC Model to the Google Trends Data*

Generally, more advanced statistical software is required to fit the TVC model. My approach is always to fit an ordinary linear regression and then use that gauge the utility of the more complex system. Data from these models are exhibited in Figure 3.9. It's clear that neither model is without a flaw but, by attempting to draw a compromise between the two data regimes, the ordinary (constant coefficients) linear model is wrong almost always whereas the TVC model is mostly right. In this model the predictors are:

(i) the log of the Google Trends search activity index;
(ii) the value of Initial Claims from the prior week;
(iii) a seasonality correction derived from the history of the differences between the SA and NSA series (when needed).

Figure 3.10 shows a close-up of the performance of the TVC model for 2020, showing the unemployment shock due to the COVID-19 outbreak and the response of the model to this change of regime. Although it stumbles in capturing the initial upwards move (on March 21), and the subsequent break back (on April 4), these are the only releases for which it was seriously in error.

Figure 3.11 shows the distribution of the standardized forward prediction errors, using the conditional means and variances generated by the model. We see a narrow, and clearly leptokurtotic distribution of errors that is decidedly non-Normal (and the two most extreme outliers are not even shown on this plot). Despite this, the sample mean error for the entire available history is -0.0035 ± 0.0558 and the sample standard deviation is 1.0019, which are exactly what would be expected.

[i] I referred to this property in Section 2.1.3.

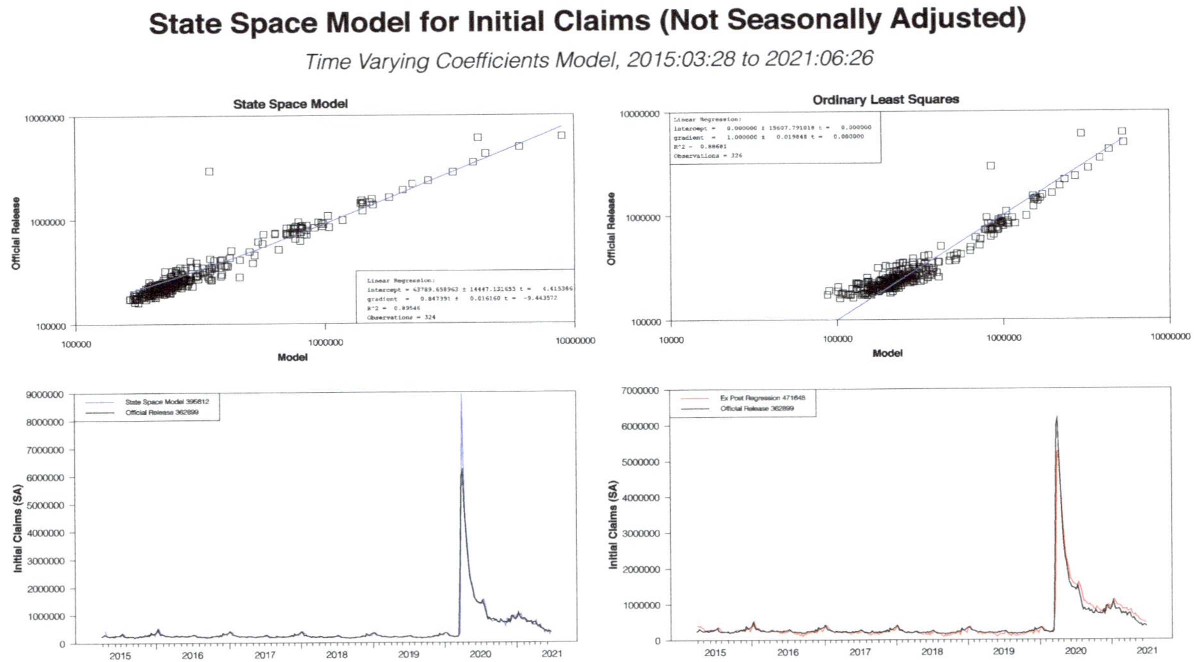

Figure 3.9: Comparison of the performance of a Time Varying Coefficients and OLS model for the regression of Initial Claims (not seasonally adjusted) onto a Google Trends index for the keyword “unemployment insurance.” The left-hand panels are for the TVC model and the right-hand for OLS The upper panels are a regression of the released data onto the predictions from each model and the lower panels time-series of the predictions and released data.

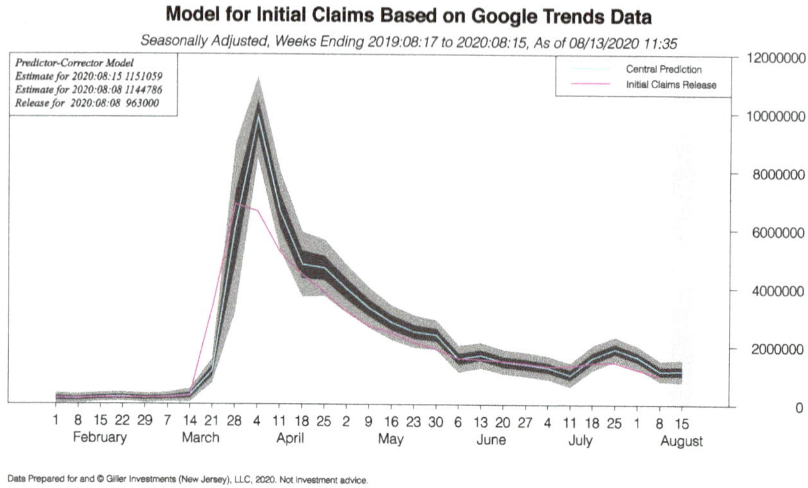

Figure 3.10: Comparison of the performance of a Time Varying Coefficients model for Initial Claims (seasonally adjusted) to the released data. The blue curve is the central prediction from the model and the shaded regions represent 68% and 99% confidence regions about the prediction. The purple curve is the actual released data, which is made available a week after the end of the reference period. The vertical bar represents a period for which a prediction is made but the actual data not yet known.

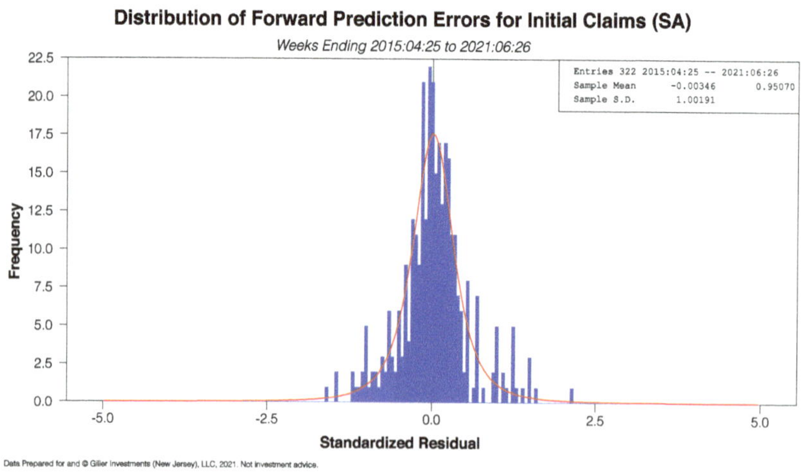

Figure 3.11: Histogram of the standardized forward prediction errors for a TVC model of Initial Claims (seasonally adjusted) from Google search trends. The blue bars are the histogram and the red curve is the best fitting Student's t distribution.

3.3. Twitter

The last section exhibited the use of "alternative data" in econometric work. This has become more and more of my focus over the years. One common thread seems to be working with Twitter. If I had been writing this book perhaps a decade ago, I would have taken time out to explain what Twitter is — but at this point I think everybody knows.[j]

Many traders look to Twitter to try to find early news about companies, to anticipate earnings surprise or M&A activity. I don't find that to be particularly useful. In fact I've not come across any reliable, automatic, processing of Twitter data that can be used *systematically* to create an advantage based on lexical sentiment or keyword triggers. Yes, we can always find examples where individually it works but, systematically, across a universe of stocks, done in a manner likely to create a durable income, I've not seen any real examples of success.[k] I think the problem is due to the nature of financial markets: at any given time there are hundreds of thousands of human beings scouring all available news sources for exactly the intelligence people are trying to find on Twitter and using it to inform the prices for which stocks are traded.

The idea that the vast trading crowd cannot find such data but a guy with a Python script and the Twitter API can is something I find implausible. Early in my tenure at Bloomberg, Carl Icahn

Figure 3.12: Tweet from known activist investor Carl Icahn announcing that he had bought Apple, Inc. shares.

[j]Go to https://www.twitter.com/StatTrader if you do not!

[k]Perhaps others have had a different experience, but I've been doing this for a long time and I think I'm quite good at it.

mentioned on television that he would be tweeting about Apple, Inc. the next day. Like many others across the street, I immediately coded systems to capture this, and was able to track the market reaction to the message that Carl had bought Apple shares.

With access to all of Bloomberg's financial data resources, I carefully studied the impact to this tweet. While the first retweet had occurred in, I recall, something like seven seconds of Carl's, Wall Street had moved the price of Apple essentially immediately — within less than a second. No statistically developed measure of "social proof," based on rate of retweets or other metric would have provided intelligence soon enough to beat the hundreds of thousands of humans who were watching Apple's stock. Indeed, nothing about the communications infrastructure operated by Twitter is comparable to the engineering done, and discussed in Section 2.9, by profit incentivized Wall Street traders. Speed is not going to be how Twitter adds value to the investment process.

3.3.1. *Do Twitter Users Believe Traders Have Hot Hands?*

3.3.1.1. *The Experiment*

In April 2009, my company, Giller Investments, began an experiment with Twitter to investigate the usage of social networking within the context of the commodity trading advisor business. The trading system I had developed for equity index futures was used to to broadcast a trade blotter[1] to any users who wish to subscribe to it. The data sent represents an historical record of trades executed by our firm for a model account and was not customized for or targeted to any individual user.

The goal of the experiment was to determine whether Twitter could be used to solicit subscriptions for a premium service without any promotional effort apart from the passive activity of broadcasting data on twitter. This was not successful although my work coincided with the emergence of the *StockTwits* website, who apparently decided in their growth stage to onboard all active accounts using the *folksonomy* of $ ticker tags into their system. My activity,

[1]Meaning a compact record of trade orders.

which was fairly low intensity, then resulted in my Twitter account, `@StatTrader`, being banned from the *StockTwits* platform — even though I never actually asked to join it!

Because of things like the *StockTwits* ban, I terminated the experiment after just a couple of months. The strategy itself was undergoing a drawdown during the period of this experiment, which likely didn't make it particularly exciting to follow. The strategy was an intraday one with low turnover. Trades were initiated at the start of the day, based on an alpha computed from the prior day's and overnight price action; held throughout the day; and, liquidated at the end of the day. Four types of tweets, in two classes, were broadcast. They were:

(i) VWAP[m] summaries, with profit and loss reports, for both open and closed trades.
(ii) Trade execution records for buy and sell trades with fill prices and quantities.

Examples are given in Table 3.5.

To an observer, the success of the strategy was contemporaneous public information which could contribute to an interested subscriber's decision to follow the account posting the trade data. That would be based upon the Twitter user's inference that past success or failure is indicative of future success or failure of the strategy — something that should not be true under the Efficient Markets Hypothesis.

3.3.1.2. *Analysis of Variance*

Data was collected from 04/20/2009 to 06/19/2009 to a Twitter account, `@StatTraderCTA`, that has subsequently been deleted. As the tweets contain profit and loss information, the success of the trading strategy was observable to interested readers of the tweets without much effort. Numbers of followers of the account were collected at the end of each day and stored, side-by-side, with a trade success indicator. In all there are just 45 data pairs and so we unable to apply the sophisticated analytical tools presented in other sections of this book.

[m] Volume Weighted Average Price

Table 3.5: Four sample formats of Twitter messages used the followers experiment.

Trade Blotter Tweets

Type	Name	Example
(a)	VWAP Summary (Closed Trade)	06/22/2009 $NQU #SHORT SLD 1442.23 BOT 1426.64, GAIN 15.58; $YMU #SHORT SLD 8368.64 BOT 8296.94, GAIN 71.70; http://is.gd/tGyI #futures #emini
(a)	VWAP Summary (Open Trade)	06/22/2009 $NQU #SHORT SLD 1451.75, LOSS 1.75; $YMU #SHORT SLD 8403.00, LOSS 2.00; http://is.gd/tGyI #futures #emini
(b)	Trade Record (Buy Trade)	16:14:47 BOT 9 $NQU 1427.5 Data delayed. In real time at http://is.gd/tGyI #futures #emini
(b)	Trade Record (Sell Trade)	08:56:14 SLD 2 $YMU 8403 Data delayed. In real time at http://is.gd/tGyI #futures #emini

Note: Note the use of an URL Shortening Service to compact the advertised hyperlink back to the Giller Investments website and the use of special characters $ and # to highlight ticker symbols and indexable content.

Instead, I will present the simplest thing possible, which is an *ANOVA* analysis.[n] There are two groups of data: those for which the trades reported upon were successful and those for which they were not. The *ANOVA* table is shown in Table 3.6.

At better than 95% confidence, but just less than 99%, we see that the success of the trade does explain the variance and the mean change in followers on days with winning trades is substantially higher, at 2.25/day, than on days with losing trades, at 0.64/day. Overall, this is not a particularly surprising or significant result but it does correlate with real human experience. Human beings, it seems, equipped with a predictive system to deal with a physical world that contains a lot of momentum — catching balls, throwing spears, etc. — seem to be unable to separate it from their financial decisions. Although, to be honest, I have no way of knowing if the impact of this experiment was anything other than the addition of a marginal

[n]Earlier, I had published a whitepaper on this strategy to the Social Science Research Network [50] which uses maximum likelihood analysis.

Table 3.6: Single factor ANOVA table for change in Twitter followers grouped by indicated trading success.

Summary Statistics					
Groups	Count	Sum	Mean	Variance	
Winning Trades	12	27	2.25	3.66	
Losing Trades	33	21	0.64	3.43	
Analysis of Variance					
Source of Variation	*SS*	*df*	*MS*	*F*	*p*-value
Between Groups	22.91	1	22.91	6.57	0.01393
Within Groups	149.89	3.49			
Total	172.8	44			

amount of lost cost spam into people's timelines. It would be a lot more relevant if it was connected to people's investment activity not their Twitter activity!

3.3.2. *#nfpguesses*

By 2014, I had been working at Bloomberg for several years, trying to bring alternative data and advanced predictive analytics into their platform. Joe Wiesenthal, first at Business Insider and after he'd joined the news team at Bloomberg, had been promoting the hashtag *#nfpguesses* for people to predict the monthly release of NFPs on what people were beginning to call "Jobs Day," every first Friday of the Month.

The concept of the "wisdom of crowds" has a long history in statistical literature, starting with Sir Francis Galton's famous article *Vox Populi* [45]. The idea is that a crowd of people with an interest in an outcome all make estimates of the likely future value of some property which is a combination of both the unknown true value and their personal error. If the errors are uncorrelated and unbiased, when averaged across the population, then the sample mean of their estimates should be an efficient and unbiased predictor of the true value of the property under discussion. This is, of course, the exact same

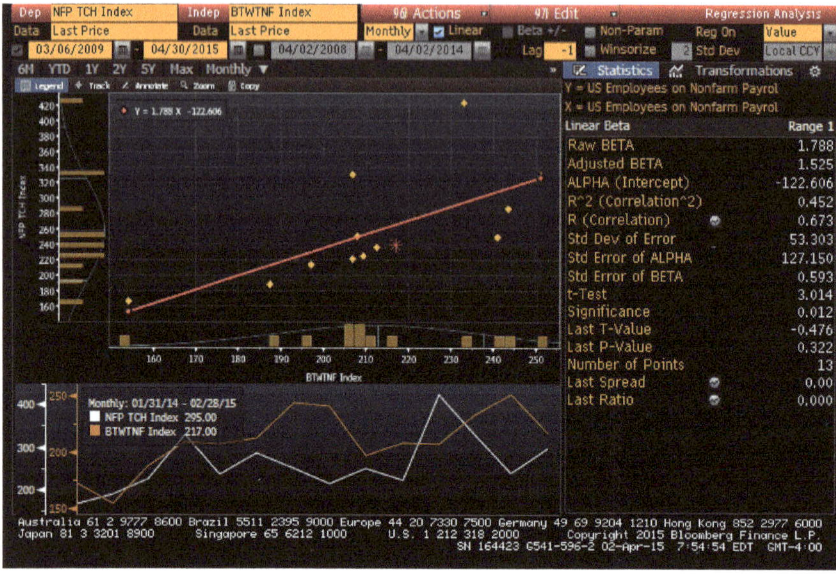

Figure 3.13: Regression analysis of Bloomberg's `BTWTNF Index` data and the release for Monthly Change in NFP (seasonally adjusted).

principal by which markets are suggested to operate and consistent with the linear additive noise framework discussed in Section 2.1.4.

I decided to track these tweets and put a summary statistic taken from them onto the terminal, which created a lot of engagement. I was told by the head of Foreign Exchange products that the first thing clients asked about when they came into Bloomberg headquarters on 731, Lexington Avenue, was our *#nfpguesses* system.

Figure 3.13 shows a regression I published using Bloomberg's `HRA`, or *Historical Regression Analysis*, function to compare our index to the official releases. At the time this was done, after just over a year of running, we had an R^2 of some 45% and a t statistic of 3.014 with a p value of 0.012. I was very proud of this system that my team put together in a few days and am pleased to see that it is still running and being used. It's a testament to the freedom to innovate that I was given by my direct manager, David Tabit. We only had one problem with collecting data from the wild internet and putting it inside the controlled Bloomberg Terminal, and that was when users `@barnejek` and `@AllThatIsSolid` decided to vandalize it by tweeting ever increasing set of numbers.

We were vulnerable to this attack because we had been unable to decide whether we should aggregate all the tweets from a single user, or just the last one, or maybe the first one? We used a robust estimator of the center of the collected data to determine the aggregate view of the crowd, and used a robust estimator of distributional width to filter outliers. From traffic online, it appeared that the vandals had been working *all night long* to try to break our system, before they succeeded in the early morning. It was my habit to arrive at Bloomberg at around 7:50 am, and I immediately noticed something was wrong. Eduardo Hermesmeyer, who had programmed the data collection code, and I rapidly decided to adopt the policy of "the last tweet from a user is the only one to be used." We removed the vandals efforts and permanently banned them from the system for good measure. This all happened in the Summer of 2014, and it has run smoothly since then.

3.3.3. *Lexical Sentiment*

From its beginnings, social media has been a consumer communication platform and people like me have been trying to get trading signals out of it. Since the dialogue, prior to the emergence of "memes based content," has has been text based, we have tried to apply the tools of Statistical Natural Language Processing (NLP), to it. Historically this meant classification of tweets by one of three methods:

(i) manual classification by humans;
(ii) the use of "sentiment dictionaries," in which numeric scores are given to particular words; and,
(iii) machine learning methods based on various NLP methods and known sentiment scores.

Often the latter step is fed output from the first two. The first method has historically been very expensive,[o] and has suffered from training sets that are small in scale. The second is crude, and often fails when a publicly available but contextually inappropriate dictionary is used.

[o]Although, now much cheaper thanks to pools of crowd workers such as Amazon's *Mechanical Turk*.

3.3.3.1. *Twitter Sentiment Analysis for Predicting the Market*

In May 2012, I ran an experiment. I built a system to collect tweets that mentioned the tickers of the S&P 400 member stocks.[p] The way Twitter's *filter* stream works is you receive all tweets that satisfy your query except that you may never receive more than 1% of the full stream — the so-called "firehose." Commercial API's permit access to more data, but I used the free service. I stored all of the tweets into a database and wrote a Python program to present me with a random selection of tweets that had no sentiment grade attached. As I worked on other things I would, from time-to-time, grade these tweets as "bullish," "bearish," or indeterminate. As I worked with this data set I rapidly discovered that retail investor activity was strongly concentrated in a small number of "momentum" stocks, and that list corresponded to those discussed on Jim Cramer's *Mad Money* T.V. show every night.

3.3.3.2. *Analysis of Twitter Users in 2012*

I sometimes characterize Twitter as offering "a whitelist for spam," due to the prevalence of accounts created solely to bombard the user with promotional messages. The first thing to look at when analyzing data from a sample of the population, are metrics that tell you how representative the sample is of the population, i.e. What do the sample demographics look like in comparison to population demographics?

For the sample of tweets gathered in this experiment, I wanted to see what the distribution of user account ages looked like. For every tweet that I had graded the sentiment of, I plotted the distribution of the age of the account (the difference between the tweet date and the `created_at` field in the `user` data provided by Twitter with each tweet). Due to the volume of data provided by Twitter, and the random sampling they use to provide this data to consumers, there were no overlaps due to accounts being collected more than once. A histogram of these ages is shown[q] in Figure 3.14.

---

[p]I had to truncate the list to 400 as the Twitter API would not accept any more.

[q]All the plots from this analysis are large "landscape" plots because I no longer have access to the raw data they were made from. I am reproducing legacy work here rather than creating new ones.

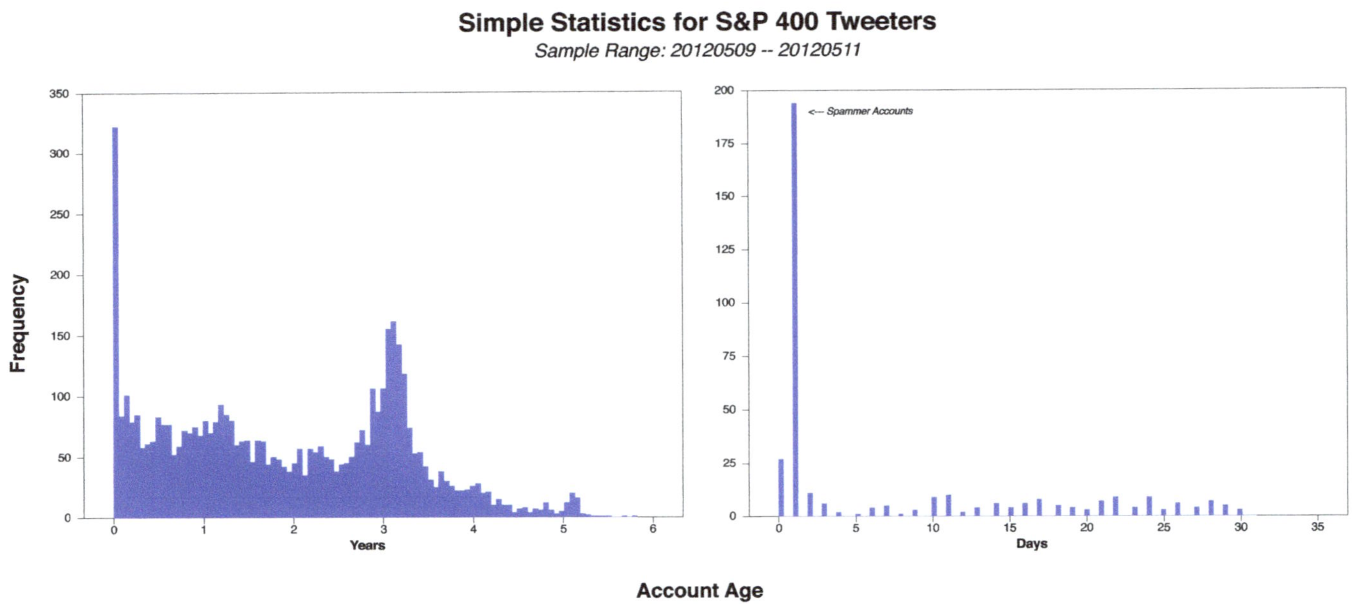

Figure 3.14: Histograms of the account age for Twitter users who were collected when listening to the streaming API for tweets mentioning stock tickers in the S&P 400 Index. The left-hand panel shows low temporal resolution data and the right-hand panel high temporal resolution at the lower end.

In this data, we see a broad peak representing a surge of account creation around three years prior to the analysis, in 2009. My account was also created in 2009, which was when Twitter began to be talked about more in the (mostly financial) press I read — that was the stimulus for my own investigation of the platform. I conjecture I was not alone in that activity.

We see a narrow peak at an age of one day! I conjectured that this was due to spammer accounts, which certainly were very prevalent on the system, being created to tout stocks in the hope of generating followers and then being shut down by Twitter's anti-spam systems. In the following work, accounts with an age of less than a week were excluded.

3.3.3.3. *Characteristics of Sentiment Graded Tweets*

Another metric of the population of graded tweets concerned how they relate to each other. Figure 3.15 shows a plot of the autocorrelation function of the graded sentiments and of the time interval between graded sentiments. The ACF is the quantity

$$\rho_k = \mathrm{Cor}[S_i, S_{i-k}], \quad k \geq 0, \tag{3.22}$$

where here i is the sequential index of the tweet and S_i is the associated sentiment grade.[r] This tweet was recorded at time t_i, and so the interval between tweets is $t_i - t_{i-1}$.

We see that there is some very weak level of positive autocorrelation that doesn't persist for long and that the intervals between tweets collected and graded are, on average, about 5 or 6 minutes. This tells us that the data represent essentially independent measurements, although not perfectly so. The fitted curve to the distribution of intervals (in hours) is a Gamma distribution, Gamma$(0.21, 0.63)$. For genuinely random events in time, such as radioactive decay, we would expect the Exponential distribution, which has a "softer" decay property, so this likely indicates some low level of clustering between events. From the properties of the distribution, the mean time between tweets is $0.21 \times 0.63 = 7.7$ minutes with standard deviation $\sqrt{0.21 \times 0.63^2} = 17$ minutes.

[r]The notation $\mathrm{Cor}[x, y]$ means the correlation of x and y.

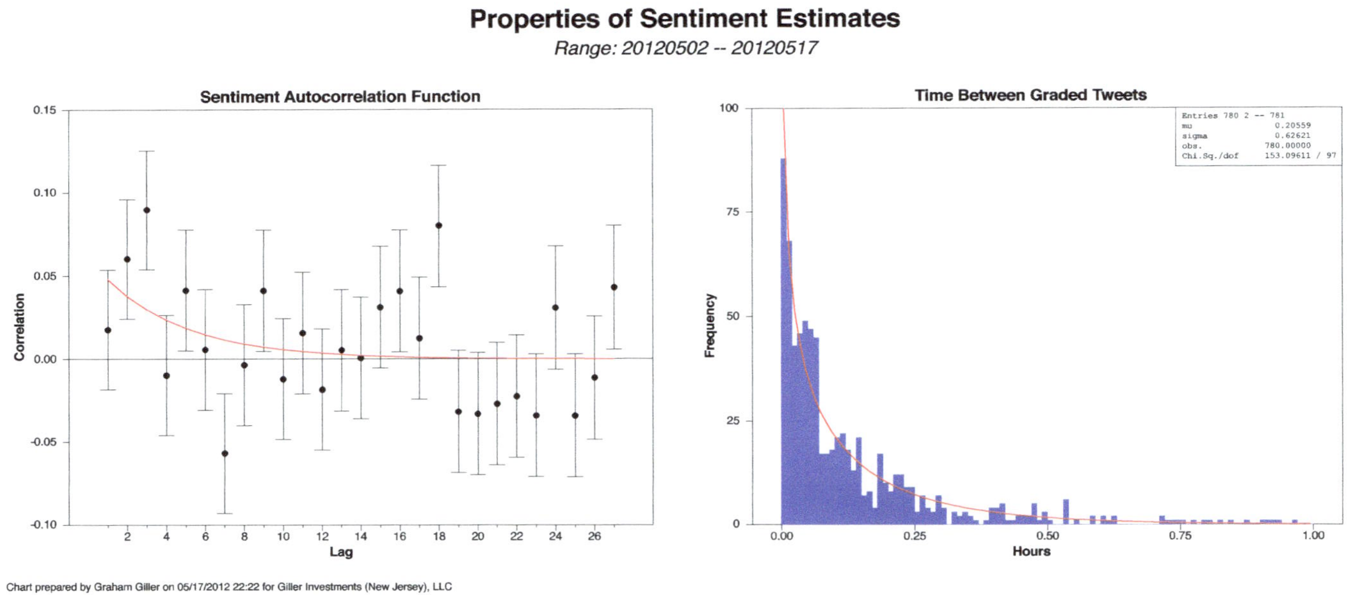

Figure 3.15: The autocorrelation function of the graded sentiments of captured tweets and the distribution of times between tweets that were captured. The left hand panel shows the autocorrelation function and a fitted, decaying, power law. It is suggestive of, perhaps, a slight momentum. The right panel shows the distribution of times between tweets and a fitted, decaying, power law. It is suggestive of a fairly random tweet generation process, but decays steeper than that for an exponential, indicating some clustering.

3.3.3.4. *Relationship of Sentiment Graded Tweets to Market Index Returns*

Having established that the tweets to be studied are not from spammers and are (essentially) independent events, we may then study how the changes in sentiment relate to changes in the market. The first analytical tool to use in this context is the *cross-correlation function* (CCF). This is an analogue to the ACF that may be used to compare two series. There are three possible scenarios:

(i) the stock market *follows* sentiment, meaning sentiment is an alpha;
(ii) the stock market *leads* sentiment, meaning retail investors (on twitter) exhibit momentum; and,
(iii) there is no correlation between the series.

The quantity computed is

$$\chi_k = \mathrm{Cor}[\Delta S_i, \Delta M_{i-k}], \tag{3.23}$$

and k may be: positive, meaning the sentiment is compared to *prior* market moves; negative, meaning sentiment is compared to *future* market moves; or zero, for *contemporaneous* data. ΔS_i and ΔM_i are the changes in sentiment and the market index respectively.[s]

From Figure 3.16, we see little apparent cross-correlation, at a wide range of lags, between the graded sentiments of captured tweets and the market. When put side-by-side the two time-series do not appear related at all, and the distribution of cross-correlation coefficients definitely appears consistent with being drawn from a distribution which is peaked around zero.

3.3.3.5. *My Opinion on Lexical Sentiment and the Market*

Based on investigations like this, and others I've performed, I've come to the conclusion that the dream of using data resources that are available at low cost and based on *consumer sentiment* to successfully predict a market in which 100,000s of well financed professional

[s]Over the time intervals considered here, there are no significant differences between the changes in the S&P 500 Index, the aggregated change of top 400 stocks in the index alone, and the *SPY* ETF itself.

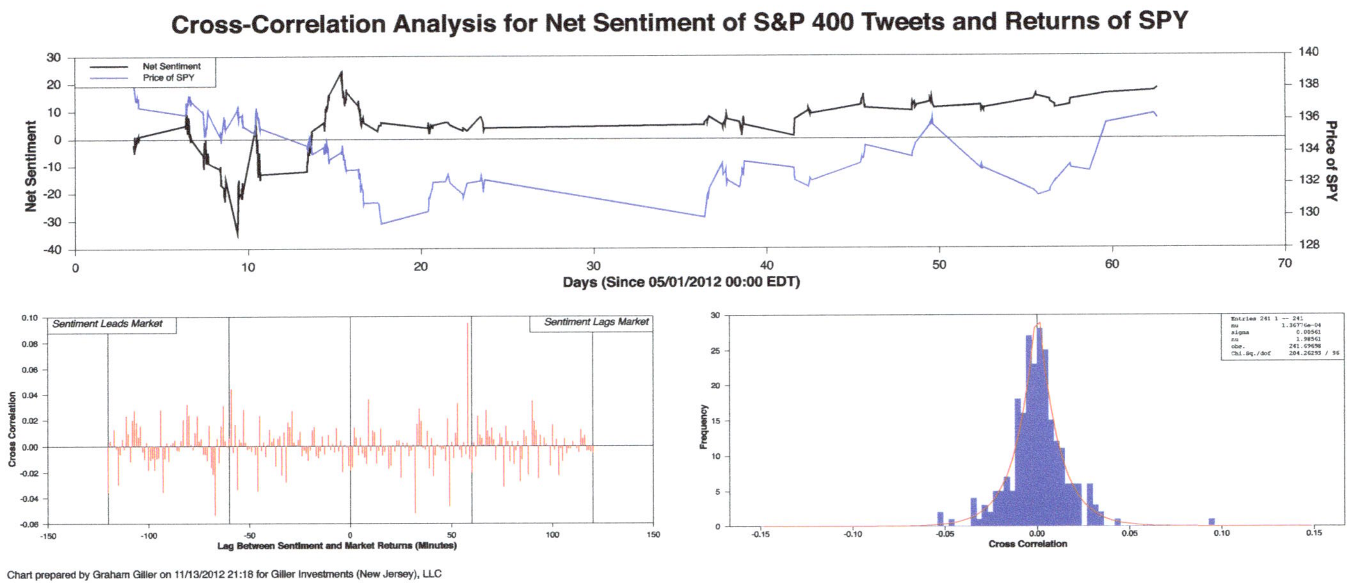

Figure 3.16: Analysis of the cross-correlation between graded sentiments of captured tweets and the returns of the S&P 500 Index for May and June 2012. The upper panel shows the time-series of the net sentiment through time and the price of the *SPY* E.T.F. (which tracks the index) at the same times. The lower left plot is the cross-correlation function of the changes in both series, and the lower right plot a histogram of the observed cross-correlation coefficients.

traders participate is likely just that — a dream. Doubtless others will disagree with me, but I've come back to this many times over the past decade and never found Twitter to be useful in a markets context. However, the resources are easy to acquire and technologies better than they were in 2012, so I encourage my readers to try it and see what they find. Just remember, use science and don't expect to create a "magic money tree" with thirty minutes' work.

3.3.4. *Sentiment and the Macroeconomy*

3.3.4.1. *Cloud Services for NLP*

Since I began my studies of Twitter in 2009 the availability of well-trained, low-cost, machine learning algorithms has dramatically changed. Whereas then one had to write and train such algorithms from scratch, they are now available as paid services from providers such as Amazon's AWS and the Google Cloud Platform. Features readily available include:

(i) machine translation;
(ii) parts of speech lexical analysis;
(iii) sentiment extraction;
(iv) summarization.

Rather than laboriously hand classifying data, as I did for the prior analysis, it is also possible to solicit classifications from crowds of workers via low cost services such as Amazon's *Mechanical Turk*.

In my experience, work done by *Turkers* is generally of low quality, as they are motivated to produce as much work in as little time as possible and compensation rates are mostly below minimum wage. I found the GCP translation and sentiment analysis offerings to offer broader coverage but less general quality than the AWS versions, and I personally concentrate on just using AWS.

3.3.4.2. *Collecting Sentiment Data from Twitter*

In 2020 I resumed collection of sentiment data on Twitter. I am interested in establishing whether the data may be used for macroeconomic insights within the United States and so selected a random subset of tweets that contain geographic location data locating it to the USA. This feature is much more prevalent than it was ten years ago. Tweets are passed to AWS for sentiment classification, which is done either in their native language, or after machine translation to English if the language is not supported for native classification.

I remove all retweets and tweets created by "blue check" verified accounts, to concentrate on original expressions of sentiment from the general population of Twitter users — I refer to this as *organic sentiment*. I have been collecting data since February 2020, and collection is ongoing. The AWS fees for the "Translate" and "Comprehend" machine learning services I use amount to a few hundred dollars a month. Although the algorithms may not be perfect, they are without doubt better than anything I could craft myself, and under continuous development. I also do what I can to eliminate accounts that are blatantly commercial or clearly bots, by manual inspection of the data.

I process the account user names to infer demographic information,[t] including age in ten year bands and gender, and then weight the users so that the demographic profile of the users matches the demographic profile of the United States as provided by the *American Community Survey* programme operated by the US Census Bureau for the year. Figure 3.17 shows the inferred population pyramid, which shows a clear over-representation of males across all age groups, which is corrected for by *ex post* weighting. Finally, as the sentiment classifications provided by A.W.S. are defined on the range $[-1, 1]$, I use Fisher's transformation to map it to the whole real line $(-\infty, \infty)$.

3.3.4.3. *Time Series of Twitter Organic Sentiment for the USA*

Figure 3.18 shows the time series of the monthly average organic Twitter sentiment, computed as described above, compared side by side with the University of Michigan's *Index of Consumer Sentiment*. This is a well known index with considerable history. It is based on traditional consumer surveys and is described in the book by Curtin [18]. From such a short time-series, it is hard to say much about whether the observed correlation of $50\% \pm 25\%$ is real or occurred by chance. Only time, which brings more data, will tell.

[t]The methodology used for this will be covered in Chapter 5.

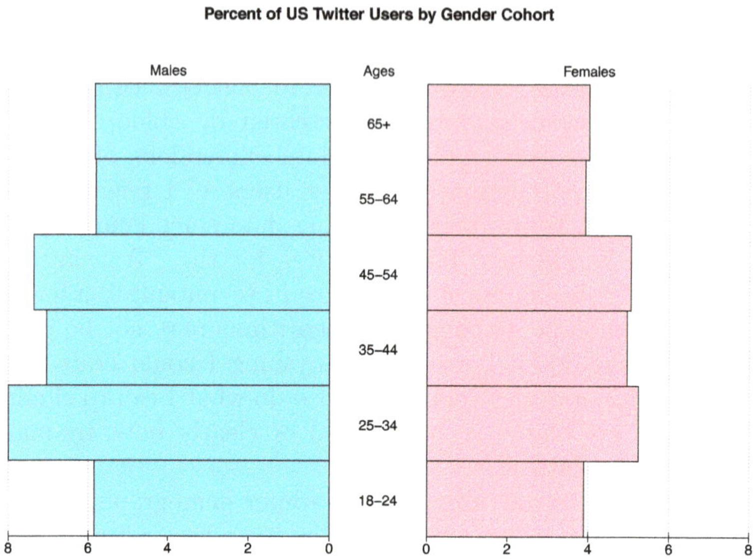

Figure 3.17: Population pyramid for Twitter users based on inferred demographics.

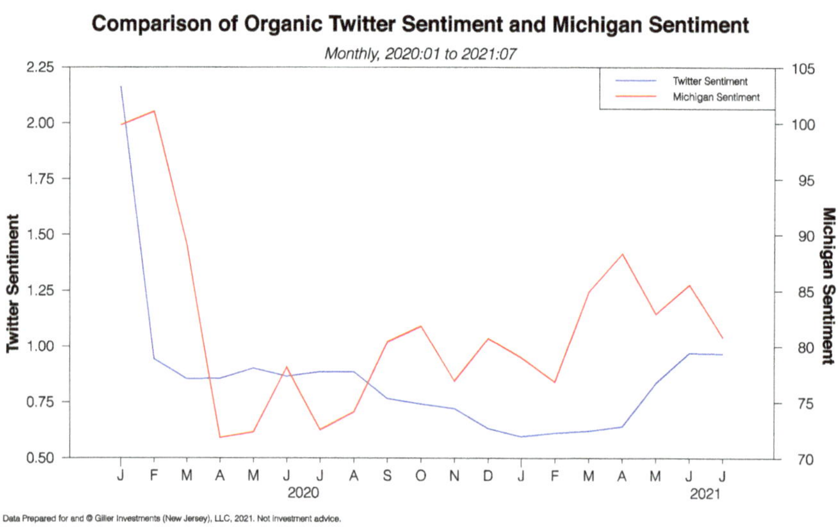

Figure 3.18: Time series of average organic Twitter sentiment for tweets geolocated to the USA and the University of Michigan's *Index of Consumer Sentiment* based on traditional consumer surveys.

3.3.4.4. *Correlation of Sentiment with Initial Claims*

We have seen that it's a struggle[u] to make Twitter sentiment tell us anything about stock returns. Until recently, that was all I was interested in. However, the reason I restarted collecting data from Twitter was to investigate whether there was any correlation with the labor markets. This arose from a conversation I had with Mike McDonough, who is Chief Economist at Bloomberg LP.[v]

Figure 3.19 shows time-series of organic Twitter sentiment tweets geolocated to the USA and Initial Claims (Seasonally Adjusted) side-by-side. I'm using the S.A. series because it seems likely that Twitter users would not be anomalously upset by seasonal unemployment that was entirely expected. The series seem to be weakly associated by eye, but we should be cautious as this might be merely a spurious linearity based on the change in dynamic range of the Initial Claims data.

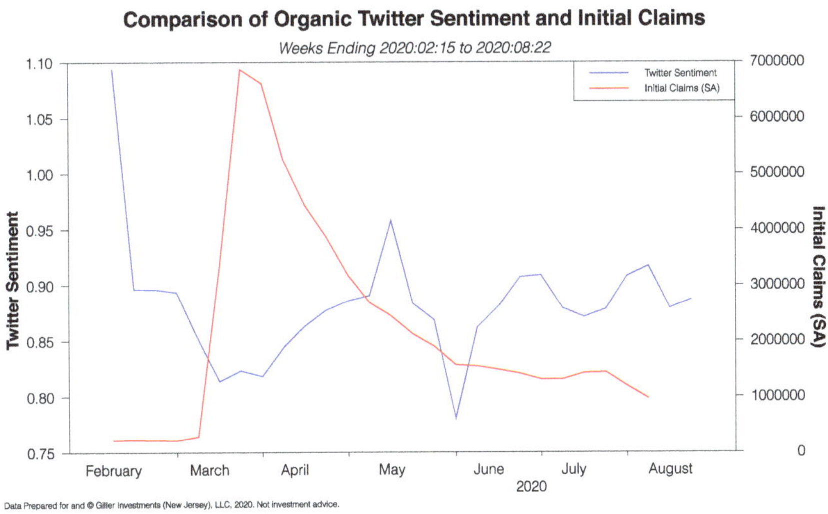

Figure 3.19: Time-series of average organic Twitter sentiment for tweets geolocated to the USA and weekly Initial Claims (for Unemployment Insurance, seasonally adjusted). The blue curve is the sentiment indicator processed as outlined in the text and the red curve is the count of Initial Claims.

[u]Or requires a data processing incantation I am not aware of.

[v]For the record, this conversation occurred in mid January 2020, before we were aware of the scale of the impact of COVID-19 on the United States.

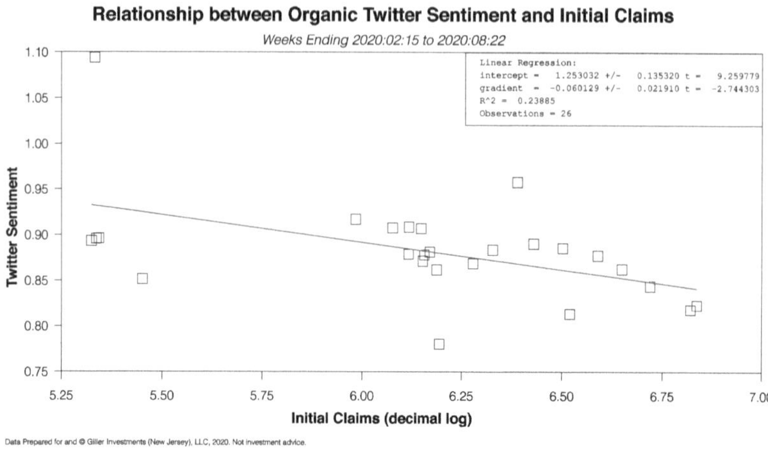

Figure 3.20: Regression between organic Twitter sentiment and the decimal log of Initial Claims (seasonally adjusted).

To deal with the extreme dynamic range of the Initial Claims data (due to the COVID-19 recession), I decided to look at the decimal log of this measure. The covariance between the data is shown in Figure 3.20. This shows a marginally significant regression with a coefficient of the right sign ($\hat{\beta} = -0.022 \pm 0.023$) and an overall significance just shy of 99% confidence (the F statistic is 7.53 with a p value of 0.011). This seems plausible, but there's not really enough data to say that it's real. More data is needed.

3.3.4.5. *Panel Regression Analysis*

One way to get more data for analysis, increasing the sample size, is to repeat it state-by-state without aggregation, providing of order 50 times more observations. If this is done just by dis-aggregating the data, then we also get 50 times as many parameters and 50 significance tests all of which will likely be more borderline than that for the global aggregate.

An alternative strategy is to run what is called a *Panel Regression Analysis*. In this, we replace the ordinary linear regression equation with an analogue that is aware of the individual identity of the various samples, i.e.

$$y_t = \alpha + \beta x_t + \varepsilon_t, \tag{3.24}$$

$$\text{becomes } y_{it} = \alpha_i + \beta x_{it} + \varepsilon_{it}, \tag{3.25}$$

where $\{\varepsilon_{it}\}$ are independent stochastic quantities. This is known as the *Fixed Effects Model* with *individual effects.*

With this structure, we model the States as each having an idiosyncratic sentiment bias, but all responding *in the same way* to their own specific signals. It is also possible to build models with common temporal covariance, known as *time effects* where α_i is replaced with δ_t, and one with both of those phenomenon. Note that there is no overall constant in the model, as this value is "swept" into the individual means. Models such as this are are discussed extensively in books such as the one by Hsiao [71]. Of course, available software is going to assume that all of the stochastics are Normally distributed, so we should examine the residuals to see how reasonable that assumption has been.

3.3.4.6. *Panel Regression of Initial Claims onto Twitter Sentiment*

In Section 3.3.4.4 we found an apparent contemporaneous relationship between total Initial Claims for the USA and average organic Twitter sentiment. The causality is not determined by the method, but it seems very clear: tens of millions of people are unhappy because they lost their jobs due to the COVID-19 crisis. It doesn't seem plausible that *tens of millions* of people lost their jobs because they created sad tweets![w]

Nevertheless, I have always been in the forecasting business, and so I would like to use data I have, $\alpha(\mathcal{I}_t)$ in my language, to predict something I care about, $E_t[m(\mathcal{I}_{t+1})]$. In this case the alpha is organic Twitter sentiment and the metric is the *late reported* Initial Claims numbers. As I am predicting something that is contemporaneous to the alpha, but unknown at the time the prediction is made, this is referred to as *nowcasting* rather than forecasting.

Over the same time-period as previously analyzed, there are now 1,127 usable observations (some states do not have sufficient Twitter data in every month) which should be plenty for reliable measurements. In order to establish *Granger Causality*, I will introduce such lagged values of the state-by-state Initial Claims data as are

[w]This is one way in which the extremities of the *Coronavirus* pandemic make analysis a little easier.

Table 3.7: Results from fixed individual effects panel regression of Initial Claims by State onto lagged values and contemporaneous organic Twitter sentiment.

Panel regression results			
Variable	Estimate	Std. error	t statistic
φ_1	0.925	0.029	31.7
φ_2	−0.268	0.028	−9.4
β	$-52,678$	12,209	−4.3
Significance tests			
Test	Statistic	Value	p-value
Causality	$F_{1,1705}$	18.6	1.8×10^{-5}

significant in the regression — this turns out to be two. Thus the model is

$$C_{it} = \alpha_i + \varphi_1 C_{it-1} + \varphi_2 C_{it-2} + \beta S_{it} + \varepsilon_{it}, \tag{3.26}$$

with C_{it} representing the Initial Claims numbers for a given State, and week, and S_{it} the organic Twitter sentiment index for the same period.

This model *is* significant, with the estimated value $\hat{\beta}$ having a t statistic of −4.3 and the Granger Causality test having a p value of 1.75×10^{-5}. However, the estimated coefficient $\hat{\beta} = -52{,}678 \pm 12{,}209$ has somewhat limited utility. As S_{it} is of order unity, a 10% change in sentiment will only move claims by about 0.5% of the current number — most of the predictive power seems to be coming from the autocorrelative terms. The results are shown in Table 3.7. Although the outcome is disappointing, hopefully the journey of learning a new methodology for our Data Scientist toolkit makes it worthwhile!

3.4. Analysis of Climate Data

In 2012, I began working as a professional data scientist, where my professional life was concentrated more on using machine learning methods to optimize business processes than forecasting financial time-series. Although it was a lot of fun, I had begun pursing some non-financial analytics for recreational purposes, and followed my curiosity. It was a relatively quiescent time for business, but changes in the global climate were becoming more well known and I wanted to see whether it was possible to "see for myself" some of these changes. Although I wasn't likely to have a significant input on the field, I felt I might pick up some useful skills.

I was also well aware that analyzing time-series is a technical skill that contains pitfalls that many people fall into *and* that human beings possess many analytical biases, and reason through heuristics, which could interfere negatively with our comprehension of small changes in temperature. In particular, *situational bias* — an assumption that current conditions are normal — is something that all traders are subject to. I have learned to fear that giddy feeling that comes when a strategy makes money at a rate more than expected, and not to execute consequential risk management decisions on the basis of a winning streak.

3.4.1. *The Central England Temperature Series*

My country's heritage has included notable works done by idiosyncratic amateur scientists. I have always been interested in *long* time-series and there are several of note. The *Central England Temperature* is a time series of mean monthly temperatures for central England from 1659 to date compiled originally by Manley [92] from many diverse records, including the notebooks of amateur scientists. It has been updated by the *Met Office* [34,35,99] and is now kept up-to-date by automatic processes. The data tabulates mean monthly temperatures in the generic location of "central England." It is clearly subject to seasonal variation and any analysis must take proper account of that variation.[x]

Although data for a single region is clearly subject to idiosyncratic variation, this data set is substantial in length and so should capture the general trends of the global climatic variation during the period

[x]In fact one of my goals in this analysis was to learn more formally about the analysis of seasonal time-series.

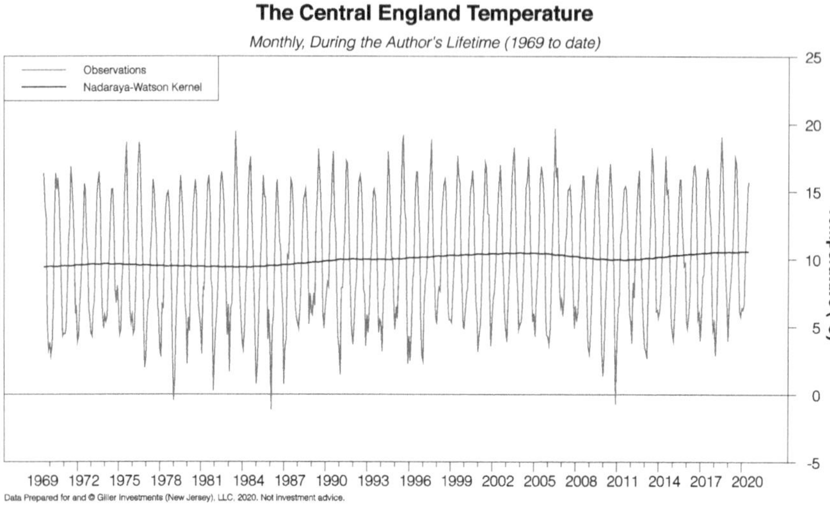

Figure 3.21: Time-series of the Central England Temperature during the author's lifetime. The blue curve is the temperature series and the black line is a non-parametric regression line computed using the Nadaraya–Watson kernel estimator with an Epanechnikov kernel of width five years.

covered. Figure 3.21 shows the Central England Temperature during the author's lifetime. It clearly shows strong annual seasonality, but it also shows extended periods of relatively warm and relatively cold Winters and Summers. In particular, the average monthly temperature in the winters of my middle childhood are notably colder than either the years afterwards (1987 onwards) and also my early childhood (prior to 1978[y]). However, there is also a sequence of cold winters in the years leading up to 2010. In fact this was a global phenomenon, and I have a clear memory of *extremely* cold days in New Jersey at this time.

I have added to this series a non-parametric regression line computed from the Nadaraya–Watson kernel estimator with an Epanechnikov kernel of width five years. This is done to bring out the general trend within the data as the eye can become distracted by the seasonal variation. It is nothing more than a form of moving average, however, and cannot be used as a predictive tool.[z] A good reference

[y]The "Winter of Discontent" [69].

[z]It is also a *less real* measure of the data than the data itself.

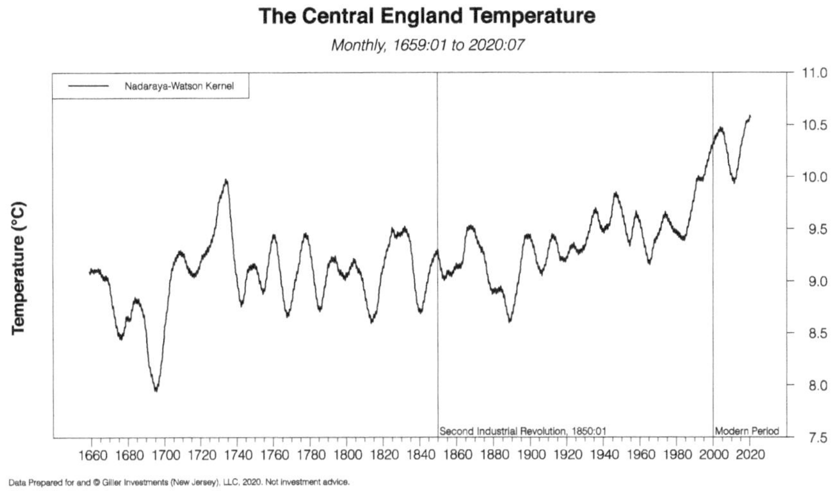

Figure 3.22: Smoothed time-series of the Central England Temperature since 1659. The line is a non-parametric regression line computed using the Nadaraya–Watson kernel estimator with an Epanechnikov kernel of width 5 years.

for this kind of model is the book by Green and Silverman [62]. The full history of this estimator is shown in Figure 3.22.

This figure leaves very little doubt that the average temperature has increased substantially in more recent times, although it also illustrates how difficult it is to analyze such time series accurately. If we were to end the plot in the 1980s, we might conclude that no real change has occurred! The magnitude of the move at the endpoint is also a fraction of the move from the 1700s to the 1750s, yet we cannot attribute that to anthropogenic global warning.

I have divided the data into three distinct regions:

(P) the "pre-industrial" period, ending in December 1849;
(I) the "industrial" period, starting in January 1850, and ending in December, 1999;
(M) the "modern" period, starting in January 2000.

The motivation for this choice is the *Second Industrial Revolution*, which is associated with the advent of large-scale industrialization, is commonly viewed as having begun in the 1860s.

This temporal classification gives two independent training sets, and a final testing set. Clearly we should find an essentially zero trend for the temperature during the pre-industrial period; a positive trend for the industrial period; and, a slight up-trend in the modern period.[aa]

3.4.1.1. *A Bootstrap Analysis of the Non-Parametric Regression*

When I first did this work, in 2012, I was interested in finding out whether the contemporaneous temperature rise was best explained as the continuation of the trend from the (I) period, or merely a statistical fluctuation consistent with the (P) period. Thus my approach was to forecast the data during the (M) period from models built independently on that data that is what my published work features [52]. The work discussed starting in Section 3.4.2 mostly follows the route I did at the time.

At that point in my career, I had not yet fully learned to exploit the power of the bootstrap method and rejected analysis such as that exhibited in Figure 3.22 on the grounds that I had absolutely no idea how to compute the sampling distribution of the curve shown, which means that although we observe swings in the average temperature computed by the non-parametric regression method we can't judge whether they are *significant* or not.

Figure 3.23 shows a small sample of bootstrap simulations of the non-parametric regression line. The method is the block bootstrap with a block width of 36 months. This means that a block is smaller than the kernel width of 60 months (5 years). Figure 3.24 shows the results of a bootstrap with 5,000 simulations.

From the figure we understand that the current rise in temperature is approximately a three standard deviation departure from the long-term mean value.[bb] So is our interpretation problem now solved? Unfortunately not, because we do not know how many random samples we have examined in this plot to compute the probability of seeing a departure from the mean at least this large.

[aa]I made these classifications in 2012 but had not made Figure 3.22 before writing this book.

[bb]The cold snap in the 1690s is even more severe, and is believed to be associated with volcanic activity [19].

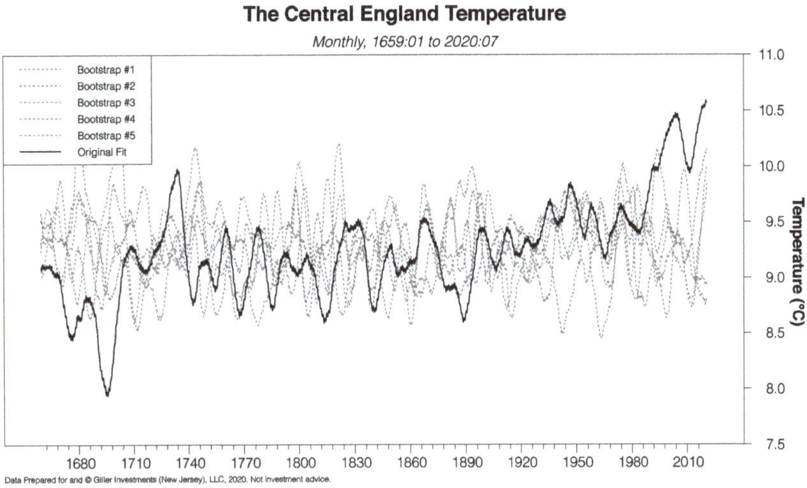

Figure 3.23: Smoothed time-series of the Central England Temperature since 1659 and five bootstrap simulations of that curve. The solid black line is a non-parametric regression line computed using the Nadaraya–Watson kernel estimator with an Epanechnikov kernel of width 5 years. The dotted gray lines are computed from block bootstrap simulations of the data.

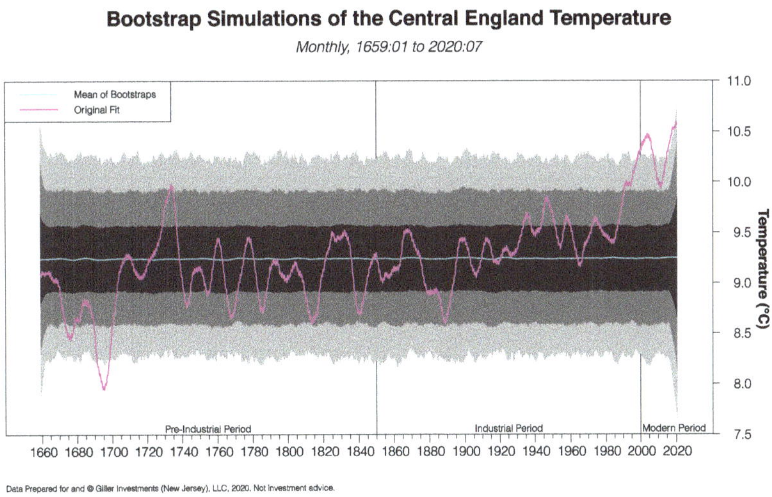

Figure 3.24: Smoothed time-series of the Central England Temperature since 1659 and the mean of 5,000 bootstrap simulations of that curve. The purple line is a non-parametric regression line computed using the Nadaraya–Watson kernel estimator with an Epanechnikov kernel of width five years. The blue line is the mean of the bootstrap simulations and the shaded regions are 68%, 95% and 99.7% confidence regions about the mean ($\pm 1\sigma$, $\pm 2\sigma$ and $\pm 3\sigma$).

Ironically, this is similar to the problem I encountered in my thesis research [47] where I was trying to search a smoothed whole-sky map of the muon flux measured in cosmic rays for local anomalies. I was fortunate that the prominent statistician David Siegmund was able to show me how to analyze this problem [113, 119]. However, that problem was a search for *point sources* in which we aggregated data over around 1° on the Celestial Sphere due to experimental resolution. This problem is about the detection of a trend, so those results will not help us. The best way I know of to tackle this problem is to use the methods of time-series analysis to model the data and ask whether the trend measured in the Industrial Era data (I) or that in the pre-Industrial Era (P) is a better descriptor the behaviour during the Modern (M) period.

3.4.2. *A Seasonal Autoregressive Model for the Central England Temperature*

In time-series analysis, a seasonal model is one which includes lagged variables with characteristic intervals, which in this case would be annual lags within a monthly series. This makes it easy to reproduce structures such as the annual temperature cycle without having to explicitly introduce *harmonic analysis*, which would anyway require many terms as the Earth's path around the Sun (the ultimate driver of seasonality) does not follow simple harmonic motion as the orbit is not circular. We just build a model that says all months bear a similarity to the same month in prior years, which then generates the seasonality from the data itself.

3.4.2.1. *Issues with Calendar Dates in Long-Time Series*

For annual data over such a long period there are even issues with counting dates.

(i) Great Britain adopted the *Gregorian Calendar*, which differs slightly in its treatment of leap years from the prior *Julian Calendar* on the day after the 2nd September, 1752. This became the 14th September, removing the effect of twelve erroneously added leap days.[cc] This date is well within our data set.

[cc]And, apparently, causing much anxiety.

(ii) Up until the late middle ages the extra, or *intracalary* date, was introduced by having 24th February occur twice, not by adding the 29th February in leap years.
(iii) From the 12th Century to 1751, England started the New Year not on the 1st January but on the 25th March.[dd] Thus applying the current Gregorian Calendar backwards, or *proleptically*, the 1st of January in the year before the adoption of that calendar would have actually been referred to as 1st January, 1750. To clarify these differences the notations "(o.s.)" and "(n.s.)," for "old style" and "new style" were added to records around this time.[ee]

It is normal practice to prevent confusion by using the Gregorian Calendar proleptically unless one is working from source documents, in which case they must be labelled properly. For the Central England Temperature, the issue are the fact that September 1752, has roughly half the observations as any other September and may have missed characteristic September activity that was subsequently labelled as occurring in October.

3.4.2.2. *A Note on Product Models and Additive Models*

In their definitive work [11], Box and Jenkins *et seq.* advocated the use of a linear additive noise model expressed in terms of the lag operator, L, defined to shift the time index, i.e. $L[a_t] = a_{t-1}$. For seasonal models, a seasonal lag operator is used where $L^s[a_t] = a_{t-s} = a_{t-12}$ for annual seasonality in monthly data. Autoregressive models are written as functions of the lag operator, so that

$$a_t = \varphi a_{t-1} + \varepsilon_t \quad \text{becomes } (1 - \varphi L)a_t = \varepsilon_t, \tag{3.27}$$

and more complex expressions have the functional form

$$\{1 - \varphi(L)\}\, a_t = \varepsilon_t, \tag{3.28}$$

[dd]This, incidentally, is why tax returns are due at the start of April — it was after the end of the year. It is also why the Roman numeric month names, September, October, November, and December, have the "wrong" numbers.
[ee]Such a notation is seen on Thomas Jefferson's gravestone in Monticello.

for some polynomial function $\varphi(L)$. In this framework, Box and Jenkins describe a model with both regular *and* seasonal autoregression via the product of operator functions. For example, $AR(1) \times SAR(1)$ is written

$$\begin{aligned}(1-\varphi L)(1-\varphi_s L^s)a_t &= \varepsilon_t \\ \Leftrightarrow\ a_t &= \varphi a_{t-1} + \varphi_s a_{t-12} - \varphi\varphi_s a_{t-13} + \varepsilon_t, \qquad (3.29)\end{aligned}$$

with parameters φ and φ_s. It is important to see that this product form has generated an autoregressive expression that includes all of the combinations of the lags in the expression and not just the simple lags themselves. This is different from the additive combination $AR(1) + SAR(1)$, which would not generate that product term in a_{t-13}.

3.4.2.3. *Selection of the Autoregressive and Seasonal Model Order for the Pre-Industrial Period*

We seek to fit an $AR(m)\times SAR(y)$ model to explain both the cyclical and short-term acyclic variations in temperature (short term trends). To this will be added a linear trend term, as a first step in explaining the rise in temperature over the years. Fully written out it is

$$\begin{aligned}C_t = \alpha + \beta(t-t_0) &+ \sum_{i=1}^{m}\varphi_i C_{t-i} + \sum_{j=1}^{y}\varphi_{12j}C_{t-12j} + \sigma\varepsilon_t \\ &- \sum_{i=1}^{m}\sum_{j=1}^{y}\varphi_i\varphi_{12j}C_{t-i-12j}, \qquad (3.30)\\ \varepsilon_t &\sim \mathrm{GED}(0,1,\kappa), \qquad (3.31)\end{aligned}$$

where C_t is the average temperature reported. If $m < 1$ or $y < 1$ the respective sum is omitted. m is not permitted to be larger than 11 so that the expression does not have *two* terms in φ_{12} *et al.*

The order of the model, (y, m), is determined by a grid search over $y \in [1, 40]$ and $m \in [1, 11]$ with the AIC(c) used as the discriminatory statistic. On the computer I had in 2012 this took a very long time to compute, so I adopted the simpler approach of fitting a Box–Jenkins model by least squares [54], implicitly assuming a Normal distribution for ε_t. This approach found a model with

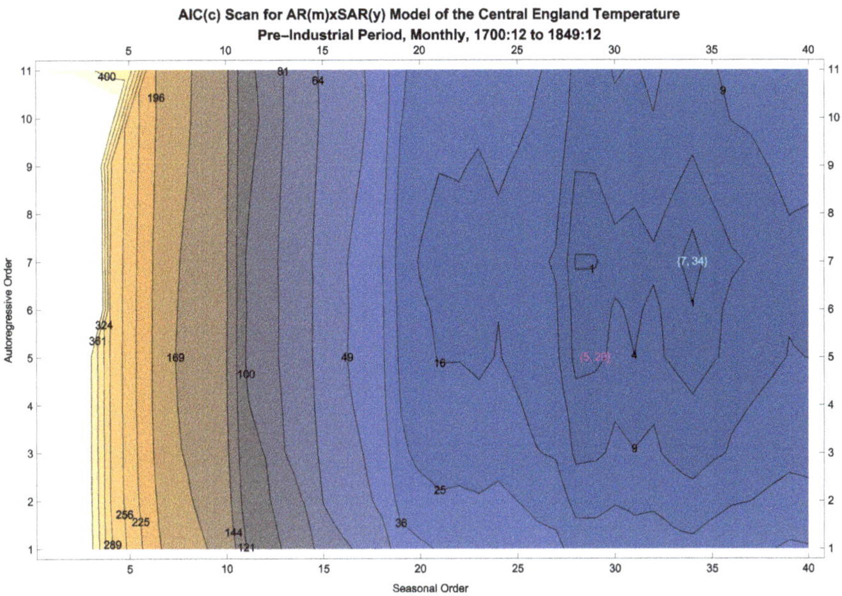

Figure 3.25: Contour plot of the ΔAIC(c) surface for fitting a leptokurtotic $AR(m) \times SAR(y)$ model to the Central England Temperature series for data from December 1700, to December 1849. Contour lines are drawn at the squares of the integers. The minimum is at $(\hat{m}, \hat{y}) = (7, 34)$ although close secondary minimum is also found at $(7, 28)$. The minimum found in the prior referenced analysis [54], which only fitted a Normal distribution, is indicated at $(5, 29)$.

$(m, y) = (5, 29)$ and the distribution of residuals was subsequently found to be non-Normal. In 2020, my computer is much faster and the more sophisticated analysis is possible.[ff]

The minimum of the AIC(c) surface is found at $(m, y) = (7, 34)$, which is a complex model with many lags. A slightly smaller model, at $(7, 28)$, is found nearby. The change in AIC(c) is less than unity. Based on the curvature of the ΔAIC(c) surface, the data strongly rejects models with low seasonal orders in favor of high seasonal orders, but only weakly discriminates between different orders for the regular autoregressive element.

[ff]Nevertheless, it is still taking over a day of compute time to execute. Although this seems like a lot, junior data scientists should not despair — it'll probably take well over a day to understand and present the results.

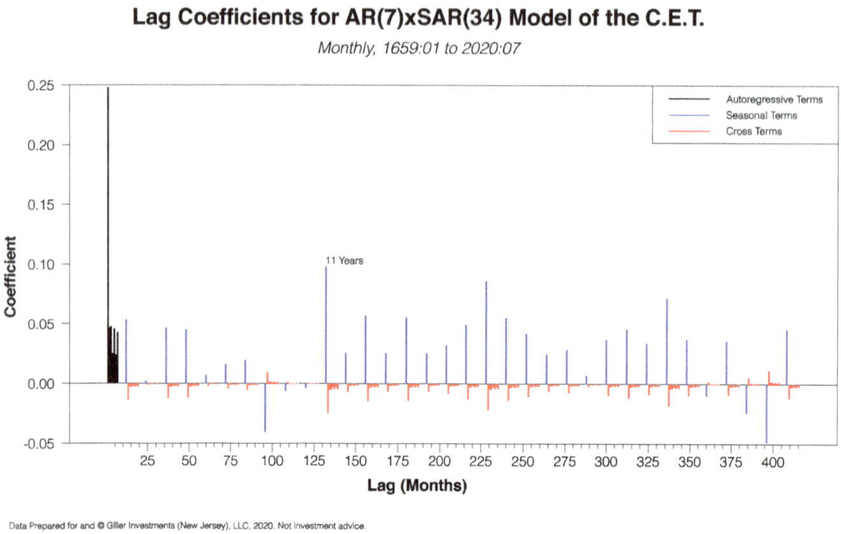

Figure 3.26: Estimated and implied weights for an $AR(7) \times SAR(34)$ model for the Central England Temperature estimated from the Pre-Industrial period data (January 1659 to December 1849). Black bars are the simple autoregressive terms, blue bars are the seasonal autoregressive terms, and red bars are the implied cross terms.

3.4.2.4. *Structure of the Optimized Model*

Figure 3.26 shows the structure of the fitted $AR(7)\times SAR(34)$ model. Notable features are the strong, 25%, momentum term at the first lag, indicating that hot months and cold months tend to follow each other. This may be indicative of the fact that weather fluctuations last for around one month but, of course, don't necessarily, line up with the calendar. Another notable feature is the relative quiescence of the seasonal terms until lag $132 = 11 \times 12$. Eleven years is a very interesting feature because the Sun is known to have an eleven year periodicity driven by changes in its magnetic field, known as the "Solar cycle." Given that zero physics has been used in this analysis, it is merely a study of the repeating structure of the numbers, this is a satisfactory coincidence. The existence of may positive coefficients at high seasonal lags implies that the temperature will undergo fairly long-period cycles compared to a human lifetime of 80 years or so. Thus any single person will likely only experience a couple of temperature regimes and should be cautious about making statements such as "it's hotter/colder now than it was when I was a child." These statements need to be based on an analysis of long term trends.

The estimated trend equation is $\hat{\alpha} = 0.20 \pm 0.08$, in °C, and $\hat{\beta} = -0.10 \pm 0.06$, in units of °/century, which is not significant and consistent with zero change in the average temperature during this period. The dispersion is estimated to be $\hat{\sigma} = 1.30 \pm 0.02$ in °/month.

3.4.2.5. *Non-Normality in the Central England Temperature*

Finally, the estimated kurtosis parameter of the Generalized Error Distribution used is $\hat{\kappa} = 0.64 \pm 0.03$, which is not consistent with $\kappa = \frac{1}{2}$ for a Normal distribution, and the Wald Test for that value has a statistic of $\chi^2_1 = 21.7$ and a p value of 3×10^{-6}. Clearly the residuals are not Normal, as can be seen from the histogram in Figure 3.27, although not as severely leptokurtotic as the data exhibited in Chapter 2.

3.4.2.6. *A Note on High Order Autoregressive Models*

When using high order models, such as the one developed in this section, to predict time-series, we need to understand the system

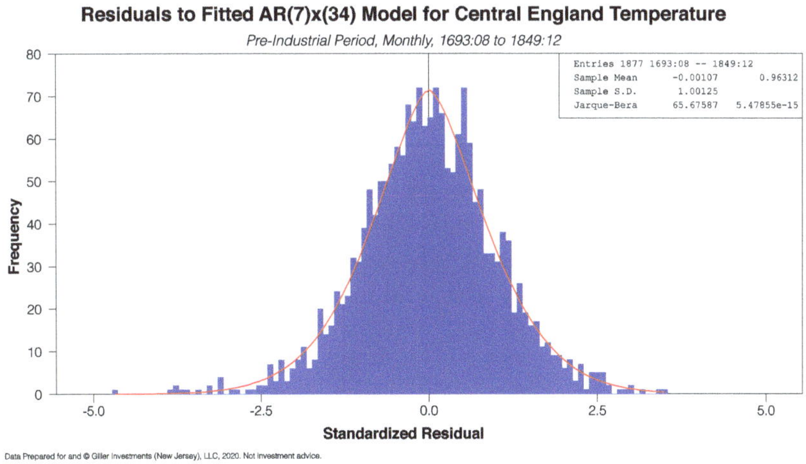

Figure 3.27: Distribution of standardized residuals from fitting a leptokurtotic $AR(7) \times SAR(34)$ model to the Central England Temperature series for data until December 1849. The blue histogram shows the distribution of standardized residuals (in sample) and the red curve is the best fitting Generalized Error Distribution, which has a kurtosis parameter of $\hat{\kappa} = 0.64 \pm 0.03$.

in the context of the "best approximating model." The time-series model is useful tool to predict the Central England Temperature, but it would be unreasonable to assert that there is a physical process that rigidly links the temperature next month to that 30 years ago. An autoregressive model describes the persistence of short-shocks and a seasonal model describes long-term regularities in the metric of interest, irrespective of their actual physical origins, and it does not seem plausible that those long-term regularities are fixated exactly on 34 lags versus 33 lags or 35 lags. It's just that, in the compromise between accuracy and reliability out-of-sample, 34 seems like a better choice.

Burnham and Anderson concretize this reasoning by describing a *multi-model inference* framework [12] in which each model is given a relative weight.[gg] Using this framework, one does not have to "bet" on the 34 lag model versus the 33 lag model — as both of them have similar weights. However, for the purposes of exposition, and to prevent confusion, I will stick to discussion of the single "best approximating model" of the data and lead it to the reader to investigate this path themselves.

3.4.3. *Heteroskedasticity in the Central England Temperature*

Having, once again, rejected the first key tenets of naïve analysis — that data are serially uncorrelated[hh] and Normally distributed — let's take a look at the other one, that of homoskedasticity. In Chapter 2, any autocorrelative structure was weak and it was generally sufficient to examine only the correlation of squared returns onto immediately prior values. The work described in Section 3.4.2.4 clearly shows a strong, complex, and extensive autocorrelative structure.

3.4.3.1. *Autocorrelation Function of the Residuals*

If a model of a time-series is able to explain fully how the data, at any time, is related to prior values, then the difference between observed

[gg]The model weight is $e^{-\frac{1}{2}\Delta}$, when Δ is the change in AIC from the minimum.
[hh]Although, in this case, nobody should have ever suggested that.

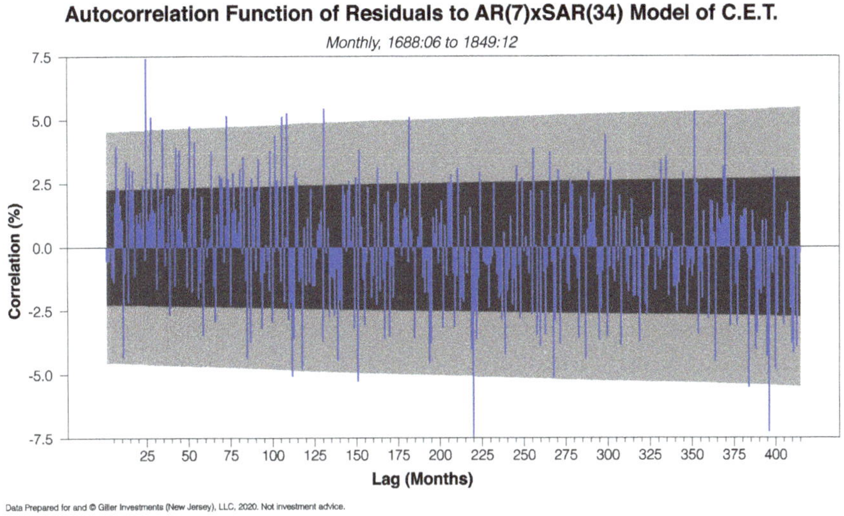

Figure 3.28: Autocorrelation function of the residuals from fitting a leptokurtotic $AR(7) \times SAR(34)$ model to the Central England Temperature series for data until December 1849. The blue bars represent the measured autocorrelation at each lag and the shaded area represents 68% and 95% confidence regions from the analysis. There are $34 \times 12 = 408$ lags for which correlations are computed from 250 years of data.

values and the model, which we call residuals, must be unpredictable from prior data — it must be noise. This means that there should be no correlation between residuals and their lagged values and, within sampling errors, the *autocorrelation function* of the residuals must show no significant structure. This is the case for the model developed here, and the ACF is illustrated in Figure 3.28.

3.4.3.2. *Autocorrelation Function of the Squared Residuals*

In a similar manner we can compute the autocorrelation function of the squared residuals. As these squared residuals are, individually, estimators of the variance of the proposed *homoskedastic* data generating process of Equation (3.30), there should similarly be no observable structure in the autocorrelation function of the squared residuals. However, this is not the case.

From the figure, it can clearly be seen that there are many lags at which the measured autocorrelation is well outside the confidence regions computed for the statistic and that there is a plainly evident periodic structure within the data. From this we must conclude that a homoskedastic noise model such as that of Equation (3.30), even though it accounts for the observed leptokurtotic nature of the data, cannot be used.

3.4.3.3. *Structural Heteroskedasticity*

The autocorrelation structure observed in Figure 3.29 is a clear signature of *seasonal heteroskedasticity*. This could be generated by either an autoregressive or a static structure, such as one in which each month has it's own idiosyncratic, but constant, variance. As the simplest hypothesis to examine is the latter, we will look for that first.

With this structure, if m_t, represents the month number corresponding to each observation period t, then our model for the CET

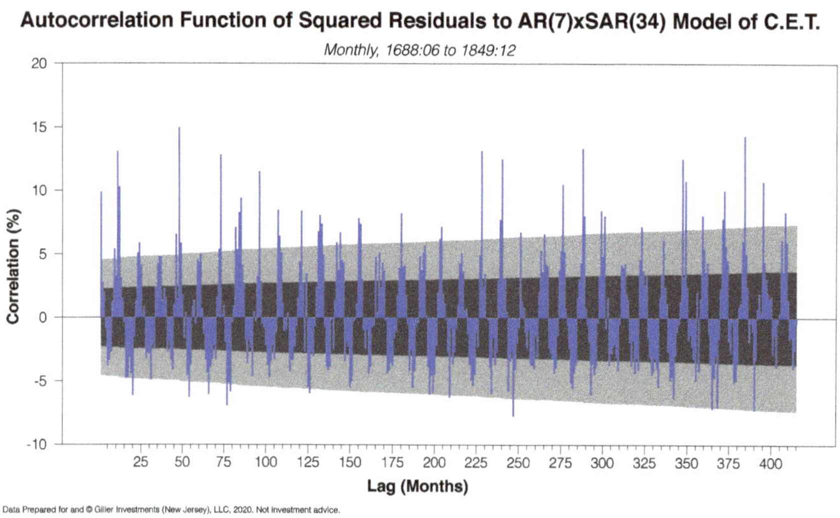

Figure 3.29: Autocorrelation function of the squared residuals from fitting a leptokurtotic $AR(7) \times SAR(34)$ model to the Central England Temperature series for data from December 1700 to December 1849. The blue bars represent the measured autocorrelation at each lag and the shaded area represents 68% and 95% confidence regions from the analysis. There are $34 \times 12 = 408$ lags for which correlations are computed from 250 years of data.

becomes

$$C_t = \alpha + \beta(t - t_0) + \sum_{i=1}^{m} \varphi_i C_{t-i} + \sum_{j=1}^{y} \varphi_{12j} C_{t-12j} + \sigma_{m_t}\varepsilon_t - \sum_{i=1}^{m}\sum_{j=1}^{y} \varphi_i \varphi_{12j} C_{t-i-12j}, \tag{3.32}$$

$$\varepsilon_t \sim \text{GED}(0, 1, \kappa). \tag{3.33}$$

The method of implementing such a structure will depend on the regression software you use.[ii] Everything else proceeds as before, with a maximum likelihood estimate of the parameters to find the best approximating model, with the autoregressive and seasonal orders fixed at the discovered values of 7 and 34, respectively.

The estimated parameters, $\{\hat{\sigma}_{m_t}\}$, are illustrated in Figure 3.30. The estimated parameters are quite clearly not consistent with the hypothesis of homoskedastic variance, i.e. $\hat{\sigma}_{m_t} = \hat{\sigma}\ \forall\ m_t$, and the Wald Test rejects that hypothesis with a test statistic of 183.2 which should be distributed as χ^2_{12} and for which the p value is vanishingly small. In general terms, the fitted coefficients indicate that the Winter average temperature is around twice as variable as that for the Summer. Since this is the standard deviation of the average monthly temperature, and there are around 30 days in a month, the Winter appears to have a daily standard deviation of approximately $2\sqrt{30} = 11°\text{C}$ whereas it is 5.5°C for the Summer months. Thus an anomalously hot New Year's Day (n.s.) should not be unexpected!

An additional, and significant, aspect of this new regression is that the kurtosis parameter is now estimated to be $\hat{\kappa} = 0.53 \pm 0.03$, which is no longer inconsistent with the Normal distribution! As I decided to try this model modification in response to the observed structure in Figure 3.29, it is important to re-examine that analysis and see if the observed structure has been remediated by the model change.

[ii]For my system, it's just a matter of replacing the reference to a parameter `sigma` with an array element `sigma(month(t))` and defining `sigma` as a vector of reals rather than a scalar quantity. `month(t)` is a function that returns the correct array index for a given observation t.

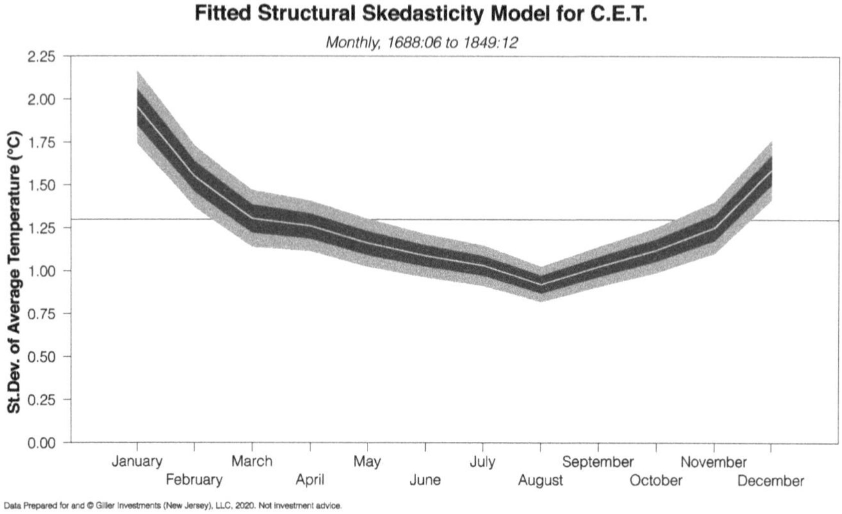

Figure 3.30: Estimated idiosyncratic standard deviations of the average monthly temperature in the Central England Temperature series when fitted to an $AR(7)\times SAR(34)$ model. The shaded areas represent the 68% and 95% confidence regions around the central estimate, which is in light blue. The horizontal line is the estimate, $\hat{\sigma}$, from the prior model with constant variance.

The results of that analysis are shown in Figure 3.31, from which it is clear that the strong structures previously observed have been eliminated. Unfortunately, a new question is raised by this structural change to the model:

> are we sure that the autoregressive structure is still optimal given the changes to the model and to the estimated kurtosis parameter?

The best way to answer that is to repeat the AIC scan. This is time-consuming, but essentially effortless, so we should not shirk from doing this task.

3.4.3.4. *Confidence Intervals and Likelihood Ratios*

I noted that the contours drawn in Figure 3.25 are at the squares of the integers, but I didn't explain why. This is actually because of the behaviour of Likelihood ratios around the optimum. Wilk's theorem

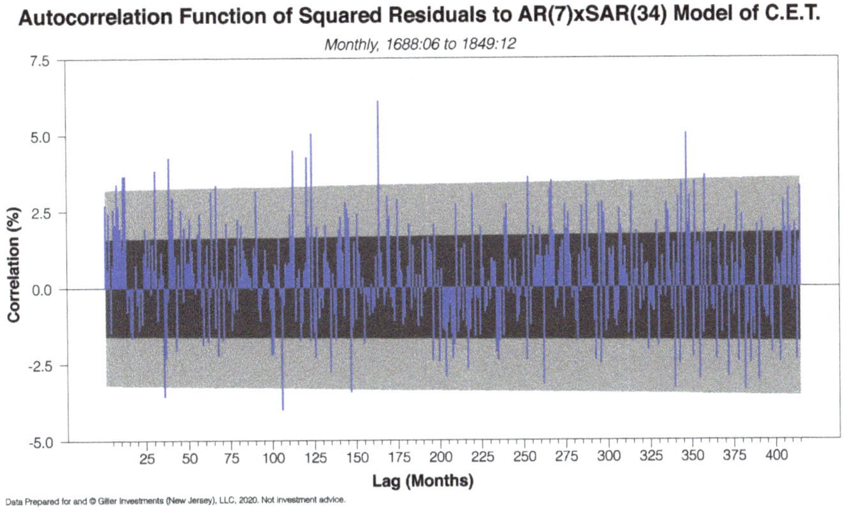

Figure 3.31: Autocorrelation function of the squared residuals from fitting a $AR(7)\times SAR(34)$ model with structural heteroskedasticity to the Central England Temperature series for data until December 1849. The blue bars represent the measured autocorrelation at each lag and the shaded area represents 68% and 95% confidence regions from the analysis. There are $34 \times 12 = 408$ lags for which correlations are computed from 250 years of data.

[139] states that for sample size n,

$$-2\ln\frac{\mathcal{L}(\hat{\boldsymbol{\theta}}_p)}{\mathcal{L}(\hat{\boldsymbol{\theta}}_q)} \xrightarrow[n\to\infty]{\mathcal{D}} \chi^2_{p-q}, \tag{3.34}$$

where there are two *nested* models, with p and q parameters respectively and for which $p > q$. $\mathcal{L}(\hat{\boldsymbol{\theta}}_p)$ is the likelihood at the maximum computed *from the same data* for each model.[jj] This likelihood ratio is also the stochastic element of the Akaike Information Criterion.

The Wald test is based on the fact that

$$\sqrt{n}(\hat{\boldsymbol{\theta}}_p - \boldsymbol{\theta}^*) \xrightarrow[n\to\infty]{\mathcal{D}} N(0, V), \tag{3.35}$$

where $V = \mathrm{Cov}[\hat{\boldsymbol{\theta}}_p]$. That is, in the large sample limit, the sampling distribution of the maximum likelihood estimators is Normally

[jj]The arrow notation is interpreted to mean "converges in distribution" for large samples.

distributed about the *unknown* true parameters, $\boldsymbol{\theta}^*$. This result, of course, is why maximum likelihood is useful.

Add to these theorems the knowledge that the sums of squares of p independent Normal variates is distributed as χ^2_p and the deeper connection between all three methods begins to be be revealed. Since the log likelihood of Normally distributed data has a simple parabolic shape around the maximum [76], it is straightforward to show that the 68% confidence region can be found by determining the contour that encloses the region where twice the log-likelihood ratio changes by 1, the 95% region by where it changes by 4, the 99.7% region by where it changes by 9, etc.

Thus the contour where the AIC changes by 4 *in the sample data* should indicate the general level of precision in which we can determine the optimal parameters, $(\hat{m}, \hat{y})$, of a model such as Equation (3.32).[kk]

3.4.3.5. *Identification of the Optimal Model with Structural Heteroskedasticity*

After this digression,[ll] let's take a look at the AIC(c) surface discovered with the more complex model of Equation (3.32). Figure 3.32 shows the surface of ΔAIC(c) computed by varying the autoregressive and seasonal orders in the model, (m, y). The minimum is at $(\hat{m}, \hat{y}) = (7, 29)$, which represents a lower order seasonal model than that previously found at $(7, 34)$ but, based on the prior section's arguments, is not greatly inconsistent with it. It is very close to the secondary minimum that was present at $(7, 28)$.

3.4.4. *Comparing Models Estimated in the Pre-Industrial and Industrial Periods*

The AIC(c) model discovery scans described here take a significant fraction of a week to execute, so are costly in computer time and

[kk]I am sweeping under the carpet here the fact that (m, y) are *discrete* parameters but the theorems as quoted are for *continuous* parameters.

[ll]From which you may conclude that I am neither a strict Bayesian, nor a strict Frequentist, but more aligned to the Information Theoretic basis for the foundations of Statistics.

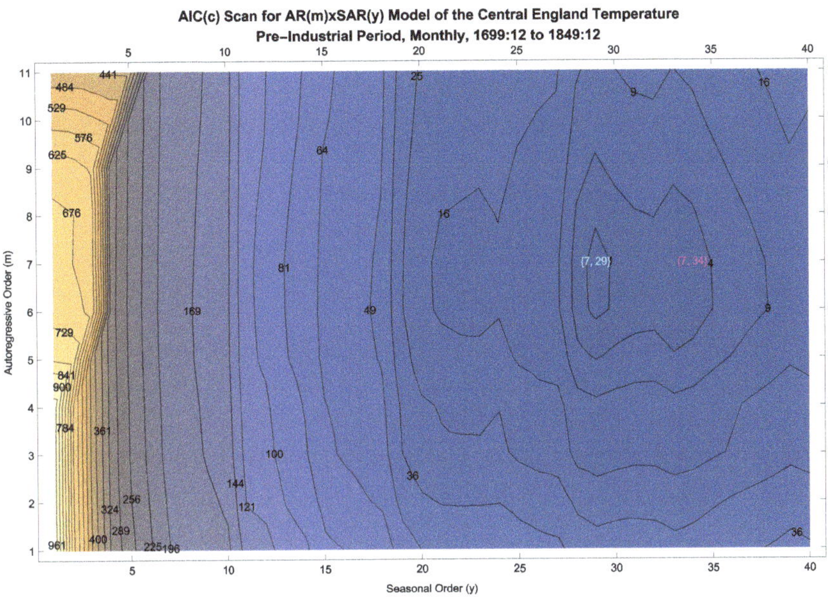

Figure 3.32: Contour plot of the ΔAIC(c) surface for fitting a leptokurtotic $AR(m) \times SAR(y)$ model to the Central England temperature series for data from December 1700, to December 1849, with Structural Heteroskedasticity. Contour lines are drawn at the squares of the integers. The minimum is at $(\hat{m}, \hat{y}) = (7, 29)$ is roughly consistent with that of $(7, 34)$ found in the prior analysis and very close to the secondary minimum found at $(7, 28)$.

actual time. Because of this, instead of repeating the entire analysis in the Industrial period, which would also deliver model score comparison without a well defined sampling distribution — and because bootstrapping would be extremely expensive to execute — I decided to take that model structure as given and re-estimate it in the second period. This allows us to compare those two sets of estimators.

3.4.4.1. *Errors in the Variables*

All of the regressions presented to date have been of the type with a *dependent variable*, y_i, which responds in some way to an *independent variable*. The independent variable, usually written x_i, is viewed as variable put precisely known, whereas the dependent variable has some stochastic element to its response. This is the message of the classic linear regression expression of Equation (3.17). However, the estimated coefficients for the Pre-Industrial period model, whatever model we are using, are not precisely known because our time-series are finite in size and so sampling error exists. When x_i itself is unknown precisely, a more accurate *linear additive noise* model may be something such as

$$y_i = \alpha + \beta x_i^* + \varepsilon_i, \tag{3.36}$$

$$x_i = x_i^* + \eta_i. \tag{3.37}$$

Here, x_i^* represents the unknown true value of the observed independent variable and both ε_i and η_i are random disturbances. If ordinary linear regression of y_i onto x_i is used, when the true model is that above, then it is easy to show that the estimate of β is biased. The estimated value will be asymptotically

$$\hat{\beta} = \frac{\beta}{1 + \text{Var}[\eta_i]/\text{Var}[\varepsilon_i]}, \tag{3.38}$$

instead of converging to the true value of β. The interpretation of this result is that the measured regression coefficient is biased *toward zero* when there are errors in the independent variable as well as the dependent variable.

3.4.4.2. *Comparing Parameters Estimated for two Distinct Periods*

Consider a linear regression of the parameter estimates from the Industrial period, $\boldsymbol{\theta}_I$, onto those from the Pre-Industrial period, $\boldsymbol{\theta}_P$. If the models are consistent, and the parameters constant, then we should have

$$\hat{\boldsymbol{\theta}}_I = \boldsymbol{\theta}^* + \boldsymbol{\varepsilon}, \tag{3.39}$$

$$\hat{\boldsymbol{\theta}}_P = \boldsymbol{\theta}^* + \boldsymbol{\eta}, \tag{3.40}$$

$$\boldsymbol{\varepsilon} \sim N(\mathbf{0}, V/T_I), \tag{3.41}$$

$$\text{and } \boldsymbol{\eta} \sim N(\mathbf{0}, V/T_P) \text{ independently.} \tag{3.42}$$

Here, $\boldsymbol{\theta}^*$ are the unknown true parameters, T_P and T_I are the lengths of the time-series in the Pre-Industrial and Industrial periods, respectively, and $N(\mathbf{0}, V/T)$ is a multivariate Normal distribution with zero mean and scaled covariance matrix V.

For maximum likelihood estimators, the covariance matrix of the estimators, V, is equal to the inverse of the Fisher Information Matrix [64], which is computable from the likelihood function. However, we don't need use this explicitly provided we fit the same model to different data sets. With this condition, the only thing that differs between the two is the sample size and so the bias factor from Equation (3.38) is known.

To correct for the bias induced by the sampling variation in the estimators we can perform an ordinary linear regression of the elements of $\hat{\boldsymbol{\theta}}_I$ onto the corresponding elements of $\hat{\boldsymbol{\theta}}_P$ and test for the hypothesis that $\hat{\alpha} = 0$ and $\hat{\beta} = 1/(1 + T_I/T_P)$.

3.4.4.3. *Consistency of the Autoregressive Models*

The Pre-Industrial period, starting $7 + 29 = 36$ months after the beginning of the data[mm] in January 1659, and ending in December 1849, contains a total of 1,937 usable observations. That from January 1850, to December 1999, contains 1,800 usable observations. Thus we should find regression with a gradient of $1/(1 + 1{,}937/1{,}800) \approx 0.48$.

This regression is exhibited in Figure 3.33. The gradient of the regression line is $\hat{\beta} = 0.47 \pm 0.12$, exactly as expected and the intercept is $\hat{\alpha} = 0.017 \pm 0.007$, consistent with zero at better than 99% confidence, although a little high. Even though some of the coefficients may have "wandered" a little between sample periods, I'm inclined to believe that the two independently estimated models are consistent.

3.4.4.4. *Consistency of the Temperature Trend*

A simple linear trend has been used to model the drift of average temperature during both the Pre-Industrial and Industrial periods. This is, at best, a crude model and I will address it in more detail later. There are two reasons to do this: one is to determine whether

[mm] Due the requirement that lagged values of the temperature be part of the model.

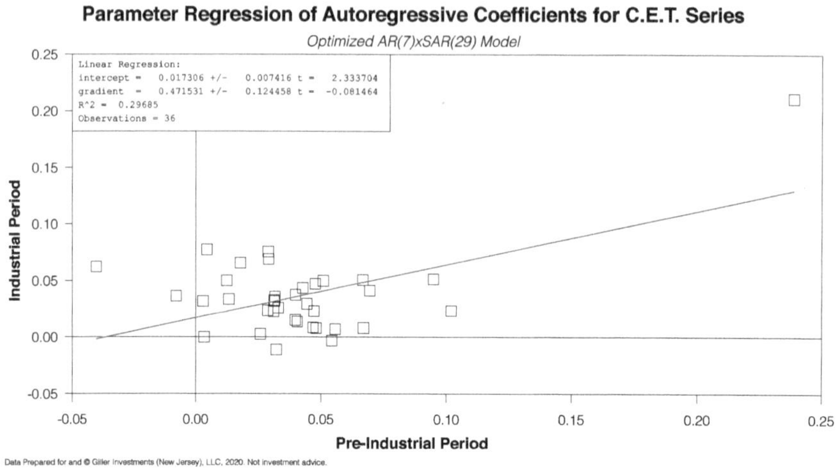

Figure 3.33: Linear regression of the autoregression and seasonal autoregressive coefficients for the Pre-Industrial period onto those of the Industrial period. As an "errors in variables" problem we expect this line to have a zero intercept and a gradient of 0.48.

the trends measured in each period are consistent and the second is to predict future temperatures. Only a model following the structure of Equation (2.4) can *predict* future values of a metric of interest, and the trend model is such a model.

The parameter that describes the trend in Equation (3.32) is β, which is regressed onto the observation number divided by twelve, so has the units of °C/annum. For the Pre-Industrial period we find $\hat{\beta} = -0.00064 \pm 0.00056$ and for the Industrial period $\hat{\beta} = 0.00078 \pm 0.00060$. Neither are individually significant, but that might be because the model is wrong! Are they consistent? Since both are quoted with errors that are Normally distributed in large samples their difference divided by the square root of the sum of the squares of the quoted errors should be Normally distributed with zero mean and unit variance. This Z score is 1.73 and the probability of Z exceeding this value[nn] is 0.082. This, alone, is unconvincing evidence for a temperature gradient change but the model is an extremely crude one.

[nn]A one sided Z Test.

3.4.5. *Forecasting the Central England Temperature in the Modern Period*

At this point in our analysis of the Central England Temperature we have discovered an $AR(7) \times SAR(29)$ model for the pre-Industrial period and re-estimated that model in the Industrial period. Although there has been much discussion of the methodology of the model search, and the consistency of the models estimated for the two individual periods, we have not yet just *looked at the models.* Such an exercise is often unsatisfactory in financial data because R^2 are low and so the model, apparently, does a terrible job of describing the data.

In markets, that's not a bad thing. If we have a model that is significant, as measured by p value, but has low utility, as measured by R^2, then it's probably *true but not obvious*, which means you're can make money from it. If it has a high R^2 it will be obvious, which means everybody can find it, and so, due to the competitive nature of markets, it will not be around for long. If it has a p value that makes it insignificant then it's likely not a real phenomenon, so won't make money outside of historic simulations.

3.4.5.1. *Forecasting Skill*

Since we have two models that predict the same data, we need a metric of their success to distinguish between them. The one in common usage in the weather forecasting industry is *forecasting skill.* If $\{f\}$ and $\{g\}$ are two forecasts of data, $\{d\}$, then the relative skill is defined to be

$$\text{SKILL}(f, g) = 1 - \frac{\text{MSE}(f, d)}{\text{MSE}(g, d)}, \tag{3.43}$$

where $\text{MSE}(f, d)$ is the *mean squared error*

$$\text{MSE}(f, d) = \frac{1}{T} \sum_{t=1}^{T} (f_t - d_t)^2. \tag{3.44}$$

This measure ranges from a maximum of 100%, which represents perfect forecasting, to $-\infty$, and is by definition a relative measure: if it is positive then it means that $\{f\}$ is a better forecast of $\{d\}$ than $\{g\}$, and if negative the reverse is true. It is not good enough to make some prediction of the data, it is necessary to make a *better* prediction than a reference forecast. This is something often forgotten by those that tout the success of "AI" in predicting financial data — you can generally make a very good prediction of a stock price from the prior price, and your machine learning algorithm needs to do better than the martingale as a forecasting system.

Looking at Equation (3.43) we see that it contains the ratio of two variance estimators. Thus we expect, if the residuals to the two forecasts are independent and Normally distributed, that it would itself be related to the F distribution. However, it's likely that our forecasts are similar and so the expected Null distribution of the statistic is not easy to compute. We can, however, use a bootstrap methodology if we assume the errors are sufficiently serially uncorrelated.

3.4.5.2. *Comparison of the Predictive Models*

Both estimated models are *out-of-sample* from 2000 onwards. Figure 3.34 shows both predictions, and the actual data, for the

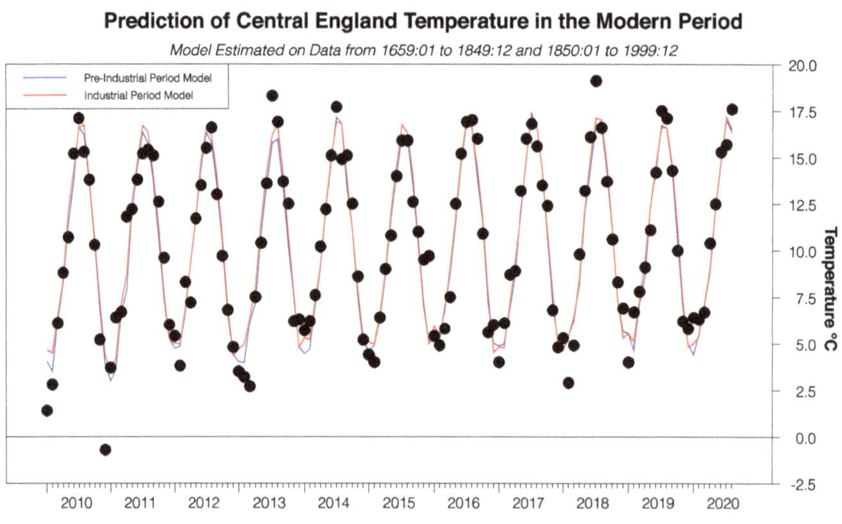

Figure 3.34: Central England Temperature in the 2010s and predicted temperature from $AR(7) \times SAR(29)$ models fitted in the Pre-Industrial and Industrial periods. The reported data are the black dots, the blue curve is the predictions from the Pre-Industrial period model and the red curve the predictions from the Industrial period model.

last decade. It's clear from this plot that the predictions made by the two models are different, but not greatly, and that they are mostly reasonable. The largest errors seem to occur at the turning points of Midsummer and Midwinter, and the forecasts from the Pre-Industrial period are generally for colder winters than those from the Industrial period.

The relative skill of the Industrial period model versus the Pre-Industrial period model is -1.58%. From a forecasting perspective, the models are essentially the same, even though the model from the Pre-Industrial period is being used to predict data observed over 150 years after it was "trained." This, to me, confirms the utility of the time-series approach.

3.4.6. *Does the Central England Temperature Support an Upward Trend?*

In the final section on the temperature *data*, let's take a look at what we get if we fit the general $AR(7) \times SAR(29)$ model with drift and structural heteroskedasticity to the entire dataset. Of interest, of course, is the estimate of the trend coefficient $\hat{\beta}$. Having demonstrated the utility of the fitted models many years out-of-sample we can be confident that they work. A better estimate of β can then be made by using the entire data set in analysis. Using all the data to date we get $\hat{\beta} = 0.073 \pm 0.026$ in units of °C/century. This has a p value of 0.0051 and so we have better than 99% confidence that it is non-zero. The effect as measured here is small and the model establishes a secular trend exists without attributing it to any cause.

3.4.7. *Do Sunspot Numbers Explain Temperature Changes?*

In Section 3.4.2.4, I noted that the autoregressive models fitted to the Central England Temperature have a significant feature at a lag of eleven years and that the Solar Cycle exhibits this periodicity.[oo] If this is so, perhaps we should introduce a measured feature of the

[oo]In fact the magnetic polarity of the Sun exhibits a 22 year cycle and it's intensity exhibits an 11 year cycle.

Sun that has a long recorded history as an explanatory variable? The Sunspot Number is the feature of the Sun with the longest recorded history and in which this cycle is observed.

3.4.7.1. *The Mean Monthly Sunspot Number*

Galileo observed sunspots when he observed the Sun through a telescope using a piece of smoked glass to reduce the light intensity.[pp] This data is the longest directly measured time-series and is readily available online. It is shown in Figure 3.35, from which I struggle to see any obvious covariance with the average temperature (from the non-parametric regression discussed on 187).

One thing that is readily apparent from this data is that it does not have the symmetrical distribution that we see in the temperature data. In fact, the Sunspot Numbers are highly right skewed, as can be

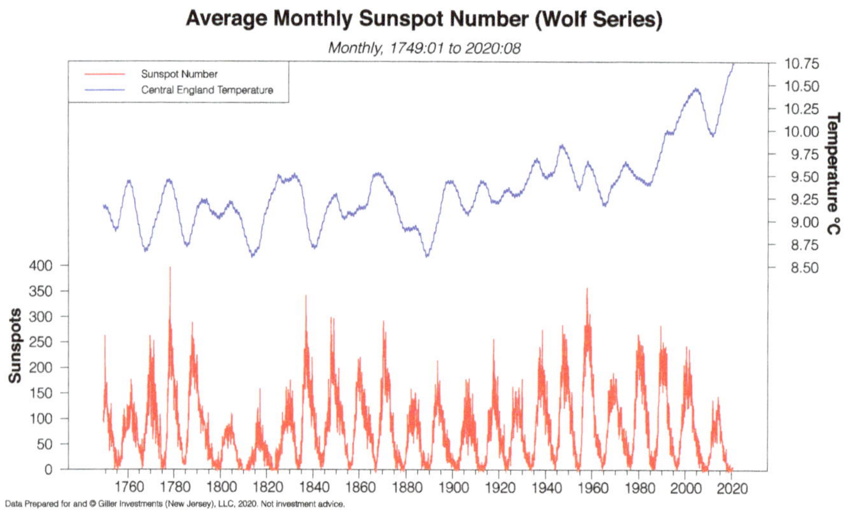

Figure 3.35: Time series of the Mean Monthly Sunspot number (the Wolf Series) and the Central England Temperature. The red line is the sunspot number and the blue line is the smoothed Central England Temperature for the same period. Data starts in 1749.

[pp]Galileo was ultimately blinded by this, but not because he didn't try to safely reduce the light intensity — he was unaware of the existence of infrared and ultraviolet light, both of which passed through his filter, and ultimately caused him to suffer from damage to his eyes.

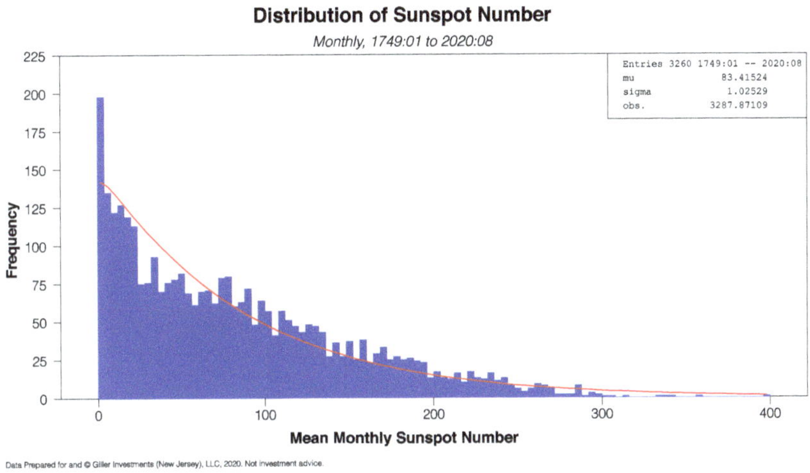

Figure 3.36: Distribution of the Monthly mean Sunspot number from 1749 to date. Blue bars are a histogram of the counts and the red line is a fitted Gamma distribution.

seen from Figure 3.36, so were we to just insert it as a predictor into our regression model (Equation (3.32)) it clearly would have issues. Fortunately my second statistical hero, George Box, had an answer to that.

3.4.7.2. *The Box–Cox Transformation*

Many distributions can be "Normalized" via a power law transformation parameterized as

$$x'_\lambda = \begin{cases} \ln x & \lambda = 0 \\ \dfrac{x^\lambda - 1}{\lambda} & \lambda \neq 0. \end{cases} \tag{3.45}$$

This is called the *Box–Cox Transformation*. It is the same transformation that turns the Geometric Brownian Motion that is alleged to model stock prices in Section 2.1.1 into regular Brownian Motion, with Normally distributed returns. The transformation can be inserted directly into any model with positive data, x, via $x \to x'_\lambda$. λ appears as an additional parameter to estimate.

Unfortunately, this often leads to very slowly converging systems so instead I take the approach of discovering the parameter, λ, that

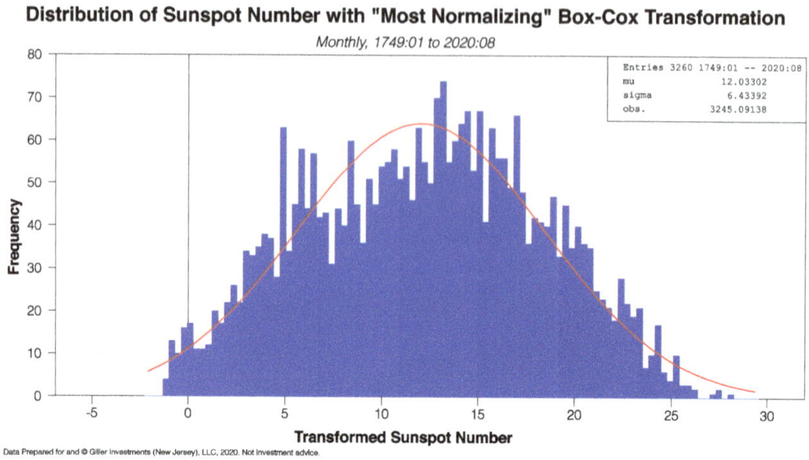

Figure 3.37: Distribution of the transformed monthly mean Sunspot number from 1749 to date. Blue bars are a histogram of the data transformed through a Box–Cox transformation with $\lambda = 0.44$ and the red line is a fitted Normal distribution.

minimizes the Jarque–Bera test statistic. For the Sunspot data this value is 0.441 to three decimal places, and the histogram of the transformed data is shown in Figure 3.37.

This data is clearly substantially more Normal, although it still fails the Jarque–Bera Test. It resembles a truncated Normal distribution, which would mean the original data follows a Box–Cox distribution. In the context of *counts* the discovered "almost square root" transformation is also interesting.

3.4.7.3. *The Statistics of Counting*

Counts of independent events follow the Poisson distribution which is described in reference works on probability and statistics such as the one by Evans *et al.* [44]. The Poisson distribution has a single parameter which determines the mean count rate. This often (also) written λ, but I will refer it here to as N to prevent confusion. The variance of the distribution is also equal to N and the minimum variance unbiased estimate of N is given by the sample mean of the observed counts.

If there is only one observation, of n events, then $\hat{N} = n$ and thus the estimated variance of the observed counts is also n. All of this is *very* familiar to Particle Physicists as we work with counts of events, such as particles produced in the detectors of machines like the Large Hadron Collider at *CERN* or in the cosmic ray experiments I worked on, all the time.

If n events are observed then we can construct a kind of pseudo t statistic by dividing the observed count rate by its expected standard deviation, which is just its own square root from the properties of the Poisson distribution given above, and so $\sqrt{n}$ is a kind of normalized measure of the significance of the observed number of counts. As Sunspot Numbers related to counts[qq] the appearance of a parameter, $\hat{\lambda} \approx 0.5$, is something that I take notice of.

3.4.7.4. *Fitting a Model with Transformed Sunspot Number*

With S_t as the Sunspot Number, our model for the Central England Temperature becomes

$$C_t = \alpha + \beta(t - t_0) + \gamma \frac{S_t^{\hat{\lambda}} - 1}{\hat{\lambda}} + \sum_{i=1}^{m} \varphi_i C_{t-i} + \sum_{j=1}^{y} \varphi_{12j} C_{t-12j} - \sum_{i=1}^{m} \sum_{j=1}^{y} \varphi_i \varphi_{12j} C_{t-i-12j} + \sigma_{m_t} \varepsilon_t, \tag{3.46}$$

$$\varepsilon_t \sim \mathrm{GED}(0, 1, \kappa), \tag{3.47}$$

where I have taken the previously discovered parameter, $\hat{\lambda}$, as fixed.

3.4.7.5. *Results*

Inserting this term does not have a notable effect: it is not significant within the reduced length data set.[rr] I find $\hat{\gamma} = 0.0055 \pm 0.0038$ (the p value is 0.15 so we are only 85% confident this is real). With a maximum transformed Sunspot Number of $\approx \sqrt{400} = 20$, the effect on the temperature of this term would be $0.0055 \times 20 = 0.1°\mathrm{C}$ *if it were true*. This does not explain the observed trend in temperature.

[qq]The Wolf number, or International Sunspot Number, is a corrected estimate taking account of individual spots and groups.

[rr]We have to start the regression in 1749, and not 1659, due to the shorter Wolf series.

3.4.8. *My Motivation for this Work and What I Learned*

As I remarked at the beginning of this section, one reason I decided to study this data was to find out if I could "see for myself" the trends being described in the popular media.[ss] The principal reason for pursuing the work at length, though, was that it required me to:

(i) gain greater experience with high order time-series models — most of the ones used in finance are very low orders;
(ii) gain a proper understanding of the use of the AIC(c) on such models; and,
(iii) learn how to properly compare the estimates of models made from different data sets.

I do believe I have achieved the three objectives outlined above. In fact, I learned some things about seasonal models *when writing up the work for this book* that I hadn't truly appreciated before. Even more than that, we have picked up skills, such as Errors in Variables Models, measuring Forecasting Skill, and the Box–Cox Transformation, that will be deployable in other venues.

The two principal facts I believe that I have developed an understanding of from this data are that the temperatures we are measuring now are notably different from those of the past and that making statements about climate based on current experience ("this year is very hot," "last year was cold") when the climate exhibits *very long horizon correlation*, such that any given observer's personal experience is limited to a few distinct regimes, is fraught with problems.

3.5. Sunspots

My friend Greg Laughlin is an Astronomer, with a side interest in high-frequency trading and quantitative finance. He is currently at Yale, but was previously at the University of California at Santa Cruz and the Lick Observatory. Greg's research has included work on

[ss]Do not conclude from this, however, that I am a "climate denier." I am not. But for me, the best way to properly understand a phenomenon has always been to work out the numbers myself.

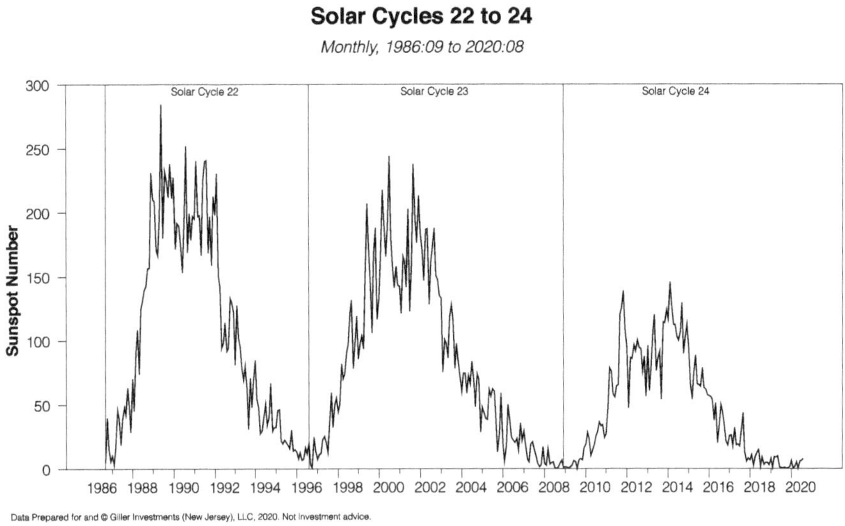

Figure 3.38: The Sunspot Number for the last three Solar cycles. The vertical lines mark the cycle boundaries, which are decided retroactively. The current cycle may be Cycle 25, or we may still be in the end of Cycle 24.

the long-term stability and evolution of the Universe [1], many exoplanet searches, and anything involving odd orbital dynamics [116] (Figure 3.38).

We started talking about Sunspots due to his desire to understand the noise fluctuations in the intensity of light from unresolved stars[tt] that are caused by *starspots* transiting the stellar surface. As Greg is involved in many exoplanet searches, understanding this process would affect his ability to find exoplanets by analyzing the variations in luminosity that occurs when a planet travels in front of a star.

I don't think there are any stars in which we can resolve spots on their surfaces, but nevertheless we hypothesize that there is nothing special about our local star and so the Sun should provide us with a laboratory with which to infer the properties of more distant stars.[uu]

[tt]Meaning those that appear as a point source in a telescope, which is almost all of them.

[uu]This Occam's Razor like reasoning is referred to as *The Copernican Principal* in physical cosmology.

3.5.1. *The Solar Cycle*

In Section 3.4.7, I breezed through the nature of the Wolf Sunspot Series quite quickly, so that I could get to the main task which was trying to ascertain their influence of the measured climate (if any). In this section I'm going to take a crack at predicting the Sunspot number directly, and so we'll look at the data in a bit more detail.

The Solar Cycle is defined to be the period between Solar Sunspot minima, which is around 11 years in length. Often the count of Sunspots reaches exactly zero for an extended period, sometimes it doesn't quite get there. After the minimum the count of Sunspots climbs until it reaches a peak, from which it decays back to zero. It is known that the rise is faster than the decay, that the rate of increase is inversely correlated with the length of the prior cycle and that the maximum Sunspot Number in a cycle is proportional to the rate of increase. To me this sounds less like an oscillator, such as a clock's pendulum where continuous motion reflects the omnipresent trade-off between inertia and gravity, and more like a system that is switching between two states: call them *accumulating* and *dissipating*.

3.5.2. *Markov Switching Models*

We can conceive of a structure in which an observable, in this case the Sunspot Number, is controlled by a hidden state variable that evolves stochastically. If there are Q states, and each observation gives an opportunity to transition from one state i to another j with probability P_{ji}, then this is a Markov Chain,[vv] such as that used in Section 2.4.1.

3.5.2.1. *General Structure*

However, let's now suppose that the dynamics of the observable are characterized by some probability distribution which, potentially, may differ from state to state, $f_i(y_t, x_t|\boldsymbol{\theta}_i)$. (Here x_t is an independent variable and y_t is the dependent variable. Both are *observable*.) If $p_{it|t-1}$ represents the probability that the system is in state i at time t given the information known at $t-1$, then the probability of

[vv]These Hidden Markov Models were referred to earlier, in Chapter 1.

an observation y_t is clearly

$$\Pr(y_t|i) = \sum_{i=1}^{Q} p_{it|t-1} f_i(y_t, x_t|\boldsymbol{\theta}_i). \tag{3.48}$$

Since we don't know what state the system is in, we also need to infer the likelihood of each state given the observed data. This may be computed through Bayes' Theorem as

$$p_{it|t} = \frac{p_{it|t-1} f_i(y_t, x_t|\boldsymbol{\theta}_i)}{\sum_{j=1}^{Q} p_{jt|t-1} f_j(y_t, x_t|\boldsymbol{\theta}_j)}. \tag{3.49}$$

A full discussion of these kinds of models is in the book by Hamilton [66] and they can be tricky to set up, but once you get the software to work, very powerful. I have used them, for example, to model the stock market as randomly switching between reversive periods, where future returns are likely to oppose prior returns, and momentum periods, where future returns are likely to follow prior returns. Such a model can be represented as an autoregression, simplistically $r_t = \varphi_i r_{t-1} + \varepsilon_t$, and if $\sum_{it} p_{it}\varphi_i \approx 0$ then a naive analyst will conclude that a market is efficient when it is not!

3.5.2.2. *Specific Model for Sunspots*

We take there to be two states, with a Markov matrix

$$P = \begin{pmatrix} p_{11} & p_{12} \\ 1 - p_{11} & 1 - p_{12} \end{pmatrix}. \tag{3.50}$$

This is a *column stochastic* matrix, meaning that the column-sums are unity. Thus p_{11} represents the probability of a system in state #1 staying in state #1, and p_{12} represents the probability of a system in state #2 transitioning to state #1.

As the Sunspot Number is a non-negative integer, I will Normalize it by a power transform. Rather than the full Box–Cox transformation of Equation (3.45), I will use the simpler form

$$X_t = S_t^r \text{ and } Y_t = X_t - X_{t-1} \tag{3.51}$$

where S_t is the Sunspot Number, X_t is its transform, which I will call the "total excitation," and Y_t is its first difference. Minimization of the Jarque–Bera test statistic leads to a value $\hat{r} = 0.44$, as before.

For both states, i, the same autoregressive structure will be used, albeit with different parameters permissible.

$$Y_t = \mu_i + \sum_{j=1}^{m} \varphi_{ij} Y_{t-j} + \sigma_i \varepsilon_t, \tag{3.52}$$

$$\varepsilon_t \sim N(0, 1). \tag{3.53}$$

The methods described in Hamilton [66] are used to fit the model. As these models are generally quite difficult to fit and may not converge easily, I strongly recommend using code that is known to work rather than writing it yourself. Note that there is no *natural* labeling of the states, and so regressions run in different periods, or with slightly different initial guesses for the parameters, might return equivalent, but differently labelled, parameters. To deal with this, where possible, I add a parameter constraint such as $\mu_1 \leq \mu_2$, etc. This permits *degeneracy* (i.e. $\hat{\mu}_1 = \hat{\mu}_2$), but requires consistency in the labels.[ww]

3.5.2.3. *Interpretation of the Model*

The model is a statement that describes a dynamical process, as are all time-series models. It says that the Sun is a machine that may occupy one of two states, that the Sunspot Number depends on the "total excitation" variable, X_t, which itself is the sum of a continually present stochastic driving factor, the nature of which may depend on the particular state, and the legacy of past "excitation." Although this is not directly linked to a defined *physical mechanism*, it clearly could be by somebody who understands the physics of the Sun better than I do.

[ww] A similar issue occurs when fitting σ in a system that is parameterized entirely in terms of σ^2. Sometimes the regression system returns a value $\hat{\sigma} < 0$ which must have its sign ignored.

3.5.3. *The Fitted Model*

As in all development of time-series models, I decided to split the data into an *in-sample* period from January 1749, to December 1999, and an *out-of-sample* period from January 2000, to date. All optimization is done in the *in-sample* period.

3.5.3.1. *Selection of the Autoregressive Model Order*

The AIC(c) was used to select the monthly autoregressive order for an AR(m) model of the data. I am not using a seasonal term, SAR(y), here because the Sunspot Number appears to not be truly periodic, meaning its oscillations do not have a *fixed* frequency, and so a seasonal lag operator cannot be easily defined. The data prefers an AR(26) model, as is illustrated in Figure 3.39. Although the minimum in AIC(c) seems fairly broad, examining the model weights in a multi-model inference scenario shows a strong preference for AR(26).

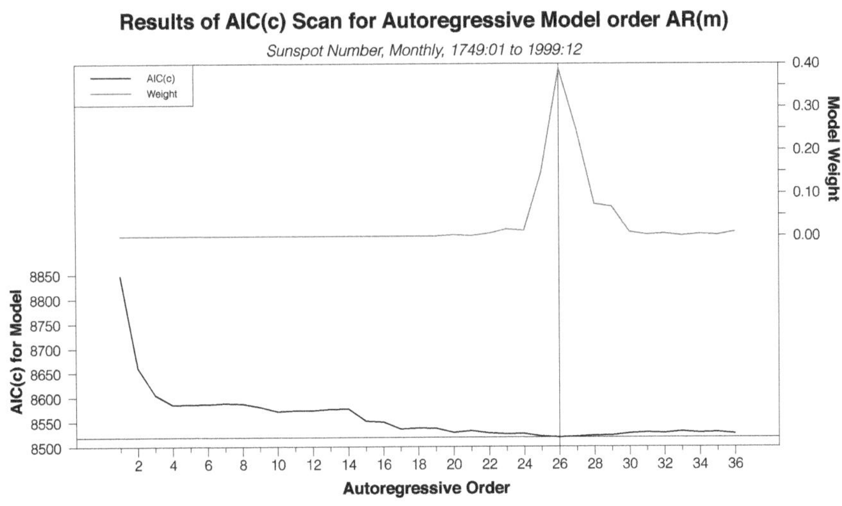

Figure 3.39: Results of scanning the model order, m, in an Markov(2) $\times$ AR(m) model of the incremental "excitation" of the Sunspot generating system. The black line shows the AIC(c) computed from the various maximum likelihood model estimations and the blue line the relative weights to be placed on each model in a multi-model inference scenario.

3.5.3.2. *Estimated Parameters for the Optimal Model*

The estimated parameters for the model are shown in Table 3.8. As these estimates are made by maximum likelihood, and not some more opaque system such as Deep Learning, we can perform the Wald Test to examine various important linear relationships between parameters.[xx] In particular, we can investigate whether all the analytical complexity brought in by the Hidden Markov Model is supported by the data.

Table 3.8: Maximum likelihood regression results for the fit of a Markov(2) × AR(6) model to the power transformed Sunspot Number.

Regression results for Sunspot Model

	State #1		State #2	
Variable	Estimate	Std. error	Estimate	Std. error
P_{11}, P_{22}	0.963	0.008	0.975*	
P_{21}, P_{12}	0.037*		0.025	0.006
μ_i	−0.199	0.031	0.094	0.030
σ_i	0.734	0.021	1.147	0.020
φ_{ij}	See Figure 3.40.			

Significance tests

Test	Statistic	Value	p-value
Diffusion	χ^2_2	7339.4	Negligible
State symmetry	χ^2_1	2.0	0.15
Equal means	χ^2_1	44.3	Negligible
Equal variance	χ^2_1	202.6	Negligible
Equal memory	χ^2_{26}	66.1	0.00002

Notes: Data is from January 1749, to August 2020; the estimated power transform index is $\hat{r} = 0.44$.
*Probabilities are implied by other estimates in stochastic matrix P.

[xx]This is one of the reasons I favor this style of analysis in circumstances when it is possible.

The first question to ask of the data is whether the Markov transition probabilities, which are estimated to be $\hat{P}_{11} = 0.963 \pm 0.008$ and $\hat{P}_{12} = 0.025 \pm 0.006$, are significantly inconsistent with the values we would expect for unconditional diffusion between states, which are 0.5 in both cases. The estimated parameters are significantly distinct from that value in both cases. A second question we can ask of the probabilities is whether the estimated and implied probabilities are actually different, i.e. Does the data support $P_{11} = P_{22}$? This implies the constraint that $\hat{P}_{11} + \hat{P}_{12} = 1$ and, in this case we find $\chi^2_1 = 2.0$ with a p value of 0.15, which is not significant, and so we should conclude that there should not be separate state transition probabilities, i.e. The Markov transition matrix is fully symmetric and should be represented as

$$P = \begin{pmatrix} p & 1-p \\ 1-p & p \end{pmatrix}. \tag{3.54}$$

Secondly, we can ask whether the estimated parameters, the various $\{\mu_i\}$, $\{\sigma_i\}$ and $\{\varphi_{ij}\}$ are significantly different between the two states. The two means, $\hat{\mu}_1 = -0.199 \pm 0.031$ and $\hat{\mu}_2 = 0.094 \pm 0.030$, have different values and the Wald test statistic of $\chi^2_1 = 44.3$ says that this difference is very significant. We note that $\hat{\mu}_1$ is negative and $\hat{\mu}_2$ is positive, suggestive of states in which the Sun is dissipating (state #1) or accumulating (state #2) its "excitation" (Figure 3.39).

The story for $\sigma_1 = \sigma_2$ is similar. With $\hat{\sigma}_1 = 0.734 \pm 0.021$ and $\hat{\sigma}_2 = 1.147 \pm 0.020$, the estimates are clearly inconsistent, and the test statistic of $\chi^2_1 = 202.6$, with negligible p value, confirms that. The same is true for the autocorrelation parameters, the various φ_{ij}. Testing all pairs together, the hypothesis that $\varphi_{1j} = \varphi_{2j}$ for all $j \in [1, 26]$, is strongly rejected with $\chi^2_{26} = 66.1$ with p value much less than 0.001.

With such a large number of lag coefficients, I find it is best to examine them graphically. They are plotted in Figure 3.40, and we see a very strong and interesting structure. Initially negative, so acting to revert the changes to the excitation due to the driving process, they become positive at around twelve lags (one year), and the state #1 coefficients remain positive for the rest of the history while the state #2 coefficients become negative again. The two curves are clearly different.

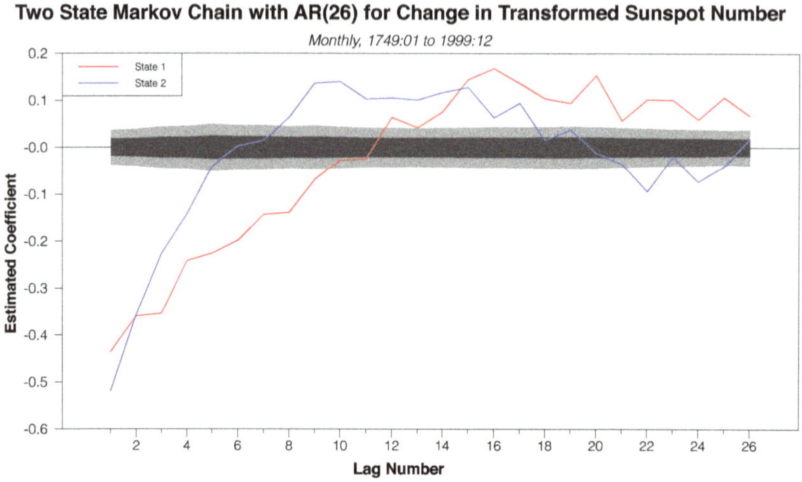

Figure 3.40: Estimated lag coefficients for a Markov(2) $\times$ AR(26) model of the incremental "excitation" of the Sunspot generating system. The red line is the state #1 coefficients and the blue line is the state #2 coefficients. The gray shading indicates the 68% and 95% confidence regions for the estimates.

3.5.3.3. *Accuracy of In-Sample Predictions*

Analysis of tables of coefficients is fairly dry, so let's look at how the predictions made have performed *in-sample*, which can be done via a linear regression of the observed data on the predictions. As this is a *classic* time-series analysis, the independent variables are always precisely known even if stochastic, so we don't need to correct for errors in variables as we did in Section 3.4.4.3. The regression should have parameters $(\alpha, \beta) = (0, 1)$, but as this is not a least squares regression they are not *guaranteed* to be exactly those values.

The regression is exhibited in Figure 3.41 and shows quite "normal" behaviour. The R^2 of 22% implies a correlation coefficient for the forecasts[yy] of 48% is quite a strong relationship, as is seen in the figure. Bear in mind that this is a forecast of *only* the immediate next datum, as more computation is required for forward forecasts. Nevertheless, *in-sample*, I see little reason to doubt the model.

[yy]Referred to as the *Information Coefficient*, or "I.C.," by many in the finance community, following Grinold and Kahn [65].

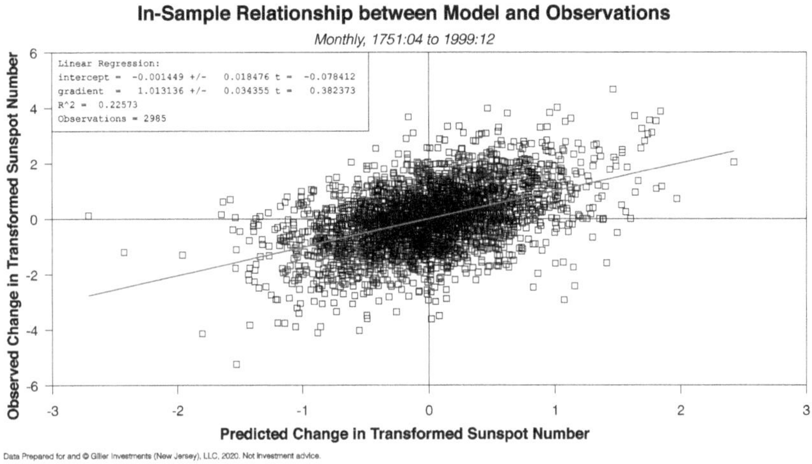

Figure 3.41: In sample regression of the model onto observations for a Markov(2) × AR(26) model of the incremental "excitation" of the Sunspot generating system. The dots are the data pairs and the blue line is the best fitting linear regression line.

3.5.3.4. *Predictions of Sunspot Number in the Modern Period*

Equation (3.52) is an autoregressive model for the change in transformed Sunspot Number. To forecast the Sunspot number one month forward we have to map its predictions back to the observed data. We compute the predicted value, $E_{t-1}[Y_t|i]$, for each state, i, and sum the state specific predictions weighted by the probabilities that the Sun is in each of the possible states. This is then added to the prior total excitation and the transformation reversed, giving

$$E_{t-1}[Y_t|i] = \mu_i + \sum_{j=1}^{m} \varphi_{ij} Y_{t-m}, \tag{3.55}$$

and

$$E_{t-1}[S_t] = \left(X_{t-1} + \sum_{i=1}^{Q} p_{it|t-1} E_{t-1}[Y_t|i] \right)^{\frac{1}{r}}. \tag{3.56}$$

These forecasts are shown in Figure 3.42.

Forecasting multiple months forward involves two steps: first the estimated state probabilities vector must be propagated forward in

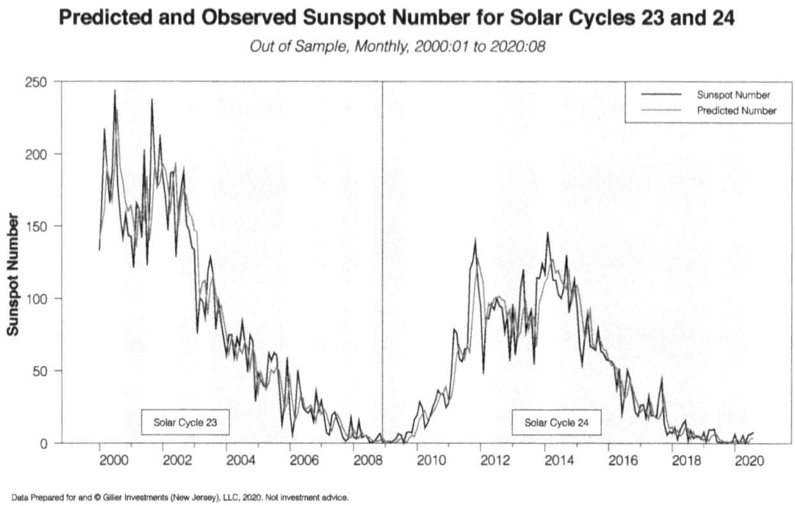

Figure 3.42: Out-of-sample predictions of a Markov(2) × AR(26) model of the incremental "excitation" of the Sunspot generating system. The black line is the observed Sunspot Number and the blue line is the prediction from the model. The gray shading indicates when the probability that the Sun is in state #1, which is characterized by innovations with a negative mean, and the alternate periods are state #2, with a positive mean.

time via the Markov transition matrix

$$p_{it+1|t-1} = \sum_{j=1}^{Q} P_{ij} p_{jt|t-1}. \tag{3.57}$$

Note that this differs from the Bayesian update, Equation (3.49), because when we forecast multiple steps into the future there is no observed data to update the state priors from. Instead we update via the expected Markovian evolution of the state chain. Then the forecasting formulae are applied with the unknown datum, X_t, replaced by its expectation (the term in parentheses in Equation (3.56)). This can then be used to forecast any number of steps into the future by applying the procedure iteratively.

The out-of-sample forecasts for the Modern period are shown in Figure 3.42. I have indicated in this plot the regions where the state #1 probability updated from the observations, $p_{1t|t}$, is over 50%. I think this model gives a convincing description of the data.

3.5.4. *Summary of This Work*

I began this project with the intention of trying to use the financial data science toolkit I had developed over the past years to tackle a problem in observational astronomy that had similarities to those I worked on when I was at Oxford. I know that this approach, of using Hidden Markov Models, and long autoregressive structures, is not one I would have followed in the past. This approach feels quite "unphysical" to me.

Nevertheless, I think I have shown that the method does work, and perhaps that reveals something interesting about the Sun. As a *financial* data scientist, there are some useful lessons. Another tool has been added to the belt, in this case the powerful method of Hidden Markov Models, and it has been done on "low risk" data — meaning data on which there are few personal consequences to a failure to build an accurate model — which contained a strong signal. It is far better to learn a method on data on which it stands a good chance of working than to bring ever more complicated methodologies to data that is essentially nothing but unpredictable noise.

Chapter 4

Politics, Schools, Public Health, and Language

In the previous chapters, the work has focused first on financial time-series, then economic and other time-series. Here, we will investigate data which, mostly, does not have a significant time-series element, meaning that the autocorrelations are weak.[a]

4.1. Presidential Elections

In October 2008, in the run up to the Presidential Election, the *New York Times* published an article on the heights and weights of various presidential candidates from 1896, to date [111]. I was interested at the time in building skills out of the traditional quantitative finance domain and this problem, the prediction of electoral outcomes, is an example of a *classification* problem.

Although this might seem like a frivolous way to assess candidates, I don't think it is necessarily so. Humans have been choosing group leaders for millenia and it's not unreasonable that a heuristic shortcut mapping "fitness to role" to "apparent physical health" might have been evolutionarily wired into our brains. A *rational voter* might ignore these primitive biases, but there's evidence that we are not such people [14].

[a]This is not totally so for the analysis of Presidential Elections, but that study seems to sit more naturally here.

4.1.1. *The New York Times Data*

The data presented for analysis contains a record of the heights and weights of Republican and Democratic candidates in the US Presidential elections from 1896 to 2004, together with the winner. I have augmented the data myself with the candidates and outcomes for the 2008, 2012 and 2016 elections, based on internet research. I will, arbitrarily,[b] label a Democratic win with $Y_t = 0$ and a Republican win with $Y_t = 1$. We can label this outcome P_t and have $P_t \in \mathbb{B}$, where $\mathbb{B}$ is the binary outcome space spanned by the values of Y_t. I augmented this data with two autoregressive variables chosen to represent both the power of incumbency and the desire for change.

4.1.1.1. *The 2016 Election*

In all of these analysis I am actually excluding the 2016 election, in which Hillary Clinton won the popular mandate and Donald Trump won the Electoral College.

Clinton, as a $5'5''$ tall woman, is substantially shorter than Donald Trump, who is listed at $6'3''$. Trump's height and weight have been the subject of controversy: he has claimed to be $6'3''$ tall but is listed at $6'2''$ in some available public records, although these may have been self-reported. He has been photographed not looking taller than others who are less than $6'3''$ tall, but these are not more than anecdotal records at best. His height is clearly in this range, whether it is exactly $6'3''$ or not.

However, these height differences between the candidates are clearly a consequence of normal gender differences and Clinton is *above average height* for a woman her age. Perhaps the right approach would be to standardize the heights and weights relative to those norms in some manner, but with just one example there is simply no way to analyze this aspect of the model reliably.

4.1.2. *Discrete Dependent Variables*

Traditional statistics has addressed these problems with the *PROBIT* method, which is a form of generalized linear model, and

[b]Actually based on the alphabetic ordering of the party names.

belongs to a class of problems that deal with *discrete dependent variables*. These have been extended to any system which may be written

$$y_i = F(\alpha + \beta x_i), \tag{4.1}$$

where F is a cumulative distribution function.

4.1.2.1. *PROBIT and Logit Models*

For the *PROBIT* Model, the distribution is taken to be the cumulative Normal distribution, which is often written $\Phi(x)$, but modern practice, for various technical reasons, is concentrated on the logistic function

$$F(x) = \frac{1}{1+e^{-x}} \Rightarrow y_i = \frac{1}{1+e^{-(\alpha+\beta x_i)}}, \tag{4.2}$$

and many popular authors in the fields of data science, machine learning, and "AI" seem unaware of the probabilistic interpretation of the problem.

4.1.2.2. *Maximum Likelihood Estimation*

The probabilistic interpretation is useful, though, as it allows the methods of maximum likelihood to be used, and all the theorems and results associated with it. y_i is taken to be the probability of variable, Y_i, taking one value of two possible choices. For convenience that choice is labelled 1 and the other 0. Such a variable is referred to as having a Bernoulli distribution, after Jacob Bernoulli the famous Swiss mathematician.

The likelihood of an outcome Y_i given logistic regression model y_i is $y_i^{Y_i}(1-y_i)^{1-Y_i}$ and so the log-likelihood for n independent observations is

$$\mathcal{L}(\{x_i\}_i, \alpha, \beta) = \sum_{i=1}^{n} \{Y_i \ln y_i + (1-Y_i)\ln(1-y_i)\} \tag{4.3}$$

$$= \sum_{i=1}^{n} \{Y_i \ln(\alpha+\beta x_i) + (1-Y_i)\ln(1-\alpha-\beta x_i)\}. \tag{4.4}$$

In machine learning this function is often referred to as the "log-loss" and it is a type of *empirical risk function*, which is a measure of the accuracy of a model.

4.1.2.3. *Other Classification Algorithms*

Many other types of classification algorithms do exist, including such things as Naïve Bayes, Neural Networks, Regression Trees and Random Forests, Support Vector Machines and Deep Learning. All of them can be represented as optimizing a response function, $y(x_i, \boldsymbol{\theta})$, over parameters, $\boldsymbol{\theta}$, that gives the probability of the event $Y_i = 1$ occurring. Which one used may depend on both user choice and data suitability.

4.1.3. *A Generalized Linear Model*

As US Presidents may serve no more than two terms,[c] I define "incumbency" simply as $I_{t+1} = P_t$, and "change"[e] as

$$C_{t+1} = \begin{cases} \neg P_t & \text{if } P_t = P_{t-1} \\ P_t & \text{otherwise.} \end{cases} \tag{4.5}$$

If H_{it} and W_{it} are the heights and weights of candidate i in the election held in year t, so the Generalized Linear Model has the structure

$$\begin{aligned} \Pr(P_{t+1} = 1) = \text{logistic}\,\{&\alpha + \eta(H_{1t} - H_{0t}) \\ &+ \omega(W_{1t} - W_{0t}) + \varphi I_t + \delta C_t\}. \end{aligned} \tag{4.6}$$

This may be estimated by maximum likelihood and, since the gradient of the function is analytic, should be quite easy to fit. The baseline Null hypothesis is that none of these factors are relevant, and so

$$\hat{\alpha} = \text{logit}\left(\frac{1}{n}\sum_{t=1}^{n} I[P_t = 1]\right), \tag{4.7}$$

where there are n elections in the data.

---

[c]Originally *de facto* following a tradition established by George Washington then, after the passage of the twenty-second amendment,[d] *de jure*.

[e]Here $\neg x = 1$ if $x = 0$ and $\neg x = 0$ if $X = 1$.

4.1.3.1. *The Baseline Model*

I find $\hat{\alpha} = 0.194 \pm 0.361$ when all other coefficients are held at zero, indicating a 55:45 preference for Republicans in the 31 elections since 1896. This is not 50:50, but how *significant* is that? Under the Null hypothesis the outcome of the election can be thought of as a Bernoulli distribution with probability $\Pr(P_t = 1) = p$. Then the variance of the sampling distribution of $\hat{p}$ is

$$\mathrm{Var}[\hat{p}] = \frac{p(1-p)}{n}, \tag{4.8}$$

for a sample of n elections. The largest this can be is for $p = 1/2$ which gives $\mathrm{Var}[\hat{p}] = 1/2\sqrt{n} \approx 9\%$ with our data. Thus any discrepancy from parity less than 20% is probably not significant.

4.1.3.2. *Testing Predictors Independently*

When faced with a bunch of independent variables that are candidates to explain the dependent variable I'm interested in, there's generally one of three approaches to take. One of:

(i) introduce all of the independent variables separately, and select those that are individually significant for a joint regression;
(ii) just introduce all the independent variables together, and remove those that that are not significant[f]; or,
(iii) introduce all the variables but use a regularization scheme, such as the *LASSO*, to pick features that are useful.

I like the *LASSO* a lot, especially as it is theoretically well supported by the work of Terrence Tao and Emmanuel Candes on *Compressed Sensing* [13], which I have spent a lot of time on personally in the context of efficient equity factor return extraction. Introducing multiple variables without regularization has many flaws, particularly when there might be strong covariance between them as this leads to unreliable estimates in-sample which means models that don't work out-of-sample. In addition, it means that the very t statistics used to

[f]This is the approach that Peter Muller favored when I was working with him.

pick the "significant" variables may have their values compromised and so the entire procedure is undermined.[g]

The approach taken here is the first one, to individually iterate though each variable as a potential enhancement to the model. Since we are doing maximum likelihood regression with a nested model this also means Wilk's Theorem applies and the Maximum Likelihood Ratio Test is valid.

4.1.3.3. *Results of the Independent Predictor Regressions*

The results of these independent regressions are shown in Table 4.1, from which we see that only the height difference and change variables are significant. Based on AIC.(c), incumbency has almost no effect whatsoever. The results are generally weak (confidence is less than 99%), but we will proceed with these two features.

Table 4.1: Independent logistic regression results to determine the predictor variables useful in explaining Presidential elections.

Independent regression results

Coefficient	Estimate	Std. error	t statistic	p-value	AIC.(c)
α	0.194	0.361			44.8
η	5.194	2.286	2.272	0.023*	38.5
ω	0.033	0.018	1.848	0.065	41.3
φ	0.799	0.747	1.069	0.285	44.7
δ	2.088	0.846	2.469	0.014*	38.9

Note: The coefficients represent (in order): general bias (α); relative height (η); relative weight (ω); incumbency (φ); and, change (δ). α is always included in the model and so its t statistic and p value are meaningless.
*Significant with 95% confidence.

[g]The reason it worked for Peter is because the models used for Statistical Arbitrage in the 1990's were extremely significant due to the presence of strong anomalies and the use of large data sets. My career has featured more marginal results and *latent* phenomena.

Table 4.2: Logistic regression results for a joint model for Presidential elections.

Joint model for Presidential elections				
Coefficient	Estimate	Std. error	t statistic	p-value
α	−0.772	0.702	−1.099	0.272
η	8.090	3.284	2.463	0.013
δ	3.074	1.230	2.498	0.013

Note: The coefficients represent (in order): general bias (α); relative height (η); and, change (δ).

4.1.3.4. *Joint Model for Elections from 1896 to 2012*

From the table, it seems that both relative height and change, treated independently, are factors in determining the outcome of Presidential elections with a moderate level of confidence. So let's repeat the logistic regression with both terms included.

When included together, both terms are significant and the joint model has a significant likelihood ratio, although that number is biased by our search for predictors. Instead I will use the Wald test against exclusion of both terms, which gives a $\chi^2_2 = 8.2$ with a p value of 0.016. Not quite at the 99% confidence level. The individual predictions are illustrated graphically in Figure 4.1, from which we can see that the *in-sample* predictions perform quite well. I actually first performed this analysis in February 2012, prior to the Republican nominating convention and at a point where it was unsure which of the three remaining candidates would win [51]. At that time, the model predicted Mitt Romney, the eventual candidate, would lose to incumbent President Barack Obama.

4.1.3.5. *Precision and Recall*

In the context of classification problems, overall predictive accuracy is not necessarily the only thing of interest. We are looking at data that is labelled in some manner, and trying to select the subset with a particular label of interest. Performance can be evaluated in terms of *precision*, meaning the proportion of the data we select that does

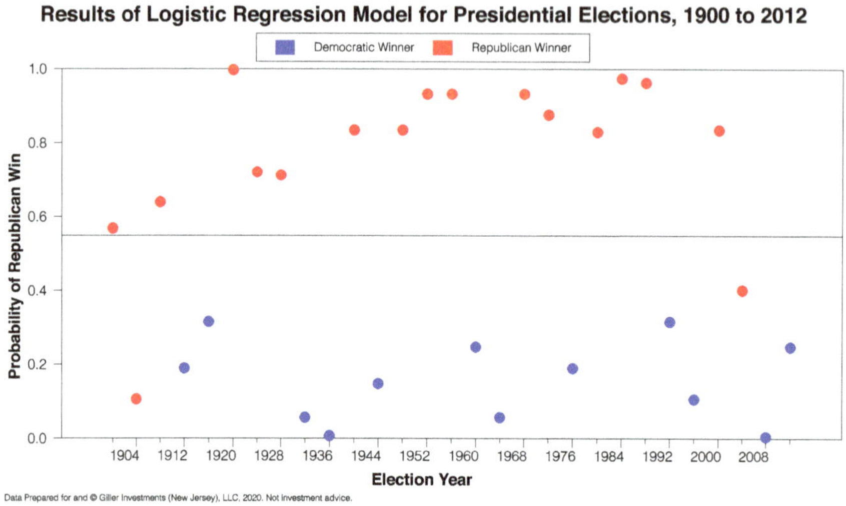

Figure 4.1: Predictions and outcomes of a logistic regression model of Presidential elections using height difference and desire for change as independent variables. The blue dots indicate that the Democratic candidate won and the red dots indicate that the Republican candidate won. The location of the dot vertically indicates the probability of a Republican win as computed from the model, and the horizontal line is drawn at the average win rate of Republicans.

have the label we are interested in, and *recall*, meaning the proportion of data with the label we are interested in that we actually select.

Writing $\hat{P}_t$ for the prediction of outcome P_t, we can define these metrics as

$$\text{precision} = \frac{\sum_t I[P_t = 1 \wedge \hat{P}_t = 1]}{\sum_t I[\hat{P}_t = 1]}, \tag{4.9}$$

$$\text{recall} = \frac{\sum_t I[P_t = 1 \wedge \hat{P}_t = 1]}{\sum_t I[P_t = 1]}. \tag{4.10}$$

This needs to be supplemented by a decision rule that converts the estimated probabilities of the logistic model of Equation (4.6) into crisp predictions. The obvious one is clearly

$$\hat{P}_t = \begin{cases} 1 & \text{if } \Pr(P_t = 1) > \beta \\ 0 & \text{otherwise,} \end{cases} \tag{4.11}$$

for some $\beta \in [0, 1]$. The choice $\beta = 0.5$ seems natural, but it depends on what whether we care most about accuracy, precision or recall.

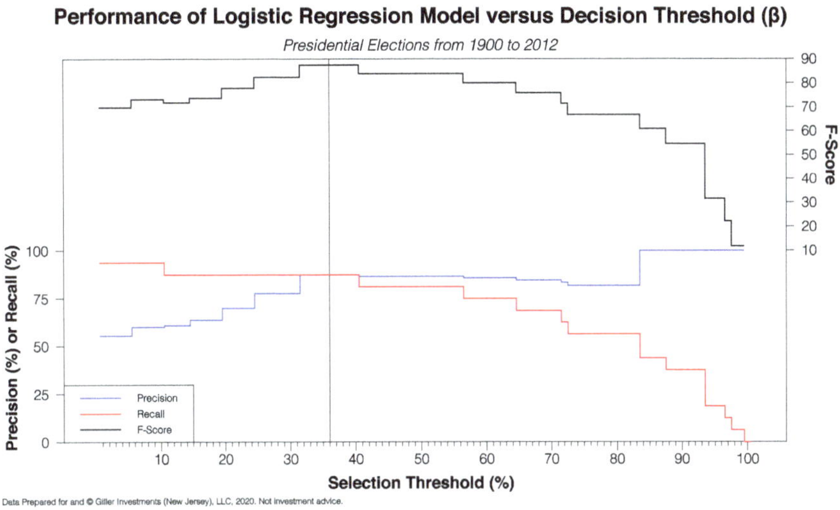

Figure 4.2: Variation of precision, recall and F-score with the decision threshold, β, for predicting a Republican President based on logistic regression. The blue curve is precision, the red curve recall, and the black curve the F-score.

$\beta = 0$ will deliver 100% recall at low precision and $\beta = 1$ will deliver 100% precision with likely zero recall.

The F-score is the harmonic mean of precision and recall, and is a commonly used "compromise" metric. We see from Figure 4.2, that the optimal choice is $\beta = 0.36$, although the naïve choice of 0.5 does not perform much differently. At the optimum, precision and recall are both 87.5%.

4.1.3.6. *Bootstrapping the F-Score Optimization*

There is enormous discussion online of precision, recall, F-score, area under ROC curves,[h] and every single one of the dozens of ways of combining the four basic statistics of a decision rule,[i] but sadly much less acknowledgement that optimizing these statistics, whichever you

[h]Another metric of decision rule performance that is used in algorithm optimization.

[i]The counts of true positives, true negatives, false positives (Type I Errors), and false negatives (Type II Errors).

choose, is an exercise in reasoning from a data sample and so is subject to sampling error.[j]

If you have continued reading to this point in my book you are no doubt not surprised that I do not take that view. Very much as one might say in mechanical engineering that "everything is a spring," I know that all inferential procedures are uncertain. However, optimizing the F-score from a logistic regression is a highly nonlinear operation: how might we compute it's sampling distribution? The obvious answer is bootstrapping!

For this dataset we do not have a lot of data and are using autocorrelated variables, so block bootstrapping might be ineffective. Instead I will use the "Markov Chain" trick of bootstrapping not the data series, P_t, but the information sets $\mathcal{I}_t$, which contain the history of every variable up to time t. With this, the procedure is straightforward: bootstrap the data, perform a logistic regression and F-score optimization, record the result and repeat. The results of 10,000 bootstraps are shown in Figure 4.3.

The lessons from the bootstrap are that:

(i) the optimal threshold is very likely below 0.5;
(ii) the reliability of any F-score optimization *on this small dataset* is quite poor.

4.1.4. *A Naïve Bayes Classifier for Presidential Elections*

In Section 4.1.2.3, I listed some of the many varieties of classifier algorithms that have been explored by researchers and practitioners over the years. One reason why such a variety of procedures exists is that performance can be quite unsatisfactory in the real world! Another reason is that the good ones are slow. With our dataset of some thirty examples, we don't have to worry about speed, however just because a generalized linear model is easy to write down and easy to compute does not mean that it is correct.

[j]This may be because many computer scientists, in my experience, have little real training in actual empirical science — there is a tendency to believe that inferential procedures are merely just another algorithm to download and apply.

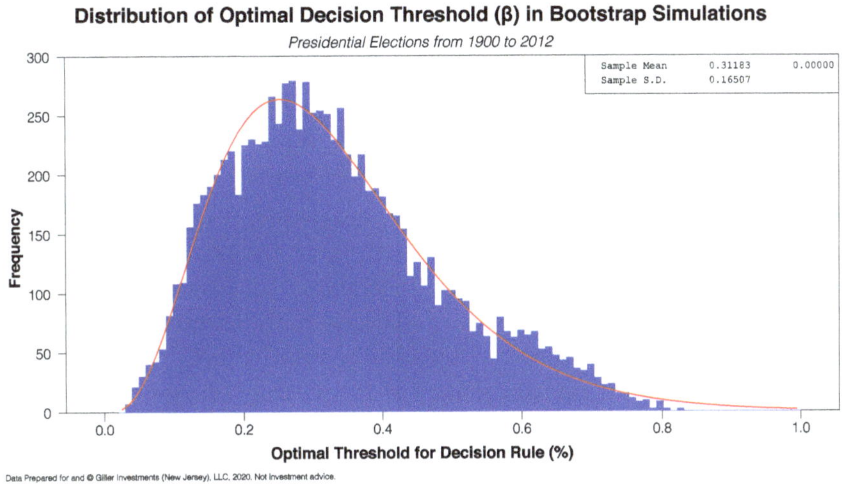

Figure 4.3: Distribution of optimal decision threshold for 10,000 bootstraps of the use of a logistic regression model to predict a Republican President based on candidate heights and desire for change. The blue bars are a histogram of the optimal thresholds selected and the red curve is the best fitting Gamma distribution.

4.1.4.1. *Naïve Bayes*

The naïve Bayes classifier is based on the assumption that we may write

$$\begin{aligned}\Pr(P_t|H_{1t}-H_{0t},W_{1t}-W_{0t},I_t,C_t) \propto{}& \Pr(H_{1t}-H_{0t}|P_t)\\ &\times\Pr(W_{1t}-W_{0t}|P_t)\\ &\times\Pr(I_t|P_t)\\ &\times\Pr(C_t|P_t),\end{aligned} \tag{4.12}$$

which arises from the rules of conditional probability, the "naïve" assumption that joint conditions may be approximated by individual conditions, and Bayes' theorem.

Equation (4.12) states that the probability of the outcome of interest jointly conditioned on all of the independent variables may be (approximately) factored into the marginal conditional probabilities for each predictor independently. To me, this is quite similar to Sklar's theorem, which states that joint probability distribution may be factored into the marginal distributions of each variable and a special function called a *copula*.[k]

4.1.4.2. *Training a Naïve Bayes Classifier*

The conditional probabilities for the independent variates that are binary in nature, I_t and C_t, may be estimated by frequency counting within the observed data. For the continuous variables, particularly with a small sample, we have to make one more assumption. As we can estimate the mean and variance of the relative height and weight data, conditioned on the two values of P_t, we may represent the conditional probabilities with those calculated from the Normal distribution. For the entire sample we then compute the relative probability that each set of variables gives rise to each possible outcome and eliminate the unconditional probabilities by dividing by the sum of those relative probabilities.

4.1.4.3. *Precision and Recall for Naïve Bayes*

As in Section 4.1.3.5, we convert the state probability estimate returned by the Naïve Bayes classifier into a decision rule by simply comparing it to a threshold, β. Figure 4.4 shows the variation of precision, recall, and F-score, with β. In comparison to Figure 4.2, it's clear that the systems, when *in-sample*, are performing at roughly the same level, which reflects the common nostrum that Naïve Bayes is not so naïve in reality.

4.1.4.4. *Correlation between Classifier Probabilities*

The similarity between the classifications from the two methods explored can be made more explicit by looking at how their covariance, which is easily done on a scatter plot. This is shown in Figure 4.5, and there is obviously strong correlation between the two methods.

---

[k]And copulas are notorious for their role in the 2008 global financial crisis [115].

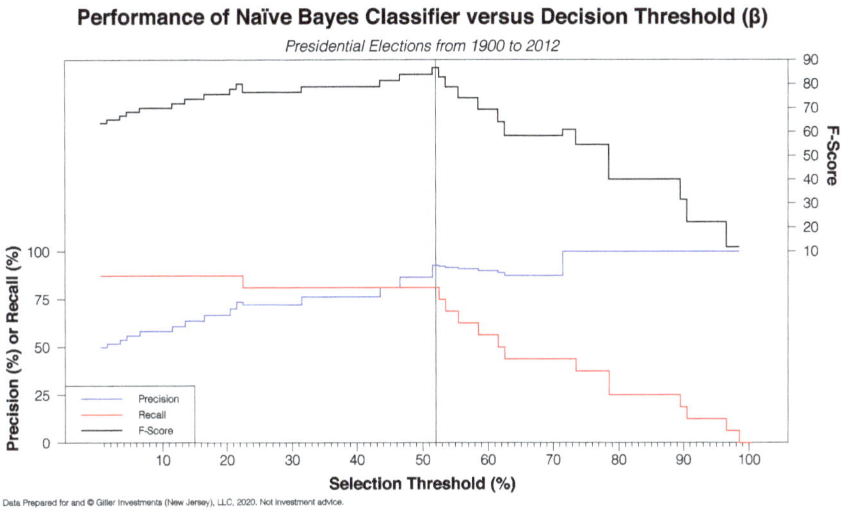

Figure 4.4: Variation of precision, recall and F-score with the decision threshold, β, for predicting a Republican President based on a Naïve Bayes classifier. The blue curve is precision, the red curve recall, and the black curve the F-score.

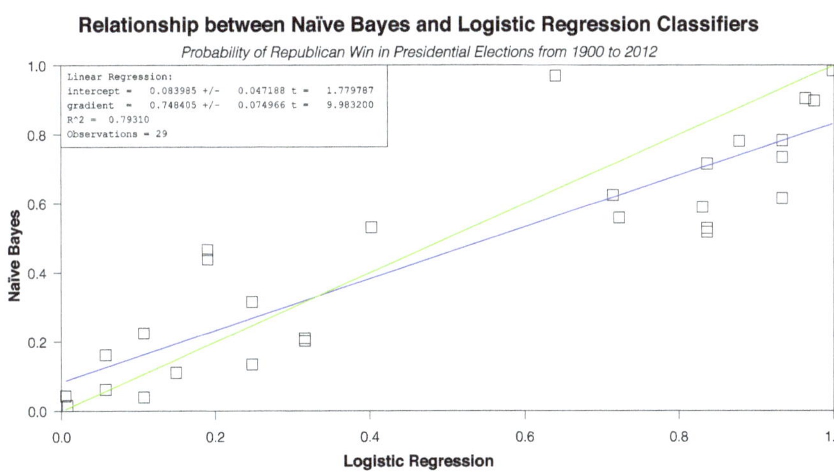

Figure 4.5: Side-by-side comparison of the probabilities for a Republican Presidential win based on a logistic regression model and a naïve Bayes classifier. The blue line is the best fitting linear regression line and the green line represents exact agreement between the two methods.

4.1.5. *The Trend Toward Taller Candidates*

If a candidate's likelihood of winning the election is a function of their relative height, and candidates are able to observe this effect themselves, then the public policy "market" for candidates should lead to the selection of those with increasing heights through time, very much as the sport of professional Basketball selects athletes with heights in excess of 7'. Progressive selection among candidates would imply upward growth in average white male height in excess of the 0.0295"/year observed in the HNES/HANES surveys during the 20th. Century[1] [81].

Treating the candidate height data as a balanced panel with individual fixed effects allows the following model to be fitted:

$$H_{it} = \mu_i + g(y_t - 1896) + \varepsilon_{it}, \tag{4.13}$$

with y_t representing the calendar year of the election at time t. The result is a significant regression with $F_{2,61} = 7.9$ and a p value of 0.0009. The estimated trend growth rate of $\hat{g} = (0.0268 \pm 0.0069)$"/year includes the survey value within the 68% confidence region, and so is entirely consistent with it. Thus we have no reason to believe that the heights of candidates of both parties have increased at a faster rate than those of the general population. However, it is clear from Figure 4.6 that most candidates are taller than the general population.

4.2. School Board Elections

In 2019, my wife decided to run for our local School Board. She was listed second on a randomized ballot and local politicians told us that this gave her a high probability of being elected in a non-partisan election. Naturally, I wanted to investigate whether this assertion was true. I also wanted to examine whether gender and age were a factor, where that data was available. Candidate heights was unlikely to be obtainable as, unlike in Presidential elections, none of our candidates are famous with their vital statistics recorded on the internet.

[1]The only two non-white male candidates being Barack Obama in 2008 and 2012, and Hillary Clinton in 2016.

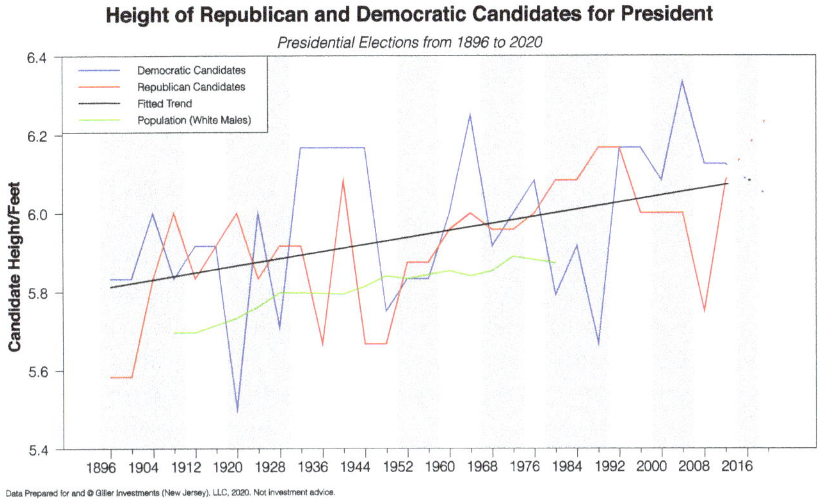

Figure 4.6: Heights of male Presidential candidates from 1896 to 2020. The blue line is the Democratic candidates, the red line the Republican candidates, the black line the fitted trend line and the green line the data from the NHES/NHANES surveys. Gray shading indicates a Republican win and 2016 is omitted as the Democratic candidate was female.

4.2.1. *How the Election Works*

Every year three seats are up for election on a nine member board that governs the local school district. In some years just three people run, but in this year there were six candidates. The elections for school boards in New Jersey operate as *multiple non-transferable vote elections*. This means multiple seats are available each year and every member of the electorate casts one vote for one person for each seat. In our home town, with three seats available, each voter may vote for up to three different candidates but may not vote more than once for any given candidate. The top three candidates, by vote count, are then awarded the seats.

The electorate are not required to allocate all of their votes and are also permitted to write in additional candidates of their choice and vote for them, so the total number of votes is not equal to product of the number of seats and the electorate size and the total of the votes for listed candidates does not equal the total votes cast.[m]

[m]Write-ins have never won in Holmdel.

The election is held at the same time as the general election across the state for municipal leadership, which is a political election.

4.2.2. *The Data*

The *Monmouth County Board of Elections* manages the electoral processes for all municipalities and executive organizations within the county, and data from past elections from 2001 to 2018 was available online, although a lot of human *scraping* was required to extract and store it — I wished I had access to Bloomberg's tools for doing this.

I also had access to the registered voter file for Holmdel, NJ, and since every candidate was required to be a resident registered voter, I could identify birthdates for all candidates, past and present, who currently resided in the community. For those that were no longer resident, either having moved out or were deceased, I decided to use *mean imputation* to complete the data. I computed the average age of the candidates for which I did have data, which was 50.464 ± 2.849 years.[n] I assigned candidate genders as I was entering it into my database based on first names or by first hand or second hand personal knowledge within the community. In the published data the candidates were listed in ballot order.[o]

Similarly, I assigned the female gender to candidates who's gender was missing as a surprisingly large set of school board candidates appeared to be female. In modeling I use the numeric codes 0 for female and 1 for male, which permits them to be treated as regression variables.[p] A positive coefficient for gender then reveals a preference for male candidates and a negative coefficient a preference for female candidates.

As all three top candidates by vote count win a seat, I used a simple binary indicator that the candidate was in the top three for

[n] A better approach is to use *random imputation* either based on the observed marginal distribution either by simulation or sampling, but I ended up having fairly complete records so I doubt it made much difference.

[o] I guessed that this was the case because the data was definitely not sorted either alphabetically or in terms of votes cast, and the data for the 2019 election exactly matched the ballot ordering we had.

[p] And in Bayesian analysis, I use a real number defined on $[0, 1]$. The *usual* convention in survey research is to code the response "male" as 1 and "female" as 2, but I find the $\{0, 1\}$ set provides a useful mnemonic.

ballot rank. In a non-negligible number of years there were not more than three candidates, so all three won.

4.2.3. *A Model for Independent Win Probabilities*

Because of the "lost votes" issue associated with both lack of complete voting and additional write-in candidates, it didn't seem reasonable to try to directly model a multicategory choice problem, but I wanted to start with something simple, so I decided to model each candidate's independent chances of winning the election based on observed features and use the existence of the lost votes as a "slack variable."

4.2.3.1. *Logistic Regression Models*

For each candidate, a logistic model is constructed for their independent win probability

$$K_{it} = \alpha + \beta B_{it} + \gamma G_{it}, \tag{4.14}$$

and

$$P_{it} = \text{logistic}\, K_{it}, \tag{4.15}$$

where P_{it} is the probability that candidate i wins the election held at time t, B_{it} is the ballot rank "top three" indicator, and G_{it} is the candidate's gender. It turns out there was very little dispersion in candidate age, so I did not include that feature — if a predictor doesn't change much its role will basically be of an additional, colinear, constant and lead to errors in estimation.

The total log likelihood was then computed as

$$\mathcal{L}(\alpha, \beta, \gamma) = \sum_{t=2001}^{2018} \sum_{i=1}^{n_t} \{W_{it} \ln P_{it} + (1 - W_{it}) \ln(1 - P_{it})\}\,. \tag{4.16}$$

n_t is the number of candidates running in the election in year t and W_{it} indicates if a candidate was a winner.

We require the constraint $\sum_i P_{it} + \omega_{it} = 3$, where ω_{it} is the probability that the write-in candidate wins. The sum is to three as three candidates will win a seat. This can be estimated with the constraint applied or it can be elided over, which is equivalent to saying that it will take whatever value necessary to satisfy the constraint. Clearly both methods are mathematically equivalent, and one is operationally much simpler.

The unaddressed flaw with this approach is that it doesn't take account of correlation and could, in theory, deliver a solution in which $\sum_i \hat{P}_{it} > 3$ and $\hat{\omega}_{it} < 0$. As vote share in historic elections seemed to be pretty evenly divided between candidates, so the maximum was around 33%, I decided to accept this limitation.

4.2.4. *Estimation Results*

With this structure, estimating the model via maximum likelihood is straightforward and the results are shown in Table 4.3.

4.2.4.1. *Results of the Independent Wins Regression*

The model is significant with better than 95% confidence, but not better than 99%. It indicates that top three ballot position is a positive factor affecting the outcome with the same level of confidence

Table 4.3: Independent wins logistic regression results to predict the outcomes of School Board elections.

Independent win regression results				
Coefficient	Estimate	Std. error	t statistic	p-value
α	0.228	0.595		
β	1.402	0.632	2.221	0.026*
γ	−1.098	0.633	−1.735	0.083

Maximum likelihood ratio test			
Test	Statistic	Value	p-value
Equiprobability	χ^2_2	8.6	0.024

Notes: The coefficients represent (in order): general bias, α; "top three" ballot placement, β; and, gender, γ. α is always included in the model and so its t statistic and p value are meaningless.
*Significant with 95% confidence.

Table 4.4: Independent wins logistic regression model predictions of the outcomes of the 2019 Holmdel School Board election.

Predicted Electoral Ranks

Candidate	Gender	Ballot rank	Win probability*
Elizabeth A. Urbanski	Female	2	0.836
Lori Ammirati†	Female	3	0.836
Joseph D. Hammer‡	Male	1	0.630
Jaimie Hynes	Female	4	0.557
John Martinez†	Male	5	0.295
Michael Sockol†	Male	6	0.295

Notes: Candidates are ordered by estimated win probability.
*Probabilities are for individual wins so do not sum to 1.
†Incumbent.
‡Prior board President.

and suggests that there may be a bias *for* female candidates with a marginal significance (92% confidence). Given that there are only eighteen elections to train the model on, this is quite a good result.

4.2.4.2. *Predicted Rankings for the 2019 Election*

Of course, as my wife was running and ranked high on the ballot, I wanted to know how this placed her! How would the two supporting forces of ballot rank and gender play out?

4.2.5. *A Poisson Model for Vote Counts*

The recorded data had the vote counts for each candidate, so I decided that I would model that directly. Total votes cast, V_t, is a statistic recorded in the electoral data, and the individual candidate votes, V_{it}, should follow a Poisson distribution. This has the *probability mass function*

$$\text{Poisson}(\lambda) \; : \; f(k|\lambda) = \frac{k^{\lambda}}{k!}e^{-\lambda}, \tag{4.17}$$

where k is the observed counts and λ the expectation.

4.2.5.1. *The Model for Candidate Vote Counts*

I model the votes cast for each candidate as

$$V_{it} \sim \text{Poisson}(K_{it}V_t/n_t), \tag{4.18}$$

$$W_t \sim \text{Poisson}(wV_t/n_t), \tag{4.19}$$

where V_{it} is the votes cast for candidate i in election year t, V_t is the total votes casts in the election, K_{it} is the linear predictive kernel of Equation (4.14), as before n_t is the number of candidates for election, and w is the expected number of votes cast for *all* write in candidates. This structure allows votes to be used for write in candidates and it also permits members of the electorate to use less than all three of their votes if they so wish. The joint log likelihood, for each year t, is then

$$\begin{aligned}\mathcal{L}_t(\alpha,\beta,\gamma,w) = {} & \frac{K_{it}V_t}{n_t}\sum_{i=1}^{n_t}(\ln V_{it}-1) - \sum_{i=1}^{n_t}\ln V_{it}! \\ & + \frac{wV_t}{n_t}(\ln W_t - 1) - \ln W_t.\end{aligned} \tag{4.20}$$

4.2.6. *Estimation Results*

4.2.6.1. *Results of the Independent Vote Counts Regression*

Again, this is a simple model with a small data sample and so the estimation results are easy to compute, although I decided to use an alternative error calculation methodology to correct for potential mispecification as the reported coefficient t statistics seemed suspiciously high. This instructed my regression software to recompute its covariance matrix and means that the Maximum Likelihood Ratio Test results were overly strong. I have used the Wald Test instead for global significance testing.

With this new model we see that the ballot rank term is significant at $\hat{\beta} = 0.092 \pm 0.032$, so we adopt this term with better than 99% confidence. The gender term is also more significant with $\hat{\gamma} = -0.144 \pm 0.058$, just shy of 99% confidence. The write in vote rate (as a proportion of total votes cast per candidate) is estimated to be $\hat{w} = 0.013 \pm 0.002$, which is strongly established. This suggests over 1% of the electorate write in at least one candidate, effectively registering a protest vote that has little actual effect.

Table 4.5: Independent vote counts regression results to predict the outcomes of School Board elections.

Independent vote count regression results

Coefficient	Estimate	Std. error	t statistic	p-value
α	1.010	0.048		
β	0.092	0.032	2.886	0.0039*
γ	−0.144	0.058	−2.487	0.0129†
w	0.013	0.002	5.98	Negligible

Wald test for zero coefficients

Test	Statistic	Value	p-value
Equiprobability	χ_2^2	19.6	0.00005

Notes: The coefficients represent (in order): general bias, α; "top three" ballot placement, β; gender, γ; and write in vote share, w. α is always included in the model and so its t statistic and p value are meaningless.
*Significant with 99% confidence.
†Significant with 95% confidence.

4.2.6.2. *Expression of the Outcome in terms of Vote Share*

The only undetermined parameter in the model of Equation (4.20) is the total votes to be cast in the 2019 election, V_{2019}. There are several approaches to fixing a value to this unknown, which must be fixed ahead of time to use this model for forecasting:

(i) use a Martingale model;
(ii) use a time-series model; or,
(iii) use a simple regression onto other features.

The easiest approach by far is the Martingale, and so that is the approach taken. However, Equations (4.18) and (4.19), introduce the vote count as a simple scalar. As outcomes are the same whether we predict vote counts or vote share, I can express my predictions that way, i.e.

$$E\left[\frac{V_{it}}{V_t}\right] = \frac{K_{it}}{n_t} = \frac{\alpha + \beta B_{it} + \gamma G_{it}}{n_t}. \qquad (4.21)$$

Mathematically this is the assumptions that $\mathrm{Cor}(V_{it}, V_t) \approx 0$ and $E_{t-1}[V_t] = V_{t-1}$.

4.2.6.3. *Predicted Vote Shares for the 2019 Election*

The predicted vote shares are shown in Table 4.6 for all named candidates, the write in candidate, and the uninformed Bayesian prior that all candidates get an equal share of the votes. We see that the predictions do not vary much from the prior, with the strongest and weakest candidates being less than 2% different from that value. One change is that the stronger gender bias term has lifted Jaimie Hynes above Joe Hammer in vote share.

4.2.7. *Election Results*

Via two different methods we came to the conclusion that my wife had two factors favoring her election, namely:

(i) her high ballot ranking;
(ii) her gender.

Table 4.6: Independent vote counts regression model predictions of the vote share for the 2019 Holmdel School Board election.

Predicted Vote Shares

Candidate	Gender	Ballot rank	Vote share (%)
Elizabeth A. Urbanski	Female	2	18.37
Lori Ammirati*	Female	3	18.37
Jaimie Hynes	Female	4	16.83
Joseph D. Hammer†	Male	1	15.96
John Martinez*	Male	5	14.43
Michael Sockol*	Male	6	14.43
Write ins			1.25
Bayesian prior			16.67

Notes: Candidates are ordered by predicted vote share.
*Incumbent.
†Prior board President.

Holmdel Township BOE (Vote For 3)		
Districts Reporting **10/10**	**Percentage**	**Votes**
NON - Joseph HAMMER	18.87%	1,760
NON - Elizabeth A. URBANSKI	18.77%	1,751
NON - Lori AMMIRATI	18.25%	1,702
NON - Jaimie HYNES	17.71%	1,652
NON - John MARTINEZ	7.73%	721
NON - Michael SOCKOL	18.39%	1,715
Write-In	0.29%	27
		9,328

Figure 4.7: Screenshot of the official election results that would be certified by the Monmouth County Clerk for the Holmdel Board of Education Election of 2019. "NON" means non-partisan.

So what were the results? We spent the evening at home eagerly refreshing the Board of Election's website. Elizabeth was the leader all though election night, until provisional ballots were added which pushed ex Board President Joe Hammer to narrowly beat her by just nine votes! The three winning candidates were: Elizabeth Urbanski, Joseph Hammer, and Michael Sockol.

The turnout was high, at 9,328 total votes cast versus 7,496 expected. The anomalous result for John Martinez may reflect that, for whatever reason, he did absolutely zero campaigning in what was a hotly contested election, and confirms that money spent on campaigning is worthwhile. The higher turnout can likely be attributed the simultaneous political election for Township Committee, which was extremely controversial and lead to recounts and lawsuits. My wife was sworn onto the Board in January 2020, and has been effective in making changes for the betterment of our town.

4.3. Analysis of Public Health Data

In 2012, I was working as a consultant for an Internet Marketing Agency, as part of their initiative to develop geospatially aware bidding algorithms for Google's search advertising product. We were seeking data on the exercise habits of the public, so that we could gain insights into where golfers lived. After some searching on the internet, I wondered if the US Government might possess data on the recreational habits of Americans, and soon came upon the *Behaviour Risk Factor Surveillance System, BRFSS*, survey, which is run annually by the CDC — the public health agency. This is a survey of around half a million people per annum that has been executed since the 1980s. It contained data from a question about exercise activity: "What type of physical activity or exercise did you spend the most time doing during the past month?" The categorical responses included 76 enumerated values, ranging from *Wii Fit* to *Yard Work*. Two variables were about golfing and auxiliary data, geographically resolved to the county level, allowed me to build the requested map of the geographic distribution of golfers.

Those who know me know that, since my teenage years, I've always been overweight and, like many, not been happy with that but have not seen much change in my situation over the years.[q] As a consumer in the United States, one is barraged by many messages regarding both diet and exercise, and so I leapt at the idea of trying to understand the effect of those variables on body weight quantitatively.

4.3.1. *The Data*

The BRFSS is a huge survey, with over 400,000 respondents per annum, that is conducted all year long. It is properly run, using both stratified sampling (*ex ante* weights) and post survey reweighting (*raking*). It provides geographic resolution to US counties and many variables of interest. The data is readily available from the CDC for download. However, unless one pursues the route of using the SAS statistical system,[r] there are annoying layout changes every year *even for critical variables*. Thus care must be taken when loading the data. It is also a very dense, mainframe-like, record format which requires processing to extract data. My usual practice has become to load it into an SQL database with one text column for an entire record, representing the encoded data for one interview, and then

[q]Apart from my time at Oxford, when I did a lot of walking.
[r]Which is very expensive.

use the feature of computed columns with persisted storage, which make them indexable, to define the feature variables of interest.

4.3.2. *Body Mass Index*

The *Body Mass Index* (BMI) originates in research by Quetelet who pioneered the statistical analysis of the population [29]. Recognizing that human body weight does not scale with the cube of height,[s] he proposed using the ratio of weight to the square of height as a measure of the "thickness" of a person, and this index has been adapted as an indicator of obesity.

4.3.2.1. *"Normal" BMI*

In my analysis of the data, I wanted to examine what recorded factors correlated with differences between observed body weight and expected body weight, recognizing that weight should scale with height. Most public health agencies regard a BMI of around 18 to 24 as indicative of a healthy body composition. This is a statement of a model for (adult) human body weight as a function of height: $E[W_i|H_i] = \beta H_i^2$, with H_i the height of an individual and W_i their weight. β is thus the measure of the ideal, so $\hat{\beta} \approx 21$ according to these authorities.

4.3.2.2. *The Relationship between Human Body Weight and Height*

The validity of the Quetelet scaling relationship can be easily examined in the data. It is quite clear from Figure 4.8 that the quadratic scaling relationship between height and weight is not supported by the data. Although weight is generally increasing with height, for both males and females the conditional mean curve flattens out at the extremities.

I have fitted the data, for males and females separately, to a logistic, linear additive noise, model which seems like a reasonable

[s]This would be the case if our bodies more resembled cubes or spheres.

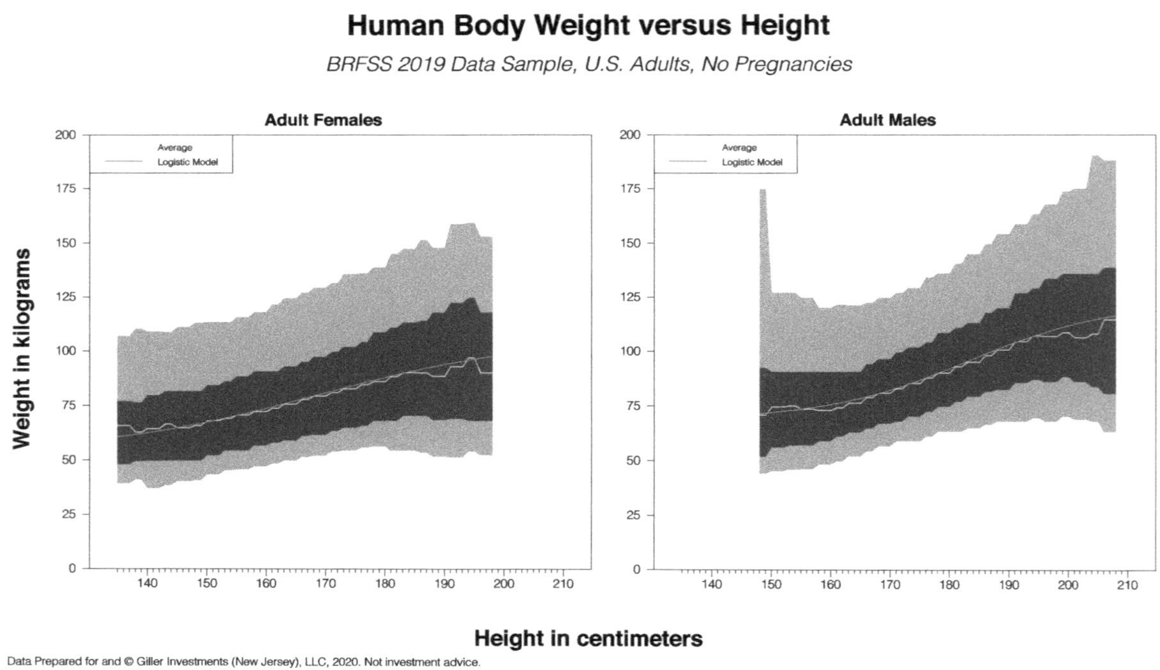

Figure 4.8: The actual relationship between human body weight and height from the BRFSS sample data for 2019. The data is for adults only (ages 18–79) and only heights where a sample of at least 100 interviews were conducted are used. The shaded regions represents 68% and 95% percentiles of the conditional distribution and blue line is the sample mean. The purple line is the best fitting logistic model.

approximating model.[t] The model is

$$W_i = \alpha_{G_i} + \beta_{G_i} \operatorname{logistic}\left(\frac{H_i - \lambda_{G_i}}{\omega_{G_i}}\right) + \varepsilon_i \tag{4.22}$$

$$\varepsilon_i \sim \mathcal{D}(G_i) \tag{4.23}$$

The distribution of the idiosyncratic errors, $\mathcal{D}(G_i)$, has mean zero and may be parameterized by the individual's gender, G_i, but, otherwise, is unspecified at this stage.

The fit was done by nonlinear least squares, which is equivalent to the assumption that $\mathcal{D}$ is the Normal distribution. However, from the figure there is obvious skew in the distributions, so the next step is to investigate what that distribution of residuals looks like (women who identified as pregnant are excluded).

4.3.2.3. *The Extreme Value Distribution (Gumbel Distribution)*

The extreme value distributions arise from the study of the extrema of samples of data, and are familiar from the financial risk management and insurance industries. For example, "what is the distribution of the worse daily loss of a portfolio in a year?"

$$\text{Gumbel}(\mu, \sigma)\colon\ f(x|\mu, \sigma) = \frac{1}{\sigma} e^{\frac{\mu - x}{\sigma} - e^{\frac{\mu - x}{\sigma}}}. \tag{4.24}$$

This parameterization has mean $\mu + \gamma\sigma$, where $\gamma \approx 0.57721$ is the *Euler-Mascheroni constant*,[u] and standard deviation $\pi\sigma/\sqrt{6}$. To the eye, it is a pretty good fit to the data, as seen in Figure 4.9, although it is not *correct* and, due to the very large data samples, fails hypothesis tests. Nevertheless, it is a better candidate than the Normal distribution, so it is worth proceeding with this analysis.

4.3.2.4. *A Model for Human Body Weight*

Incorporating what we've learned from the previous sections, I can now propose a model for human body weight as a function of height

[t] It was chosen by inspection.

[u] Which is a fundamental number that arises in Number Theory, similar to π and e.

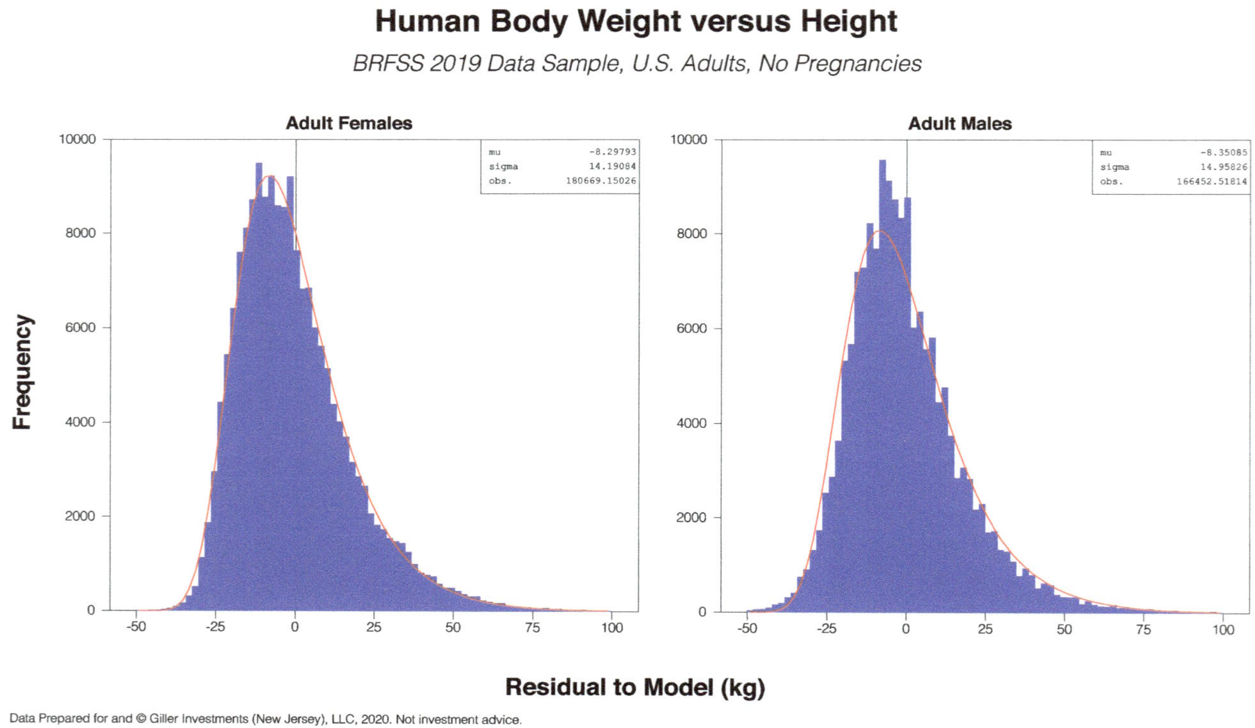

Figure 4.9: Distribution of the residuals to a fitted logistic model for human body weight as a function of height for the BRFSS sample data for 2019. The data is for adults only (ages 18–79). The blue bars are a histogram of the residuals and the red line is the best fitting extreme value distribution model.

that will be the kernel from which further models may be developed.

$$\mu_i = \alpha_{G_i} + \beta_{G_i} \operatorname{logistic}\left(\frac{H_i - \lambda_{G_i}}{\omega_{G_i}}\right) - \gamma\sigma_{G_i} \tag{4.25}$$

$$W_i \sim \operatorname{Gumbel}(\mu_i, \sigma_{G_i}) \tag{4.26}$$

4.3.2.5. *Estimated Parameters*

The parameters in Equation (4.25) may be estimated together, although it is really two separable systems due to the structure of the model. The results are shown in Table 4.7. Assuming the distributional assumption is correct, the estimated coefficients are inconsistent between genders apart from the parameters $\{\hat{\omega}_{G_i}\}$, which seem to agree. This parameter determines the width of the inflection region in the logistic function.

Specifically, but not surprisingly, females have a lower average weight, $\hat{\alpha}$, a smaller weight range, $\hat{\beta}$, and the transition between the regions with positive curvature and negative curvature occurs at a smaller height, $\hat{\lambda}$. The width of the transition, $\hat{\omega}$, is apparently similar. Females have slightly less dispersion, $\hat{\sigma}$, in their weight given their height.

Table 4.7: Estimated parameters and consistency test for logistic model to relationship between human body weight and height.

Fit of logistic model to BRFSS 2019 data

	Adult males		Adult females		Neutrality	
Coefficient	Parameter	Std. error	Parameter	Std. error	χ^2_2	p-value
α	70.2658	1.0987	62.7936	0.5588	36.75	0.1×10^{-7}
β	36.4658	2.1340	26.0657	0.9868	19.57	0.5×10^{-4}
λ	1.7475	0.0040	1.6243	0.0042	449.57	Negligible
ω	0.1020	0.0074	0.1022	0.0046	0.00	0.9999
σ	15.3595	0.0492	14.5175	0.0288	218.31	Negligible

Note: Data is from the BRFSS 2019 survey for adult respondents.

4.3.2.6. *Correcting for the Dependence of Weight on Age*

One key demographic variable that has not been used to explain weight is age. Given that we are restricting our analysis to adults, we should see just the tail end of the pubescent growth spurt in the younger sample and the known decline of stature with age in the older sample. Thus, we might expect to see some negative curvature in the distribution of residuals when conditioned on survey respondent age. This is relatively easy to examine, and the results are shown in Figure 4.10.

The data do show a soft curvature peaking, in middle ages, and so I decided to augment the structure of Equation (4.25) with additional terms to represent this. The model then becomes

$$\mu_i = \alpha_{G_i} + \beta_{G_i} \operatorname{logistic}\left(\frac{H_i - \lambda_{G_i}}{\omega_{G_i}}\right) - \gamma\sigma_{G_i} + a_{G_i}A_i^2 + b_{G_i}A_i \tag{4.27}$$

$$W_i \sim \operatorname{Gumbel}(\mu_i, \sigma_{G_i}), \tag{4.28}$$

where A_i is the respondent's reported age. As before, we structure the model to permit gender differences in the parameters. There is no constant in the quadratic part of the model because the values $\{\alpha_{G_i}\}$ already play this role.

The estimates for the adjusted model are shown in Table 4.8. A notable change to the parameters is that the values of $\hat{\alpha}_{G_i}$ have changed and are no longer inconsistent by gender. Examination of the empirical distribution functions of the residuals shows little disagreement between the data and the model, either in the tails or core of the distributions. The distributions for females passes the Kolmogorov–Smirnov Test, but that for males doesn't. However, as the errors are nowhere near as gross as those discussed in Chapter 2, and as I don't have an alternative to propose, I feel it is worthwhile to continue with the present structure.

In summary, we can fit a model to explain the variation of human body weight with height. That model:

(1) is *not* the Body Mass Index;
(2) does not involve Normally distributed errors.

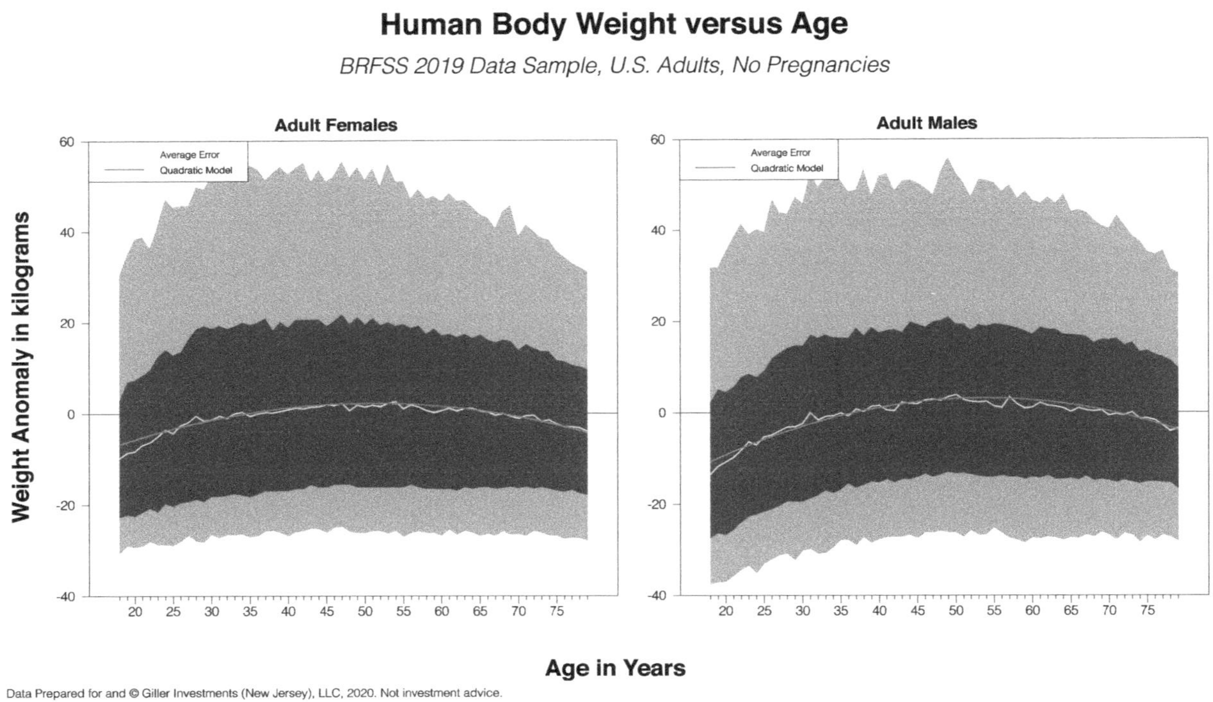

Figure 4.10: Moments of the conditional distributions of the residuals to the model for human body weight versus age. The data is for adults only (ages 18 to 79) and a sample of at least 100 interviews were conducted is required. The shaded regions represents 68% and 95% percentiles of the conditional distribution and blue line is the sample mean. The purple line is the best fitting quadratic model.

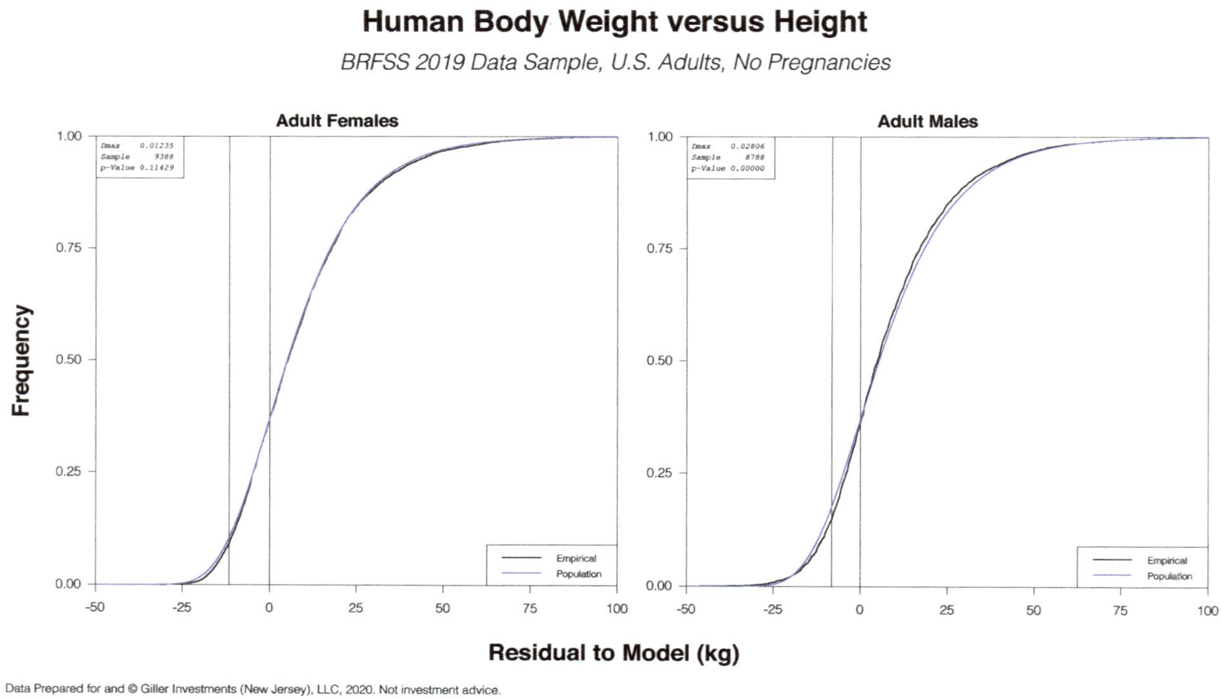

Figure 4.11: Empirical distribution functions for a fitted logistic model for human body weight as a function of height for the BRFSS sample data for 2019. The data is for adults only (ages 18–80). The black line is the observed empirical distribution function and the blue line the expected cumulative distribution function for a Gumbel distribution. Charts are made from a random subsample of 10,000 observed values.

Table 4.8: Estimated parameters and consistency test for logistic model to relationship between human body weight and height and age.

Fit of logistic model to BRFSS 2019 data

	Adult males		Adult females		Neutrality	
Coefficient	Parameter	Std. error	Parameter	Std. error	χ^2_2	p-value
α	46.7523	1.0659	48.4619	0.7655	1.70	0.4280
β	37.4307	1.8992	27.9036	1.2483	17.57	0.0002
λ	1.7565	0.0048	1.6378	0.0052	280.34	Negligible
ω	0.0996	0.0062	0.1054	0.0054	0.50	0.7781
a	−0.0085	0.0002	−0.0052	0.0001	296.86	Negligible
b	0.9484	0.0150	0.5598	0.0122	403.01	Negligible
σ	14.7689	0.0604	14.0865	0.0308	101.33	Negligible

Note: Data is from the BRFSS 2019 survey for adult respondents.

4.3.3. *Testing Dietary and Activity Variables*

My interest in body weight is to gain insight into the often repeated tropes regarding diet and exercise. I would like to know if they work! Some authors, such as Gary Taubes[v] [129] have suggested that the field of nutrition is full of counterintuitive results. For example, that exercise, when assessed across a population, does not cause weight loss. The reason proposed is that exercise causes increased energy consumption by the body and that causes increased calorific intake by the body — put simply, exercise makes you hungry. I'll confess, I like food and I dislike exercise, and you can tell from the work I've written about here that I like to engage in analysis that contrasts with conventional wisdom.

4.3.3.1. *Analytical Approach*

Since the BRFSS is not a *longitudinal survey*, meaning one that tracks the same people through time, it cannot address issues of causality, either indirectly through Granger's time-series analysis or directly via randomized controlled trials. However, we can identify

[v]Who happens to be the husband of one of my wife's friends.

significant correlation which is either consistent, or inconsistent, with theoretical priors.

In the rest of this section, I will introduce variables for dietary and exercise habits into our logistic-quadratic model for bodyweight as a function of height and age. I use this method as it provides not only a model for the expected bodyweight but also a realistic description of the distribution of residuals which allows the use of significance tests derived from maximum likelihood estimation without appeals to Normal distributions that are not present in the data.

4.3.3.2. *Alcohol Consumption*

Beer contains a lot of calories. I spent some of my childhood on a *Council Estate* in Coventry,[w] and my friends' fathers were obese men who worked in car factories and drank beer in quantity at the end of their work days and work weeks.

The BRFSS includes two variables related to alcohol consumption:

(1) `ALCDAY5` asks how many days-per-week, or days-per-month, the respondent has consumed at least one alcoholic drink;
(2) `AVEDRNK2` asks how many "standard measure" drinks are consumed on average on each drinking day.

The average number of drinks per day is then the product of these two variables and, remarkably, the survey is able to code answers up to *seventy-six drinks per day* and responses reach up to that number too! This is roughly equivalent to having a drink every twelve minutes, all day long. This data is shown in Figure 4.12, which is a histogram which uses the raking weights to sum to the total population size (rather than the sample size). The data roughly follows the shape of a Gamma distribution, but is very irregular due to the quantized nature of the survey responses.

In the model of Equation (4.27), the conditional mean is modified to

$$\mu_i = \alpha_{G_i} + \delta_{G_i} D_i + LQ, \tag{4.29}$$

[w]The US name for this is a *Housing Project*.

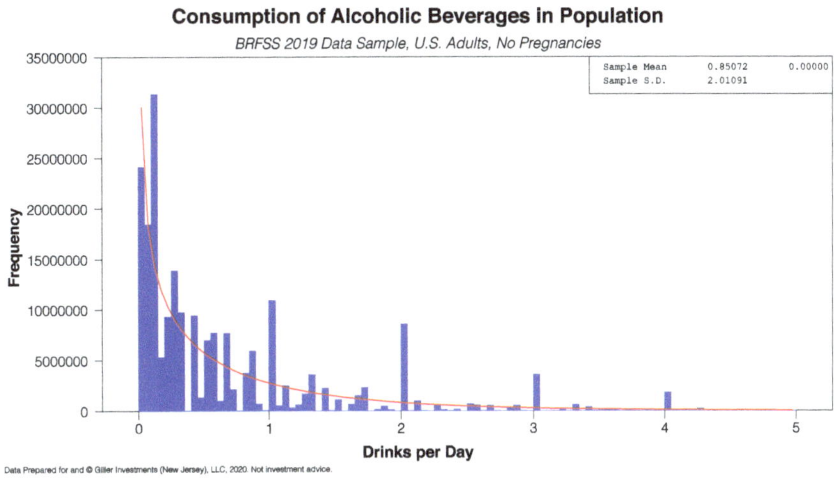

Figure 4.12: Distribution of consumption of alcoholic drinks per day for the BRFSS sample data for 2019. The data is for adults only (Ages 18–80). The blue bars are a histogram, weighted to sum to the proportion within the total population, and the red line is the best fitting Gamma distribution.

where D_i is the reported number of drinks per day, with analysis restricted to exclude interviews where this datum was missing, and LQ representing the rest of the logistic-quadratic model.

The estimated parameters, in units of kilograms per daily drink, are $\hat{\delta}_1 = -0.272 \pm 0.025$, for males, and $\hat{\delta}_0 = -0.638 \pm 0.057$, for females, and both terms are highly significant with negligible p values. To test whether the coefficients should be different we can use the Wald Test to estimate whether $\hat{\delta}_1 - \hat{\delta}_0$ is significantly different from zero. The result is a χ^2_1 of 33.5, so difference between the estimated coefficients is likely real.

The message of the data is that people who drink more weigh less than expected, and this is over twice as strong for women as men. Due to the inability to investigate causality, however, the message is most definitely not that if you want to lose weight you should become a drunk! Why would alcohol consumption correlate with negative body weight anomaly? There is, in fact, a possible physical mechanism in that alcohol has a diuretic effect resulting drinkers perhaps having a systematically less hydrated body.

4.3.3.3. *Exercise*

Not unsurprisingly, the BRFSS has long asked about exercise habits. The variable with the most consistent history of being asked seems to be `EXERANY2`, which asks whether the respondent has done any exercise not part of their work over the last month. As is normal in survey research, encoding is "1" for yes and "2" for two, with the added values "7" for "don't know/not sure" and "9" for "refused." In 2019, around 1% of respondents said that they didn't know or were unsure but only 525 are included when we require that the height, weight and age also be reported.

Equation (4.27) is again modified to

$$\mu_i = \alpha_{G_i} + \delta_{G_i} D_i + \xi_{G_i} X_i + LQ \tag{4.30}$$

with X_i representing $I[\texttt{EXERANY2}_i = 1] + 0.05I[\texttt{EXERANY2}_i = 7]$. Thus ξ gives the impact of exercise on body weight anomaly and I, arbitrarily, gave the response "maybe" a 5% chance of meaning "yes."

Again we see a strong difference between the results for men and women, with $\hat{\xi}_1 = -0.494 \pm 0.140$ and $\hat{\xi}_0 = -3.042 \pm 0.161$ in units of kilograms. The coefficients themselves, and the differences between them, are all significant. Women who exercise are, on average, over six pounds lighter than those that don't.

4.3.3.4. *French Fries*

In 2017 and 2019, the BRFSS survey has included the question:

> "How often did you eat any kind of fried potatoes, including french fries, home fries, or hash browns?"

with the results encoded into the variable `FRENCHF1` in the manner of `ALCDAY5`.

As is true for many Britons, I grew up in a community with a *chip shop*, and grew up eating them around once per week. Sometimes, when I had to buy my own lunch because it was not provided in school for some reason, I would walk to the chip shop and get a scallop[x] and chips, a 100% fried potato meal. It was delicious!

[x]In the West Midlands, a slice of potato, covered in fish'n'chip batter and deep fried.

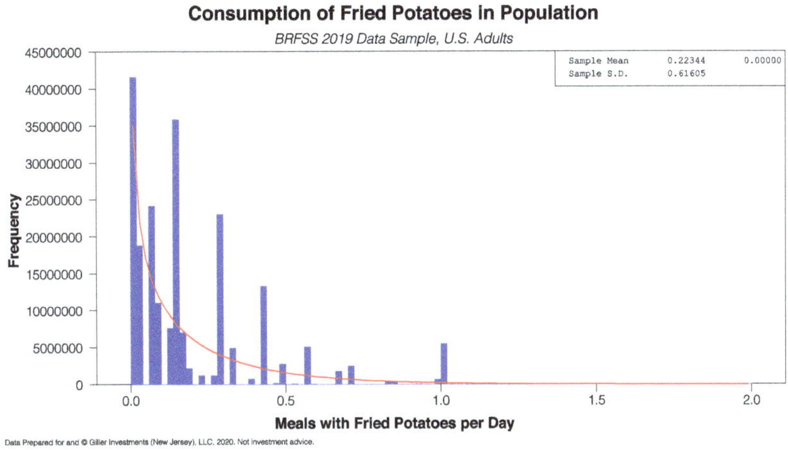

Figure 4.13: Distribution of consumption of meals including fried potatoes per day for the BRFSS sample data for 2019. The data is for adults only (ages 18–80). The blue bars are a histogram, weighted to sum to the proportion within the total population, and the red line is the best fitting Gamma distribution.

Analysis proceeds as before. In the model of Equation (4.25), the conditional mean is modified to

$$\mu_i = \alpha_{G_i} + \delta_{G_i} D_i + \xi_{G_i} X_i + \phi_{G_i} F_i + LQ, \tag{4.31}$$

where F_i is the reported number of fried potato meals per day and the data are restricted to exclude interviews where this datum was missing.

The estimated parameters, in units of kilograms per meal, are $\hat{\phi}_1 = 0.074 \pm 0.057$, for males, with p value 0.19 and $\hat{\phi}_0 = 0.392 \pm 0.082$, for females, with p value 1.6×10^{-6}. The coefficient for males is not significantly different from zero, but that for females is highly significant, and they are not consistent with each other. These results suggest women gain approaching an extra pound per fried potato meal per day, relative to those that don't eat any.

4.3.3.5. *What Should My Weight Be?*

The above suggests that diet and exercise do affect body weight, and in exactly the way expected, but much more strongly for women than for men. The alcohol result may be counterintuitive, but clearing up this kind of thing is exactly why randomized controlled trials exist.

I know I am overweight, but how significant is that? At the time of writing, my vital statistics are as follows:

(i) my weight is 227 lbs., or 103 kg;
(ii) my height is 5′10″ or 1.79 m;
(iii) I am 51 years old;
(iv) I drink an average of two alcoholic drinks a day;
(v) I do exercise regularly every month.
(vi) I eat fried potatoes about twice a week;

So what should my weight be? Plugging this data into the model, I get:

(i) baseline expected weight of 74.0 kg, or 163.3 lbs;
(ii) a contribution from drinking of −0.6 kg, or −1.3 lbs;
(iii) a contribution from exercise of −0.6 kg, or −1.3 lbs;
(iv) a contribution from eating fried potatoes of 0.02 kg, or 0.05 lbs;
(v) giving a final expected weight of 72.9 ± 14.0 kg, or 160.7 ± 30.9 lbs.

Based on these figures, I am 30 kg, or 66.4 lbs, overweight, and these numbers place me in the upper 11% of the population. My personal Z score is $+2.1\sigma_1$, so I am in the *fatter tail* of the distribution. Whether the mean represents an "ideal" weight cannot be decided from this analysis, but it is certainly true that I am above average even in America.

4.3.4. *Survey Design and Causality*

There are many fascinating variables in the BRFSS survey, but its utility as anything other than a measurement device is limited by the lack of structure to support causal inference. This is a very expensive public health exercise. The 450,000 odd phone interviews may cost around $45 each to complete,[y] which gives an interviewing budget alone of some $20 million. The likely total costs could be several times that amount, representing a massive public investment in measuring the health of Americans, yet no attempt is made to follow up with interviewees in later years. Due to the size of the US

[y]Based on typical costs in the consumer survey industry.

population, the chances of re-encountering a subject in later years is vanishingly small, yet the cost of following up with a small subset of respondents *just one year later* is relatively small. If as few as 10,000 were called back, with 50% compliance,[z] that would already represent an extremely large sample compared to some contemporary medical research. Such a follow up strategy would allow some knowledge of causality to be extracted from this vitally useful information. I think it is a mistake to assume that such surveys should be either 100% longitudinal or not at all, with no intermediate design.

As analysis based on panel regression, following individuals through time, or randomized controlled trials are unavailable the only solution is time-series analysis of the aggregate properties of the distributions of all survey respondents. It was Clive Granger's genius[aa] to realize that time-series provide a kind of *natural experiment* which can be used to substitute for RCT's in some circumstances.

4.3.5. *Variation of Parameter Estimates with Survey Year*

4.3.5.1. *Demographic Parameters*

Figure 4.14 shows the estimated parameters for the logistic-quadratic model of Equation (4.27) for survey years[bb] 2004 to 2019. The regressions are run independently and there is no way for the estimates in a given year to influence those in another year unless the model is measuring a genuinely true property of the data. In the figure we see that some of the parameters show strong trends and others seem to be consistent with a constant.

For the logistic part of the model, which describes the dependence of expected weight on height, the parameter that determines the mean weight for each gender, $\hat{\alpha}_{it}$, starts far apart but the two estimates converge post 2015. The scale of the variation from those with below average height to those with above average height, $\hat{\beta}_{it}$ seems

[z] After all, these people have already shown their willingness to undergo a long public health interview.
[aa] For which he won the Nobel Prize.
[bb] Frequently, a small number of interviews are performed in the calendar year following the survey year.

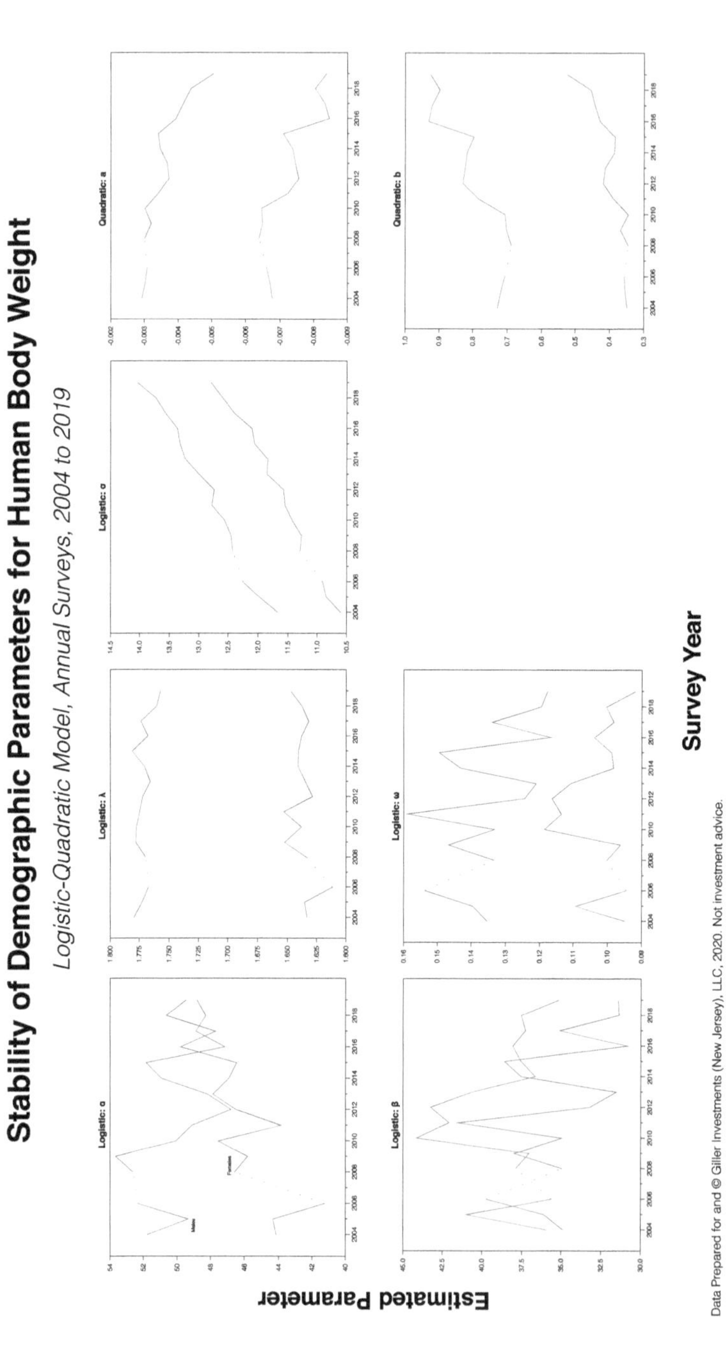

Figure 4.14: Time-series of parameter estimates for a logistic-quadratic model of human body weight as a function of height and age. These are the *demographic* parameters, meaning those that describe the relationship of weight to gender, age, and height.

generally stable as is the parameter that determines the location of the transition, $\hat{\lambda}_{it}$. We see from the charts that the measured statistically insignificant difference between the parameters that determine the width of the transition, $\hat{\omega}_{it}$, in the 2019 sample doesn't hold up when all of the data are examined, and that the parameter determining the scale of the dispersion in weights, $\hat{\sigma}_{it}$, shows a strong up trend. The quadratic terms, that describes the dependence of expected height anomaly on age, both show trends throughout the data period.

In all, I find these results reassuring that the structures discovered aren't *idiosyncratic* to 2019. Other demographic changes have occurred to the population, such as an increase in the average age of respondents, which will be discussed in the next section.

4.3.5.2. *Behavioural Parameters*

Perhaps more important to examine than the demographic parameters, which to an extent merely "are what they are," are the *behavioral* parameters that relate body weight anomaly to exercise and diet. Unfortunately, the variable `FRENCHF1` only exists in the 2017 and 2019 survey years, and the CDC do not recommend comparing the food consumption related variables in prior years to those post 2016. Thus we are restricted to looking at the terms in exercise and drinking, both of which are included in all of the surveys from 2004 to 2019. These data are shown in Figure 4.15.

From the charts we see that the effect of drinking on body weight anomaly is fairly stable which, to me, enhances its believably. For exercise, the message is different. There appears to be a trend in the size of the effect for both men and women, which is moderated post 2010 for men. Although the demographic parameters are describing the general *structure* of the distribution of human body weight, these parameters describe the *effect* of a given behavior. Is it possible that the effect of exercise on the human body would change over the timescale of a few years? Yes, it is, but my prior is that such changes take place over larger periods. Furthermore the question asked about exercise has stayed exactly the same for the entire period studied.[cc]

[cc]The variable name, `EXERANY2`, includes the number 2 to indicate that it is the second version of the question, but that number stays the same throughout the whole period.

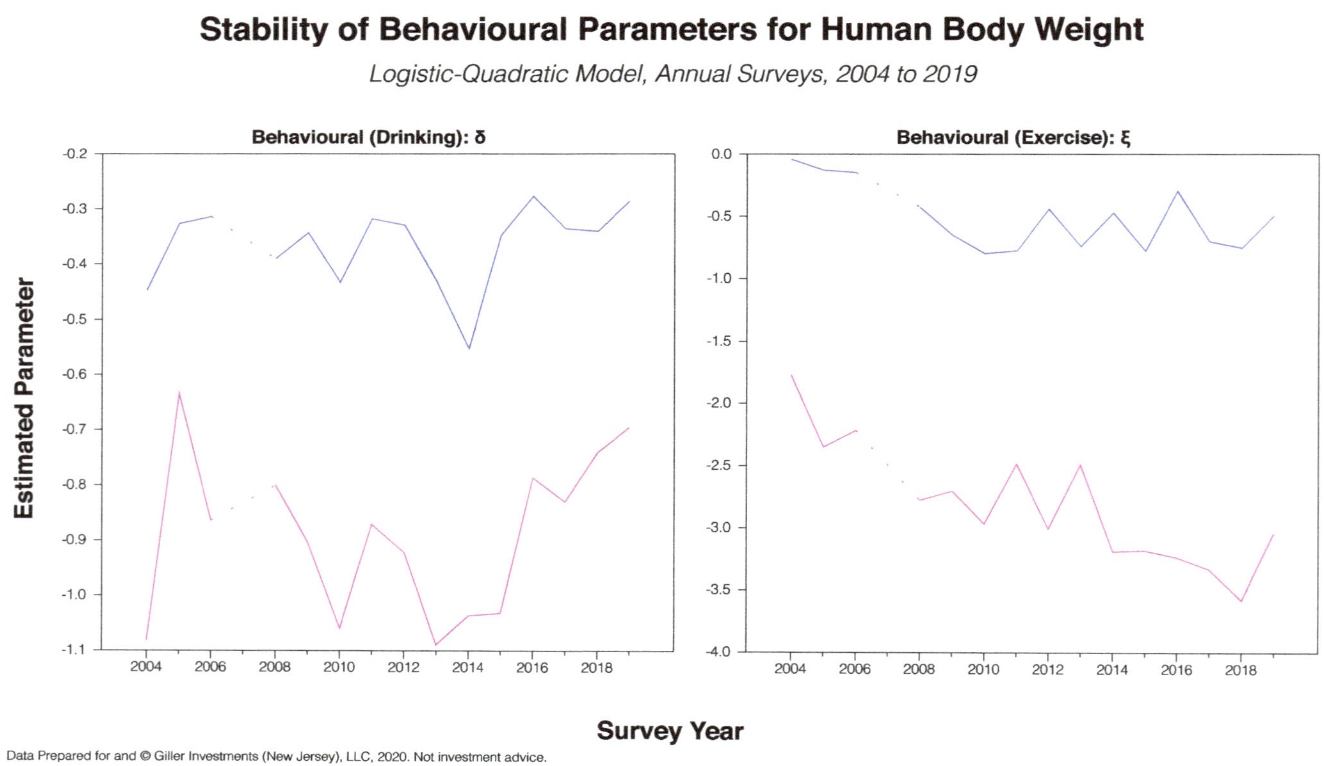

Figure 4.15: Time-series of parameter estimates for linear adjustments to the logistic-quadratic model for human body weight based on exercise and drinking habits.

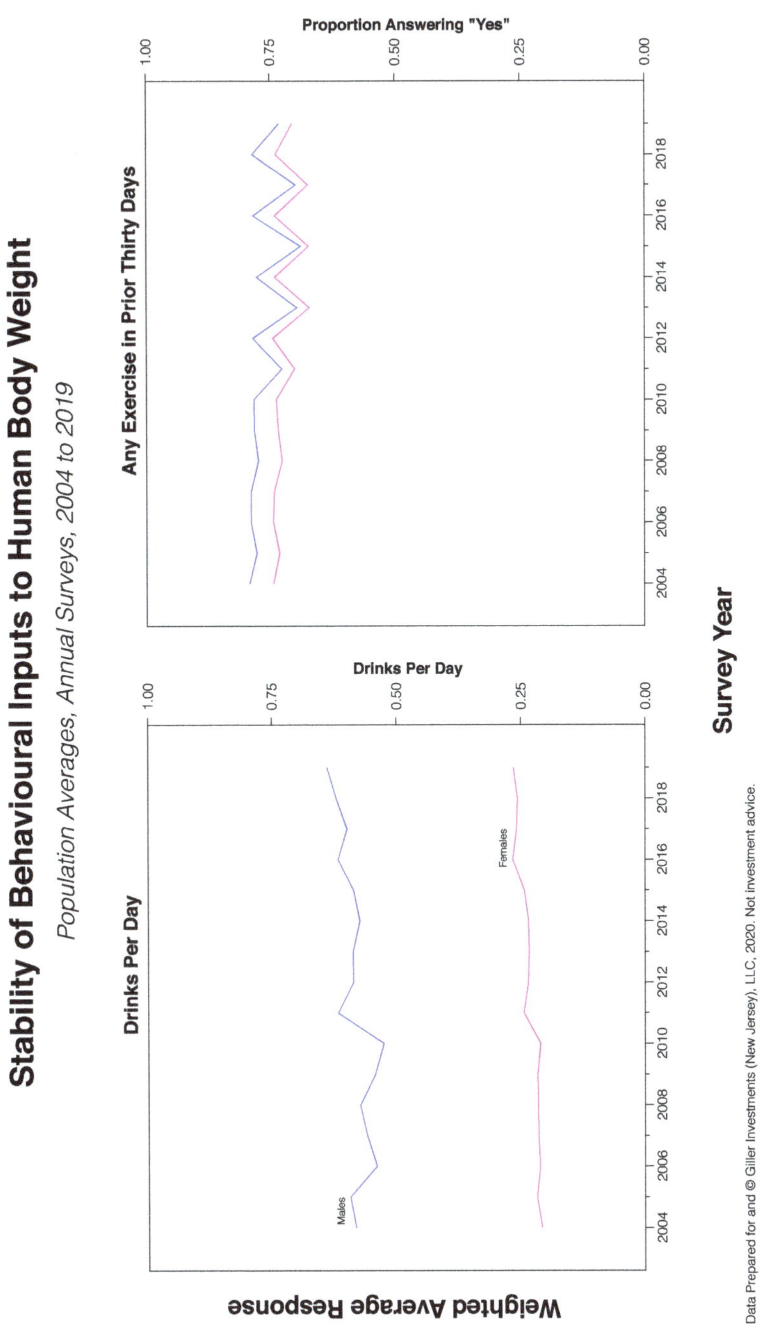

Figure 4.16: Time-series of weighted averages of inputs to model for human body weight. Data are averages weighted by raking weights to align results with the population rather than the sample.

This data demonstrates clearly that *some exercise* leads to lower body weight anomaly but, from a physical point of view it seems likely that the *amount* of exercise should determine the size of the effect. If this is the real phenomenon then, clearly, there must be a positive correlation between the response of `EXERANY2` and the unknown true factor that measures the quantity of exercise performed over a standard period. In such a scenario, an increase in the number of people answering "yes" and a concurrent increase in the amount of exercise done by those people would lead to the effect observed.

Even more simply, though, if the true phenomenon is a response to quantity of exercise done regularly, *and* the probability of answering "yes" to a question stated in terms of exercise done in the last month is clearly an increasing function of the same metric, then that would also explain the phenomenon as the covariance is implicit in the answers. Obviously this question needs to be structured to permit more quantitative responses.

4.3.6. *Variation of Population Aggregates with Survey Year*

Given the observations above, it's interesting to look at the behaviour of the *inputs* to the model as well as the coefficients. Although not perfectly flat, these show remarkably stable responses. The number of drinks per day seems to have increased a little over the past 15 years, with a disruption around 2011.

The proportion of the population responding "yes" to the question of `EXERANY2` appears to be much flatter, although some oscillation shows up after 2011. This result refutes the suggestion that more people are exercising than before, so the strengthening coefficients must imply that those that exercise are doing more exercise than before thus leading to a larger *negative* body weight anomaly for those who do *any* exercise in the past thirty days.

4.3.7. *What I Learned from this Analysis*

I originally began to work with the BRFSS survey data in 2011, to support my work in the internet marketing industry. As I got the hang of it, I feel that I learned a lot about population demographics and how to process survey data. These skills would turn out to be very valuable when I was asked to create a unit based on Primary Research for Deutsche Bank, as it meant that I could talk intelligently to the survey professionals who worked for me at that time. In general terms, I learned some good disciplines around how to load and process US Government provided data, which is often delivered in dense text files encoded very much as the BRFSS data is. This is a very useful skill as this data is seldom distributed in the formats that entry level data scientists would prefer. There are no `JSON` documents, or "pickle" files, or even `.CSV`s. The files are dense and the ETL.[dd] process is burdensome.

Regarding the data itself, I confirmed that it's likely true that exercise is a contributor to decreased body weight. That isn't the answer I wanted because, as I pointed out, I don't particularly like exercise, but it is one that caused me to change my behaviour. On that basis alone, it was worthwhile doing this work.

4.4. Statistical Analysis of Language

The work I featured on using Twitter in Chapter 3 relied on my understanding of *Statistical Natural Language Processing*. I do not claim to be an expert in this field, but my skills are non-zero, and in the past I've used NLP in other venues, such as on predicting earnings surprise based on conference call transcripts.

One problem with using language counts in predictive analysis is that there are a lot more words in the language than are used in any given document. Thus, any regression, or machine learning task, that attempts to use frequency counts[ee] of words, or compound phrases, as independent variables likely has many more variables present than data examples, and would be insoluble without some form of *regularization* scheme to reduce this count. Such a procedure is sometimes known as *dimensional reduction*.

4.4.1. *Zipf's Law and Random Composition*

Statistically, a sentence in a language is representable as a sequence of tokens which contain both unconditional and conditional frequency

[dd] *Extract-transform-load.*

[ee] Or some function of them. Using raw counts is called "bag of words" analysis.

distributions. Many are aware of the strategies used to break codes based on the observed frequencies of either letters or words, which are characteristic of a particular language.

The unconditional distribution of words in the English language was discovered to possess a surprising regularity now known as Zipf's Law [114]. An observed power law exists in the relationship between the frequency of a word's use and its rank based on frequency: $f_r \propto r^{-\alpha}$ for $r \in [1, 2, 3, \ldots]$ and some positive α. Empirically $\hat{\alpha}$ was measured to be a little larger than unity. This result dates from the 1930s and was done with punched card sorting machines.

Benoit Mandelbrot, the inventor of *fractals*, spent a lot of time studying the frequency distributions found in Nature,[ff] and particularly the suprising regularity with which we find power laws such as Zipf's Law. With better processing tools,[gg] he extended Zipf's Law to a more accurate version [90].

$$f_r = \frac{C}{(r+B)^\alpha}. \tag{4.32}$$

Much later, Wentian Li discovered [87] that a typography composed of M symbols and a space character, when composed randomly into *pseudowords*, exhibited the Zipf–Mandelbrot rule with a index of $\alpha = \ln(M+1)/\ln M \approx 1.01158$ for $M = 26$, very close to the estimate.

4.4.2. *Empirical Distributions of Words in English Language Corpora*

My approach to analysis has not changed much since I started out at Oxford. When entering a new field, I try to find a text-book that "works for me," and then reproduce the results it describes for myself. Not by literally copying code, as *I* learn nothing from cut-and-paste operations, but by acquiring the data and attempting, where possible, to repeat the analysis myself. Thus, when I learned about Zipf's Law, I wanted to reproduce the work myself.

[ff] I wholeheartedly recommend reading his book *Fractals and Scaling in Finance* [91].

[gg] He was working at the IBM research laboratories.

Furthermore, we know that Li's analysis, suggesting that Zipf's Law was a *meaningless* aspect of the existence of sentences and words, is not entirely correct. Simulation of Li's pseudowords often generates sequences of symbols *much longer* than the longest words found in the English language.[hh] If the probability of getting a space during word composition is $p = 1/27$ then word lengths, L, should follow a Geometric distribution and so

$$\Pr(L \geq 29) = \sum_{l=29}^{\infty} p(1-p)^l \approx 0.335. \tag{4.33}$$

Yet no such words exist.

4.4.2.1. *The Natural Language Toolkit (NLTK)*

Most of my work on language has been via the NLTK, developed as a teaching tool and implemented in the Python computer language [7]. As NLP has become more important in the internet economy faster and more efficient tools have been developed, but it remains a minority interest for me so I stick to this package when I am doing *hands on* analytics. For production systems, such as those used in the Twitter analysis earlier, I'm using API's provided by Amazon and Google.

4.4.2.2. *The Corpora*

A collection of documents is called a Corpus, and a collection of collections are corpora. NLTK comes with many public domain corpora built in. They are:

(i) *The Brown Corpus*: A collection of English language writing put together by the titular institution. In it I found a total of 1,024,054 words (tokens) in the Brown Corpus, of which 43,732 are distinct (types).
(ii) *The Reuters Corpus*: A collection of articles from the Reuters news service. I find a total of 1,476,860 words in the Reuters

[hh] *Antidisestablishmentarianism* (28 letters) and *floccinaucinihilipilification* (29 letters) are middle-school favorites for the longest words in English.

Corpus, of which 30,952 are distinct. Thus we see that Reuters is less *lexically diverse* than Brown.

(iii) *Genesis*: A translation of the book of Genesis included with NLTK, in which there are a total of 278,448 words, and 22,036 are distinct.

(iv) *The State of the Union*: A Corpus consisting of transcriptions of the *State of the Union* addresses, delivered by American Presidents each year. This contains 355,357 words, of which 12,675 are distinct.

(v) *Movie Reviews*: A set of online movie reviews. This has a total of 1,337,066 words of which 39,708 are distinct.

Full details of this data are in the *NLTK Book*.

4.4.2.3. *An Extended Zipf–Mandelbrot Law*

Visual inspection of the frequency-rank plots for the various corpora suggest a modified relationship might apply. I extend the Zipf–Mandelbrot Law as

$$\ln f(r) = \beta - \alpha \ln\left(1 + \gamma_1 r + \frac{1}{2!}\gamma_2 r^2 + \cdots\right). \tag{4.34}$$

If $\gamma_2 = 0$ then the Zipf–Mandelbrot Law is recovered, so this may be used as a hypothesis test to determine whether the structure in the frequency-rank plot arises from pseudoword composition, in the manner suggested by Li, or whether the generative process differs from that.

4.4.2.4. *Frequency Analysis*

For all corpora considered we fit a pure power law, the original Zipf's Law form; a linear correction to the pure power law, the Zipf–Mandelbrot Law; and, a quadratic extension to the pure power law, the lowest rank nonlinear model formed from Equation (4.34). We fit using weighted nonlinear least squares, where the weights are the frequency counts themselves. That is assuming that the raw counts are Poissonian in nature and thus the variance of the frequency count is the frequency count itself. On the basis of the variance assumption, the AIC(c) may be computed from the weighted least-squares regressions in the large sample approximation

$$\lim_{\lambda \to \infty} \text{Poisson}(\lambda) = \text{Normal}(\lambda, \lambda). \tag{4.35}$$

4.4.2.5. *Empirical Results*

The frequency-rank plot for the Brown Corpus, with fitted lines according to Zipf's Law, the Zipf–Mandelbrot Law, and the extension of Equation (4.34) is shown in Figure 4.17. It can clearly be seen that Zipf is good, Zipf–Mandelbrot is better, but the quadratic extension is excellent. This is also true for the other corpora.

Full results are given in Table 4.9. The customary nomenclature of "types," meaning distinct words, and "tokens," meaning all words are used, with T representing the number of types and N the number of words.

4.4.2.6. *Conclusions from Frequency Analysis*

The fit of frequency-rank distributions to power laws is well known. This analysis demonstrates that a novel polynomial extension to the Zipf–Mandelbrot form leads to a much better approximating distribution than other, simpler forms. The corpora on which this has been tried are disparate, both in antiquity (and therefore, presumably, the *style* of the written language) and also in length, but the conclusion has been the same. On a rigorous information-theory based metric the quadratic fits we have made are superior to the other forms. To the eye, their description of the data is clearly better.

4.4.3. *Simulation of the Frequency-Rank Distribution for Naive Pseudowords Generated from the Brown Corpus*

To help understand the sampling distribution of the estimators $\hat{\gamma}_2$ under the naive Li hypothesis, we can generate pseudowords by random draws from the symbol alphabet of a Corpus and produce a frequency-rank analysis for that data. We use the Brown Corpus as it is extensively researched. This procedure is well known and its output are pseudowords that are *not at all like* real words — but

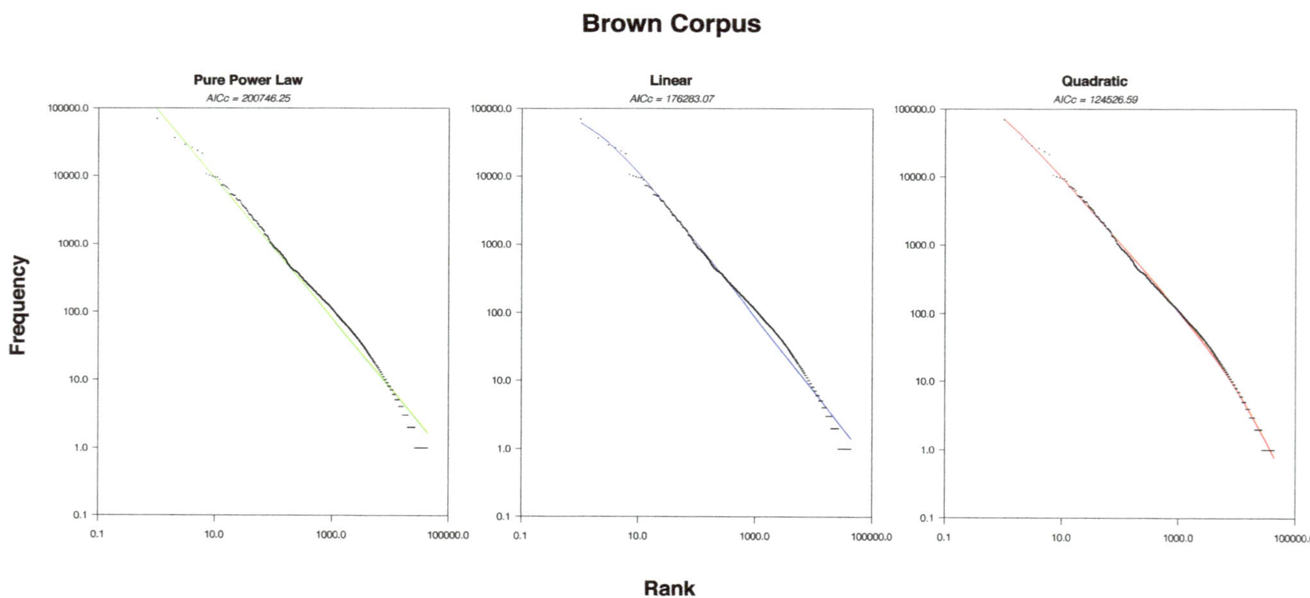

Figure 4.17: Frequency-rank analysis for the Brown Corpus illustrating the best fitting models. A pure power law (Zipf's Law); a linear modification to the power law (the Zipf–Mandelbrot Law); and, a quadratic modification to the power law are considered. The quadratic model is the best approximating model based upon the Akaike Information Criterion (corrected).

Table 4.9: Basic statistics and regression results for the corpora analyzed.

Corpus	Tokens	Types	*TTR*%	*R*	β	α	γ_1	γ_2
Genesis	278 448	22 036	7.9	42	8.6	1.008	0.12	0.00003
State of the Union	355 357	12 675	3.6	21	10.8	0.947	1.25	0.00108
Brown	1 024 054	43 732	4.3	43	12.5	0.969	3.09	0.00043
Movie reviews	1 337 066	39 708	3.0	34	11.8	1.006	0.79	0.00014
Reuters	1 476 860	30 952	2.1	26	11.5	0.910	0.72	0.00073

Note: The data are ranked in order of increasing token count. *TTR* refers to the "types to tokens" ratio, or T/N, and R to Guiraud's lexical diversity index, $T/\sqrt{N}$.

that is not our object (to create *convincing pseudowords* we would require a much more sophisticated generation procedure).

4.4.3.1. *Alphabet Statistics*

The discovered alphabet frequencies are given in Table 4.10. This table was generated from the Brown Corpus by replacing all non-alphanumeric characters with spaces and removing any duplicated spaces. The symbol frequencies within the generated token stream are then counted. We tabulate the letters in three classes: when they are the *first* letter of a word; when they are within the *rest* of the word; and also their frequency within the *entire* body of the corpus. It is well known that these frequencies differ.[ii] It is readily apparent that the symbol frequencies *in no way* resemble the equiprobable assumption of the Li hypothesis.

4.4.3.2. *Pseudoword Generation*

Pseudoword generation is straightforward. Characters are picked from Table 4.10 according to the frequencies observed within the Corpus. If the picked character is the delimiter, represented by $\cdot$ in the table, a new word is started; otherwise, the character is added to the end of the current word. The word is completed when the next delimiter is generated.

[ii] Our table is ranked by first letter frequency, which is why it doesn't spell out `etaoin shrdlu` [123], or anything similar to that.

Table 4.10: Symbol statistics for the alphabet discovered in the Brown Corpus after processing.

Rank	Symbol	First	Entire	Rest	Rank	Symbol	First	Entire	Rest
1	t	161 185	438 960	277 775	21	v	6 644	47 261	40 617
2	a	117 546	382 803	265 257	22	j	5 560	7 756	2 196
3	o	72 374	360 287	287 913	23	k	5 184	31 179	25 995
4	s	70 866	310 753	239 887	24	1	4 129	5 182	1 053
5	i	68 747	345 755	277 008	25	q	2 013	5 103	3 090
6	w	61 873	89 140	27 267	26	2	1 701	2 621	920
7	h	55 036	257 234	202 198	27	3	1 059	1 732	673
8	c	49 495	147 210	97 715	28	0	653	4 458	3 805
9	b	46 900	72 804	25 904	29	4	652	1 452	800
10	f	41 706	110 672	68 966	30	5	632	2 144	1 512
11	m	40 476	120 641	80 165	31	$	579	579	0
12	p	40 124	95 932	55 808	32	6	414	1 451	1 037
13	d	30 994	188 295	157 301	33	7	396	1 065	669
14	r	26 710	291 000	264 290	34	8	324	1 265	941
15	e	24 965	593 146	568 181	35	z	271	4 553	4 282
16	l	24 265	196 146	171 881	36	9	206	2 125	1 919
17	n	22 087	336 706	314 619	37	x	66	9 435	9 369
18	g	17 550	92 584	75 034	38	·	0	1 024 053	1 024 053
19	u	11 889	128 799	116 910					
20	y	8 782	81 774	72 992					

Note: In the above table the symbol · is used as a placeholder for the whitespace symbol (token delimiter).

We propose two distinct and simplistic, or *naïve*, pseudoword generation methods:

(i) Most similar to Li's method, the character frequencies are drawn according to the entire Corpus letter frequencies. I call these *unordered* pseudowords as the letter choice probability is independent of its position within the word.
(ii) More realistically: if the character is to be the first letter of a new word it is drawn according to the *first* letter frequencies; if it is to be another letter in an existing word, it is drawn according to the *rest* of the word frequencies. I call these *semi-ordered* pseudowords as some slight account of the ordering is made.

For the first method, a typical run of 10 pseudowords is given by

$$\{\texttt{k}, \texttt{aidt}, \texttt{yyutnon}, \texttt{epoemcwtinfe}, \texttt{tc}, \\ \texttt{vaer7ei}, \texttt{kgntiv}, \texttt{oftr}, \texttt{nn}, \texttt{inpreae}\}; \tag{4.36}$$

whereas, for the second method, a typical run of 10 pseudowords is given by

$$\{\texttt{teul}, \texttt{aneaseauwish}, \texttt{ol1nta}, \texttt{chue}, \texttt{te}, \\ \texttt{welef}, \texttt{tm}, \texttt{a}, \texttt{at}, \texttt{ehhs}\}. \tag{4.37}$$

Exactly 1,024,054 pseudowords were generated for this study, which is the same number of words as in the actual Brown Corpus when processed as above.

I refer to both methods as *naïve* pseudoword generation as they take only slight account or, in the case of the first method, no account of the conditional probabilities in character selection that are present in actual Corpus words and which turn the generation process into something more resembling a Markov Chain.

4.4.3.3. *Bootstrapping the Brown Corpus Pseudowords*

In order that we may assess the standard error of the estimators of the frequency-rank distribution shape parameters, $\{\hat{\alpha}, \hat{\beta}, \hat{\gamma}_1, \hat{\gamma}_2\}$, I use a bootstrap procedure. For computational efficiency, rather than repeatedly creating large samples of pseudowords for analysis, I draw with replacement from a single, but large, set of pseudowords. This sample of pseudowords are then sorted, ranked, and counted just as the original Brown Corpus was.

4.4.3.4. *Analysis of Unordered Pseudowords*

In Figure 4.18, the frequency-rank plot for four runs of the bootstrap on a full sample of 1,024,054 unordered pseudowords is shown. It is readily apparent that, although the random process does generate some curvature in the log-log plot, these curves do not look like those for the real Corpus. Most notable is that the frequencies appear to flatten out at the tail end of the curves, not rapidly attenuate as is present in the distributions for actual English language corpora. In fact, in three of the four plots the curvature is positive. To the eye, no fit is as convincing as the fit to real data.

Sample statistics for the bootstrapped estimators are given in Table 4.11. On average, $\bar{\gamma}_2$ has a slightly negative value for this data, indicating positive curvature at the tail-end of the distribution. However, it is very close to zero for unordered pseudowords, as predicted by Li.

The actual regression coefficients for the Brown Corpus (without standard errors) are given in Table 4.9. It is very clear that the hypothesis of Li-type word construction is very strongly rejected by this data with vanishingly small p-values. In the Brown Corpus itself the value of $\hat{\gamma}_2 = 0.00043$ has a t statistic of 1,300, as estimated from the bootstraps. We can unequivocally conclude that the observed frequency-rank distribution for words in the Brown Corpus is not generated by the sort of unordered pseudowords constructed according to the Li-*like* algorithm, even when corrected for the actual symbol frequencies observed within this data.

4.4.3.5. *Analysis of Semi-Ordered Pseudowords*

Recognizing that the unordered pseudoword process might be too simplistic, I also repeated the procedures described above for the more realistic algorithm. The summary statistics for the fits to the pseudoword distributions in this case are exhibited in Table 4.12. Four bootstrap samples are illustrated in Figure 4.19.

Again we find that the negative curvature ($\hat{\gamma}_2 > 0$) found in the actual Brown Corpus does not occur. We also see a steeper spectral index, $\bar{\alpha} = 1.093$ versus 1.045 above; however, the linear terms do appear to be consistent within the sampling errors: $\bar{\gamma}_1 = 0.43 \pm 0.02$

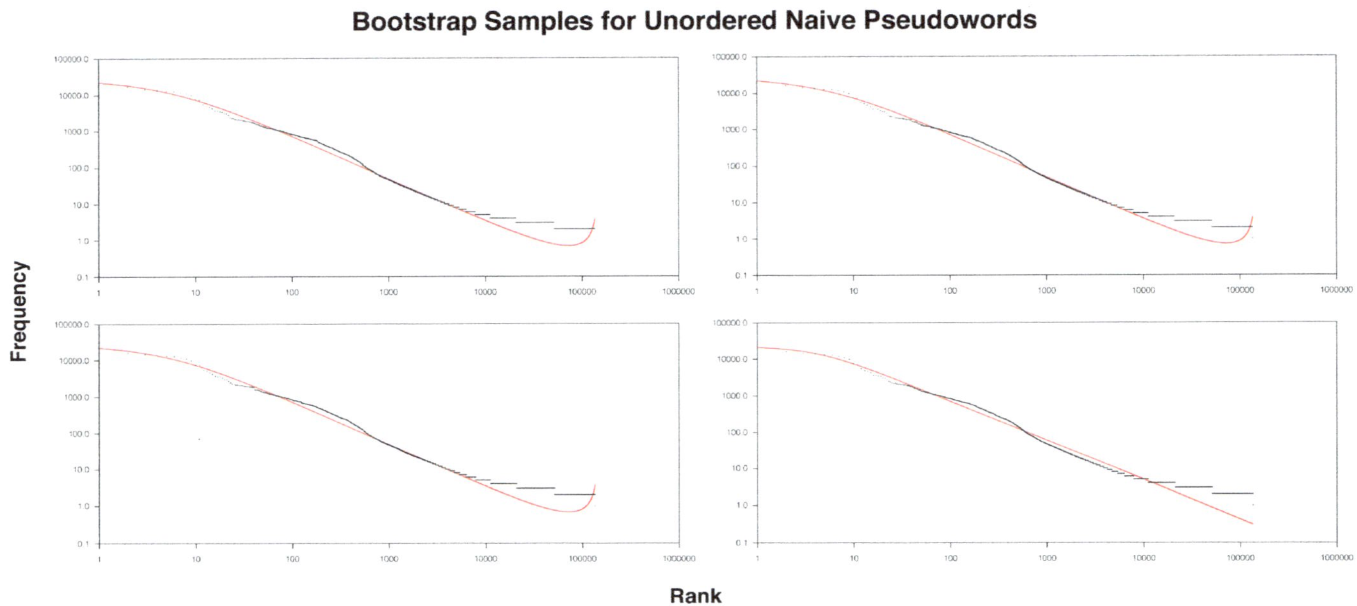

Figure 4.18: Frequency-Rank analysis for four bootstrap samples of unordered pseudowords drawn according to the entire Brown Corpus character frequencies of the discovered alphabet.

Table 4.11: Sample statistics for the bootstrapped estimators of the frequency-rank distribution parameters for unordered pseudowords generated from the Brown Corpus.

Parameter	Mean	Std. dev.
α	1.04537	0.00234
β	10.51877	0.03697
γ_1	0.45285	0.02671
γ_2	-5.80949×10^{-6}	3.35248×10^{-7}

Table 4.12: Sample statistics for the bootstrapped estimators of the frequency-rank distribution parameters for semi-ordered pseudowords generated from the Brown Corpus.

Parameter	Mean	Std. dev.
α	1.09300	0.00216
β	10.80191	0.03166
γ_1	0.43060	0.01997
γ_2	-6.51812×10^{-6}	2.94066×10^{-7}

versus 0.45 ± 0.03. As before, the measured curvature parameter is massively distant from the simulation estimate, with $\hat{\gamma}_2 = +0.0043$ versus $\bar{\gamma}_2 = -6.5 \times 10^{-6} \pm 2.9 \times 10^{-7}$. This more realistic pseudoword construction methodology does not reproduce the characteristics of the data.

4.4.3.6. *Summary of the Pseudoword Studies*

In summary, neither of the pseudoword methods attempted here can create the negative curvature observed in frequency-rank plots made from Brown Corpus (or the other corpora). My conclusion is that the structures of words is not completely arbitrary. I doubt that this is a startling revelation, although it is interesting to see how subtle this result is in practice.

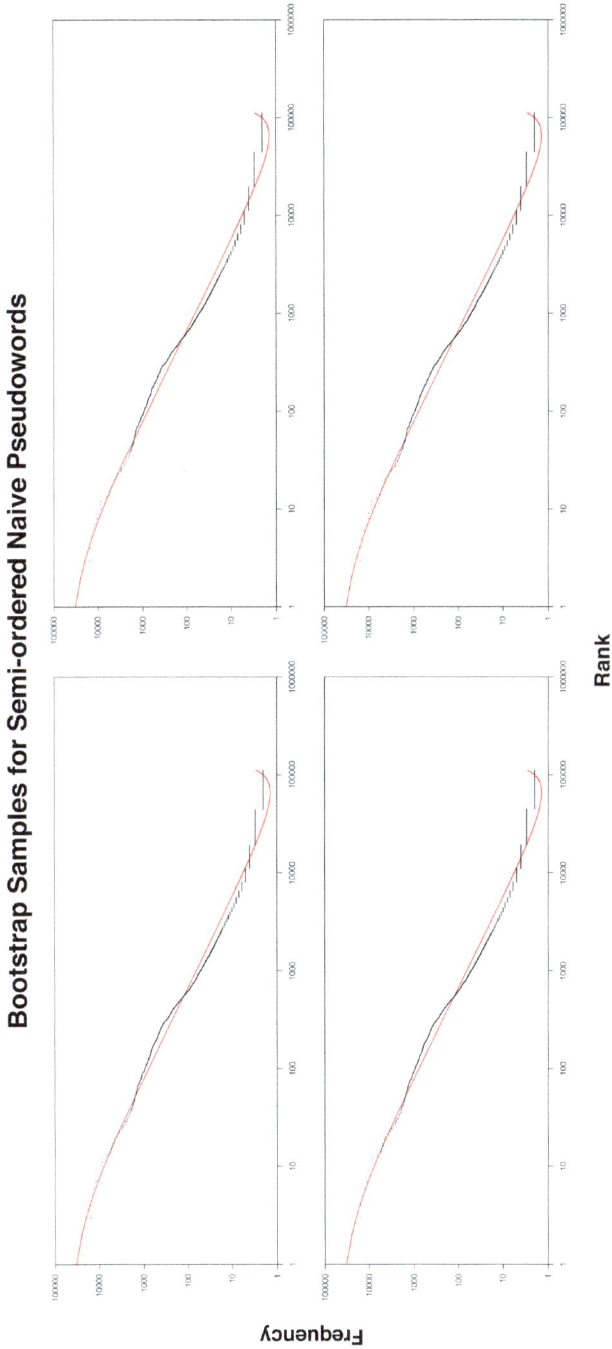

Figure 4.19: Frequency-rank analysis for four bootstrap samples of semi-ordered pseudowords drawn according to the entire Brown Corpus character frequencies of the discovered alphabet.

4.5. Learning from a Mixed Bag of Studies

The work described in this section are small studies drawn from a variety of subjects not aligned with either my traditional field of particle physics or my professional field of financial and economic data analysis. There are also other topics I've looked at, but the work didn't seem sufficiently completed to include here. It is worth asking: what's the point? The common thread here is curiosity: I examined these data sets because I could and because I wanted to build knowledge and skills. I do not flatter myself that I have broken new analytical ground in subjects where I am a stranger, but nevertheless I want to demonstrate that skills built in one area can be used in another. The work I've done on language, including that above, put me in position to do the work I've done on Twitter. My rules are: Do not be afraid to dive into data you don't know, but do not forget others have made their life's work working in these fields and that means they probably know what they're talking about.

Chapter 5

Demographics and Survey Research

The work in this chapter focuses on modeling people. This is something I started to get involved with when I began working in Internet Marketing, and later informed my work on Primary Research. I have found it quite stimulating to enter this field and to use its results in my own one.

5.1. Machine Learning Models for Gender Assignment

One of the key tasks involved, and which I've repeated many times subsequently, is imputing demographics from the sort of identity data one gets through internet marketing packages. We would like to know gender, age, and possibly race and heritage. In many cases the chances of getting these inferences *right* are low, but if posterior probabilities are computed accurately then population aggregates will be correct.

The first task I tackled was how to figure out gender for email names such as `joe@gmail.com` or `mary@icloud.com`. You and I both, immediately, know the answer to this question,[a] but how do we do it at scale? In Section 4.2.2, I hand classified gender based on names for the candidates for the School Board Election, but such hand classification won't work when databases contain thousands of names, so how do we teach a computer to do it automatically?

[a]And there's a fairly small probability that we're wrong.

5.1.1. *The Data*

Any analysis begins and ends with data. While working in internet marketing, I had become pretty adept at figuring out how to find public data to address questions about human populations, and with a little work I found that the Social Security Administration in the United States publishes a database of baby names. This contains summary data by state for every year since 1910 and for every name that occurs more than once. Going forward I will refer to it as the *Baby Names Database*. This data is compiled from birth registrations and so we can assume that the data are (almost) exact.

In all there are 32,684 distinct names, representing 21,595 identified as males and 14,145 identified as females. Note that these sums add up to more than the whole because some names are not gender specific.

5.1.1.1. *Creating Features*

For those schooled in numerical analysis of data, perhaps the biggest step to get to working with textual data is to realize that you can *just do it*. Any lexical token can be converted to a binary variable regarding its presence, or a categorical variable, and both traditional statistics and machine learning have plenty of methods available to deal with objects of this type.

For my analysis I decided to create the following features[b]:

(i) the first letter of the name;
(ii) the second letter of the name;
(iii) the penultimate letter;
(iv) the final letter;
(v) the length of the name;
(vi) an indicator if the first letter is a vowel[c];
(vii) an indicator if the last letter is a vowel.

Only the regular roman alphabet is used, `A...Z`. Although these variables are not all distinct, I intended to either exclude overlapping

---

[b]A more detailed analysis is certainly possible.
[c]Actually, in the set $\{\mathtt{A}, \mathtt{E}, \mathtt{I}, \mathtt{O}, \mathtt{U}, \mathtt{Y}\}$.

features or use a method that would remove the least useful by some form of regularization.

The dependent variable is the gender of the name, taken to be the proportion of the records indicating a registered male gender for each name to the total number of records. These values are mostly 0 or 1, but some names have more ambiguous results such as "Marion" and "Leslie."

5.1.1.2. *Random Subsampling*

In time-series analysis we can use the arrow of time, and the new data it brings, to test hypotheses derived from data and validated from those same data. In studying something like language, we don't have the ability to do that. Instead we need to rely on tools like bootstrapping, and cross-validation, to validate our analysis.

It is common practice in machine learning to use five-fold cross validation, meaning to divide the data into five groups, test in one and train our models in the rest, iterating over every combination. This is similar to a "blocked" version of the *Jackknife* method used in statistics to establish bias within analysis [27]. This 4:1 division of the data is certainly an operational norm in many teams, but I am not aware of any work similar to either the Nyquist–Shannon Sampling Theorem [117], or the results of Tao and Candès [13], that address the size of a sample required to deliver an accurate model of a given complexity and conclude that five-fold is the correct answer. I personally prefer the approach of bootstrapping, which is based on the well established convergence of the empirical distribution function to the population cumulative distribution function.

For this analysis, I chose to draw a random sample of 20% of the data for training and another random sample of 20% for testing.[d] With a data set of this size, the number of ways in which these samples may be drawn are vast, and the probability of testing on the same data used for training is low. This procedure can then be repeated many times, as a bootstrap subsample.

---

[d]I actually started with 10% but that gave rise to testing data in which contained feature values not present in the training data.

5.1.2. *Logistic Regression*

I started with a logistic regression for the observed relative gender frequencies, G_i, of each distinct name i.

$$\Pr(I[G_i \geq 1/2]) = \text{logistic}(\alpha + \beta_1 V_i + \beta_2 W_i), \tag{5.1}$$

where $V_i = 1$ when the first letter of the name is a vowel and 0 otherwise. W_i plays the same role for the last letter. I am using an indirect model via the indicator function because the observed gender identities are not binary. The purpose of beginning with such a simple model is to establish whether a mathematical analysis of such data could possibly be meaningful at all. It is clearly influenced by the observation that many female names do end in a vowel whereas male names end in a consonant.

With this transformation of the gender identity variable, the training sample has 40% male names and 60% female names. This training set is unbalanced and the parameters, $\hat{\alpha}$, will take a value necessary to deliver that bias on average. To control for that, I again randomly subsample the data in such a manner that we have a 60% probability of selecting a male identified name and 40% probability of selecting a female identified name.

We find $\hat{\alpha} = 1.068 \pm 0.063$. The first letter being a vowel does not seem to be informative, with $\hat{\beta}_1 = -0.046 \pm 0.099$ which is insignificant, but the last letter being a vowel is strongly indicative of a female gender assignment, at $\hat{\beta}_2 = -1.976 \pm 0.081$ with vanishing p value. Setting the decision threshold to be the average value of the logistic function in the training set gives a precision and recall of 74% and 55%, respectively. The F-score is 63%.

With the procedure of drawing independent testing sets, I am able to examine sampling distribution of the performance metrics in the testing sets. The precision and recall have means of $(64 \pm 1)\%$ and $(56 \pm 1)\%$ respectively, with an F-score of $(60 \pm 1)\%$. This is not bad for a model based essentially on just one feature, the loss in precision when going out-of-sample is 10% and of recall is indistinguishable from zero. These data are shown in Figure 5.1.

5.1.3. *A Regression Tree Model*

In this book, the majority of the models proposed are for *continuous* dependent variables and are *locally smooth.* Even the kernel

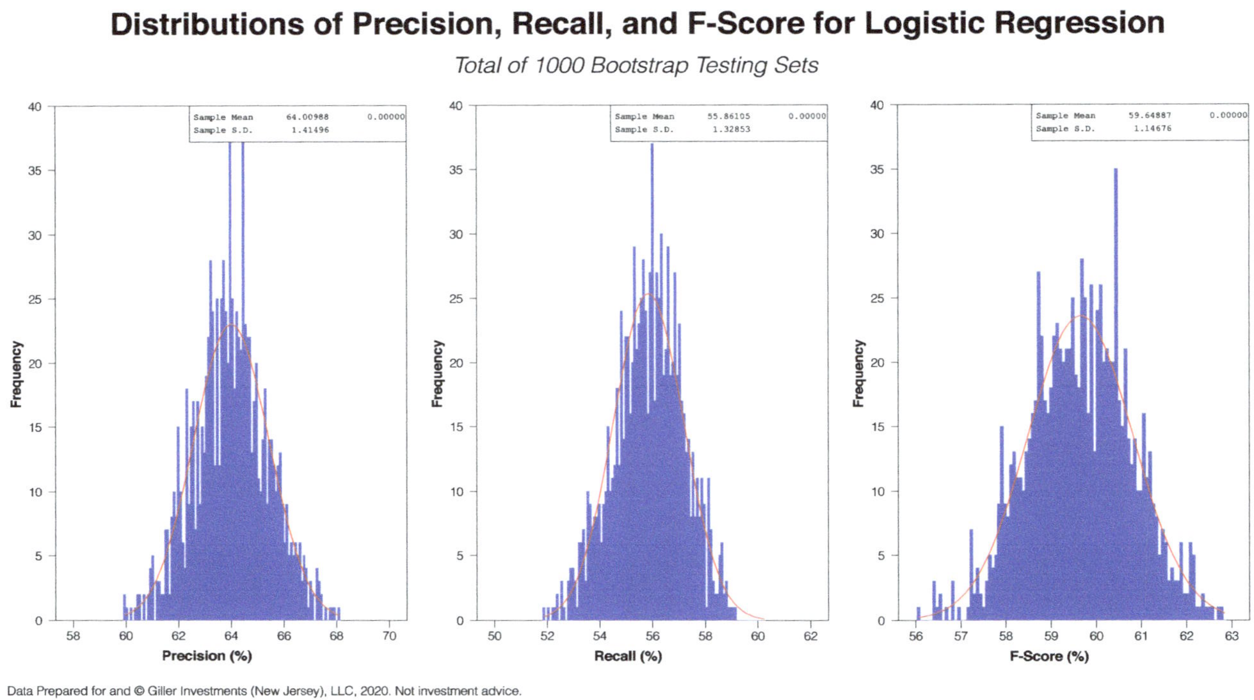

Figure 5.1: Distribution of precision, recall and F-score for a logistic regression model of gender based on vowels within a first name. The data is from 1,000 randomly sampled testing sets based on a model trained on one random sample. The blue bars are a histogram and the red curves are the best fitting Normal distribution.

smoothing used in Section 3.4.1 delivers such a model. However, there is no reason to believe that the best model, *empirically*, is composed in such a way. Statistical methods have been developed since the beginning to deal with categorical variables, including Fisher's work on *ANOVA* and contingency tables, but it wasn't until the influential statistician Leo Breiman introduced *Classification and Regression Trees*, or *CART*, that we got a practical method based on piecewise constant response functions built out of a sequence of contingent binary decisions [127].

The *CART* method builds a decision tree from a sequence of splits that are chosen to optimize variance separation in the dependent variable. The tree built is then *pruned* in a manner that promotes robustness. Once the data has been separated appropriately the response is computed as the mean value of all the responses within each partition. I most frequently use the package `rpart` in the *R* statistical system to evaluate trees, but many other frameworks exist. Figure 5.2 shows such a tree computed from a random sample of 20% of the Baby Names Database. Unlike the logistic model of Equation (5.1), this tree is evaluated by the "kitchen sink" method of giving it all possible features to reason from. The algorithm itself selects the relevant ones.

One of the advantages of tree models is that they are extremely easy to parse into decision rules. The model built here is a *regression* tree because the dependent variable is the proportion of males with a given name. Computer scientist Judea Pearl, says that

> [artificial intelligence is about] creating simple rules for dumb robots. — Judea Pearl

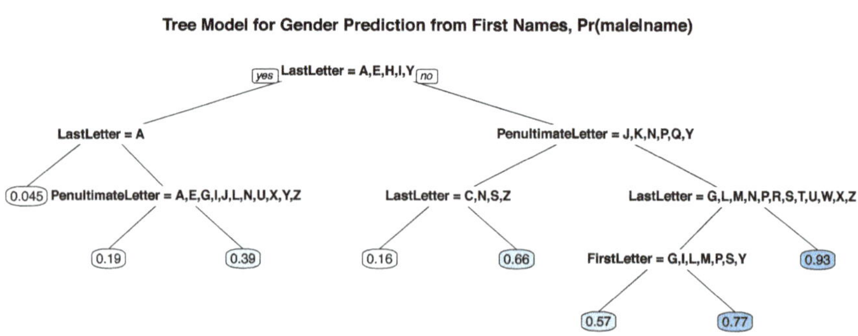

Figure 5.2: Regression tree to predict assigned gender from first names based upon a random sample of 20% of the SSA's Baby Names Database.

To evaluate the precision and recall, so that there are commensurable statistics, we have to covert to binary decisions, which I do by using a threshold of 0.5 for both the prediction and the result. In-sample the model has a precision of 74% and a recall of 74%, giving an F-score of 75%. Compared to the logistic regression model the precision is basically the same but the recall is over twenty points better. For the out-of-sample bootstraps the results are $(73 \pm 2)\%$ and $(74 \pm 1)\%$, eliminating the training loss observed with the logistic regression. The distributions are in Figure 5.3. Clearly this model performs better out of sample.

5.1.4. *Machine Learning and Language*

The work of this section demonstrates that it is possible, with reasonably high precision, to assign gender *at scale* to data containing just first names. It is not intended to exhibit the *best approximating model* discoverable via machine learning methods. Other algorithms, such as *Support Vector Regression* or some form of enhanced tree algorithm may do better. Obviously this analysis is customized to the United States, but I don't doubt that similar work can be done in other nations. The logistic regression describes a tendency of association, whereby names ending in vowel sounds are more associated with female gender, but the tree model gives us much deeper insight into a decision making process that comes to conclusions about gender from name. It's not too much of a leap, I think, to conjecture a *learning* process being evolutionarily created in our minds to replicate this statistically discovered reasoning.

Furthermore, this demonstrates the power of tree models that use response functions which are piecewise constant. Although they may be less "physically real" in some circumstances, there's no reason to believe they are empirically less useful than models built from continuous variables.

5.1.5. *A Note on Non-Binary Gender*

In all of my work involving demographic variables I work with the traditional, *binary*, characterization of gender. The simple reason for this is that all of the official government data I have access to, whether it is the Census data, the BRFSS data discussed in Chapter 4, or the Baby Names database used here, *all* use those classifications.

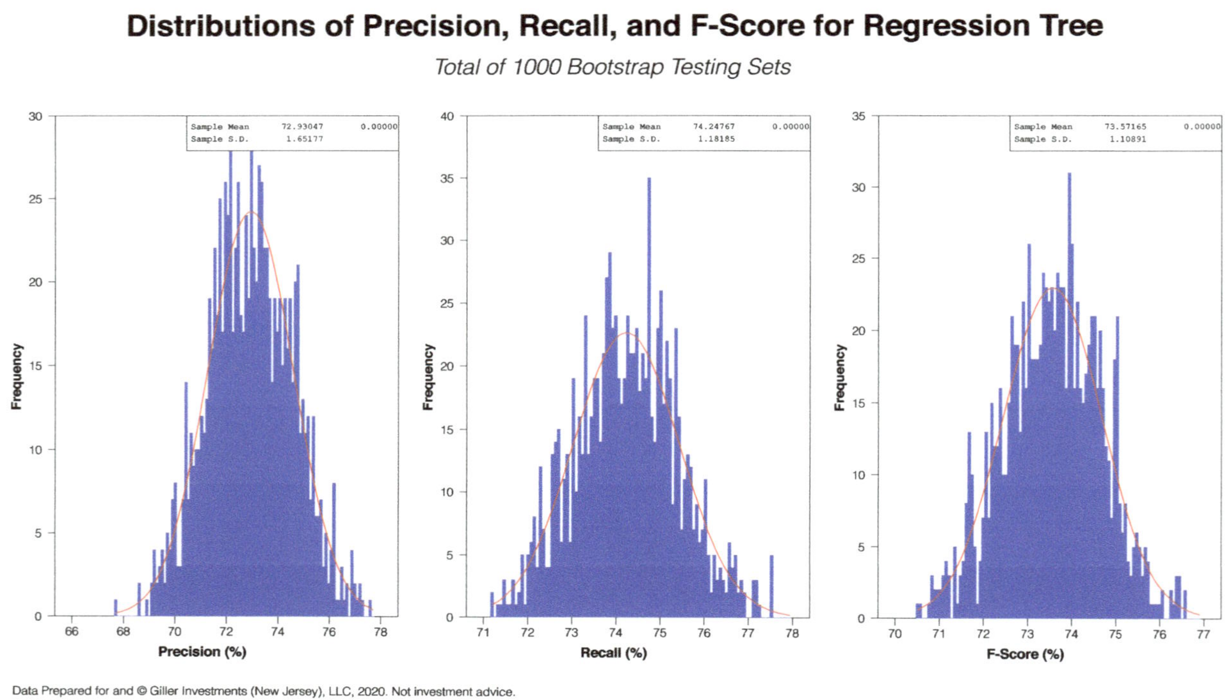

Figure 5.3: Distribution of precision, recall and F-score for a regression tree model of gender based on vowels within a first name. The data is from 1,000 randomly sampled testing sets based on a model trained on one random sample. The blue bars are a histogram and the red curves are the best fitting Normal distribution.

Unfortunately, any survey I ran that permitted answers other than "male" or "female" for gender would not be alignable to the census populations and any gender identity chosen would be processed *as if* it were equivalent to "not disclosed" and be given zero weight. Consequently, those selecting non-binary gender would be given *no voice* when the opinions of the survey panel are aggregated — and this applies to almost all scientific opinion polling being done today. The solution to this, I feel, has to start with the practices of the Census Bureau, which is an agency of the US Department of Commerce, because they are the definitive voice defining the measurement of the identities of Americans.

5.2. Bayesian Estimation of Demographics

My work on algorithmic models for demographic imputation dates from 2012. When I returned to this later I started to think about the logical conclusions of using a tree model on a dataset such as the Baby Names Database. The features I have created are derivatives of the actual data, picking apart names according to rules I presupposed would work based on my own experiences in, and biases from, a mostly Anglo-Saxon culture.

In his book *Statistical Learning Theory*, Vladimir Vapnik writes:

> one should solve the problem directly and never solve a more general problem as an intermediate step. — Vladimir Vapnik [136]

In this analysis the goal is *not* to discover how language describes concepts[e] but to simply predict whether "George," "Amit," or "Leslie" are male or female. Thus the question could, in fact, be answered directly by frequency counting within the database and this would also allow us to track how these assignments are related to birth year.

5.2.1. *Methodology*

If we knew a person's birth year we could directly look up that year's data from the Baby Names Database and measure the relative

[e] Although that *is* a worthwhile goal.

frequency of both gender assignments, male and female. However, the task we are tackling is often to build up a demographic profile from as little information as the first and last name, without knowledge of their birth year.

Fortunately, we do know how many people of a given age and gender are living in the United States for any given year. This data comes from the Census Bureau and their annual survey program *The American Community Survey*, and provides both national and regional population pyramids. The population pyramid gives an unconditional probability that a person picked at random in the United States has a given age and gender and the Baby Names Database gives a conditional probability of gender given age and name. Together they may be used to estimate gender by summing over the marginal dimension of age weighted by the probabilities inferred from the census data.

Explicitly, if $\Lambda(a, g, y)$ is the proportion of the population in known year, y, with a given age, a, and gender,[f] g, and $B(g, b, n)$ is the proportion of babies born with gender g in birth year b with name n then, since $a = y - b$, we have

$$\Pr(G_i = g|N_i) = \frac{\sum_a B(g, y - a, N_i)\Lambda(a, g, y)}{\sum_{a,g} B(g, y - a, N_i)\Lambda(a, g, y)}, \tag{5.2}$$

as a Bayesian estimate of the gender of a given person, G_i, given their first name N_i. Similarly,

$$\Pr(A_i = a|N_i) = \frac{\sum_g B(g, y - a, N_i)\Lambda(a, g, y)}{\sum_{a,g} B(g, y - a, N_i)\Lambda(a, g, y)}, \tag{5.3}$$

for the age. Furthermore, we can condition on a or g and estimate marginal probabilities:

$$\Pr(G_i = g|N_i, a) = \frac{B(g, y - a, N_i)\Lambda(a, g, y)}{\sum_g B(g, y - a, N_i)\Lambda(a, g, y)}, \tag{5.4}$$

and

$$\Pr(A_i = a|N_i, g) = \frac{B(g, y - a, N_i)\Lambda(a, g, y)}{\sum_a B(g, y - a, N_i)\Lambda(a, g, y)}. \tag{5.5}$$

Technically all these expressions are *estimates* of the probabilities, not the exact values, however, the maximum likelihood estimator of

[f]That is, Λ is the population pyramid for a given year.

a population proportion is equal to the sample proportion and, as the Baby Names Database and American Community Survey are both compiled from many thousands of records, sampling errors are relatively small.

5.2.2. *Interesting Marginal Results*

The marginal probabilities are available from machine learning models, but what is required, essentially, is to build a model for each marginal that we desire to examine. The Bayesian approach featured here feels more direct.

5.2.2.1. *The Probable Age of "Veronica"*

There is an Elvis Costello song *Veronica*, which describes someone suffering from Alzheimer's disease. This name is not one that you hear much of at the time of writing, but it is an old name derived from a Latinization of ancient Greek.[g] The data shows that if I were to meet Veronica, she is likely to be about my age.

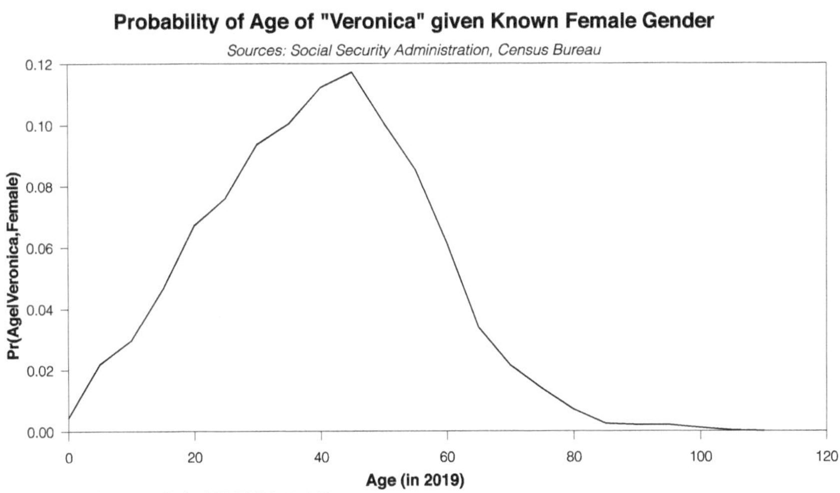

Figure 5.4: The probable age of a woman called Veronica given known age and gender, derived from the BRFSS and ACS data.

[g]It is important in Christianity due to the relic of the *Veil of Veronica*.

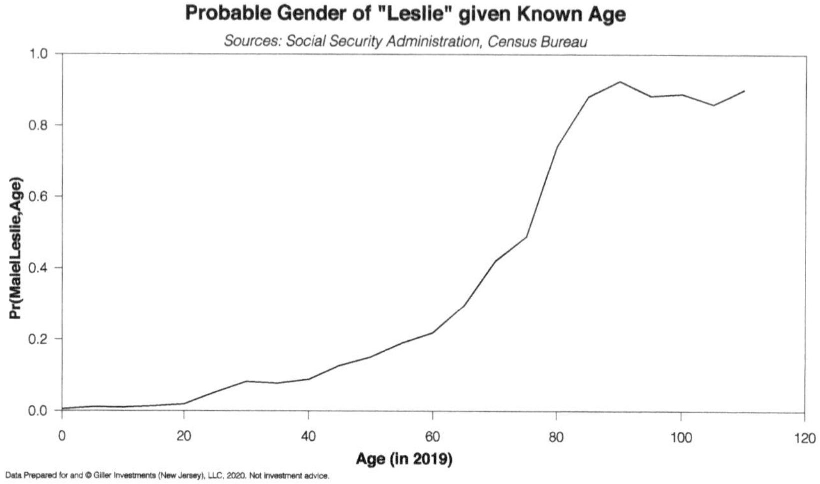

Figure 5.5: The probability that Leslie is male given their age, derived from the BRFSS and ACS data.

5.2.2.2. *The Likely Gender of "Leslie"*

My father's first name is Leslie, and it is my middle name. When I was little, my parents carefully explained that *Leslie* was the *male* version and *Lesley*[h] the *female* version. In fact, Leslie is an example of a name that has changed gender over the years. Figure 5.5 shows how the probable gender of Leslie varies with the age of the person.

My father's 80th birthday was in the Summer of 2020, and I was unable to visit due to the Coronavirus pandemic. The data shows that for his generation, and also for *his parents*' generation, it was almost exclusively a male name but, after the Second World War it began to shift and now it is unambiguously a female name. Both of these results rather neatly confirm the utility of the Bayesian approach, over the discrete classification into categories pursued earlier.

5.3. Working with Patreon

In the 21st century, many of us have turned away from broadcast radio and television to social media and streaming services in search

[h]Note the different spelling of the final syllable.

of entertainment and informative content. A downside of this is the model of advertising funded entertainment that has been adopted, and has lead to algorithmically targeted recommendations, autoplay, "infinite scrolling," and other aspects of online viewing that, we are beginning to learn, may have a negative effect on our shared society.

Patreon is a company that permits the public to eschew advertising funded media, instead offering subscriptions to fund creators in their work. Often this work also appears on sites like *YouTube*, but the patrons get early, advertising free, access without the associated "doomscrolling" facilitated by algorithmic recommendations. Patreon also facilitates the production of works in media other than online video, allowing creators to connect directly to consumers and displacing intermediaries who rely on algorithmic advertising. Those who fund the works are called *Patrons*.

As a subscriber to some woodworking and metalworking creators, I am a user of Patreon. When I deleted a pledge to one creator, whose work I was no longer interested in, I was presented with a survey asking why I had taken the action I did. As one of the reasons offered was due to a change in economic circumstances, and I have been involved in using consumer surveys to predict economic variables, I was fascinated by the opportunity this presented to, perhaps, get early insights into possible causes of such actions like unemployment and consumer expectations of a contracting economy.

I approached Patreon and spent some time talking to Maura Church, their Head of Data Science, about opportunities to work on their data. I explained how survey research worked, including reweighting data to match a given demographic profile, and Maura surprised me by stating that they had very little demographic data and so did not know how I would go about doing this. I explained the Bayesian assignment of demographics just presented in the prior section, and we agreed that I could use these techniques to create a demographic profile for them and then take a look at how their data might relate to macroeconomic variables.

5.3.1. *The Data*

After signing an NDA, Patreon gave me access to some 5,010,637 anonymized deletion surveys and account names for 3,935,623 distinct Patrons. From these, I was able to assign genders and ages to 3,124,563 US based users by the methods described above.

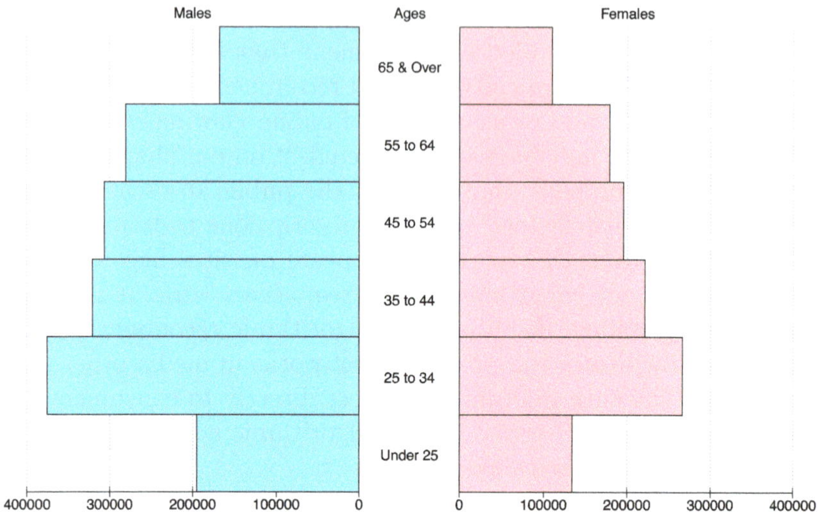

Figure 5.6: Estimated population pyramid for Patreon users. Derived from data provided by Patreon, Inc. and published with their permission.

This allowed me to create a population pyramid for Patrons which was found to exhibit a strong male bias and a noticeable deficit of under 25s and over 65s. In comparison, the US population as a whole is much more balanced in age and gender. The data is shown in Figure 5.6.

5.3.2. *Raking Weights*

With gender and age assignments done, I could compute raking weights to adjust the population to match the desired demographic, which was the population estimates from the American Community Survey. This procedure, named "raking" as one adjusts the data to match a population one marginal dimension at a time, is relatively straightforward. We assign to every individual, i, a weight which is a function of their age, gender, and geographic location. The sum of the weights is then required to match the demographic profile of the population, known via census data, when computed along the marginal dimensions. When this is done the normalization can either be fixed to the total population count, so each weight is typically quite large, or to the total sample size, so the average weight is unity. The BRFSS follows the former convention, but I used the latter in this work.

There are two principal ways to adjust the weights from their initial values to deliver the target demographic profile. The first is known as *Iterative Proportional Fitting* and the second is a simple least-squares based approach. In the latter, which I followed, the weight for a given user is assumed to be factorable into marginal functions for each dimension, i.e.

$$w(A_i, G_i, R_i) = w_a(A_i) w_g(G_i) w_r(R_i) \tag{5.6}$$

for age, A_i, gender, G_i, and region, R_i.

As the demographic variables in use, (A_i, G_i, R_i), are all categorical, these functions are all, in fact, piecewise constant and, with the standard marginal cohorts used throughout such work,[i] there are $2 + 6 + 4 = 12$ weight parameters to estimate. For example,

$$w_g(G_i) = \begin{cases} w_0 & \text{if } G_i = \text{female} \\ w_1 & \text{if } G_i = \text{male}, \end{cases} \tag{5.7}$$

if the genders are known precisely. When they are known probabilistically we must sum over the parameters weighted by those probabilities.

$$w_g(G_i) = w_0 \times \Pr(G_i = \text{female}) + w_1 \times \Pr(G_i = \text{male}). \tag{5.8}$$

This is a relatively simple model to compute, and I wrote a custom `Python` script to execute it. With weights estimated, as in all survey research, analysis may proceed with weighted statistics used wherever normal statistics would be. The resulting inferences are then about the *population* as a whole and not the sample alone.

5.3.3. *Patreon Cancellation Surveys and Consumer Sentiment*

I concentrated on the prevalence of the answer "financial instability" as the reason for the cancellation of a pledge to a creator. I did not get any success with unemployment variables I had originally tried, but was able to find that general consumer sentiment was important.

[i] $G_i \in \{\text{male}, \text{female}\}$, $A_i \in \{\text{under } 25, 25\text{-}34, 35\text{-}44, 45\text{-}54, 55\text{-}64, 65 \ \& \ \text{over}\}$ and $R_i \in \{\text{north east}, \text{south}, \text{south west}, \text{west}\}$.

5.3.3.1. *The University of Michigan's Index of Consumer Sentiment*

The University of Michigan publishes the results of regularly run survey of consumers every month. A preliminary release gives an early peek into the numbers half way into the month, and a final release, usually published on the last Friday of the week in which the month ends, encompasses all the responses used for the preliminary datum, so they are not independent statistics.[j] The releases are not bi-weekly in nature, as there are never more than two releases per calendar month, so I refer to its cadence as "semi-monthly." The data takes the form of a "diffusion index" representing the proportion of respondents who answer positively to a set of five questions that generally permit four types of answer:

(i) conditions/expectations are positive;
(ii) conditions/expectations are negative;
(iii) conditions/expectations are neutral;
(iv) I don't know how to answer/don't have an opinion.

I assume that each final release, F_t, is an equally weighted average of the preliminary release, P_t, and an unknown interim value, U_t, representing the statistic that would be computed for the period between the last survey used in the preliminary release and the last survey used in the final release. Thus

$$F_t = \frac{U_t + P_t}{2} \Rightarrow U_t = 2F_t - P_t \tag{5.9}$$

and the survey data may be rendered as the semi-monthly sequence $C = \{U_t, P_t, U_{t-1}, P_{t-1}, \ldots\}$ indexed by the year and release number within the year (i.e. $t = (y, n)$), with 24 releases per year. This is the time-series used in this analysis as the dependent variable.

5.3.3.2. *"Not Financial Instability"*

With the data provided on Patron deletion surveys, and the demographic raking weights computed for each Patron, we are able to compute the proportion of responses who selected the answer that

[j]We will learn more about this survey later in this chapter.

"Financial Instability" was the reason for their pledge deletion as a simple weighted average for responses computed during the intervals defined by the University of Michigan's survey dates.

Specifically, I divide the month into two periods based on the three dates:

(i) the first day of the month;
(ii) the day before the preliminary release by the University of Michigan;
(iii) the last day of the month.

For all surveys within each period I compute

$$N_t = 100 - 100\frac{\sum_i w_i I_{it}[\text{Fin. Inst.}]}{\sum_i w_i I_{it}[\text{Survey}]}, \tag{5.10}$$

where the indicator function $I_{it}[\text{Fin.Inst.}]$ takes the value 1 if Patron i selected the "Financial Instability" response in the cancellation survey question asking why the pledge was deleted during time period t, and 0 otherwise, and the indicator function $I_{it}[\text{Survey}]$ takes the value 1 if they took the survey, and 0 otherwise. This series is computed as the complementary value, "Not Financial Instability," based on the heuristic that financial instability will be negatively correlated with consumer sentiment in general.

5.3.3.3. *The Relationship between Consumer Sentiment and Pledge Cancellation*

We are now in a position to directly investigate whether there is any covariance between pledge deletion by Patrons and general consumer sentiment. As is usual, my exploratory data analysis starts with simply looking at the data, which is shown in Figure 5.7. The data shows that Patreon's business has grown steadily, at more or less constant rate, over the 5 years for which the indicator N_t can be computed. There is a weak but highly significant linear relationship between the Patreon index and consumer sentiment, with an R^2 of 21% and an $F_{1,93}$ statistic of 24.6, which has a p value of 3.2×10^{-6}.

In the figure two regression lines are drawn: the blue one represents that for the entire data set and the green one for the data with the last two points, concurrent with the initial onset of the recession due to the Coronavirus outbreak in the USA, excluded. There is

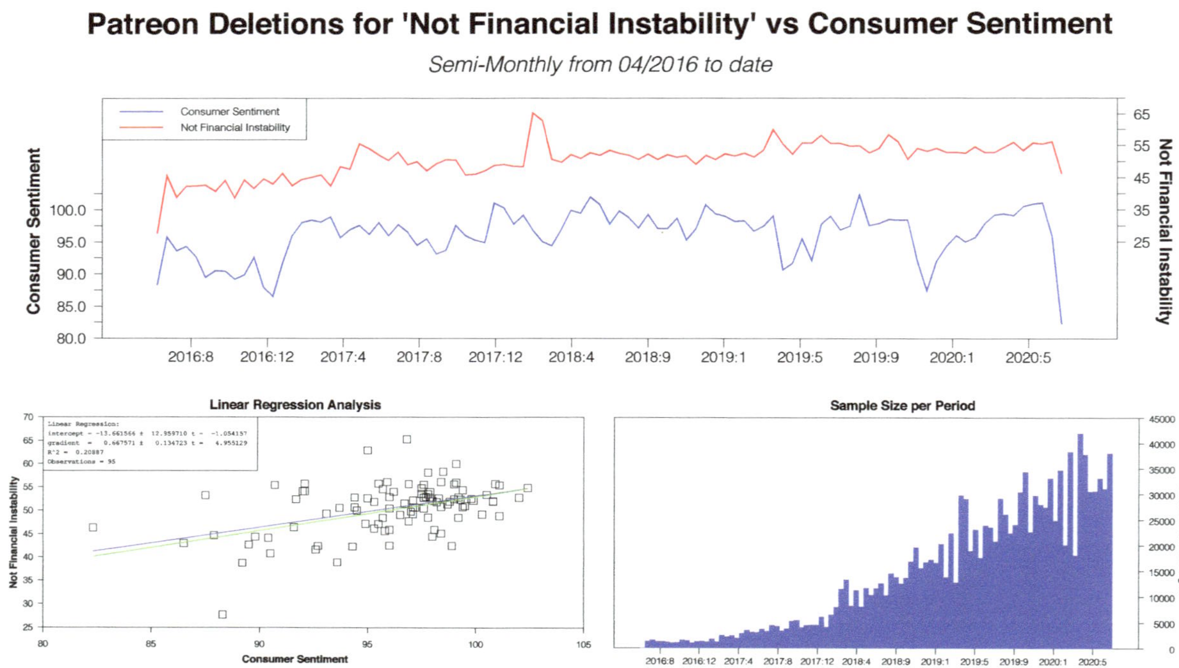

Source: Patreon, Inc, The University of Michigan, Giller Investments (New Jersey), LLC

Figure 5.7: Comparison of the Patreon "Not Financial Instability" index and the University of Michigan's Index of Consumer Sentiment. Upper panel: the two series side by side. Lower left panel: scatter plot and linear regression. Lower right panel: total counts of Patrons. Derived from data provided by Patreon, Inc. and published with their permission. The history of the sentiment data is obtained from public sources.

clearly very little difference between them, and so this result is not driven by accommodating that disruption.

5.3.3.4. *A Granger Causality Analysis of Patreon Data*

Although the goal for Patreon in our collaboration was to understand their data, and I was happy to help with that, I was also very interested in seeing whether such "alternative data" could be used in understanding public metrics of the economy and markets. I decided to pursue this analysis in an orthodox manner, which meant investigating whether Patreon's data could be used to anticipate general consumer sentiment. Formally, this is is establishing whether the Patreon index is a *predictive cause* of the University of Michigan's data.

Of course, I don't really think that people cancelling Patreon pledges for reasons of financial instability actually *causes* the University of Michigan's index to change, as in a country the size of the United States the probability of a Patreon user being interviewed by the University of Michigan's team is vanishingly small. Clearly both series respond to an unknown common factor which, for the sake of simplicity, we can just label *consumer sentiment*, in potentially biased and inefficient manner. However, having advanced knowledge of a predictive cause of a market moving data release is exactly the business I've been in for most of my career, and so this is a good framework within which the data may be examined.

5.3.3.5. *A Linear Predictive Model*

The linear predictive model we seek to fit is

$$S_t = \alpha + \sum_{i=1}^{a} \varphi_i S_{t-i} + \sum_{i=0}^{c} \beta_i N_{t-i} + \varepsilon_t, \tag{5.11}$$

$$\varepsilon_t \sim N(0, \sigma^2), \tag{5.12}$$

where S_t is the University of Michigan's Index of Consumer Sentiment and N_t is the index computed from the Patreon data as defined in Equation (5.10). The Granger algorithm follows three steps:

(i) establish the autoregressive order, a, by "step regression" — meaning increasing a from 1 until the last added coefficient is not significant, which we assess by applying the Wald test to each additional predictor;
(ii) establish the cross-regressive order, c, in the same manner, but in this time starting at 0;
(iii) perform the Wald Test on the exclusion of the cross-regressive terms.

In the above, I use a critical value of 0.01, corresponding to 99% confidence. This is stronger than typical practice, which would be to use 95% confidence. If the added cross-terms pass the applied test, we conclude that the tested series, which in this case is the Patreon index, is a *causal predictor* of the dependent variable. Note that we start the cross-regression at 0th. order on the assumption that the Michigan index is reported late and that the user of this model has access to the Patreon index data for the contemporaneous period *before* that data is released.

5.3.3.6. *Results of the Granger Test*

This procedure selects $(a, c) = (1, 0)$, with the fitted autoregressive coefficient of $\hat{\varphi}_1 = 0.602 \pm 0.093$, which is extremely significant. The cross-term $\hat{\beta}_1 = 0.119 \pm 0.065$, which has a p value of 0.07 and is therefore not introduced into the model and is not found to be a predictive cause of consumer sentiment.

In my experience, this is typical of analysis in a financial and econometric context. The predictor makes sense, is correlated in the manner desired, but is not sufficiently strong to adopt on the basis of the hypothesis testing formalism. We keenly want to assert that "it's probably true," and accept the model despite this. That is a bet that many may make, but I would rather wait until there is more data before staking money on such a proposition. If the phenomenon is real it will strengthen as more data is added, and if not it will remain insignificant.

There is a better way to approach this, though. As I have remarked, the Golden Rule of Prediction permits me to use *any causal predictor I want.* This will be examined in the next section.

5.4. Survey and Opinion Research

One of the things that I realized as my thoughts turned toward using alternative data to predict financial and economic metrics of interest was that *many* economic indicators are actually the direct product of what we now label alternative data. In fact, many such metrics are the product of consumer surveys and many economists actively pursue such research in their work. In the 21st century, the practice of market research has changed, and embraced the cost-savings provided by the internet. We have moved from an environment in which surveys may cost \$60–\$100 per interview, performed in person on the street or by telephone, to one in which they are executed for \$1–\$5 per interview, executed online.

This change in delivery channel has also brought changes in the nature of the response. In person and telephone interviews permit the interviewer to clarify the meaning of questions to respondents, and refine ambiguous answers. The script for the University of Michigan's interviews includes extensive instructions on how to do this [132]. Online surveys permit no interaction between the interviewer and the interviewee and, as they are generally compensated by some form of "microreward" such as entry into a lottery for an Amazon gift card or a small payment of order 50¢, respondents are motivated to complete the survey as fast as possible. This mode of interaction promotes the activation of Kahneman and Tversky's "System 1" reasoning, based on heuristics, rather than "System 2," based on thoughtful decision making [78].

I initiated a research programme to measure many aspects of the macroeconomy by direct consumer research while working at Deutsche Bank. Since leaving I have been able to resume this program, and to initiate a trading strategy based on these results. As I am using a low-cost, online, survey provider I cannot replicate the detailed script that the University of Michigan provides to its interviewers, but I can ask questions that address the same issues in the same manner and process the results to the same end. Because of the reduced costs available, I can also run a survey of equivalent size.

The probability of my process interviewing the same people, or a sufficient fraction of the same people, as the University of Michigan is vanishingly small in a population so large as the United States.

Thus any significant covariance between my results and theirs is not because the same people are present in the surveys, it must be because we are both measuring, with associated errors and biases, the same underlying factor that drives responses in each independent panel.

5.4.1. *Consumer Sentiment*

The first series I decided to investigate was the one most commonly reported, which is consumer sentiment. As noted, the survey procedure is essentially the same as the University of Michigan's, albeit delivered via a different channel. I run surveys weekly, collating the data to predict both the interim and final monthly data released to the public, recompute raking weights against the *nationally representative* population demographic profile obtained from the most recent American Community Survey data published by the Census Bureau, and directly compare the two series. The University of Michigan's sample size is stated to be "a minimum of 500 interviews," whereas mine is around 400 on average.[k]

5.4.1.1. *Exploratory Data Analysis*

The published *Index of Consumer Sentiment* is actually composed of two independent sub-indices: one called the *Index of Current Conditions* and the other the *Index of Consumer Expectations*. I will label these S_t, C_t and X_t, respectively. My estimates of the indices will be $\hat{S}_t$, $\hat{C}_t$ and $\hat{X}_t$.

Figure 5.8 shows good *ex-ante* correspondence between my analogues of the University of Michigan's data and the published sentiment series. The ordinary linear regression of S_t onto $\hat{S}_t$ has a coefficient of 0.710 ± 0.072, with a vanishing p value. It is significantly different from unity.

[k]With an online survey there is no ability to prevent a respondent abandoning the interview midway, but we can use partially complete interviews if they answer all the needed questions on a particular topic.

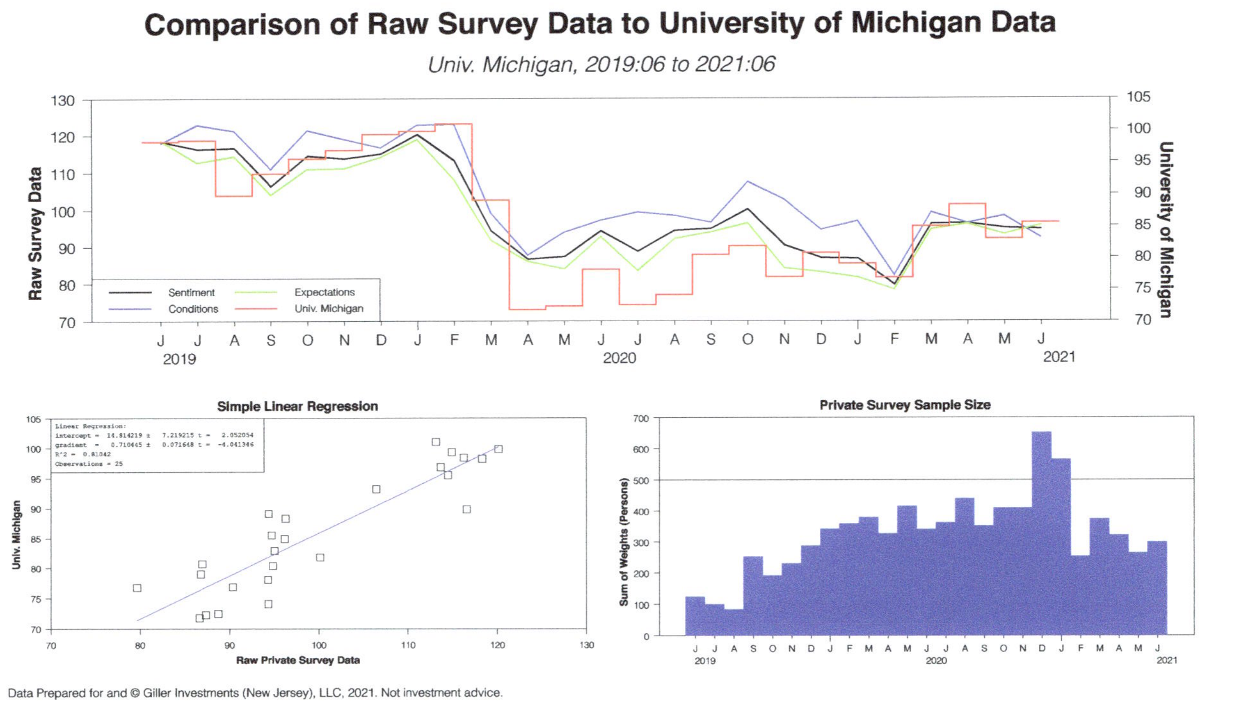

Figure 5.8: Comparison of the University of Michigan's Index of Consumer Sentiment and my own data. Upper panel: the steps are the official series and the lines my private estimates of the series and its components. Lower left panel: scatter plot and linear regression between S_t and $\hat{S}_t$. Lower right panel: total counts of interviewees in my sample. The history of the sentiment data is obtained from public sources.

5.4.1.2. *A Time-Varying Coefficients Model*

Assuming that the relationship between the University of Michigan's data, and my data, to the true, unobservable, sentiment factor possesses bias and inefficiency that may drift with time, I propose a time-varying coefficients model to capture the relationship between the two observed series.

$$\begin{aligned} S_t &= \alpha_t + \beta_{Ct}\hat{C}_t + \beta_{Xt}\hat{X}_t + \varepsilon_t\sigma_0 \\ \alpha_t &= \alpha_{t-1} + \eta_{1t}\sigma_1 \\ \beta_{Ct} &= \beta_{Ct-1} + \eta_{2t}\sigma_2 \\ \beta_{Xt} &= \beta_{Xt-1} + \eta_{3t}\sigma_3 \end{aligned} \tag{5.13}$$

All stochastic quantities, ε_t and η_{it}, are required to be Normally distributed for the system to be solvable. The regression procedure outputs not only the current prediction of the observed data, but also the time-series of coefficients, which are shown in Figure 5.9, and an estimate of the variance of the system through time. This permits confidence bounds[l] to be placed around the predicted series.

From the chart we see that at the beginning of the data the predictors are largely ignored and the model is largely dominated by a local-level, or random walk, term so that $\hat{\alpha}_t \approx S_{t-1}$. When the sentiment series begins to shift downwards, around the beginning of the Coronavirus outbreak in early 2020, the system learns that it can do better by listening to my private survey indices and rejects a non-zero constant in favor of that data. At the time of writing the model is placing approximately 20% weight on the private "conditions" series value and 45% weight on the "expectations" series value, with a small constant.

The time-series of the estimated index and the actual public data, for the Index of Consumer Sentiment, are shown in Figure 5.10. This data includes the value forecast from the model at the time of writing,[m] after the publication of the public index data. Clearly the two series are within the quoted errors. Their correlation over this period is 85%.

[l]Assuming a Normal distribution of errors.
[m]June 2021.

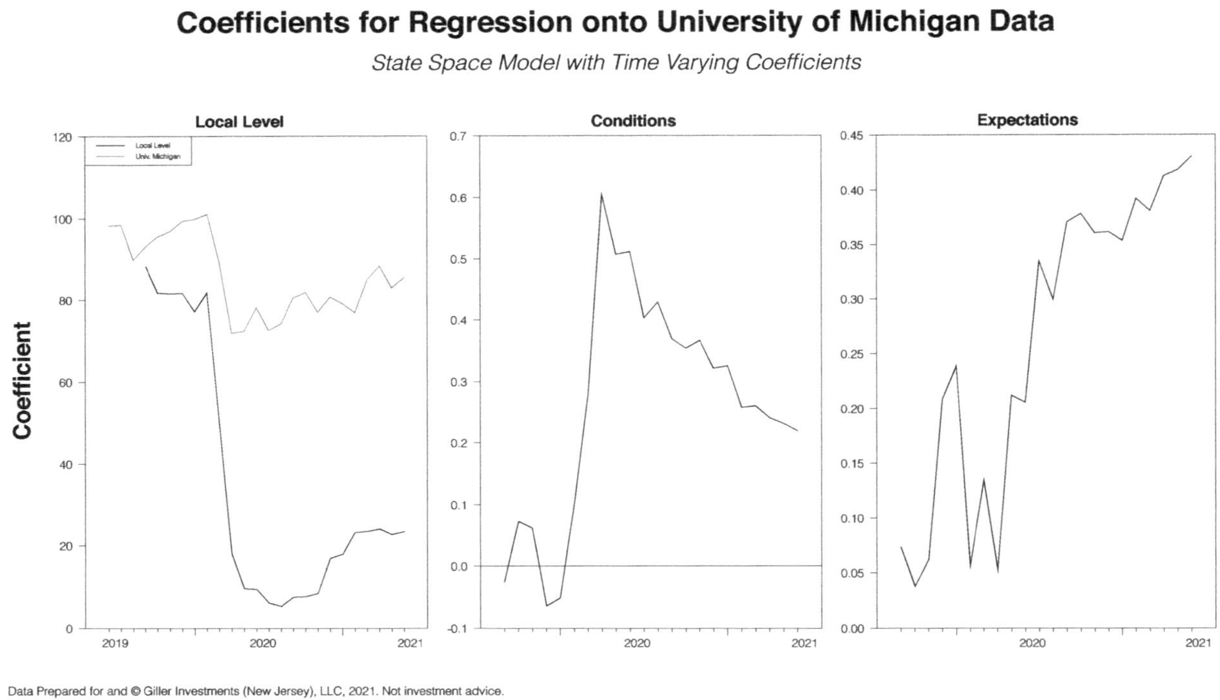

Figure 5.9: Estimates of the time-varying coefficients in the regression of Equation (5.13). Left panel: estimated "local level" parameter, α_t (black) and the official series, S_t (blue); middle panel: coefficient onto the private consumer conditions series, $\hat{C}_t$; right panel: coefficient onto the private consumer expectations series, $\hat{X}_t$. The history of the sentiment data is obtained from public sources.

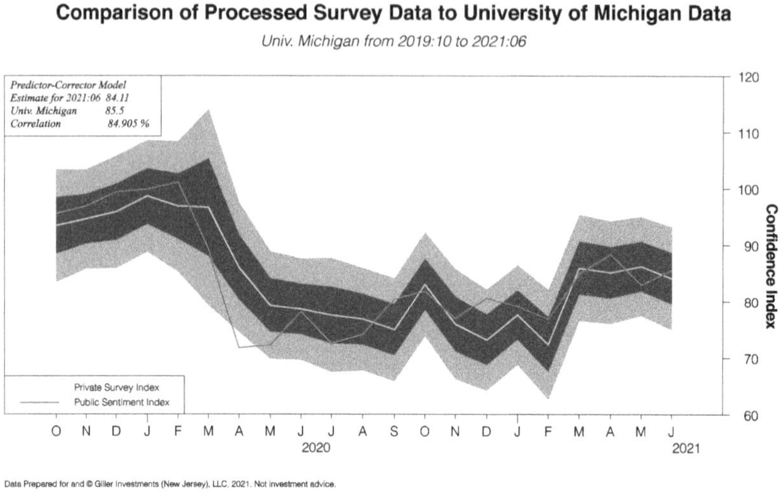

Figure 5.10: Estimated value of the Index of Consumer Sentiment based on private survey data and the public series. Magenta: official series; blue: private model; gray: 68% and 95% confidence regions.

5.4.2. *Consumer Expectations of Inflation*

Additional series derived from the University of Michigan's surveys represent consumer expectations of inflation. In their book *Animal Spirits*, Nobel Prize winners George Akerlof and Robert Shiller discuss the pernicious effects of inflation in the context that human beings seem to struggle to understand it *intellectually* [2].

The University of Michigan has, for many years, asked interviewees for their personal estimates of price changes over one and 5–10-year horizons. I do the same, supplementing this with a question specifically tied to the missing 2–5-year interval. The answers for the University of Michigan are numerical estimates, whereas I ask which of a given set of ranges the interviewee would select. In both cases we assume that the respondent properly understands not only the concept of inflation but how to judge a likely percentage growth rate for prices not due to changes in supply and demand. Akerlof and Shiller might think we are asking a lot of the public.

5.4.2.1. *Exploratory Data Analysis*

These concerns notwithstanding, let's take a look at whether we can also reproduce this index through private consumer survey research.

If so, this is another piece of evidence supporting the idea that our private surveys are meaningfully measuring the same data as that recorded by the University of Michigan.

In Figure 5.11, we see that the private survey estimates of inflation expectations over three horizons are well ordered with short term rates exceeding long term rates. If expected rates of inflation have this kind of term-structure it implies that the forward rates[n] are expected to be declining and so represents a forecast of short-term inflation reverting to a lower average rate in the long-term. This is not the case for the University of Michigan data, where the two curves lie essentially on top of each other for the period considered. Also exhibited is a scatter plot and linear regression between the private survey and officially released versions of the one year expected inflation rate. From a linear regression, this has an estimated slope coefficient of 0.691 ± 0.105 with a p value of 0.000001 and so we can conclude that the data are associated with high confidence.

5.4.2.2. *A Time-Varying Coefficients Model*

As in Section 5.4.1.2, I build a time-varying coefficients model to predict the released short term inflation expectations, S_t, from the observed short, medium, and long-term rates estimated from the private survey while allowing the relationship between the series to possess bias and inefficiencies that drift through time. Rather than model the rates directly, however, I use the implied forward rates so that covariance between the predictors is reduced. Writing these as $\hat{S}_t$, $\hat{M}_t$, and $\hat{L}_t$ respectively, the model is

$$S_t = \alpha_t + \beta_{St}\hat{S}_t + \beta_{Mt}\hat{M}_t + \beta_{Lt}\hat{L}_t + \varepsilon_t\sigma_0. \tag{5.14}$$

The coefficients are assumed to follow random walks in the manner of the prior model.

The time-series of the consumer expectations of inflation for the next year and the associated predicted value from the time-varying coefficients model are shown in Figure 5.12. Again the correlation is positive, and strong, at 75%.

[n]Meaning the 2–5-year rate with the effect of the 1-year rate removed and the 5–10 year rate with the effect of both of the others removed.

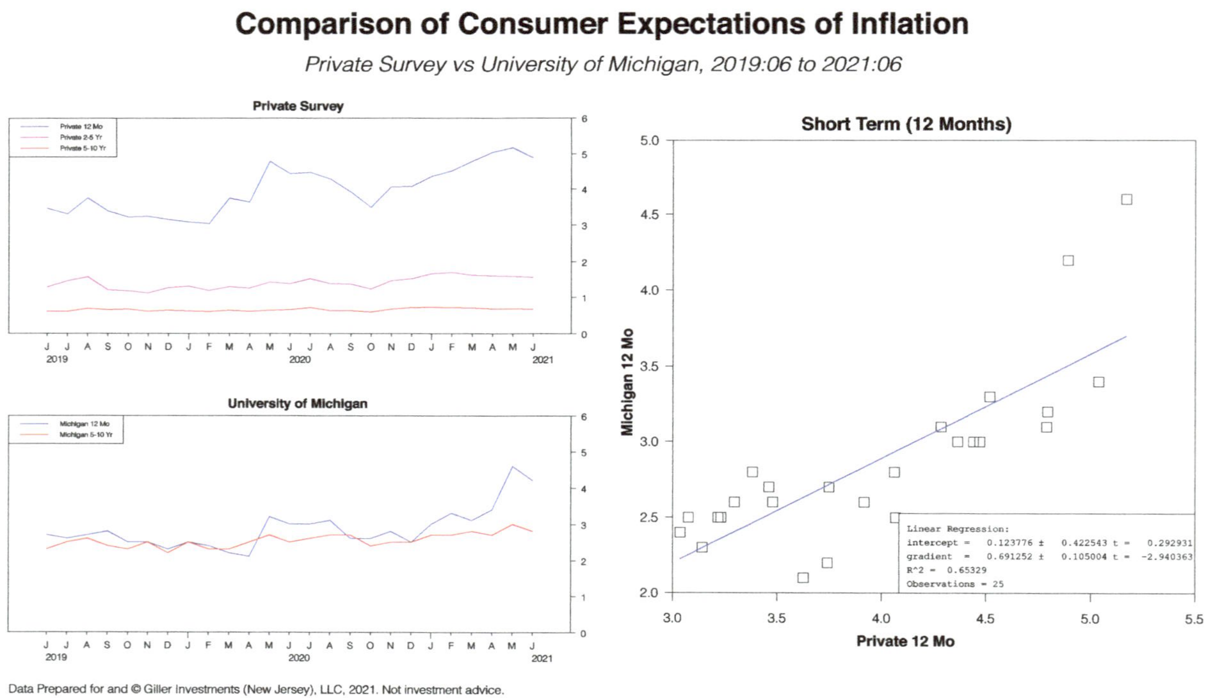

Figure 5.11: Comparison of consumer expectations of inflation from private surveys and the University of Michigan's data. Upper left panel: the three private time-series; lower left panel: the two Michigan time-series; right panel: scatter plot and regression of the short horizon (1 year) data. The history of the sentiment data is obtained from public sources.

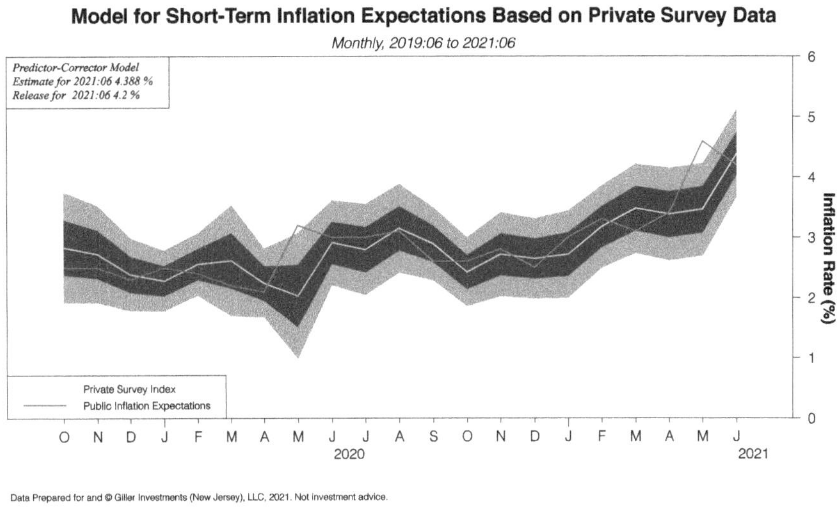

Figure 5.12: Estimated value of expectations of short-term inflation based on private survey data and the results of the University of Michigan's survey. Magenta: official series; blue: private model; gray: 68% and 95% confidence regions.

5.4.3. *The Residuals to the Time-Varying Coefficients Model*

Although the time-varying coefficients model is a powerful framework, relatively easy to use once you get the hang of it, and has built in a non-stationarity in the values of the regression coefficients, it suffers from the drawback that it demands the use of the Normal distribution to be readily solvable. It is therefore incumbent on the user of the models to validate whether this is an accurate assumption. We have seen in earlier chapters that such an assumption should not be taken for granted. Fortunately, in addition to forecasting the center of the distribution of future values of the dependent variable, the framework permits the extraction of a covariance matrix for the estimators. From this a Z score for the forecasts can be computed and its distribution compared to the Normal.

Figure 5.13 shows the empirical distribution function for the Z scores for all estimates I've made of various University of Michigan data series since I started this survey program in July 2019. In all there are 43 and the statistic for the Kolmogorov–Smirnov Test evaluates to 0.09 with a p value of 0.88. Therefore, I conclude that these

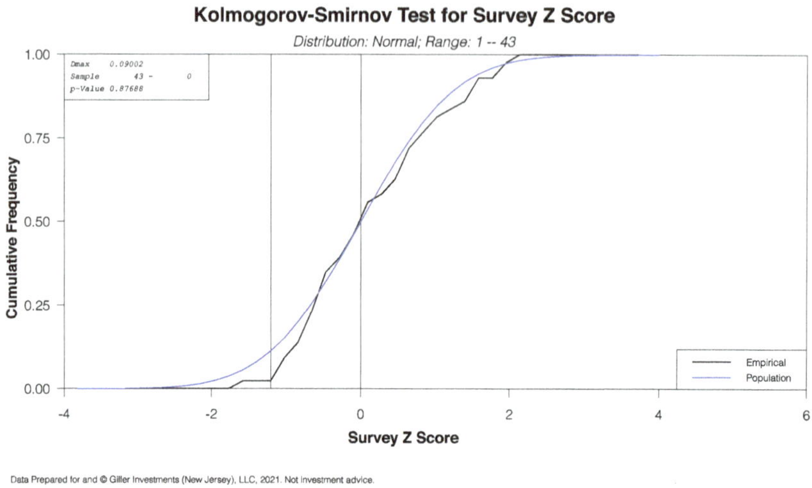

Figure 5.13: Empirical distribution function for Z score variables to University of Michigan data and the cumulative probability distribution of the Normal distribution. The University of Michigan data is obtained from public sources.

standardized residuals *are* all consistent with being drawn from a Normal distribution. On that basis I may also apply the Student's t test for Zero Mean, obtaining a value of $\bar{Z} = 0.115$ which has a t statistic of 0.81 and is not significantly different from zero. These results support the idea that the framework based on the Normal distribution *is* appropriate in this context, and validate the use of these methods for the work described.

5.4.4. *Response Times and Question Complexity*

As I noted above, the format of online survey presentation is quite different to that of traditional "man on the street" interviews. Figure 5.14 shows screenshots from the iPhone apps provided by two leading participants in this space: YouGov and SurveyMonkey. The advent of *gamification* and microtasks is clear.

The form of question shown is known in the survey business as "multiple-choice, single-answer" and requires two button clicks, the selection of the answer and the clicking of a progress button, to get the respondent one step closer to their microreward. We generally control for so-called "speeders," who just click the first, or last, answer regardless of opinion by both randomizing the positions

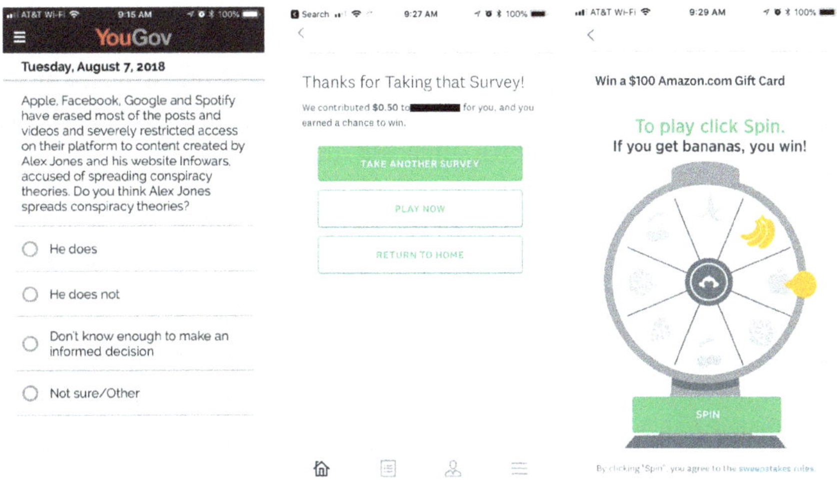

Figure 5.14: Screenshots showing the delivery of online surveys and microrewards to participants. Left: a survey in progress from YouGov; middle: payment of a microreward to a participant's charity of choice by SurveyMonkey; right: entry into a lottery for a gift card with a win probability of 1/60000 (from terms and conditions at time of capture) by SurveyMonkey.

of the questions and by timing responses and rejecting ones that are improbably quick. Human reaction time is, in fact, well studied.

5.4.4.1. *Hick's Law*

Hick's Law is a result from experiments run in the 1950s to understand human reaction times [70]. When placed in laboratory situation and asked to choose one of n options it was found that the time taken scaled as

$$T(n) = b \log_2(n+1). \tag{5.15}$$

The binary logarithm appears due to a hypothesized "divide and conquer" strategy employed by the brain to solve the problem presented, which was to click a button with the label indicated by a lamp that would light up at random.

5.4.4.2. *Empirical Results*

Because of results like Hick's Law, it is reasonable to expect an interviewee, speeding through a questionnaire to obtain a microreward, to exhibit a reaction time that depends on the number of choices. It is also reasonable to expect excessive question complexity to deter response.

I have not specifically run surveys that would address this issue, but I have run surveys with differing numbers of mutiple-choice single-answer questions and use a provider that indicates response time for each question answered. The data I have is shown in Figure 5.15.

The fitted curve is the Hick's Law relationship with an added constant term, a. With such a small quantity of data, there is little that can be said about the quality of the fit. The fit is by nonlinear least squares and finds the constant is $\hat{a} = 8.573 \pm 2.674$ and the scale factor $\hat{b} = 1.369 \pm 1.250$. Neither term is significant with better than 99% confidence, although the p value for the constant is close at 0.03. Although the data is *not inconsistent* with the Hick's Law curve I drew on the chart, the truth is many functional forms would fit and there is insufficient data to discriminate accurately between them. My data doesn't refute Hicks Law, but I can't emphatically say that it supports it either.

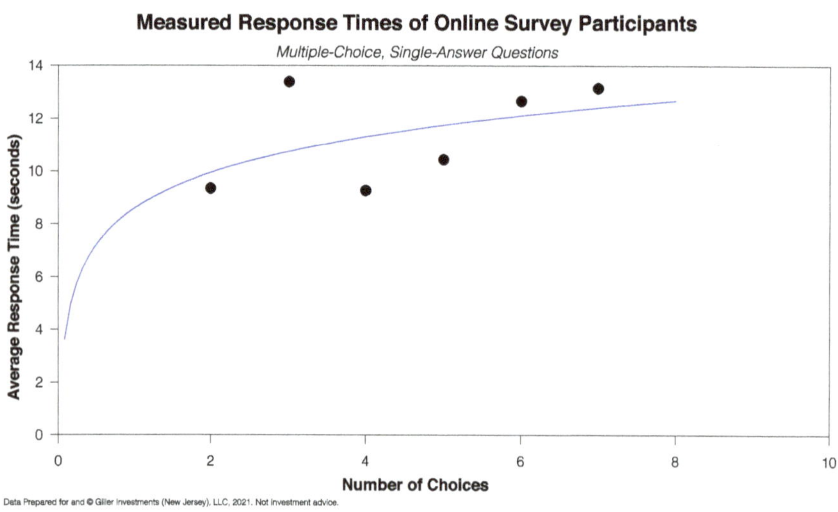

Figure 5.15: Scaling of question response time with number of choices. Data from consumer sentiment surveys run by Giller Investments, units are in seconds.

5.4.5. *Respondent Honesty*

Randomization of answer order prevents answers given with malintent from biasing the inferences from a survey, but they still have to be paid for and included in the results, which decreases the accuracy of the inferences from the survey. It also does not prevent a respondent from deliberately entering essentially random answers.

One of the most common reactions I find to analysis of survey data is a statement along the lines of:

> "you don't seriously believe these people are telling the truth?"

In fact I do, for several reasons:

(1) it is hard work to be consistently dishonest, it's actually a lot easier to be honest; and,
(2) the results of Section 5.4.3 show that my data is not significantly different from that of the University of Michigan, and I find it implausible that a grand conspiracy to coordinate dishonest answers across such a vast population would exist.

Nevertheless, it is incumbent on me to examine respondent honesty.

5.4.5.1. *The Giller Investments Employment Situation Survey*

It is impossible to know the *honesty* of respondents to online surveys, because it is impossible to know the *intent* of their answers. However, it is possible to examine their *reliability* by examining cross-tabulation between different answers that may be contradictory. The survey I run asks several questions that can be used for this purpose[o]:

(Q1) Which of the following categories best describes your *current* employment situation?

- Employed, working full-time.
- Employed, working part-time.
- Retired.
- Disabled, not able to work.
- Not employed, looking for work.

[o]Emphasis as presented to the respondent.

- Not employed, NOT looking for work.
- Homemaker, or full time carer, or student.[p]

  (These responses presented in a fully randomized manner.)

(Q2) *Approximately* how many hours do you work *for pay or profit* each week? (One full work day is usually 8 hours)

- None, I'm not currently working.
- No more than 8 hours.
- Between 9 and 16 hours.
- Between 17 and 24 hours.
- Between 25 and 32 hours.
- Between 33 and 40 hours.
- More than 40 hours.

  (These responses presented in order or reversed, with the direction selected at random.)

(Q3) For what kind of organization do you work *for pay or profit* each week?

- None, I'm not currently working.
- A for profit business I don't own.
- A for profit business I own.[q]
- A public entity (a government, school etc.)
- As an independent professional.
- A not-for-profit organization.
- A farm.

  (These responses presented in a fully randomized manner.)

These questions present an opportunity to validate consistency because the offered options "None, I'm not currently working."/"Nothing, I don't get paid to work." are clearly inconsistent with answers such as "Employed, working full-time."/"Employed, working part-time."

5.4.5.2. *Analysis of Cross-tabulations*

As I use the *Google Surveys* platform, in which surveys are presented as a task for internet users and the micro-reward for completion is

[p]This category added in response to an observation in which women aged 25–34 identified as "retired."

[q]Referred to as "self employed" in the cross-tabulations of Table 5.1.

access to "premium" content [126], I have to rely entirely on the respondents' *own* interpretations of what the questions mean, unlike a phone survey in which the meaning of responses can be confirmed and ambiguities resolved. It is plausible that a retiree or homemaker is also doing some side work, for example, and it also ambiguous to what extent "working full-time" correlates with a specific number of hours worked per week. It is less likely, however, that someone who answers "Employed, working full-time" also legitimately answers "None, I'm not currently working."

The relevant cross-tabulations are illustrated in Table 5.1. The table of Q1 versus Q2 shows that 22 of 2,511 people who indicated that they were employed full-time in their response to Q1 subsequently chose the option that they were not working *at all* when asked about their average weekly working hours. This is 0.9%. In addition, the table of Q1 versus Q3 shows that 41 of 2,353 people who had already indicated that they were employed full-time in Q1 subsequently chose the answer that they were not working when asked about the type of employer organization they worked for. This is 1.7%. These counts are not independent, and 360 of the people who answered Q1 and Q2 failed to answer Q3.

This analysis seems to suggest that around 1% of answers are unreliable, which is not bad at all. Of course, one important question is whether those answers are actually significant or just represent sampling error. Traditional statistical science has a long history of the analysis of such *contingency tables*. A key assumption is that the counting statistics are sufficiently large to permit the approximation of a Poisson distribution with a Normal distribution. In these circumstances Pearson's χ^2 Test may be used to assess significance[r] of departures from independence across the entire table.

The test addresses the statistical independence of both types of categorical variable featured in the cross-tabulation, and proceeds by estimating the *expected* counts for each element of the table as the product of their implied marginal rates multiplied by the sample size and then summing the squares of all of the observed standardized errors.

[r]The test is named after statistical pioneer Karl Pearson, who introduced it.

Table 5.1: Cross-tabulation of employment situation versus weekly hours worked and employer type from a private consumer survey.

	Average weekly working hours (Q2)							
Status (Q1)	Not working	Under 9	9–16	17–24	25–32	33–40	Over 40	Totals
Employed full-time	22	92	88	15	57	684	1554	2511
Retired	753	39	26	18	10	15	37	898
Employed part-time	13	32	70	105	102	41	42	405
Not employed	189	7	3	12	7	3	26	246
Homemaker	138	25	20	5	8	13	31	238
Unemployed	102	17	5	10	7	13	28	182
Disabled	146	12	5	2	0	1	13	180
Totals	1363	224	217	167	190	770	1730	4661

	Employer type (Q3)							
Status (Q1)	Not working	Farm	Independent	Not-for-profit	Public	Business	Self. empl.	Totals
Employed full-time	41	49	153	337	573	1015	1200	2353
Retired	610	38	29	41	30	28	52	799
Employed part-time	14	7	59	59	54	160	188	381
Not employed	128	18	17	19	10	14	25	216
Homemaker	116	15	17	18	18	20	33	217
Unemployed	96	18	17	7	9	18	27	173
Disabled	116	5	6	6	9	5	20	162
Totals	1121	149	297	486	703	1259	1545	4301

Note: Data from a survey run by Giller Investments through the *Google Surveys*. Counts are sums of raking weights. Tabulations are *not* independent.

For the Q1 versus Q2 table, the expected "confusion rate" for the data pair of interest is

$$\frac{E[\text{not working}|\text{employed full-time}]}{4661} = \frac{2511}{4661} \times \frac{1363}{4661} = \frac{734}{4661}. \quad (5.16)$$

The data are obviously not consistent with the assumption of independence on the basis of this coordinate alone.

However, this rejection of the lack of association between the responses doesn't help us figure out what that response rate ought to be. For this, assuming a "speeding" respondent clicks the first response in the list irrespective of its contents,[s] we can compute the expected rate as

$$E[\text{not working}|\text{employed full-time}] = 4661 \times \frac{1}{7} \times \frac{1}{2} \times \Pr(\text{speeding}). \quad (5.17)$$

Given an observation of 22 counts where $333 \times \Pr(\text{speeding})$ are expected, this suggests $\Pr(\text{speeding}) \approx 7\%$. Although this is not a great result, it does suggest that the overwhelming majority (93%) of the answers are legitimate.

5.5. Working with China Beige Book

The economic statistics published by the *National Bureau of Statistics of China* are viewed with some skepticism by many in the West. *China Beige Book* is a company that runs unique surveys assessing the state of the Chinese economy directly. The respondents are businesses based in China, so this data offers unique insights.

I met Shehzad Qazi through an ex Deutsche Bank colleague in late 2019, and we agreed it would be interesting to take a look at predicting Chinese economic statistics and the performance of China-exposed companies from their data. We signed an NDA and I started diving into their data, using the methods presented here to learn the relationships between their data and other series. In this section I'm going to give the example of using CBB's data to predict the

[s]And, presumably, all the while thinking to themselves what a fool I am to offer payment to them for filling out a "bogus" survey.

earnings of the casino operator *Wynn Resorts*. This is not the only piece of work I did for them, however, and, to be fully up front, it does represent a *good result*.

I have not yet had success at building a model for Chinese economic statistics, such as the *Purchasing Managers' Index* which is of great interest to investors. I believe this is because the official series are very severely disrupted by the COVID-19 crisis in the first quarter of 2020. Models developed prior to that period do fine, but they are impacted when the affected period is used and we don't really have enough additional data to figure out whether Q1 should just be ignored, or whether it should be allowed to alter inferences.[t]

5.5.1. *Modeling Fundamental Company Data*

There are many nuances to modeling company data, by which we mean things like sales, earnings and revenues. For American companies they are released quarterly but sequential quarters are generally not comparable. For example, many retailers do the majority of their business around the year end holiday period and the quarterly sales reported for this period are not really related to those of the next period or the previous one, which is a quiet one. It is also the reason why retailers such as *Home Depot* end their fiscal year in January.

Instead, in the *fundamental analysis* of companies we use the concept of the most recent comparable quarter. For most companies this is the fiscal period 1 year ago, so the fourth fiscal quarter for 2020, which covers November 2019, December 2019, and January 2020 for Home Depot, is more properly comparable to the fourth fiscal quarter for 2019 than the third fiscal quarter of 2020.

5.5.2. *The China Beige Book Data*

China Beige Book runs quarterly surveys that are available before the end of each calendar quarter to subscribers. As mentioned, the data comes from businesses based in China and takes the form of *diffusion indices* computed from questions that generally permit four answers. Does the respondent expect or observe a particular metric to:

[t]This is an issue that will apply to *Western* economic statistics as well. It is not specific to China!

(i) increase;
(ii) decrease;
(iii) stay the same; or,
(iv) they don't know or can't answer.

This is exactly the same structure as the University of Michigan data, studied earlier in this chapter. A diffusion index is usually computed as

$$100 \times \frac{\sum_i I_{it}[\text{up}]}{\sum_i (I_{it}[\text{up}] + I_{it}[\text{down}] + I_{it}[\text{no change}])}, \tag{5.18}$$

and represents the proportion of respondents indicating growth during the period examined.

In my work, I prefer an alternate statistic

$$\frac{\sum_i (I_{it}[\text{up}] - I_{it}[\text{down}])}{\sqrt{\sum_i I_{it}[\text{up}] + I_{it}[\text{down}]}}. \tag{5.19}$$

If there is no actual difference between the expected counts of up and down responses then this statistic is asymptotically distributed as Normal$(0, 1)$. The limit is usable when the "large sample" approximation of Poisson(λ) by Normal(λ, λ) is appropriate, which is often taken to be $\lambda \approx 10$. My first step was to compute this statistic from the China Beige Book data. This was done for all industrial sectors: agriculture, commodities, manufacturing, real estate and construction, retail, and services; for all regions; and for all indicators of which there are around 75 including such things as: backlog of work, export orders, and workforce.

5.5.3. *Predicting the Quarterly Revenues of Wynn Resorts*

Wynn Resorts is a casino and hotel operator with a substantial business interests in Macao. Their quarterly revenues are available from many public sources. The health of the Chinese economy would likely affect Wynn by increasing or decreasing visitors to their hotels based in Macao, and so the specific variables we looked at were aggregated across all industrial sectors so that they measured the state of the Chinese economy *as a whole*.

5.5.3.1. *A Simple Model*

If R_t represents the quarterly revenues of Wynn Resorts, in billions of dollars, and C_{it} an index computed from China Beige Book data of type i, then a linear additive noise model can be built, such as

$$R_t = \alpha + \beta_i C_{it} + \varphi R_{t-4} + \varepsilon_t \sigma \tag{5.20}$$

$$\varepsilon_t \sim \text{Student}(0, 1, \nu). \tag{5.21}$$

5.5.3.2. *Results*

As always, I begin my analysis by looking at the data. This is shown in the upper panel of Figure 5.16. I followed this by a robust regression, which is relatively immune to distributional choice, and then a maximum likelihood estimation of the parameters in Equation (5.20).

Five indicators were examined: sales, workforce, output, inventory, and wages. These are standardized directional indicators computed across all industrial sectors in China. The strongest results are for workforce, where positive numbers indicate companies are hiring and negative numbers indicate companies are laying off workers. The data very strongly favors the addition of China Beige Book data to a seasonal autoregression for the quarterly earnings, and the term is significant with $\hat{\beta}_w = 0.0165 \pm 0.0026$ and a p value less than 10^{-7}. The degrees of freedom parameter of the Student's t distribution is 3.1337 ± 1.7893 which is very far from the value that would indicate the distribution of residuals is consistent with a Normal distribution.

5.5.3.3. *The Effect of Coronavirus*

It's clear from Figure 5.16 that the largest errors for the model are for the period after the effective end of the Coronavirus outbreak in China. The China Beige Book data shows a substantial rebound that does not appear to lift Wynn Resorts with it. Whether this represents a paradigm shift or a temporary disruption remains to be seen. The only way to answer this question is with more data.

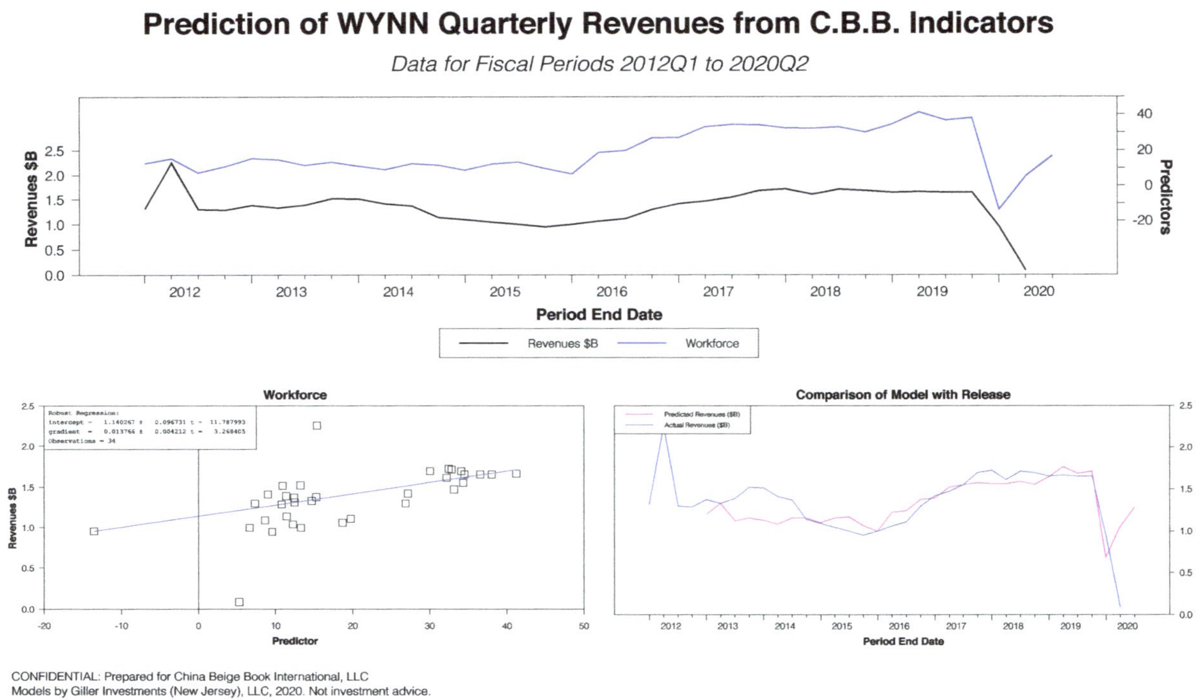

Figure 5.16: Analysis of the China Beige Book all sectors workforce change index and quarterly revenues for Wynn Resorts, Limited. Top panel: time series of CBB indicator and WYNN earnings; lower left: scatter plot of linear model and revenues plus robust regression line; lower right comparison of forecast revenues and reported revenues.

Table 5.2: Maximum likelihood regression of the quarterly revenues of Wynn Resorts, Limited on the national workforce indicator computed from China Beige Book data.

Regression results for Wynn resorts			
Variable	Estimate	Std. error	t statistic
α	0.7192	0.1582	4.5
β_w	0.0165	0.0026	6.2
φ	0.2173	0.0834	2.6
σ	0.0535	0.0512	
ν	3.1337	1.7893	

5.6. Generalized Autoregressive Dirichlet Multinomial Models

In this section, I am going to develop a model for an autoregressive time-series that may be used to model survey participants' responses to multiple-choice single-answer questions. This is necessary to understand the model I use to analyze and forecast Presidential Approval data in Section 5.7. The formal development of the model is necessary because this is not something you can find in text books. It unifies the continuous response variable time-series analysis presented in earlier sections with the static analysis usually done on survey data. I believe it is an entirely novel presentation, which I previously shared a preprint of [55]. It may be freely omitted for those do not wish to dive into the weeds of analyzing the stability of an autoregressive time-series model for opinion polls, and skip ahead to Section 5.7 to see the results of using the process on real data.

The structure of the process developed is a *state-space* representation of linked Dirichlet–Multinomial distributions in which the *concentration* vector, $\boldsymbol{\alpha}_t$ undergoes a strongly autocorrelated evolution and acts as a stochastic driver for a set of resulting multinomial counts, $\boldsymbol{n}_t$. The state-space structure is chosen to match the simple structure of the $GARCH(1,1)$ model of Engle [31] and Bollerslev [9] and for this reason the process is labeled the *Generalized Autoregressive Dirichlet–Multinomial Model.*

5.6.1. *The Dirichlet Distribution*

The Dirichlet distribution, which is sometimes called the *stick-breaking distribution*, is used to model random vectors, $\boldsymbol{p}$, that are constrained so that the sum of their elements is equal to a constant value and that each individual element lies between zero and their total. These constraints match those on the lengths of the parts of a stick which is randomly broken into a two pieces, and then the second piece randomly broken again, etc. until there are a fixed number of pieces, K, created. These are also the constraints that apply to the probabilities of an event and, without any loss of generality, we may take $p = \boldsymbol{p}^T\mathbf{1} = 1$ and $0 < p_i < 1$. It is a multivariate version of the Beta distribution, and the marginal distributions are Beta distributions. It has the probability density function

$$\text{Dirichlet}(\boldsymbol{\alpha}) \; : \; f(\boldsymbol{p}|\boldsymbol{\alpha}) = \frac{\Gamma(\alpha)}{\prod_{i=1}^{K}\Gamma(\alpha_i)}\prod_{i=1}^{K} p_i^{\alpha_i - 1}. \tag{5.22}$$

The parameter $\boldsymbol{\alpha}$ is called the concentration vector and has positive definite elements. The larger the value of an element, α_i, the more certain is it that the associated random number, p_i, will take the value α_i/α, where $\alpha = \boldsymbol{\alpha}^T\mathbf{1}$.

5.6.2. *The Multinomial Distribution*

The multinomial distribution describes the probability that we may obtain a set of counts of different types of objects when each individual trial involves picking one of K objects once. If the vector $\boldsymbol{p}$ represents the probabilities of those objects being chosen in one trial, and there are a total of n trials, then we expect a vector of counts $\boldsymbol{n}$ which has the property that the sums of the individual counts equals the total number of trials, or $\boldsymbol{n}^T\mathbf{1} = n$ and $0 < n_i < n$.

The multinomial distribution is very much a kind of discrete version of the Dirichlet distribution, expressed in terms of counts not proportions, and the Dirichlet is its *conjugate prior* in Bayesian analysis. It has the probability mass function[u]

$$\text{Multinomial}(\boldsymbol{p}) \,:\, f(\boldsymbol{n}) = \frac{n!}{\prod_{i=1}^{K} n_i!} \prod_{i=1}^{K} p_i^{n_i}. \tag{5.23}$$

5.6.3. *The Dirichlet–Multinomial Distribution*

The multinomial distribution is clearly highly suitable for modeling the responses to opinion polls that ask the public multiple-choice single-answer questions. If the public has a propensity to answer such a question by selecting option i with probability p_i then, in a panel of n people we should find the option selected $n_i = np_i$ times. However, when real world data is examined we often find the phenomenon of *overdispersion*, meaning that the variance of the counts, n_i, exceeds that expected, $np_i(1-p_i)$, even though the mean np_i is correct. This is a "fat tail" phenomenon similar to that observed in Chapter 2, where the variances of market returns was found to exceed that expected of the Normal distribution.

The analogue to the Generalized Error Distribution in this space of counting preferences is the *Dirichlet–Multinomial* distribution. In this we hypothesize that the probability vector, $\boldsymbol{p}$, of a multinomial distribution of counts, $\boldsymbol{n}$, is *itself* a random draw from a Dirichlet distribution, with concentration $\boldsymbol{\alpha}$. The $\boldsymbol{p}$ may be integrated out of the formulæ, to give an overdispersed distribution of counts expressed with the probability mass function

$$\text{DirMult}(\boldsymbol{\alpha}) \,:\, f(\boldsymbol{n}) = \frac{\Gamma(n+1)\Gamma(\alpha)}{\Gamma(n+\alpha)} \prod_{i=1}^{K} \frac{\Gamma(n_i+\alpha_i)}{\Gamma(n_i+1)\Gamma(\alpha_i)}. \tag{5.24}$$

[u]Some authors write $n!$ rather than $\Gamma(n+1)$ to emphasize the fact that the n's are discrete and the α's are continuous variables. The expressions are identical because $z! = \Gamma(z+1)$ from the properties of the Euler Gamma function. It is also possible to write it in terms of Euler's Beta function since $B(x,y) = \Gamma(x+y)/\{\Gamma(x)\Gamma(y)\}$ and $\Gamma(z+1) = z\,\Gamma(z)$.

5.6.4. *The Temporal Evolution of Opinion and Sentiment*

After defining several multivariate probability distributions, let's see how they can be used. Multicategory choice is often the procedure used to examine the opinion and sentiment of the general public and interviewees are asked questions with multiple-choice single-answer questions, such as those already discussed in this chapter.

The following is a question included in the well regarded Monmouth University polls:

> Do you approve or disapprove of the job Donald Trump is doing as president? [105]
>
> - approve;
> - disapprove; or
> - no opinion.

Polls typically have a predetermined, although possibly variable, sample size, n_t, and measure the number of responses n_{it} observed in each category, i, over a short interval (ending) at time t. This is assumed to be a statistically independent "snapshot" from which one can estimate the general population allocation probability, $\boldsymbol{p}_t$, as $\hat{\boldsymbol{p}}_t = \boldsymbol{n}_t/n_t$ and it is straightforward to show that this is the MLE of $\boldsymbol{p}_t$.

Traditional polling, whether by random-digit-dialed telephone call or in-person interview, is typically slow and expensive to operate. For an independent multinomial allocation, the variance of the proportion of responses in category i, σ_{it}^2, is given by

$$\sigma_{it}^2 = \frac{p_{it}(1 - p_{it})}{n_t}. \tag{5.25}$$

This is the equation that leads to the typically quoted "margin-of-error" in the results of opinion polls. The Monmouth University poll cited above has a sample size of 800 and a margin-of-error of 3.5%. For a roughly 50:50 proposition, such as a current presidential approval ratings, Equation (5.25) leads to a "worse case" standard deviation of $\sqrt{0.5 \times 0.5/800} \approx 1.8\%$ and a 95% confidence region as quoted.

However, many opinion pollsters measure the same aspects of consumer sentiment and all opinion pollsters repeat their samples frequently. Even a cursory examination of the time-series of polls from multiple vendors[v] shows that there is considerable serial correlation of their estimates of $\hat{\boldsymbol{p}}_t$ through time. This supports not only the idea that a true, underlying, state-space process generating the allocation probability $\boldsymbol{p}_t$ does actually exist (i.e. it is not an *idiosyncratic* to the polling organization but a general *systemic* property of the population itself) but also that it should be modeled with a process that naturally generates autocorrelation.

The introduction of explicit models for the temporal evolution of the allocation probability, $\boldsymbol{p}_t$, as distinct from *ad hoc* processing such as moving averages, kernel density estimation, or varieties of local linear regression [120], and which are known to be an inefficient procedure when observations are not independent in time,[w] allow less biased models to be estimated and, critically, for those estimated models to be used for forecasting purposes.

5.6.5. *Differing Time-Horizons*

Explicit models for the temporal evolution of the allocation probability also permit analysis to proceed in circumstances when the frequency of observation differs from the frequency of calibration. An example of this might be a "predictor–corrector" model where a higher resolution estimate of a more slowly reported statistic is required such as a private survey that is executed daily but calibrated to public data that is only released monthly. Classic state-space time-series models (as described in [25]) and estimated via the Kalman Filter [67] may be used for such modeling, yet they assume fundamentally Gaussian processes that do not apply in this case. The essential constraints that "the sum of the parts must equal the whole," and that all observations be non-negative, will be violated *almost certainly* by the use of a surrogate Gaussian model.

Market research surveys and opinion polls can be slow and costly to produce at high volume. In addition, to maintain continuity of

[v]See, for example, the collections of opinion polls hosted by *The Huffington Post* [72] or Nate Silver's *538* [121].

[w]See any of the classic works on time series analysis such as [11].

methodology within the series, methods in use *today* are more likely to correspond to the "state-of-the-art" several decades ago than the most efficient collection procedures available to contemporary analysts. Thus official government agencies, such as the Bureau of Labor Statistics (BLS) for the USA, tend to produce market moving data with low temporal frequency (e.g. monthly) and significant latency (such as a week after the end of the reference period).[x] This data is highly informative about the economy and so many market participants are interested in advance knowledge of the likely change in such statistics, provided they can calibrate any private data to agree with the official statistic over the long term. The process model described in this work may be used for such a purpose.

5.6.6. *Use of the Dirichlet–Multinomial Distribution*

In the following, a discrete time framework to model counts of categorical responses to survey questions that are collected sequentially is developed. The basic structure is that categorical responses are controlled by an unknown K-dimensional state vector, $\boldsymbol{\alpha}_t \in (\mathbb{R}^+)^K \ \forall\ t \in \mathbb{Z}^+$, that evolves through time in response to a stochastic input but also with a substantial memory element. This state vector is unknowable directly but may be estimated from observed data. It is interpreted as the "concentration parameter" of a Dirichlet distribution from which the probability vector, $\boldsymbol{p}_t$ is drawn. This probability vector then generates the allocation of n_t answers into K categories and the observation of category counts $\boldsymbol{n}_t$ via a draw from a multinomial distribution. The observed counts then affect the (otherwise deterministic) future evolution of the state vector and thus the resultant process is stochastic and autocorrelated.

An analogy to the properties of the variance process, $\boldsymbol{h}_t$, in the GARCH$(1,1)$ model of Bollerslev [9] is quite straightforward. The total number of responses, n_t, is assumed to be an exogenous factor without much fundamental interest and the goal of the experimenter is to estimate and forecast $\boldsymbol{p}_t$, a general property of the population, and not merely $\boldsymbol{n}_t$, the preferences of the sample.

[x]These metrics are for the *Employment Situation* release of the BLS.

There are several properties of the Dirichlet–Multinomial distribution that make it attractive to build such a model around. Although the probability vector has two strong constraints *for all* t,

$$\mathbf{0} < \boldsymbol{p}_t < \mathbf{1} \quad \text{and} \quad \boldsymbol{p}_t^T \mathbf{1} = 1, \tag{5.26}$$

the constraint on $\boldsymbol{\alpha}_t$ itself is weaker

$$\boldsymbol{\alpha}_t > \mathbf{0}, \tag{5.27}$$

and it generates a random draw that necessarily satisfies Equation (5.26) by construction.[y] The work of Bollerslev [9] *et seq.* on modeling variance processes shows that the constraint of Equation (5.27) is, in fact, fairly easy to "bake in" to the structure when the stochastic driver is non-negative definite.

The fundamentally stochastic nature of $\boldsymbol{p}_t$ facilitates the construction of overdispersed multinomial counts that are often found "in the field"[z] and the natural ability of the Dirichlet–Multinomial to generate overdispersion is an attractive feature of the distribution.[aa]

5.6.7. *Simple ARMA*(1, 1) *Models*

Let $\boldsymbol{n}_t$ be the set of counts of responses to a "choose one of K" multiple choice survey question conditioned on the information set of the population, $\mathcal{I}_t$, at time t and let n_t be the total survey sample size and require $n_t \in \mathbb{Z}^+$.

The process is defined by:

$$\mathcal{I}_{t+1} \supseteq \mathcal{I}_t \cup \boldsymbol{n}_t \tag{5.28}$$

$$\boldsymbol{n}_t | \mathcal{I}_t \sim \text{Multinomial}\left(\boldsymbol{p}_t, n_t\right) \tag{5.29}$$

$$\boldsymbol{p}_t \sim \text{Dirichlet}\left(\boldsymbol{\alpha}_t\right) \tag{5.30}$$

$$\boldsymbol{\alpha}_t = \boldsymbol{\alpha}_0 + \varphi \boldsymbol{\alpha}_{t-1} + \psi \boldsymbol{n}_{t-1} \; \forall \, t > 1 \tag{5.31}$$

$$\mathcal{I}_1 = \{\varphi, \psi, \boldsymbol{\alpha}_0, \boldsymbol{\alpha}_1\}. \tag{5.32}$$

---

[y] Vector inequalities are to be interpreted as elementwise inequalities.

[z] See Lindsley [88] and others.

[aa] A fuller discussion of the Dirichlet–Multinomial may be found in works such as that of Mossiman[103].

From the definition of the multinomial distribution and Equation (5.29), it follows that:

$$\boldsymbol{n}_t \geq \mathbf{0} \tag{5.33}$$

and

$$\boldsymbol{n}_t^T \mathbf{1} = n_t. \tag{5.34}$$

(The unit-norms of non-negative vectors[bb] $||\boldsymbol{x}||_1$ will be written simply as x thus $||\boldsymbol{n}_t||_1 = n_t$ and $||\boldsymbol{p}_t||_1 = 1$ and those quantities will be referred to as "the norm" of the vector.)

From the definition of the Dirichlet distribution and Equation (5.30) the properties of $\boldsymbol{p}_t$ in Equation (5.26) follows and thus the elements of $\boldsymbol{p}_t$ may be interpreted as giving the probabilities that a single respondent picks choice i for $i \in [1, K]$. In the above $\boldsymbol{\alpha}_0$ is *not* interpreted as "the value of $\boldsymbol{\alpha}_t$ at time $t = 0$" as $t > 0$. $\boldsymbol{\alpha}_0$ is a fundamental parameter of the process definition as are ϕ and ψ.

5.6.8. *Special Cases*

Equation (5.31) has a number of special cases that are interesting.

(1) *Stochastic Trend*: if $\boldsymbol{\alpha}_0 = \mathbf{0}$, $\varphi = 0$, and $\psi = 1$, then $\boldsymbol{\alpha}_t = \sum_{u=1}^{t} \boldsymbol{n}_u$ represents the cumulative counts in each category at time t. Due to the nature of the stochastic fluctuations of counting processes, this system will tend to concentrate around the allocation that arises by chance in its early stages.
(2) *Linear Filter*: if $\boldsymbol{\alpha}_0 = \mathbf{0}$, and $\varphi + \psi = 1$, then $\boldsymbol{\alpha}_t$ is an exponentially weighted moving average of $\{\boldsymbol{n}_u\}_{u=1}^{t}$ with memory scale $1/\psi$ observations.
(3) *Mean Reversion*: if $\boldsymbol{\alpha}_0 > \mathbf{0}$, then the system is mean reverting with a central tendency in the direction of $\boldsymbol{\alpha}_0$. The discussion below will concentrate on this choice.

5.6.9. *Properties of the Dirichlet Distribution and the Dirichlet Multinomial Distribution*

As a draw from the Dirichlet distribution, the properties of $\boldsymbol{p}_t$ are well known and the distribution is discussed in many works on

[bb]That is, $||\boldsymbol{x}||_1 = \sum_{i=1}^{K} |x_i| \Rightarrow ||\boldsymbol{x}||_1 = \boldsymbol{x}^T\mathbf{1}$ iff $\boldsymbol{x} > \mathbf{0}$.

multivariate analysis such as Mardia [93]. The elementary expression for the expectation in terms of the concentration vector and its norm

$$E_t[\boldsymbol{p}_t] = \frac{\boldsymbol{\alpha}_t}{\alpha_t}. \tag{5.35}$$

is important. The compound distribution is analytically tractable due to the strong structural similarity between the Dirichlet and Multinomial distributions. Of particular note is the reduction of Equation 5.24 when the Gamma functions are folded into Beta functions and the values for $n_{jk} = 0$ are removed (which is possible since $\Gamma(1) = 1$). This gives the probability of an outcome $\boldsymbol{n}_t$, as a product over only the non-zero counts and given by

$$\Pr(\boldsymbol{n}_t|\boldsymbol{\alpha}_t) = \frac{n_t B(n_t, \alpha_t)}{\prod_{i:n_{it}>0} n_{it} B(n_{it}, \alpha_{it})}, \tag{5.36}$$

where $B(x, y)$ is the Euler Beta function. From Equation (5.35), assuming that n_t is either non-stochastic or independent of $\boldsymbol{p}_t$, it follows that

$$E_t[\boldsymbol{n_t}] = E_t[n_t \boldsymbol{p}_t] = n_t E_t[\boldsymbol{p}_t] = n_t \frac{\boldsymbol{\alpha}_t}{\alpha_t}. \tag{5.37}$$

and so we see that central tendency of the count vector $\boldsymbol{n_t}$ is directly proportional to the *direction* of the concentration vector but not its magnitude.

5.6.10. *Unconditional Means*

Taking the process definition of Equation (5.31) and requiring that at some sufficient distance $s > 0$ away from the start of the process there exist an unconditional mean for the concentration, $\boldsymbol{\alpha} = E[\boldsymbol{\alpha}_t]\ \forall\, t > s$, gives

$$\boldsymbol{\alpha} = \frac{\boldsymbol{\alpha}_0 + \psi E[\boldsymbol{n}_{t-1}]}{1 - \varphi}\ \forall\, t > s. \tag{5.38}$$

as a condition for the existence of the unconditional mean of the concentration.

5.6.11. *Unconditional Mean of the Norm of the Concentration Vector*

The existence of the unconditional mean of a vector with strictly positive elements requires the existence of the unconditional mean of its 1-norm as the norm is linear on such a vector. That is $(E[\boldsymbol{x}])^T\mathbf{1} = E[\boldsymbol{x}^T\mathbf{1}] = E[x]$, meaning that

$$\exists(\boldsymbol{\alpha} = E[\boldsymbol{\alpha}_t]) \Rightarrow \exists(\alpha = E[\alpha_t]) \text{ and } \alpha = \boldsymbol{\alpha}^T\mathbf{1}. \tag{5.39}$$

Specializing to the case of constant sample size ($n_t = n$) gives the condition

$$\alpha = \frac{\alpha_0 + \psi n}{1 - \varphi} > 0, \tag{5.40}$$

for the unconditional mean of the norm of the concentration to exist. Since α_0 and n are strictly positive, this reduces to

$$\varphi < 1 \quad \text{and} \quad \psi > -\frac{\alpha_0}{n}, \tag{5.41}$$

$$\text{or} \quad \varphi > 1 \quad \text{and} \quad \psi < -\frac{\alpha_0}{n}. \tag{5.42}$$

5.6.12. *Lead 1 Forecasting*

With the simple linear learning model of Equation (5.31), forecasting at lead 1 is elementary. Equation (5.37) gives

$$E[\boldsymbol{n}_{t+1}|\boldsymbol{\alpha}_{t+1}] = n_{t+1}\frac{\boldsymbol{\alpha}_{t+1}}{\alpha_{t+1}} \tag{5.43}$$

for time $t+1$ and non-stochastic (but not necessarily constant) n_{t+1}. Since the concentration at time $t+1$ is a deterministic function of the prior state and prior innovation

$$\boldsymbol{\alpha}_{t+1} = \boldsymbol{\alpha}_0 + \varphi\boldsymbol{\alpha}_t + \psi\boldsymbol{n}_t, \tag{5.44}$$

$$\alpha_{t+1} = \alpha_0 + \varphi\alpha_t + \psi n_t, \tag{5.45}$$

$$\Rightarrow E_t[\boldsymbol{n}_{t+1}] = n_{t+1}\frac{\boldsymbol{\alpha}_0 + \varphi\boldsymbol{\alpha}_t + \psi\boldsymbol{n}_t}{\alpha_0 + \varphi\alpha_t + \psi n_t}. \tag{5.46}$$

Note that, trivially, $E_t[n_{t+1}] = n_{t+1}$, as must be the case for non-stochastic n_{t+1}.

5.6.13. *Lead m Forecasting and Stationarity*

The prior section shows a forecasting formula constructed directly. More generally, forecasting concentration at lead m can be done by taking the conditional expectation of Equation (5.31), repeatedly resubstituting into that expression, and applying the law of iterated expectations, i.e. that $E_t E_u = E_t$ if $t \geq u$. The first order expressions are:

$$E_t[\boldsymbol{\alpha}_{t+m}] = \boldsymbol{\alpha}_0 + \varphi E_t[\boldsymbol{\alpha}_{t+m-1}] + \psi E_t[\boldsymbol{n}_{t+m-1}], \tag{5.47}$$

and

$$E_t[\alpha_{t+m}] = \alpha_0 + \varphi E_t[\alpha_{t+m-1}] + \psi n_{t+m-1}. \tag{5.48}$$

If resubstitution is done a total of $v - 1$ times, the concentration scale forecast (Equation 5.48) becomes

$$E_t[\alpha_{t+m}] = \alpha_0 \sum_{u=1}^{v} \varphi^{u-1} + \varphi^v E_t[\alpha_{t+m-v}] + \psi \sum_{u=1}^{v} \varphi^{u-1} n_{t+m-u}, \tag{5.49}$$

$$= (\alpha_0 + \psi \bar{n}_v) \frac{1 - \varphi^v}{1 - \varphi} + \varphi^v E_t[\alpha_{t+m-v}], \tag{5.50}$$

where

$$\bar{n}_v = \frac{1 - \varphi}{1 - \varphi^v} \sum_{u=1}^{v} \varphi^{u-1} n_{t+m-u} \tag{5.51}$$

is an exponentially weighted moving average of the sample sizes (and the expectation operator $E_u[\cdot]$ becomes unity for $u \leq t$). This expression shows a classic time-series forecast structure of decaying initial conditions, averaged shocks, and a steady state bias.

For the *semi-infinite* time domain considered here, clearly iteration backwards must stop at time $t+m-v = 1 \Rightarrow \max v = t+m-1$. Convergence of the geometric series in the limit $m \to \infty$ requires that $|\varphi| < 1$ and, with these conditions,

$$\lim_{m\to\infty} E_t[\alpha_{t+m}] = \frac{\alpha_0 + \psi \bar{n}}{1 - \varphi} \text{ with } \bar{n} = \lim_{m\to\infty} \bar{n}_{t+m-1}. \tag{5.52}$$

In the above, $\bar{n}$, if it exists, is the limit of the sequence of exponentially weighted averages of the set of sample sizes. For the simple case of fixed sample sizes, $n_t = n \; \forall \; t > 0$, it clearly does exist under the same conditions on φ. The existence of Equation (5.52) is a precise statement that the concentration scale is stationary in expectation and, in the case of constant sample sizes, is equal to Equation (5.40). Thus, in this case, the expected value of the norm of the concentration at large leads is equal to its unconditional mean. The condition on φ for convergence of the forecasts eliminates half of the parameter space permitted in Section 5.6.11 as it is inconsistent with Equation (5.42).

Equation (5.47) can similarly be iteratively resubstituted into itself, leading to an analogue expression to Equation (5.52) with similar conditions and so that does not advance the solution. Alternately, the "delta method" of Oehlert [110] can be used for non-stochastic sample size to write

$$E_t[\boldsymbol{\alpha}_{t+m}] = \boldsymbol{\alpha}_0 + \varphi E_t[\boldsymbol{\alpha}_{t+m-1}] + \psi n_{t+m-1} E_t\left[\frac{\boldsymbol{\alpha}_{t+m-1}}{\alpha_{t+m-1}}\right], \tag{5.53}$$

$$\simeq \boldsymbol{\alpha}_0 + \left(\varphi + \frac{\psi n_{t+m-1}}{E_t[\alpha_{t+m-1}]}\right) E_t[\boldsymbol{\alpha}_{t+m-1}]. \tag{5.54}$$

(In the above the delta method to first order is used to express the expectation of a ratio in terms of the ratio of expected values.) Equation 5.50 on 336 at the extremum $v = t + m - 1$ takes the value

$$E_t[\alpha_{t+m}] = (\alpha_0 + \psi \bar{n}_{t+m-1}) \frac{1 - \varphi^{t+m-1}}{1 - \varphi} + \varphi^{t+m-1} \alpha_1, \tag{5.55}$$

$$\simeq \frac{\alpha_0 + \psi \bar{n}_{t+m-1}}{1 - \varphi}, \tag{5.56}$$

at large m. If variation in n_t is relatively small, such that $n_t \approx \bar{n} \; \forall \; t$, then

$$E_t[\boldsymbol{\alpha}_{t+m}] \simeq \boldsymbol{\alpha}_0 + \left(\frac{\alpha_0 \varphi + \psi \bar{n}}{\alpha_0 + \psi \bar{n}}\right) E_t[\boldsymbol{\alpha}_{t+m-1}]. \tag{5.57}$$

Using this expression and iterating back to $t = 1$, gives

$$E_t[\boldsymbol{\alpha}_{t+m}] \approx \boldsymbol{\alpha}_0 \frac{1 - \beta^{t+m-1}}{1 - \beta} + \beta^{t+m-1} \boldsymbol{\alpha}_1, \tag{5.58}$$

$$\text{where } \beta = \frac{\alpha_0 \varphi + \psi \bar{n}}{\alpha_0 + \psi \bar{n}}, \tag{5.59}$$

and convergence in the limit $m \to \infty$ requires $|\beta| < 1$ giving

$$\lim_{m\to\infty} E_t[\boldsymbol{\alpha}_{t+m}] = \frac{\boldsymbol{\alpha}_0}{1-\beta}. \tag{5.60}$$

If this limit exists then the concentration vector itself is stationary in the mean and, from that, it follows that the sample counts themselves are stationary in the mean.

5.6.14. *Aggregate Conditions for Stationarity of the Process*

Collecting all the conditions discussed above, in aggregate, stationarity in expectation when the sample size is constant or deterministic with low variability requires

$$|\varphi| < 1 \quad \text{and} \quad \psi > -\frac{\alpha_0}{2\bar{n}}(1+\varphi) \tag{5.61}$$

with α_0 and $\bar{n}$ strictly positive by construction. This region is illustrated in Figure 5.17.

5.6.15. *In Conclusion*

The work of this section has demonstrated that a process that models the autoregressive evolution of multicategory choice preferences through time can be constructed and that, under demonstrated combinations of parameters, it is stationary in expectation. Due to the nature of the conditional probability distribution constructed it follows from this that it is also stationary in other higher moments, particularly in variance. This kind of process is suitable to model data from venues such as public opinion polling and consumer choice surveys, and others, and by the method of construction will never violate necessary conditions for such data, such that the category counts be whole numbers and that the sum of the category counts equal the total sample size. Approximations based upon the Normal distribution will violate these constraints almost certainly. The method will also model "unpopular" choices with the appropriate skew and covariance, again unlike approximations based on the Normal distribution.

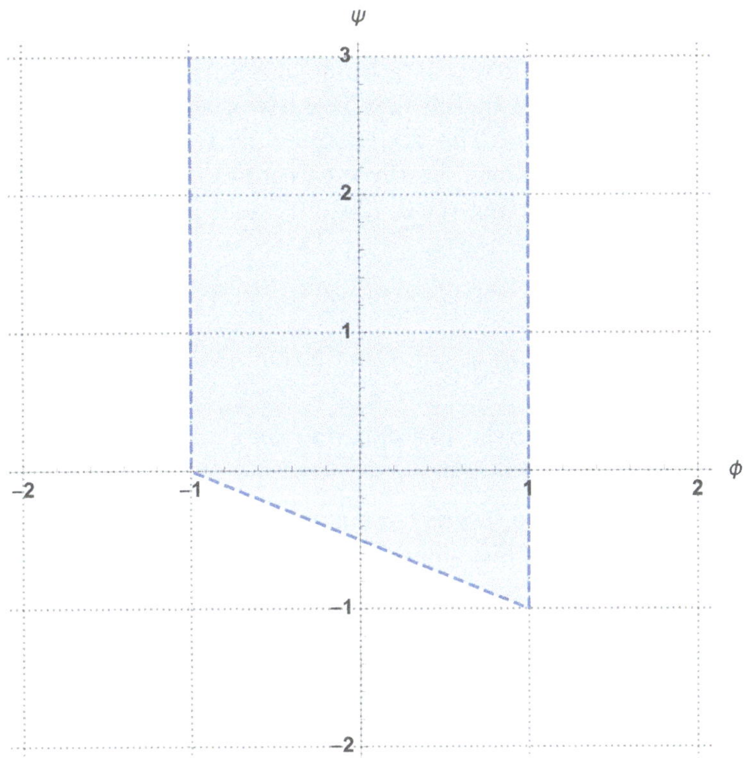

Figure 5.17: Region of stationarity in expectation for the case $\alpha_0 = \bar{n}$. The region is open for positive ψ provided $|\varphi| < 1$.

5.7. Presidential Approval Ratings

Like many others, I am interested in the political situation in the country I reside in and, although I am not a US Citizen, I keenly follow *data driven* analysis sites like Nate Silver's *538* and *Plural Vote*. Many regular opinion polls monitor presidential approval ratings, and the coverage of the approval of Donald Trump has been more active than ever before. My understanding of the business model behind *public* opinion polling is that it draws respondents in with questions about political issues before following up with questions about issues more relevant to consumer brands that pay to be included on these surveys.

5.7.1. *The Data*

I am currently taking survey data from Nate Silver's *538*,[cc] although this work was initiated in the first months of the Trump administration using data from *The Huffington Post's Pollster*. The data consists of approval counts, for three categories of response, for 107 different pollsters, starting on 01/20/2017 and updated daily. The data fields covered are:

(i) questions[dd];
(ii) population polled;
(iii) start and end date;
(iv) sample size;
(v) number of approves, disapproves, and don't knows (when present).[ee]

As is my usual practice, I wrote a custom Python script to capture the data and upload it into my database and I run that script automatically, every day.

The data as processed by *538* is published on their website [121]. At the time of writing it looked like that shown in Figure 5.18, which is a direct capture from publicly available data published on their website. It is very clear from the chart that the underlying factor driving these responses changes dynamically through time but does not look like mere noise.

5.7.2. *Combining Opinion Polls*

When we face the problem of combining multiple opinion polls there is a spectrum of views on the appropriate methodology. Many use some variant of Nate Silver's methodology, as outlined on their website [120]. These methods use the estimates of the proportions of responses from various polls, $\{\hat{\boldsymbol{p}}_i\}$, as inputs to some kind of smoothing algorithm that is essentially

$$\hat{\boldsymbol{p}}^* = \frac{\sum_i \hat{\boldsymbol{p}}_i w_i}{\sum_i w_i}, \tag{5.62}$$

with the weights, $\{w_i\}$, chosen in some manner.

[cc]Details of data sources may be found in the appendix on 395.
[dd]Some polls don't include a "don't know" options.
[ee]In some cases these counts are reconstructed from reported percentages.

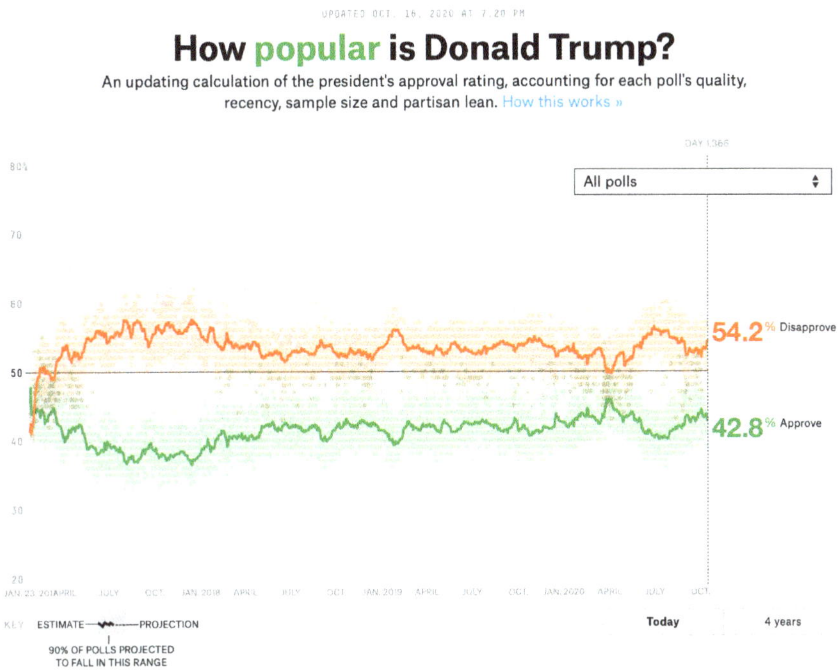

Figure 5.18: Presidential approval ratings data as processed by Nate Silver's *538*. The image is a screenshot from their publicly available page https://projects.fivethirtyeight.com/trump-approval-ratings/.

I chose to use a different methodology for several reasons:

(i) since actual response counts are knowable for all polls considered, we can accumulate counts across pollsters provided we can align their question set,
(ii) by aligning counts of responses rather than proportions we can incorporate results from polls that do and that don't include a "don't know" question,
(iii) few of the polls cited are single-day "snapshots" of opinion — they are typically collected over three or four days,
(iv) I wanted to have access to an algorithm that permitted *forecasting* intrinsically in its construction.

This latter item is most important: algorithms such as moving averages, kernel smoothing, or local linear or polynomial regression, cannot be used for forecasting because they contain no recipe for constructing the expected value of a *future* information set in terms of currently observed data. Many commentators like to draw historic averages on time series but these lines *provide no additional information that is not contained in the data itself*, they just allow us to pretend that the data is less stochastic than it actually is. All of my modeling work is directed toward predicting the values of unobserved data and all contains some variant of the now familiar linear additive noise model of Equation (2.4).

As few polls are single day snapshots, and many overlap without being entirely coincident, I needed a recipe to deal with this. I decided to divide the responses from each poll *equally* over the days it was in the field. If a given poll took four days and sampled 1,500 people I would assign the responses of 375 to each day and allocate those counts to the permitted answers in a manner proportionate to the final result, e.g. if 800 answered "yes," and 600 "no," in the final counts I would allocate 200 per day to "yes" and 150 per day to "no." Although this is *arbitrary* post hoc processing I feel that it is, nevertheless, a reasonable and justifiable way to deal with the data.

The model of Section 5.6.7 was explicitly designed to be usable to solve this problem. In addition to smoothing and combining data it also allowed me to forecast future values of the metric of interest, $E_s[\boldsymbol{p}_t]$ for $s < t$. The work of the prior section was then necessary to demonstrate that such a construction was *meaningful*.

5.7.3. *The Model*

To be concrete, the process to be estimated is:

$$\boldsymbol{\alpha}_t = \boldsymbol{\alpha}_0 + \varphi\boldsymbol{\alpha}_{t-1} + \psi\boldsymbol{n}_{t-1}, \tag{5.63}$$

$$\boldsymbol{n}_t \sim \text{DirMul}(\boldsymbol{\alpha}_t), \tag{5.64}$$

$$\boldsymbol{p}_t = \frac{\boldsymbol{\alpha}_t}{\alpha_t}, \tag{5.65}$$

with $\boldsymbol{n}_t$ representing the aggregated counts for three categories (approve, disapprove, and don't know) computed as described above. I model three states such that the vector $\boldsymbol{n}_t$ represents total counts of respondents indicating that they approve, disapprove, or are undecided about President Trump, summed over all surveys that were active on date t, and with the total counts for each survey divided by the number of days for which the survey was in the field. $\boldsymbol{p}_t$ is the metric we are interested in, as it represents the probability that a respondent chosen at random from the population would choose each response:

$$\boldsymbol{p}_t = \begin{pmatrix} \Pr(\text{approve}) \\ \Pr(\text{disapprove}) \\ \Pr(\text{don't know}) \end{pmatrix}. \tag{5.66}$$

Estimation is done by maximum likelihood, which is straightforward to compute using Equation (5.36). The log likelihood is

$$\mathcal{L}(\boldsymbol{\alpha}_0, \varphi, \psi) = \sum_t \Bigg[\ln n_t + \ln B(n_t, \alpha_t) - \sum_{i:n_{it}>0} \{\ln n_{it} + \ln B(n_{it}, \alpha_{it})\} \Bigg], \tag{5.67}$$

and efficient routines exist to compute the log of the Beta function quickly.

5.7.4. *Estimated Parameters*

The first polls were taken on 01/02/2017, before Donald Trump's inauguration on 01/20/2017, and the data presented here terminates on 10/18/2020. The end time-series of imputed probabilities for 2020, which are estimates of the population approval ratings, for the fitted model are shown in Figure 5.19. This chart also shows forecasts made out to election day, 11/03/2020, with 95% confidence regions. These confidence regions are computed from the marginal Beta distributions for each parameter and, for the "don't know" choice, clearly show the asymmetry which exists close to the zero bound.

The estimated parameters are listed in Table 5.3 (t statistics are with quoted with respect to zero null hypothesis values). There are several interesting hypotheses to test from this data.

Firstly we should examine whether the data is consistent with a "constant preferences" model in which $\hat{\boldsymbol{\alpha}}_0 > \mathbf{0}$ and $\hat{\varphi} = \hat{\psi} = 0$. This can be done via the Maximum Likelihood Ratio Test for the introduced parameters from the autoregressive model. This gives $\chi^2_2 = 5,978$ which has a vanishingly small p value. The hypothesis is strongly rejected, the approval ratings are not constant.

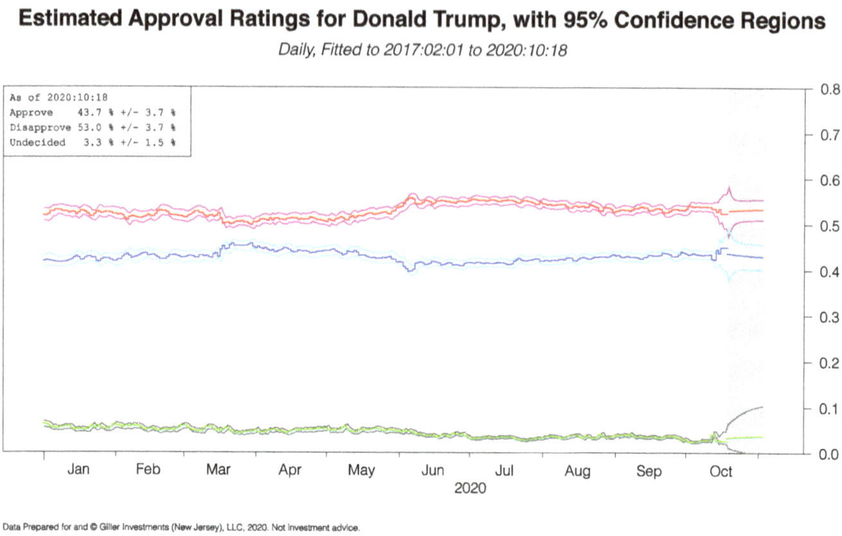

Figure 5.19: Time-series of estimated approval ratings for President Trump during 2020 with confidence regions and forecasts. The red line represents "disapprove," and the magenta lines the edge of the 95% confidence regions; the blue line represents "approve," and the cyan lines the 95% confidence regions; and the green line is "don't know" with gray for the confidence region. The shaded regions are the forecasts, which end on election day 11/03/2020.

Table 5.3: Maximum likelihood estimates of the parameters for the generalized autoregressive Dirichlet multinomial model for Presidential approval ratings.

Regression results for Trump approval ratings

Variable		Estimate	Std. error	t statistic	p-value
	Approve	178.9	33.1	5.4	0.7×10^{-7}
α_0	Disapprove	224.9	42.2	5.3	1.0×10^{-7}
	Don't know	16.5	3.4	4.9	1.0×10^{-6}
φ		−0.054	0.022	−2.3	0.019
ψ		0.369	0.029	12.7	Negligible

Secondly, we can examine whether the data is consistent with a Martingale model in which $\hat{\boldsymbol{\alpha}}_0 = \mathbf{0}$, $\hat{\varphi} = 0$ and $\hat{\psi} = 1$. This can be done with the Wald test, which has test statistic $\chi^2_5 = 1,417$, again with vanishing p value. The best forecast of tomorrow's polls is not just today's polls.

5.7.5. *Interpretation of the Model*

On the basis of either of these proposed null hypotheses, we chose the proposed model. The model mixes just over one third of any new data from polls into its current moving estimate of the approval ratings vector. It has a slight "error correcting" tendency in the small negative value for $\hat{\varphi}$, although that is borderline significant, with only confidence of 98% that it is non-zero. The other terms are considerably stronger.

The message of this model is that preferences do wander through time but we should not read too much into the most recent poll results. This can be seen in the forecasts done in Figure 5.19, which indicate a reversal from the most recent measurements to the longer term average values.

5.7.6. *Validation of the Framework*

As I wrote in Section 5.6, I believe that the multivariate discrete choice time-series model developed herein is a novel formalism. I derived the conditions under which it would be stationary and the work of this section validates that it is a *useful* way to describe real data and to permit hypothesis tests and forecasting to be done with the results of regularly repeated surveys featuring multiple-choice, single-answer, questions.

Acknowledgements

This chapter has featured two pieces of work that I did with other businesses, bringing my methods and understanding to their data. I know I benefited from this collaboration and I hope the two businesses featured, Patreon and China Beige Book, did as well. I am very grateful to both Maura Church at Patreon and Shehzad Qazi at China Beige Book for their willingness to spend time working with me and for permitting me to publish work originally covered by non-disclosure agreements. In addition the support of Andre Bach at Patreon and Leland Miller, C.E.O. of China Beige Book, should be noted.

Chapter 6

Coronavirus

This brief chapter contains the work I did on the Coronavirus outbreak in 2020. Fortunately, at this point, my only real exposure has been to be locked down and concerned about my family. Like many people involved in data science, I reacted to this by trying to understand better the data being reported to me. In particular, I was seeking information about the likely severity of the outbreak and its estimated end date.

Initially, having experienced prior outbreaks, such as the *MERS*, *SARS*, and the *H1N1/9* "Swine Flu," in a largely passive manner from the comfort of a developed Western nation, I didn't really pay much attention. I didn't expect it to reach the United States or bring the entire world to its knees. I didn't expect my children to be working from home half of the year or for the US economy to fall off a massive cliff, experiencing a recession with unprecedented levels of unemployment. It was very much unexpected to me that the United States would become one of the worse cases in the world. At the time of writing,[a] it appears that the US and Western Europe are beginning to experience a "third wave" of infections.

As I started putting this work together I began publishing articles on the website *Medium*, a home for creative writing, as I wanted to share what I was learning. I am not an epidemiologist, and do not claim to be, but was not entirely unfamiliar with the *compartment models* used to model disease propagation having studied them

[a]October 2020.

recreationally in the past. As I wrote and learned things about the data I modified my models, and so some of those articles have become outdated. Here I will attempt to update them as best as is possible using the data that has been observed since they were originally written.

6.1. Discrete Stochastic Compartment Models

6.1.1. *Continuous Time Compartment Models*

The standard analysis of epidemics uses a set of coupled ordinary differential equations called the *S-I-R Model.* This divides the population into three "compartments," comprising *susceptible*, *infected* and *removed.* The equations are expressed in continuous time, which the data is not, and contain no elements that are stochastic.

The model is

$$F = \beta I, \tag{6.1}$$

$$\frac{dS}{dt} = -\frac{FS}{N}, \tag{6.2}$$

$$\frac{dI}{dt} = \frac{FS}{N} - \gamma I, \tag{6.3}$$

$$\frac{dR}{dt} = \gamma I. \tag{6.4}$$

Walking through the equations, we start with the "force of infection," $F = \beta I$, which essentially says that a fixed proportion of the infected, $I(t)$, are able to propagate the disease. As only the susceptible may become infected the next term describes that infection process: it says that the rate of change in the susceptible is proportional to the probability that the infectious, F/N, encounters someone who is susceptible multiplied by the count of those people, $S(t)$. Here N is the population size, which is viewed as fixed from the beginning of the process.[b] This number subtracts from the count of the susceptible and adds to the count of the infected, which is also changed by the

[b]We are assuming that both the birth rate and death rate are small compared to the population over the timescales that the outbreak is active.

proportion of the infected that are permanently removed from the susceptible population.

This "removal" can be either due to recovery, and associated immunity, or death. To separate those terms, Equation (6.3) is modified to

$$\frac{dI}{dt} = \frac{FS}{N} - \gamma I - \mu I, \tag{6.5}$$

and the count of the deceased, $D(t)$, is added:

$$\frac{dD}{dt} = \mu I. \tag{6.6}$$

This makes the *S-I-R-D Model* and γ and μ represents the recovery rate and mortality rate respectively.

6.1.2. *Discrete Time Stochastic Models*

Models such as these are made in continuous time for two major reasons:

(i) the quantities *genuinely* evolve in continuous, or very finely dividable time; or
(ii) differential equations such as the above are generally more easy to deal with than difference equations.

Differential equations are also usually introduced via the limiting process

$$\frac{dI}{dt} = \lim_{\delta t \to 0} \frac{I(t + \delta t) - I(t)}{\delta t}. \tag{6.7}$$

The data we will be looking at are *daily counts* of the cumulative numbers of the infected and the deceased. The limit $\delta t \to 0$ must, in fact, stop at $\delta t = 1$ day and the changes, $I(t + \delta t) - I(t) = I_{t+1} - I_t$, are macroscopic in nature. Over those large intervals the changes in counts will be:

(i) large;
(ii) stochastic;
(iii) follow a right skewed distribution.

This latter item follows because the basic variables all represent *counts* of persons and so are defined on non-negative integers. Although the Normal distribution to the Poisson limit may be reasonable for very large populations it will not be suitable in the early stages of the outbreak.

6.1.2.1. *Defining the Model*

The model I'm using to fit to the data is[c]

$$f_t N \sim \text{Poisson}(\beta I_{t-1}), \tag{6.8}$$

$$m_t I_{t-1} \sim \text{Poisson}(\mu I_{t-1}), \tag{6.9}$$

$$S_t = S_{t-1} - f_t S_{t-1} \tag{6.10}$$

$$I_t = I_{t-1} + f_t S_{t-1} - \gamma I_{t-1} - m_t I_{t-1}, \tag{6.11}$$

$$R_t = R_{t-1} + \gamma I_{t-1} \tag{6.12}$$

$$D_t = D_{t-1} + m_t I_{t-1}. \tag{6.13}$$

This starts with a Poisson draw of the number of infectious people which has a mean proportional to the prior count of the infected. The ratio of that number to the total population gives the probability that an infectious person is encountered by the susceptible. The next step is a second Poisson draw, which determines the number of the infected who die in each iteration. The ratio of that number to the infected is the "force of mortality." The rest of the equations are then the book-keeping that follows from these numbers.

6.1.2.2. *The Data*

The data I am going to be using is the data published to *GitHub* by *The New York Times*.[d] It contains counts of total cases and total deaths for the United States as a whole, the individual States and Territories, and the Counties or equivalent areas within the States.

[c]This is *not* the original model I published on *Medium*. As I worked with the data, my understanding of how to process it evolved, which is my usual experience.

[d]The URL for this data is in the appendix.

Some large metropolitan areas, such as New York City which comprises five counties,[e] are also aggregated and reported separately. The data is daily and published with a one day latency. I wrote a custom Python script to capture this data daily and upload it into my database.

6.1.2.3. *Estimating the Model*

To estimate the unknown parameters of the model, $\{\beta, \gamma, \mu\}$, and the inferred time series, $\{S_t, I_t, R_t\}$, the expressions of Section 6.1.2.1 need to be tied to the observables, which are the counts of total cases, C_t, and deaths, D_t. The count of cases is simply

$$C_t = I_t + R_t + D_t \tag{6.14}$$

and the force of infection, in terms of observables and inferred quantities, is

$$f_t = \frac{I_t - I_{t-1}(1 - \gamma - m_t)}{S_{t-1}}, \tag{6.15}$$

$$= \frac{C_t - R_t - D_t - I_{t-1}(1 - \gamma - m_t)}{S_{t-1}}. \tag{6.16}$$

The metric I'm *really* interested in is $\hat{I}_t$, the estimated number of infected people in the community and this is indicative of the likelihood of any member of the public encountering a person whose disease puts them at risk. This is not reported in the data, either by the *New York Times* or other sources.

As we are dealing with non-Normally distributed data, I will estimate the parameters of the process by maximum likelihood. The log likelihood is

$$\mathcal{L}(\beta, \gamma, \mu) = \ln \prod_t \Pr(f_t N | \beta I_{t-1}) \Pr(m_t I_{t-1} | \mu I_{t-1}). \tag{6.17}$$

With the specified process, the probabilities are computable from the probability mass function of the Poisson distribution, given in

[e]New York County (Manhattan), Kings County (Brooklyn), Bronx County (The Bronx), Richmond County (Staten Island), and Queens County (Queens).

Equation (4.17). The time-series, $\{S_t, I_t, R_t\}$, are all computed *on the fly* as part of the estimation process. For forecasting, as is usual, stochastic quantities, such as $f_t N$, are replaced with their expected values, $\hat{\beta}\hat{I}_{t-1}$, and the system is updated iteratively.

6.1.2.4. *The Reproduction Ratio and Case Fatality Rate*

The *Reproduction Ratio* for such a system, $R_0 = \beta/(\gamma + \mu)$, may be estimated from parameters. The *Case Fatality Rate*, or C.F.R., is usually treated as something determined "long after the outbreak." It is the final ratio of the fatalities to cases, which we may estimate as:

$$\text{C.F.R.} = \lim_{t \to \infty} \frac{\hat{D}_t}{\hat{C}_t}. \tag{6.18}$$

6.2. Fitting Coronavirus in New Jersey

After a pretty long preamble, let's get down to estimating this model in my home state of New Jersey. I will examine both Monmouth County, where I live, and the entire state.

6.2.1. *Early Models and Predictions*

The first article I published [57] was based on data obtained up to 04/01/2020 and so I will reproduce the analytics for that period first.[f] The Governor of New Jersey, Phil Murphy, had issued an executive order 107, shutting down the State with effect on 03/21/2020 [104], which was just a week before that analysis was executed. My children had begun remote schooling two weeks earlier, and my wife and I had scrambled to set up desks for them with my outdated computers and stacked toilet paper and other consumables in our basement.

The trajectory of the outbreak is shown in Figure 6.1. There isn't really a null hypothesis to test, but the parameter estimates are: $\hat{\beta} = 0.4582 \pm 0.0025$; $\hat{\gamma} = 0.2996 \pm 0.0023$; and, $\hat{\mu} = 0.0085 \pm 0.0015$. From the point of view of 04/02/2020, the data is projecting a severe outbreak in which a peak of 34,975 of 623,387 people in Monmouth

[f] Any discrepancies between the published results and these now discussed are due to the fact that my understanding of how to work with these models has improved over time, and I've also had the luxury of time to do some bug-fixes.

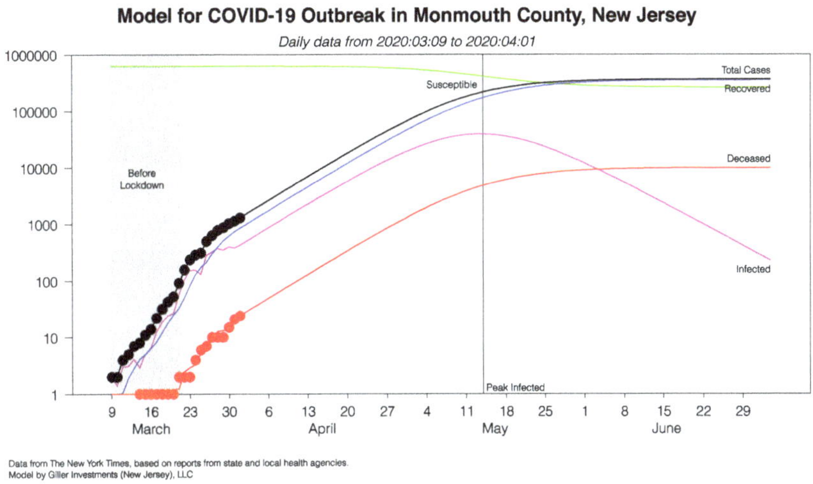

Figure 6.1: Early results of fitting a Stochastic Discrete Compartment Model to the Coronavirus outbreak in Monmouth County, NJ. The black curve and dots are the estimated and actual total case count; the red lines and dots are the estimated and total deaths. Other curves are: susceptible in green; infected in magenta; and, recovered in blue. Data is from the *New York Times*.

County, or 5.6% of the population, are infected. With the estimated CFR, 944 people would die from COVID-19. The projected outbreak peaks on 05/14/2020, and is essentially burned out by Independence Day, 07/04/2020.

The estimated Reproduction Ratio is $\hat{R}_0 = 1.49$, within the 1.4–2.5 range originally quoted by the World Health Organization, and the CFR is 2.7%. At the time of writing,[g] the Johns Hopkins gives a global deaths to cases ratio of 2.7%. This means that, at this point in time, Monmouth County, NJ, was experiencing an outbreak that was behaving entirely as it had played out elsewhere.

6.2.2. *Modeling Coronavirus with Piecewise Constant Parameters*

The results of Section 6.2.1 were both disturbing and reassuring. I was able to reproduce the data being quoted in the media, which

[g]Global totals of 1,127,797 deaths for 41,033,709 cases from their dashboard [16] on 10/21/2020.

was very reassuring, but the consequences of the data were quite horrifying — many people would die in my county alone.

Of course, the disease outbreak was not unchecked. The Governors of New Jersey, and New York, acted to dramatically curtail person-to-person contact within the states by shutting down many parts of our economies. Fortunately, many people in this area work in relatively technologically advanced industries and were able to switch to remote working from home, just as my children were able to study from home.

This should decrease the *Effective Reproduction Ratio*, R, below the value, $\hat{R}_0 = 1.49$ found above. Without a *model* for this parameter, we can fit a *piecewise constant* function $\beta_t = \beta_{M_t}$, for month number M_t counted sequentially from the beginning of the data. Few changes to the analysis procedure are required to accommodate this change. I decided not to modify the other parameters, γ and μ, in the same manner on the assumption that recovery and mortality rates would not have dramatically changed in response to the lockdown.

6.2.2.1. *Monmouth County*

From Figure 6.2, it's clear that the first month is quite different from the rest. Due to not having to accommodate the April data, the estimate $\hat{R}_0$ rises to 1.66. Using the mean and standard deviation of the observed estimates of R_t for April, 2020, onwards, we find that the estimate for March has a Z score of 8.9 relative to those values. It is significantly inconsistent with them. The model for the outbreak itself is shown in Figure 6.3. This illustrates the decline in the count of infected persons, following a peak now estimated to lie on 04/10/2020, and a resurgence beginning around late August. This model gives an expected final count of 1,289 deceased, with an final CFR of 6.6%.

6.2.2.2. *New Jersey*

The next step in this analysis is to "scale out" to the data for the entire State of New Jersey. The model is the same, but the daily incremental changes in counts are larger, so the use of the Poisson distribution is less critical. Nevertheless, since the code is written, the same code can be used.

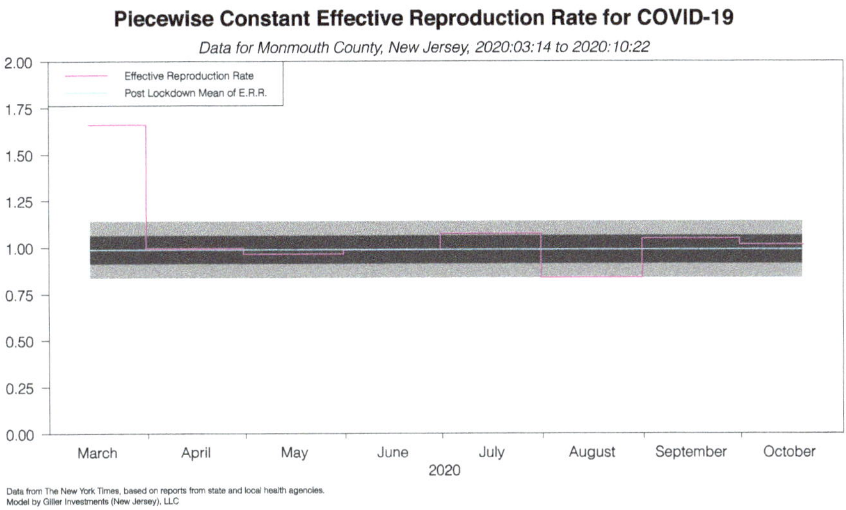

Figure 6.2: Estimated values for the piecewise constant Effective Reproduction Rate of the Coronavirus outbreak in Monmouth County, NJ. The blue line is the mean of the post lockdown estimates and the gray shading illustrates 68% and 95% confidence regions about that value. The purple line is the individual *per month* estimates. Data is from the *New York Times*.

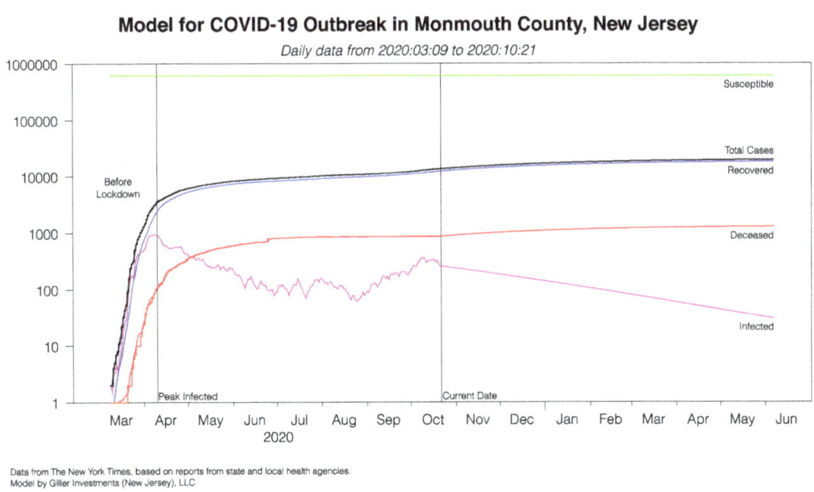

Figure 6.3: Current results of fitting a Stochastic Discrete Compartment Model, with piecewise constant β_t, to the Coronavirus outbreak in Monmouth County, NJ. The black lines are the estimated and actual total case count; the red lines are the estimated and total deaths. Other curves are: susceptible in green; infected in magenta; and, recovered in blue. Data is from the *New York Times*.

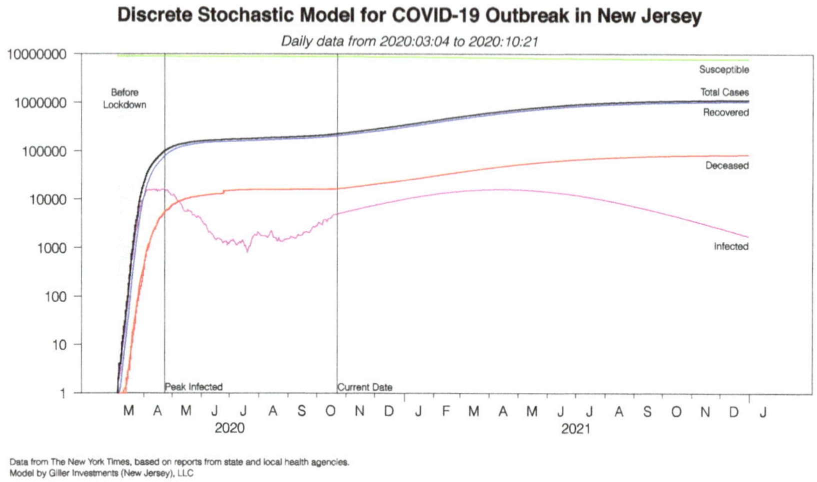

Figure 6.4: Current results of fitting a Stochastic Discrete Compartment Model in New Jersey. Key is as for Figure 6.3. Data is from the *New York Times*.

This data tells a similar story, although when the whole State's data is aggregated the estimate of the basic reproduction rate for March is increased to $\hat{R}_0 = 1.91$ and the CFR is 7.4%. Again, month-by-month data can be used to estimate the discrepancy of $\hat{R}_0$ from the means of the estimates of $\hat{R}$ for other months, and the t statistic is even larger at 9.4.

The curves that estimate the trajectory of the outbreak are show in Figure 6.4. Again, we see a resurgence of the count of the infected within the community that starts in late August. The curves are visually quite similar to those for Figure 6.3, although the State data is not showing evidence of having exited the Summer surge and, unlike the Monmouth County data, we are expecting the secondary peak to occur *next* Summer.

6.2.2.3. *United States*

Scaled out again, we can model the entire United States. The data begins on 01/21/2020 but no deaths were reported prior to 02/29/2020. There were no reported infections within New Jersey before March. The regression coefficients are listed in Table 6.1, along with those for Monmouth County and New Jersey. This data clearly

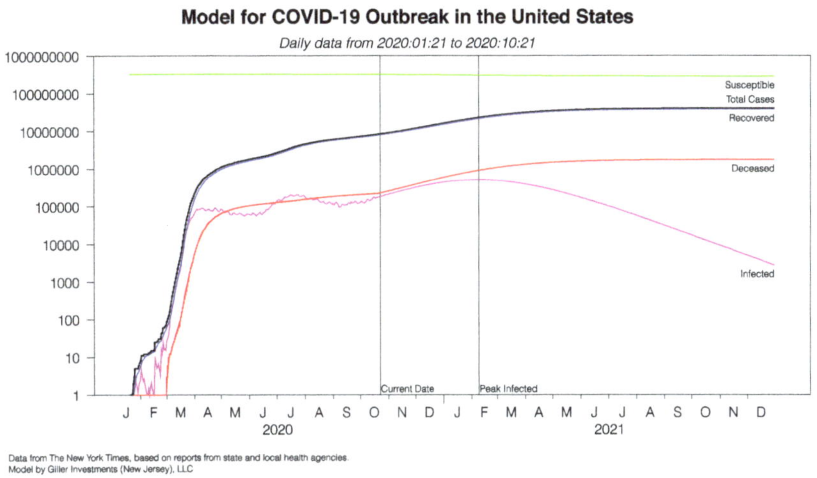

Figure 6.5: Current results of fitting a model for the Coronavirus outbreak in the entire United States. Key is as for Figure 6.3. Data is from the *New York Times*.

Table 6.1: Estimated parameters for discrete stochastic compartment model for Coronavirus outbreaks.

Regression Coefficients for Coronavirus Models

	Monmouth County		New Jersey		United States	
Coefficient	Parameter	Std. error	Parameter	Std. error	Parameter	Std. error
β_1					0.3303	0.0561
β_2					0.1217	0.1143
β_3	0.4051	0.0833	0.4185	0.0764	0.5105	0.0231
β_4	0.2448	0.0765	0.2269	0.0600	0.3582	0.0052
β_5	0.2380	0.0747	0.1893	0.0649	0.3445	0.0049
β_6	0.2439	0.0769	0.2143	0.0640	0.3798	0.0079
β_7	0.2649	0.0738	0.2469	0.0688	0.3672	0.0029
β_8	0.2074	0.0636	0.1982	0.0605	0.3382	0.0054
β_9	0.2572	0.0649	0.2326	0.0574	0.3598	0.0030
β_{10}	0.2438	0.0630	0.2368	0.0573	0.3765	0.0034
γ	0.2302	0.0635	0.2029	0.0550	0.3331	0.0001
μ	0.0163	0.0040	0.0163	0.0038	0.0169	$<10^{-4}$

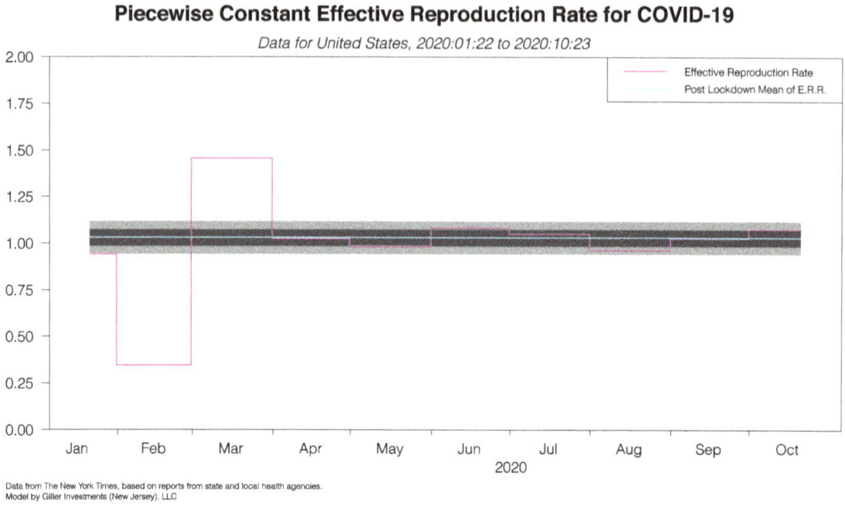

Figure 6.6: Estimated values for the piecewise constant in the United States. Key is as for Figure 6.2. Data is from the *New York Times*.

shows three waves of infection, with the current one set to peak in February 2021. In computing these curves the last value of the fitted β_t coefficient is used for forecasting, so this may change as we enter November.

Figure 6.6 shows how the estimated effective reproduction rate has varied since January 2020. In this, the mean value of the coefficients, $\{\hat{\beta}_t\}$, is computed from the data from April onwards. Two months, February and March, are clearly out of line indicating that the virus was spreading differently during those periods.

6.3. Independent Models by State

In Section 6.2.2, a model for the entire United States is presented *as a monolith*. Clearly the models need to take account of geography as that is a key factor in the transmission of a disease.

6.3.1. *Independent Analysis of the States*

Table 6.2 shows the results of fitting the model of Section 6.2.2 State-by-State (independently). The value of R_0 quoted is the largest value

Table 6.2: Estimated parameters for discrete stochastic compartment model for Coronavirus outbreaks in the United States by State.

State by State Results

State	R_0	CFR(%)	State	R_0	CFR(%)
Alabama	2.44	1.70	Mississippi	1.36	0.46
Alaska	1.39	0.06	Missouri	4.63	1.91
Arizona	2.67	2.57	Montana	1.50	1.19
Arkansas	1.62	0.23	Nebraska	1.52	0.11
California	1.48	1.95	Nevada	1.88	1.94
Colorado	2.05	2.70	New Jersey	1.91	7.40
Connecticut	3.50	7.48	New Mexico	2.19	2.70
Delaware	1.55	0.92	New York	1.28	6.75
District of Columbia	1.68	2.37	North Dakota	4.18	1.74
Florida	2.20	2.16	Ohio	1.20	2.76
Georgia	2.51	2.34	Oklahoma	3.21	1.21
Hawaii	1.48	1.15	Oregon	2.08	1.66
Idaho	1.51	1.05	Pennsylvania	2.20	4.67
Illinois	2.08	2.83	Puerto Rico	1.53	0.86
Indiana	2.74	2.81	Rhode Island	2.75	0.14
Iowa	2.85	1.57	South Carolina	2.96	2.36
Kansas	1.34	0.09	South Dakota	2.05	1.10
Kentucky	1.50	0.19	Tennessee	3.51	1.42
Louisiana	1.78	0.62	Texas	2.22	2.07
Maine	1.88	0.58	Utah	1.40	0.13
Maryland	2.06	3.00	Vermont	1.71	0.03
Massachusetts	1.47	6.57	Virginia	2.75	2.16
Michigan	2.93	4.84	Washington	9.71	0.43
Minnesota	1.52	1.93	West Virginia	1.48	0.12

Note: Regression did not converge for regions not listed.

of the individual month estimates for each State, i.e. the *worst* value, and the value of the effective reproduction ratio, R, is the latest value. From the table, sample averages are $\hat{R}_0 = 2.28 \pm 0.19$, $\hat{R} = 1.14 \pm 0.02$, CFR $= 2.02\% \pm 0.27\%$.

6.3.1.1. *Variation of Reproduction Rate by State*

We may augment the data of Table 6.2 with various causal variables of interest. In a polarized and divisive electoral period,[h] much interest

[h] I am writing this ten days before the election of November 3, 2020.

is directed to the differing responses of the States to the COVID-19 outbreak, and whether that is driven by party politics.

Figure 6.7 exhibits scatter plots and regression lines of the peak fitted effective reproduction rate, which is used as a proxy for R_0, and the final fitted reproduction rate, R, versus the surveyed approval rates for President Trump. The survey data is taken from a Morning Consult analysis [102], dated February 2020, which is *before* the full outbreak of Coronavirus in the United States. The statistic examined is the ratio of the difference between the proportion who approve and disapprove divided by their sum.

Two facts are readily apparent from this data:

(i) there is no apparent relationship between Presidential approval, which we may treat as a proxy for majority statewide partisanship, and the reproduction ratio of the disease, as estimated above;
(ii) the final reproduction ratio is very much more tightly distributed, around a mean value of $\bar{R} = 1.15 \pm 0.03$, than the peak value, $\bar{R}_0 = 2.27 \pm 0.19$.

This data should serve to support the following inferences:

(1) responses to the disease *have* had the effect of reducing the rate at which it propagates;
(2) Coronavirus is affecting all the States, in essentially the same manner.

Given the degree of partisanship current in American politics, these results may be dismissed as based on public opinion surveys that are viewed skeptically by many. Instead, let's examine the effect of the party allegiance of the executive leadership of the States.[i] As the US is operationally a bipartisan system, we can perform an ANOVA analysis of both $\hat{R}_0$ and $\hat{R}$ with respect to the party of the Governors' of the States.

[i]The Governors of the States and Puerto Rico, and the Mayor of Washington, DC.

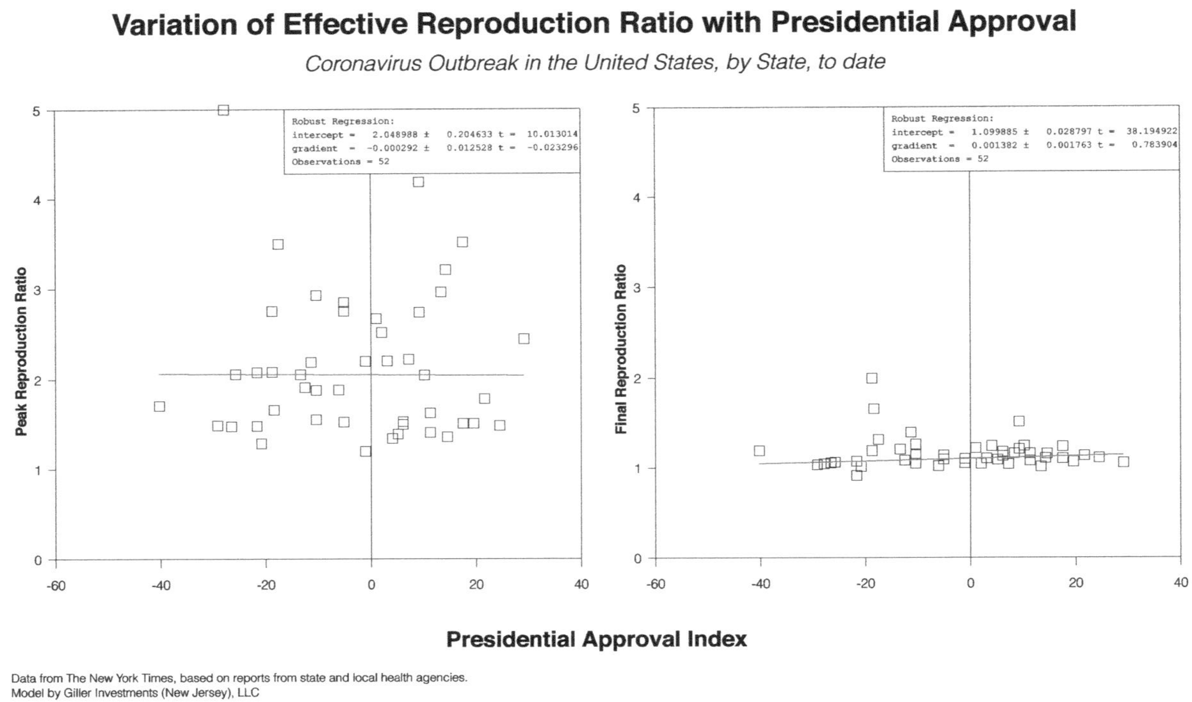

Figure 6.7: Observed covariance of the estimates $\hat{R}_0$ and $\hat{R}$, from Table 6.2 and Presidential Approval ratings by State for Donald Trump. The approvals data is from Morning Consult surveys (see text). The left panel is for the peak fitted effective reproduction rate, which I use as a proxy for R_0, and the right panel the final fitted effective reproduction rate, R.

Table 6.3: Single factor ANOVA table for the estimated values of $\hat{R}_0$ dependent on the party of the Governor of the States.

Summary statistics

Groups	Count	Sum	Mean	Variance	
Democratic	23	53.01	2.30	2.92	
Republican	26	58.06	2.23	0.82	

Analysis of variance

Source of variation	*SS*	*df*	*MS*	*F*	*p*-value
Between groups	0.06	1	0.06	0.03	0.85
Within groups	84.76	47	1.80		
Total	84.8261	48			

Table 6.4: Single factor ANOVA table for the estimated final values of $\hat{R}$ dependent on the party of the Governor of the States.

Summary statistics

Groups	Count	Sum	Mean	Variance	
Democratic	23	26.61	1.16	0.04	
Republican	26	29.78	1.15	0.02	

Analysis of variance

Source of variation	*SS*	*df*	*MS*	*F*	*p*-value
Between groups	0.002	1	0.002	0.05	0.83
Within groups	1.56	47	0.03		
Total	1.57	48			

Table 6.3 shows the ANOVA analysis of $\hat{R}_0$ versus party. This analysis does not support the hypothesis that the party of the Governor of the State affected the value of R_0, or even marginally suggest that it was a factor. The same conclusion applies to the estimates of

the effective reproduction number, $\hat{R}$. There is no apparent connection to the party of the Governor, who is the executive coordinating the response to the pandemic.

6.3.1.2. *The Effect of Population on Reproduction Rate*

Turning to more demographic data, we can look at the effect of population and population density. COVID-19 is, after all, an infectious disease and human interaction is required for it to propagate.

Although the data in Figure 6.7 are essentially "flatlines," with respect to Presidential approval ratings, those in Figure 6.8 do show some covariance. I could construct an explanatory narrative for the observed weak trends, but the relationship is not statistically significant and so such an exercise is essentially meaningless. The fair conclusion from this analysis is that the propagation of the virus has not been idiosyncratically different in any particular state.

6.3.1.3. *The Effect of Population Size on Case Fatality Rate*

Having not found any real effects for the reproduction rate of the disease, let's take a look at the Case Fatality Rate. In this it is important to note that *this* CFR is my estimate, based on extrapolating the model of Equations (6.8) to (6.13), and not official estimates *or* the current ratio of deaths to cases, D_t/C_t for t =10/21/2020.

Figure 6.9 shows a scatter plot between the estimated CFR, according to our method, and the decimal log of the State populations from the Census. Here, we do see a significant relationship, with an estimated slope of 2.03 ± 0.56, which has a t statistic of 3.62 and a p value of 0.0007. The R^2 is 22%, so the explanatory power of the model is low, but we see four outliers from east coast states: New York, New Jersey, Connecticut and Massachusetts. This result may be telling us many things, one of which may be that high population densities create poor outcomes, but we should note that these states are also connected geographically.

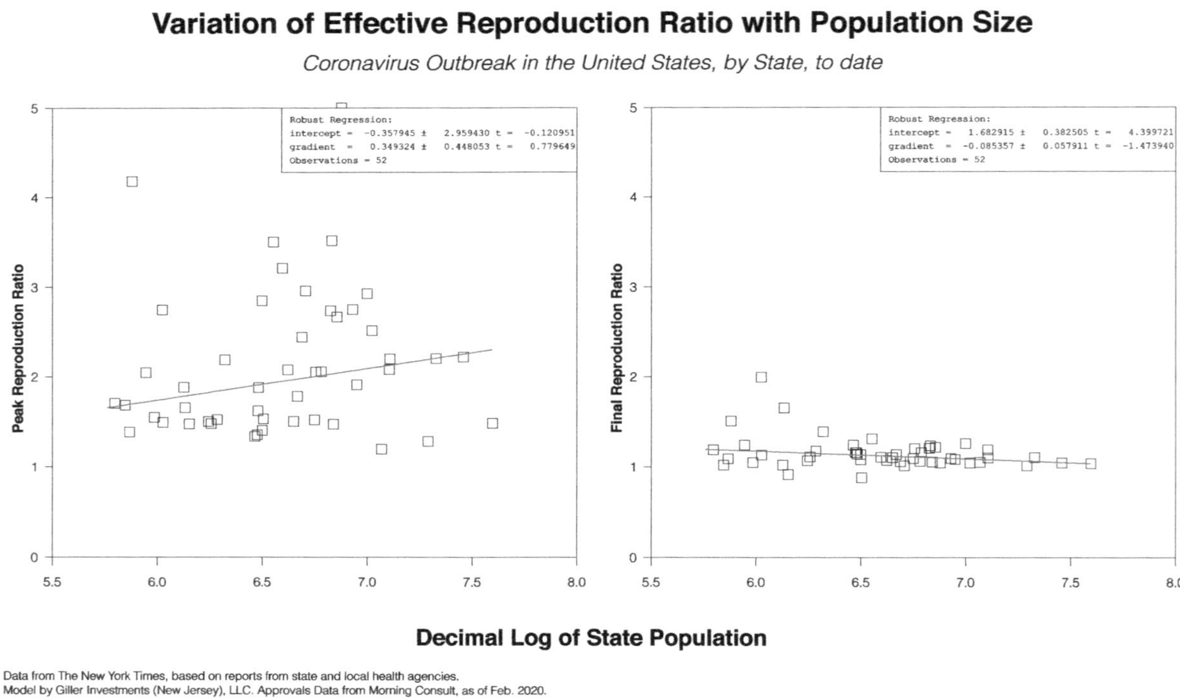

Figure 6.8: Observed covariance of the estimates $\hat{R}_0$ and $\hat{R}$, from Table 6.2 and the decimal log of the population counts of the States. The populations are from Census data for 2019. The left panel is for the peak fitted effective reproduction rate, which I use as a proxy for R_0, and the right panel the final fitted effective reproduction rate, R.

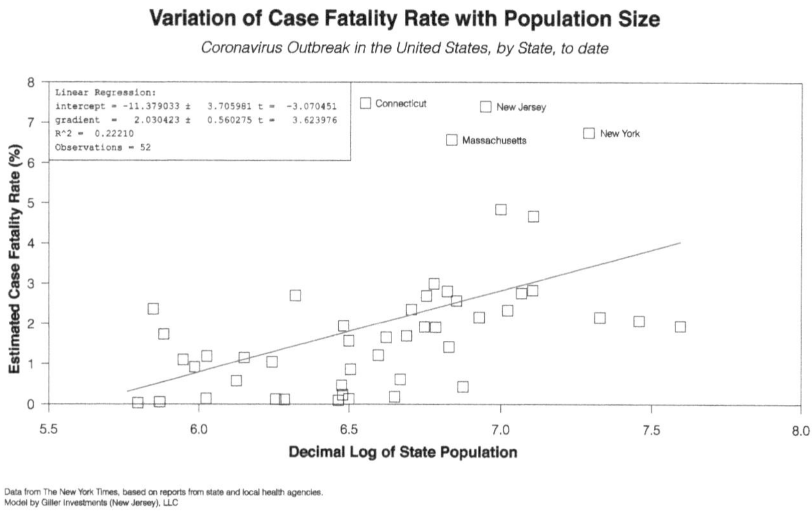

Figure 6.9: Observed covariance of estimated Case Fatality Rates for the States and the decimal log of the population. The populations are from Census data for 2019 and the CFR are estimated from the *New York Times* data and the model of Equations (6.8) to (6.13).

6.4. Geospatial and Topological Models

Physics knows how to deal with interactions between spatially separated regions. For coordinates $\boldsymbol{r} = (x, y, z)$, we define functions of the coordinate, $f(\boldsymbol{r})$. These functions are generally required to be differentiable, even *smooth*, which means that their values in the neighborhood of the original coordinate are similar and vary in a manner described by a gradient, $\nabla f(\boldsymbol{r})$. From the perspective of a model builder this means likely response functions are characterized by fairly small numbers of parameters, and so analytically tractable, but geographers and geophysicists know that these assumptions are not always valid "on the ground."

6.4.1. *Topology versus Geography*

I live in a town that has, over the last 100 years, been transformed from the sleepy farming community my wife's grandparents moved into, to a commuter suburb that still retains a distinctly rural character. I live on a farm, but for much of my recent time here I've taken public transport into New York City to work in various investment banks. Although living on a farm is rare these days commuting to work in New York is not, and I brushed shoulders daily with hundreds of people, many of whom don't live where I do, but live in neighboring towns or counties and congregate around the same transport hubs. COVID-19 is an infectious disease, meaning that it's spread by human-to-human contact. Thus, from the beginning, I knew I needed to make my models "geospatially aware," meaning having the geographic attributes of proximity and having parameters that vary by location and as a function of the relationship between regions.

In mathematics, we have a lot of tools to deal with "spaces" and the one most people are familiar with is Euclidean Geometry. This means that we have coordinates (x, y, z) that locate points in space, and that there are concepts of neighborhoods around those points, and that there is a meaningful concept of distance with well-understood properties and that obeys laws such as Pythagoras's Theorem. When thinking about how to model the contacts of commuters within a data set indexed by states and counties, Euclidean geometry's concept of distance is, perhaps, not the most useful tool. Our network of connectivity clusters around roads and railways between towns and the shortest path between two points is not necessarily the literal distance "as the crow flies."

Let's consider a literal example of this, which is the way many of my colleagues used to commute to Midtown Manhattan. If I am living a suburban town, say Middletown, NJ, I might drive from my home to Highlands, NJ, and board a ferry, which would sail into New York Bay from the Jersey Shore, finally docking on the east side of Manhattan. From there I might board a bus to Grand Central Station before walking to the office. The quickest public transport route, as computed by *Apple Maps*, is shown in Figure 6.10. From personal experience, I can tell you that this is much quicker than driving! A key feature of this route, though, is that the closeness of the regions is not equal to their Euclidean separation, and it also involves segments in which we are transiting in the wrong direction, geographically speaking, actually increasing the distance between ourselves and our destination. It appears we need to step away from the geometry of metric spaces, toward something that merely reflects the point-to-point connectivity of the regions for which I have data. This is a

Figure 6.10: Computed "shortest time" route between Middletown, NJ, and Midtown, Manhattan. Routing recommended by *Apple Maps*.

topological space, which possesses the concept of "neighborhood" but not, necessarily, of "distance."

6.4.2. *A Map of New Jersey Based on Connectivity*

If we concentrate solely on the *connectivity* of regions, and not their *physical proximity*, there are plenty of tools to assist us. Graph theory and geography have been related right from the beginning. When Leonard Euler was solving the famous *Seven Bridges of Königsburg* problem, he realized that what was important was not the geography but the connectivity of the two islands, through the seven bridges that linked them. We now call the methods he developed to solve the problem "graph theory" and the definition of regions linked by their membership of "neighborhoods" a "topological space."

Assuming few New Jersey commuters are *flying* to work,[j] we can create a map of the connectivity of the counties of the State based on those that share borders. The NBER has a list of all counties[k] that share a physical border, which may be downloaded from their website [107]. This data, which is of the form

"county i shares a border with county j," or $A_{ij} = 1$,

defines what is called the *adjacency matrix* of an *undirected graph*, which is represented in Figure 6.11.

Such analysis allows the spatial models of physics to be represented with simple matrices based on the indices of the nodes of the

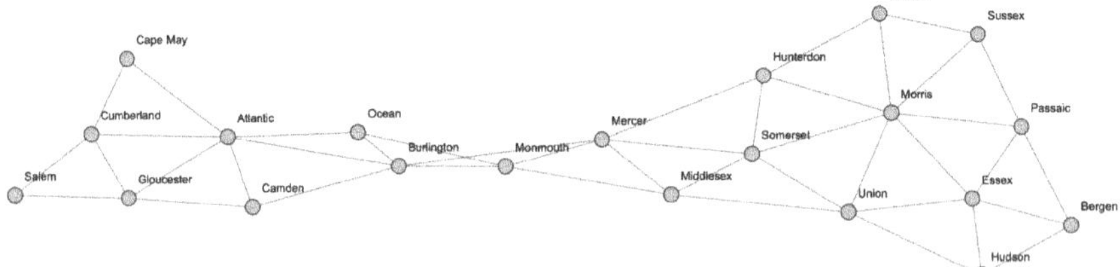

Figure 6.11: Undirected graph for the connectivity of New Jersey counties as output by *Mathematica*.

[j]I'm sure a few do, but most don't.

[k]Or equivalent places in other States.

graph. Graph theory provides additional tools to analyze these networks, and one tool that many people have become familiar with is *eigenvector centrality*, since it played a critical role in the development of Google's earlier *PageRank* algorithms [85]. Eigenvector centrality can be understood as a measure of how much time a traveler, who randomly explores the graph, spends on each node of the graph. If I were to start in my home county of Monmouth and randomly pick a bordering county to travel to, in my case one of Mercer, Middlesex, Ocean and Burlington counties, and then repeated the process from where I landed, and never stopped, then on average how much of my time would I be spending in each county? This is one way to measure their relative importance.

A lot of the tools in graph theory are directed at understanding social networks and one particularly interesting tool is based on the idea of identifying communities. Software allows us easily to compute the "communities" of a graph, and the results for the New Jersey graph of Figure 6.11 are shown in Figure 6.12. Algorithms to do this are discussed in references such as Newman and Girven's article [109]. Quite interestingly, the groups identified seem to make sense, and I have labeled them Northern, Southern, and Central Jersey.

6.4.3. *A Topological Compartment Model for COVID-19*

To create a topological model for disease propagation we have to think through the process established by Equations (6.8) to (6.13).

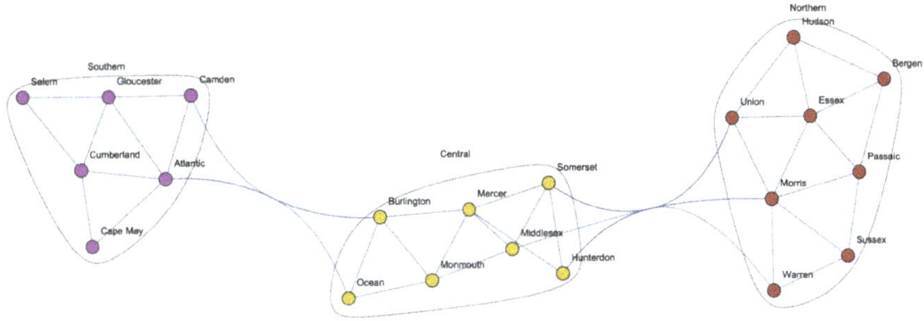

Figure 6.12: Undirected graph for the communities of New Jersey counties as output by *Mathematica*, with labels assigned by the author.

6.4.3.1. *Defining the Model*

The modifications I propose are:

$$f_{it}N_i \sim \text{Poisson}\left[|\det\beta|^{1/c} I_{it-1}\right], \tag{6.19}$$

$$m_{it}I_{it-1} \sim \text{Poisson}[\mu_i I_{it-1}], \tag{6.20}$$

$$S_{it} = S_{it-1} - S_{it-1}\sum_{j=1}^{c}\beta_{ij}f_{jt}, \tag{6.21}$$

$$I_{it} = I_{it-1} + S_{it-1}\sum_{j=1}^{c}\beta_{ij}f_{jt} - \gamma_i I_{it-1} - m_{it}I_{it-1}, \tag{6.22}$$

$$R_{it} = R_{it-1} + \gamma I_{it-1}, \tag{6.23}$$

$$D_{it} = D_{it-1} + m_{it}I_{it-1}. \tag{6.24}$$

This structure links the count of the infected in a given region, i, to the infected in all connected regions, j, via the parameters, β_{ij}, i.e. the β parameter of Equation (6.8) is now a matrix indexed by the counties, $[1 \ldots c]$. By definition, it's a symmetric matrix, because infectious contact is not "directed," and involves replacing the single parameter of Equation (6.8), with an array of $c(c+1)/2$ parameters, for c interacting regions. This change generates the sums over j in the third and fourth equations.

With this modification, we need to find a way for β to still play the role of governing the expected number of infectious, which is the role it has in the first equation. I tried introducing a separate term for that, but this introduced the problem of bilinearity, and I ultimately realized that the form given was correct.[1] For any matrix, the determinant is a scalar quantity that measures the size of the "volume it spans." This is easiest to see if we consider the cuboid, or rectangular prism, defined by the vectors $(x, 0, 0)$, $(0, y, 0)$, and $(0, 0, z)$, and for which the determinant of the matrix made from those vectors is xyz. This is the volume of that cuboid. In general, for a non-diagonal three-dimensional matrix, the volume is that of a parallelepiped formed from all combinations of the vectors and, in an

[1]By which I mean I used up many days of computer time on models that did not converge, or gave absurd results, until I finally figured out the above structure.

arbitrary number of dimensions, it is the hypervolume of the "parallelope" formed by the vectors. As a hypervolume in c dimensions, associated with a c-dimensional matrix for c regions, the determinant itself takes a value that varies in magnitude with the power of the number of dimensions (very much as the volume of a cube of side s is s^3, whereas the "volume" of a square, we call "area," is s^2 and of a line, which we call "length" is just s itself).

If all of the elements of β are similar in scale, we should expect that $|\det\beta|$ itself to be approximately the size of β^c. Using $|\det\beta|$ as the scale factor that governs the rate of infection would give a model in which the rate of infection depends on the number of regions involved in the model, which isn't a desirable property, so I use the term $|\det\beta|^{1/c}$ which is a c-dimensional measure of the "size" of the β matrix.

6.4.3.2. *Estimating the Model*

Having established a model structure that seems viable and meaningful, it's now time to talk about how to estimate the values of the parameters. One reason that I decided to specify discrete stochastic models in this chapter, instead of ordinary differential equations (ODE) or stochastic differential equations (SDE), is that the method of estimation follows immediately from the basic structure.

I maximize the log likelihood given by the joint probabilities of the stochastic terms given the observed data. As before, this is

$$\mathcal{L}(\beta,\gamma,\mu) = \ln\prod_{it}\Pr\left[f_{it}N_i\,\middle|\,|\det\beta|^{1/c}I_{it-1}\right]\Pr\left[m_{it}I_{it-1}\,|\mu I_{it-1}\right], \tag{6.25}$$

with additional products over the regions, i. To compute the likelihood we require the Force of Infection, f_{it}, which is computed from

$$Q_{it} = \frac{I_{it} - I_{it-1}(1-\gamma_i - m_i)}{S_{it-1}}, \tag{6.26}$$

$$= \frac{C_{it} - R_{it} - D_{it} - I_{it-1}(1-\gamma_i - m_i)}{S_{it-1}}, \tag{6.27}$$

$$\Rightarrow \; Q_{it} = \sum_{j=1}^{c} \beta_{ij} f_{jt}, \tag{6.28}$$

$$\Rightarrow \; f_{it} = \sum_{j=1}^{c} \alpha_{ij} Q_{jt} \text{ where } \sum_{j=1}^{c} \alpha_{ij}\beta_{jk} = \delta_{ik} \text{ (Kronecker delta).} \tag{6.29}$$

(That is, the matrix α is the inverse of β.)

Now, I don't *know* this is the right form, in the sense that it was taken from peer-reviewed papers that I found online. It wasn't: I searched, but didn't find any references that were useful. It makes sense *to me*[m] and it does seem to work empirically, but readers may find it *quite complicated.*

6.4.3.3. *Adding Piecewise Continuous Propagation*

The remaining key feature of the model from Section 6.2.2 is the time-varying nature of the propagation matrix, β. This may be introduced with a time dependent scale factor:

$$\beta \rightarrow \beta_t = \frac{\lambda_{M_t}\beta}{\bar{\lambda}} \quad \text{where } \bar{\lambda} = \frac{1}{M}\sum_{M} \lambda_M. \tag{6.30}$$

Here, λ_{M_t} is varied by month M_t, and a Null hypothesis is $\boldsymbol{\lambda} = \mathbf{1}$. As both λ_t and β carry scale, we must constrain one of them to be fixed in aggregate to avoid collinearity.

6.4.4. *Estimating the Topological Model for Central Jersey*

As I mentioned above, the model is quite complicated. To reduce the complexity, for this single state model I did not require there to be separate recovery and mortality rates *per county*. This assumption is based on the idea that the standards of care and public policies are uniform within the States, even though they may vary between the States. In all, there are $c(c + 1)/2 + m + 1$ free parameters, where c

[m]But perhaps I am insufficiently self-critical?

is the count of regions and m is the number of months. I could not get models including Hunterdon Country to converge meaningfully, so decided to omit it from the first analysis phase. For the remaining six counties in Central Jersey, that's $6 \times 7/2 + 9 = 30$ parameters to estimate.

I could not get the model to converge using gradient based solvers such as BFGS[n] and so used the *Simplex* algorithm of Nelder and Mead.[o] Both methods are described in books such such as Fletcher's [43]. The downside of not computing the Hessian matrix of second derivatives is that it is used to estimate the covariance matrix of the estimators and is part of creating a confidence region for the location of the maximum in the space of parameters. We can, still, use the maximum likelihood ratio (MLR) test to determine the overall significance of the regression.

6.4.4.1. *Results of the Regression*

The results of the regression are shown in Figure 6.13. For all of the counties covered, the model closely tracks the data for total cases and total reported deaths and shows a decline in the proportion of the county populations that are infected beginning at the end of the data. It should be noted the press at the time of writing was full of stories of the growing outbreak in the heartland of the USA, but that New Jersey *still* seemed to have COVID-19 under control.

The time-series of the time-series of the scale factor, λ_t, is compared to its own history in Figure 6.14. As before, the March estimate is clearly distinct from the other periods, which are all relatively consistent within their own mean and standard deviation. The t statistic for this discrepancy is 4.9 with a p value of 0.0045, but the data sample is too small for the distribution

[n]The Broyden–Fletcher–Goldfarb–Shanno algorithm is a "hill climbing" method of optimization utilizing estimated second derivatives that is considerably more advanced than simple "steepest ascent" methods.

[o]This method doesn't explicitly use derivatives, although it does assume that the objective function is locally smooth in some manner so that the location of the true extremum may be inferred from recent samples of the objective function.

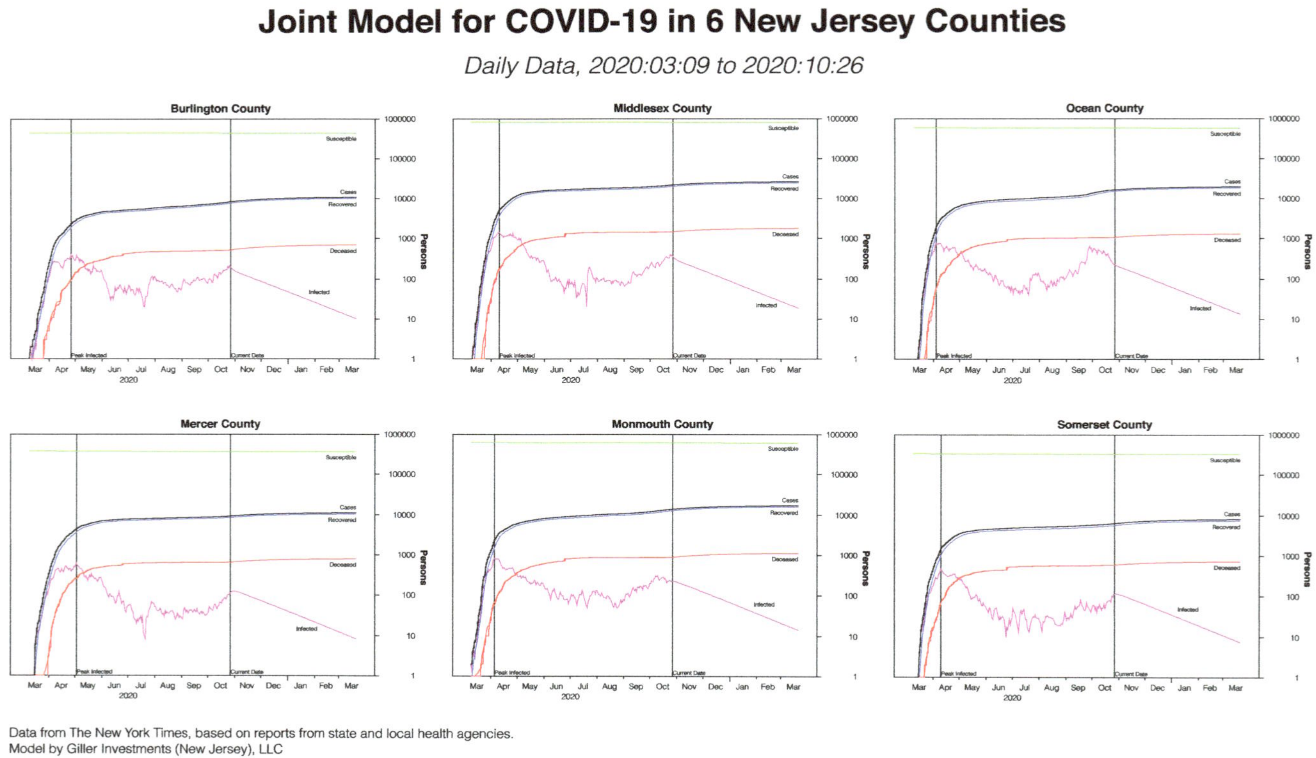

Figure 6.13: Current results of fitting a topological model for the Coronavirus outbreak in six counties in central New Jersey. Key is as for Figure 6.3. Data is from the *New York Times*.

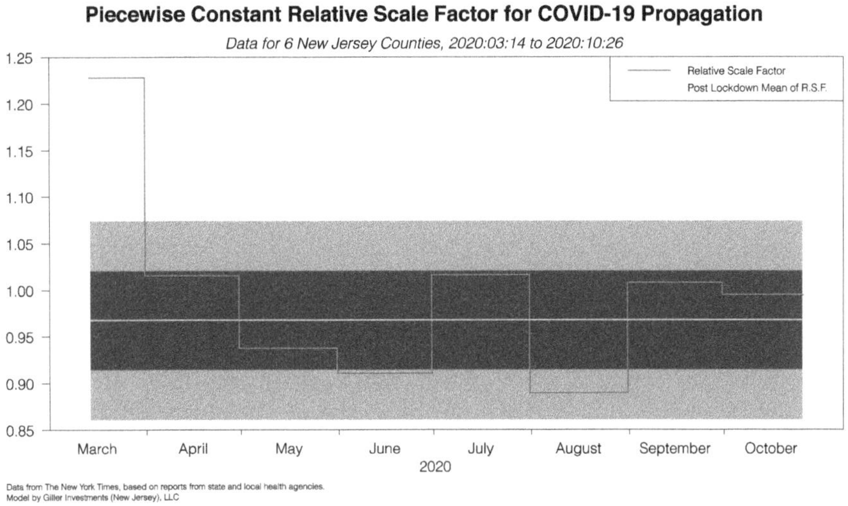

Figure 6.14: Estimated values for the time-varying scale factor, λ_t, in topological model for the Coronavirus outbreak in six counties in central New Jersey. Key is as for Figure 6.2. Data is from the *New York Times*.

to be overly confident in the accuracy of that value.[p] However, the implied claim that March was the worst month to date is not really controversial!

6.4.4.2. *Comparison of the Models for Monmouth County, New Jersey*

Having looked at a lot of these plots over the past six months, it's apparent to me that the count of infected persons in each county is declining *faster* with this model than the values estimated for the single county models presented earlier. The two series can be compared directly, which is done in Figure 6.15. This plot shows two regions, the first one when the estimate is responding to the daily fluctuations in the counts of cases and deaths, which we are modeling as drawn from the Poisson distribution, and the second after the end of the measured data, where we extrapolate the series based on the model estimated from the prior data.

[p]The Central Limit Theorem can't be confidently assumed to apply to a sample of just eight values.

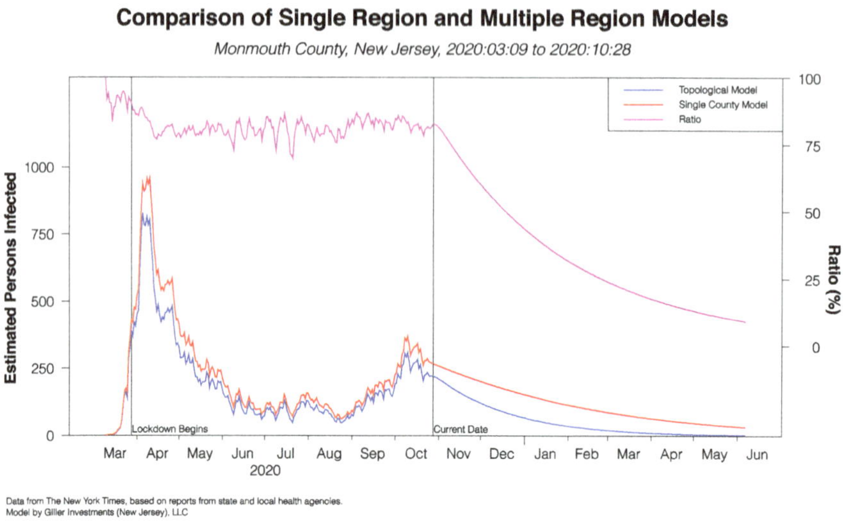

Figure 6.15: Estimated time-series of the number of infected persons in Monmouth County, New Jersey, based on the single county and topological models. Data is from the *New York Times*.

We see that for the period with daily data the estimated count of the infected from the topological model is around 83% of that from the single county model. This relationship is mostly stable. In the second period, where the counts are forecast from the prior data, the count from the topological model is declining faster than that of the single county model.

6.4.5. *A Map of the United States Based on Connectivity*

The map of the political geography of the United States is likely familiar to most readers of this book. As in Section 6.4.2, a graph of the United States may be constructed from the relationship "shares a border with," although this necessarily excludes Alaska, Hawaii, Puerto Rico and the other territories. Such a graph is shown in Figure 6.16 and, to some extent, resembles a turkey! In this graph the States are highlighted by their eigenvector centrality weighting. On that basis, the most "connected" States in the Union are Missouri

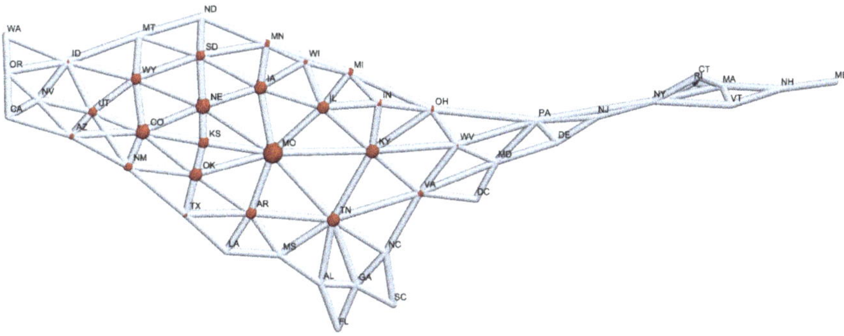

Figure 6.16: Undirected graph for the connectivity of the United States as output by *Mathematica*. Node sizes are proportional to eigenvector centrality.

and Kentucky, and it should be no surprise that the UPS worldwide air hub is based in Louisville, KY.

From that graph the same processing to identify communities may be applied, and the results are in Figure 6.17. One of the reasons for doing this analysis is to permit models to be fitted that are regionally restricted, and that is necessary due to the growing complexity of the topological model. With 49 connected regions in the mainland USA,[q] there are now $s(s+1)/2 + 2s + m$ parameters to estimate where s is the count of States included and m the number of months. This is $49 \times 50/2 + 2 \times 49 + 10 = 1,333$ parameters, compared to just thirteen with one State alone, or 102 times as many parameters when there is just 49 times as much data.

There are two impacts to this "curse of dimensionality":

(i) the statistical precision of our estimates, which scales with the square-root of the sample size, per degree of freedom in the model, is rapidly deteriorating;
(ii) the analysis requires the computation of matrix inverses, the computational complexity of which scales with the cube of the matrix dimension.

Put simply, the code executes painfully more slowly and delivers notably less reliable output when it (finally) ends. The restriction of

[q]Excluding Alaska, Hawaii and Puerto Rico and including Washington, DC.

analysis to the defined communities creates a much needed "dimensional reduction," which delivers tractable systems that may be solved in realistic amounts of computer time.

6.4.6. *Estimating the Topological Model for the Midwest*

Just as in Section 6.4.4, I will estimate the Topological Model for COVID-19 propagation in part of the United States rather than all of the United States. The Midwest, from Figure 6.17, is defined to be the eight states: North Dakota, South Dakota, Minnesota, Iowa, Nebraska, Missouri, Kansas, and Oklahoma.

6.4.6.1. *Individual Time Series for the States*

Figure 6.19 shows the results of fitting this model jointly to the eight states selected. All states show a peak count of infected persons within the State just before the end of 2020. The "fuzz" in this time-series for Kansas likely indicates errors in the cumulative counts of cases which are subsequently corrected. This would induce sudden drops in the implied number of infected to accommodate the

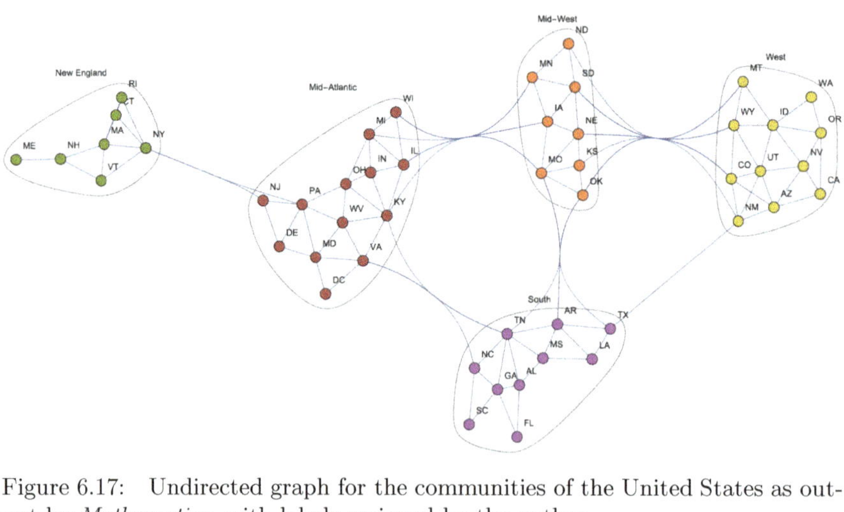

Figure 6.17: Undirected graph for the communities of the United States as output by *Mathematica*, with labels assigned by the author.

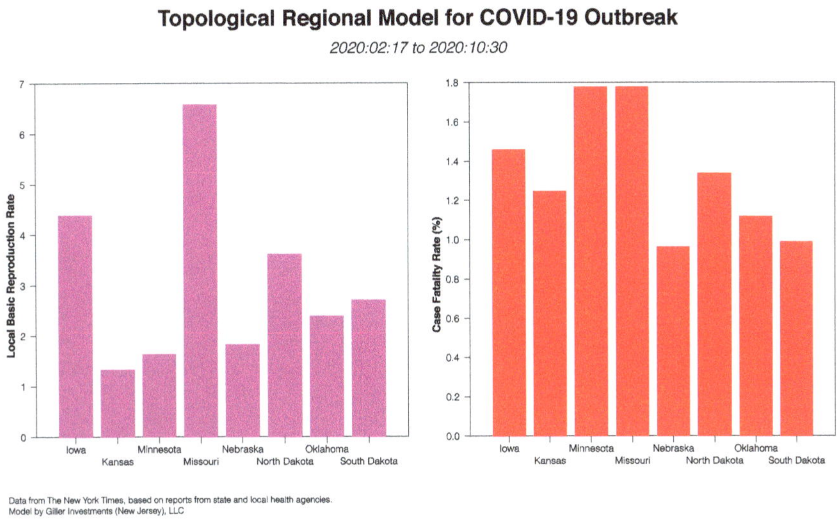

Figure 6.18: Results of fitting a topological model for the Coronavirus outbreak in the Midwest. Left panel is the basic reproduction rate, $\hat{R}_0$, and the right panel is the CFR, for each region individually. Data is from the *New York Times*.

error, resulting in the observed noise. As a passive consumer of data prepared by others, I am not an expert on the particular series nor sufficiently influential to get it "fixed."

6.4.6.2. *The Regional Reproduction Rate and Case Fatality Rate*

The regional basic reproduction rate, R_{0i}, is computed as

$$R_{0i} = \frac{|\det \beta|^{1/c}\beta_{ii}}{\gamma_i + \mu_i}, \tag{6.31}$$

which modifies the canonical expression as a consequence of the structure of Equations (6.19) and (6.21), (6.21). The CFR is defined as before but indexed by the state. The basic reproduction rate shows data clustered around $\hat{R}_{0i} \approx 1$–2 for most of the states, with outliers seen for Iowa, Missouri, and North Dakota. There is dispersion in the CFR, but no striking outliers.

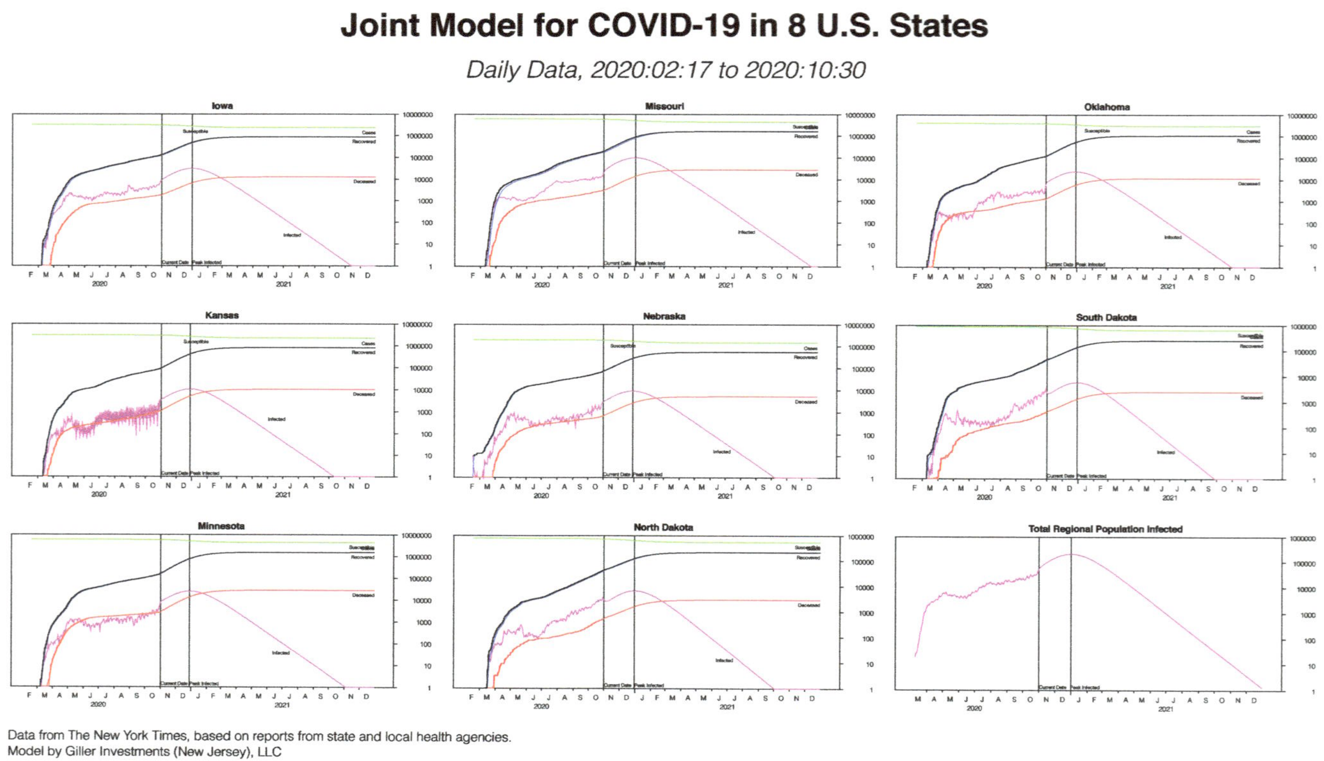

Figure 6.19: Results of fitting a topological model for the Coronavirus outbreak in the Midwest. Key is as for Figure 6.3. Data is from the *New York Times*.

Table 6.5: Estimated characteristic rates for COVID-19 in the Midwest.

Implied rates		
State	R_{0i}	CFR (%)
Iowa	4.39	1.46
Kansas	1.33	1.25
Minnesota	1.64	1.78
Missouri	6.58	1.78
Nebraska	1.83	0.96
North Dakota	3.63	1.34
Oklahoma	2.40	1.12
South Dakota	2.71	0.99

6.4.6.3. *Piecewise Constant Scale for the Reproduction Rate*

A region-wide piecewise constant scale factor for the reproduction rate is defined by Equation (6.30). It probably makes sense for this also *to vary by region*, but that would introduce an additional $8 \times 9 = 72$ parameters to the static model so I decided to stick with a single structure for the average scale factor applied jointly to the entire Midwest.

As before, bounds on these values may be created from their own history with the outlier month excluded. In this case that is May, not March as it was in New Jersey. In Figure 6.20 we see substantial, significant, enhancement of that month's disease propagation rate Overall, the May number of $\hat{R}/\hat{R}_0 = 1.25$ is a $t = 2.8$ discrepancy from the average of the other months, which is 1.10. The p value is 0.038, representing better than 95% confidence that this month *is different*, but my prior comment about the lack of Normality of small samples still applies.

6.4.6.4. *Comparison of Estimates of the Number of Infected People in Nebraska*

Figure 6.21 shows the time-series of the number of people infected with COVID-19 in Nebraska as computed from the multi-region topological model for the Midwest and the single state model of the form of Equation (6.8). As before, for the models estimated for Monmouth

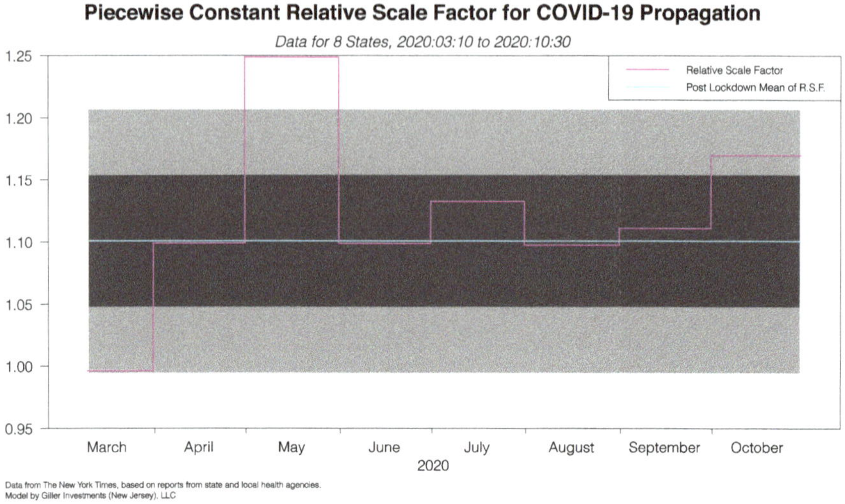

Figure 6.20: Effective reproduction rate scale-factor implied by a topological model for the Coronavirus outbreak in the Midwest. Key is as for Figure 6.2. Data is from the *New York Times*.

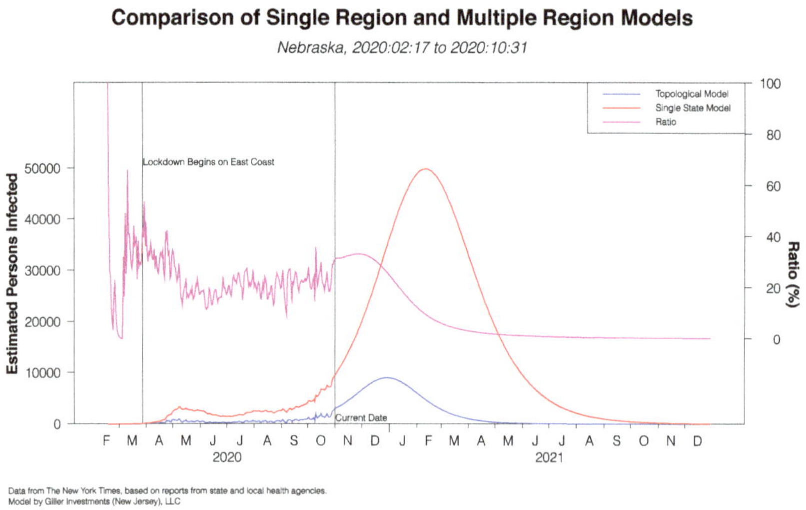

Figure 6.21: Estimates of the number of people infected with COVID-19 in Nebraska based on a single state model and a topological model for eight states in the midwest. Key is as for Figure 6.2. Data is from the *New York Times*.

County, the topological model predicts a smaller outbreak than that from the single-state models. In the case of Nebraska, it is *substantially smaller*. The outbreak also ends earlier, roughly at the end of 2020, rather than surging into the spring of 2021.

I believe that the explanation for this is that a smaller count of the infected *within the state* is needed to explain the observed counts of cases when infections arise from contact with people from out of the state. The impact of each infected person is greater with the multi-regional model.

6.4.6.5. *Estimate of the Propagation Matrix* β

The parameter β in the model of Equation (6.21) is a symmetric matrix. The estimated coefficients of this matrix for the Midwest are

$$\hat{\beta} = \left(\begin{array}{ccccccccc} & \text{IA} & \text{KS} & \text{MN} & \text{MO} & \text{NE} & \text{ND} & \text{OK} & \text{SD} \\ \text{IA} & \mathbf{1.097} & & & & & & & \\ \text{KS} & 1.012 & \mathbf{0.994} & & & & & & \\ \text{MN} & \mathbf{0.969} & 0.984 & \mathbf{0.992} & & & & & \\ \text{MO} & \mathbf{0.945} & \mathbf{0.963} & 0.981 & \mathbf{0.995} & & & & \\ \text{NE} & \mathbf{0.936} & \mathbf{0.949} & 0.959 & \mathbf{0.970} & \mathbf{0.995} & & & \\ \text{ND} & 0.921 & 0.946 & \mathbf{0.953} & 0.954 & 0.990 & \mathbf{1.022} & & \\ \text{OK} & 0.913 & \mathbf{0.945} & 0.956 & \mathbf{0.947} & 0.966 & 0.974 & \mathbf{0.969} & \\ \text{SD} & \mathbf{0.930} & 0.935 & 0.925 & 0.938 & \mathbf{0.944} & \mathbf{0.962} & 1.075 & \mathbf{1.023} \end{array}\right) \tag{6.32}$$

and the scale factor from the determinant has value $|\det\beta|^{1/8} = 0.03743$. Matrix elements where the relationship "shares a border with" is true are boldened, as is the diagonal.

The first observation we make of this matrix is that all of the values are about one, but most of them are below one. The 36 matrix elements have a mean of 0.97 ± 0.04. Using the notion of "direct contact," meaning "shares a border" or is the state itself, allows an ANOVA analysis[r] to be done for that factor, the results of which are in Table 6.6. The ANOVA analysis indicates that "direct connection"

[r]This, of course, is contingent on the assumption that the coefficients are Normally distributed.

Table 6.6: Single factor ANOVA table for the variation of estimated values of $\hat{\beta}_{ij}$ dependent on the level of contact between the States, with contact defined by the connectivity graph of Figure 6.17.

Summary statistics

Groups	Count	Sum	Mean	Variance
Indirect contact	15	14.44	0.96	0.0017
Direct contact	21	20.49	0.98	0.0015

Analysis of variance

Source of variation	SS	df	MS	F	p value
Between groups	0.0014	1	0.0014	0.88	0.36
Within groups	0.053	34	0.0016		
Total	0.0546	35			

is not a factor in determining the values of the β coefficients. My conclusion from this is that topology is not affecting Coronavirus propagation: it is everywhere.

6.5. Looking Back at this Work

As I stated at the beginning of this chapter, I am not an epidemiologist and I do not expect the work described herein to compare to that done by real experts on what is a very complicated, and critically important, subject. I decided to reproduce the work I have done here because I wanted to share my thoughts about, and methods for modeling, a complex system for which data is available to the general public. It was emotionally better for me to do this than just worry about the world my children are exposed to.

To me, the important aspects of my work are the use of discrete time-series models rather than differential equations and the use of the Poisson distribution to model changes in total counts. In doing this I have made the subject of quantitative epidemiology resemble the other work I am familiar with, which is time-series analysis with non-Normal distributions of innovations.

6.5.1. *How Public Coronavirus Data has Changed*

When I first started downloading *The New York Times*'s data on the COVID-19 outbreak they were providing only total counts of cases and total counts of deaths. I have stuck with these data, but since then we have gained access to time-series of the number of tests performed and the positivity rates of those tests. One would assume that this is now sufficient data to measure the statistic that I truly cared about, the number of *infectious* people within the community and the probability that the people I would encounter on my trips to the grocery store, or walking on the beach with my wife, were able to infect me with the disease.

However, that is still not the case: we do not know who is infected because we do not perform testing on random samples of the population. Only people who think they have symptoms, or work for an employer that demands it, are tested. Thus the product of the number of tests done and the test positivity rate likely overstates the proportion of the population that are infected. And we must also draw a distinction between *infected* and *infectious*. One compartment means "having active virus" and the other adds "and able to transmit it." A person in isolation is not infectious even when they are infected!

6.5.2. *Ex Post Analysis of My Coronavirus Predictions*

This chapter contains many charts with projected traces of the counts of total cases and total deaths broken down by region: for Monmouth County, and several other counties, in New Jersey; for New Jersey itself, and several other states; and, for the United States as a whole. Most of these predictions were made in October 2020, and extrapolated day-by-day to the end of 2021. Thus we can look up the predicted numbers for a day a few days earlier than this date[s] and compare them to the data we now have available. For clarity I will examine predictions for December 31, 2020, and June 30, 2021. Some of the earlier models I built were not extrapolated this far into the future so I will not include them here.

[s]August 16, 2021.

The models I have built are time-series models. These are structured as the familiar linear additive noise expressions introduced earlier in this book by Equation (2.4). Time series models of *integrated quantities* are generally very accurate when used to forecast small intervals into the future, but when used to forecast a long way into the future they often go wrong. They are *adaptive learning systems*: they incorporate updates of newly observed data into the forecasts made from that data and this is how they keep their forecasts *dialed in* to the trends within the data. A forecast made for June 1, 2021, on May 31, 2021 is likely quite accurate and quite a bit more accurate than one made on May 1, or in October 2020. Even before beginning this analysis I fully expect the projections to have made significant errors, for that is often the nature of time-series forecasting with this kind of model. In Chapter 3, we saw models to predict the Central England Temperature that were very accurate when used *decades* after the date they were constructed for. That data is seasonal, and not integrated, and easier to forecast by these methods.

For a *Null hypothesis* I can assume that the counts of total cases and total deaths are those given by my models and that the differences between these numbers and the corresponding values on the forecast date are drawn from a Poisson distribution with a mean taken from the models. If the counts in those numbers are sufficiently high, the Normal approximation to the Poisson should be reliable and we can construct a 95% confidence region around those numbers based on twice the change in the expected counts. The actual probability content of such a region can be determined from the Poisson distribution's probability mass function. Specifically:

$$D_t - D_p \sim \text{Poisson}(\hat{D}_t - D_p), \tag{6.33}$$

and

$$C_t - C_p \sim \text{Poisson}(\hat{C}_t - C_p), \tag{6.34}$$

where p is the prediction date and t is the test date. These data are not independent[t] but, since Case Fatality Rates are of order a

[t]Since one cannot die of COVID-19 if one is not infected by the Coronavirus and so $D_t \leq C_t$ always.

percent or so,[u] the bias arising from treating them as independent measurements should not be too large.

6.5.2.1. Ex Ante *Predictions*

My predictions are tabulated in Table 6.7. These were calculated from the data known at 10/21/2020.[v] Projections are made for the end of that year, 12/31/2020, and for six months later. Before the start of this latter interval, of course, the Coronavirus vaccines were approved by the FDA [135] and delivered to millions of people within the United States in the following months.

6.5.2.2. Ex Post *Analysis*

I will follow Rutherford, again, in the analysis of this data. Given the simple Poisson model defined above, the errors between my predictions and the observed data should have implausibly low probabilities of occurring. The Poisson model is plainly ruled out. That is, clearly, a very naïve model when used to extrapolate months into the future.

Looking at the data in Table 6.7, I must ask myself whether the exercise was worthwhile? For the United States as a whole, looking at the errors in the total counts of cases, the errors are −18% for the end of 2020 and +16% at the midpoint of 2021. For New Jersey it is less accurate, with errors of −28% and −11% respectively, and for Monmouth County, New Jersey, alone, even less accurate, with errors of −47% and −74%. The relevant questions are:

(i) how well do these errors compare to "typical" errors; and,
(ii) how well do these errors compare to other forecasting methods?

The literature on forward forecasting of epidemiological models, especially the long horizons such as those considered here of 71 days and 252 days respectively, does not seem to be deep. In their review of COVID-19 forecasting in Chile, Barría-Sandoval *et al.* consider the mean absolute percentage errors a variety of time-series forecasting techniques and find a best case M.A.P.E. of 17.5% for an ARIMA

---

[u] And improving.

[v] This was the date of writing of this section in the 1st edition of the book.

Table 6.7: Table of predicted total counts of cases and deaths for the Coronavirus ourbreak in various regions of the United States.

		Cases		Deaths	
Region	Date	Model	Data	Model	Data
Monmouth County	10/21/2020		13,569		870
	12/31/2020	16,921	31,937	1,101	1,040
	06/30/2021	19,826	76,104	1,299	1,638
New Jersey	10/21/2020		225,012		16,245
	12/31/2020	342,946	479,381	24,696	19,042
	06/30/2021	907,233	1,023,395	66,524	26,452
United States	10/21/2020		8,404,635		222,195
	12/31/2020	16,373,899	20,024,801	631,419	346,050
	06/30/2021	38,949,623	33,639,764	1,843,830	604,446

Notes: All forecasts were made for the dates indicated on 10/21/2020, and the actual reported data are for the indicated dates. Data is from the *New York Times* via GitHub.

model with a horizon of just six days [5]. They do not seem to think this is a remarkably bad outcome and my national results are consistent in magnitude with theirs, especially when scaled by a factor of $O(\sqrt{71/6}) \approx 3.5$ or $O(\sqrt{252/6}) \approx 6.5$ to account for the much larger forecast horizon! On this basis, I think my results for total cases are quite acceptable, although those for total deaths are not.

6.6. COVID Partisanship in the United States

In the opening section of this chapter I wrote[w] that the United States appeared to be entering a third wave of the Coronavirus epidemic. At this time,[x] we have seen that wave of the original variant come and go, and learned that it would be replaced by a much more virulent δ-variant. Throughout the time that the Coronavirus has been actively spreading within the United States, it has been treated in a

[w]In October 2020.
[x]August 2021.

highly partisan manner, even to the extent that some communities deny its reality or the utility of measures to combat it [75].

In Section 6.3.1.1, I examined whether the effective reproduction rate, $\hat{R}$, of COVID-19 showed variation by state that could be explained by party partisanship and found no evidence for that. Since then, the United States went through the fiercely partisan election of November 2020, and we have a new metric of partisanship in terms of the official results of that election [131]. To re-examine that proposition in the light of this new data, I repeated the procedure of that section by fitting the piecewise constant stochastic model developed in Section 6.2.2 to the new data now available[y] state-by-state.

6.6.1. *State by State Results*

The time-series of the implied effective reproduction rates, by month and state, $\hat{R}_{it} = \hat{\beta}_{it}/(\hat{\gamma}_i + \hat{\mu}_i)$, are illustrated in Figure 6.22. The data have been colored by the majority *Electoral College* assignment from the 2020 Presidential Election, with red for Republican states

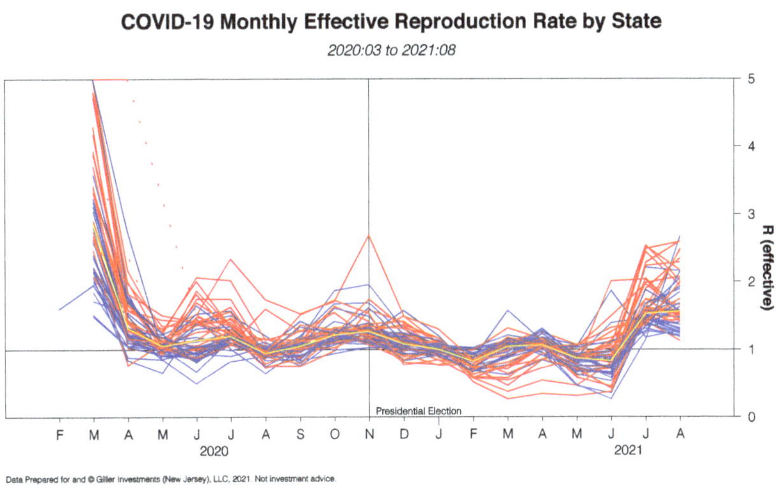

Figure 6.22: Time series of estimated effective reproduction rate, by state, for the United States. Curves colored in blue were majority Democratic in the Presidential Election of 2020 and those in red were majority Republican, in both cases by counts of Electors. The yellow line is the median.

[y]That is data including August 2020.

and blue for Democratic states. To my eye, this data shows that the US had contained the virus propagation by the measures taken in 2020 and, finally, broken it in the new year of 2021, with the median effective reproduction rate dropping below unity at that time. There is a clear resurgence, associated with the δ-variant, in the Summer of 2021. It seems to be clear from the coloring of the individual state time-series that the "red states" had enhanced propagation during the earliest part of the pandemic, and are also playing that role during the current "δ-pandemic," but also that outlying low-propagation rate states during the Spring of 2021 were Republican and not Democratic in nature. Figure 6.23 shows a map of the implied effective reproduction rates, by state, for July, 2021. All states are now showing a reproduction rate in excess of unity, with the largest values concentrated in the traditional South of the United States.[z]

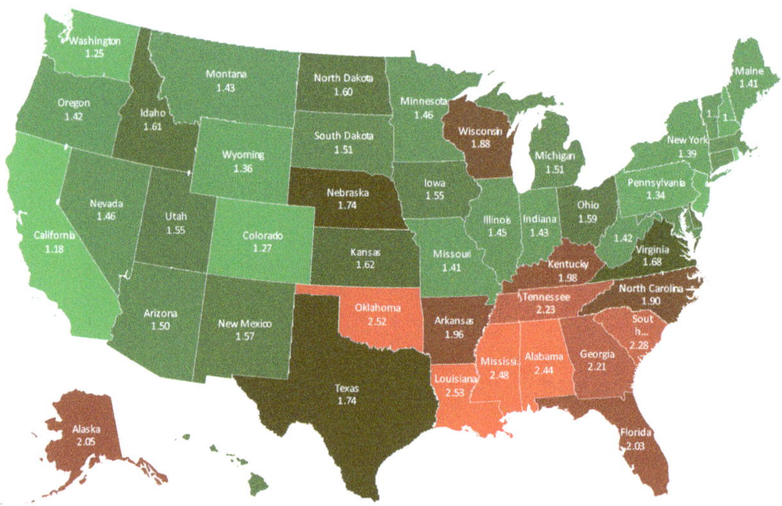

Figure 6.23: Map of the effective reproduction number by state for the COVID-19 epidemic in July 2021. Color indicates the virulence of the disease which, at this time, is dominated by the δ-variant.

[z]That is, the geographic South–East.

6.6.2. *Meta-Analysis of the Reproduction Rate*

To make this discussion more quantitative we can execute various statistical analyzes on the *estimated* effective reproduction rate data. I refer to this as *meta-analysis* as it is the analysis of the results of an analysis, not the analysis of primary source data.

6.6.2.1. *ANOVA Analysis*

The simplest thing to do with this data, having asserted that the factor "partisanship" is described by the results of the election conducted on 11/03/2021, is to divide the results for a sample period by that indicator and perform an *ANOVA* analysis. I'm using the Electoral College results in this analysis as they are the officially certified, and precisely known, independent variable. For the states that execute some form of *proportional representation*,[aa] I will round the Electoral College assignments to either completely Republican or completely Democratic. Puerto Rico is excluded from this analysis as it does not vote in the Electoral College, but the District of Columbia *is* included even though it does not have Congressional representation.

The results of the *ANOVA* analysis are in Table 6.8, and they clearly support the hypothesis that the party affiliation of a state contributes to the value of effective reproduction rate for the δ-variant in that state. This is troubling as it suggests the virus *is* affected by human behavioural patterns[bb] and so it is within our power to control it.

6.6.2.2. *Panel Regression Analysis*

To drill deeper into this analysis we can construct a fixed-effects panel regression with time effects. That would be the model

$$\hat{R}_{it} = R_t + \rho P_{it} + \varepsilon_{it}, \tag{6.35}$$

where P_{it} is the proportion of Republican Electoral College votes for a given state and time and ρ is the coefficient of partisanship.

[aa]Maine and Nebraska.

[bb]Which should not really be a surprise for an infectious disease which, by definition, is spread from person to person.

Table 6.8: Single factor ANOVA table for the variation of estimated values of $\hat{R}_{it}$ dependent on the level of partisanship of the States as defined by their Electoral College results in the Presidential Election of 11/03/2020.

Summary statistics

Groups	Count	Sum	Mean	Variance
Democratic	27	39.9	1.48	0.045
Republican	25	46.0	1.84	0.151

Analysis of variance

Source of variation	*SS*	*df*	*MS*	*F*	*p*-value
Between groups	1.69	1	1.69	17.78	0.0001
Within groups	4.78	50	0.10		
Total	6.47	51			

Note: t is taken to be July 2021.

This model is similar to that explored in Section 3.3.4 except that the *individual effects*, represented by a per-individual coefficient α_i, are replaced by *time effects*, represented by the per-month coefficient R_t. It is still a *fixed effects* model because the time depended element, R_t, is modeled as a set of constants to be estimated and not as a stochastic process. P_{it} is taken to be the share of a states Electoral College vote given to the Republican Party in the most recent election before the given month but, as the most recent the election was on 3, November 2021, I take it to have occurred "at the start" of the data analysis month and so the P_{it} data will exhibit a step discontinuity for some states for November, 2021. Panel regression analysis typically assumes the Normal distribution for the independent residuals, ε_{it}. Since our dependent data are themselves maximum likelihood estimators from a large sample that is likely a reasonable assumption.

The regression is straightforward to execute and estimates $\hat{\rho} = 0.146 \pm 0.039$ with a t statistic of 3.74 and a p value of 0.0002. Thus this data strongly supports the idea that Republican party partisanship has lead to an increased value of the effective reproduction rate in many states. The individual state effective reproduction rates for

Table 6.9: Estimated value of the effective reproduction rate, $\hat{R}_{it}$ of COVID-19 for July 2021, by State, and the value corrected for partisanship, $\hat{R}'_{it}$.

State by State results

State	$\hat{R}_{it}$	$\hat{R}'_{it}$	State	$\hat{R}_{it}$	$\hat{R}'_{it}$
Alabama	2.44	2.29	Montana	1.43	1.29
Alaska	2.05	1.90	Nebraska	1.74	1.62
Arizona	1.50	1.50	Nevada	1.46	1.46
Arkansas	1.96	1.82	New Hampshire	1.34	1.34
California	1.18	1.18	New Jersey	1.31	1.31
Colorado	1.27	1.27	New Mexico	1.57	1.57
Connecticut	1.50	1.50	New York	1.39	1.39
Delaware	1.60	1.60	North Carolina	1.90	1.75
District of Columbia	1.57	1.57	North Dakota	1.60	1.46
Florida	2.03	1.89	Ohio	1.59	1.45
Georgia	2.21	2.21	Oklahoma	2.52	2.38
Hawaii	1.57	1.57	Oregon	1.42	1.42
Idaho	1.61	1.46	Pennsylvania	1.34	1.34
Illinois	1.45	1.45	Puerto Rico	1.45	
Indiana	1.43	1.28	Rhode Island	1.15	1.15
Iowa	1.55	1.41	South Carolina	2.28	2.13
Kansas	1.62	1.48	South Dakota	1.51	1.37
Kentucky	1.98	1.84	Tennessee	2.23	2.08
Louisiana	2.53	2.39	Texas	1.74	1.60
Maine	1.41	1.37	Utah	1.55	1.40
Maryland	1.50	1.50	Vermont	1.44	1.44
Massachusetts	1.48	1.48	Virginia	1.68	1.68
Michigan	1.51	1.51	Washington	1.25	1.25
Minnesota	1.46	1.46	West Virginia	1.42	1.28
Mississippi	2.48	2.34	Wisconsin	1.88	1.88
Missouri	1.41	1.27	Wyoming	1.36	1.22

July 2021, and the value corrected for partisanship, are shown in Table 6.9.

6.7. Final Conclusions

Revisiting this work I have established that forecasting errors for the compartment models of the Coronavirus outbreak I developed are not small but they are consistent with other teams' results and not so large as to make the forecasting procedure totally pointless. We have, sadly, also seen that party partisanship is an active factor in aggravating the propagation of the disease in the United States having measured its impact in an entirely dispassionate, and I believe credible, manner.

Chapter 7

Theory

In this chapter, I am going to present the contents of some white-papers I have written which are mostly theoretical in nature but motivated by the empirical work I was doing. I needed to fully understand, or extend, some of the concepts I was working with and felt it would be useful to encapsulate each piece of work into a single document. It has become my practice to publish such work on the *Social Science Research Network* (SSRN), where you may find them under my author page [125], and these sections more-or-less directly echo those works.

7.1. Some Remarks on the PDT Trading Algorithm

While I was at Morgan Stanley, in PDT, I solved the stochastic programming problem that represented the trading algorithm in use by the PDT group at the time. I learned a lot from that process. It took two years to get that done, but not two years of work. I would sporadically think about the problem, and from time-to-time re-hash the math that didn't work, until one weekend I realized the approach necessary to get it done. It was working with my team-mate Paul Schimmel, trying to understand the solutions he was observing in simulation for a simpler problem, that connected the dots for me, and I was able to put the work together in the space of two or three days. I am proud of this piece of work, although it has never been published. I have reached out to Morgan Stanley to ask for permission to publish it, as I believe it would be regarded as "work for hire," but they have not replied to me. My most recent work on trading strategy analysis will be in *Essays on Trading Strategy* [58].

7.2. Cosine Similarity

I began studying cosine similarity while I was working in internet marketing, and rapidly realized that, like many things in the emerging discipline of data science and machine learning, the statistic was used without any idea of its sampling distribution — under any assumptions. The empirical practice I learned in physics is that all measures are meaningless unless they are quoted within a margin of error, so I set out to compute this. The white-paper is Reference [53].

7.2.1. *Definition of Random Bitstreams*

A random bitstream (N, p) is a vector $\boldsymbol{B}$ in $\mathbb{B}^N$ where each component of the vector is independently drawn from the Bernoulli distribution, Bernoulli(p), i.e.

$$b_i = \boldsymbol{B} \cdot \boldsymbol{e}_i \sim \text{Bernoulli}(p) \quad \forall\, i \in [1, N], \tag{7.1}$$

for basis vectors, $\boldsymbol{e}_i$. I will represent this as the notation $\boldsymbol{B} \sim \text{Bitstream}(N, p)$. Two bitstreams of equal length, $\boldsymbol{A} \sim \text{Bitstream}(N, p)$ and $\boldsymbol{B} \sim \text{Bitstream}(N, q)$, are *independent* if $E(a_i b_j) = E(a_i)E(b_j)\ \forall\, i, j \in [1, N]$. From this it follows that

$$\boldsymbol{A} \wedge \boldsymbol{B} \sim \text{Bitstream}(N, pq), \tag{7.2}$$

where $\boldsymbol{A} \wedge \boldsymbol{B}$ represents the Boolean *and* operation performed pairwise on bitstream elements and is identically equal to the vector of the pairwise products of the bitstream elements, i.e.

$$(\boldsymbol{A} \wedge \boldsymbol{B}) \cdot \boldsymbol{e}_i = a_i b_i. \tag{7.3}$$

Trivially, $\boldsymbol{A} \wedge \boldsymbol{A} = \boldsymbol{A}$ for any bitstream, $\boldsymbol{A}$.

7.2.2. *The Support and Inner Product of Bitstreams*

7.2.2.1. *Definition*

In market basket and collaborative filtering analysis it is common to introduce a term called the "support"[a] [122] of the bitstream which represents the count of the bits that are non-zero divided by the length of the bitstream, N.

$$\operatorname{supp} \boldsymbol{B} = \frac{1}{N}\sum_{i=1}^{N} b_i = \bar{b}. \tag{7.4}$$

7.2.2.2. *Distribution*

From Equation (7.1) we see that

$$\boldsymbol{B} \sim \text{Bitstream}(N, p) \Rightarrow N \operatorname{supp} \boldsymbol{B} \sim \text{Binomial}(N, p). \tag{7.5}$$

As a scaled Binomial distribution, we immediately have

$$\begin{aligned} &E[\operatorname{supp} \boldsymbol{B}] = p \\ &\text{and} \\ &\operatorname{Var}[\operatorname{supp} \boldsymbol{B}] = \frac{p(1-p)}{N}. \end{aligned} \tag{7.6}$$

and it immediately follows that the distribution of $\operatorname{supp} \boldsymbol{B}$ has a well understood limiting Normal distribution defined solely by these moments.

7.2.2.3. *Relationship to the Inner Product*

From Equation (7.4), we see that the inner product of two bitstreams is proportional to the support of their logical product, i.e.

$$\boldsymbol{A} \cdot \boldsymbol{B} = N \operatorname{supp} \boldsymbol{A} \wedge \boldsymbol{B} \sim \text{Binomial}(N, pq), \tag{7.7}$$

where $\boldsymbol{A} \sim \text{Bitstream}(N, p)$ and $\boldsymbol{B} \sim \text{Bitstream}(N, q)$.

---

[a] The usage has some commonalities with, but is not identical to, the usage of the term in measure theory.

7.2.2.4. *Covariance of the Inner Product with its Arguments*

Let $\boldsymbol{A}$ and $\boldsymbol{B}$ be independent bitstreams of equal length as defined above. Then the inner products $\boldsymbol{A} \cdot \boldsymbol{B}$ and $\boldsymbol{A} \cdot \boldsymbol{A}$ are both Binomial random variables but they are not independent. Suppose for some $\boldsymbol{A}$, $N \operatorname{supp} \boldsymbol{A} = n \sim \text{Binomial}(N, p)$ i.e. there are n non-zero bits where n is a Binomial variate. The elements of $\boldsymbol{B}$ at the unsupported bits are irrelevant as $x \wedge 0 = 0 \; \forall \; x \in \mathbb{B}$ and so $\boldsymbol{A} \cdot \boldsymbol{B} \leq n$.

We may reorder the *arbitrary* indices of *both* vectors so that $\boldsymbol{A} = (\boldsymbol{1}_n, \boldsymbol{0}_{N-n})$ and $\boldsymbol{B} = (\boldsymbol{B}_n, \boldsymbol{B}_{N-n})$ where the subscripted vectors, represent the partition of a vector in the first n bits, $\boldsymbol{B}_n$, and the remaining $N - n$ bits, $\boldsymbol{B}_{N-n}$ and $\boldsymbol{1}$ and $\boldsymbol{0}$ are the unit and zero vectors, respectively. Clearly, $\boldsymbol{A} \cdot \boldsymbol{B} = \boldsymbol{B}_n \cdot \boldsymbol{1}_n = n \operatorname{supp} \boldsymbol{B}_n$. Since the full length vectors are independent then any similar partition of them must also be independent and so $n \operatorname{supp} \boldsymbol{B}_n \sim \text{Binomial}(n, q)$ and *independent* of $\boldsymbol{A}$ except for the dependence on n. Therefore,

$$\begin{gathered} \boldsymbol{A} \cdot \boldsymbol{B} \mid \boldsymbol{A} \cdot \boldsymbol{A} \sim \text{Binomial}(\boldsymbol{A} \cdot \boldsymbol{A}, q) \\ \text{where } \boldsymbol{A} \cdot \boldsymbol{A} \sim \text{Binomial}(N, p). \end{gathered} \tag{7.8}$$

Thus, $\boldsymbol{A} \cdot \boldsymbol{B}$ is seen to be drawn from a *nested* Binomial distribution with parameters (N, p, q).

The covariance of $\boldsymbol{A} \cdot \boldsymbol{B}$ and $\boldsymbol{A} \cdot \boldsymbol{A}$ is given by

$$\operatorname{Cov}[\boldsymbol{A} \cdot \boldsymbol{B}, \boldsymbol{A} \cdot \boldsymbol{A}] = E[\boldsymbol{A} \cdot \boldsymbol{B} \times \boldsymbol{A} \cdot \boldsymbol{A}] - E[\boldsymbol{A} \cdot \boldsymbol{B}] \times E[\boldsymbol{A} \cdot \boldsymbol{A}]. \tag{7.9}$$

The latter two terms are known to be Npq and Np, respectively. The cross term may be evaluated as

$$\begin{aligned} E[\boldsymbol{A} \cdot \boldsymbol{B} \times \boldsymbol{A} \cdot \boldsymbol{A}] = &\sum_{\boldsymbol{A} \cdot \boldsymbol{A}=0}^{N} \boldsymbol{A} \cdot \boldsymbol{A} \Pr(\boldsymbol{A} \cdot \boldsymbol{A} | N, p) \\ &\times \sum_{\boldsymbol{A} \cdot \boldsymbol{B}=0}^{\boldsymbol{A} \cdot \boldsymbol{A}} \boldsymbol{A} \cdot \boldsymbol{B} \Pr(\boldsymbol{A} \cdot \boldsymbol{B} | \boldsymbol{A} \cdot \boldsymbol{A}, q) \end{aligned} \tag{7.10}$$

and (remarkably) the entire expression reduces[b] to

$$\operatorname{Cov}[\boldsymbol{A} \cdot \boldsymbol{B}, \boldsymbol{A} \cdot \boldsymbol{A}] = Np(1 - p)q. \tag{7.11}$$

[b]This was simplified using *Mathematica* as the expression `FullSimplify[Sum[AA Pr[AA,N,p] Sum[AB Pr[AB,AA,q],{AB,0,AA}],{AA,0,N}]]` where `Pr[n_,N_,p_] :=PDF[BinomialDistribution[N,p],n]`.

Similarly

$$\text{Cov}[\boldsymbol{A} \cdot \boldsymbol{B}, \boldsymbol{B} \cdot \boldsymbol{B}] = Npq(1-q). \tag{7.12}$$

7.2.3. *The Cosine Similarity of two Bitstreams*

7.2.3.1. *Definition*

We define the *cosine similarity* of two bitstreams of equal length as

$$\cos(\boldsymbol{A}, \boldsymbol{B}) = \frac{\boldsymbol{A} \cdot \boldsymbol{B}}{\sqrt{\boldsymbol{A} \cdot \boldsymbol{A} \times \boldsymbol{B} \cdot \boldsymbol{B}}}, \tag{7.13}$$

following the usual definition for an inner product space. Some properties of this metric are discussed in [141]. Unlike the cosine in Euclidean inner product space, this statistic is bounded below at 0.

7.2.3.2. *Relationship to the Support*

The properties of the support then allow us to write

$$\cos(\boldsymbol{A}, \boldsymbol{B}) = \frac{\operatorname{supp} \boldsymbol{A} \wedge \boldsymbol{B}}{\sqrt{\operatorname{supp} \boldsymbol{A} \times \operatorname{supp} \boldsymbol{B}}}. \tag{7.14}$$

7.2.3.3. *A Tighter Upper Bound*

The authors of [141] point out that it also follows from the definition of support that

$$\cos(\boldsymbol{A}, \boldsymbol{B}) \leq \sqrt{\frac{\operatorname{supp} \boldsymbol{A}}{\operatorname{supp} \boldsymbol{B}}}, \tag{7.15}$$

when $\operatorname{supp} \boldsymbol{A} \leq \operatorname{supp} \boldsymbol{B}$.

7.2.3.4. *A Normal Approximation to the Sampling Distribution of the Cosine Similarity*

We will approximate the sampling distribution of the cosine similarity of equal length independent bitstreams by using the well-known "Delta Method" [110] of taking the expectations of the first-order

Taylor expansion of a function of random variables about the means of the underlying variables, i.e.

$$E[f(\boldsymbol{r})] \simeq f(E[\boldsymbol{r}]) + (\boldsymbol{\nabla} f) \cdot E[\delta \boldsymbol{r}], \tag{7.16}$$

$$\text{and } \mathrm{Var}[f] \simeq (\boldsymbol{\nabla} f) \cdot \mathrm{Var}[\boldsymbol{r}] \cdot \boldsymbol{\nabla} f \tag{7.17}$$

Consider

$$f(\boldsymbol{r}) = \frac{x}{\sqrt{yz}}, \tag{7.18}$$

where $\boldsymbol{r} = (x\,y\,z)^T$ and x, y, and z are correlated asymptotically normal random variables with a known mean vector and covariance matrix. In this case we have

$$\frac{\partial f}{\partial x} = \frac{f}{x}, \quad \frac{\partial f}{\partial y} = -\frac{f}{2y} \quad \text{and} \quad \frac{\partial f}{\partial z} = -\frac{f}{2z} \tag{7.19}$$

and so

$$E[\cos(\boldsymbol{A}, \boldsymbol{B})] \simeq \sqrt{pq} = \mu, \tag{7.20}$$

$$\mathrm{Var}[\cos(\boldsymbol{A}, \boldsymbol{B})] \simeq \frac{4 - 3p - 3q + 2pq}{4N} = \sigma^2, \tag{7.21}$$

where we have substituted in the previously developed values of the inner product expectations, variances and covariances using $x = \boldsymbol{A} \cdot \boldsymbol{B}$, $y = \boldsymbol{A} \cdot \boldsymbol{A}$ and $z = \boldsymbol{B} \cdot \boldsymbol{B}$. Therefore, we model $\cos(\boldsymbol{A}, \boldsymbol{B})$ as asymptotically distributed as $N(\mu, \sigma^2)$ where μ is given by Equation (7.20) and σ^2 is given by Equation (7.21).

The expected value of the cosine similarity for fully independent bitstreams may be quite large, for example if $p = q = 0.5$ then it is 0.5 but for internet scale bitstreams of large lengths, e.g. $N = 10,000$, the sampling error about this number is quite small in comparison (0.006 in this case). Note that as $p, q \to 1$ then $\sigma^2 \to 0$ whereas $p, q \to 0$ then $\sigma^2 \to 1/N$.

7.2.3.5. *Numerical Simulations*

To verify the formulae of Section 7.2.3.4 we conducted a small number of Monte Carlo experiments in *Mathematica*. We generate a random bitstream with the function

$$\texttt{RandomBitstream[N\_, p\_]} := \texttt{Table[If[Random[]} \leq \texttt{p, 1, 0], \{N\}]} \tag{7.22}$$

and generate the of cosine similarity of two independent bitstreams with

$$\begin{aligned}\texttt{Cosine[N\_, p\_, q\_]} := \texttt{Module[\{A, B\},A} &= \texttt{RandomBitstream[N, p];}\\ \texttt{B} &= \texttt{RandomBitstream[N, q];}\\ &\texttt{(A.B)/Sqrt[(A.A)(B.B)]].}\end{aligned} \tag{7.23}$$

One thousand trials of the cosine similarity were then generated for bitstreams of length 10,000, 100 and 10 bits and various combinations of p and q. The sample mean and variance for these trials were then compared with the predicted values. This results are show in Table 7.1. Without performing any precise statistical testing, it seems fair to conclude that the formulae established are reasonable estimates of the first two moments of the sampling distribution of the cosine similarity of independent random bitmaps.

Table 7.1: Results of numerical simulations of the cosine similarity between independent random bitmaps of length 10 000, 100 and 10 bits.

N	p	q	Exp. mean	Obs. mean	Exp. var.	Obs. var.
10 000	0.5	0.5	0.5	0.500091	0.000038	0.000039
10 000	0.5	0.25	0.353553	0.353659	0.000050	0.000049
10 000	0.5	0.125	0.25	0.249839	0.000056	0.000053
10 000	0.5	0.0625	0.176777	0.176880	0.000059	0.000058
100	0.5	0.5	0.5	0.499110	0.00375	0.003740
100	0.5	0.25	0.353553	0.347558	0.005	0.005328
100	0.5	0.125	0.25	0.248546	0.005625	0.005876
100	0.5	0.0625	0.176777	0.175621	0.005938	0.006224
10	0.5	0.5	0.5	0.485566	0.0375	0.041569
10	0.5	0.25	0.353553	0.330916	0.05	0.049284
10	0.5	0.125	0.25	0.287991	0.05625	0.055474
10	0.5	0.0625	0.176777	0.254209	0.059375	0.056185

Note: For each parameter set, 1000 trials were generated.

7.2.3.6. *Support Adjusted Cosine Similarity*

To compensate for the bias in the cosine similarity as discussed in Section 7.2.3.4, we propose adjusting the formula of Equation (7.13) by subtracting the asymptotic expected value, i.e.

$$\operatorname{sacos}(\boldsymbol{A}, \boldsymbol{B}) = \cos(\boldsymbol{A}, \boldsymbol{B}) - \sqrt{\operatorname{supp} \boldsymbol{A} \times \operatorname{supp} \boldsymbol{B}} \tag{7.24}$$

$$= \frac{\operatorname{supp} \boldsymbol{A} \wedge \boldsymbol{B} - \operatorname{supp} \boldsymbol{A} \operatorname{supp} \boldsymbol{B}}{\sqrt{\operatorname{supp} \boldsymbol{A} \times \operatorname{supp} \boldsymbol{B}}} \tag{7.25}$$

where Equation (7.14) has been substituted into Equation (7.24) to give (7.25). We note there is a parallel between the structure of this equation and that of the Pearson correlation coefficient.

7.3. The Construction and Properties of Ellipsoidal Probability Density Functions

I began investigating methods for the construction of multivariate probability distributions because I wanted to measure the value-at-risk I was exposed to while trading portfolios of Eurodollar Futures. I needed a probability distribution function that matched financial data reasonably well, could model realistic leptokurtosis in price changes, and could describe strongly correlated assets. At the time of writing this work, I was unaware of the concept of "copulas," which also provide a recipe for constructing multivariate distributions. This work is from the white-paper I wrote describing these methods, which is Reference [48].

7.3.1. *The Distance Metric Framework*

7.3.1.1. *Normal and Multinormal Distributions*

The mathematical form of the Normal probability density function has a number of remarkably useful properties. In particular, it has a very natural generalization from a univariate form to a multivariate form. If $f(x|\mu, \sigma)$ represents the univariate p.d.f.

$$f(x|\mu, \sigma) = \frac{1}{\sqrt{2\pi}\sigma} \exp -\frac{1}{2}\left(\frac{x-\mu}{\sigma}\right)^2, \tag{7.26}$$

we find that the joint probability for n variables has the form [80, p. 267].

$$f(\boldsymbol{x}|\boldsymbol{\mu},\Sigma) = \frac{1}{(2\pi)^{\frac{n}{2}}|\Sigma|^{\frac{1}{2}}} \exp -\frac{1}{2}(\boldsymbol{x}-\boldsymbol{\mu})^T \Sigma^{-1} (\boldsymbol{x}-\boldsymbol{\mu}). \tag{7.27}$$

It is notable that the functional form of Equation (7.27) is the same as that of Equation (7.26), with the univariate "standardized distance" measure $(x-\mu)/\sigma$ replaced by multivariate metric $(\boldsymbol{x}-\boldsymbol{\mu})^T \Sigma^{-1} (\boldsymbol{x}-\boldsymbol{\mu})$ and the normalization scale σ replaced by the square root of the determinant of the covariance matrix $|\Sigma|^{\frac{1}{2}}$. This form of Equation (7.27) arises from directly constructing the multivariate p.d.f. from the combination of univariate functions, according to the rules of joint probability [80, p. 20].

7.3.1.2. *A Method for Generalization from Other Univariate Distributions*

Unfortunately, the majority of univariate densities do not posses this appealing property of the Normal distribution.[c] In fact, the choice of "natural" multivariate distributions available to the analyst is quite constrained. In order to generate a workable family of multivariate distributions, we therefore choose to follow the suggestion of Equations (7.26) and (7.27) by writing the argument of a univariate p.d.f. in terms of a standardized distance measure and then replacing that measure itself with a multivariate metric.

At this point we will limit our analysis to symmetrical distributions, i.e. Functions for which we can make the transformation:

$$f(x^2)\,dx \to f\{(\boldsymbol{x}-\boldsymbol{\mu})^T \Sigma^{-1} (\boldsymbol{x}-\boldsymbol{\mu})\}\, d^n\boldsymbol{x}. \tag{7.28}$$

Furthermore, for clarity of exposition in the following section, we shall put the multivariate location term, $\boldsymbol{\mu}$, to $\mathbf{0}$. (This term is trivial to reintroduce by translation.)

Therefore, our procedure to generate a multivariate p.d.f.suitable for study is to take a parent univariate p.d.f., $f(x^2)$, and transform it to the multivariate p.d.f., $f(\boldsymbol{x}^T\Sigma^{-1}\boldsymbol{x})$. An additional normalization

[c]That the joint distribution of multiple variables has the same functional form as the individual conditional distributions from which it is built.

term, $\mathcal{A}$, is introduced to restore the normalization of the p.d.f. to unity,[d] i.e.

$$f(x^2)\,dx \to \mathcal{A} f(\boldsymbol{x}^T\Sigma^{-1}\boldsymbol{x})\,d^n\boldsymbol{x}. \tag{7.29}$$

To establish the value of $\mathcal{A}$, we must perform the integral

$$\int \cdots \int_{\boldsymbol{\Omega}} f(\boldsymbol{x}^T\Sigma^{-1}\boldsymbol{x})\,d^n\boldsymbol{x} \tag{7.30}$$

over the region $\boldsymbol{\Omega}$ for which the p.d.f. is defined. From experience with the multinormal distribution, we know that for an infinite domain this integral can be done in polar coordinates [80, pp. 374–375]. The correlated variables $\boldsymbol{x}$ can easily be transformed into uncorrelated variables $\boldsymbol{f}$ (sometimes called *factors* or *principal components*) via an orthogonal transformation $\boldsymbol{f} = R\boldsymbol{x}$. (The required matrix, R, is a rotation into a coordinate system in which the matrix $R\Sigma R^T$ is diagonal — i.e. it is the matrix of the eigenvectors of Σ.) The inverse of such a matrix is trivially equal to the matrix with each diagonal term replaced by its reciprocal. The distance metric is then reduced to a scaled sum-of-squares.

$$\boldsymbol{x}^T\Sigma^{-1}\boldsymbol{x} \to \boldsymbol{f}^T\boldsymbol{\lambda}^{-1}\boldsymbol{f} = \sum_{i=1}^{n} \frac{f_i^2}{\sigma_i^2}. \tag{7.31}$$

The matrix $\boldsymbol{\lambda}$ is the diagonal matrix $(\sigma_1^2, \sigma_2^2, \ldots, \sigma_n^2)$ of the eigenvalues of Σ. For a Multinormal model, the term σ_i^2 represents the variance of factor i.

Transforming into an n-dimensional elliptical polar coordinate system (i.e. one with one length, r, and $n-1$ hyper-angles, θ_i) allows the n-dimensional hyper-volume integral $\int \cdots \int_\Omega d^n\boldsymbol{x}$ to be replaced with a single distance integral and $n-1$ hyper-angle integrals. As the scaled sum-of-squares has no angular dependence in this coordinate system, the hyper-angular integrals are trivial and we have reduced the multiple integral of Equation (7.30) to a single integral.

The following section will discuss the general form of n-dimensional spherical polar coordinates,[e] to be used in this analysis.

---

[d] The normalization of the original p.d.f. is disrupted by replacing single integrals with multiple integrals in n-dimensional space.

[e] The generalization to elliptical polar is trivial.

7.3.2. *A Generalization of Spherical Polar Coordinates to an Arbitrary Number of Dimensions*

At a graduate level, the analyst should be very familiar with operations involving integration in one, two and three dimensions in a number of coordinate systems in addition to simple Cartesian coordinates. However, less of us have any intuition or experience with generalizing those operations into four, five, or more dimensions in any coordinate system other than the Cartesian system. In this section we illustrate how to extend "polar" systems into higher dimensions, and then present a general method for the construction of a "polar" system in an arbitrary number of dimensions.

7.3.2.1. *The Lower Dimensions*

Let us consider the coordinate of a point on a hyper-sphere in each of 1, 2, 3, 4 and 5 dimensions. A sphere is defined to be the locus of all points at a given distance from the origin. We will define "distance," r, to be the square root of the sum of the squares of the coordinates (i.e. $r^2 = \sum_{i=1}^{n} x_i^2$). Therefore, a "1d" sphere is the pair of points $\{+r, -r\}$; a "2d" sphere is the circle with radius r; a "3d" sphere is a normal sphere of radius r; and so forth.

In one dimension, there is no difference between the Cartesian coordinate (x) and the polar coordinate (r). In two dimensions, we take the "x" axis to be primary, and define the angle θ to be the angle between that axis and the line from the origin to a point on the circle of radius r. Thus $(x, y) \to r(\cos\theta, \sin\theta)$ for $\theta \in [0, 2\pi]$. Similarly, in three dimensions, we take the "z" axis to be principal and project a point on the sphere onto the axis and onto the $x - y$ plane. In the plane, we reapply the method for two dimensions. This leads to the familiar expression $(x, y, z) \to r(\sin\theta\cos\phi, \sin\theta\sin\phi, \cos\theta)$ with $\theta \in [0, \pi]$ and $\phi \in [0, 2\pi]$.

In each higher dimension we follow the same procedure: first project a point on the sphere onto a primary axis (this gives a "$r\cos\theta$" coordinate with $\theta \in [0, \pi]$); then project the point into the "plane" spanned by the other coordinates (leading to a "$r\sin\theta$" factor in all the other coordinates); then, we apply the result for the $n-1$th. dimension and iterate until the plane we are projecting into

Table 7.2: Cartesian and polar coordinates for 1 to 5 dimensions.

n	Cartesian	Polar
1	(x)	(r)
2	(y, x)	$r(\sin\alpha, \cos\alpha)$
3	(y, x, z)	$r(\sin\alpha\sin\beta, \sin\alpha\cos\beta, \cos\alpha)$
4	(y, x, z, u)	$r(\sin\alpha\sin\beta\sin\gamma, \sin\alpha\sin\beta\cos\gamma, \sin\alpha\cos\beta, \cos\alpha)$
5	(y, x, z, u, v)	$r(\sin\alpha\sin\beta\sin\gamma\sin\delta, \sin\alpha\sin\beta\sin\gamma\cos\delta,$ $\sin\alpha\sin\beta\cos\gamma, \sin\alpha\cos\beta, \cos\alpha)$

is actually a two dimensional plane. This is the sole angle which does not have a redundancy[f] and so this final angle is defined on $[0, 2\pi]$.

The results for the first five dimensions are summarized in Table 7.2. In the table, angles are represented by Greek letters and distances by Roman. The ordering of x and y are reversed to help emphasize the pattern produced by iterative projection into lower dimensions.[g] It can be readily verified that the sum of the squares of the coordinates is r^2 in each case.

7.3.2.2. *A General Scheme*

From Table 7.2 we can infer a general scheme for n dimensions. Let the Cartesian coordinates be $\{x_i\}_{i=1}^{n}$. Let the polar distance coordinate be r and the $n-1$ angles be $\{\theta_i\}_{i=1}^{n-1}$. Choosing the *primary* axis arbitrarily to be x_n, we write[h]

$$x_1 = r\prod_{i=1}^{n-1}\sin\theta_i. \tag{7.32}$$

For the remaining coordinates, x_i where $i > 1$, we have

$$x_i = r\cos\theta_{n-i+1}\prod_{j=1}^{n-i}\sin\theta_j. \tag{7.33}$$

[f] Angles in $[\pi, 2\pi]$ can be mapped into angles in $[0, \pi]$ by a rotation in the subplane about the axis we are projecting onto.

[g] From this table, it would appear that our conventional assignment of x and y are the wrong way around!

[h] When the product term $\prod_{i=j}^{k}$ appears for $k < j$ we take it's value to be unity.

The domains of the polar coordinates are

$$r \in [0, \infty];\ \theta_i \in [0, \pi]\,\forall\, 1 < i < n-1;\ \theta_{n-1} \in [0, 2\pi]. \tag{7.34}$$

7.3.2.3. *Transformation of the Volume Integral*

The transformation of the hyper-volume integral,[i] given the coordinate transformation specified by Equations (7.32) and (7.33), is given by Equation (7.35)

$$\int_{x_1=-\infty}^{\infty} \cdots \int_{x_n=-\infty}^{\infty} d^n\boldsymbol{x} = \int_{r=0}^{\infty} \int_{\theta_1=0}^{\pi} \int_{\theta_2=0}^{\pi} \cdots \int_{\theta_{n-1}=0}^{2\pi} |J_n| dr \prod_{i=1}^{n-1} d\theta_i, \tag{7.35}$$

where J_n represents the *Jacobian* of the transformation. J_n is defined to be the determinant given by Equation (7.36).

$$J_n = \frac{\partial(x_1, x_2 \ldots x_n)}{\partial(r, \theta_1, \theta_2, \ldots \theta_{n-1})} = \begin{vmatrix} \frac{\partial x_1}{\partial r} & \frac{\partial x_1}{\partial \theta_1} & \cdots & \frac{\partial x_1}{\partial \theta_{n-1}} \\ \frac{\partial x_2}{\partial r} & \frac{\partial x_2}{\partial \theta_1} & \cdots & \frac{\partial x_2}{\partial \theta_{n-1}} \\ \vdots & \vdots & \ddots & \vdots \\ \frac{\partial x_n}{\partial r} & \frac{\partial x_n}{\partial \theta_1} & \cdots & \frac{\partial x_n}{\partial \theta_{n-1}} \end{vmatrix} \tag{7.36}$$

From our definition of the coordinate transformations, we find:

$$\frac{\partial x_1}{\partial r} = \prod_{i=1}^{n-1} \sin\theta_i = \frac{x_1}{r}; \tag{7.37}$$

and,

$$\frac{\partial x_1}{\partial \theta_i} = r\cos\theta_i \prod_{\substack{j=1 \\ j\neq i}}^{n-1} \sin\theta_j = x_1 \cot\theta_i; \tag{7.38}$$

for the first row of the determinant, and

$$\frac{\partial x_i}{\partial r} = \cos\theta_{n-i+1} \prod_{j=1}^{n-i} \sin\theta_j = \frac{x_i}{r}; \tag{7.39}$$

[i] The argument followed here is well known in the literature. See Reference [80, pp. 374–375], for example.

$$\left.\frac{\partial x_i}{\partial \theta_j}\right|_{\substack{i>1\\ j<n-i+1}} = r\cos\theta_{n-i+1}\cos\theta_j\prod_{\substack{k=1\\ k\neq j}}^{n-i}\sin\theta_k = x_i\cot\theta_j; \tag{7.40}$$

$$\left.\frac{\partial x_i}{\partial \theta_{n-i+1}}\right|_{i>1} = -r\sin\theta_{n-i+1}\prod_{j=1}^{n-i}\sin\theta_j = -x_i\tan\theta_{n-i+1}; \tag{7.41}$$

and,

$$\left.\frac{\partial x_i}{\partial \theta_j}\right|_{\substack{i>1\\ j>n-i+1}} = 0; \tag{7.42}$$

for the remaining rows. The Jacobian therefore has the value

$$J_n = \begin{vmatrix} \frac{x_1}{r} & x_1\cot\theta_1 & x_1\cot\theta_2 & \cdots & x_1\cot\theta_{n-2} & x_1\cot\theta_{n-1} \\ \frac{x_2}{r} & x_2\cot\theta_1 & x_2\cot\theta_2 & \cdots & x_2\cot\theta_{n-2} & -x_2\tan\theta_{n-1} \\ \frac{x_3}{r} & x_3\cot\theta_1 & x_3\cot\theta_2 & \cdots & -x_3\tan\theta_{n-2} & 0 \\ \frac{x_4}{r} & x_4\cot\theta_1 & x_4\cot\theta_2 & \cdots & 0 & \vdots \\ \vdots & \vdots & \vdots & \ddots & \vdots & \vdots \\ \frac{x_n}{r} & -x_n\tan\theta_1 & 0 & \cdots & 0 & 0 \end{vmatrix}. \tag{7.43}$$

We may take out common factors in each row or column, giving

$$J_n = \frac{\prod_{i=1}^n x_i}{r}\begin{vmatrix} 1 & \cot\theta_1 & \cot\theta_2 & \cdots & \cot\theta_{n-2} & \cot\theta_{n-1} \\ 1 & \cot\theta_1 & \cot\theta_2 & \cdots & \cot\theta_{n-2} & -\tan\theta_{n-1} \\ 1 & \cot\theta_1 & \cot\theta_2 & \cdots & -\tan\theta_{n-2} & 0 \\ 1 & \cot\theta_1 & \cot\theta_2 & \cdots & 0 & \vdots \\ \vdots & \vdots & \vdots & \ddots & \vdots & \vdots \\ 1 & -\tan\theta_1 & 0 & \cdots & 0 & 0 \end{vmatrix}. \tag{7.44}$$

Substituting Equations (7.32) and (7.33) into the scale factor of Equation (7.44), we see that this term is equal to

$$r^{n-1} \prod_{i=1}^{n-1} \sin^{n-i} \theta_i \prod_{i=1}^{n-1} \cos \theta_i. \tag{7.45}$$

We may now reduce the determinant by using the property of determinants that adding any multiple of one row to another row leaves the value of the determinant unchanged. In Equation (7.44), we successively subtract row k from row $k-1$ to reduce the determinant as follows:

$$\begin{aligned}
\text{row } 1 - \text{row } 2 &\Rightarrow \text{row } 1 \rightarrow (0, 0, 0 \ldots 0, \cot \theta_{n-1} + \tan \theta_{n-1}) \\
\text{row } 2 - \text{row } 3 &\Rightarrow \text{row } 2 \rightarrow (0, 0, 0 \ldots \cot \theta_{n-2} + \tan \theta_{n-2}, 0) \\
&\ \ \vdots \\
\text{row}(n-2) - \text{row}(n-1) &\Rightarrow \text{row}(n-2) \rightarrow (0, \cot \theta_1 + \tan \theta_1, 0 \ldots, 0)
\end{aligned} \tag{7.46}$$

Applying the results of Equation (7.46) to the determinant of Equation (7.44) gives the determinant

$$\begin{vmatrix}
0 & 0 & 0 & \cdots & 0 & \cot \theta_{n-1} + \tan \theta_{n-1} \\
0 & 0 & 0 & \cdots & \cot \theta_{n-2} + \tan \theta_{n-2} & 0 \\
\vdots & \vdots & \vdots & \ddots & 0 & \vdots \\
0 & \cot \theta_1 + \tan \theta_1 & 0 & \cdots & \vdots & \vdots \\
1 & -\tan \theta_1 & 0 & \cdots & 0 & 0
\end{vmatrix}. \tag{7.47}$$

This evaluates to

$$\prod_{i=1}^{n-1} \frac{1}{\cos \theta_i \sin \theta_i}. \tag{7.48}$$

Substituting Equations (7.45) and (7.48) into Equation (7.43), we have the final expression for the Jacobian of this transformation.

$$J_n = r^{n-1} \prod_{i=1}^{n-2} \sin^{n-i-1} \theta_i. \tag{7.49}$$

We can easily verify that this expression gives the correct result for the well known lower dimensions: $dx \to dr$; $dx\,dy \to r\,dr\,d\theta$; and, $dx\,dy\,dz \to r^2 \sin\theta\,dr\,d\theta\,d\phi$. Note that in Equation (7.49), the sine of angles θ_i is only ever taken for $1 < i < n-2$ which is the set of angles for which $\theta_i \in [0,\pi]$. Therefore, $\sin\theta_i$ is never negative, and the absolute value $|J_n|$ from Equation (7.35) can be replaced with just J_n itself.

If we are integrating a function, $f(r)$, which depends solely on the radial distance, r, in two or more dimensions ($n > 1$) we see that the angular integrals in Equation (7.36) are trivial.

$$\int \cdots \int_{\mathbb{R}^n} f(r)\,d^n\boldsymbol{x} = \int_0^{\infty} f(r)\,r^{n-1}\,dr \prod_{i=1}^{n-2} \int_{\theta_i=0}^{\pi} \sin^{n-i-1}\theta_i\,d\theta_i \int_{\theta_{n-1}=0}^{2\pi} d\theta_{n-1}. \tag{7.50}$$

The Beta function has the integral representation of Equation (7.51), (see [61, p. 389]).

$$\int_0^{\pi/2} \sin^{\mu-1} x \cos^{\nu-1} x\,dx = \frac{1}{2} B\Big(\frac{\mu}{2}, \frac{\nu}{2}\Big) \text{ where } \Re\mu > 0, \Re\nu > 0. \tag{7.51}$$

Therefore, the integrals containing sine terms in Equation (7.50) may be written

$$\int_{\theta_i=0}^{\pi} \sin^{n-i-1}\theta_i\,d\theta_i = B\left(\frac{n-i}{2}, \frac{1}{2}\right) = \pi^{\frac{1}{2}} \frac{\Gamma\big(\frac{n-i}{2}\big)}{\Gamma\big(\frac{n-i+1}{2}\big)}. \tag{7.52}$$

Substituting these results into Equation (7.50), we have

$$\int \cdots \int_{\mathbb{R}^n} f(r^2)\,d^n\boldsymbol{x} = 2\pi^{\frac{n}{2}} \prod_{i=1}^{n-2} \frac{\Gamma\big(\frac{n-i}{2}\big)}{\Gamma\big(\frac{n-i+1}{2}\big)} \int_{r=0}^{\infty} f(r^2)\,r^{n-1}\,dr. \tag{7.53}$$

7.3.3. *The Normalization of a Multivariate Distribution based on a Distance Metric Transformation of a Univariate Distribution*

In this section, the results of Sections 7.3.1 and 7.3.2 are combined to yield a full expression for the normalization constant introduced when we construct a multivariate distribution using the method presented here.

7.3.3.1. *Solution for a General Distribution*

We consider a symmetric parent univariate distribution, normalized over an infinite domain.

$$\int_{-\infty}^{\infty} f(x^2)\, dx = 1. \tag{7.54}$$

Following Equation (7.28), we construct a multivariate distribution using the distance metric and must evaluate the new normalization constant, $\mathcal{A}$.

$$\frac{1}{\mathcal{A}} = \int_{x_1=-\infty}^{\infty} \cdots \int_{x_n=-\infty}^{\infty} f\{(\boldsymbol{x}-\boldsymbol{\mu})^T \Sigma^{-1} (\boldsymbol{x}-\boldsymbol{\mu})\}\, d^n\boldsymbol{x}. \tag{7.55}$$

The first step in performing this integral is the simple translation $\boldsymbol{y} = \boldsymbol{x} - \boldsymbol{\mu}$. Since the domain of integration is infinite, and writing $\mathcal{N}$ for $1/\mathcal{A}$, we have

$$\mathcal{N} = \int_{y_1=-\infty}^{\infty} \cdots \int_{y_n=-\infty}^{\infty} f(\boldsymbol{y}^T \Sigma^{-1} \boldsymbol{y})\, d^n\boldsymbol{y}. \tag{7.56}$$

We know from the analysis sketch of Section 7.3.1 that this expression should be further reduced by diagonalizing the coordinate system through an orthogonal rotation. This leaves an elliptical polar system which may be transformed into a spherical polar system via simple scaling operations. Such operations lead to a normalization constant that is proportional to the square root of the product of the eigenvalues of the matrix Σ.

We require that Σ be a symmetric positive definite matrix. (This is consistent with the parallel we are drawing with the multinormal distribution, for which Σ is equal to the covariance matrix of $\boldsymbol{x}$ and is s.p.d. by definition.) The matrix of eigenvalues of such a matrix may be factored as $\boldsymbol{\lambda} = D^2 = DD^T = D^T D$, where D is a diagonal matrix with positive definite elements σ_i. Furthermore, we know that the inverse $\boldsymbol{\lambda}^{-1} = (D^2)^{-1} = (D^{-1})^2$ is trivial.

If R is the matrix of eigenvectors of Σ, then we may define the matrix D by

$$R^T \Sigma R = D^2. \tag{7.57}$$

From Equation (7.57) and the definitions of D and R, it follows that

$$R^T \Sigma^{-1} R = (D^{-1})^2. \tag{7.58}$$

Therefore, rather than the transformation $\boldsymbol{f} = R\boldsymbol{y}$ (suggested in Section 7.3.1, we shall make the transformation

$$\boldsymbol{g} = D^{-1} R \boldsymbol{y}. \tag{7.59}$$

Equation (7.59) implies that $\boldsymbol{y} = R^T D\boldsymbol{g}$ and $\boldsymbol{y}^T = \boldsymbol{g}^T DR$. The distance metric may now be written

$$\begin{aligned} \boldsymbol{y}^T \Sigma^{-1} \boldsymbol{y} &= \boldsymbol{g}^T DR\Sigma^{-1} R^T D\boldsymbol{g} \\ &= \boldsymbol{g}^T D(R^T \Sigma R)^{-1} D\boldsymbol{g} \\ &= \boldsymbol{g}^T D(D^2)^{-1} D\boldsymbol{g} \\ &= g^2. \end{aligned} \tag{7.60}$$

Using the transformation of Equation (7.59), Equation (7.56) becomes

$$\mathcal{N} = \int_{g_1=-\infty}^{\infty} \cdots \int_{g_n=-\infty}^{\infty} f(g^2)\, |K_n|\, d^n \boldsymbol{g}, \tag{7.61}$$

where K_n is the Jacobian

$$K_n = \frac{\partial(y_1 \ldots y_n)}{\partial(g_1 \ldots g_n)} = \begin{vmatrix} \frac{\partial y_1}{\partial g_1} & \cdots & \frac{\partial y_1}{\partial g_n} \\ \vdots & \ddots & \vdots \\ \frac{\partial y_n}{\partial g_1} & \cdots & \frac{\partial y_n}{\partial g_n} \end{vmatrix}. \tag{7.62}$$

From Equation (7.59) we have $\frac{\partial y_i}{\partial g_j} = (R^T D)_{ij}$, therefore $K_n = |R^T D| = |D|$. Since $|D^2| = |\Sigma|$ (from Equation (7.58)), we have $|D| = |\Sigma|^{\frac{1}{2}}$. Furthermore, since Σ is s.p.d. by construction, the determinant of Σ is positive definite and we may replace $|K_n|$ by K_n in Equation (7.61). We may now make the spherical polar transformation of Section 7.3.2, to give

$$\mathcal{N} = 2\pi^{\frac{n}{2}} |\Sigma|^{\frac{1}{2}} \prod_{i=1}^{n-2} \frac{\Gamma\left(\frac{n-i}{2}\right)}{\Gamma\left(\frac{n-i+1}{2}\right)} \int_{g=0}^{\infty} f(g^2)\, g^{n-1}\, dg. \tag{7.63}$$

7.3.3.2. *Evaluation of the Product Factor*

We have shown above that the normalization factor $\mathcal{A}$ is proportional to $|\Sigma|^{-\frac{1}{2}}$. The full expression, Equation (7.63), also contains a term dependent on the precise p.d.f. in use and a term that is the product of a series of ratios of gamma functions. In this section, we will use the known result of Equation (7.27) to derive a more compact expression for this factor.

Let us represent this gamma function factor as P_n, i.e.

$$P_n = \prod_{i=1}^{n-2} \frac{\Gamma\left(\frac{n-i}{2}\right)}{\Gamma\left(\frac{n-i+1}{2}\right)} \tag{7.64}$$

Equation (7.63) now becomes

$$\mathcal{N} = 2\pi^{\frac{n}{2}} |\Sigma|^{\frac{1}{2}} P_n \int_{g=0}^{\infty} f(g^2)\, g^{n-1}\, dg. \tag{7.65}$$

For the standardized distribution $N(0,1)$, we have

$$f(x^2) = \frac{e^{-\frac{1}{2}x^2}}{\sqrt{2\pi}}. \tag{7.66}$$

Substituting this into Equation (7.65) gives

$$\mathcal{N} = \sqrt{2\pi^{n-1}|\Sigma|} P_n \int_0^{\infty} e^{-\frac{1}{2}g^2} g^{n-1}\, dg. \tag{7.67}$$

The integral in this expression is recognized as a representation of the gamma function [61, p. 884]. Substituting this result into Equation (7.67) gives an expression for $\mathcal{N}$ in terms of $|\Sigma|$ and P_n.

$$\mathcal{N} = \sqrt{(2\pi)^{n-1}|\Sigma|} P_n \Gamma\left(\frac{n}{2}\right). \tag{7.68}$$

Comparing Equation (7.27) and Equation (7.68), we must have

$$P_n = \frac{1}{\Gamma\left(\frac{n}{2}\right)}. \tag{7.69}$$

Therefore

$$\mathcal{N} = \frac{2\pi^{\frac{n}{2}} |\Sigma|^{\frac{1}{2}}}{\Gamma\left(\frac{n}{2}\right)} \int_0^{\infty} f(g^2)\, g^{n-1}\, dg. \tag{7.70}$$

The normalized univariate p.d.f. $f(x^2)$ is renormalized by dividing by this factor when the distance metric transformation is used to generate a multivariate p.d.f.

7.3.4. *A Test Statistic for the Identification of Multivariate Distributions*

7.3.4.1. *Definition*

In this section, we propose a statistic that may be used to aid testing the hypothesis that a given dataset is drawn from a multivariate distribution such as one derived using the methodology outlined in this document.

For univariate distributions, powerful tests for distribution identification can be constructed using either the Kolmogorov statistic or a statistics from the Smirnov-Cramér-von Mises Group [26, pp. 268–269]. Both of these methods rely on the comparison of the empirical distribution function (or "order statistics") with the actual distribution function. This comparison is well defined in one dimension, but it is problematic to generalize to arbitrary numbers of dimensions. The problems arise from defining the direction in n-space through which one travels to define the order statistic. Another way of stating this is that no simple analog of the transformation to convert an arbitary univariate distribution into a uniform distribution may be defined for a multivariate distribution. Some authors have suggested examining every possible ordering of the transformation to uniformity [77]; however, for n dimensions there are $n!$ such orderings and the procedure clearly can only be performed for n of order 2 to 4. Problems involving twenty or more dimensions are out of the question!

Therefore, we propose using the Kolmogorov test on the distance metric itself. This test has the advantages that it is easy to define, understand, and execute. It has the drawback that it is not the most powerful test we could define (for example, it is possible that the conditional distribution of variable x_i has excess kurtosis and that the conditional distribution of variable x_j has insufficient kurtosis in such a way that when they are combined in the distance metric this effect is exactly cancelled and the test proposed has zero power to identify such a defect).

Define g^2 as the value of the distance metric, and the density function and distribution function of g^2 as $f'(g^2)$ and $F'(g^2)$, respectively. The probability that $g^2 < G^2$, where G^2 is a particular sample value of the distance metric, is equal to the probability that $\boldsymbol{x}$ lies within the region Ω_G defined to be the hypervolume enclosed by the hyperellipsoidal shell parameterized by particular value of the distance metric, i.e.

$$F'(G^2) = \Pr(g^2 < G^2) = \Pr(\boldsymbol{x} \in \Omega_G) \text{ where } G^2 = (\boldsymbol{x}-\boldsymbol{\mu})^T\Sigma^{-1}(\boldsymbol{x}-\boldsymbol{\mu}). \tag{7.71}$$

Therefore,

$$F'(G^2) = \int \cdots \int_{\Omega_G} \mathcal{A} f\{(\boldsymbol{x}-\boldsymbol{\mu})^T\Sigma^{-1}(\boldsymbol{x}-\boldsymbol{\mu})\}\, d^n\boldsymbol{x}. \tag{7.72}$$

Applying the results of Section 7.3.3, we have

$$F'(G^2) = \frac{\int_{g=0}^{G} f(g^2)\, g^{n-1}\, dg}{\int_{g=0}^{\infty} f(g^2)\, g^{n-1}\, dg}. \tag{7.73}$$

7.3.4.2. *An Example: The Multinormal Statistic*

To illustrate the use of the statistic, we will evaluate its p.d.f. for the case of the multinormal distribution. Using Equation (7.66) to define the univariate p.d.f., we have

$$\int_{g=0}^{G} e^{-\frac{1}{2}g^2} g^{n-1}\, dg = 2^{\frac{n}{2}-1} \int_{u=0}^{\frac{1}{2}G^2} e^{-u} u^{\frac{n}{2}-1}\, du. \tag{7.74}$$

This integral is the "lower" incomplete gamma function [61, p. 890], $\gamma(\cdot)$. Therefore,

$$F'(G^2) = \frac{\gamma(\frac{n}{2}, \frac{1}{2}G^2)}{\Gamma(\frac{n}{2})}. \tag{7.75}$$

For an integral argument, n, the incomplete gamma function has the simple series expansion ([61, p. 890]):

$$\gamma(n, x) = \Gamma(n)\left(1 - e^{-x}\sum_{k=0}^{n-1}\frac{x^k}{k!}\right). \tag{7.76}$$

For an even number of dimensions, $n \in \{2, 4, 6, \ldots\}$, we have

$$F'(G^2) = 1 - e^{-\frac{1}{2}G^2} \sum_{k=0}^{\frac{n}{2}-1} \frac{G^{2k}}{2^k k!}. \tag{7.77}$$

The density $f'(G^2)$ is given by

$$f'(G^2) = \frac{dF'(G^2)}{dG^2} = \frac{1}{\Gamma(\frac{n}{2})} \frac{\partial\gamma(\frac{n}{2}, \frac{1}{2}G^2)}{\partial G^2}. \tag{7.78}$$

The derivative of $\gamma(\alpha, x)$ w.r.t. x is $x^{\alpha-1}e^{-x}$ ([61, p. 891]). Using this result, Equation (7.78) becomes

$$f'(z) = \frac{1}{2^{\frac{n}{2}}\Gamma(\frac{n}{2})} z^{\frac{n}{2}-1} e^{-\frac{1}{2}z} \tag{7.79}$$

(where we have written z for G^2). This is, of course, the well known χ^2 distribution for n degrees of freedom ([80, p. 376]). It has the mean n and variance $2n$.

7.3.5. *Measures of Location, Dispersion and Shape for Multivariate Distributions with Ellipsoidal Symmetry*

7.3.5.1. *The Population Mean, Mode and Median*

The population mean and mode are the simplest measures of location to define. The mean is given by

$$E[\boldsymbol{x}] = \mathcal{A} \int \cdots \int_{\Omega} \boldsymbol{x} f\{(\boldsymbol{x} - \boldsymbol{\mu})^T \Sigma^{-1} (\boldsymbol{x} - \boldsymbol{\mu})\}\, d^n\boldsymbol{x}. \tag{7.80}$$

Using the transformations discussed above, we may write Equation (7.80) as

$$E[\boldsymbol{x}] = \boldsymbol{\mu} + \mathcal{A} R^T D |D| \int \cdots \int_{\Omega} \boldsymbol{g} f(g^2)\, d^n\boldsymbol{g}. \tag{7.81}$$

The integral on the r.h.s. of Equation (7.81) clearly vanishes by virtue of our definition of $f(g^2)$, leaving the simple result $E[\boldsymbol{x}] = \boldsymbol{\mu}$.

The population mode is the most likely value of the coordinate vector $\boldsymbol{x}$, i.e.

$$\boldsymbol{m} = \arg\max_{\boldsymbol{x}\in\Omega} f\{(\boldsymbol{x}-\boldsymbol{\mu})^T\Sigma^{-1}(\boldsymbol{x}-\boldsymbol{\mu})\}. \tag{7.82}$$

If the p.d.f. is differentiable everywhere, then $\boldsymbol{m}$ is a solution of

$$\boldsymbol{\nabla} f\{(\boldsymbol{x}-\boldsymbol{\mu})^T\Sigma^{-1}(\boldsymbol{x}-\boldsymbol{\mu})\} = \frac{df}{dz}\,\boldsymbol{\nabla} z = \boldsymbol{0} \text{ where } z = (\boldsymbol{x}-\boldsymbol{\mu})^T\Sigma^{-1}(\boldsymbol{x}-\boldsymbol{\mu}). \tag{7.83}$$

z is clearly minimized at $\boldsymbol{x} = \boldsymbol{\mu}$. If f is a monotonic decreasing function of z, then the p.d.f. will be unimodal with $\boldsymbol{m} = \boldsymbol{\mu}$. If f is a monotonic increasing function of z, for a finite domain Ω, then $\boldsymbol{m}$ must be a region of the surface S bounding Ω. If f is not a monotonic function then $\boldsymbol{m}$ is any point on the elliptical shell $z = z_0$ where z_0 is the global maximum of $f(z)$ within Ω.

The median, M, of a continuous univariate p.d.f. may be defined to be the solution of the equation

$$\int_{-\infty}^{M} f(x)\,dx = \int_{M}^{\infty} f(x)\,dx. \tag{7.84}$$

For a multivariate p.d.f., we may similarly define the median to be the surface S_M that divides the domain into two distinct sets of regions $\Omega_1 = \cup_i\Omega_{1i}$ and $\Omega_2 = \cup_i\Omega_{2i}$. (Note that S_M is not necessarily simply connected.) S_M must satisfy

$$\int\cdots\int_{\Omega_1} f(g^2)\,d^n\boldsymbol{g} = \int\cdots\int_{\Omega_2} f(g^2)\,d^n\boldsymbol{g}. \tag{7.85}$$

There is clearly no unique solution to this equation in terms of S_M when $n > 1$; however, a choice that makes sense for unimodal distributions is the ellipsoidal shell S_M enclosing the region Ω_M centered on $\boldsymbol{\mu}$. M^2 is defined by Equation (7.71) and its particular value is chosen to satisfy Equation (7.85) with $\Omega_1 = \Omega_M$ (and Ω_2 its complement).

Using the ellipsoidal symmetry of a multivariate p.d.f. constructed using the methodology presented here, Equation (7.85) then becomes

$$\int_{g=0}^{M} f(g^2)\,g^{n-1}\,dg = \int_{g=M}^{\infty} f(g^2)\,g^{n-1}\,dg. \tag{7.86}$$

7.3.5.2. *The Population Covariance Matrix*

Let V be the population covariance matrix for our constructed multivariate p.d.f. Using the notation developed above, we may write the ijth. element of this matrix as

$$V_{ij} = \mathcal{A} \int \cdots \int_{\Omega} y_i y_j f(\boldsymbol{y}^T \Sigma^{-1} \boldsymbol{y}) \, d^n \boldsymbol{y}. \tag{7.87}$$

Using the transformation of Equation (7.59), Equation (7.87) may be written

$$V_{ij} = \mathcal{A}|D| \sum_{klpq} R_{ki} D_{kl} R_{pj} D_{pq} \int_{g_1=-\infty}^{\infty} \cdots \int_{g_n=-\infty}^{\infty} g_l g_q f(g^2) \, d^n \boldsymbol{g}. \tag{7.88}$$

Due to the symmetry of $f(g^2)$, the integral in Equation (7.88) may be written

$$\begin{aligned} &\int_{g_1=-\infty}^{\infty} \cdots \int_{g_n=-\infty}^{\infty} g_l g_q f(g^2) \, d^n \boldsymbol{g} \\ &\quad = \delta_{lq} \int_{g_1=-\infty}^{\infty} \cdots \int_{g_n=-\infty}^{\infty} g_q^2 f(g^2) \, d^n \boldsymbol{g} \\ &\quad = \frac{\delta_{lq}}{n} \int_{g_1=-\infty}^{\infty} \cdots \int_{g_n=-\infty}^{\infty} g^2 f(g^2) \, d^n \boldsymbol{g} \\ &\quad = \frac{2\pi^{\frac{n}{2}} \delta_{lq}}{n\Gamma(\frac{n}{2})} \int_{g=0}^{\infty} f(g^2) \, g^{n+1} \, dg. \end{aligned} \tag{7.89}$$

Here, δ_{lq} is the Kronecker delta. (Note that the final step in Equation (7.89) is a transformation to a polar integral. This introduces the $\pi^{n/2}$ and gamma function terms.) Substituting this expression into Equation (7.88) and summing over the index q, gives

$$V_{ij} = \frac{2\pi^{\frac{n}{2}} \mathcal{A}|D|}{n\Gamma(\frac{n}{2})} \sum_{klp} R_{ki} D_{kl} R_{pj} D_{pl} \int_{g=0}^{\infty} f(g^2) \, g^{n+1} \, dg. \tag{7.90}$$

From Equation (7.57), we see that the summation in Equation (7.90) is equal to Σ_{ij}. After Substituting the value of $\mathcal{A}$ from

Equation (7.70), we have

$$V_{ij} = \frac{\Sigma_{ij}}{n} \frac{\int_{g=0}^{\infty} f(g^2)\, g^{n+1}\, dg}{\int_{g=0}^{\infty} f(g^2)\, g^{n-1}\, dg}. \tag{7.91}$$

The covariance matrix for the constructed distribution is seen to be proportional to the matrix used to define the metric distance. Obviously, this factor can be eliminated by rescaling the matrix Σ. When a metric distance is defined with the covariance matrix itself, then this distance is referred to as the Mahalanobis distance[j] [93, p. 31], $\Delta_V^2(\boldsymbol{x}, \boldsymbol{\mu})$. Equation (7.91) shows that the metric distance defined here is always proportional to the Mahalanobis distance between the random vector $\boldsymbol{x}$ and its expectation.

For the multinormal distribution, the ratio of integrals in Equation (7.91) is equal to n and so, for this distribution, we have the required result that $V = \Sigma$.

7.3.5.3. *Measures of Distributional Shape*

In additional to the location and width of a distribution, we are interested in characterising the dispersion of probability density between distributions after standardizing with respect to these two factors. For univariate distributions this is commonly done using the skew and kurtosis parameters, which are computed from the third and fourth central moments of the p.d.f., respectively.

Pearson proposed the ratio of the distance from the mean to the mode in units of the population standard deviation [80, p. 108], as a measure of the asymmetry of a p.d.f. A multivariate extension of this concept would be a vector proportional to the Mahalanobis distance between the mean and the mode and directed parallel to that vector, e.g.

$$\boldsymbol{s} = \frac{\Delta_V(\boldsymbol{\mu}, \boldsymbol{m})}{\Delta_I(\boldsymbol{\mu}, \boldsymbol{m})}(\boldsymbol{\mu} - \boldsymbol{m}). \tag{7.92}$$

(In the case of a multimodal p.d.f., it would make sense to average this quantity over all of the modes.) Mardia [93] defines an alternate

[j] The subscript V indicates that the distance is calculated using the matrix V^{-1}.

measure based upon multivariate generalizations of the β_1 and β_2 parameters that arise in discussion of the Pearson System of distributions [80, pp. 215–240]. Mardia's skewness is

$$\beta_{1,n} = E\left[\{(\boldsymbol{x}-\boldsymbol{\mu})^T V^{-1}(\boldsymbol{y}-\boldsymbol{\mu})\}^3\right], \tag{7.93}$$

where $\boldsymbol{x}$ and $\boldsymbol{y}$ are i.i.d. with covariance matrix V. Both of these measures vanish in the case of ellipsoidal symmetry.

The role of the kurtosis measure is to parameterize the way in which the probability density is spread within the domain of definition of the p.d.f. The β_2 parameter, defined to be the ratio of the fourth central moment to the square of the second central moment [80, p. 108], is generally taken to be indicative of this spread (often "standardized" to relative to the Normal by subtracting 3). Many univariate distributions with positive kurtosis exhibit a functional form with a sharper peak at the mean and with heavy tails. Those with a negative kurtosis exhibit a broad flat shape near the mean and light tails.[k] Mardia defines the measure

$$\beta_{2,n} = E\left[\{(\boldsymbol{x}-\boldsymbol{\mu})^T V^{-1}(\boldsymbol{x}-\boldsymbol{\mu})\}^2\right], \tag{7.94}$$

as a multivariate generalization of the kurtosis parameter. If we write the constant of proportionality from Equation (7.91) as $1/\xi$, then we have $\beta_{2,n} = \xi^2 E[g^4]$.

In Section 7.3.4.1, we obtained an expression for the c.d.f. of the metric distance. Using the z variable defined above, Equation (7.73) can be written

$$F'(z) = \frac{1}{2}\frac{\int_0^z f(u)\,u^{\frac{n}{2}-1}\,du}{\int_0^\infty f(g^2)\,g^{n-1}\,dg}. \tag{7.95}$$

Differentiating w.r.t. z gives the p.d.f. of z:

$$f'(z) = \frac{1}{2}\frac{f(z)\,z^{\frac{n}{2}-1}}{\int_0^\infty f(g^2)\,g^{n-1}\,dg}. \tag{7.96}$$

[k]Although there are many counter examples to this generalization within the literature, it is a useful description of these functional shapes.

Evaluating $E[z^2] = \int_0^\infty z^2 f'(z)\,dz$, and transforming back to the g variable, gives

$$E[g^4] = \frac{\int_0^\infty f(g^2)\,g^{n+3}\,dg}{\int_0^\infty f(g^2)\,g^{n-1}\,dg} \Rightarrow \beta_{2,n}$$
$$= n^2 \frac{\int_0^\infty f(g^2)\,g^{n+3}\,dg \int_0^\infty f(g^2)\,g^{n-1}\,dg}{\left\{\int_0^\infty f(g^2)\,g^{n+1}\,dg\right\}^2}. \quad (7.97)$$

As in Section 7.3.5.2, this expression has a particularly simple form for multinormal distribution. In this case, we have $\beta_{2,n}^N = n(n+2)$. (Note that, for the univariate case, $\beta_{2,1}^N = 3$). We may also define a multivariate generalization of the *excess* kurtosis as $\beta_{2,n} - \beta_{2,n}^N$.

7.3.5.4. *Invariance Under Affine Transformations*

An Affine transformation is one of the form $\boldsymbol{x} \to A\boldsymbol{x} + \boldsymbol{b}$ where A is a non-singular matrix and $\boldsymbol{b}$ is a vector. The Mahalanobis distance is invariant under an Affine transformation, i.e.

$$(\boldsymbol{x}' - \boldsymbol{\mu}')^T \Sigma'^{-1} (\boldsymbol{x}' - \boldsymbol{\mu}')$$
$$= (\boldsymbol{x} - \boldsymbol{\mu})^T \Sigma^{-1} (\boldsymbol{x} - \boldsymbol{\mu}) \text{ where } \begin{cases} \boldsymbol{x}' = A\boldsymbol{x} + \boldsymbol{b} \\ \boldsymbol{\mu}' = A\boldsymbol{\mu} + \boldsymbol{b}\,. \\ \Sigma' = A\Sigma A^T \end{cases} \quad (7.98)$$

The normalized elemental volume is also invariant under the associated transformation of the matrix Σ, i.e. $d^n\boldsymbol{x}/|\Sigma|^{1/2} = d^n\boldsymbol{x}'/|\Sigma'|^{1/2}$.

Any p.d.f. constructed in the manner described above[1] may be written in the form: $f\{\Delta_\Sigma(\boldsymbol{x}, \boldsymbol{\mu})\}\,d^n\boldsymbol{x}/|\Sigma|^{1/2}$. It follows that any such distribution is invariant under an Affine transformation, i.e. $dF(\boldsymbol{x}'|\boldsymbol{\mu}', \Sigma') = dF(\boldsymbol{x}|\boldsymbol{\mu}, \Sigma)$, meaning that if $\boldsymbol{x}$ is drawn from some particular p.d.f., then $\boldsymbol{x}'$ will also be drawn from that same p.d.f. (albeit with transformed parameters). Furthermore, it is also clearly true that any statistic which is a function of the Mahalanobis distance is also invariant under an Affine transformation.

[1]In fact, any p.d.f. with ellipsoidal symmetry.

7.3.6. The Characteristic Function and the Moment Generating Function

7.3.6.1. The Characteristic Function

A function derived from a multivariate density that has many useful applications is the characteristic function, $\phi(\boldsymbol{k}) = E[e^{i\boldsymbol{k}\cdot\boldsymbol{x}}]$. For a general p.d.f., defined as above, we have

$$\phi(\boldsymbol{k}) = \mathcal{A} \int_{x_1=-\infty}^{\infty} \cdots \int_{x_n=-\infty}^{\infty} e^{i\boldsymbol{k}\cdot\boldsymbol{x}} f\{(\boldsymbol{x}-\boldsymbol{\mu})^T \Sigma^{-1} (\boldsymbol{x}-\boldsymbol{\mu})\}\, d^n\boldsymbol{x}. \tag{7.99}$$

Making same change of variables as previously, we may write Equation (7.99)

$$\phi(\boldsymbol{k}) = \mathcal{A}|\Sigma|^{\frac{1}{2}} e^{i\boldsymbol{k}\cdot\boldsymbol{\mu}} \int_{g_1=-\infty}^{\infty} \cdots \int_{g_n=-\infty}^{\infty} e^{i\boldsymbol{k}\cdot R^T D\boldsymbol{g}} f(g^2)\, d^n\boldsymbol{g}. \tag{7.100}$$

It is a well-known result that the n-dimensional Fourier transform of a radial function is equivalent to a one dimensional Hankel transform [74]. For space-vector $\boldsymbol{x}$ and wave-vector $\boldsymbol{y}$, the result is

$$\begin{aligned}\mathcal{F}[u](\boldsymbol{y}) &= \frac{1}{2\pi^{\frac{n}{2}}} \int_{x_1=0}^{\infty} \cdots \int_{x_n=0}^{\infty} e^{i\boldsymbol{x}\cdot\boldsymbol{y}} u(x)\, d^n\boldsymbol{x} \\ &= y^{1-\frac{n}{2}} \int_{x=0}^{\infty} u(x) J_{\frac{n}{2}-1}(xy)\, x^{\frac{n}{2}}\, dx,\end{aligned} \tag{7.101}$$

where $J_\nu(x)$ is the Bessel function of the first kind, $\mathcal{F}[u](\cdot)$ is the Fourier Transform of $u(\cdot)$, and $x = \sqrt{\boldsymbol{x}^T\boldsymbol{x}}$ and $y = \sqrt{\boldsymbol{y}^T\boldsymbol{y}}$. Clearly

$$\phi(\boldsymbol{k}) = (2\pi)^{\frac{n}{2}} \mathcal{A}|\Sigma|^{\frac{1}{2}} e^{i\boldsymbol{k}\cdot\boldsymbol{\mu}} \mathcal{F}[f](DR\boldsymbol{k}). \tag{7.102}$$

Let $\boldsymbol{s} = DR\boldsymbol{k} \Rightarrow s^2 = \boldsymbol{s}^T\boldsymbol{s} = \boldsymbol{k}^T R^T D^2 R\boldsymbol{k} = \Delta^2_{\Sigma^{-1}}(\boldsymbol{k}, \boldsymbol{0})$. Substituting this value into Equation (7.102) gives

$$\begin{aligned}\phi(\boldsymbol{k}) &= e^{i\boldsymbol{k}\cdot\boldsymbol{\mu}} \Gamma\left(\frac{n}{2}\right) \left\{\frac{2}{\Delta_{\Sigma^{-1}}(\boldsymbol{k}, \boldsymbol{0})}\right\}^{\frac{n}{2}-1} \\ &\quad \times \frac{\int_0^\infty f(g^2) J_{\frac{n}{2}-1}\{g\Delta_{\Sigma^{-1}}(\boldsymbol{k}, \boldsymbol{0})\}\, g^{\frac{n}{2}}\, dg}{\int_0^\infty f(g^2)\, g^{n-1}\, dg}.\end{aligned} \tag{7.103}$$

7.3.6.2. *The Moment Generating Function*

Another useful function is the moment generating function, defined to be $E[e^{-\boldsymbol{k}\cdot\boldsymbol{x}}]$. This is clearly given by the characteristic function evaluated for a purely imaginary argument, $i\boldsymbol{k}$. We recognize it as the Bilateral Laplace Transformation. Making the substitution $\boldsymbol{k} \to i\boldsymbol{k}$ in Equation (7.103), and using $\Delta_M(i\boldsymbol{x}, i\boldsymbol{y}) = i\Delta_M(\boldsymbol{x}, \boldsymbol{y})$, gives

$$\phi(i\boldsymbol{k}) = e^{-\boldsymbol{k}\cdot\boldsymbol{\mu}}\Gamma\left(\frac{n}{2}\right)\left\{\frac{2}{\Delta_{\Sigma^{-1}}(\boldsymbol{k}, \boldsymbol{0})}\right\}^{\frac{n}{2}-1} \times \frac{\int_0^\infty f(g^2) I_{\frac{n}{2}-1}\{g\Delta_{\Sigma^{-1}}(\boldsymbol{k}, \boldsymbol{0})\}\, g^{\frac{n}{2}}\, dg}{\int_0^\infty f(g^2)\, g^{n-1}\, dg}, \tag{7.104}$$

where $I_\nu(x) = i^{-\nu} J_\nu(ix)$ is the modified Bessel function of the first kind.

In making the transformation above we have glossed over the convergence criteria for the upper integral. In the direction $-\boldsymbol{\mu}$ the transform kernel is diverging exponentially and so the p.d.f. must converge faster than this and in the direction $\boldsymbol{\mu}$ the kernel is converging exponentially and so the p.d.f. cannot diverge faster than this. If these criteria are not met, the m.g.f. will not exist, although the c.f. may.

However, in view of the formula above, we can directly specify the convergence criteria in terms of the g variable alone. From the series expansion of $I_\nu(x)$ [61, p. 909], we see that all the functions of half integral order converge at the origin, except for the function $I_{-1/2}(x)$ which diverges as $x^{-1/2}$ and this divergence is cancelled by the $x^{1/2}$ term in the corresponding integrand. For large x the all of the functions converge to $e^x/\sqrt{2\pi x}$ and therefore they diverge slower than exponentially.

7.3.6.3. *The Roots of the Gradient of the Moment Generating Function*

In some circumstances (e.g. asset allocation problems) it is useful to evaluate the roots of the gradient of the m.g.f. Removing all of the extraneous scale factors and writing $\Delta(\boldsymbol{k})$ for $\Delta_{\Sigma^{-1}}(\boldsymbol{k}, \boldsymbol{0})$, we may define a modified m.g.f. as

$$\psi_{\frac{n}{2}}(\boldsymbol{k}) = e^{-\boldsymbol{k}\cdot\boldsymbol{\mu}}\{\Delta(\boldsymbol{k})\}^{1-\frac{n}{2}} \int_0^\infty f(g^2) I_{\frac{n}{2}-1}\{g\Delta(\boldsymbol{k})\}\, g^{\frac{n}{2}}\, dg. \quad (7.105)$$

Let $\boldsymbol{\nabla}_{\boldsymbol{k}}$ be the vector with components $\partial/\partial k_i$. When taking the gradient of Equation (7.105), we note that the symmetry of Σ means that $\boldsymbol{\nabla}_{\boldsymbol{k}}\Delta(\boldsymbol{k}) = \Sigma\boldsymbol{k}/\Delta(\boldsymbol{k})$.

Solving for the roots of the gradient of $\psi(\cdot)$, we find that the solution may be written

$$\boldsymbol{k}\Psi_{\frac{n}{2}}\{\Delta(\boldsymbol{k})\} = \Sigma^{-1}\boldsymbol{\mu}, \quad (7.106)$$

where $\Psi_\nu(x)$ is a scalar function. This shows that, when $\Psi(\cdot)$ is convergent, the root is always in the direction $\Sigma^{-1}\boldsymbol{\mu}$. When $\Psi(\cdot)$ diverges for finite $\boldsymbol{k}$ the root is at the origin. The function $\Psi_\nu(x)$ from Equation (7.106) is defined to be

$$\Psi_\nu(x) = \frac{1}{x}\frac{\int_0^\infty f(g^2) I_\nu(gx)\, g^{\nu+1}\, dg}{\int_0^\infty f(g^2) I_{\nu-1}(gx)\, g^{\nu}\, dg} \quad (7.107)$$

for non-negative x and $\nu \geq 1/2$. If Equation (7.106) has a non-trivial root, it is simple to show that the value of $\Delta(\boldsymbol{k})$ at the root is the solution to

$$x\Psi_{\frac{n}{2}}(x) = \sqrt{\boldsymbol{\mu}^T\Sigma^{-1}\boldsymbol{\mu}}. \quad (7.108)$$

7.3.6.4. *Example: The Multinormal Solution*

For the multinormal distribution the integral of Equation (7.105) is well known[m] and is independent of n.

$$\psi(\boldsymbol{k}) = \frac{1}{\sqrt{2\pi}} e^{-\boldsymbol{k}^T\boldsymbol{\mu} + \frac{1}{2}\boldsymbol{k}^T\Sigma\boldsymbol{k}}. \quad (7.109)$$

For this p.d.f., the $\Psi(\cdot)$ function is identically equal to unity and the root of the gradient of $\psi(\cdot)$ is always $\boldsymbol{k} = \Sigma^{-1}\boldsymbol{\mu}$. Therefore the function $\Psi(\cdot)$ can be thought of a factor scaling the solution for the Normal distribution in a manner controlled by the actual distribution in use.

[m] In fact, for this case, the Fourier transform is straightforward in Cartesian coordinates.

7.3.7. *Maximum Likelihood Estimation*

In this section, we will derive an expression for the maximum likelihood estimator of $\boldsymbol{\mu}$, written $\hat{\boldsymbol{\mu}}$, and that of Σ, written $\hat{\Sigma}$. Let the multivariate p.d.f. under study be parameterized by the set $\{\boldsymbol{\mu}, \Sigma, \boldsymbol{\theta}\}$. The vector $\boldsymbol{\theta}$ represents all distributional parameters not specified by $\boldsymbol{\mu}$ and Σ and is not to be interpreted as a vector within the coordinate space that defines $\boldsymbol{\mu}$ and Σ.

Let $\{\boldsymbol{x}_i\}_{i=1}^N$ be a set of N observations drawn from a p.d.f. with ellipsoidal symmetry. The probability density associated with observation i may be written

$$dF(\boldsymbol{x}_i) = \mathcal{A}(\Sigma, \boldsymbol{\theta}) f(g_i^2, \boldsymbol{\theta})\, d^n\boldsymbol{x}_i \text{ where } g_i^2 = (\boldsymbol{x}_i - \boldsymbol{\mu})^T \Sigma^{-1} (\boldsymbol{x}_i - \boldsymbol{\mu}). \tag{7.110}$$

Therefore, the log-likelihood for the entire sample, $\{\boldsymbol{x}_i\}$, is

$$L(\boldsymbol{\mu}, \Sigma, \boldsymbol{\theta}) = N \ln \mathcal{A}(\Sigma, \boldsymbol{\theta}) + \sum_{i=1}^{N} \ln f(g_i^2, \boldsymbol{\theta}). \tag{7.111}$$

7.3.7.1. *The Maximum Likelihood Estimator of the Population Mean*

The maximum likelihood estimator of $\boldsymbol{\mu}$ is defined to be the value of $\boldsymbol{\mu}$ that maximizes Equation (7.111). If the first derivative of the log-likelihood is continuous everywhere within the region where the p.d.f. is defined, then this is equal to the root of $\boldsymbol{\nabla}_{\boldsymbol{\mu}} L(\boldsymbol{\mu}, \Sigma, \boldsymbol{\theta})$. ($\boldsymbol{\nabla}_{\boldsymbol{\mu}}$ is the vector with components $\partial/\partial\mu_i$.) The gradient of the log-likelihood is

$$\boldsymbol{\nabla}_{\boldsymbol{\mu}} L = \sum_{i=1}^{N} \boldsymbol{\nabla}_{\boldsymbol{\mu}} \ln f(g_i^2, \boldsymbol{\theta}) = \sum_{i=1}^{N} \frac{f'(g_i^2, \boldsymbol{\theta})}{f(g_i^2, \boldsymbol{\theta})} \boldsymbol{\nabla}_{\boldsymbol{\mu}} g_i^2, \tag{7.112}$$

where $f'(\cdot)$ is the first derivative of $f(\cdot)$ w.r.t. g_i^2. Since Σ is symmetric by definition, we have $\boldsymbol{\nabla}_{\boldsymbol{\mu}} g_i^2 = 2\Sigma^{-1}(\boldsymbol{\mu} - \boldsymbol{x}_i)$. Substituting this result into Equation (7.112) gives

$$\boldsymbol{\nabla}_{\boldsymbol{\mu}} L = 2\Sigma^{-1} \left\{ \boldsymbol{\mu} \sum_{i=1}^{N} \frac{f'(g_i^2, \boldsymbol{\theta})}{f(g_i^2, \boldsymbol{\theta})} - \sum_{i=1}^{N} \frac{f'(g_i^2, \boldsymbol{\theta})}{f(g_i^2, \boldsymbol{\theta})} \boldsymbol{x}_i \right\}. \tag{7.113}$$

Therefore, the maximum likelihood estimator $\hat{\boldsymbol{\mu}}$ is the solution to

$$\boldsymbol{\mu} \sum_{i=1}^{N} \frac{f'(g_i^2, \boldsymbol{\theta})}{f(g_i^2, \boldsymbol{\theta})} = \sum_{i=1}^{N} \frac{f'(g_i^2, \boldsymbol{\theta})}{f(g_i^2, \boldsymbol{\theta})} \boldsymbol{x}_i. \tag{7.114}$$

This expression clearly shows that the maximum likelihood estimator of the population mean is a "weighted mean" of the sample vectors.

7.3.7.2. *The Sample Mean Differential Equation*

If the function $f(\cdot)$ satisfies the partial differential equation:

$$\frac{\partial f(z,\boldsymbol{\theta})}{\partial z} = f(z,\boldsymbol{\theta})h(\boldsymbol{\theta}), \tag{7.115}$$

where $h(\boldsymbol{\theta})$ is an unknown function that is not dependent on $\boldsymbol{x}_i$, $\boldsymbol{\mu}$ or Σ, then the ratio $f'(\cdot)/f(\cdot)$ is invariant under the sums of Equation (7.114). Under these conditions, the root of the equation is

$$\hat{\boldsymbol{\mu}} = \frac{1}{N}\sum_{i=1}^{N} \boldsymbol{x}_i. \tag{7.116}$$

So for a p.d.f. that satisfies Equation (7.115), the maximum likelihood estimator of the population mean is the sample mean.

7.3.7.3. *A General Solution to the Sample Mean Differential Equation*

Let $f(z,\boldsymbol{\theta})$ have the form $a(\boldsymbol{\theta})e^{b(z,\boldsymbol{\theta})}$. Then differentiating w.r.t. z gives

$$\frac{\partial f(z,\boldsymbol{\theta})}{\partial z} = f(z,\boldsymbol{\theta})\frac{\partial b(z,\boldsymbol{\theta})}{\partial z}. \tag{7.117}$$

Comparing this expression with Equation (7.115) shows that the function $b(\cdot)$ must be linear in z, i.e. that $b(z,\boldsymbol{\theta}) = h(\boldsymbol{\theta})z + c(\boldsymbol{\theta})$. Absorbing the constant of partial integration, $c(\boldsymbol{\theta})$, into the definition of the function $a(\boldsymbol{\theta})$, leads to the following general solution to the p.d.e. of Equation (7.115):

$$f(z,\boldsymbol{\theta}) = a(\boldsymbol{\theta})e^{h(\boldsymbol{\theta})z}. \tag{7.118}$$

Our definition of $f(x^2,\boldsymbol{\theta})$ as a univariate probability density function imposes the constraint that

$$\int_{x=-\infty}^{\infty} f(x^2,\boldsymbol{\theta})\,dx = 1 \Rightarrow f(z,\boldsymbol{\theta}) = \sqrt{\frac{-h(\boldsymbol{\theta})}{\pi}}\,e^{h(\boldsymbol{\theta})z}. \tag{7.119}$$

For convergence of the normalization integral in Equation (7.119), $h(\boldsymbol{\theta})$ must be everywhere real and negative. Clearly a particular solution to Equation (7.115) is

$$h(\boldsymbol{\theta}) = -\frac{1}{2} \Rightarrow f(x^2) = \frac{e^{-\frac{1}{2}x^2}}{\sqrt{2\pi}}. \tag{7.120}$$

7.3.7.4. *The Maximum Likelihood Estimator of the Covariance Parameter*

As in Section 7.3.7.1, the maximum likelihood estimator of the covariance parameter, $\hat{\Sigma}$ is defined to be the root of $\nabla_\Sigma L(\boldsymbol{\mu}, \Sigma, \boldsymbol{\theta})$, where ∇_Σ is the matrix with elements $\partial/\partial\Sigma_{ij}$.

Using Equation 7.70, we see that Equation (7.111) may be written

$$L(\boldsymbol{\mu}, \Sigma, \boldsymbol{\theta}) = N \ln \mathcal{B}(\boldsymbol{\theta}) - \frac{N}{2} \ln|\Sigma| + \sum_{i=1}^{N} \ln f(g_i^2, \boldsymbol{\theta}). \tag{7.121}$$

Therefore,

$$\nabla_\Sigma L = \sum_{i=1}^{N} \frac{f'(g_i^2, \boldsymbol{\theta})}{f(g_i^2, \boldsymbol{\theta})} \nabla_\Sigma g_i^2 - \frac{1}{2} N \nabla_\Sigma \ln|\Sigma|. \tag{7.122}$$

Now, Jacobi's formula for the derivative of the determinant of an invertible matrix is $d|A| = |A| \operatorname{tr}(A^{-1}dA)$, so for a symmetric invertible matrix we have the remarkably compact result $\nabla_A \ln|A| = A^{-1}$. Additionally, $dA^{-1} = -A^{-1}\, dA\, A^{-1}$, which gives the result $\nabla_A(\boldsymbol{a}^T A^{-1}\boldsymbol{b}) = -A^{-1}\boldsymbol{a}\boldsymbol{b}^T A^{-1}$. Using these expressions in Equation (7.122), gives

$$\hat{\Sigma} = -\frac{2}{N} \sum_{i=1}^{N} \frac{f'(g_i^2, \boldsymbol{\theta})}{f(g_i^2, \boldsymbol{\theta})} (\boldsymbol{x}_i - \boldsymbol{\mu})(\boldsymbol{x}_i - \boldsymbol{\mu})^T. \tag{7.123}$$

For the special case of the multinormal distribution, the we see that this becomes the familiar result

$$\hat{V} = \frac{1}{N} \sum_{i=1}^{N} (\boldsymbol{x}_i - \boldsymbol{\mu})(\boldsymbol{x}_i - \boldsymbol{\mu})^T. \tag{7.124}$$

7.3.7.5. The Maximum Likelihood Estimator of the Distributional Parameters

Finally, we define the maximum likelihood estimator of the additional distributional parameter set, $\hat{\boldsymbol{\theta}}$, as the root of $\boldsymbol{\nabla}_{\boldsymbol{\theta}} L(\boldsymbol{\mu}, \Sigma, \boldsymbol{\theta})$. Differentiating Equation (7.121), we see that $\hat{\boldsymbol{\theta}}$ is the solution of

$$\frac{\boldsymbol{\nabla}_{\boldsymbol{\theta}} \mathcal{B}(\boldsymbol{\theta})}{\mathcal{B}(\boldsymbol{\theta})} = -\frac{1}{N} \sum_{i=1}^{N} \frac{\boldsymbol{\nabla}_{\boldsymbol{\theta}} f(g_i^2, \boldsymbol{\theta})}{f(g_i^2, \boldsymbol{\theta})}. \tag{7.125}$$

7.3.8. *The Simulation of Multivariate Distributions*

Analysis of the results of Monte Carlo simulation of data drawn from a given p.d.f. is a powerful technique in applied probability and statistics. In this section, we will briefly consider a method that may be used to generate a distribution with ellipsoidal symmetry.

7.3.8.1. General Methodology

For the ellipsoidal distributions discussed here, this simulation is a relatively straightforward procedure. We may follow the procedure of Marsaglia [96] to pick points uniformly distributed on a hypersphere in n-space. Remarkably, this procedure is to simply pick a vector $\hat{\boldsymbol{f}} \sim N(\mathbf{0}, \mathbf{1}_n)$ and then normalize the vector to unity, i.e. $\hat{\boldsymbol{g}} = \hat{\boldsymbol{f}}/|\hat{\boldsymbol{f}}|$ is uniformly distributed on the surface of an $(n-1)$-sphere. To generate a vector with the appropriate covariance matrix we reverse the transformation of Equation (7.59) to generate the hyperellipsoid $\hat{\boldsymbol{y}} = R^T D \hat{\boldsymbol{g}}$. Since the radial and angular motions are independent for an ellipsoidal variate, a vector drawn from the full p.d.f. may then be computed as

$$\boldsymbol{x} = \boldsymbol{\mu} + R^T D g \hat{\boldsymbol{g}}, \tag{7.126}$$

where g is a scale factor drawn from the p.d.f. of the Mahalanobis distance $\Delta_{\mathbf{1}_n}$.

The distribution of $F''(G) = \Pr(g < G)$ represents the probability that a random vector $\boldsymbol{g}$ lies within the volume enclosed by a hyperspherical shell, Ω_G, with radius G. Since the radius of a sphere is non-negative by definition we see that $\Pr(g < G) = \Pr(g^2 < G^2)$.

This latter expression has already been evaluated in general in connection with the Kolmogorov statistic of Section 7.3.4.1. Hence, we have

$$F''(G) = \frac{\int_{g=0}^{G} f(g^2)\, g^{n-1}\, dg}{\int_{g=0}^{\infty} f(g^2)\, g^{n-1}\, dg} \quad \text{and} \quad f''(G) = \frac{f(G^2)\, G^{n-1}}{\int_{g=0}^{\infty} f(g^2)\, g^{n-1}\, dg}. \tag{7.127}$$

(The expression for the density has been obtained by differentiating the p.d.f. w.r.t. the upper limit of the integral in the numerator.) Once the univariate distribution is known it is a simple matter to generate a variate with the associated univariate density by the standard technique of drawing u from the uniform distribution $U(0,1)$ and solving $F''(g) = u$ for g.

7.3.8.2. *An Example: Generation of Multinormal Variates*

To give a verifiable example of the method we will evaluate the p.d.f. $f''(G)$ for the multinormal case.[n] Substituting $f(g^2) = e^{-\frac{1}{2}g^2}/\sqrt{2\pi}$ into Equation (7.127), it is straightforward to demonstrate that

$$f''(g) = \frac{1}{2^{\frac{n}{2}-1}\Gamma(\frac{n}{2})} g^{n-1} e^{-\frac{1}{2}g^2}. \tag{7.128}$$

This is recognizable as the density for the χ_n distribution, which is the distribution of the square root of a χ_n^2 variate [44, p. 57]. This is clearly the definition of the normalization factor removed in Section 7.3.8.1. For the univariate case it is trivial to verify that this identical to the p.d.f. of $|x|$ where $x \sim N(0,1)$.

7.4. The Generalized Error Distribution

I started using the Generalized Error Distribution to investigate the effect on optimal trading strategies in the presence of leptokurtotic, or "fat tailed," distributions of returns. Subsequently, I learned that it also does a very good job of describing equity prices, and other

[n]Of course, there are more efficient methods available to generate variates drawn from the multinormal distribution should that be the p.d.f. the analyst wishes to simulate.

financial assets, as featured in Chapter 2. The following is from the white-paper of Reference [49], which describes the general properties of the univariate and multivariate Generalized Error Distributions.

7.4.1. *The Univariate Generalized Error Distribution*

7.4.1.1. *Definition*

The Generalized Error Distribution is a symmetrical unimodal member of the exponential family. The domain of the p.d.f. is $x \in [-\infty, \infty]$ and the distribution is defined by three parameters: $\mu \in (-\infty, \infty)$, which locates the mode of the distribution; $\sigma \in (0, \infty)$, which defines the dispersion of the distribution; and, $\kappa \in (0, \infty)$, which controls the skewness. We will use the notation $x \sim \text{GED}(\mu, \sigma^2, \kappa)$ to define x as a variate drawn from this distribution. A suitable reference for this distribution is Evans *et al.* [44, pp. 74–76].

The probability density function, $f(x)$, is given by

$$\text{GED}(\mu, \sigma, \kappa) \ : \ f(x|\mu, \sigma, \kappa) = \frac{e^{-\frac{1}{2}\left|\frac{x-\mu}{\sigma}\right|^{\frac{1}{\kappa}}}}{2^{\kappa+1}\sigma\Gamma(\kappa+1)}. \tag{7.129}$$

This function is represented in Figure 7.1. It is clear from this definition that the mode of the p.d.f. is μ and that it is unimodal and symmetrical about the mode. Therefore the median and the mean are also equal to μ.

If we choose $\kappa = \frac{1}{2}$ then Equation (7.129) is recognized as the p.d.f. for the univariate Normal Distribution, i.e. $\text{GED}(\mu, \sigma^2, \frac{1}{2}) = N(\mu, \sigma^2)$. If we choose $\kappa = 1$ then Equation (7.129) is recognized as the p.d.f. for the Double Exponential, or Laplace, distribution, i.e. $\text{GED}(\mu, \sigma^2, 1) = \text{Laplace}(\mu, 4\sigma^2)$. In the limit $\kappa \to 0$ the p.d.f. tends to the uniform distribution $\text{Uniform}(\mu - \sigma, \mu + \sigma)$.

7.4.1.2. *The Central Moments*

The central moments are defined by Equation (7.130).

$$\mu_r = E[(x-\mu)^r] = \frac{1}{2^{\kappa+1}\sigma\Gamma(\kappa+1)} \int_{x=-\infty}^{\infty} (x-\mu)^r e^{-\frac{1}{2}\left|\frac{x-\mu}{\sigma}\right|^{\frac{1}{k}}} \, dx. \tag{7.130}$$

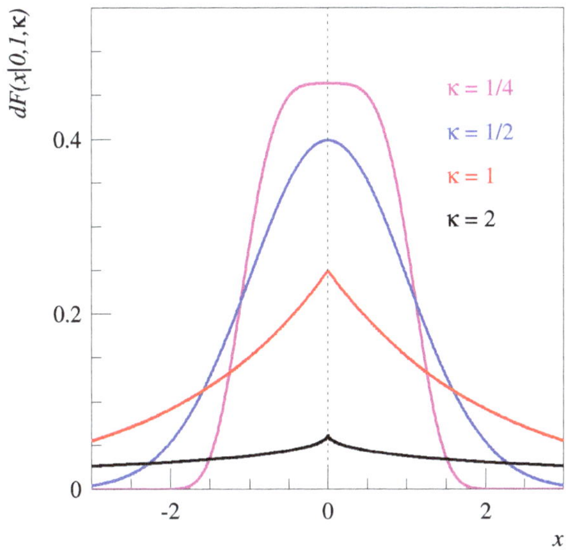

Figure 7.1: The Generalized Error Distribution probability density function for various values of the kurtosis parameter, κ.

The odd moments clearly all vanish by symmetry. For the even moments, Equation (7.130) may be written as Equation (7.131), in which we recognize that the integral is a representation of the gamma function.

$$\mu_r = \frac{2^{r\kappa}\sigma^r}{\Gamma(\kappa)}\int_0^\infty t^{\kappa(r+1)-1}e^{-t}\,dt = 2^{r\kappa}\sigma^r\frac{\Gamma\{\kappa(r+1)\}}{\Gamma(\kappa)} \tag{7.131}$$

Therefore, the distribution has the parameters:

$$\text{mean} = \mu; \tag{7.132}$$

$$\text{variance} = 2^{2\kappa}\sigma^2\frac{\Gamma(3\kappa)}{\Gamma(\kappa)}; \tag{7.133}$$

$$\text{skew, } \beta_1 = 0; \tag{7.134}$$

and

$$\text{kurtosis, } \beta_2 = \frac{\Gamma(5\kappa)\Gamma(\kappa)}{\Gamma^2(3\kappa)}. \tag{7.135}$$

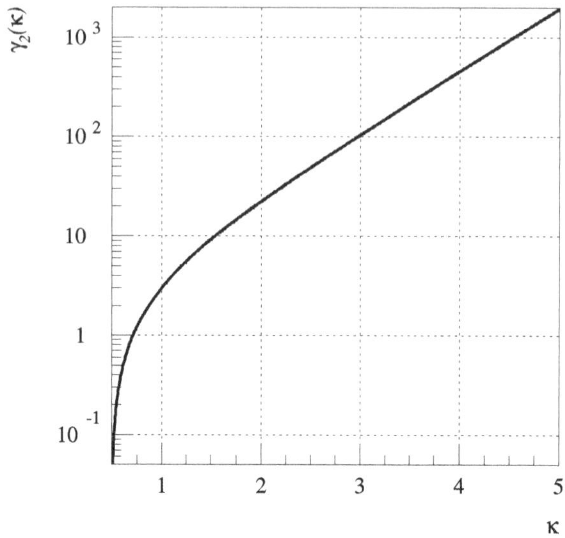

Figure 7.2: Excess kurtosis measure γ_2 of the Generalized Error Distribution, for $\kappa > \frac{1}{2}$.

For $\kappa < \frac{1}{2}$ the distribution is platykurtotic and for $\kappa > \frac{1}{2}$ it is leptokurtotic.[o] The excess kurtosis, γ_2, is tends to $-6/5$ as $\kappa \to 0$ and is unbounded for $\kappa > \frac{1}{2}$. The leptokurtotic region is illustrated in Figure 7.2. We may use Stirling's formula for $\Gamma(z)$ to obtain the following approximation for the kurtosis:

$$\gamma_2(\kappa) \simeq \frac{3}{\sqrt{5}} \left(\frac{3125}{729} \right)^{\kappa} \approx 1.3 \times 4.3^{\kappa}. \tag{7.136}$$

7.4.2. *A Standardized Generalized Error Distribution*

It is often convenient to work with the p.d.f. which is "standardized." By this it is meant that that population mean is zero and the population variance is unity. We see from Equation (7.133) that the variance of the G.E.D. p.d.f., as defined in Equation (7.129), is a very strong function of κ.

[o]For this reason, some authors write $c/2$ for κ, parameterizing the Normal distribution as $c = 1$.

However, it is trivial to rescale the variance to transform Equation (7.129) into an equivalent p.d.f. with constant variance σ^2. Let us introduce the scaling parameter ξ and make the substitution $\sigma \to \sigma\xi^\kappa$ in Equation (7.129). The normalized p.d.f. now has the form

$$f(x|\mu, \sigma, \kappa; \xi) = \frac{e^{-\frac{1}{2\xi}\left|\frac{x-\mu}{\sigma}\right|^{\frac{1}{\kappa}}}}{2^{\kappa+1}\sigma\xi^\kappa\Gamma(\kappa+1)}. \tag{7.137}$$

This p.d.f. has the variance

$$2^{2\kappa}\sigma^2\xi^{2\kappa}\frac{\Gamma(3\kappa)}{\Gamma(\kappa)}. \tag{7.138}$$

If we choose ξ to eliminate all dependence of the variance on κ, then we may define a homoskedastic p.d.f. as

$$f_H(x|\mu, \sigma, \kappa) = \left\{\frac{\Gamma(3\kappa)}{\Gamma(\kappa)}\right\}^{\frac{1}{2}} \frac{e^{-\left\{\frac{\Gamma(3\kappa)}{\Gamma(\kappa)}\left(\frac{x-\mu}{\sigma}\right)^2\right\}^{\frac{1}{2\kappa}}}}{2\sigma\Gamma(\kappa+1)}. \tag{7.139}$$

A standardized p.d.f. is therefore trivially given by $f_S(x|\kappa) = f_H(x|0, 1, \kappa)$.

With this formulation the extremely rapid increase in kurtosis, as κ is increased from the Normal reference value of $\frac{1}{2}$, is clearly demonstrated in Figure 7.3.

7.4.3. *A Multivariate Generalization*

7.4.3.1. *Construction of a Multivariate Distribution*

The p.d.f. of Equation (7.129) is of the form suitable for the construction of a multivariate p.d.f. using the recipe of Reference [48]. This procedure is applied to the standardized univariate p.d.f., $f(x^2)$, defined for our distribution as

$$f(x^2) = f_S(x^2|\kappa) = \frac{1}{2\Gamma(\kappa+1)}\left\{\frac{\Gamma(3\kappa)}{\Gamma(\kappa)}\right\}^{\frac{1}{2}} e^{-\left\{\frac{\Gamma(3\kappa)}{\Gamma(\kappa)}x^2\right\}^{\frac{1}{2\kappa}}}. \tag{7.140}$$

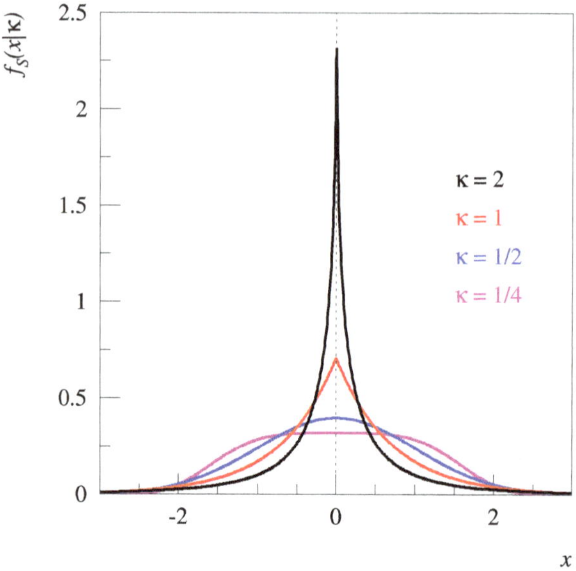

Figure 7.3: Univariate standardized Generalized Error Distribution for several values of the kurtosis parameter, κ.

Replacing x^2 in Equation (7.140) by the Mahalanobis distance $\Delta^2_\Sigma(\boldsymbol{x}, \boldsymbol{\mu})$, gives

$$f(\boldsymbol{x}|\boldsymbol{\mu}, \Sigma, \kappa) = \frac{\mathcal{A}}{2\Gamma(\kappa+1)} \left\{ \frac{\Gamma(3\kappa)}{\Gamma(\kappa)} \right\}^{\frac{1}{2}} \times \exp - \left\{ \frac{\Gamma(3\kappa)}{\Gamma(\kappa)} (\boldsymbol{x}-\boldsymbol{\mu})^T \Sigma^{-1} (\boldsymbol{x}-\boldsymbol{\mu}) \right\}^{\frac{1}{2\kappa}}. \quad (7.141)$$

The constant $\mathcal{A}$ is introduced to maintain the normalization of the new function. It is given by

$$\frac{1}{\mathcal{A}} = \frac{\sqrt{\pi^n |\Sigma|}}{\Gamma(\kappa+1)\Gamma(\frac{n}{2})} \left\{ \frac{\Gamma(3\kappa)}{\Gamma(\kappa)} \right\}^{\frac{1}{2}} \int_0^\infty e^{-\left\{\frac{\Gamma(3\kappa)}{\Gamma(\kappa)}\right\}^{\frac{1}{2\kappa}} g^{\frac{1}{\kappa}}} g^{n-1}\, dg = \sqrt{\pi^n |\Sigma|} \frac{\Gamma(n\kappa)}{\Gamma(\kappa)\Gamma(\frac{n}{2})} \left\{ \frac{\Gamma(\kappa)}{\Gamma(3\kappa)} \right\}^{\frac{n-1}{2}}. \quad (7.142)$$

Substituting this result into Equation (7.141) gives

$$f(\boldsymbol{x}|\boldsymbol{\mu},\Sigma,\kappa) = \frac{1}{\sqrt{\pi^n|\Sigma|}}\frac{\Gamma(1+\frac{n}{2})}{\Gamma(1+n\kappa)}\left\{\frac{\Gamma(3\kappa)}{\Gamma(\kappa)}\right\}^{\frac{n}{2}}$$
$$\times \exp -\left\{\frac{\Gamma(3\kappa)}{\Gamma(\kappa)}(\boldsymbol{x}-\boldsymbol{\mu})^T\Sigma^{-1}(\boldsymbol{x}-\boldsymbol{\mu})\right\}^{\frac{1}{2\kappa}}. \quad (7.143)$$

7.4.3.2. *Moments of the Constructed Distribution*

Using results of Reference [48], we see that the p.d.f. of Equation (7.141) is unimodal with mode $\boldsymbol{\mu}$. This is also equal to the mean of the distribution. The covariance matrix, V, is equal to the matrix Σ multiplied by the scale factor

$$\frac{1}{n}\frac{\int_0^\infty e^{-\left\{\frac{\Gamma(3\kappa)}{\Gamma(\kappa)}\right\}^{\frac{1}{2\kappa}}g^{\frac{1}{\kappa}}}g^{n+1}\,dg}{\int_0^\infty e^{-\left\{\frac{\Gamma(3\kappa)}{\Gamma(\kappa)}\right\}^{\frac{1}{2\kappa}}g^{\frac{1}{\kappa}}}g^{n-1}\,dg} = \frac{\Gamma\{(n+2)\kappa\}\Gamma(1+\kappa)}{\Gamma(3\kappa)\Gamma(1+n\kappa)}. \quad (7.144)$$

Note that in the limit $\kappa \to 0$ this becomes $\frac{3}{n+2}$. The strong dependence of this factor on κ, for several values of n, is shown in Figure 7.4.

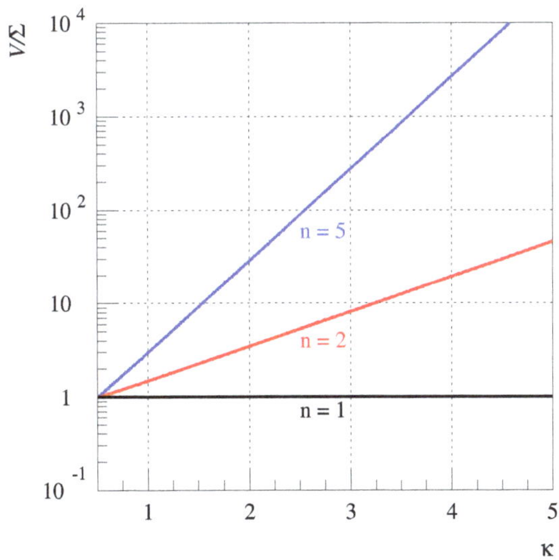

Figure 7.4: Variance scale factor for constructed multivariate Generalized Error Distributions as a function of the kurtosis parameter, κ, for various numbers of dimensions, n.

The skew of the distribution is zero by construction ($\beta_{1,n} = 0$) and the multivariate kurtosis parameter is

$$\begin{aligned}\beta_{2,n} &= n^2 \frac{\int_0^\infty e^{-\left\{\frac{\Gamma(3\kappa)}{\Gamma(\kappa)}\right\}^{\frac{1}{2\kappa}} g^{\frac{1}{\kappa}}} g^{n+3}\, dg \int_0^\infty e^{-\left\{\frac{\Gamma(3\kappa)}{\Gamma(\kappa)}\right\}^{\frac{1}{2\kappa}} g^{\frac{1}{\kappa}}} g^{n-1}\, dg}{\left[\int_0^\infty e^{-\left\{\frac{\Gamma(3\kappa)}{\Gamma(\kappa)}\right\}^{\frac{1}{2\kappa}} g^{\frac{1}{\kappa}}} g^{n+1}\, dg\right]^2} \\ &= n^2 \frac{\Gamma\{(n+4)\kappa\}\Gamma(n\kappa)}{\Gamma^2\{(n+2)\kappa\}}. \end{aligned} \tag{7.145}$$

The leptokurtotic region is illustrated in Figure 7.5.

7.4.3.3. *The Multivariate Kolmogorov Test Statistic*

Let $\{G_i^2\}_{i=1}^N$ represent an ordered set of sample values of $\Delta_\Sigma^2(\boldsymbol{x}, \boldsymbol{\mu})$. From Reference [48], we know that

$$\Pr(g^2 < G^2) = F'(G^2) = \frac{\int_{g=0}^{G} f(g^2)\, g^{n-1}\, dg}{\int_{g=0}^{\infty} f(g^2)\, g^{n-1}\, dg}. \tag{7.146}$$

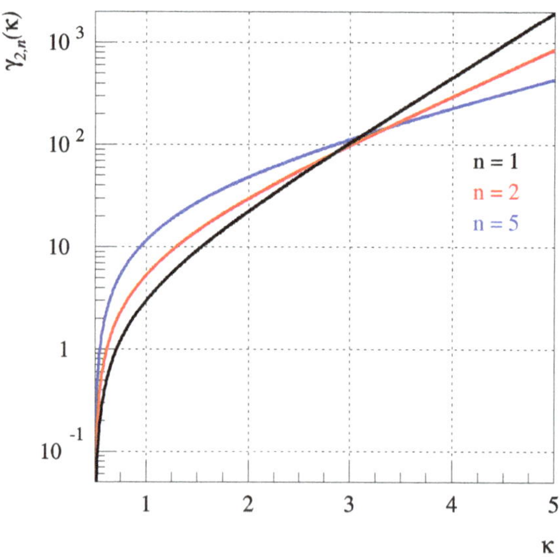

Figure 7.5: Excess kurtosis measure $\gamma_{2,n}$ multivariate Generalized Error Distributions as a function of the kurtosis parameter, κ, with $\kappa > \frac{1}{2}$ and various number of dimensions, n.

Substituting our expression for $f(\cdot)$, Equation (7.140), gives

$$F'(G^2) = \frac{\gamma\left[n\kappa, \left\{\frac{\Gamma(3\kappa)}{\Gamma(\kappa)}G^2\right\}^{\frac{1}{2\kappa}}\right]}{\Gamma(n\kappa)}, \tag{7.147}$$

where $\gamma(\cdot)$ is the lower incomplete gamma function [61]. We may use the Kolmogorov–Smirnov Test influenced statistic

$$d_N = \max_i |S_i - F'(G_i^2)|, \tag{7.148}$$

where $\{S_i\}_{i=1}^N$ are the order statistics associated with the sample, to test the null hypothesis that a given dataset is represented by Equation (7.143).

7.4.3.4. *Maximum Likelihood Regression*

Given a set of N i.i.d. random vectors, $\{\boldsymbol{X}_i\}_{i=1}^N$, each drawn from the Generalized Error Distribution, the joint probability, or likelihood, of a particular realization, $\{\boldsymbol{x}_i\}_{i=1}^N$, is given by

$$L(\boldsymbol{\mu}, \Sigma, \kappa) = \prod_{i=1}^N f(\boldsymbol{x}_i|\boldsymbol{\mu}, \Sigma, \kappa). \tag{7.149}$$

The commonly used likelihood function, $\mathcal{L} = -\ln L$, is therefore given by

$$\mathcal{L}(\boldsymbol{\mu}, \Sigma, \kappa) = \sum_{i=1}^N \left\{\frac{\Gamma(3\kappa)}{\Gamma(\kappa)}(\boldsymbol{x}_i - \boldsymbol{\mu})^T\Sigma^{-1}(\boldsymbol{x}_i - \boldsymbol{\mu})\right\}^{\frac{1}{2\kappa}} + \frac{N}{2}\ln|\Sigma| + \frac{Nn}{2}\ln\frac{\pi\Gamma(\kappa)}{\Gamma(3\kappa)} + N\ln\frac{\Gamma(1+n\kappa)}{\Gamma(1+\frac{n}{2})}. \tag{7.150}$$

We may also write this expression in terms of the covariance matrix, V, as below

$$\mathcal{L}(\boldsymbol{\mu}, V, \kappa) = \sum_{i=1}^N \left[\kappa\frac{\Gamma\{(n+2)\kappa)\}}{\Gamma(1+n\kappa)}(\boldsymbol{x}_i - \boldsymbol{\mu})^T V^{-1}(\boldsymbol{x}_i - \boldsymbol{\mu})\right]^{\frac{1}{2\kappa}} + \frac{N}{2}\ln|V| + \frac{Nn}{2}\ln\frac{\pi\Gamma(1+n\kappa)}{\kappa\Gamma\{(n+2)\kappa\}} + N\ln\frac{\Gamma(1+n\kappa)}{\Gamma(1+\frac{n}{2})}. \tag{7.151}$$

7.5. Frictionless Asset Allocation with Ellipsoidal Distributions

7.5.1. *Utility Theory and Portfolio Choice*

7.5.1.1. *Asset Allocation Under Uncertainty*

The *Utility Hypothesis* explains risk aversion by asserting that the value a person places on their wealth is described by an increasing function, $U(W)$, with negative curvature. Due to Jensen's Inequality, when future wealth is uncertain the expected utility of future wealth is less than that which would be expected without the uncertainty, i.e.

$$E_s[U(W_t)] < U(E_s[W_t]) \text{ if } \frac{dU}{dW} > 0 \text{ and } \frac{d^2U}{dW^2} < 0, \tag{7.152}$$

for times $s < t$. This condition can be very simply derived by taking the expectation of the Taylor series expansion of the utility function around the current wealth[p]:

$$\begin{aligned} E_s[U(W_t)] &\simeq U(W_s) + \frac{dU}{dW} E_s[W_t - W_s] \\ &\quad + \frac{1}{2}\frac{d^2U}{dW^2} E[(W_t - W_s)^2] + \cdots \qquad (7.153) \\ &= U(W_s) + \frac{dU}{dW}\alpha + \frac{1}{2}\frac{d^2U}{dW^2}(\sigma^2 + \alpha^2) + \cdots, \qquad (7.154) \end{aligned}$$

where α is the expected change in wealth and σ^2 the variance of the change in wealth.

Under this framework, the approach to an asset allocation problem is straightforward. An agent purchases a portfolio, $\boldsymbol{C}$, of risky assets available for investment. Let the intertemporal change in the asset prices be $\boldsymbol{p}_t$, and ignore transaction costs, funding costs, etc. The optimal choice of investment, $\hat{\boldsymbol{C}}$, is the holding that maximizes the expected future utility, i.e.

$$\hat{\boldsymbol{C}}_s = \arg\max_{\boldsymbol{C}} E_s[U\{W_t(\boldsymbol{C})\}]\,. \tag{7.155}$$

---

[p]This assumes that the utility is a differentiable function of the wealth.

7.5.1.2. *Negative Exponential Utility and Frictionless Trading*

To *actually* solve this problem, we must specify a form for $U(W)$. A common choice is *constant absolute risk aversion*, for which the utility function takes on the Pratt form $U(W) = -e^{-\lambda W}$. The parameter λ determines the degree of risk aversion.

Due to the assumption of negligible trading and funding costs,[q] the solution is

$$\hat{\boldsymbol{C}}_s = \arg\min_{\boldsymbol{C}} E_s[e^{-\lambda \boldsymbol{C}\cdot\boldsymbol{p}_t}]. \tag{7.156}$$

From the prior section, we recognize this as the minimum of the moment generating function for the p.d.f. of $\boldsymbol{p}_t$.

7.5.2. *Ellipsoidal Distributions*

7.5.2.1. *General Considerations*

In this section, we specialize our discussion to probability distributions with ellipsoidal symmetry. This is the set of continuous multivariate distributions that are constructed from a normalized symmetrical univariate distribution $f(x^2)$ by the substitution $\{x \to \boldsymbol{x}, f(x^2) \to \mathcal{A}f(g^2)\}$, where g is the Mahalanobis distance $\Delta_\Sigma(\boldsymbol{x}, \boldsymbol{\alpha}) = \sqrt{(\boldsymbol{x}-\boldsymbol{\alpha})^T\Sigma^{-1}(\boldsymbol{x}-\boldsymbol{\alpha})}$ and $\mathcal{A}$ is a constant introduced to normalize the constructed distribution over $\mathbb{R}^n$. These distributions are discussed extensively in Section 7.3 and [48].

7.5.2.2. *The Scaling Functions*

The m.g.f. of such a distribution is proportional to the function [48]

$$\psi_{\frac{n}{2}}(\boldsymbol{k}) = e^{-\boldsymbol{k}\cdot\boldsymbol{\mu}}\{\Delta(\boldsymbol{k})\}^{1-\frac{n}{2}} \int_0^\infty f(g^2) I_{\frac{n}{2}-1}\{g\Delta(\boldsymbol{k})\}\, g^{\frac{n}{2}}\, dg, \tag{7.157}$$

where $\boldsymbol{k} = \lambda\boldsymbol{C}$, $\Delta(\boldsymbol{k}) = \Delta_{\Sigma^{-1}}(\boldsymbol{k}, \boldsymbol{0}) = \sqrt{\boldsymbol{k}^T\Sigma\boldsymbol{k}}$ and n is the number of risky assets. $I_\nu(x)$ is the modified Bessel function of the first kind.

---

[q]This is what makes the trading *frictionless* in the jargon of the subject.

The root of the gradient of this function is shown to be the solution of

$$\lambda \boldsymbol{C}\Psi_{\frac{n}{2}}\{\lambda\Delta(\boldsymbol{C})\} = \Sigma^{-1}\boldsymbol{\alpha} \text{ where } \Psi_\nu(x) = \frac{1}{x}\frac{\int_0^\infty f(g^2)I_\nu(gx)\,g^{\nu+1}\,dg}{\int_0^\infty f(g^2)I_{\nu-1}(gx)\,g^\nu\,dg}. \tag{7.158}$$

For the case of the multivariate normal distribution, the function $\Psi_\nu(x) = 1$ for all values of its arguments. The "scaling" function $\Psi_\nu(x)$ is a function that is sensitive to the behaviour of the p.d.f. in the tails and measures that behaviour relative to the Normal.

The value of $\lambda\Delta(\boldsymbol{C})$ at the solution is the value $\hat{x}$ that solves

$$x\Psi_{\frac{n}{2}}(x) = \sqrt{\boldsymbol{\alpha}^T\Sigma^{-1}\boldsymbol{\alpha}}. \tag{7.159}$$

If it exists, we define the "inverting" function $\Phi_\nu(x)$ to be the root with respect to y of $y\Psi_\nu(y) = x$. Thus $\hat{x} = \Phi_\nu(\sqrt{\boldsymbol{\mu}^T\Sigma^{-1}\boldsymbol{\alpha}})$ and the value to be used in Equation (7.158) is $\Psi_{\frac{n}{2}}\{\Phi_{\frac{n}{2}}(\sqrt{\boldsymbol{\alpha}^T\Sigma^{-1}\boldsymbol{\alpha}})\}$.

7.5.2.3. *The Optimal Portfolio*

The optimal portfolio is then given by

$$\hat{\boldsymbol{C}} = \frac{\Sigma^{-1}\boldsymbol{\alpha}}{\lambda\Psi_{\frac{n}{2}}(\hat{x})}, \tag{7.160}$$

and the expected return on the portfolio is

$$\hat{\boldsymbol{C}}^T E_s[\boldsymbol{x}] = \frac{\boldsymbol{\alpha}^T\Sigma^{-1}\boldsymbol{\alpha}}{\lambda\Psi_{\frac{n}{2}}(\hat{x})}. \tag{7.161}$$

This expression has several interesting properties. Firstly, the optimal portfolio is always proportional to the portfolio $\Sigma^{-1}\boldsymbol{\alpha}$, which is also the solution to Markowitz's mean-variance optimization problem [95] Secondly, the dependence on the parameter λ is a simple inverse scaling, which means that all investors with access to public information will be interested in obtaining the same portfolio in some proportion, i.e. A "market" portfolio can exist with these distributions and a C.A.P.M. style model will be constructable. Thirdly, the solution is completely independent of the wealth, W_s (which is the result of specifying constant absolute risk aversion via the negative exponential utility function).

7.5.3. *The Generalized Error Distribution*

At this point it should be no surprise to the reader that we seek to find the optimal portfolio to hold when price changes are drawn from a multivariate Generalized Error Distribution with mean $\boldsymbol{\alpha}$, mixing matrix Σ, and kurtosis parameter κ, i.e.

$$\boldsymbol{p}_t \sim \mathrm{GED}(\boldsymbol{\alpha}, \Sigma, \kappa). \tag{7.162}$$

The previous section shows that this is equal to $\Sigma^{-1}\boldsymbol{\alpha}$ divided by a scale factor that depends on the size of the alpha.

7.5.3.1. *Calculation of the Scaling Functions for a Single Asset*

Using the definition of Equation (7.139), we may write down an explicit form for the scaling function of Equation (7.157):

$$\Psi_\nu(x) = \frac{1}{x}\frac{\int_0^\infty e^{-\eta g^{\frac{1}{\kappa}}} I_\nu(gx) g^{\nu+1}\, dg}{\int_0^\infty e^{-\eta g^{\frac{1}{\kappa}}} I_{\nu-1}(gx) g^{\nu}\, dg} \quad \text{where } \eta = \left\{\frac{\Gamma(3\kappa)}{\Gamma(\kappa)}\right\}^{\frac{1}{2\kappa}}. \tag{7.163}$$

Both of the integrands in Equation (7.163) contain a modified Bessel function factor and this function converges to $e^{gx}/\sqrt{2\pi gx}$ for large gx ([61, p. 909]). The rate of convergence depends on the order, ν, of the Bessel function but is true for all orders. This means that this Bessel function factor generally leads to exponential divergence of the integral. However, the divergence may be controlled by the exponential term arising from the p.d.f. as this is a convergent factor. Specifically, if $gx - \eta g^{1/\kappa} > 0$ then the integral will diverge exponentially and if this term is negative then the integral will converge exponentially. Therefore, we can conclude that the integrals will converge for all $0 < \kappa < 1$ and will converge for $\kappa = 1$ (Laplace distribution) if $x < \sqrt{2}$, but will diverge otherwise. This behaviour is illustrated for $\nu = \frac{1}{2}$ in Figure 7.6.

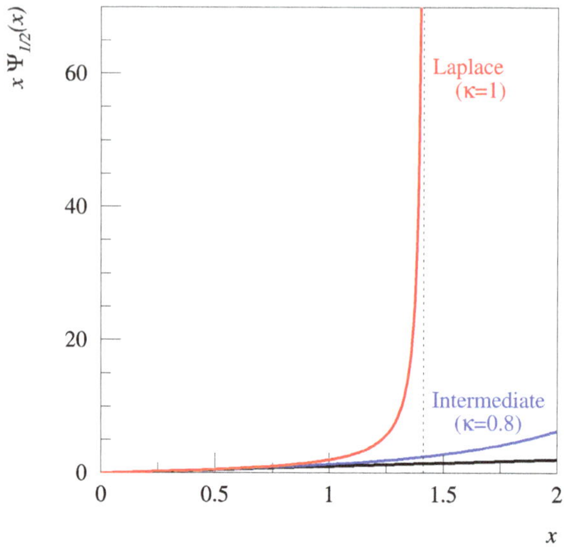

Figure 7.6: Behavior of the scaling function $x\Psi_{1/2}(x)$ for $\kappa = 0.5, 0.8$ and 1.

The sharp divergence illustrated for the Laplace distribution as $x \to \sqrt{2}$ has practical consequences for the computation of the inverting function, $\Phi_\nu(x)$. For the "regular" distributions (i.e. $0 < \kappa < 1$), $\Phi_\nu(x)$ is an unbounded increasing function of x. As $\kappa \to 1$ the function converges toward the value for the Laplace distribution, but it is never bounded above. For $\kappa = 1$ the function possesses an asymptote to $\sqrt{2}$ and is bounded below that level. This function is illustrated in Figure 7.7.

The optimal portfolio is computed by scaling the Normal distribution based portfolio $\Sigma^{-1}\boldsymbol{\alpha}$ by the factor $1/\Psi_{n/2}(\hat{x})$. This scaling factor is illustrated in Figure 7.8, and shows that for $\kappa > \frac{1}{2}$ the optimal portfolio for is never as heavily invested as the normal theory portfolio and is progressively less invested as risk/reward metric $(x = \boldsymbol{\alpha}^T\Sigma^{-1}\boldsymbol{\alpha})$ increases.

The reason for this *scaleback* is clearly shown by Figure 7.9. Here the expected portfolio return (assuming $\lambda = 1$) is plotted as $\kappa \to 1$. We see that for Normal distributions the expected portfolio return is a quadratically increasing function of the risk/reward metric leading to heavy bets on large expected relative returns. These bets then dominate the profit stream from trading the asset. For non-Normal

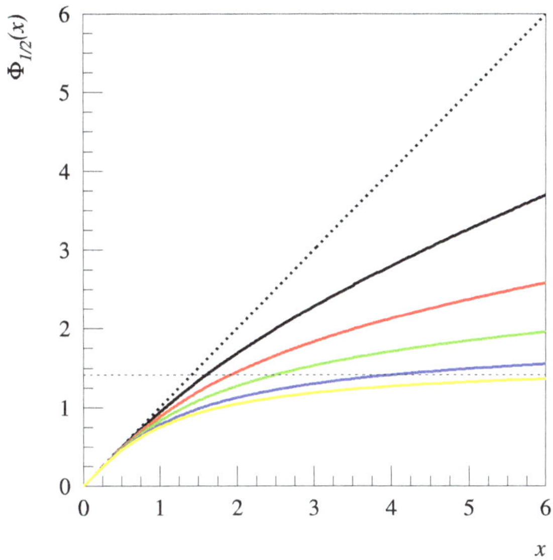

Figure 7.7: Behavior of the Inverting Function $\Phi_{1/2}(x)$ as $\kappa \to 1$. The dotted diagonal line represents the Normal distribution theory $\Phi_\nu(x) = 1$ and the dotted horizontal line shows the upper bound $\Phi_{1/2}(x) < \sqrt{2}$ for $\kappa = 1$.

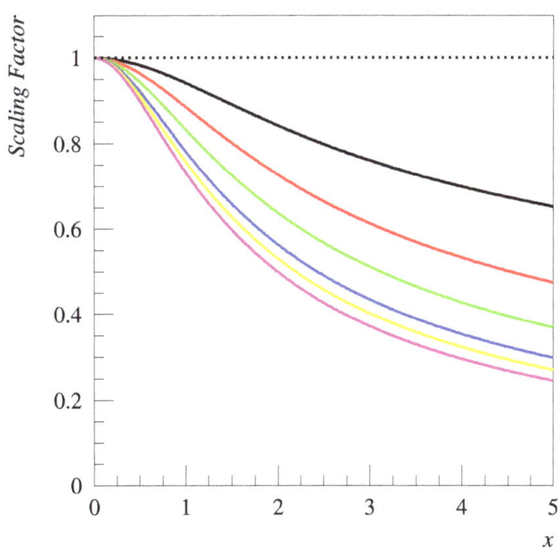

Figure 7.8: Portfolio scaling factors $1/\Psi_{1/2}\{\Phi_{\frac{1}{2}}(x)\}$ for a single asset as $\kappa \to 1$. The dotted line represents the Normal distribution theory.

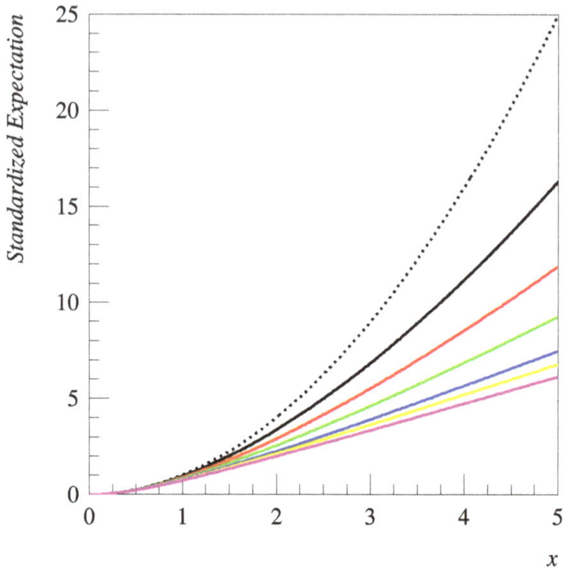

Figure 7.9: Standardized portfolio expected return $x^2/\Psi_{\frac{1}{2}}\{\Phi_{\frac{1}{2}}(x)\}$ for a single asset as $\kappa \to 1$. The dotted line represents the Normal distribution theory.

distributions, these bets are dramatically curtailed, due to the progressively less "interesting"[r] nature of high risk/reward portfolios. We also see that a trader that implemented the Normal distribution theory-based portfolio in a more leptokurtotic market could be making a substantial overallocation of risk to reward and dramatically increasing their risk of ruin.

7.6. Asset Allocation with Realistic Distributions of Returns

The previous three sections represent my investigations into the area of asset allocation with realistic distributions of returns. Coming out

[r]By "interesting" we are talking about the nominal statistical significance of the risk/reward metric. For the normal distribution ($\kappa = \frac{1}{2}$) a "5σ" expected return is very significant, and the trader's response is to make a heavy bet in those circumstances. For the Laplace distribution ($\kappa = 1$), such an expected return is much less significant and the trader in fact makes a smaller bet on the return.

of proprietary trading at Morgan Stanley, in 2000, I was convinced that:

(i) the idea that trading strategy was subject to scientific investigation was sound;
(ii) the classical Markowitz theory didn't work in practice; and
(iii) the returns of asset prices in the real world were not Normally distributed.

7.6.1. *Markowitz Style Mean-Variance Efficient Portfolios*

Harry Markowitz won the Nobel Prize in Economics for his work on constructing mean-variance efficient portfolios [95]. I referred to these results in the prior section, but will go through them in more detail here.

7.6.1.1. *Mean Variance Efficient Portfolio Selection*

For a set of assets for which we expect the *future* distribution of returns to be Normally distributed we seek to chose a portfolio $\boldsymbol{C}$ that maximizes the expected return $\boldsymbol{C}^T\boldsymbol{r}$ and minimizes the expected variance $\boldsymbol{C}^T\Sigma\boldsymbol{C}$, i.e.

$$\hat{\boldsymbol{C}} = \arg\max_{\boldsymbol{C}} \boldsymbol{C}^T\boldsymbol{\alpha} - \lambda\boldsymbol{C}^T\Sigma\boldsymbol{C} \tag{7.164}$$

$$\text{as } \boldsymbol{r} \sim N(\alpha, \Sigma). \tag{7.165}$$

If the distribution of returns is Normal then no other moments need be considered. λ is a *Lagrange multiplier* which also plays the role of the *Market Price of Risk*. If portfolio holdings are assumed to be *infinitely divisible*,[s] then we may differentiate Equation (7.164) w.r.t. $\boldsymbol{C}$ and find the root of the gradient of the objective. This is

$$\hat{\boldsymbol{C}} = \frac{\Sigma^{-1}\boldsymbol{\alpha}}{2\lambda}, \tag{7.166}$$

which is Equation (7.160) *without* the scaling function $\Psi_{\frac{n}{2}}(\hat{x})$, which evaluates to unity for the Normal distribution, within the scale factor of 2 which may be absorbed into λ.

[s]They're not, but it's not that bad an assumption for a large asset manager.

7.6.2. *Portfolio Selection in the Real World*

Equation (7.166) tells us to align a portfolio in the direction $\Sigma^{-1}\boldsymbol{\alpha}$ and to size the positions proportional to $|\boldsymbol{\alpha}|$, i.e. the bigger the expected return the larger the position, without limit. The parameter λ is essentially undetermined by this procedure and merely allows different investors to scale their positions differently, based on the way they *personally* trade off risk and return, but they will all want to chose the same basic portfolio — which has come to be known as the *Market Portfolio* in capital markets theory.

In my personal experience, trading using the Markowitz theory *almost always* underperformed trading with simple "barrier" rules. In particular the rule

$$\boldsymbol{C} \propto \begin{cases} \operatorname{sgn} \boldsymbol{\alpha} & \text{if } |\boldsymbol{\alpha}| \geq \boldsymbol{b} \\ 0 & \text{otherwise} \end{cases} \tag{7.167}$$

generally delivers better performance, where operations are applied *element by element* for vectors. Figure 7.10 compares this kind of trading rule to the Markowitz rule for a single asset.

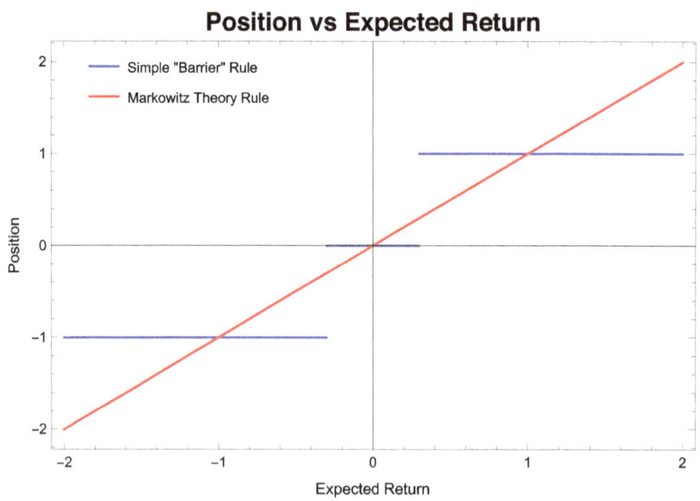

Figure 7.10: Illustration of the form of the Markowitz trading rule and the simple barrier rule of Equation (7.167). The red line is the Markowitz theory rule and the blue lines the simple barrier rule.

7.6.3. *The Motivation for this Work*

Believing, as I do, that investment practice is subject to scientific analysis, an observation such as that above *must* be attributed to a flaw in the assumptions we have made and I do not believe that this flaw is that scientific analysis is useless. Having worked through the analysis of Section 7.5, I hope you can see that the simple barrier rule is, in some sense, a crude approximation to the theory developed for asset allocation under the Generalized Error Distribution in Section 7.5.3. To me, this indicates that the flaw is the assumption that the returns are drawn from the Normal distribution. Given the empirical results of Chapter 2, that's not exactly a hard sell.

So, this work was done to find out how to trade in markets that are not well described by Normal distribution theory; in markets where specifying the expected return and expected variance of the returns on the assets you are going to invest in is not enough to allow you to determine the portfolio to hold. Markets are probably not exactly described by a multivariate Generalized Error Distribution — but it's a much better tool to work with than those offered by canonical theory.

Epilogue

In this book I've told you some tales about my life and experiences adventuring in data science in the financial services industry. As I am now in the latter part of my career, and have just documented many of the things that interest me, it's appropriate to step back and reflect on this. Time and tide wait for no man [24], and my tides have begun to run out.

E.1. The Nature of Business

Within large corporations I have found not only brilliant minds and lifelong friends but also mendacious fools. The intellectual experience I had working in proprietary trading at Morgan Stanley was equivalent, on a personal level, to that I had as an undergraduate and graduate student in Oxford. Sadly, I feel that the Global Financial Crisis of 2008 has purged people of this quality of people from the *sell side* of the industry. There seem to be less intellectuals in the business than before, although I have had the privilege of some of my superiors, peers, and juniors turning from colleagues into friends.

Personally, I have always approached my investigations as an adventure in understanding the riddles wrapped up within the data that Nature presents us with. I have never been the person to deliver a bad model to hit a performance benchmark and have experienced the consequences of revealing the truth about shoddy work to powerful people who didn't want to hear it. I have always thought that honesty was more important than internal marketing and seen businesses prosper when they deploy scientists into decision making roles.

E.2. The Analysis of Data

Turning to the analysis of data, I believe *making models* is an essential aspect of human intelligence and a key part of the successful prediction of future information. Non-parametric systems, whether they are simple kernel density estimators or the heights of *Deep Learning*, simply cannot extrapolate into unexplored parts of the Universe — you need a model to do that and you cannot build such a system by combining massively large interpolation systems, no matter how accurate they are. A successful model is a representation of reality that reflects some of Nature's truths and from which we can learn. We learn nothing when we approach analytical work merely an exercise in software engineering and the models we construct as merely algorithms to download.

As I've remarked, in physics, we propose a model which asserts that *fundamentally random events* dictate the evolution of the Universe. This model performs spectacularly well, and I see no reason to believe that it is not applicable to the world of social sciences or that I am engaged in some kind of mystical pursuit by following an analytical approach based on likelihood methods. Strict Bayesians ridicule the "multiverse" model of frequentist statisticians, but physics seems to favor the multiverse. Bayesian analysis does provide an extremely useful method for the calculus of information and the evolution of belief, and has many spectacularly useful applications in the real world. However, the assertion that no future events are random, and that the "true" probabilities of events were always either 0 if they don't happen and 1 if they do, actually stands in contrast to my understanding of the teachings of Quantum Mechanics.

Both the Schrödinger's Cat and Einstein–Podelsky–Rosen thought experiments address the modeled evolution of the Universe through quantum wave functions,[a] $\psi(\boldsymbol{r}, t)$, that are interpretable as frequentist probabilities when the absolute value is squared

[a] Actually, we have moved beyond simple wave functions to interacting Quantum Fields, but the reasoning is the same.

i.e. $|\psi(\boldsymbol{r}, t)|^2$. A key feature of this math is that it depends on the linear combinations of wave function amplitudes, which are then squared to obtain probabilities, and not the linear combination of probabilities, which we might expect if the Universe was strictly Bayesian.

Billions of dollars have been spent on experiments that depend on this framework and the model has not failed us yet. It provides the most empirically accurate and useful descriptions of the Universe we've ever had, and makes billions of predictions every day that are proved right time and time again. But one does not have to get to abstractions of Quantum Mechanics to experience repeatable experiments that deliver results that are unpredictable yet describable by the concepts of frequency distributions and random variables. This also happens every day, on race tracks all over the world, where the frequencies at which horses win races are very well described by betting odds.

E.3. Summing Things Up

On a practical level, I hope you will end this book sharing my belief that the use of the Normal distribution is, in some important cases, extremely flawed, but that does not mean that the data described is not subject to *any* analysis. There are plenty of alternatives to the Normal distribution and, in many cases, not only are they much more accurate descriptions of data but they are also no more complex to use analytically. As a stable distribution the Normal will show itself in many places, but that doesn't mean that, fundamentally, other distributions will not be useful too.

It appears to me that many critiques of the Neyman–Pearson approach to hypothesis testing are confusing failure of the Normal distribution to adequately describe real data, and the eagerness to report results based on weak critical values, with problems in the entire framework. Based on my experience in both experimental physics and finance, I have no doubt that, when applied in circumstances where the behaviour of variables is accurately described, then these frameworks do perform as theoretically expected.

I also hope you will have shared in some of the joy I have developed from "finding things out," and to be spurred to do similar work. Perhaps it is not obvious why I decided to dive deeply into some particular subject? The truth is often that I was just curious about it. To misquote Edmund Hillary, in many cases my motivation to study some data was because it was there. Your adventures in data science will likely be quite different from mine, but if you have learned one or two things here that help you out then I am happy. As I remarked in the introductory chapter: we learn as we go. Many of the things I now know about data analysis I did not know when I was awarded my doctorate at Oxford University. In fact, I think I learned some new things just while writing this book. I think I am a better and more skilled analyst now than at any time in the past 25 years. New problems may require new solutions, and learning how to find them creates the most important and durable skills: the ability to think flexibly and creatively. If you learn just one thing from your day's work, it has been a day well spent.

Appendix A

How I Store and Process Data

A.1. Databases

Data science begins and ends with data. I am a power user of the latest version the *MySQL* open source database. My approach is to store *all data* into a monolithic database, which I sometimes refer to as *Sauron's database* as there is "one [database] to rule them all." This stems from a belief that the value of a the data you have access to should grow more rapidly than the size of the data stored, i.e. If $\mathcal{D}$ represents the database and $|\mathcal{D}|$ its "size," however that is defined, then

$$\text{value}(\mathcal{D}) \propto |\mathcal{D}|^k \quad \text{where } k > 1. \tag{A.1}$$

This is important because it means that the value of incremental data is more than its incremental size. It is achievable when the data is thoroughly cross-referenced, so links between different data items may be explored. Note that this doesn't require a single technology to be used, it just requires that there be consistent foreign key references between the data. Data is made valuable by curation that permits cross-referencing.

Most of the work I do doesn't require specialized time-series databases — in fact you don't really need these unless you're in the world of high-frequency "trades and quotes" data. Time-series data that is well indexed can be performatively served by a relational database on good server hardware. Over the last 5 years or so, most relational database platforms have rapidly incorporated the innovations of the "NoSQL" technologies, such as column storage, direct JSON, XML, and text blob storage, geospatial functions, etc. Unless you have a very specialized use case, something like MySQL should be effective as a tool for you. It is *far superior* to managing a vast and poorly curated set of `.csv` files or `pickle` storage.

A.2. Programming and Analytical Languages

I am an extensive user of *R*, *Python*, but also some commercial statistical software designed specifically for time-series analysis. I use *Mathematica* quite a bit. I strongly prefer "script oriented" analysis over "notebook oriented" analysis due to the inherent *repeatability* of the scripting workflow. I do some file munging in shell scripts, principally *bash* and *zsh*, with some work in *Perl*. I used to work in *Fortran*, *C*, *C++*, and *Java*, but haven't really done so for a while. *Python* has become my *procedural* language of choice. I do still use *Excel* on an almost daily basis. It is a powerful tool and using it doesn't make you a bad person.

The overall theme here is there are many tools, each of which may be good for a particular task, so you need to use a lot and learn how to string their results together. In my experience, those who evangelize a single "power tool" for all tasks are likely more interested in software engineering than learning the truths hidden by Nature within data, and data scientists make *terrible* software engineers.[a]

A.3. Analytical Workflows

I refer to the analytical workflow I uses as *REPS*. This stands for the four tasks:

R render;
E extract;
P process; and
S store.

An analytical task will likely require multiple *REPS*.

[a]In my personal experience, of course. The same is also true of quants.

Firstly, do data-management heavy work, such as cross-referencing, organization, and aggregation, inside the engine optimized for that purpose — your database. Then extract this data into your analytical system. Next do compute heavy work, which is statistical analysis, modeling, and prediction, inside the engine optimized for that purpose — which in many cases is your desktop workstation. Finally, take the results of your processing and use it to *decorate* your stored data with value added inferences. This way your single primary data store becomes a resource that is ever increasing in value.

A.4. Hardware Choices

Every time I've priced hardware for use I've come to the conclusion that the best thing for a data analyst to use is a high performance desktop workstation. Laptops to not have enough storage or processing power and cloud, since it is for data, becomes quite expensive should you wish to persist terabytes of data indefinitely. We have recently seen the provision of useful, and complex, analytical services via *cloud API's*. I am an enthusiastic user of these.

Appendix B

Some of the Data Sources I've Used for This Book

B.1. Financial Data

- *EODData*:
  https://www.eoddata.com (commercial service)
- *Yahoo! Finance*:
  https://finance.yahoo.com (advertiser supported) and the Python package `yfinance`
- *Cboe Data Shop*:
  https://datashop.cboe.com (commercial service)

B.2. Economic Data

- *The Federal Reserve Economic Database* (FRED):
  https://fred.stlouisfed.org
- *The University of Michigan*:
  http://www.sca.isr.umich.edu
- *The Bureau of Labor Statistics*:
  https://www.bls.gov/data/tools.htm
- *China Beige Book*:
  https://www.chinabeigebook.com (commercial service)

B.3. Social Media and Internet Activity

- *Twitter*:
  https://developer.twitter.com
- *Google Trends*:
  https://trends.google.com/trends
- *Patreon*:
  https://www.patreon.com

B.4. Physical Data

- The Central England Temperature Series:
  https://www.metoffice.gov.uk/hadobs/hadcet
- The International Sunspot Number:
  http://www.sidc.be/silso/datafiles

B.5. Health and Demographics Data

- The Census Bureau:
  https://www.census.gov
- Baby Names Database:
  https://www.ssa.gov/OACT/babynames/limits.html
- B.R.F.S.S.:
  https://www.cdc.gov/brfss/annual_data/annual_data.htm
- N.H.A.N.E.S.:
  https://www.cdc.gov/nchs/nhanes/index.htm
- *The New York Times*' Coronavirus data is on *GitHub* here:
  https://github.com/nytimes/covid-19-data

B.6. Political Data

- *The New York Times*' Presidential stature data:
  https://archive.nytimes.com/www.nytimes.com/interactive/2008/10/06/opinion/06opchart.html

- *538*'s Presidential Approval Data:
  https://projects.fivethirtyeight.com/trump-approval-ratings/polls.json
- *Monmouth County Board of Elections*:
  https://www.monmouthcountyvotes.com

Bibliography

[1] F. C. Adams and G. Laughlin. *The Five Ages of the Universe: Inside the Physics of Eternity*. Simon and Schuster, 2016.

[2] G. A. Akerlof and R. J. Shiller. *Animal Spirits: How Human Psychology Drives the Economy, and Why it Matters for Global Capitalism*. Princeton University Press, 2010.

[3] L. Bachelier. Théorie de la spéculation. *Annales scientifiques de l'École normale supérieure*, 17:21–86, 1900.

[4] N. T. J. Bailey. *Mathematical Approach to Biology and Medicine*. Wiley, 1967.

[5] C. Barría-Sandoval, G. Ferreira, K. Benz-Parra, and P. López-Flores. Prediction of confirmed cases of and deaths caused by covid-19 in chile through time series techniques: A comparative study. *Plos One*, 16(4):e0245414, 2021.

[6] P. Billingsley. Statistical methods in Markov Chains. Technical report, RAND Corporation, 1960.

[7] S. Bird, E. Klein, and E. Loper. *Natural Language Processing with Python: Analyzing Text with the Natural Language Toolkit*. O'Reilly Media, Inc., 2009.

[8] F. Black and M. Scholes. The pricing of options and contingent claims. *Journal of Political Economy*, 81(3):9, 1973.

[9] T. Bollerslev. Generalized autoregressive conditional heteroskedasticity. *Journal of Econometrics*, 31(3): 307–327, 1986.

[10] G. E. P Box, William Gordon Hunter, J Stuart Hunter, *et al. Statistics for Experimenters*, p. 681. John Wiley & sons New York, 1978.

[11] G. E. P Box, G. M. Jenkins, G. C. Reinsel, and G. M. Ljung. *Time Series Analysis: Forecasting and Control*. John Wiley & Sons, 2015.

[12] K. P. Burnham and D. R. Anderson. *Model Selection and Multimodel Inference*. Springer-Verlag, 2002.

[13] E. Candes, T. Tao, *et al.* The dantzig selector: Statistical estimation when p is much larger than n. *The Annals of Statistics*, 35(6):2313–2351, 2007.

[14] B. Caplan. *The Myth of the Rational Voter: Why Democracies Choose Bad Policies-New Edition.* Princeton University Press, 2011.

[15] M. M. Carhart. On persistence in mutual fund performance. *The Journal of Finance*, 52(1):57–82, 1997.

[16] Center for Systems Science and Engineering at Johns Hopkins University. COVID-19 Dashboard, 2020.

[17] Crowdsourced. Wikipedia: Short-rate models. Website, 06 2020.

[18] R. T. Curtin. *Consumer Expectations: Micro Foundations and Macro Impact.* Cambridge University Press, 2019.

[19] R. D'Arrigo, P. Klinger, T. Newfield, M. Rydval, and R. Wilson. Complexity in crisis: The volcanic cold pulse of the 1690s and the consequences of Scotland's failure to cope. *Journal of Volcanology and Geothermal Research*, 389:106746, 2020.

[20] K. Demeterfi, E. Derman, M. Kamal, and J. Zou. More than you ever wanted to know about volatility swaps. *Goldman Sachs Quantitative Strategies Research Notes*, 41:1–56, 1999.

[21] P. A. M. Dirac. A new notation for quantum mechanics. In *Mathematical Proceedings of the Cambridge Philosophical Society*, Volume 35, 416–418. Cambridge University Press, 1939.

[22] Y. Dodge and D. Commenges. *The Oxford Dictionary of Statistical Terms.* Oxford University Press on Demand, 2006.

[23] A. C. Doyle. *The Sign of Four.* Broadview Press, 2010.

[24] B. Duckett. Mcgraw-hill's dictionary of american idioms and phrasal verbs. *Reference Reviews*, 2007.

[25] J. Durbin and S. J. Koopman. *Time Series Analysis by State Space Methods*, Volume 38, Oxford University Press, 2012.

[26] W. T. Eadie, D. Drijard, F. E. James, M. Roos, and B. Sadoulet. *Statistical Methods in Experimental Physics.* Amsterdam: North-Holland, 1971.

[27] B. Efron. *The Jackknife, the Bootstrap and Other Resampling Plans.* SIAM, 1982.

[28] A. Einstein. *Investigations on the Theory of the Brownian Movement.* Courier Corporation, 1956.

[29] G. Eknoyan. Adolphe quetelet (1796–1874) — the average man and indices of obesity, 2008.

[30] R. F. Engle. *Autoregressive Conditional Heteroscedasticity with Estimates of the Variance of Inflationary Expectations.* School of Economics, 1979.

[31] R. F. Engle. Autoregressive conditional heteroscedasticity with estimates of the variance of United Kingdom inflation. *Econometrica*, 50(4):987–1007, 1982.

[32] R. F. Engle. GARCH 101: The use of ARCH/GARCH models in applied econometrics. *Journal of Economic Perspectives*, 15(4):157–168, 2001.

[33] D. Enrich. *The Spider Network: The Wild Story of a Maths Genius, a Gang of Backstabbing Bankers, and One of the Greatest Scams in Financial History*. Random House, 2017.

[34] Parker *et al.* Monthly mean central england temperature (Degrees C) 1974. *International Journal of Climatology*, 1992.

[35] Parker *et al.* Monthly mean central england temperature (Degrees C) 1974. *International Journal of Climatology*, 2005.

[36] F. J. Fabozzi and S. V. Mann. *The Handbook of Fixed Income Securities*. McGraw-Hill Education, 2012.

[37] E. F. Fama and J. D. MacBeth. Risk, return, and equilibrium: Empirical tests. *Journal of Political Economy*, 81(3):607–636, 1973.

[38] Federal Open Market Committee. Federal reserve issues FOMC statement. *Press Release*, December 2015.

[39] J. Fesenmaier and G. Smith. The nifty-fifty re-revisited. *The Journal of Investing*, 11(3):86–90, 2002.

[40] R. P. Feynman. *The Pleasure of Finding Things Out: The Best Short Works of Richard P. Feynman*. Helix Books, 2005.

[41] R. A. Fisher. Frequency distribution of the values of the correlation coefficient in samples of an indefinitely large population. *Biometrika*, 10(4):507–521, 1915.

[42] R. A. Fisher *et al. The Design of Experiments*; 7th edition. Edinburgh: Oliver and Boyd. London, 1960.

[43] R. Fletcher. *Practical Methods of Optimization*. John Wiley & Sons, 2013.

[44] C. Forbes, M. Evans, N. Hastings, and B. Peacock. *Statistical Distributions*. John Wiley & Sons, 2011.

[45] F. Galton. V. Populi. *Nature*, 75(1949):450–451, 1907.

[46] G. Giller. *Electronics: Principles and Applications*. Sigma Press, 1991.

[47] G. L. Giller. *The Construction and Analysis of a Whole-Sky Map Using Underground Muons*. PhD thesis, University of Oxford, 1994.

[48] G. L. Giller. The construction and properties of ellipsoidal probability density functions. Available at SSRN 1300689, 2003.

[49] G. L. Giller. A generalized error distribution. *Social Science Research Network*, 2005.

[50] G. L. Giller. Maximum likelihood estimation of a poissonian count rate function for the followers of a twitter account making directional forecasts of the stock market. Available at SSRN 1423628, 2009.
[51] G. L. Giller. A probit model for presidential elections in terms of relative height and desire for change. Available at SSRN 2010078, 2012.
[52] G. L. Giller. A seasonal autoregressive model for the central england temperature series. Available at SSRN 1997813, 2012.
[53] G. L. Giller. The statistical properties of random bitstreams and the sampling distribution of cosine similarity. Available at SSRN 2167044, 2012.
[54] G. L. Giller. The accuracy of autoregressive forecasts of the average monthly temperatures in Central England, Central Park and New Jersey. Central Park and New Jersey (2013), 2013.
[55] G. L. Giller. Generalized autoregressive Dirichlet multinomial models: Definition and stability. Available at SSRN 3512527, 2020.
[56] G. L. Giller. Google Scholar profile page, June 2020.
[57] G. L. Giller. *Modeling COVID-19 Across the United States*. Medium, 2020.
[58] G. L. Giller. *Essays on Trading Strategy*. World Scientific, Expected 2022.
[59] L. R. Glosten, R. Jagannathan, and D. E. Runkle. On the relation between the expected value and the volatility of the nominal excess return on stocks. *The journal of finance*, 48(5):1779–1801, 1993.
[60] M. Goodfriend and R. G. King. The incredible volcker disinflation. *Journal of Monetary Economics*, 52(5):981–1015, 2005.
[61] I. S. Gradsteyn and I. M. Ryzhik. Tables of Integrals, etc., 1965.
[62] P. J. Green and B. W. Silverman. *Nonparametric Regression and Generalized Linear Models: A Roughness Penalty Approach*. CRC Press, 1993.
[63] W. H. Greene. *Econometric Analysis*. Pearson Education India, 2003.
[64] Z. Griliches, R. Engle, M. D. Intriligator, J. J. Heckman, D. McFadden, and E. E. Leamer. *Handbook of Econometrics*. Elsevier, 1983.
[65] R. C. Grinold and R. N. Kahn. *Active Portfolio Management*. New York, NY, McGraw Hill 2000.
[66] J. D. Hamilton. Time Series Analysis, 1994.
[67] Andrew C Harvey. *Forecasting, Structural Time Series Models and the Kalman Filter*. Cambridge University Press, 1990.
[68] D. B Hausch and W. T. Ziemba. Transactions costs, extent of inefficiencies, entries and multiple wagers in a racetrack betting model.

In *The Kelly Capital Growth Investment Criterion: Theory and Practice*, pp. 681–694. World Scientific, 2011.

[69] C. Hay. The winter of discontent thirty years on. *The Political Quarterly*, 80(4):545–552, 2009.

[70] W. E. Hick. On the rate of gain of information. *Quarterly Journal of Experimental Psychology*, 4(1):11–26, 1952.

[71] C. Hsiao. *Analysis of Panel Data*. Cambridge University Press, 2014.

[72] The Huffington-Post/pollster. Presidential approval ratings. Website, 2009–date. http://www.huffingtonpost.com/2009/01/06/jobapproval-obama_n_726319.html.

[73] J. Hull *et al. Options, Futures and Other Derivatives*. Upper Saddle River, NJ: Prentice Hall, 2009.

[74] K. Itō. *Encyclopedic Dictionary of Mathematics*, Volume 1, MIT Press, 1993.

[75] J. Jaiswal, C. LoSchiavo, and D. C. Perlman. Disinformation, misinformation and inequality-driven mistrust in the time of covid-19: lessons unlearned from aids denialism. *AIDS and Behavior*, 24:2776–2780, 2020.

[76] F. James. *Statistical Methods in Experimental Physics*. World Scientific Publishing Company, 2006.

[77] A. Justel, D. Peña, and R. Zamar. A multivariate Kolmogorov-Smirnov test of goodness of fit. *Statistics & Probability Letters*, 35(3):251–259, 1997.

[78] D. Kahneman. *Thinking, Fast and Slow*. Farrar, Straus and Giroux, 2011.

[79] G. Kasparov. *Deep Thinking: Where Machine Intelligence Ends and Human Creativity Begins*. Hachette UK, 2017.

[80] M. G. Kendall *et al.* The advanced theory of statistics. volumes. In 4th edition, *The Advanced Theory of Statistics*. Volume 1, 1948.

[81] J. Komlos and B. E. Lauderdale. The mysterious trend in american heights in the 20th century. *Annals of Human Biology*, 34(2):206–215, 2007.

[82] D. A. Kuhe and S. D. Audu. Modelling volatility mean reversion in stock market prices: Implications for long-term investment. *Nigerious Journal of Science Reserach*, 15(1):131–139, 2016.

[83] A. S Kyle. Continuous Auctions and Insider Trading. *Econometrica: Journal of the Econometric Society*, 1315–1335, 1985.

[84] A. S. Kyle. "All alphas are betas onto risk factors not yet named." Private Communication, 1998.

[85] A. N. Langville and C. D. Meyer. *Google's PageRank and Beyond: The Science of Search Engine Rankings*. Princeton University Press, 2011.

[86] M. Lewis. *Liar's Poker*. WW Norton & Company, 2010.
[87] W. Li. Random texts exhibit zipf's-law-like word frequency distribution. *IEEE Transactions on Information Theory*, 38(6):1842–1845, 1992.
[88] J. K. Lindsey and P. M. E. Altham. Analysis of the human sex ratio by using overdispersion models. *Journal of the Royal Statistical Society: Series C (Applied Statistics)*, 47(1):149–157, 1998.
[89] B. G. Malkiel and E. F. Fama. Efficient capital markets: A review of theory and empirical work. *The Journal of Finance*, 25(2):383–417, 1970.
[90] B. B. Mandelbrot. The fractal geometry of nature/revised and enlarged edition. *WHF*, 1983.
[91] B. B. Mandelbrot. *Fractals and Scaling in Finance: Discontinuity, Concentration, Risk. Selecta Volume E*, Springer Science & Business Media, 2013.
[92] G. Manley. Monthly mean central england temperature, 1659–1973. *QJR Meteorological Society*, 100:389–405, 1974.
[93] K. V. Mardia, J. T. Kent, and J. M. Bibby. *Multivariate Analysis*. Academic Press, 1979.
[94] H. Markowitz, W. F. Sharpe, and M. H. Miller. The Founders of Modern Finance: Their Prize-Winning Concepts and 1990 Nobel Lectures. Cfa Inst, 1991.
[95] H. M. Markowitz. Portfolio Selection. *Journal of Finance*, 7(1), 1952.
[96] G. Marsaglia *et al.* Choosing a point from the surface of a sphere. *The Annals of Mathematical Statistics*, 43(2):645–646, 1972.
[97] F. J. Massey Jr. The kolmogorov-smirnov test for goodness of fit. *Journal of the American Statistical Association*, 46(253):68–78, 1951.
[98] R. C. Merton and P. A. Samuelson. *Continuous Time Finance*. Blackwell Boston, 1992.
[99] Met Office. The central england temperature series (Degrees C) 1659–date. Website, updated monthly. http://www.metoffice.gov.uk/hadobs/hadcet/cetml1659on.dat.
[100] B. Monsell. The X-13A-S Seasonal Adjustment Program. In *Proceedings of the 2007 Federal Committee on Statistical Methodology Research Conference*. U.S. Census Bureau, 2009.
[101] T. Mori. Five years of lep experiments. Technical Report, SCAN-9506039, 1995.
[102] Morning Consult. Presidential Approval by State. Website, February 2020.
[103] J. E. Mosimann. On the compound multinomial distribution, the multivariate β-distribution, and correlations among proportions. *Biometrika*, 49(1/2):65–82, 1962.

[104] P. D. Murphy. *Executive Order 107.* The State of New Jersey, 2020.

[105] P. Murray. Monmouth University Poll. Press-release, August 2019.

[106] Name withheld. "in machine learning these methods aren't relevant." Private Communication, 2016.

[107] N.B.E.R. County Adjacencies File. Website, 10 2020.

[108] W. Newey. Large sample estimation and hypothesis testing, Ch. 36 in handbook of econometrics, Vol. 4, rf engle and d. mcfadden eds., 1994.

[109] M. E. J. Newman and M. Girvan. Finding and evaluating community structure in networks. *Physical Review E*, 69(2):026113, 2004.

[110] G. W. Oehlert. A note on the delta method. *The American Statistician*, 46(1):27–29, 1992.

[111] Open NY. The Measure of a President, October 2008.

[112] S. Patterson. The quants: How a new breed of math whizzes conquered wall street and nearly destroyed it. *Currency*, 2010.

[113] D. Rabinowit and D. Siegmund. The approximate distribution of the maximum of a smoothed poisson random field. *Statistica Sinica*, 7(1):167–180, 1997.

[114] R. Rousseau. George kingsley zipf: Life, ideas, his law and informetrics. *Glottometrics*, 3(1):11–18, 2002.

[115] F. Salmon. The formula that killed wall street. *Significance*, 9(1):16–20, 2012.

[116] D. Seligman, G. Laughlin, and K. Batygin. On the anomalous acceleration of 1i/2017 u1 'oumuamua. *The Astrophysical Journal Letters*, 876(2):L26, 2019.

[117] C. E. Shannon and W. Weaver. *The Mathematical Theory of Communication.* University of Illinois Press, 1962.

[118] J. Siegel. *Stocks for the Long Run*, Volume 40, New York: McGraw-Hill, 1998.

[119] D. Siegmund, B. Yakir *et al.* Tail probabilities for the null distribution of scanning statistics. *Bernoulli*, 6(2):191–213, 2000.

[120] N. Silver. How We're Tracking Donald Trump's Approval Ratings. Website, March 2017. https://fivethirtyeight.com/features/how-were-tracking-donald-trumps-approval-ratings/.

[121] N. Silver. How Popular/Unpopular is Donald Trump? Website (Updated daily), August 2019. https://projects.fivethirtyeight.com/trump-approval-ratings.

[122] C. Silverstein, S. Brin, and R. Motwani. Beyond market baskets: Generalizing association rules to dependence rules. *Data Mining and Knowledge Discovery*, 2(1):39–68, 1998.

[123] T. Silvey. Farewell etaoin shrdlu: An age-old printing process gives way to modern technology. *Laboratory Studies Journal*, 8:160, 1983.

[124] J. H. Simons. "Sometimes it's just random." Private Communication, 1999.
[125] Social Science Research Network. Graham Giller: S.S.R.N. Author Page. Website, 2020.
[126] K. Sostek and B. Slatkin. How Google Surveys Works. Website, 2017. http://services.google.com/fh/files/misc/google-surveys-whitepaper.pdf.
[127] D. Steinberg and P. Colla. Cart: classification and regression trees. *The Top Ten Algorithms in Data Mining*, 9:179, 2009.
[128] D. Stirzaker and D. Grimmett. *Probability and Random Processes.* Clarendon Press, 1992.
[129] G. Taubes. *Good Calories, Bad Calories.* Anchor, 2007.
[130] T. Thadewald and H. Büning. Jarque-bera Test and its Competitors for Testing Normality — a Power Comparison. *Journal of Applied Statistics*, 34(1):87–105, 2007.
[131] The National Archives. 2020 Electoral College Results. Technical report, The National Archives, January 2021. https://www.archives.gov/electoral-college/2020.
[132] The University of Michigan. Surveys of Consumers: Questionnaire. https://data.sca.isr.umich.edu/fetchdoc.php?docid=24776, 2020.
[133] M. Tyldum and G. Moore. The imitation game. Movie, 2014.
[134] UB40 (band). One In Ten. Record Album (Present Arms, 1981), May 1981.
[135] U.S. Food & Drug Administration. FDA Takes Key Action in Fight Against COVID-19 By Issuing Emergency Use Authorization for First COVID-19 Vaccine. Press-release, 12 2020.
[136] V. Vapnik. *The Nature of Statistical Learning Theory.* Springer Science & Business Media, 2013.
[137] O. Vasicek. An equilibrium characterization of the term structure. *Journal of Financial Economics*, 5(2):177–188, 1977.
[138] M. D. Ward and J. S. Ahlquist. *Maximum Likelihood for Social Science: Strategies for Analysis.* Cambridge University Press, 2018.
[139] S. S. Wilks. The large-sample distribution of the likelihood ratio for testing composite hypotheses. *The Annals of Mathematical Statistics*, 9(1):60–62, 1938.
[140] R. Wilner. Maria is no longer sweet on 'Honey'. *The New York Post*, March 2010.
[141] S. Zhu, J. Wu, H. Xiong, and G. Xia. Scaling up top-k cosine similarity search. *Data & Knowledge Engineering*, 70:60–83, 2011.
[142] G. Zuckerman. *The Man Who Solved the Market: How Jim Simons Launched the Quant Revolution.* Penguin, 2019.

Index

L

M

N

X

Y

Z

Milton Keynes UK
Ingram Content Group UK Ltd.
UKHW052141230224
438368UK00002B/5